ADVANCED TOPICS IN
BIOMETRICS

ADVANCED TOPICS IN
BIOMETRICS

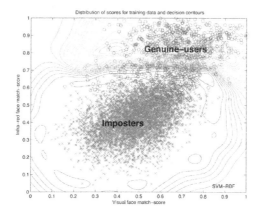

Haizhou Li
Institute for Infocomm Research, Singapore

Kar-Ann Toh
Yonsei University, Korea

Liyuan Li
Institute for Infocomm Research, Singapore

 **World Scientific**

NEW JERSEY · LONDON · SINGAPORE · BEIJING · SHANGHAI · HONG KONG · TAIPEI · CHENNAI

Published by

World Scientific Publishing Co. Pte. Ltd.

5 Toh Tuck Link, Singapore 596224

USA office: 27 Warren Street, Suite 401-402, Hackensack, NJ 07601

UK office: 57 Shelton Street, Covent Garden, London WC2H 9HE

British Library Cataloguing-in-Publication Data
A catalogue record for this book is available from the British Library.

ADVANCED TOPICS IN BIOMETRICS

ISBN-13 978-981-4287-84-5
ISBN-10 981-4287-84-9

Desk Editor: Tjan Kwang Wei

Typeset by Stallion Press
Email: enquiries@stallionpress.com

Printed in Singapore.

PREFACE

Man has long believed in his ability to establish or verify one's identity based on physiological or behavioural characteristic. According to Quintillian (35–96 AD), "the voice of the speaker is as easily distinguished by the ear as the face is by the eye." As another instance, there had been archaeological evidence of fingerprint being used as an identifier in ancient time. Such human skills belong to the field of biometric authentication. The quest to improve such an ability has never stopped. The invention of digital computers makes possible biometric authentication through computing. The question is how to scientifically measure the individuality of such physiological or behavioural characteristics. Today, biometric technologies are not just in fiction movies. We have seen many of them being deployed for practical use. For example, the fingerprint system has become a low cost and high performance access control tool. Biometric authentication is also called biometrics in general, which is known to be an interdisciplinary research built upon foundations across digital signal processing, pattern recognition, machine learning and human-machine interface. This book documents the recent advances of various technical approaches. Like all other technologies, biometric technologies become useful only when they meet operational goals in real-world applications. This book also provides an account of fusion, decision, and security methodologies that are critical to system deployment.

This book brings together 35 among the most respected researchers and scientists to provide both a concise and accessible introduction to the field as well as a detailed coverage on unique research problems with their solutions in nine parts, namely Voice, Face, Fingerprint, Gait, Hand Geometry, Handwriting, Human Behavior Analysis, Multibiometrics, Security and Others. The contributions present the pioneering efforts, international benchmarking, and state-of-the-art results, with special focus on practical issues concerning system development.

In the past decade, we have witnessed an intensive technological progress spurred on by community initiatives such as international benchmarking and standardization, with increasingly fast and affordable computing facilities. The editors had its first meeting in 2008 to find it was timely and beneficial to the community to have a collective documentation on the recent advances in biometrics. It has not been an easy task putting together an extensive volume within a short time frame. The editors would like to express their sincere gratitude to all distinguished contributors who make this book possible, and the group of reviewers who have offered invaluable comments to improve the quality of each and every chapter. A special thank is extended to Professor John Daugman for his comment on the listing of topics. A dedicated team at World Scientific Publishing has also assisted the editors continuously from the inception to the final production of the book. We thank them for their painstaking efforts in all stages of production.

Haizhou Li
Kar-Ann Toh
Liyuan Li
August 2011

CONTENTS

LIST OF CONTRIBUTORS

Eliathamby Ambikairajah
School of Electrical Engineering and Telecommunications,
University of New South Wales, Australia
E-mail: ambi@ee.unsw.edu.au

Jeung-Yoon Choi
School of Electrical & Electronic Engineering
Yonsei University, Seoul, Korea
E-mail: jychoi@yonsei.ac.kr

How-Lung Eng
Institute for Infocomm Research,
1 Fusionopolis Way, #21-01 Connexis,
Singapore
E-mail: hleng@i2r.a-star.edu.sg

Julien Epps
School of Electrical Engineering and Telecommunications,
University of New South Wales, Australia
E-mail: j.epps@ee.unsw.edu.au

Yongsheng Gao
School of Engineering,
Griffith University, Australia
E-mail: yongsheng.gao@griffith.edu.au

David K. Han
Office Naval Research,
Washington D.C. USA
E-mail: david.k.han@navy.mil

Fengling Han
School of Computer Science and Information Technology,
Royal Melbourne Institute of Technology, VIC 3001, Australia
E-mail: fengling.han@rmit.edu.au

Sungjun Hong
School of Electrical & Electronic Engineering,
Yonsei University, Seoul, Korea
E-mail: imjune@yonsei.ac.kr

Jiankun Hu
School of Computer Science and Information Technology,
Royal Melbourne Institute of Technology, VIC 3001, Australia
E-mail: jiankun@cs.rmit.edu.au

Vivek Kanhangad
Department of Computing,
The Hong Kong Polytechnic University,
Hung Hom, Kowloon, Hong Kong
E-mail: csvivek@comp.polyu.edu.hk

Ashraf Kassim
Department of Electrical and Computer Engineering,
National University of Singapore, Singapore
E-mail: eleashra@nus.edu.sg

Euntai Kim
School of Electrical & Electronic Engineering,
Yonsei University, Seoul, Korea
E-mail: etkim@yonsei.ac.kr

Hanseok Ko
School of Electrical Engineering,
Korea University,
Seoul, Korea
E-mail: hsko@korea.ac.kr

Ramamohanarao Kotagiri
Department of Computer Science and Software Engineering,
University of Melbourne, Australia
E-mail: kotagiri@unimelb.edu.au

Ajay Kumar
Department of Computing,
The Hong Kong Polytechnic University,
Hung Hom, Kowloon, Hong Kong
E-mail: csajaykr@comp.polyu.edu.hk

Heesung Lee
School of Electrical & Electronic Engineering,
Yonsei University, Seoul, Korea

Haizhou Li
Institute for Infocomm Research,
1 Fusionopolis Way, #21-01 Connexis,
Singapore
E-mail: hli@i2r.a-star.edu.sg

Jun Li
Institute for Infocomm Research,
1 Fusionopolis Way, #21-01 Connexis,
Singapore
E-mail: jli@i2r.a-star.edu.sg

Liyuan Li
Institute for Infocomm Research,
1 Fusionopolis Way, #21-01 Connexis,
Singapore
E-mail: lyli@i2r.a-star.edu.sg

Qingshan Liu
Department of Computer Science,
Rutgers University,
Piscataway, New Jersey, 08904 USA
E-mail: qsliu@cs.rutgers.edu
National Laboratory of Pattern Recognition,
Chinese Academy of Sciences,
Beijing, China
E-mail: qsliu@nlpr.ia.ac.cn

Hanqing Lu
National Laboratory of Pattern Recognition,
Chinese Academy of Sciences,
Beijing, China
E-mail: luhq@nlpr.ia.ac.cn

Bin Ma
Institute for Infocomm Research,
1 Fusionopolis Way, #21-01 Connexis,
Singapore
E-mail: mabin@i2r.a-star.edu.sg

Dimitris N. Metaxas
Department of Computer Science,
Rutgers University,
Piscataway, New Jersey, 08904 USA
E-mail: dnm@cs.rutgers.edu

Bingbing Ni
Department of Electrical and Computer Engineering,
National University of Singapore, Singapore
E-mail: g0501096@nus.edu.sg

Junbum Park
School of Electrical Engineering,
Korea University,
Seoul, Korea
E-mail: jbpark@ispl.korea.ac.kr

Norman Poh
University of Surrey,
Guildford, GU2 7XH, Surrey, UK
E-mail: normanpoh@ieee.org

Jagath C. Rajapakse
School of Computer Engineering and BioInformatics Research Centre,
Nanyang Technological University,
Singapore
E-mail: asjagath@ntu.edu.sg

Andrew Beng Jin Teoh
Biometrics Engineering Research Center (BERC),
Yonsei University, Seoul, Korea
E-mail: bjteoh@yonsei.ac.kr

Kar-Ann Toh
Biometrics Engineering Research Center,
School of Electrical & Electronic Engineering, Yonsei University,
Seoul, Korea
E-mail: katoh@yonsei.ac.kr

Michael Wagner
National Centre for Biometric Studies,
Faculty of Information Sciences & Engineering,
University of Canberra, ACT 2601, Australia,
E-mail: michael.wagner@canberra.edu.au

Yang Wang
Neville Roach Laboratory,
National ICT, Australia
E-mail: yang.wang@nicta.com.au

Shuicheng Yan
Department of Electrical and Computer Engineering,
National University of Singapore, Singapore
E-mail: eleyans@nus.edu.sg

Wei-Yun Yau
Institute for Infocomm Research,
1 Fusionopolis Way, #21-01 Connexis,
Singapore
E-mail: wyyau@i2r.a-star.edu.sg

Bailing Zhang
Department of Computer Science and Software Engineering,
Xi'an Jiaotong-Liverpool University, Suzhou, China
E-mail: bailing.zhang@xjtlu.edu.cn

Yanchun Zhang
Centre for Applied Informatics Research,
School of Engineering and Science,
Victoria University, Australia

Part I

Voice

Chapter 1

TEXT-INDEPENDENT SPEAKER RECOGNITION

Bin Ma and Haizhou Li
Institute for Infocomm Research
1 Fusionopolis Way, #21-01 Connexis (South Tower)
Singapore 138632
mabin,hli@i2r.a-star.edu.sg

1.1 Introduction

The fundamental issues of automatic speaker recognition include speaker characterization, classifier design, channel- and session-compensation techniques, and score normalization algorithms for a robust speaker recognition decision. In this chapter, an overview on text-independent speaker recognition systems is first given. Then, the acoustic feature extraction and the state-of-the-art speaker classification approaches are described. A further discussion on compensation of session variability and score normalization for robust speaker recognition then follows. Finally, a performance assessment is provided, as a case study, on the National Institute of Standards and Technology (NIST) 2008 Speaker Recognition Evaluation corpus.

1.2 Overview of Speaker Recognition

Automatic speaker recognition is a technology that identifies a speaker, based on his/her speech, using a computer system. Just like any other pattern recognition problem, it involves feature extraction, speaker modeling, or speaker characterization, and classification decision strategy, as shown in Fig. 1.1. Speaker recognition is often referred to as voiceprint or voice biometrics in applications where a speaker's identity is required, for example, in access control and forensic investigation. As opposed to other biometric technologies, such as biometric recognition with fingerprint, face and iris, an advantage of speaker recognition is that it does not require any specialized hardware for the user interface. The only requirement is a microphone, which has been made widely available in pervasive telephone infrastructure. Over the telephone, speaker enrollment and recognition can be carried out remotely.

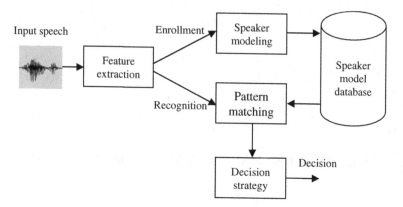

Fig. 1.1. A speaker recognition system.

1.2.1 *Text-dependent and text-independent speaker recognition*

If a speaker recognition system operates on speech of pre-defined text, it is called a text-dependent system, otherwise, it is a text-independent one. A text-dependent speaker recognition system can work with fixed text, such as passwords, credit card numbers, or telephone numbers, as well as with prompted text, which is given by the system at the point of use. It works well in situations where the speakers are cooperative. A text-independent speaker recognition system, on the other hand, does not specify any speech content. It accepts speech with any content and even in different languages. The latter provides great flexibility especially when the speakers of interest are not available to provide speech samples.

In general, a text-dependent speaker recognition system, with comparable speech content, is more accurate than a text-independent one. Although a speaker can say any words during enrolment, a text-dependent speaker recognition system usually assumes that the words spoken during run-time tests have already been enrolled and are known to the system. In this way, a verbatim comparison using hidden Markov model (HMM) (Rabiner and Juang, 1993), a commonly used acoustic model structure in automatic speech recognition (ASR), becomes possible and has shown promising results (Naik *et al.*, 1989; Matsui and Furui, 1993; Che *et al.*, 1996; Parthasarathy and Rosenberg, 1996).

Text-independent speaker recognition provides a more flexible application scenario because it does not require information about the words spoken. Among the research activities in this area, the National Institute of Standards and Technology (NIST, US) has conducted a series of speaker recognition evaluations (SREs) since 1996 (NIST, 1996), which provide a common platform for text-independent speaker recognition technology benchmarking. The NIST SRE has seen an increasing participation in the recent years.

1.2.2 *Speaker identification and verification*

In practice, speaker recognition is implemented as either an identification or a verification task. Speaker identification is the process of determining who speaks among a list of speakers who are known to the system. Speaker verification, on the other hand, is the process of a binary decision, accepting or rejecting the identity claim of a speaker, given an input speech.

Speaker identification can be regarded as a one-to-many problem, identifying the person as one of the many in the speaker database, while speaker verification can be regarded as one-to-one problem, answering the question: "Is the person who he claims to be?." While the two tasks are formulated differently to address application need, they share some common technical challenges. Fundamentally, they are just different applications of the same speaker modeling and classification techniques, which are studied in this chapter. For simplicity, they are presented only in relation to speaker verification applications.

1.2.3 *Speaker verification framework*

Just like any other problem in pattern recognition, both speaker identification and speaker verification require a training process for each speaker to register with the system before a test can be conducted. A typical example of a speaker verification system is shown in Fig. 1.2.

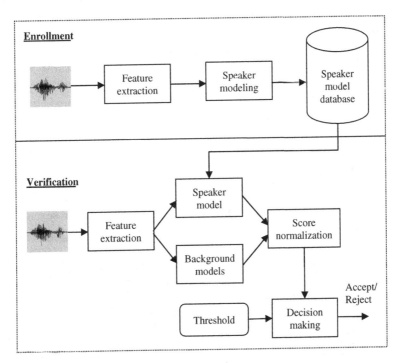

Fig. 1.2. A speaker verification system.

During enrollment, a feature extraction process converts the speech samples into speech feature vectors. A speaker model, such as Gaussian mixture models (GMMs) or support vector machines (SVMs), is then built to characterize a speaker from his/her speech features. The resulting speaker models are kept in a speaker database for future verification tests.

During verification, the same feature extraction process is employed. The speech feature vectors are then evaluated against the claimed speaker model. To make a robust decision, a score normalization algorithm is a crucial component in speaker verification system. It scales the matching score against the scores given by a group of background speakers, to make a calibrated decision. Finally, a decision can be made by comparing the normalized score with a decision threshold, which is estimated from a development database. Figure 1.2 shows the fundamental components of a speaker verification system. Each of these components is reviewed and then a case study of performance evaluation is carried out on the NIST 2008 Speaker Recognition Evaluations (SREs) corpus.

1.3 Feature Extraction

It is believed that digital speech signal carries substantially redundant information as far as speech or speaker recognition is concerned. Transforming the input speech signal into a sequence of feature vectors is called feature extraction. The resulting feature vectors are expected to be discriminative among speakers and robust against any distortion and noise. Low-level acoustic feature extraction is also a data-reduction process that attempts to capture the essential characteristics of the speaker and provides a more stable and compact representation of the input speech than the raw speech signals. The popular acoustic features adopted in ASR, such as Mel-frequency cepstral coefficients (MFCCs) (Atal, 1974), perceptual linear predictive (PLP) (Hermansky, 1990) coefficients and linear predictive cepstral coefficients (LPCCs) (Davis and Mermelstein, 1980) are also effective in speaker recognition.

1.3.1 *Spectral analysis*

The spectral analysis consists of several processing steps. The input speech signals pass a low-pass filter to remove high-frequency components and are segmented into frames. Each frame is a time slice, which is short enough so that the speech wave can be considered stationary within the frame. For example, a typical practice is to segment the speech into frames by a 20 ms window at a 10 ms frame rate. A Hamming window is typically used to window each frame by minimizing the signal discontinuities at the frame boundaries.

Voice activity detection (VAD) is used to detect the presence of human voice in the signal. It plays an important role as a pre-processing stage in almost all speech-processing applications including speaker recognition. It improves the performance of speaker recognition by excluding silence and noise.

Among the different ways of determining the short-time spectral representation of speech, MFCC was originally developed for speech recognition but also found to be effective in speaker recognition. The choice of center frequencies and bandwidths of the filter bank used in MFCC is determined by the properties of the human auditory system. In particular, a Fourier transform is applied to the windowed speech signals and a set of bandpass filters is used. These filters are normally equally spaced in the Mel scale. The output of each filter can be considered as representing the energy of the signal within the passband of the filter. A discrete cosine transform can be applied to the log-energy outputs of these filters, in order to calculate the MFCC as follows

$$c_i = \sum_{j=1}^{P} m_j \cos \left(\frac{i(j - 0.5)\pi}{P} \right), \quad 1 \le i \le M \tag{1.1}$$

where c_i is the ith MFCC, P is the order of analysis, m_j is the logarithm of the jth filter bank output, and M is the number of output parameters. Normally the first- and second-order derivatives of MFCC features are included in the feature vector for speaker recognition.

1.3.2 *Cepstral feature normalization*

Since speech signals may be transmitted through different channels, for example different telephone lines and telephone handsets, the spectral features will include characteristics other than those of the speakers. To normalize the undesired channel effects, the cepstral mean normalization (CMN) (Atal, 1974) and RASTA filtering methods (Hermansky *et al.*, 1992) were proposed. Besides normalizing the mean vector, scaling by the standard deviation of the feature vectors may help further.

The CMN is simple and straightforward. However, it does not remove all the channel characteristics. More sophisticated normalization techniques have been studied. Feature warping (Pelecanos and Sridharan, 2001) aims to construct a more robust representation of each cepstral feature distribution, for linear channel effects and slowly varying additive noise, by conditioning and conforming the individual elements of cepstral feature vectors such that they follow a specific target distribution over a speech window. In practice, feature warping can be effectively conducted by mapping each cepstral element in the speech feature vector to a normal distribution. The distribution of a normal curve is given as

$$h(c) = \frac{1}{\sqrt{2\pi}} \exp \left(-\frac{c^2}{2} \right) \tag{1.2}$$

where c is the variable representing an element in a cepstral feature vector, and $h(c)$ is the target distribution. Each cepstral feature is treated independently in its own element of features. A window of N features in the feature element is isolated and their values are sorted in descending order. To determine a single warped feature given the cepstral feature that exists in the center of the current sliding window,

the ranking of the cepstral feature within the sorted list is calculated. This ranking
is used as an index in a lookup table to determine the warped feature value. The
lookup table is devised so as to map a rank order determined from the sorted
cepstral feature to a warped feature using the desired warping target distribution.
The process is repeated for each frame shift of the sliding window.

Another cepstral feature normalization technique is feature mapping (Reynolds,
2003), which transforms the features coming from particular channels into channel-
independent features. First, a channel-independent GMM is trained using an
aggregation of speech data from many different channels, and then channel-
dependent GMMs are trained using channel-dependent data to adapt the channel-
independent GMM. Given an input speech, the most likely channel is detected and
each feature vector $\mathbf{x}$ in the speech is mapped to the channel-independent space
based on its most likely Gaussian component in the channel-dependent GMM as
follows

$$\mathbf{y} = (\mathbf{x} - \boldsymbol{\mu}^{\text{CD}}) \frac{\boldsymbol{\sigma}^{\text{CI}}}{\boldsymbol{\sigma}^{\text{CD}}} + \boldsymbol{\mu}^{\text{CI}} \tag{1.3}$$

where $\boldsymbol{\mu}^{\text{CD}}$, $\boldsymbol{\sigma}^{\text{CD}}$ are the mean and deviation vectors of the most likely Gaussian
component in the channel-dependent GMM, and $\boldsymbol{\mu}^{\text{CI}}$, $\boldsymbol{\mu}^{\text{CI}}$ are the mean and
deviation vectors of the corresponding Gaussian component in the channel-
independent GMM.

1.3.3 *Prosodic and token features*

While the spectral features have been the dominating features, other types of
features, such as prosodic features and the features extracted from token systems
are also applied in speaker recognition. These features, as opposed to the spectral
features, have low speaker recognition accuracy alone, while generally providing
a complementary gain when they are combined with acoustic systems of spectral
features (Campbell *et al.*, 2003).

The most common prosodic features for speaker recognition (Adami *et al.*, 2003;
Sonmez *et al.*, 2004) are the pitch features, which are believed to be more robust
against channel distortions and noise than spectral features. However, they do still
suffer from other problems, such as invalidation in unvoiced frames of the speech and
difficulty in normalization. Due to the large gap in speaker recognition performance
between spectral features and prosodic features, a careful fusion strategy is necessary
for the fusion system to be effective (Long *et al.*, 2009).

In token feature extraction, the input speech is converted into a sequence of
tokens that can be words (Doddington, 2001), phones (Campbell *et al.*, 2004), and
even frame-based GMM indexes (Ma *et al.*, 2006). The tokens are represented by
discrete symbols in an ordered sequence, and the rules governing the sequences
of admissible tokens carry discriminative information among different speakers.
Modeling of the token sequence is usually conducted based on the statistic

probabilities of the n-grams of the tokens. Although the token features have been adopted in some of the speaker recognition systems, they are not as effective as they are in spoken language recognition. In language recognition, it is the belief that although common sounds are shared considerably across spoken languages, the statistics of the sounds, such as phone n-grams, differ very much from one language to another.

1.4 Classifier Design

Speaker verification is the task to decide whether an input speech sample is spoken by a given claimant or not. It is, therefore, also known as speaker detection. The claimant is known as the target speaker. For this to happen, we need to train a model for each speaker, which characterizes the speaker's individuality. We also need to build a background model, which characterizes the cohort of reference speakers, that serves as the reference in making speaker detection decision. If we use one reference model for all the target speakers, then we call such a model universal background model (UBM). It is understandable that if a test sample is very close to a target speaker model, but very different from its background model, then there is a good chance that the test sample belongs to the target speaker; otherwise, the test sample does not. This influences many different speaker verification paradigms.

The training of speaker models and background models can be summarized into two main categories generative modeling, such as HMM and GMM, and discriminative modeling, such as SVM and artificial neural networks (ANNs). While both techniques are to support a reliable speaker verification decision, the former focuses on building speaker model that best characterizes the speakers; while the latter makes effort to understand the difference between the speakers. We discuss some of the techniques next.

1.4.1 *Gaussian mixture modeling*

The GMM is one of the successful techniques based on generative modeling for text-independent speaker verification (Reynolds and Rose, 1995; Gish and Schmidt, 1994). Since no prior knowledge about speech content is available, a large number of mixture Gaussian density functions based on the stochastic modeling become a good choice as they are advantageous in modeling the statistical variations of speech signals over other sophisticated likelihood functions, such as HMM, which makes use of the prior knowledge about speech content in a text-dependent task.

For a D-dimensional feature vector, $\mathbf{x} \in X$, with M Gaussian mixture density functions, the likelihood function of a GMM is a weighted linear combination:

$$p(\mathbf{x}|\lambda) = \sum_{i=1}^{M} w_i p_i(\mathbf{x}) \tag{1.4}$$

Each of the Gaussian density functions is parameterized by a D-dimensional mean vector, $\boldsymbol{\mu}_i$, and a $D \times D$ covariance matrix Σ_i while a diagonal covariance matrix is normally adopted for the computation efficiency and good performance especially when there is only limited training data available. The Gaussian density function is then represented as follows

$$p_i(\mathbf{x}) = \frac{1}{(2\pi)^{D/2}|\Sigma_i|^{1/2}} \exp\left[-\frac{1}{2}(\mathbf{x} - \boldsymbol{\mu}_i)^t \Sigma_i^{-1}(\mathbf{x} - \boldsymbol{\mu}_i)\right] \tag{1.5}$$

where the mixture weights satisfy the constraint $\sum_{i=1}^{M} w_i = 1$, and the Gaussian mixture models are denoted by $\lambda = \{w_i, \boldsymbol{\mu}_i, \Sigma_i\}$, $i = 1, \ldots, M$.

One of the advantages of using a GMM for speaker recognition is that it is based on a well-understood statistical model and is computationally inexpensive. Another advantage is that a large number of Gaussian mixtures are used to model diversified sound components or clusters based on their underlying distribution of acoustic observations from a speaker. Furthermore, a GMM is not sensitive to the temporal dynamics of the speech signals.

The training of a GMM, given a collection of training feature vectors, is generally conducted using the expectation-maximization (EM) algorithm (Dumpster *et al.*, 1977) to estimate the model parameters with maximum likelihood (ML) criterion. The EM is an iterative method which alternates between performing an expectation step, which computes an expectation of the log likelihood with respect to the current estimate of the GMM parameters and a maximization step, which computes the parameters which maximize the expected log likelihood found on the expectation step. These parameters are then used to determine the parameters of the models in the next expectation step. An example of GMM training for speaker recognition can be found in (Reynolds, 1995).

1.4.1.1 *Likelihood ratio test*

Given an input speech, X, and a hypothesized speaker S, speaker verification is the task of making decision as to whether X is spoken by S. It can be formulated as a hypothesis test between

H_0: X is spoken by the hypothesized speaker; and
H_1: X is not spoken by the hypothesized speaker.

A likelihood ratio test is used in obtaining the decision, in an optimal manner, between these two hypotheses:

$$\frac{p(X|H_0)}{p(X|H_1)} \begin{cases} \geq \theta \text{ accept } H_0 \\ < \theta \text{ accept } H_1 \end{cases} \tag{1.6}$$

where $p(X|H_i)$, $i = 0, 1$ are the probability density functions (PDFs) for the hypotheses H_0 and H_1 with the input speech X.

With generative modeling, the likelihoods are explicitly represented by probability models, i.e., H_0 by a model denoted as λ_{spk} for the claimant speaker and H_1 by a model denoted as λ_{bg} for the background speakers, as shown in Fig. 1.2. The likelihood ratio score is then calculated as follows

$$\frac{p(X|H_0)}{p(X|H_1)} = \frac{p(X|\lambda_{\text{spk}})}{p(X|\lambda_{\text{bg}})} \tag{1.7}$$

The higher the likelihood ratio score is, the more probable the H_0 overtakes H_1. The likelihood ratio is often represented in the log-likelihood ratio (LLR) score for the final speaker recognition decision:

$$\Lambda(X) = \log p(X|\lambda_{\text{spk}}) - \log p(X|\lambda_{\text{bg}}) \tag{1.8}$$

1.4.1.2 *Universal background model*

In the likelihood ratio detector shown in Eq. (1.8), there are two models, λ_{spk} and λ_{bg}, respectively that need to be estimated. The model λ_{spk} is estimated using the training speech from the claimant speaker, while the model for the alternative hypothesis λ_{bg} should be estimated using the training speech of many speakers, representing the entire space of all possible alternative speakers, or speaker-independent feature space. Therefore, the model λ_{bg} is also called the universal background model (UBM) (Reynolds *et al.*, 2000).

Given a large collection of training feature vectors, a large number of mixtures, from 512 to 2048, are normally adopted for the UBM modeling to achieve a high performance. Such a GMM–UBM is supposed to represent the speaker-independent distribution of speaker features. Although a single UBM can be trained for all the speaker clusters and feature clusters, when certain prior knowledge, such as gender information, is available, more than one UBM, such as gender-dependent UBMs, may be trained to represent different speaker/feature clusters. Gender-dependent UBMs generally can give a better performance in speaker recognition.

Since the UBM is supposed to represent the distribution of all speakers in the feature space, a large database, from a sizeable population of speakers and a variety of acoustic channels, is necessary to characterize the speaker and acoustic conditions. As such, the choice of training database is paramount, because inappropriate training data could adversely affect the speaker recognition performance. Typically, a UBM training database is selected based on some assumptions and heuristic evidences. The selection of such a database remains a challenge in many real-world applications.

1.4.1.3 *Adaptation of speaker model*

In the GMM–UBM paradigm, training a GMM speaker model directly from the speaker's samples may not be the best practice, due to the limited training samples from individual speakers. The Bayesian learning of maximum a posterior

(MAP) (Gauvain and Lee, 1994) is commonly used to adapt the parameters of the UBM for a speaker model using the speaker's samples. The MAP adaptation takes into account the prior knowledge of UBM, which is used to improve the adaptation procedure. Unlike the ML estimation, which views the GMM parameters as quantities whose values are fixed but unknown, and the best estimate is defined to be the one that maximizes the probability of actually observed samples, Bayesian estimation views the parameters as random variables having some known prior distribution. Observation of the samples converts this to a posterior density, which hopefully is sharply peaked about the true values of the parameters.

Consider a GMM with the parameters, $\lambda = \{w_i, \boldsymbol{\mu}_i, \Sigma_i\}$, $i = 1, \ldots, M$, and let $X = (\mathbf{x}_1, \ldots, \mathbf{x}_T)$ be a sequence of observations. The observation PDF of GMM is

$$p(X|\lambda) = \prod_{t=1}^{T} \sum_{i=1}^{M} w_i p_i(\mathbf{x}_t|\boldsymbol{\mu}_i, \Sigma_i) \tag{1.9}$$

where $p_i(\mathbf{x}_t|\boldsymbol{\mu}_i, \Sigma_i)$ is shown in Eq. (1.5).

In MAP estimation, the GMM parameter λ is assumed randomly with a prior distribution function $g(\lambda)$. Using Bayes theorem, the MAP estimate $\tilde{\lambda}$ is found by solving

$$p(\lambda|X) = \frac{p(X|\lambda)g(\lambda)}{p(X)} \tag{1.10}$$

and

$$\tilde{\lambda} = \arg \max_{\lambda} p(X|\lambda)g(\lambda) \tag{1.11}$$

Here $g(\lambda)$ is an informative prior, i.e., the distribution of the parameters to be estimated. This is a key that allows MAP learning. If we consider λ to be fixed but unknown, we assume no prior knowledge about λ; in other words, we assume a non-informative prior. In this case, Eq. (1.11) will be reduced to the ML formulation.

Having defined the appropriate prior densities, the MAP estimates of the Gaussian mixture parameters can be found by applying the EM algorithm. Through the maximization of the auxiliary function $Q(\lambda, \tilde{\lambda})$ at each iteration, where $\tilde{\lambda}$ is the current fit for λ, the estimation of the Gaussian mixture parameters can be achieved (Gauvain and Lee, 1994). In a speaker recognition practice, only the mean vectors are adapted while the mixture weights and covariance matrices are unchanged. The mean vectors are adapted as follows

$$\tilde{\boldsymbol{\mu}}_i = \frac{\tau_i \mathbf{m}_i + \sum_{t=1}^{T} c_{it} \mathbf{x}_t}{\tau_i + \sum_{t=1}^{T} c_{it}} \tag{1.12}$$

where

$$c_{it} = \frac{w_i p_i(\mathbf{x}_i|\boldsymbol{\mu}_i, \Sigma_i)}{\sum_{i=1}^{M} w_i p_i(\mathbf{x}_i|\boldsymbol{\mu}_i, \Sigma_i)} \tag{1.13}$$

The τ_i is the control parameter for the amount of adaptation from the UBM, and $\mathbf{m}_i$ is the multivariate normal prior density parameters. (Reynolds *et al.*, 2000; Lee and Gauvain, 1993).

1.4.2 *Support vector machines*

The SVM is a technique for pattern classification, effective especially for high-dimensional feature vectors. It is optimized based on a structural risk minimization principle (Vapnik, 1995). Because of its distribution-free property, it is suitable for designing vector-based classifiers. Further, SVM is typically designed to separate vectors in a 2-class problem, also referred to as a binary classification, in which SVM projects an input vector $\mathbf{x}$ into a scalar value $f(\mathbf{x})$

$$f(\mathbf{x}) = \sum_{i=1}^{N} a_i y_i K(\mathbf{x}, \mathbf{x}_i) + b \qquad (1.14)$$

where $y_i = \{-1, 1\}$ are the ideal outputs, the vectors $\mathbf{x}_i$ are support vectors, N is the number of support vectors, the function $K(\cdot, \cdot)$ is the kernel, a_i is an adjustable weight, and b is a bias. Note that $\sum_{i=1}^{N} a_i y_i = 0$. The kernel $K(\cdot, \cdot)$ is subject to certain properties (the Mercer condition), so that it can be expressed as

$$K(\mathbf{x}, \mathbf{y}) = \phi(\mathbf{x})^t \phi(\mathbf{y}) \qquad (1.15)$$

where $\phi(\mathbf{x})$ is a mapping from the input space to a possibly infinite dimensional space.

Since SVM is a binary classifier, speaker verification task is normally conducted through a one-versus-rest training strategy in which the training vectors of target speaker are labeled as $\mathbf{x}_+$ and the training vectors of other speakers, also called as background speakers, are labeled as $\mathbf{x}_-$. The SVM adopts the discriminative learning for the optimization problem with the goal of maximizing the margin, i.e., the distance between the separating hyperplane, $f(\mathbf{x}) = \sum_{i=1}^{N} a_i y_i K(\mathbf{x}, \mathbf{x}_i) + b = 0$, and the nearest training vectors, or if $f(\mathbf{x}) > 0$, then $\mathbf{x} \in \mathbf{x}_+$, and if $f(\mathbf{x}) \leq 0$, then $\mathbf{x} \in \mathbf{x}_-$.

The key to apply SVM to speaker recognition is to find an effective and efficient kernel function. Several successful attempts have been made to propose kernels for spectral features, GMM parameters, as well as the transformations that project a speaker-independent space to speaker-dependent space. Next, several of the recent techniques are described.

1.4.2.1 *Sequence kernel for speaker recognition*

To apply an SVM to speaker recognition, using the spectral feature vectors of spoken utterances as the input, there needs to be a way of taking a sequence of input feature vectors, calculating a kernel operation $K(\{\mathbf{x}_i\}, \{\mathbf{y}_i\})$ for two input sequences, and computing the SVM output, as shown in Fig. 1.3.

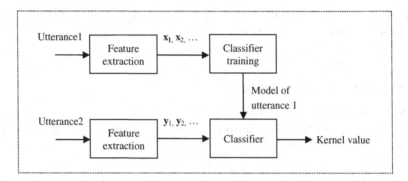

Fig. 1.3.   Sequence kernel.

A successful approach using the sequence kernel is the generalized linear discriminative sequence (GLDS) (Campbell *et al.*, 2006a). It takes the explicit polynomial expansion up to certain degree for the input feature vector and applies sequence kernel based on generalized linear discriminants. Polynomial expansion is to include all the monomials of the features in the feature vector. As an example, suppose there are two features in the input feature vector, $\mathbf{x} = [x_1, x_2]^t$, the monomials with degree 2 are

$$\mathbf{b}(\mathbf{x}) = [1 \; x_1 \; x_2 \; x_1^2 \; x_1 x_2 \; x_2^2]^t \tag{1.16}$$

Suppose that the two sequences of input feature vectors are $\{\mathbf{x}_i\}$ and $\{\mathbf{y}_i\}$. The polynomial discriminant can be obtained using mean-squared error training and the GLDS kernel can be given as follows

$$K(\{\mathbf{x}_i\}, \{\mathbf{y}_i\}) = \bar{\mathbf{b}}_x^t \bar{R}^{-1} \bar{\mathbf{b}}_y \tag{1.17}$$

where

$$\bar{\mathbf{b}}_x = \frac{1}{N_x} \sum_i \mathbf{b}(\mathbf{x}_i) \tag{1.18}$$

$\bar{\mathbf{b}}_x$ is the average expansion over all the feature vectors of the input utterance. $\bar{\mathbf{b}}_y$ can be obtained similarly from the feature vector sequence $\{\mathbf{y}_j\}$. $\bar{R}$ is the correlation matrix of a background data set. An approximation of $\bar{R}$ can be applied to calculate only the diagonal terms (Campbell *et al.*, 2006a).

Another example of sequence kernel is the GMM-based probabilistic sequence kernel (PSK) (Lee *et al.*, 2007), which is built upon a set of Gaussian basis functions, where half of the basis functions contain speaker-specific information while the other half implicates the common characteristics of the competing background speakers. A speech utterance having a varying number of feature vectors will be mapped into a single probabilistic vector, in which each element represents the probability of the Gaussian components.

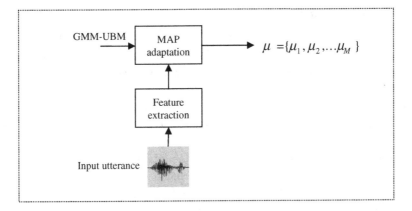

Fig. 1.4. A GMM supervector.

1.4.2.2 *GMM–SVM*

Unlike the sequential kernels, recent studies also explore the use of model parameters, such as GMM in the GMM–UBM paradigm as discussed in Sec. 1.4.1, to construct supervectors for the SVM classifier.

Suppose that there is a GMM-based UBM (GMM–UBM), denoted by $\lambda = \{w_i, \boldsymbol{\mu}_i, \Sigma_i\}$, $i = 1, \ldots, M$. With a speech utterance for a speaker, MAP adaptation can be applied to obtain the speaker model with a mixture of Gaussian components. From the adapted speaker model, a GMM supervector $\boldsymbol{\mu} = \{\boldsymbol{\mu}_1, \boldsymbol{\mu}_2, \ldots, \boldsymbol{\mu}_M\}$ (Campbell *et al.*, 2006b), can be formed as shown in Fig. 1.4.

With two speech utterances, a and b, two GMMs can be trained using MAP adaptation to obtain two sets of mean vectors, $\boldsymbol{\mu}^a = \{\boldsymbol{\mu}_1^a, \boldsymbol{\mu}_2^a, \ldots, \boldsymbol{\mu}_M^a\}$ and $\boldsymbol{\mu}^b = \{\boldsymbol{\mu}_1^b, \boldsymbol{\mu}_2^b, \ldots, \boldsymbol{\mu}_M^b\}$. A Kullback-Leibler (KL) divergence between the two utterances can be calculated as

$$d(\boldsymbol{\mu}^a, \boldsymbol{\mu}^b) = \frac{1}{2} \sum_{i=1}^{M} w_i (\boldsymbol{\mu}_i^a - \boldsymbol{\mu}_i^b)^t \Sigma_i^{-1} (\boldsymbol{\mu}_i^a - \boldsymbol{\mu}_i^b) \qquad (1.19)$$

to approximate the distance where we can find the corresponding inner product that serves as the kernel function:

$$K(a, b) = \sum_{i=1}^{M} w_i (\boldsymbol{\mu}_i^a)^t \Sigma_i^{-1} \boldsymbol{\mu}_i^b = \sum_{i=1}^{M} \left(\sqrt{w_i} \Sigma_i^{-1/2} \boldsymbol{\mu}_i^a \right)^t \left(\sqrt{w_i} \Sigma_i^{-1/2} \boldsymbol{\mu}_i^b \right) \qquad (1.20)$$

As a linear transform is applied on the GMM supervectors, we call this kernel a linear kernel. To take into consideration of both the mean and variance of a GMM model, a Bhattacharyya kernel was proposed (You *et al.*, 2009) which shows improved performance.

1.4.2.3 Maximum likelihood linear regression

Maximum likelihood linear regression (MLLR) (Leggetter and Woodland, 1995) and constrained MLLR (Digalakis *et al.*, 1995) are the two widely used techniques for speaker adaptation in larger vocabulary continuous speech recognition (LVCSR) systems. The affine transforms describe the difference between the target speaker and the speaker-independent model, thus characterizing the target speaker. This motivates the use of MLLR transformation matrices as the vectors to characterize speakers in an SVM classification.

The MLLR uses a set of linear transforms to adapt the HMM mean parameters based on the ML criterion. Consider a set of mean vectors, $\boldsymbol{\mu}_i$, $i = 1, \ldots, M$, in a set of Gaussian mixture HMMs λ. For each of the mean vector $\boldsymbol{\mu}_i$, the adaptation is achieved by applying a transformation matrix W_i to the extended mean vector $\boldsymbol{\xi}_i = [\mathbf{1} \, \boldsymbol{\mu}_{i1} \cdots \boldsymbol{\mu}_{iD}]$ to obtain the adapted mean vector $\tilde{\boldsymbol{\mu}}_i$:

$$\tilde{\boldsymbol{\mu}}_i = W_i \boldsymbol{\xi}_i = A\boldsymbol{\mu}_i + \mathbf{b}_i \tag{1.21}$$

where $W_i = [\mathbf{b}_i, A_i]$ is the $D \times (D+1)$ transformation matrix and D is the dimension of spectral feature vector. The PDF with observation $\mathbf{x}_t$ for the adapted Gaussian component becomes

$$p_i(\mathbf{x}_t) = \frac{1}{(2\pi)^{D/2}|\Sigma_i|^{1/2}} \exp\left[-\frac{1}{2}(\mathbf{x}_t - W_i\boldsymbol{\xi}_i)^t \Sigma_i^{-1}(\mathbf{x}_t - W_i\boldsymbol{\xi}_i)\right] \tag{1.22}$$

To estimate the transforms, the EM algorithm is used and the auxiliary function can be written as

$$Q(\lambda, \tilde{\lambda}) = K - \frac{1}{2}\sum_{i=1}^{M}\sum_{t=1}^{T} \gamma_i(t) \left[K_i + \log|\Sigma_i| + (\mathbf{x}_t - \tilde{\boldsymbol{\mu}}_i)^t \Sigma_i^{-1}(\mathbf{x}_t - \tilde{\boldsymbol{\mu}}_i)\right] \tag{1.23}$$

where K is a constant dependent only on the transition probability of HMMs, K_i is the normalization constant associated with ith Gaussian, $X = (\mathbf{x}_1, \ldots, \mathbf{x}_T)$ is the adaptation data, and $\gamma_i(t) = P(\mathbf{x}_t \in \lambda_i | \lambda, X)$.

As described above, an MLLR transformation matrix is estimated for a set of mean vectors, called a cluster. Such a cluster-based MLLR speaker adaptation transformation matrix can be used as a supervector for speaker recognition (Stolcke *et al.*, 2005). It is noted that one needs the speech transcript to obtain the MLLR supervectors.

Although in practice only mean vectors are adapted, optionally covariance matrices of HMMs can also be transformed by affine transforms, with the aim to maximize the likelihood function (Gales and Woodland, 1996). Constrained MLLR (CMLLR) (Digalakis *et al.*, 1995) forces the transform to be the same for both mean vector and covariance matrix:

$$\begin{cases} \tilde{\boldsymbol{\mu}}_i = A\boldsymbol{\mu}_i + \mathbf{b}_i \\ \tilde{\Sigma}_i = A_i \Sigma_i A_i^t \end{cases} \tag{1.24}$$

It can be proved that the model-level adaptation with CMLLR is equivalent to the feature-level feature compensation:

$$\tilde{\mathbf{x}}_t = A_i^{-1} \mathbf{x}_t + A_i^{-1} \mathbf{b}_i \tag{1.25}$$

As an attempt to get rid of the speech transcripts, a single-class constrained MLLR transformation based on a GMM–UBM model was recently studied (Ferras *et al.*, 2007).

1.4.2.4 *Feature transformation (FT) with MAP estimation*

In the previous section, it has been shown that the feature transforms, which project the speaker-independent features to speaker-dependent features, can be used to characterize speakers. Such transformation matrices are estimated based on the ML criterion.

In ML estimation, we assume the parameters are fixed but unknown without any prior knowledge; instead, in MAP estimation, we assume the parameters belong to some prior PDFs, which have been proved as an effective way in dealing with sparse training data. A recent piece of research, which formulates the joint estimation of both the mean vectors and covariance matrices in a single process (Zhu *et al.*, 2008), has benefited from the MAP learning.

Let us assume that a speech utterance spoken by a speaker has been converted into a sequence of feature vectors, $X = (\mathbf{x}_1, \ldots, \mathbf{x}_T)$, where $\mathbf{x}_t$ is a D-dimensional vector. An FT function is defined to map the speaker's feature vector $\mathbf{x}$ to a speaker-independent feature vector $\tilde{\mathbf{x}}$ as follows

$$\tilde{\mathbf{x}} \triangleq \mathrm{F}(\mathbf{x}; \Theta) = A_k \mathbf{x} + \mathbf{b}_l \tag{1.26}$$

where A_k is a non-singular $D \times D$ matrix, $\mathbf{b}_l$ is a D-dimensional vector, $\Theta = \{A_k, \mathbf{b}_l; k = 1, \ldots, K; l = 1, \ldots, L\}$ includes two sets of parameters, the transform matrices and bias vectors, which can be vectorized to form a supervector for SVM classification.

With the GMM–UBM $\lambda = \{w_i, \boldsymbol{\mu}_i, \Sigma_i\}$, $i = 1, \ldots, M$, the two separate classes of feature transform parameters, $C_{A_k} = \{A_k, k = 1, \ldots, K\}$ and $C_{b_l} = \{b_l, l = 1, \ldots, L\}$ are constructed by clustering the transformation components for the parameter sharing. The objection function that trains the feature transforms based on the MAP criterion is defined as

$$L(\Theta, \lambda) = p(\mathrm{F}(\mathbf{x}; \Theta)|\lambda) \prod_{k=1}^{K} p(A_k) \prod_{l=1}^{L} p(\mathbf{b}_l) \tag{1.27}$$

where $p(A_k)$ and $p(\mathbf{b}_l)$ are the prior PDF of A_k and $\mathbf{b}_l$, respectively.

The FT technique rides on the GMM–UBM framework. Unlike the MLLR transform, it does not require speech transcripts to estimate the transformation matrices. This technique was shown to consistently outperform the GMM–UBM baseline.

1.5 Modeling of Session Variability

Like other applications in speech processing, the recording variability between the enrollment and recognition poses a major challenge to a speaker recognition system. The term "session variability" has been adopted to refer to all the phenomena that cause the enrollment and recognition recordings to sound different from each other. These include channel effects, environment factors, such as noise and room acoustics, and the aging effect over time.

The session variability in speaker recognition can be handled in three levels, namely feature level, model level, and score level. Spectral feature normalization has been described in the previous section. Two model-level compensation approaches, joint factor analysis (JFA) (Kenny *et al.*, 2007; Vogt and Sridharan, 2008) and nuisance attribute projection (NAP) (Solomonoff *et al.*, 2005), are described in this section. We discuss score-level normalization in the next section.

1.5.1 *Joint factor analysis*

The JFA (Kenny *et al.*, 2007) aims to model both the speaker variability and the channel variability in speaker recognition. It is assumed that a speaker- and channel-dependent supervector $\mathbf{M}$, which is concatenated from the mean vectors of all the Gaussian components in the GMM, can be decomposed into a sum of two supervectors, $\mathbf{s}$, representing the speaker factor, and $\mathbf{c}$, representing the channel factor

$$\mathbf{M} = \mathbf{s} + \mathbf{c} \tag{1.28}$$

where $\mathbf{s}$ and $\mathbf{c}$ are statistically independent and normally distributed.

The estimation of $\mathbf{s}$ involves both classical MAP and eigenvoice MAP (Kenny *et al.*, 2005), which constrains the speaker supervectors to lie in a low-dimensional space using principal components analysis so that a very rapid speaker adaptation can be made since only a small number of free parameters need to be estimated. The speaker supervector $\mathbf{s}$ is estimated as follows

$$\mathbf{s} = \mathbf{m} + \mathbf{v}\mathbf{y} + \mathbf{d}\mathbf{z} \tag{1.29}$$

where $\mathbf{m}$ is the speaker- and channel-independent supervector, $\mathbf{v}$ is a rectangular matrix of low rank, $\mathbf{d}$ is a diagonal matrix, and $\mathbf{y}$ and $\mathbf{z}$ are independent random vectors having standard normal distributions. The elements of $\mathbf{y}$ refer to common speaker factors, which reflect the variation of the entire speaker acoustic space, while the elements of $\mathbf{z}$ refer to speaker factor which reflects the speaker-specific information.

In order to compensate for channel effects, eigenchannel modeling is applied for the channel compensation supervector $\mathbf{c}$, which is normally distributed in a low-dimensional subspace of the supervector space:

$$\mathbf{c} = \mathbf{ux} \tag{1.30}$$

where the common channel factor $\mathbf{x}$ has a standard normal distribution and $\mathbf{u}$ is a rectangular matrix of low rank (Kenny *et al.*, 2007).

The JFA has been effectively used in GMM–UBM-based speaker recognition to compensate the session variability.

1.5.2 *Nuisance attribute projection*

The NAP aims to compensate the channel effects in the high-dimensional SVM space. The basic idea of an NAP is to remove some subspaces from SVM expansion, which are irrelevant to the speaker recognition problem, by using a modified kernel to project out the channel effects (Solomonoff *et al.*, 2005; Campbell *et al.*, 2006b). An appropriate project matrix $\mathbf{P}$ in the expansion space is introduced to do this job.

Given two speech utterances, a and b, we can derive two supervectors, $\mathbf{m}^a$ and $\mathbf{m}^b$, in the same way as in Sec. 1.4.2.2. The NAP works by removing subspaces that cause variability in the kernel by constructing a new kernel:

$$\begin{aligned} K(\mathbf{m}^a, \mathbf{m}^b) &= [\mathbf{P}b(\mathbf{m}^a)][\mathbf{P}b(\mathbf{m}^b)] \\ &= b(\mathbf{m}^a)^t \mathbf{P} b(\mathbf{m}^b) \\ &= b(\mathbf{m}^a)^t (I - \mathbf{v}\mathbf{v}^t) b(\mathbf{m}^b) \end{aligned} \tag{1.31}$$

where $\mathbf{P}$ is a projection ($\mathbf{P}^2 = \mathbf{P}$), $\mathbf{v}$ is the direction being removed from the SVM expansion space, $b(\cdot)$ is the SVM expansion, and $\|\mathbf{v}\|_2 = 1$. The design criterion for $\mathbf{P}$ and correspondingly $\mathbf{v}$ is

$$\mathbf{v}^* = \arg \min_{\mathbf{v}, \|\mathbf{v}\|_2 = 1} \sum_{ij} W_{i,j} \|\mathbf{P}b(\mathbf{m}^i) - \mathbf{P}b(\mathbf{m}^j)\|_2^2 \tag{1.32}$$

where the $\{\mathbf{m}^i\}$ and $\{\mathbf{m}^j\}$ are typically a background dataset. The elements of the symmetric matrix W can be designed as positive for the pairs of training utterances that are to be pulled together, negative for pairs that are to be pushed apart, and zero for pairs that are of no concern.

1.6 Score Normalization

Another important issue in the statistical approaches to speaker verification is that of score normalization, which applies a scaling to the likelihood score distribution of different speakers. The score normalization allows us to overcome some of the undesired score variations due to speech content or test conditions, and to make a sound decision at run time. The score normalization can be either conducted with a UBM shown in Eq. (1.8), which represents a distribution over a large number of speakers, or with cohort normalization, which simulates the imposter distribution. The cohort normalization has shown a better performance.

Several cohort score normalization approaches, for example Z-norm (Li and Porter, 1988), T-norm (Auckenthaler *et al.*, 2000), and H-norm (Reynolds, 1997), have been proposed to compensate the LLR score as follows

$$\Lambda^{\text{norm}}(X) = \frac{\Lambda(X) - \mu(X, S)}{\sigma(X, S)} \qquad (1.33)$$

where $\mu(X, S)$ and $\sigma(X, S)$ are the speaker-specific mean and variance, respectively for the imposter distribution.

The main difference in these score normalization techniques lies in the way the bias, $\mu(X, S)$, and the scale factor, $\sigma(X, S)$, are estimated. In the Z-norm, a speaker model is tested against a set of imposter utterances and the log-likelihood scores are used to estimate a speaker-specific mean and variance for the imposter distribution. The advantage of Z-norm is that the estimation of the normalization parameters can be performed offline during training. In the T-norm, a set of imposter speaker models is used to calculate imposter log-likelihood scores for a test utterance. The advantage of T-norm is that the estimation of the distribution parameters is carried out on the same utterance as the target speaker test. Hence, the mismatch between the test utterance and normalization utterances can be avoided. In the H-norm, handset-microphone-dependent values of the bias and scale factors are estimated, therefore, the normalization is carried out with regard to the test condition instead of the speaker.

1.7 Performance Measurement

The NIST has conducted a series of SREs since 1996. The goal of the NIST SRE is to contribute to the direction of research efforts and the calibration of technical capabilities of text-independent speaker recognition. Most recently, there were over 40 research sites participating in the NIST 2008 SRE (NIST, 2008). As a case study for the techniques discussed in this chapter, this section describes a state-of-the-art speaker recognition system, the I4U submission (Li *et al.*, 2009), in the NIST 2008 SRE (SRE08).

The SRE08 is distinguished from previous evaluations by including, in the training and test conditions of the core test, not only conversational telephone speech data (telephone data) but also (1) conversational telephone speech data recorded over a microphone channel (microphone data), and (2) conversational speech recorded over a microphone channel involving an interview scenario

Table 1.1: Acoustic features and classifier techniques (both generative[+] and discriminative[*])

Classifier	Acoustic features
GMM–UBM–EIG[+]	SFLW
GMM–UBM–JFA[+]	PLP
GLDS–SVM[*]	Channel-compensated MFCC
GMM–SVM[*]	MFCC, FM
FT–SVM[*]	MFCC
PSK–SVM[*]	MFCC
Bhattacharyya kernel[*]	LPCC

(interview data). This prompted participants to apply effective channel compensation techniques and to adopt adequate system-development strategies.

1.7.1 *System description*

The I4U system consists of three main modules, namely (1) feature extraction, (2) a parallel of seven speaker classifiers, and (3) classifier fusion. Two of the classifiers are based on the generative GMM–UBM approach, while the other five are based on discriminative SVM techniques. Different acoustic features were implemented in combination with various classifiers, to achieve subsystem diversity, as summarized in Table 1.1.

1.7.1.1 *Feature extraction*

In feature extraction, an energy-based VAD was first applied to remove silence frames and to retain only the high-quality speech frames. An input utterance was then converted to a sequence of feature vectors. Finally, the feature vectors were processed by mean-variance-normalization (MVN), RASTA, and feature warping. Five different types of cepstral features and one frequency modulation (FM) feature were used (Thiruvaran *et al.*, 2008), as shown in Table 1.1. Both the MFCC and LPCC features have 36 dimensions. The short-time frequency with long-time window (SFLW) (Huang *et al.*, 2008) is specially designed to account for both the short-time spectral characteristics and long-time resolution. The FM features capture dominant frequency deviation in sub-bands. Feature-level channel compensation was performed on MFCCs as in (Castaldo *et al.*, 2007), where channel adaptation factors were computed using probabilistic subspace adaptation (Lucey and Chen, 2003).

1.7.1.2 *Classifiers*

The development datasets are also summarized in Table 1.2, and the classifier specifications and strategies are described as follows.

Table 1.2:   Classifier development datasets

Classifier	Development dataset		
	UBM/Background	Channel space	*T*-norm/*Z*-norm
GMM–UBM–EIG	SRE04	SRE04,05,06, Mixer5	SRE05(T), SRE06(Z)
GMM–UBM–JFA	SRE04	SRE04,05,06, Mixer5	SRE05(T), SRE06(Z)
GLDS–SVM	SRE04	SRE04,05,06, Mixer5	SRE05(T)
GMM–SVM	SRE04	SRE04,05,06, Mixer5	SRE05(T)
FT–SVM	SRE04	SRE04,05,06, Mixer5	SRE05(T)
PSK–SVM	SRE04	SRE04,05,06, Mixer5	SRE05(T)
Bhattacharyya kernel	SRE04	SRE04,05,06, Mixer5	SRE05(T)

GMM–UBM–EIG   The GMM–UBM–EIG is a GMM–UBM (Reynolds and Rose, 1995) with eigenchannel adaptation (Kenny *et al.*, 2007). The NIST 2004 SRE (SRE04) 1conv4w (1 conversation) data was used to train the gender-dependent UBMs, each having 512 Gaussian mixture components. The telephone data from SRE04 and SRE06, together with the microphone data of SRE05, SRE06 and the interview data recorded in the LDC Mixer 5 project (distributed by the NIST to participants), were used for eigenchannel adaptation. The number of eigenchannels was set to 30 empirically. The telephone data of SRE05 and SRE06 were used for score normalization of *T*-norm (Auckenthaler *et al.*, 2000) and *Z*-norm (Li and Porter, 1988) in both GMM–UBM–EIG and GMM–UBM–JFA classifiers.

GMM–UBM–JFA   Another GMM–UBM classifier is equipped with JFA as the main channel compensation technique (Kenny *et al.*, 2007). The SRE04 1conv4w data was used to train the gender-dependent UBMs, each having 1024 Gaussian mixture components. Switchboard II and SRE04 data were used to train the speaker space with 300 speaker factors. For channel space training, telephone data from SRE04, SRE05, and SRE06 were used to train the telephone channel space (100 channel factors), microphone data from SRE05 and SRE06 to train the microphone channel space (50 channel factors), and the Mixer 5 interview data to train the interview channel space (50 channel factors). The channel factors for different channel conditions were trained independently. These three subspaces were then combined to obtain a channel space of 200 channel factors. This subspace training scheme was motivated by considering that there was considerably less training data for the interview channel. Experimental results showed that the scheme was a wise and an effective attempt to create a balanced representation of the three different channels.

GLDS–SVM   The GLDS–SVM classifier follows the architecture in (Campbell *et al.*, 2006a). The 36-dimension feature vectors extracted from an utterance were expanded to a higher-dimensional space by employing all monomials up to order 3, thus resulting in a feature space of 9139 dimensions. The expanded features were then averaged to form a single vector for each of the utterances. It is also assumed that the kernel inner product matrix is diagonal for computational simplicity. The same development dataset was used for all the five SVM classifiers (Table 1.2). The SRE04 data was used as the background dataset; the telephone and microphone data from SRE04, SRE05, and SRE06, and the interview data of Mixer 5 were applied for NAP training; and the 1conv4w telephone data of SRE05 were used for T-norm. For the NAP training, the same scheme of individual channel space training and subspace combination as that for JFA was adopted.

GMM–SVM This classifier uses GMM supervectors to construct SVM kernels (Campbell *et al.*, 2006b). Given a speaker's utterance, a GMM is estimated by using MAP-adapted means of the UBM of 512 Gaussian mixture components. The mean vectors of mixture components in the GMM are then concatenated to form a supervector, which is used in the SVM kernels. The NAP was used to compensate for the channel effects.

FT–SVM This classifier uses parameters of an FT function to form the supervectors (Zhu *et al.*, 2008). An iterative training procedure is carried out for the MAP estimation of the FT parameters from the UBM model. The UBM is a gender-dependent GMM with 512 Gaussian mixture components. The FT function has one transformation matrix and 512 bias vectors.

PSK–SVM In the PSK SVM classifier (Lee *et al.*, 2007), the front-end bases were obtained by aggregating the GMMs of 72 speakers selected from a background dataset, which gave the largest scattering measure. Each GMM speaker model has 256 Gaussian components, resulting in $72 \times 256 = 18{,}432$ Gaussian bases. The background speakers' GMMs were pooled together with equal weights to form an ensemble of front-end bases.

Bhattacharyya kernel In the GMM–SVM system with the Bhattacharyya kernel (You *et al.*, 2009), both mean and covariance statistics are taken into account through the Bhattacharyya distance, which measures the discrepancy between two probability distributions. A UBM of 512 GMM components, SVM background, and NAP projection matrix was trained on SRE04 data.

1.7.2 *Classifier fusion*

The I4U Primary submission adopted the linear fusion

$$\hat{s} = \sum_{i=1}^{N} w_i s_i + w_0 \tag{1.34}$$

where s_i is the score from the ith classifiers and $N = 7$ is the total number of classifiers. The weights are optimized for minimum decision cost function (DCF) on the development set:

$$(\hat{w}_i, \hat{w}_0) = \arg \min_{w_i, w_0} \text{DCF} \left(\sum_{i=1}^{N} w_i s_i + w_0 \right) \tag{1.35}$$

where w_i is adjusted iteratively using numerical optimization, subject to the sum of 1.0 and w_0 is given by the threshold, which yields minimum DCF.

The core test of SRE08 was designed to have a *short2* training condition, which involves either telephone or interview speech, and a *short3* test segment condition, which involves telephone, microphone, or interview speech. As interview-microphone condition is not included, there were 5 training-test conditions in combination. A development dataset was created for system fusion and threshold setting using SRE06 1conv4w (telephone data), SRE06 1convmic (microphone data), and Mixer 5 (interview data) datasets. There are only 6 speakers (3 males and 3 females) in the Mixer 5 dataset, with each speaker having 6 sessions, and each session having 9 recordings of around 30 minutes. Each Mixer 5 recording was split into 6 trials in the development dataset.

A development dataset was created to cover the imposter and genuine trials of telephone-telephone, telephone-microphone, and interview-interview conditions, and imposter trials only for telephone-interview and interview-telephone conditions. The whole development dataset was divided into two disjoint halves, one as a *tuning set* for calibrating fusion weights and another as an *evaluation set* for evaluating the performance. The fusion weights and thresholds were estimated for each *short2–short3* pair separately. For those pairs for which there was only imposter trials, the fusion parameters estimated from the telephone-telephone development dataset were adopted.

1.7.3 *Evaluation results*

Table 1.3 reports the performance of the seven individual classifiers as well as the fused system on the telephone-telephone development dataset. The performance is reported in terms of equal error rate (EER) and minimum DCF score (minDCF). It is worth noting that GMM–UBM–JFA demonstrates an outstanding performance, which is attributed to the effective channel space training (Kenny *et al.*, 2007).

Figure 1.5 illustrates the detection error tradeoff (DET) curves of all seven classifiers and the fusion system in SRE08 on telephone-telephone condition. Table 1.4 summarizes the performance in terms of minDCF in the SRE08 core test with all short2-short3 trials being pooled together in the 5 training-test conditions. For reference, the performance of the evaluation set in the development dataset is also reported. It is observed that a 22.3% minDCF reduction over the best individual classifier was achieved by the fusion system.

Table 1.3:   Performance of individual classifiers and the fused system on the telephone-telephone development dataset

	Tuning set		Evaluation set	
	EER(%)	minDCF	EER(%)	minDCF
GMM–UBM–EIG	5.47	0.0270	5.22	0.0243
GMM–UBM–JFA	3.19	0.0168	3.11	0.0160
GLDS–SVM	4.30	0.0238	4.44	0.0208
GMM–SVM	4.47	0.0238	4.43	0.0205
FT–SVM	4.20	0.0222	3.66	0.0189
PSK–SVM	5.29	0.0266	4.77	0.0230
Bhattacharyya kernel	4.46	0.0246	5.16	0.0242
Best individual	3.19	0.0168	3.11	0.0160
Fusion	2.49	0.0122	2.05	0.0122
Improvement	21.94	27.38	34.08	23.75

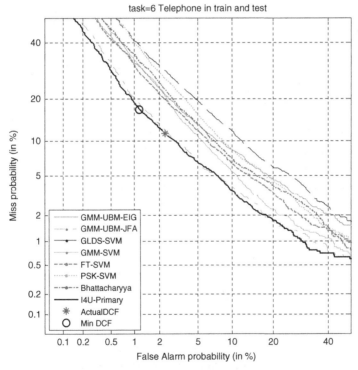

Fig. 1.5.   DET curves of individual classifiers and the fused system on the SRE08 telephone-telephone condition.

1.8 Summary

In the past decade, the performance of text-independent speaker recognition technique has been improved tremendously, which can be attributed to the

Table 1.4: Performance of individual classifiers and the fused system on the *Evaluation Set* and SRE08 *short2–short3* core test

	Evaluation set	SRE08 (short2–short3)	
	minDCF	minDCF	Actual DCF
GMM–UBM–EIG	0.0330	0.0347	—
GMM–UBM–JFA	0.0223	0.0260	—
GLDS–SVM	0.0475	0.0447	—
GMM–SVM	0.0290	0.0382	—
FT–SVM	0.0310	0.0416	—
PSK–SVM	0.0527	0.0475	—
Bhattacharyya kernel	0.0405	0.0442	—
Best individual	0.0223	0.0260	—
Fusion	0.0073	0.0202	**0.0239**
Improvement	67.26%	22.30%	—

advancement of many new techniques around GMMs and SVMs. The recent progress features the use of high-dimensional feature vectors, which are also called supervectors (Kinnunen and Li, 2010). It should be noted that the compensation of the session variability plays a critical role in system design. With the invention of JFA and NAP, the speaker recognition performance in mismatched acoustic environments has been greatly enhanced.

Despite much success, many challenges remain ahead of us. The performance gap between the text-independent speaker recognition and text-dependent speaker recognition is still large. Applications of speaker recognition need to overcome the mismatch of acoustic environment between enrollment and testing, which is still a major hurdle, because most of the current compensation techniques work well only for known acoustic environments and with sufficient training data. The selection of background speaker data has shown to be critical to system performance and it is often application dependent, which means much fine tuning is needed during system development. It is encouraging that text-independent speaker recognition has made major progress for long test speech samples. However, the state-of-the-art performance for short test samples (less than 10 seconds) proves that the technology still fall short of people's expectation.

References

Adami, A. G., Mihaescu, R., Reynolds, D. A., and Godfrey, J. J. Modeling prosodic dynamics for speaker recognition, in *Proc. ICASSP*, pp. 788–791, 2003.

Atal, B. S. Effectiveness of linear prediction characteristics of the speech wave for automatic speaker identification and verification, *J. Acoust. Soc. Am.* **55**, 1304–1312, 1974.

Auckenthaler, R., Carey, M., and Lloyd-Thomas, H. Score normalization for text-independent speaker verification systems, *Digital Signal Processing* **10**, 1–3, 42–54, 2000.

Campbell, W. M., Campbell, J. P., Reynolds, D. A., Jones, D. A., and Leek, T. R. High-level speaker verification with support vector machines, in *Proc. ICASSP*, pp. 1:73–76, 2004.

Campbell, W. M., Campbell, J. P., Reynolds, D. A., Singer, E., and Torres-Carrasquillo. Support vector machines for speaker and language recognition, *Computer Speech Language* **20**, 210–229, 2006a.

Campbell, W. M., Sturim, D. E., Reynolds, D. A., and Solomonoff, A. SVM-based speaker verification using a GMM supervector kernel and NAP variability compensation, in *Proc. ICASSP*, pp. 1:97–100, 2006b.

Campbell, J. P., Reynolds, D. A., and Dunn, R. B. Fusing high- and low- features for speaker recognition, in *Proc. Eurospeech*, pp. 2665–2668, 2003.

Castaldo, F., Colibro, D., Dalmasso, E., Laface, P., and Vair, C. Compensation of nuisance factors for speaker and language recognition, *IEEE Trans. Audio, Speech, and Language Processing* **15**, 7, 1969–1978, 2007.

Che, C. W., Lin, Q., and Yuk, D. S. An HMM approach to text-prompted speaker verification, in *Proc. ICASSP*, pp. 673–676, 1996.

Davis, S. and Mermelstein, P. Comparison of parametric representation for monosyllabic word recognition in continuous spoken sentence, *IEEE Trans. Acoustic and Speech Signal Processing* **28**, 357–366, 1980.

Digalakis, V., Rtischev, D., and Neumeyer, L. G. Speaker adaptation using constrained estimation of Gaussian mixtures, *IEEE Trans. Speech and Audio Processing* **3**, 5, 357–366, 1995.

Doddington, G. Speaker recognition based on idiolectal differences between speakers, in *Proc. Eurospeech*, pp. 2521–2524, 2001.

Dumpster, A., Laird, N., and Rubin, D. Maximum likelihood from incomplete data via the EM algorithm, *J. Royal Statistical Soc.* **39**, 1–38, 1977.

Ferras, M., Leung, C. C., Barras, C., and Gauvain, J.-L. Constrained MLLR for speaker recognition, in *Proc. ICASSP*, pp. 4:53–56, 2007.

Gales, M. J. F. and Woodland, P. C. Mean and variance adaptation within the MLLR framework, *Computer Speech and Language* **10**, 249–264, 1996.

Gauvain, J. L. and Lee, C.-H. Maximum a posterior estimation for multivariate Gaussian mixture observations of Markov chains, *IEEE Trans. Speech and Audio Processing* **2**, 2, 291–298, 1994.

Gish, H. and Schmidt, M. Text independent speaker identification, *IEEE Signal Processing Magazine* **11**, 4, 18–32, 1994.

Hermansky, H. Perceptual linear predictive (PLP) analysis of speech, *J. Acoust. Soc. Am.* **87**, 1738–1752, 1990.

Hermansky, H., Morgan, N., Bayya, A., and Kohn, P. Rasta-PLP speech analysis technique, in *Proc. ICASSP*, pp. 1:121–124, 1992.

Huang, C.-L., Ma, B., Wu, C.-H., Mak, B., and Li, H. Robust speaker verification using short-time frequency with long-time window and fusion of multi-resolutions, in *Proc. Interspeech*, pp. 1897–1900, 2008.

Kenny, P., Boulianne, G., and Dumouchel, P. Eigenvoice modelling with sparse training data, *IEEE Trans. Speech and Audio Processing* **13**, 4, 345–354, 2005.

Kenny, P., Boulianne, G., Ouellet, P., and Dumouchel, P. Joint factor analysis versus eigenchannels in speaker recognition, *IEEE Trans. Audio, Speech, and Language Processing* **15**, 4, 1435–1447, 2007.

Kinnunen, T. and Li, H. An overview of text-independent speaker recognition: from features to supervectors, *Speech Communication* **52**, 12–40, 2010.

Lee, C.-H. and Gauvain, J.-L. Speaker adaptation based on MAP estimation of hmm parameters, in *Proc. ICASSP*, pp. 2:558–561, 1993.

Lee, K. A., You, C., Li, H., and Kinnunen, T. A GMM-based probabilistic sequence kernel for speaker verification, in *Proc. Interspeech*, pp. 294–297, 2007.

Leggetter, C. J. and Woodland, P. C. Maximum likelihood linear regression for speaker adaptation of continuous density hidden Markov models, *Computer Speech and Language* **9**, 171–185, 1995.

Li, H., Ma, B., Lee, K. A., Sun, H., Zhu, D., Sim, K. C., You, C., Tong, R., Karkainen, I., Huang, C.-L., Pervouchine, V., Guo, W., Li, Y., Dai, L., Nosratighods, M., Thiruvaran, T., Epps, J., Ambikairajah, E., Chng, E.-S., Schultz, T., and Jin, Q. The 14U system in NIST 2008 speaker recognition evaluation, in *Proc. ICASSP*, pp. 4201–4204, 2009.

Li, K. P. and Porter, J. E. Normalizations and selection of speech segments for speaker recognition scoring, in *Proc. ICASSP*, pp. 1:595–598, 1988.

Long, Y., Ma, B., Li, H., Guo, W., Chng, E.-S., and Dai, L. Exploiting prosodic information for speaker recognition, in *Proc. ICASSP*, pp. 4225–4228, 2009.

Lucey, S. and Chen, T. Improved speaker verification through probabilistic subspace adaptation, in *Proc. Eurospeech*, pp. 2021–2024, 2003.

Ma, B., Zhu, D., Tong, R., and Li, H. Speaker cluster based GMM tokenization for speaker recognition, in *Proc. Interspeech*, pp. 505–508, 2006.

Matsui, T. and Furui, S. Concatenated phoneme models for text-variable speaker recognition, in *Proc. ICASSP*, pp. 391–394, 1993.

Naik, J. M., P., N. L., and Doddington, G. R. Speaker verification over long distance telephone lines, in *Proc. ICASSP*, pp. 524–527, 1989.

NIST (1996). The speaker recognition evaluation (SRE), http://www.itl.nist.gov/iad/mig//tests/sre/index.html.

NIST (2008). The 2008 NIST speaker recognition evaluation plan, http://www.itl.nist.gov/iad/mig/tests/sre/2008/sre08_evalplan_release4.pdf.

Parthasarathy, S. and Rosenberg, A. E. General phrase speaker verification using sub-word background models and likelihood ratio scoring, in *Proc. ICASSP*, pp. 2403–2406, 1996.

Pelecanos, J. and Sridharan, S. Feature warping for robust speaker verification, in *Proc. Odyssey*, pp. 213–218, 2001.

Rabiner, L. R. and Juang, B.-H. *Fundamental of Speech Recognition* (Prentice-Hall, Englewood Cliffs), 1993.

Reynolds, D. A. Speaker identification and verification using Gaussian mixture models, *Speech Communication* **17**, 1–2, 91–108, 1995.

Reynolds, D. A. Comparison of background normalization methods for text-independent speaker verification, in *Proc. Eurospeech*, pp. 2:963–966, 1997.

Reynolds, D. A. Channel robust speaker verification via feature mapping, in *Proc. ICASSP*, pp. 2:6–10, 2003.

Reynolds, D. A., Quatieri, T. F., and Dunn, R. B. Speaker verification using adapted Gaussian mixture modeling, *Digital Signal Processing* **10**, 19–41, 2000.

Reynolds, D. A. and Rose, R. Robust text-independent speaker identification using Gaussian mixture speaker models, *IEEE Trans. Speech and Audio Processing* **3**, 1, 72–83, 1995.

Solomonoff, A., Campbell, W. M., and Boardman, I. Advances in channel compensation for SVM speaker recognition, in *Proc. ICASSP*, pp. 1:629–632, 2005.

Sonmez, K., Zheng, J., Shriberg, E., Kajarekar, S., Ferrer, L., and Stolcke, A. Modeling nerfs for speaker recognition, in *Proc. Odyssey*, pp. 51–56, 2004.

Stolcke, A., Ferrer, L., Kajarekar, S., Shriberg, E., and Venkataraman, A. MLLR transforms as features in speaker recognition, in *Proc. Eurospeech*, pp. 2425–2428, 2005.

Thiruvaran, T., Ambikairajah, E., and Epps, J. Extraction of FM components from speech signals using an all-pole model, *IET Electronics Letters* **44**, 6, 449–450, 2008.

Vapnik, V. *The Nature of Statistical Learning Theory* (Springer-Verlag), 1995.

Vogt, R. and Sridharan, S. Explicit modelling of session variability for speaker verification, *Computer Speech and Language* **22**, 17–38, 2008.

You, C.-H., Lee, K.-A., and Li, H. A GMM supervector kernel with the Bhattacharyya distance for SVM based speaker recognition, in *Proc. ICASSP*, pp. 4221–4224, 2009.

Zhu, D., Ma, B., and Li, H. Using MAP estimation for feature transformation for speaker recognition, in *Proc. Interspeech*, pp. 849–852, 2008.

Chapter 2

DISTINCTIVE FEATURES IN THE REPRESENTATION OF SPEECH AND ACOUSTIC CORRELATES

Jeung-Yoon Choi
School of Electrical & Electronic Engineering
Yonsei University, Seoul, Korea
jychoi@yonsei.ac.kr

2.1 Introduction

Speech communication may be broadly described as a process that conveys ideas between speakers and listeners, using sound that can be produced by the human articulatory system. Generally, a speaker formulates a message in his or her mind and manipulates articulators in his or her vocal tract to produce speech sounds. This acoustic signal is radiated through the air and is picked up by the auditory system of a listener, and the message is decoded from the speech signal. In order to communicate between each other, both the speaker and the listener must have a common representation of speech. This representation should allow speech information to be easily "encoded" during speech production and "decoded" during speech perception.

The representation of an utterance of speech has been described at various levels. Higher levels may include semantic and syntactic information, and lower levels may specify lexical and segmental information. At the lowest level, a *segment*, or more commonly, a *phoneme*, is a speech unit such as the consonant /t/ or the vowel /aa/. A segment is specified in an efficient manner by a set of *distinctive features*, or simply, *features*, which describe the characteristics of the segment (Fant, 1973; Halle, 1992). These abstract linguistic units termed segments have been found to have corresponding *landmarks* in the speech signal, which indicate when and how a segment has been produced. Landmarks are generally manifested as maxima/minima or discontinuities in the speech signal, and can be interpreted to yield a subset of distinctive features related to broad classes of articulation types, for example, vowels or consonants. Further *acoustic correlates*, or *acoustic cues*, for extracting the remaining distinctive features for the segment can be found around the landmarks (Stevens, 1998). Often during speech production, the features of a segment may be modified due to contextual effects (Chomsky and Halle, 1968). The process of extracting and marking landmarks and features from a speech signal using machines is called *labeling*. Incorporating distinctive features into segments, and further, into *words*, constitutes the first steps in designing speech recognition systems that make use of distinctive features. Such speech recognition systems are often termed *knowledge-based* speech recognition systems.

There has been an effort in recent years to construct speech recognition systems based on distinctive features and acoustic correlates, as described in this chapter. Such a knowledge-based speech recognition system will begin by attempting to extract the presence of landmarks in a speech signal, i.e., *landmark detection*. Next, distinctive features from the speech signal will be found by searching for acoustic cues around landmarks. The extracted distinctive features will then be consolidated into segments. These segments will not always be directly identifiable as canonical phonemes; further processing to deduce any modifications that may have occurred, and to infer the underlying phonemes, will be required next. These segments will then be integrated into word units. This process has been termed *lexical access*. To find higher level structures, and finally to deduce the meaning of an utterance, the application of grammatical parsing and semantic analysis methods will need to be implemented as well. Methods related to finding higher level structures, however, are beyond the scope of what can be covered here, and the reader is referred to related literature.

In this chapter, a description of the distinctive feature representation of speech is presented, followed by the detailed descriptions of corresponding acoustic cues that can be extracted from the speech signal to infer the presence of these features. In the last section, several common forms of variation in the speech signal are described in terms of feature modifications, as an illustration of the ease of explicitly describing variations that occur in speech using distinctive features.

2.2 The Distinctive Feature Representation of Speech

Distinctive features describe a segment of speech, and can be thought of abstractly as being arranged in a column for a particular segment. Although there is some controversy over the exact list of distinctive features that describe speech, we adopt here a generally used set that is closely related to the articulatory processes that occur during speech production. Standard features for segments in English are shown in Tables 2.1 and 2.2. The phonetic symbols mainly follow the ARPABET convention. The distinctive features that describe a segment can be classified into three types: articulator-free features, articulator features, and articulator-bound features.

2.2.1 *Articulator-free features*

Articulator-free features describe the type of sound being produced — vowels, glides, consonants, and the particular types of consonants. There are six articulator-free

Table 2.1: Standard distinctive feature sets for vowels and glides in English

symbol	iy	ih	ey	eh	ae	aa	ao	ow	ah	uw	uh	rr	ex	au	ai	oi	h	w	y	r
Vowel	+	+	+	+	+	+	+	+	+	+	+	+	+	+	+	+				
Glide														+	+	+	+	+	+	+
Consonant																				
Sonorant																				
Continuant																				
Strident																				
Stiff																				
Slack																				
Spread																	+			
Constricted																				
Advanced Tongue Root	+	−	+	−	−	−	−	+	−	+	−			−	−	−		+	+	
Constricted Tongue Root			−	−	−	+	+	−	−	−	−			+	+	+				
Nasal																				
Body																				
Blade																				
Lips																				
High	+	+	−	−	−	−	−	−	−	+	+	−	−	−	+	+		+	+	−
Low	−	−	−	−	+	+	+	−	−	−	−	−	−	+	−	−				
Back	−	−	−	−	−	+	+	+	+	+	+	+		+	−	−		+	−	
Anterior																				
Distributed																				
Lateral																				
Rhotic												+									+
Round							+	+		+	+			+		+		+		

Table 2.2: Standard distinctive feature sets for consonants in English

symbol	l	m	n	ng	v	dh	z	zh	f	th	s	sh	b	d	g	p	t	k	dj	ch
Vowel																				
Glide																				
Consonant	+	+	+	+	+	+	+	+	+	+	+	+	+	+	+	+	+	+	+	+
Sonorant	+	+	+	+	−	−	−	−	−	−	−	−	−	−	−	−	−	−	−	−
Continuant	−	−	−	−	+	+	+	+	+	+	+	+	−	−	−	−	−	−	− +	− +
Strident					+	−	+	+	+	−	+	+							+	+
Stiff									+	+	+	+				+	+	+		+
Slack					+	+	+	+					+	+	+				+	
Spread																				
Constricted																				
Advanced Tongue Root																				
Constricted Tongue Root																				
Nasal	−	+	+	+																
Body				+											+			+		
Blade	+		+			+	+	+		+	+	+		+			+		+	+
Lips		+			+				+				+			+				
High				+											+			+		
Low				−											−			−		
Back	+			+											+			+		
Anterior	+		+			+	+	−		+	+	−		+			+		−	−
Distributed	−		−			+	−	+		+	−	+		−			−		+	+
Lateral	+																			
Rhotic	−																			
Round	−	−			−				−				−			−				

features: *vowel, glide, consonant, sonorant, continuant*, and *strident*. Vowels are marked [+vowel] and glides (e.g., /h/, /w/, /r/, etc.) are marked [+glide]. In this scheme, sounds are classified as glides if they are produced with narrowing in the vocal tract that is not significant enough to produce turbulence or a complete blockage in the oral tract. If the narrowing is significant, the sound is classified as a consonant. Consonants, in addition to being [+consonant] (or [+cons]), are further specified using the remaining articulator-free features. The liquid /l/ and the nasal sounds /m/, /n/, and /ng/ are [+sonorant, −continuant] (or [+son, −cont]). Sonorant consonants are accompanied by sustained vibration in the vocal folds. Continuant consonants do not show a complete constriction along the midsagittal plane of the vocal tract. Strident consonants produce turbulence noise that is comparable in amplitude to surrounding vowels. Fricatives (e.g., /v/, /dh/, /z/, /zh/, etc.) are [−sonorant, +continuant]. Of the fricatives, the alveolar and palatal fricatives /z/, /zh/, /s/, and /sh/ are additionally assigned the [+strident] (or [+strid]) feature. Stops (e.g., /b/, /t/, etc.) are [−sonorant, −continuant]. Affricates have the attributes of both stops and fricatives, and are [−sonorant, −/+continuant]; in addition, they are also [+strident]. The articulator-free features are also called *manner features*.

2.2.2 *Articulator features*

Articulator features describe which articulator is used to produce the sound. There are seven articulators that may be specified: *vocal folds, glottis, pharynx, soft palate*, (tongue) *body*, (tongue) *blade*, and the *lips*. The last three articulators function as *primary articulators* for consonants, and specify the location of the constriction in the oral tract. These articulators indicate the *place of articulation*, or *place*, for a segment. The lips are used to produce labial sounds, such as /b/, /m/, /f/, etc. The [+blade] feature is assigned to sounds produced using the tip of the tongue (e.g., /t/, /z/, /l/, etc.). These include the *dental* (produced behind the front teeth), *alveolar* (produced at the alveolar ridge), and *palatal* (produced at the roof of the mouth behind the alveolar ridge) sounds. Sounds produced using the body of the tongue, such as /g/ and /ng/ are [+body]. The remaining four articulators are used to further define the sound produced, and may be regarded as *secondary articulators* for consonants. For example, the vocal folds and glottis are used to characterize voicing in consonants. The [+pharynx] features may be used to describe the difference between tense and lax sounds, although it is not distinctive in consonants in English. When the soft palate, or *velum*, is lowered, as in the nasal consonants /m/, /n/, and /ng/, the feature [+soft palate] is used. The secondary articulators are usually indicated only by marking their associated articulator-bound features. In this case, instead of [+soft palate], the segment may simply be marked [+nasal], or [−nasal], depending on whether the soft palate is lowered or raised, respectively. Similarly, the [+pharynx] features may be marked with relevant values for [advanced tongue root] and [constricted tongue root] (or [atr] and [ctr]). The [glottis] feature is equivalently marked by [spread] and [constricted] (or [constr]); the [vocal folds] feature is marked by [stiff] and [slack].

2.2.3 *Articulator-bound features*

Articulator-bound features specifically describe how the articulators are used to produce a sound. [+Round] denotes rounded lips. [+Anterior] (or [+ant]) denotes tongue blade contact with the roof of the mouth anterior to the alveolar ridge, and [+distributed] (or [+dist]) shows that a broad portion of the tongue blade makes contact. The anterior and distributed features are used to distinguish the [+blade] consonants into the dental, alveolar, and palatal consonants. Configuration of the tongue blade so that air is able to flow around the constriction it makes is described by the feature [+lateral] (or [+lat]), and rounding it to produce sounds such as /r/ is marked [+rhotic] (or [+rhot]). The features [anterior], [distributed], [lateral], and [rhotic] are associated with the [+blade] articulator feature. The features [+high], [+low], and [+back] describe the general position of the tongue in the oral cavity, and are associated with the [+body] articulator. [+Advanced tongue root] and [+constricted tongue root] show the positioning of the pharynx, and are associated roughly with non-back, tense vowels and with back vowels, respectively. Nasal segments, in which sounds are produced with the passage into the nasal tract open, are [+nasal]. An open glottis is [+spread], while [+constricted] shows a glottis that is pressed together. [+Stiff] and [+slack] describe the state of the vocal folds, and are associated with descriptions of consonant voicing.

2.2.4 *Prosody and stress features*

In addition to the articulator-related features above, the features related to *prosody* and *stress* describe how syllables are emphasized or grouped into phrase units. A *syllable* consists of one or more segments, and can be divided into a *nucleus*, and possibly an *onset* or a *coda*. A syllabic segment, which is usually a vowel, forms the nucleus of a syllable. (Syllabic segments also include syllabic liquids and syllabic nasals, such as the second syllables in "bottle" and "button," respectively.) Consonants and/or glides constitute the onset or coda; segments that appear before the nucleus make up the onset, and those that appear after the nucleus form the coda. Prosody features include markers for *accent* and *boundary* levels. As for stress features, three degrees of stress may be labeled: [+stressed, −reduced], [−stressed, −reduced], and [−stressed, +reduced], in order of emphasis. The vowels in the word "potato" are, in order, [−stressed, +reduced], [+stressed, −reduced], and [−stressed, −reduced]. Prosody and stress features are usually assigned to the syllabic segment that form the nucleus, but acoustic cues for these features may be found in the onset and coda, as well as in the nucleus. Acoustic cues for prosody and stress are currently being studied actively, but a discussion of these cues is not presented in this chapter.

2.3 Acoustics Correlates of Distinctive Features

This section describes the acoustic correlates of distinctive features that appear in the speech signal. Acoustic correlates of articulator-free features give rise to various landmarks in the signal (Liu, 1996). Examination of the signal around these landmarks allows the extraction of articulator and articulator-bound features that are associated with the articulator-free features.

2.3.1 *Landmarks*

Vowels are produced with no narrowing of the vocal tract (maximally open), approximating a resonant tube. For vowels, spectral energy is concentrated in frequency bands, called *formants*. A vowel landmark is placed at a time when the amplitude of the first formant (F1) is a maximum (Howitt, 2000). The articulator-free feature for a vowel is marked [+vowel]. Diphthongs, such as /ai/, /au/, and /oi/, exhibit different vowel qualities at the start and at the end of the sound. These sounds may be described as vowels with *off-glides*. A separate off-glide landmark is thus assigned to a time near the end of the sound. This event is marked [+glide], and is assigned articulator-bound features associated with the off-glide.

Glides are produced with an intermediate narrowing of the vocal tract, so that there are no abrupt discontinuities from an adjacent vowel. Glide landmarks are chosen at times where the signal amplitude becomes a minimum (Sun, 1996). The [+glide] feature is marked for those times.

Consonants are produced with an extreme narrowing or complete closing of the vocal tract, resulting in abrupt changes in the signal when the vocal tract closes (*closure*) and opens (*release*). The region between the closure and the release is also called the *closure interval*. Accordingly, there are usually two places in the signal that correspond to an underlying consonant. These times are marked [+consonantal]. The sonorant consonants show a continuation of quasi-periodic low frequency energy during the closure interval ([+sonorant]); the closure and release themselves are signaled by an abrupt decrease in high frequency energy ([−continuant]).

A fricative shows a dropoff of low-frequency energy ([−sonorant]), but is characterized by the continuation of high-frequency "noise" (*frication*) throughout the closure interval ([+continuant]).

Stops also show a dropoff in low-frequency energy ([−sonorant]), but in addition, there is a sharp drop in high frequencies ([−continuant]) — a silence-like region after the closure and an abrupt burst of energy at the release can be observed.

Affricates are similar to a combination of stops and fricatives: they are produced with a complete closure, a partial release (burst release), and a complete release (frication release). The first two landmarks are [−sonorant, −continuant], and the final one is [−sonorant, +continuant]. If the amplitude of the frication is comparable to the amplitude of adjacent vowels, it is marked as [+strident]. The articulator and articulator-bound features are the same for landmarks produced by the same consonant.

Other events of interest in the signal, which are not landmarks, include voicing onset/offset, soft palate opening/closing, and the regions of glottalization (forceful constriction of the larynx). Although these do not classify as landmarks (they do not specify any underlying segment), they can be used to infer changes in the configuration of the secondary articulators.

2.3.2 *Acoustic correlates of articulator-bound features*

The acoustic correlates for articulator-bound features may be extracted by examining the speech signal around the landmarks corresponding to the related articulator-free features. The various types of sounds — vowels, glides, and consonants — have acoustic correlates that are found in specific spectral and temporal regions in the speech signal. Representative acoustic correlates for phonemes in English are described below.

2.3.2.1 *Vowels*

Vowels are associated with one [+vowel] landmark, with an additional [+glide] landmark for diphthongs. The articulator-bound features for vowels are largely found by examining the F1 (first formant) and F2 (second formant) values at the landmarks. The overall range of formant values for the speaker should be taken into account when determining the features.

A low F1 corresponds to the feature [+high] and a high F1 to [+low]. An intermediate value of F1 is marked [−high, −low]. The feature [+back] is marked for low values of F2, and [−back] for mid or high values of F2. Vowels produced with an advanced or constricted tongue root are called *tense* vowels; those that are not are called *lax* vowels. Tense vowels have formant values that are relatively higher or lower than average values for the speaker. Of these, the [−low] vowels are marked [+atr], while the [+low, +back] vowels are marked [+ctr] (Syrdal and Gopal, 1986).

The vowels /ao/, /ow/, /uw/, and /uh/ are produced with the lips rounded, and are denoted [+round]. The vowel /rr/ has a very low F3, similar to the glide /r/, and the tongue blade features are marked for [+rhotic]. The vowel /ex/ (schwa) is typically very short and has neutral formant values; it is left unmarked for the feature [back]. The features for the glide landmark in diphthongs are similar to the glides /w/ and /y/, with the difference that off-glides are [−atr].

In addition to the features discussed above, the features [spread], [constr], and [nasal] may additionally be marked for a vowel landmark. An aspirated vowel exhibits noisy formant structure similar to the glide /h/, and may be marked [+spread]. A glottalized vowel, which is expected to show irregular pitch, is [+constr]. A nasalized vowel, with is expected to have an extra pole-zero pair around 1 KHz due to nasal coupling, is [+nasal] (Chen, 1997).

2.3.2.2 *Glides*

Glides are marked with a [+glide] landmark, and that region is first examined for formant values. Some glides are produced with the tongue body as well as another articulator. In this case, both sets of articulator-bound features are marked.

The glide /h/ is produced with the glottis spread open, and is recognized by a characteristic "noise-like" spectrum, with energy around the F3 and F4 regions comparable in amplitude to that around F1 and F2. This sound is marked as [+spread].

The glide /w/ has low F1 and F2, corresponding to the features [+high, −low, +back]. The very low formant values point to the [+atr] feature. This segment is also produced with rounded lips, marked [+round]. It is similar to the tense back vowel /uw/.

The glide /y/ has very low F1 and high F2, so that the features [+high, −low, −back, +atr] are marked. A high F3 suggests articulation with the tongue blade; high F2 and F3 are consistent with the configuration [−ant, +dist]. This segment is similar to the tense high vowel /iy/ (Espy-Wilson, 1992).

Lax variants of the segments /w/ and /y/ appear as off-glides in the diphthongs /au/, /ai/, and /oi/. Off-glide segments are [−atr].

The glide /r/ is recognized by an extremely low F3. At the same time, F1 has an intermediate value, and F2 is low. The segment is produced with a narrowing using a rounded tongue. Air is able to flow over the constriction, but not around it. The features are thus marked [−high, −low, +back], [−ant, −dist, −lat, +rhot].

In addition to these standard glide segments in English, other glide sounds are frequently produced as the modifications of consonant segments. For example, a glottal stop (which may be written /q/) may be produced in place of an unvoiced syllable-final stop consonant. The segment is produced by pressing the glottis together, so that the formant structure is visible, but the pitch is irregular. A glottal stop is marked [+constr]. Another example is the flapped /t/ (which may be written /dd/ or /dx/). The tongue blade briefly contacts the alveolar ridge, but there is no true constriction of the vocal tract, and should be denoted [+glide]. This articulation is similar to that for /r/, but F3 is not as low. This segment is also typically very short in duration. The articulator-bound features for the flapped /t/ may be marked [−ant, −dist].

2.3.2.3 *Sonorants*

Sonorant consonants usually exhibit one closure and one release landmark, similar to fricatives and stops.

The liquid segment /l/, with a low F1 and F2, is marked with the features [+blade, +ant, −dist]. It is marked [−nasal], to emphasize that it is a non-nasal sonorant consonant.

The nasal consonants are produced by lowering the soft palate ([+nasal]) while forming a constriction with a primary articulator. Nasal consonants show a sudden decrease in high-frequency energy and a broadening of the F1 bandwidth during the closure interval (Chen, 2000). The three nasal consonants in English differ in the place of articulation. The labial /m/ is produced with the lips and is marked [+lips], [−round]. The alveolar /n/ is marked [+blade], [+ant, −dist]. The velar /ng/ is marked [+body], [+high, −low, +back], but the feature [back] for the velar is variable, according to context.

The place of articulation can be found by examining formant transitions into the closure and out of the release. Typically, a labial segment shows F1 and F2 falling into and rising out of the segment. An alveolar segment has a falling F1, but the F2 heads toward a locus at about 1.8 KHz at the closure. A velar segment shows a characteristic "pinching" of F2 and F3 into and out of the closure interval.

2.3.2.4 *Fricatives*

Fricatives usually produce one closure and one release landmark.

Fricatives are associated with "noise"-like high-frequency energy (frication) during the interval from the closure to the release.

There are roughly four distinct places of articulation for fricatives, resulting in labial (/f/ and /v/), dental (/th/ and /dh/), alveolar (/s/ and /z/), and palatal (/sh/ and /zh/) fricatives. There are no velar fricatives in English. Usually, only the alveolar and palatal fricatives are [+strid].

The place of articulation may be found by examining formant transitions at the closure and release, similar to nasal consonants (Kewley-Port, 1982). This is especially effective for distinguishing between sounds produced with the lips as opposed to produced with the tongue blade. The place of articulation may also be determined by looking at the spectral distribution of frication energy during the closure interval. The spectrum for the labial ([+lips], [−round]) segments show frication energy that is lower in all frequencies in relation to adjacent vowels and has a relatively flat spectral shape. The burst spectrum for a dental ([+blade], [+ant, +dist]) segment also has low-spectral energy with a slight concentration around F5 or F6. Alveolar ([+blade], [+ant, −dist]) bursts show energy concentration around F4 or F5. Bursts for palatal ([+blade], [−ant, +dist]) fricatives show the most energy at the lower F3 or F4 regions (Stevens, 2000).

In addition to the place of articulation, fricatives are distinguished by the voicing features [stiff] and [slack]. Voiced sounds ([+slack]) show a relatively long continuation of low-frequency energy near the fundamental frequency (F0) of the speaker for a portion of the closure interval. Voiceless sounds ([+stiff]) have a sharp falloff of low frequency energy (Choi, 1999).

2.3.2.5 *Stops*

Similar to fricatives, stop consonants also produce one closure and one release landmark.

The stop consonants are distinguished by place of articulation and by voicing. As described above for fricatives, the place of articulation is found by tracing the formant transitions into the closure and out of the release. It can also be found by looking at the burst spectrum at the release (Sussman *et al.*, 1991; Suchato, 2004). The characteristic spectra for labial, alveolar, and velar stops are similar to those for the frication spectra for the respective fricatives. Similar to fricatives, labial stops are marked [+lips], [−round]. Alveolars are marked [+blade], [+ant, −dist], and velars are marked [+body], [+high, −low, +back]. The [back] feature may vary depending on context.

Voicing in stop consonants can also be determined by the rate of decrease of fundamental frequency energy around the closure and release landmarks, as described for fricatives. The corresponding [+slack] or [+stiff] feature is marked for voiced and unvoiced stops, respectively. An additional cue for detecting the voicing features for stops is the degree of aspiration after the release. If aspiration noise (as for /h/) is observable, the segment is marked [+spread], which is another marker for unvoiced stops in English. If aspiration is present, there will be an interval of time between the burst release and the onset of voicing of the next vowel. This time interval is called the *voice onset time* (VOT). The VOT will be longer at the release of unvoiced stops than those of voiced stops.

2.3.2.6 *Affricates*

Affricate consonants are associated with one closure and two releases, the first being a burst release, and the second, a frication release.

There are two affricates in English, /dj/ and /ch/. Both can be thought of as consisting of a modified alveolar stop followed by a palatal fricative. Accordingly, both affricates are assigned the features [+strid, +blade]. All the affricate landmarks are marked [−ant, +dist]. The initial alveolar stop becomes more "backed," so that the affricate is mainly considered a palatal segment. The formant transitions and the burst and frication spectra may be examined to confirm the place of articulation and the corresponding articulator-bound features.

The two affricates differ in voicing, and this is determined by examining the falloff of fundamental frequency energy at the closure, as described for fricatives and stops. The features are marked [+slack] or [+stiff] as before, for /dj/ and /ch/, respectively.

2.3.3 *Modifications*

The distinctive features extracted from analysis of the speech signal will not always be identical to the standard set of features for English phonemes. Modifications may occur in the articulator, articulator-bound, or articulator-free features. A change in the articulator-free features means that the landmarks for that segment have been changed. Features may be deleted or inserted, or a set may be substituted for another. Similarly, a landmark itself may be deleted or inserted, or changed to another type (Zue *et al.*, 1990; Gow Jr., 2001). Several examples are discussed below.

An example of distinctive feature deletion occurs in the instance where a tense vowel such as /iy/ is "reduced" to a lax vowel such as /ih/, as in an utterance such as "··· today we will ···," where the /iy/ in "we" is often pronounced as /ih/.

Feature insertion can occur when the vowel /rr/ becomes glottalized ([+constr]) in the word "water" for an utterance that ends in "··· the water." The remaining features for the /rr/ are unchanged from the standard form.

In the utterance "··· balloon before ···," the final nasal in "balloon" may be modified into a labial nasal, due to assimilation effects of the following labial /b/. In this case, the articulator and articulator-bound feature set [+blade, +and, −dist] undergoes substitution into the feature set [+lips, −round].

A larger change may be observed in an utterance such as "··· small and Debby ···," where the sequence of landmarks consisting of the /n/ release, the /d/ closure, /d/ release, and the subsequent /d/ closure occurring across the word boundary between the two words in "and Debby" are all unobservable in casual pronunciation of this utterance.

As an example of landmark insertion, a glottal stop (marked by a glide landmark) can appear across the word boundary between the two words in the utterance "··· woman in ···."

Landmark substitution can also occur in cases such as in the utterance "··· balloon before ···," where the [+consonantal] /l/ closure in "balloon" may be modified into a lateral glide. The /l/ release usually retains the [+consonantal] feature since it appears before a [+stressed] vowel, i.e., the /uw/, in the word "balloon."

2.4 Speech Recognition Based on Distinctive Features Representation of Speech and Acoustic Correlates

There has been an effort in recent years to construct speech recognition systems based on distinctive features and acoustic correlates, as described in this chapter (Bitar and Espy-Wilson, 1996; Salomon *et al.*, 2003; Hasegawa-Johnson *et al.*, 2005; Espy-Wilson *et al.*, 2007; Juneja and Espy-Wilson, 2008). Such a knowledge-based speech recognition system will begin by attempting to extract the presence of landmarks in a speech signal, i.e., landmark detection. Then, distinctive features from the speech signal will be found by searching for acoustic cues around landmarks. The extracted distinctive features will then be consolidated into segments. These segments will not always be of the canonical form presented in Tables 2.1 and 2.2; further processing to deduce the modifications that have occurred, and to infer the underlying phonemes will be required next. These segments will then be integrated into word units. This process has been termed *lexical access* (Stevens, 2002). To find higher level structures, and finally to deduce the meaning of an utterance, application of grammatical parsing and semantic analysis methods will need to be implemented as well. These methods are beyond the scope of what can be covered here, and the reader is referred to related literature.

2.5 Summary

A description of speech based on distinctive features and their acoustic correlates has been outlined in this chapter. The distinctive features are grouped into articulator-free, articulator, and articulator-bound features, and describe the articulatory processes that occur when the sounds are produced. These features can be extracted from the speech signal and integrated into segments to form words; this process forms the basis of knowledge-based speech recognition systems. Further higher-level processing will be needed to find syntactic and semantic information. It is hoped that further research into such systems will lead to efficient and robust methods for recognizing speech.

References

Bitar, N. and Espy-Wilson, C. Knowledge based parameters for HMM speech recognition, in *Proc. ICASSP*, pp. 1:29–32, 1996.

Chen, M. Y. Acoustic correlates of English and French nasalized vowels, *J. Acoust. Soc. Am.* **102**, 2360–2370, 1997.

Chen, M. Y. Nasal detection model for a knowledge-based speech recognition system, in *Proc. ICSLP*, pp. 4:636–639, 2000.

Choi, J. Y. *Detection of consonant voicing: a module for a hierarchical speech recognition system*, Ph.D. thesis, Massachusetts Institute of Technology, MA, USA, 1999.

Chomsky, N. and Halle, M. *The Sound Pattern of English* (Harper and Row, New York), 1968.

Espy-Wilson, C. Acoustic measures for linguistic features distinguishing the semivowels / w j r l / in American English, *J. Acoust. Soc. Am.* **92**, 736–757, 1992.

Espy-Wilson, C., Pruthi, T., Juneja, A., and Deshmukh, O. Landmark-based approach to speech recognition: an alternative to HMMs, in *Proc. Interspeech*, pp. 886–889, 2007.

Fant, G. *Speech Sounds and Features* (MIT Press, Cambridge, MA.), 1973.

Gow Jr., D. W. Assimilation and anticipation in continuous spoken word recognition, *J. Memory Lang.* **45**, 133–159, 2001.

Halle, M. Phonetic features, in W. Bright (ed.), *International Encyclopedia of Linguistics* (Oxford University Press, New York), pp. 207–212, 1992.

Hasegawa-Johnson, M., Baker, J., Borys, S., Chen, K., Coogan, E., Greenberg, S., Juneja, A., Kirchoff, K., Livescu, K., Mohan, S., Muller, J., Sonmez, K., and Wang, T. Landmark-based speech recognition: report of the 2004 Johns

Hopkins summer workshop, in *Proc. IEEE Int. Conf. Acoustics, Speech, and Signal Processing*, pp. 213–216, 2005.

Howitt, A. W. *Automatic syllable detection for vowel landmarks*, Ph.D. thesis, Massachusetts Institute of Technology, MA, USA, 2000.

Juneja, A. and Espy-Wilson, C. A probabilistic framework for landmark detection based on phonetic features for automatic speech recognition, *J. Acoust. Soc. Am.* **123**, 1154–1168, 2008.

Kewley-Port, D. Measurement of formant transitions in naturally produced stop consonant-vowel syllables, *J. Acoust. Soc. Am.* **72**, 379–389, 1982.

Liu, S. A. Landmark detection for distinctive feature-based speech recognition, *J. Acoust. Soc. Am.* **100**, 3417–3430, 1996.

Salomon, A., Espy-Wilson, C., and Deshmukh, O. Detection of speech landmarks: use of temporal information, *J. Acoust. Soc. Am.* **115**(3), 1296–1305, 2003.

Stevens, K. N. *Acoustic Phonetics* (MIT Press, Cambridge, MA), 1998.

Stevens, K. N. Diverse acoustic cues at consonantal landmarks, *Phonetica* **57**, pp. 139–151, 2000.

Stevens, K. N. Toward a model for lexical access based on acoustic landmarks and distinctive features, *J. Acoust. Soc. Am.* **111**, 1872–1891, 2002.

Suchato, A. *Classification of stop consonant place of articulation*, Ph.D. thesis, Massachusetts Institute of Technology, MA, USA, 2004.

Sun, W. *Analysis and interpretation of glide characteristics in pursuit of an algorithm for recognition*, Master's thesis, Massachusetts Institute of Technology, MA. USA, 1996.

Sussman, H. M., McCaffrey, H., and Matthews, S. An investigation of locus equations as a source of relational invariance for stop place categorization, *J. Acoust. Soc. Am.* **90**, 1309–1325, 1991.

Syrdal, A. K. and Gopal, H. S. A perceptual model of vowel recognition based on the auditory representation of American English vowels, *J. Acoust. Soc. Am.* **79**, 1086–1100, 1986.

Zue, V. W., Glass, J. R., Goodine, D., Phillips, M., and Seneff, S. The SUMMIT speech recognition system: phonological modeling and lexical access, in *Proc. IEEE Int. Conf. Acoustics, Speech, and Signal Processing*, pp. 49–52, 1990.

Chapter 3

SPEECH CHARACTERIZATION AND FEATURE EXTRACTION FOR SPEAKER RECOGNITION

Julien Epps[*,†,‡] and Eliathamby Ambikairajah[*,†,§]

*School of Electrical Engineering and Telecommunications
University of New South Wales, Australia

†ATP Laboratory, National ICT Australia, Eveleigh, Australia

‡j.epps@ee.unsw.edu.au

§ambi@ee.unsw.edu.au

3.1 Speech Production and Characterization

Spoken language abounds in a variety of types of information: the words themselves, the speaker's identity, the language, the emotion expressed by the speaker, and other non-linguistic cues concerning the speaker's current mental state and intent. When performing recognition of speaker identity, some of this information is speaker specific and must be parameterized efficiently to achieve good classification performance, while the remaining information represents a source of unwanted variability, which must be modeled, compensated for, or removed. In this chapter, we focus on where speaker-specific information resides in the speech signal and how it can be captured in a compact set of features, while modeling and classification are discussed in Chapter 1 of this book.

3.1.1 The source-filter model of speech production

The simplest model of speech production describes the speech sound pressure wave $x(t)$ as the output of a filter with impulse response $h(t)$, excited by an input source $e(t)$ (Fant, 1960)

$$x(t) = h(t) * e(t) \tag{3.1}$$

as shown in Fig. 3.1.

The vocal tract filter is physically determined by the shape of the vocal tract acoustic tube, while the excitation is physically determined by the variations in air pressure produced by the vibrations of the vocal cords. This model is significant for a number of reasons, of which perhaps the most relevant here is that by modeling

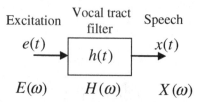

Fig. 3.1.   The source-filter model of speech production.

the vocal tract filter, the excitation signal can be estimated. The excitation and vocal tract filter

(1) have important roles in speech production, related to the pitch of the speech signal and the sound being produced, respectively; and
(2) can be compactly parameterized, so that to a reasonable approximation, speech can be accurately characterized using just a few tens of parameters for short durations.

During speech production in which the vocal cords are vibrating, known as voiced speech, the rate of vibration determines the fundamental frequency $F_0 = 1/T_0$ of the speech, and hence the pitch perceived by a listener. A simplistic but not inaccurate model of the excitation source for voiced speech is a periodic impulse train

$$e(t) = \sum_{k=0}^{\infty} \delta(t - kT_0) \tag{3.2}$$

whose spectrum $E(\omega)$ is harmonic with fundamental frequency $2\pi F_0$. During speech production in which the vocal cords are not vibrating, known as unvoiced speech, the excitation is often represented as white noise, which physically corresponds to air passing through a constriction at some point in the vocal tract.

Acoustic resonances due to the shape of the vocal tract give rise to peaks in the magnitude spectrum of the vocal tract filter $|H(\omega)|$, which can be observed as broad peaks in the amplitude spectrum of speech $|X(\omega)|$ when the filter is excited by $E(\omega)$. The frequencies of these peaks are known as formant frequencies $F_1, F_2, F_3, \ldots$, which comprise one method of parametric description of the vocal tract filter shape. Another theoretically and practically important parametric description of $h(t)$ can be obtained via linear prediction (Atal, 1974). Changes in the formant frequencies, in particular F_1 and F_2, are well understood to account for the different sounds perceived during speech. The effects of different pitch and formant frequencies for voiced and unvoiced speech can be observed in Fig. 3.2(a–d).

Although historically some researchers have attempted to deconvolve the speech signal directly into $h(t)$ and $e(t)$ using homomorphic deconvolution (Oppenheim and Schafer, 1968), the process of estimating the vocal tract filter can be simplified by assuming that the excitation spectrum $|E(\omega)|$ is flat, which is reasonable for either the periodic impulse train or white noise models discussed above. Then, it is

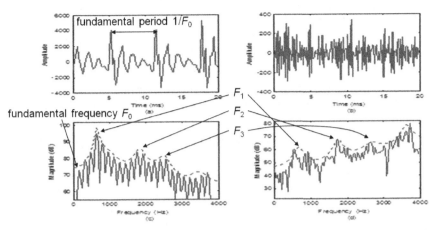

Fig. 3.2. Examples of (a) voiced and (b) unvoiced speech signals, and their spectra (c) and (d) respectively, with a 10th order linear prediction filter shown as an approximation to $|H(\omega)|$ (dashed line).

sufficient to describe $H(\omega)$ in terms of the (amplitude) spectral envelope of $|X(\omega)|$, which can be determined from the Fourier transform. A further critical assumption is required here, however, since speech is clearly a time-varying signal. In order to permit use of the Fourier transform generally an assumption of local stationarity is applied, in practise by analysing short (20–30 ms) frames of speech. This assumption is weak during transients (i.e., the onset of the word "don't"), but more reasonable during sustained voiced or unvoiced sounds (e.g., during /o/ in "don't"), for which it has been shown that vocal tract articulators are not physically capable of changing much faster than every 20–30 ms (Davis and Mermelstein, 1980).

3.1.2 *Speaker-specific characteristics of speech*

Differences in speech production arise due to both variation in physiology and in learned speech traits. An example of the former is the scaling of the frequency axis due to vocal tract length, e.g., producing formant frequencies approximately 20% higher in female than male speakers. An example of the latter is the variations to the vowel sounds produced by speakers with different accents. Of interest here are variations that are large across different speakers but small within individual speakers.

Relatively few studies have investigated intraspeaker and interspeaker variations in the physical properties of the speech production system and the corresponding effects on the speech signal. A small-scale study by Kitamura *et al.* (2005) of the hypopharyngeal cavities (the laryngeal tube and piriform fossa, located just above the vocal cords) found that during speech these vary significantly between speakers and very little within individual speakers' speech. This effect was also reflected in the speech spectra, particularly those above about 2.5 kHz.

Historically, the short-term speech spectral envelope became the primary basis for speaker-recognition features (Campbell, 1997; Doddington, 1985), due to its improved performance over features derived from other information, such as the fundamental frequency. A primary problem for speaker recognition is that characterizations of the speech signal in terms of vocal tract filter models do not exclusively distinguish speaker identity; they all contain other information, in particular phonetic information. Reynolds has even commented that there are no features that exclusively contain speaker-specific information (Reynolds and Rose, 1995).

Early speaker-recognition research recognized that long-term features contain speaker-specific attributes. Short-term features including pitch, intensity, formants and predictor coefficients (LP) were modeled as contours, which were successfully used to distinguish speakers (Rosenburg, 1976). Examples of more recent work of this kind include the use of prosodic information such as intonation (variation in F_0), which produced a 7–10% improvement in speaker-recognition accuracy when parameters from simple linear models of the long-term F_0 variation were employed jointly with cepstral features (Sönmez *et al.*, 1998).

In forensic speaker recognition, features are usually extracted manually or semi-manually, and must contain sufficient discrimination to facilitate decision-making in a legal context. Vocal cord-related features have been identified as significant, in particular the vibration rate (fundamental frequency F_0), which is relatively robust under noise or distortion, and the mode of vibration (e.g., "creaky" or "breathy") (Rose, 2002). Nasal consonants also receive interest, due to their dependence on the physical characteristics of the nasal cavity, which are rigid and specific to an individual (Rose, 2002). Vowel sounds from stressed syllables are identified as being less prone to within-speaker variation than those from unstressed syllables (Rose, 2002). Formant frequencies are typically used to characterize voiced speech for forensic purposes, and recently their time trajectories have been shown to be more sensitive to speaker identity than other features traditionally used in forensics (Morrison, 2009).

Psychoacoustic experiments present yet another interesting perspective on speaker recognition. A study of human speaker-identification accuracies for the vowel sound /a/ following modifications to F_0, the glottal wave and the vocal tract filter by Lavner *et al.* (2000) revealed that the shape of the glottal wave was a less important factor than other contributions, perhaps in contrast to the significance attributed to it in forensic speaker recognition. On the other hand, vocal tract characteristics appeared to have the strongest bearing on speaker identity (Lavner *et al.*, 2000). Shifting formant frequencies provided a significant degradation in listener identification accuracy, and in particular this was observed for F_3 and F_4 more than for F_1 and F_2 (Lavner *et al.*, 2000). It is reasonable to assume, as the authors suggest, that these higher formants are able to characterize speaker identity with fewer constraints from the phonetic content of the speech. A further significant result from this study is that the vowel sound for each speaker seemed to be sensitive to different features (Lavner *et al.*, 2000), suggesting that no single feature (known or as yet unknown) may generally be able to characterize speaker identity.

3.2 Feature Extraction

Having reviewed speaker-specific characteristics in speech, we now turn our attention to methods by which this information can be efficiently extracted and compactly represented. In this section, particular emphasis is given to acoustic feature extraction methods, due to their prevalence among contemporary state-of-the-art speaker-recognition systems.

3.2.1 *Voice activity detection*

Voice activity detectors (VADs) are a key component in most speech-processing applications, serving the purpose of segmenting the signal into speech and non-speech regions, of which the latter are discarded before subsequent processing.

Energy is an obvious feature for voice activity classification, and has been shown to outperform other features for voiced/silence classification as far back as 1976 (Atal and Rabiner, 1976). The key consideration in energy-based VADs then becomes the choice of energy threshold. In speaker-recognition systems, where test utterances may be very short and/or noisy, the threshold choice may be based on one or more of (1) retaining a specific minimum number of frames, to allow reasonable speaker modeling, (2) rejecting a predetermined percentage of frames ranked lowest using an energy criterion, and (3) rejecting all frames with energies below the maximum energy within the utterance minus a preset energy difference. It is also interesting to note that the energy of voiced speech is generally greater than that of unvoiced speech (Atal and Rabiner, 1976), so that a more severe choice of threshold will tend to have the effect of preserving mainly voiced speech frames.

An example of more sophisticated voice activity detection is the GSM VAD (Benyassine *et al.*, 1997), which employs log energy, lowband (0–1 kHz) log energy (large for voiced speech), zero-crossing rate (large for unvoiced speech), and line spectral frequencies, which are a transformation of linear prediction parameters, discussed below. These parameters are then compared with similar parameters extracted from background noise. Often the start of a speech recording contains only background noise, and can be used for this purpose. In the GSM VAD, "difference parameters" are calculated between parameter values extracted for each frame of speech and the background noise parameters. The resulting difference parameters are combined into a four-dimensional feature, and a multi-boundary initial voicing activity decision is made for a particular frame based on the position of the feature relative to 14 hyperplanes (constructed based on labeled training data).

Finally, decision smoothing is applied to ensure that the voicing decisions are conservative and match our intuitive understanding of speech activity, in particular to avoid "cutting off" voice-active frames too soon at the end of speech and to avoid isolated frames for which the voicing decision is inconsistent with that of the frames around them (Benyassine *et al.*, 1997). For example, if previous frames are found to be voice active and the energy of the current frame is sufficiently large, then the current frame is also labeled as voice active; alternatively if the previous 10 frames are found to be voice inactive and the energy of the current frame is similar, then it is also labeled as voice inactive.

3.2.2 *Acoustic features*

3.2.2.1 *Linear prediction-based features*

The acoustic resonances that give rise to the formants discussed in Sec. 3.2.1 can be modeled as a discrete-time all-pole filter:

$$H(z) = \frac{X(z)}{E(z)} = \frac{1}{1 + \sum_{k=1}^{p} a_k z^{-k}} \tag{3.3}$$

where $z = e^{j\theta}$, $\theta = \omega/f_s$ is the discrete-time frequency, f_s is the sampling frequency, a_k are real coefficients, and p is the model order. The acoustic resonances then correspond to conjugate pole-pair factors of $H(z)$, and the problem becomes one of estimating the a_k from the discrete-time (sampled) version of the speech signal $x(t)$. Taking the inverse z-transform of Eq. (3.3), we have

$$x[n] = -\sum_{k=1}^{p} a_k x[n-k] + e[n] \tag{3.4}$$

i.e., $x[n]$ can be approximated by an autoregressive process, where the excitation $e[n]$ is the "error" in the approximation. Since the parameters a_k are linear in $x[n-k]$, a least squares solution can be found by setting

$$\frac{\partial}{\partial a_m} E\{e^2[n]\} = 0 \tag{3.5}$$

under the assumption that the "error" term $e[n]$ is spectrally flat and Gaussian distributed. This produces p equations for $m = 1, 2, \ldots, p$:

$$E\{e^2[n]\} = E\{x[n]x[n-m]\} + \sum_{k=1}^{p} a_k E\{x[n-k]x[n-m]\}$$

$$= \gamma_{xx}[m] + \sum_{k=1}^{p} a_k \gamma_{xx}[m-k] \tag{3.6}$$

where $\gamma_{xx}[m]$ can be approximated by

$$\gamma_{xx}[m] \simeq \sum_{n=0}^{N-1-m} x[n]x[n-m] \tag{3.7}$$

where N is the length of the signal. Finally, applying Eq. (3.5) leads to

$$\sum_{k=1}^{p} a_k \gamma_{xx}[m-k] = \gamma_{xx}[m], \quad m = 1, 2, \ldots, p \qquad (3.8)$$

which are known as the normal equations. Since in matrix form, the equations take on a Toeplitz structure, they can be efficiently solved using the Levinson-Durbin algorithm for the linear predictor (LP) parameters a_k.

The linear predictive representation of the speech signal is significant for a number of reasons apart from the important fact that the poles have a physical correlate in the acoustic resonances of the vocal tract. These include the fact that for a low order (typically $p = 10$), $|H(z)|$ provides an excellent approximation to the speech spectral envelope, the fact that the a_k therefore form a compact representation of the speech signal (or at least its spectral envelope), and the fact that inverting $H(z)$ produces a stable filter, allowing estimation of the excitation signal $e[n]$ from speech $x[n]$ (Atal and Hanauer, 1971). These properties hold in practice despite the fact that the excitation signal $e[n]$ does not usually obey the above assumptions of having a flat spectrum or being Gaussian distributed.

As features, however, the parameters a_k have proven inferior to other representations that can be derived directly from them. The linear predictive cepstral coefficients (LPCCs) are one example, and it has been shown (Atal, 1974) that these outperform other LP-based features in a speaker-recognition task. The LPCCs can be derived from the parameters a_k using a simple recursion (Atal, 1974):

$$C_l^{\text{LP}} = a_p + \sum_{i=1}^{p-1} \frac{i}{p} C_i^{\text{LP}} a_{p-i} \qquad (3.9)$$

Another widely used variation of linear prediction is known as perceptual linear prediction (PLP). In the extraction of PLP features (Hermansky *et al.*, 1992), the FFT spectrum is warped to the Bark frequency scale, which is derived from empirical psychoacoustic data. The equal-loudness (human hearing sensitivity) curve is then used to pre-emphasize the warped amplitude spectrum, and a cubic root power-law compression is applied (analogous to the logarithm in Eq. (3.11)). An inverse FFT permits the creation of an all-pole (linear predictive) model, which is then taken as the PLP feature. The PLPs thus contain a better approximation to human auditory perception than the LP parameters.

3.2.2.2 *mel cepstral-based features*

Without question, the most important features in speech classification generally are the mel frequency cepstral coefficients (MFCCs). The MFCC extraction method begins with a filterbank analysis of the short-term speech signal, implemented in the frequency domain, for reasons of computational efficiency. The filters are usually taken as triangular, with center frequencies following the auditory mel scale, each overlapped by 50%, as seen in Fig. 3.3.

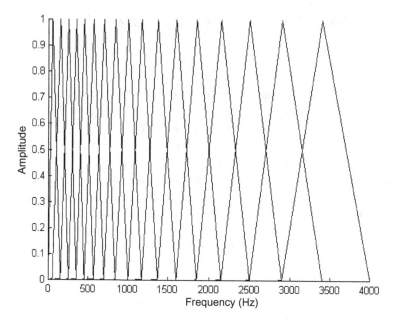

Fig. 3.3. mel-scale triangular filterbank.

The energies of each subband output are thus calculated as

$$E_m = \sum_{k=k_L}^{k_H} w_k^m |X^2[k]| \tag{3.10}$$

where w_k^m are the weights corresponding to the magnitude response of the mth subband triangular filter at the frequencies $k \in \{k_L, \ldots, k_H\}$. The energies E_m are thus a compact approximation to the short-term spectral envelope, with the possible exception of the first few, which may reflect some pitch information, depending on the value of F_0. To account for the logarithmic loudness perception of the human auditory system, the E_m are then log transformed.

The final step in the MFCC extraction method is the application of a discrete cosine transformation to the log energies:

$$MFCC_l = 2 \sum_{m=1}^{M} \log E_m \cos \left(\frac{(2m+1)l\pi}{2M} \right) \tag{3.11}$$

where $l = 0, 1, \ldots, M$, and M is the number of mel-scaled filters in the speech bandwidth. The original motivation for this transformation was dimensionality reduction, due to the near-optimal decorrelating properties of the DCT, however further benefits of the DCT include: (1) features that are approximately decorrelated can be modeled more simply (e.g., using diagonal covariance matrices) and (2) the near-Gaussian distribution of the resulting MFCC feature elements is well matched to modeling techniques such as Gaussian mixture modeling (GMM) (refer to Chapter 1).

Since the MFCCs are transformed features, it is helpful to interpret them in a physical manner to obtain insight into why they make good speech features:

- The MFCCs are the DCT of *log* energies: a change in scaling of the speech amplitude merely shifts the entire log energy spectrum up or down, without changing the amplitude variations.
- $MFCC_0$ is the mean of the log filterbank energies, and can usually be discarded because it is affected only by the level of the speech signal and not by its spectral shape.
- $MFCC_1$ is the amplitude of the component in the log energy spectral shape that looks like a cosine of period $2M$. In other words, $MFCC_1$ describes the average spectral tilt.
- $MFCC_2$ is the amplitude of the component in the log energy spectral shape that looks like a cosine of period M. Note that again its value is unaffected by the amplitude of the speech signal, and only describes the shape of the speech spectrum.
- Higher-order MFCCs are similarly related to shorter period cosine variations in the shape of the spectrum. Very high order coefficients represent fine detail in the spectrum that may be due to pitch harmonics or noise. These latter coefficients are highly variable, and are removed in many applications.

Originally developed for speech recognition, the consistently high performance of MFCCs in this domain, since Davis and Mermelstein empirically compared them with various alternatives in 1980 (Davis and Mermelstein, 1980), has seen them become a standard feature [8]. Then, MFCCs were subsequently introduced to speaker recognition, where they were shown to be more robust than LP parameters (Reynolds and Rose, 1995). The success of MFCCs in speech recognition points to effective characterization of the phonetic content of short-term speech, which is a source of variability for the speaker-recognition problem. This variability is nearly always modeled using GMMs, so that speaker-specific information within MFCCs is modeled on a per-mixture basis, in terms of variations from the Gaussian mixture mean. However, it is reasonable to question the MFCC extraction method as a feature for speaker-recognition applications, since the mel scale concentrates the modeling power of the MFCCs in the low frequencies, while speaker-specific information is thought by some to be predominantly concentrated at higher frequencies, as discussed in Sec. 3.1.2.

3.2.2.3 *Group delay features*

Since the MFCC features are extracted purely from the magnitude spectrum of the speech signal, it is of interest to consider information derived from the phase spectrum, which may be expected to possess complementary characteristics.

Group delay $\tau(\omega)$ is the time delay experienced by a signal component of frequency ω at the output of a filter $H(\omega)$ relative to the input, or

$$\tau(\omega) = -\frac{d\phi(H(\omega))}{d\omega} \tag{3.12}$$

where $\phi(H(\omega))$ denotes the phase response of the filter. Speech, as the output of a stable filter, exhibits characteristics in the magnitude and phase spectra due to the vocal tract filter poles and zeroes, of which the poles are of most interest. The phase spectrum of the speech signal $\phi(X(\omega))$ has properties similar to the phase response of the vocal tract spectrum (Murthy and Gadde, 2003), which can be expressed as a linear term via the following identity

$$\log(X(\omega)) = \log(|X(\omega)|) + j\phi(X(\omega)) \tag{3.13}$$

Taking the negative derivative of Eq. (3.13) with respect to ω and considering only the imaginary term leads to the following expression for group delay (Murthy and Gadde, 2003):

$$\tau(\omega) = \frac{X_R(\omega)Y_R(\omega) + Y_I(\omega)X_I(\omega)}{|X(\omega)|^2} \tag{3.14}$$

where $X_R(\omega)$ and $X_I(\omega)$ are the real and imaginary parts of $X(\omega)$ respectively, and $Y(\omega)$ is the Fourier transform of $tx(t)$. In practice, Eq. (3.14) suffers from large-value "spikes" generated by noise and window effects that cause the denominator to approach zero at some frequencies. To reduce the effect of these, smoothing of the denominator term and the application of two empirically tuned power-law parameters were proposed, resulting in a formulation known as the modified group delay function (MODGDF) (Murthy and Gadde, 2003).

Recently, an alternative method for group delay calculation was proposed that addresses the numerical issues of Eq. (3.14) in a less heuristic manner (Kua *et al.*, 2009). Based on empirical values of the numerator and denominator expressions at discrete frequencies ω_k, the expression

$$X_R(\omega_k)Y_R(\omega_k) + Y_I(\omega_k)X_I(\omega_k) \approx \tau_{LS}(\omega_k)|X(\omega_k)|^2 \tag{3.15}$$

can be posed, where $\tau_{LS}(\omega_k)$ is an estimate based on frequencies $\{\omega_l | l = k - \frac{M-1}{2}, \ldots, k, k+1, \ldots, k + \frac{M-1}{2}\}$ of the group delay using least squares (Kua *et al.*, 2009). Thus, if we define vectors for the numerator

$$\mathbf{n} = \begin{bmatrix} X_R(\omega_{k-\frac{M-1}{2}})Y_R(\omega_{k-\frac{M-1}{2}}) + Y_I(\omega_{k-\frac{M-1}{2}})X_I(\omega_{k-\frac{M-1}{2}}) \\ \vdots \\ X_R(\omega_{k+\frac{M-1}{2}})Y_R(\omega_{k+\frac{M-1}{2}}) + Y_I(\omega_{k+\frac{M-1}{2}})X_I(\omega_{k+\frac{M-1}{2}}) \end{bmatrix} \tag{3.16}$$

and denominator

$$\mathbf{d} = \begin{bmatrix} |X(\omega_{k-\frac{M-1}{2}})|^2 \\ |X(\omega_{k+\frac{M-1}{2}})|^2 \end{bmatrix} \tag{3.17}$$

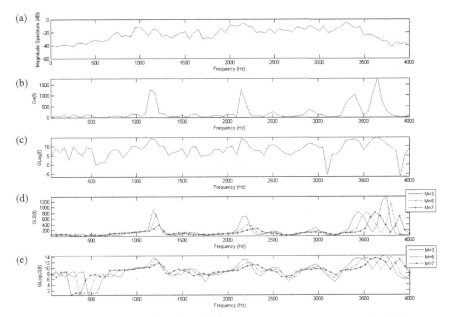

Fig. 3.4. Comparison of group delay spectra for an example frame of the sound /r/: (a) magnitude spectrum, (b) MODGDF spectrum (Murthy and Gadde, 2003), (c) log MODGDF spectrum (Thiruvaran *et al.*, 2007), (d) least square MODGDF (Kua *et al.*, 2009), and (e) log least square MODGDF.

then

$$\tau_{LS}(\omega_k) = [\mathbf{d}^T\mathbf{d}]^{-1}\mathbf{d}^T\mathbf{n} \qquad (3.18)$$

where T denotes vector transpose (Kua *et al.*, 2009). The least squares regularization of group delay helps to reduce the dynamic range of the group delay, while preserving the essential characteristics, as seen in Fig. 3.4.

An alternative method for compressing the dynamic range of the group delay is to apply the logarithm (Thiruvaran *et al.*, 2007). This greatly attenuates "spikes" resulting from denominator values near zero in Eq. (3.14), but also has the effect of increasing the dynamic range of group delay values close to zero.

As seen in Fig. 3.4, the group delay spectrum contains information concerning both the pitch harmonics and the formant structure. Typical extraction of features from the group delay applies the DCT to the MODGDF, and the lowest-order coefficients are then taken as the feature vector (Kua *et al.*, 2009; Murthy and Gadde, 2003; Thiruvaran *et al.*, 2007).

3.2.2.4 *Frequency modulation features*

The previous two subsections have discussed a decomposition of the speech signal in terms of its magnitude and phase spectra, respectively. The AM–FM model is an alternative representation of the speech signal, which has been shown to provide an accurate model of speech for analysis and synthesis purposes and which accounts for some nonlinearities in the speech-production process (Maragos *et al.*, 1993). In this model, speech is represented as the sum of AM–FM components, each considered to represent a resonance (Maragos *et al.*, 1993):

$$x(t) = \sum_{k=1}^{K} a_k(t) \cos\left(\omega_{c_k}t + \int_0^t q_k(\tau)d\tau\right) \tag{3.19}$$

where $a_k(t)$, $q_k(t)$, and ω_{c_k} represent the AM component, FM phase component, and carrier frequency of the kth AM–FM component, respectively and K is the number of AM–FM components in the speech bandwidth. By analogy with the (linear) all-pole model of speech, in which resonances are modeled using conjugate pole-pairs with impulse response

$$h_k(t) = A_k e^{-\rho_k t} \cos(\Omega_k t) \tag{3.20}$$

where A_k is the amplitude of the exponential decay, and ρ_k and Ω_k are the pole radius and angle respectively, a number of different methods for extracting the AM- and FM components may be developed.

The discrete energy separation algorithm (Maragos *et al.*, 1993) employs a differential approach, defining an energy operator

$$\Psi_c[x(t)] = [\dot{x}(t)]^2 - x(t)\ddot{x}(t) \tag{3.21}$$

for which $\Psi_c[A\cos(\Omega t)] = (A\Omega)^2$, if A and Ω are constant. If the kth component has time-varying amplitude, the energy operator alone will not allow separation of the amplitude and frequency components, so the ratio $\Psi_c[\dot{x}(t)]/\Psi_c[x(t)]$, termed the energy separation algorithm (Maragos *et al.*, 1993), is instead employed. From this estimate of Ω_k, the FM component may be estimated for a given instant by comparing the phase terms of (17) and (18) to obtain

$$q_k = \Omega_k - \omega_{c_k} \tag{3.22}$$

as shown in Fig. 3.5. When the AM and FM components are time-varying rather than constant, clearly the energy separation algorithm is an approximation whose validity degrades as longer signal segments are used during the signal derivative estimation process. Nonetheless, this approach has been used to accurately extract the FM component from various types of signals, using segment sizes of down to around 1 ms.

A recently proposed alternative method for FM extraction models the kth AM–FM speech component as a second-order autoregressive process, effectively fitting a two-pole resonator impulse response of the kind shown in Eq. (3.20) (Thiruvaran *et al.*, 2008). Using second-order linear prediction, the parameters ρ_k and Ω_k can be estimated as the pole radius and angle of the linear predictive transfer function, i.e.,

$$\hat{\Omega}_k = f_s \tan^{-1}\left(\frac{-a_1}{2\sqrt{a_2}}\right) \tag{3.23}$$

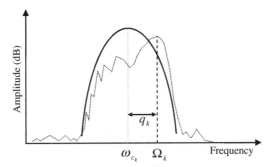

Fig. 3.5. Frequency domain representation of FM extraction from a bandpass signal. Solid line: filter magnitude response, dashed line: pole angle (frequency), and dotted line: bandpass signal amplitude spectrum.

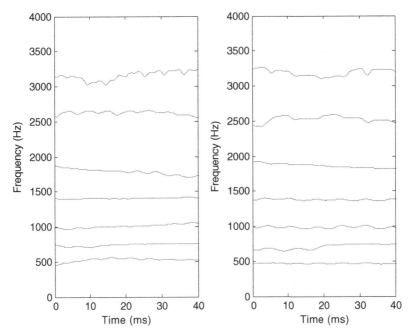

Fig. 3.6. FM contours, extracted using the all-pole method, for two speakers each uttering the vowel /aa/.

where f_s is the sampling frequency, and from this estimate, the FM component may be determined as given in Eq. (3.22). For this method, which we term all-pole FM extraction, the key parameter of interest is the length N of the discrete-time speech signal $x[n]$ used to estimate the autocorrelation (Fig. 3.6). The minimum value of N for this application is just three samples, which is attractive from the perspective of estimating an "instantaneous" value of the FM component; however, such a small value is associated with a large variance in the autocorrelation and hence also the estimated parameters.

A more computationally efficient approximation to the all-pole FM extraction technique is to simply count the number of zero crossings N_{ZC} over a given segment of an AM–FM speech component, and estimate its frequency as (Thiruvaran *et al.*, 2009)

$$\hat{\Omega}_k = \frac{\pi N_{ZC}}{t_{\text{last}} - t_{\text{first}}} \tag{3.24}$$

where t_{first} and t_{last} are the first and last zero crossings in the segment, respectively. Empirical results show that features extracted using the zero-crossing technique require a fraction of the processing time and are able to produce comparable results to the all-pole FM extraction method (Thiruvaran *et al.*, 2009).

When applying the above FM extraction methods to a speech signal, two important practical considerations must be made:

(1) Since resonance frequency extraction and tracking is a difficult and error-prone process, and the number of resonances within a fixed bandwidth may vary, while a fixed-dimension feature is needed, it is more practical for feature extraction to instead apply a filter bank, and assume that each subband signal comprises a single AM–FM component.

(2) Unlike for communications signals, in speech components the carrier frequency ω_c is unknown. In a filter bank FM feature extraction configuration, it is convenient to assume that ω_c is equal to the filter center frequency, while the remaining (time-varying) frequency component is attributed to the frequency modulation.

A further consideration of key practical importance is that although very short-term estimates of the FM components can be made, resulting in accurate analysis-synthesis, there remains the issue of how to summarize these into more typical frame lengths of around 20–30 ms for speech feature extraction. As discussed in (Thiruvaran *et al.*, 2008), this has historically been achieved by representing the very short-term estimates in terms of their mean or median, i.e., performing averaging on the extracted FM estimates.

A key insight of (Thiruvaran *et al.*, 2008), however, is that for the purposes of feature extraction, it is significantly more advantageous to perform the averaging *during* the process of FM extraction. In the case of the all-pole extraction method, this can be easily achieved by increasing the window length N used to estimate the autocorrelation, effectively averaging the contribution of shorter subsegments of the window even before the FM component is estimated from the two-pole model. The price paid for this is clearly that as N is increased, only successively more slowly varying frequency modulation can be reliably tracked. Although FM extraction methods such as those presented above can produce FM estimates with fine temporal resolution, empirical work suggests that this is not necessary, and even produces unwanted variability in the process of summarizing very short-term estimates into a single feature per frame (Thiruvaran *et al.*, 2008).

3.2.2.5 *Frequency scales for speaker recognition features*

The foregoing discussion of speaker-specific characteristics of speech in Sec. 3.1.2 has suggested the importance of pitch and higher formants, while the first two formants have been strongly identified with phonetic characteristics. A question might thus be posed concerning whether features for speaker-recognition purposes should be extracted according to a different frequency scale from that employed for features in other applications of speech processing. Lu and Dang (2008) have recently addressed this question, showing empirically that a significantly different filterbank design to the mel scale, emphasising the 0–400 Hz and 4–5.5 kHz regions of the spectrum, is able to produce substantial reductions in speaker-recognition error rate compared with the conventional MFCCs. Although their design emphasizes frequency regions above and below the F_1 and F_2 ranges, it did not exclude spectral content in the range of the first two formants. A likely reason for this is that implicit phonetic classification (performed during speaker modeling, typically using Gaussian mixture models) is a key component of the speaker-recognition process.

3.2.3 *Dynamic information*

The features described in Secs. 3.2.1 and 3.2.2 are examples of static features, in the sense that they describe the speech signal at a particular instant in time, but do not provide any information about the trajectory of the signal. Since the arrangement of short-term sounds by the speaker during speech production is highly structured and purposeful, clearly such trajectory information (referred to as dynamic features) should be useful, and recent forensic speaker-recognition investigations support this (Morrison, 2009). The questions of interest here are how the information should be captured and over what duration of the signal.

The first derivative of the feature vector with respect to time is an important indicator of the feature trajectory, and is often approximated as

$$\Delta v_l^t = \frac{1}{K(K+1)} \sum_{k=-K}^{K} k v_l^{t+k} \qquad (3.25)$$

where v_l^t is the lth element of the feature vector at frame number t. These features are generally referred to as "delta features". Repeating equation Eq. (3.25) on the delta features Δv_l^t produces delta–delta features $\Delta\Delta v_l^t$, which are sometimes referred to as acceleration features.

By extracting delta features over multiple frames, it is possible to describe longer feature contours. A popular framework for this, known as shifted delta cepstra (SDC) (Torres-Carrasquillo *et al.*, 2002), is specified in terms of how many delta features (k) are used, the spacing between each (P), the span of each delta (d), and the static feature dimensionality (N), abbreviated as $N - d - p - k$. The SDCs are calculated using a first-order approximation to the derivative

(Torres-Carrasquillo *et al.*, 2002):

$$\Delta C_l^t = C_l^{t+iP+d} - C_l^{t+iP-d} \qquad (3.26)$$

where i varies between 0 and $k - 1$. The SDC is a high-dimensional feature, but one that is capable of representing some of the kind of long-term features discussed in Sec. 3.1.2 in the context of an acoustic feature-based speaker-recognition system. This "shifted delta" approach can be applied to any feature other than cepstra.

3.2.4 *Prosodic features*

As discussed in Sec. 3.1.2, long-term, prosodic information is an effective approach for characterizing the speaking style of an individual. Extracting features to describe this information requires (1) short-term estimates of the fundamental frequency F_0 (via pitch estimation and tracking) and/or energy, and (2) methods for compactly representing the longer-term variation of F_0 and/or energy. Accurate pitch estimation is a long-standing research problem, however in the scope of this chapter a brief introduction to the autocorrelation method can be made.

For a frame of voiced speech $x[n]$ of length N with period $1/F_0$ sampled at frequency f_s, like that shown in Fig. 3.1(a), the autocorrelation $\gamma_{xx}[m]$ of the sampled speech signal $x[n]$ will exhibit a strong peak at the value of m closest to f_s/F_0. The short-term pitch estimate may then be further refined using more sophisticated methods. Pitch tracking refers to the arrangement of short-term pitch estimates across multiples frames so as to eliminate any unvoiced regions and remove or correct pitch estimation errors (typically pitch doubling or halving), and results in a pitch contour.

Finally, the pitch contour may be modeled, for example using least squares to produce a piecewise linear stylization (Sönmez *et al.*, 1998). In this stylization, each voiced segment is represented by its median pitch value, contour slope, and voiced segment duration, and these three parameters form a prosodic feature capable of substantially augmenting the accuracy of acoustic speaker-recognition systems (Sönmez *et al.*, 1998). Alternative methods for characterizing prosodic information include statistics derived from F_0 or energy distributions (Reynolds *et al.*, 2003). Note that speaker-recognition systems based on prosodic features are not language independent, due to the existence of tone languages such as Mandarin.

3.2.5 *Phonetic features*

Although this chapter concentrates mainly on acoustic features, it is important to note that pronunciation has strong speaker-specific aspects. Like prosodic features, phonetic features contain information concerning the speaking style of an individual. Use of phonetic features depends on the application of a trained phoneme recognizer to label individual frames of speech as belonging to phonetic classes, usually specific to that language. Statistics on the sequence of phoneme labels are then used to derive features (Reynolds *et al.*, 2003), for example using n-grams. An n-gram is a conditional probability model that predicts the probability of a particular phoneme given the knowledge of the (ordered) sequence of $n - 1$ previous phonemes. In practice, trigrams ($n = 3$) or more likely bigrams ($n = 2$) must be used due to the requirement for sufficient training and particularly test data to accumulate n-gram statistics. Given a test utterance, the phoneme labels for successive groups of n frames are assigned by the phoneme recognizer (which generally uses MFCC features). Then, the probability of that sequence of n phoneme labels, given the n-gram model for the speaker under test, can be used to indicate the similarity of the phonetic content of the test utterance to that speaker's speaking style. Phonetic features of this kind show particular promise when augmented with acoustic features such as MFCCs (Reynolds *et al.*, 2003).

Interestingly, while the precision of the phoneme recognizer might intuitively be assumed to have an important bearing on the speaker-recognition performance, recent work seems to suggest otherwise. In a study of speaker recognition on English and Spanish databases (Toledano *et al.*, 2005), the use of phoneme recognizers trained on other languages was found to be as good as or slightly better than a phoneme recognizer trained on the same language, in terms of recognizing phonemes for use as n-gram features in speaker recognition.

3.2.6 *Feature normalization*

All features discussed in this chapter are subject to variation due to sources other than speaker identity. Consider for example the first MFCC element, C_0, extracted first on clean speech, and then on the same speech but with noise added. Clearly the distribution of C_0 will be shifted (higher) for the noisy speech relative to that of the original speech, creating a mismatch between the two conditions. If one of the conditions were used for training and one for testing, the mismatch will manifest itself as a reduction in classification accuracy. Hence, without any *a priori* knowledge of the source of non-speaker-specific variability in feature distributions, an important approach to improving the robustness of features is to reduce the mismatch by normalizing the feature distribution.

The simplest approach to feature normalization was introduced in the context of the MFCC as cepstral mean subtraction, and is applied to the lth element of a feature vector v_l^t at time t as

$$\tilde{v}_l^t = v_l^t - \frac{1}{T} \sum_{t=1}^{T} v_l^t \qquad (3.27)$$

where T is the number of frames over which normalization is to be applied. In practice, T is often taken as the number of frames in the utterance.

Adjusting the feature distribution simply by removing the mean may not be sufficient if the shape or variance of the feature distribution is also significantly

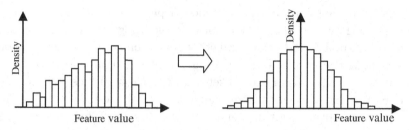

Fig. 3.7.   Cumulative distribution mapping of an arbitrary feature distribution (left) to a Gaussian distribution (right) using Eq. (3.28).

mismatched. Mean and variance normalization can be applied to remedy this problem, by dividing the result of Eq. (3.27) by the standard deviation of v_l^t over $t \in \{1, 2, \ldots, T\}$.

Alternatively, to better match the shape of the distribution, cumulative distribution mapping (also known as feature warping) can be applied (Segura *et al.*, 2002). In this approach, the feature distribution is modified by an invertible transformation such that the cumulative distribution is preserved, i.e.,

$$\int_{-\infty}^{\alpha} q(v)dv = \int_{-\infty}^{\beta} p(x)dx \qquad (3.28)$$

where $q(v)$ is the probability density function of the feature v and $p(x)$ is the target (desired) probability density function. In Eq. (3.28), the feature value is nonlinearly mapped from α to β. For multidimensional features, the mapping is performed on a dimension-by-dimension basis.

To achieve this in practice, where $q(v)$ is unknown, quantile histogram equalization is used. Given a series of T speech frames to be mapped, all feature values are calculated, then sorted into ascending order. For each feature, its rank r, as a percentage of the number of frames in the utterance, is used to determine which point of the function $p(x)$ it should be mapped onto. $p(x)$ is typically stored as a look-up table for some predefined number of points N_p uniformly spaced along the x-axis, ranked in ascending order of x-value. The position rN_p is then used to look up the required value of $p(x)$, using linear interpolation if it falls between two pre-stored values of $p(x)$. The resulting density mapping is illustrated in Fig. 3.7. In speech-processing applications, $p(x)$ is chosen as the Gaussian distribution, which provides a good match to Gaussian mixture model backends, but also performs well with other classifiers.

3.3 Comparison of Features for Speaker Recognition

Having described a selection of acoustic feature extraction techniques, in this section a number of experimental comparisons are reported. First, to give an illustrative indication of the relative importance of aspects of the feature extraction process, voice activity detection, dynamic information and normalization are incrementally added to the process of an MFCC extraction. Second, a selection of popular contemporary acoustic features are compared empirically. Finally, an evaluation of recently proposed frequency modulation and group delay-based features is conducted, demonstrating the potential for improving the conventional MFCC-based feature extraction process.

3.3.1 *System description and experimental configuration*

Speaker-recognition experiments in this section were conducted using the male speaker subset of the NIST 2008 SRE database, with telephone/telephone data for training/evaluation. This comprises 648 speakers for training and 895 speakers for testing, with a total of 12511 trials. The duration of training and testing utterances was 5 minutes.

The speaker modeling and classification components of the recognition system for the first two experiments were based on training a 512-mixture Gaussian mixture model (GMM) universal background model (UBM) from 400 utterances of the NIST2004 database. The training data from the evaluation set was then used to adapt speaker models from the UBM. Finally, classification was performed on the test data of the evaluation set, by detecting the target speaker as the model having the maximum likelihood for the given test segment. The classification back-end is not typical of contemporary systems, but is convenient for comparing multiple front-ends and has been employed here for illustrative purposes.

For the third experiment (Sec. 3.3.4), a GMM–SVM back-end was used, with 512 mixtures, where NIST 2004 data were used to train the UBM and to compose the set of background speakers for SVM training. Nuisance attribute projection, derived from NIST 2005 data, was also applied to the GMM supervectors before SVM classification, for compensation of channel variability. Finally, T-norm based on 75 speakers from the NIST 2005 dataset was applied to the resulting scores. This classification back-end is more typical of speaker-recognition systems at the time of writing.

Two evaluation metrics employed by the National Institute of Standards and Technology (NIST), and widely used in the literature, are the equal error rate (EER) and minimum detection cost function (DCF). The DCF is defined as a weighted sum of the miss- and false-alarm probabilities. A helpful visualization tool, which shows the speaker-recognition performance as a function of different classification threshold choices, is the detection error trade-off (DET) curve, which is based on classifier decisions during the evaluation.

3.3.2 *Effect of VAD, dynamic information, and normalization*

This experiment commenced with the ETSI standard front-end [8], based on the mel cepstral coefficients described in Eq. (3.11), without voice activity detection. An energy-based VAD, similar to that described in Sec. 3.2.1, was then included in the feature extraction process, an experimental condition denoted as V + MFCC. Delta and delta–delta MFCCs were then successively calculated according to Eq. (3.25) and appended, creating conditions V+MFCC+D and V+MFCC+DD, respectively. Utterance-based feature normalization, using cepstral mean subtraction (V + MFCC+CMS+DD) and cumulative distribution mapping (V+MFCC+CDM+DD), were then evaluated. Finally, shifted delta cepstra, calculated according to Eq. (3.26) with the parameter settings 7-1-3-7, were then applied (V+MFCC+CDM+SDC) for comparison with the delta-MFCC features.

From the results shown in Fig. 3.8, several key observations can be made:

(1) VAD is an important component of speaker-recognition systems. This result is even more convincing if the speech data contain noise, rather than being noise free (as in Fig. 3.8).
(2) Dynamic features are able to capture some of the speaker-specific temporal information in the speech signal. Both delta features and particularly the SDCs significantly increase the feature dimension, so careful choice of the dimensionality of the delta features helps in the tradeoff between system performance and computational complexity. In the above comparison, the poorer performance of SDCs relative to delta and delta–delta features is attributed to the higher feature dimension (the number of GMM mixtures was kept constant at 512, but could be increased to improve the performance of SDC).

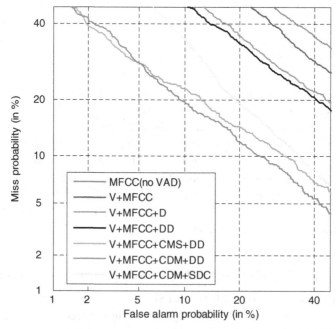

Fig. 3.8. Comparison of DET curves for feature extraction configurations combining various conventional system components.

(3) Normalization of any kind is extremely beneficial to speaker recognition, helping to reduce the mismatch in feature distributions between training and test conditions. Feature warping using cumulative distribution mapping produces the greatest benefits.

Hence, in the ensuing comparisons, all systems evaluated include VAD, dynamic features, and normalization.

3.3.3 *Comparison of speaker-recognition feature types*

In this experiment, a baseline mel cepstral-based front-end similar to the current state-of-the-art (V + MFCC + CDM + DD, referred to henceforth as BaseMFCC) was compared with selected other commonly used amplitude-based features (LPCC, PLP) and selected phase-based features (MODGDF, LogGD, LogLSGD, FM-DESA, FM-AP, FM-ZCC).

The least squares group delay was applied over an interval of $M = 3$. The smooth DESA (also known as SEOSA) and all-pole FM extraction both employed 14 Bark-spaced Gabor filters, from which an FM estimate was extracted from each subband signal once per 30 ms frame, with a 10-ms-frame advance. Delta features were appended following feature warping, producing a 28-dimensional feature.

Results, shown in Fig. 3.9, indicate that correctly extracted group delay and frequency modulation features can produce error rates approaching those of a conventional MFCC-based system, although this is more convincingly seen in

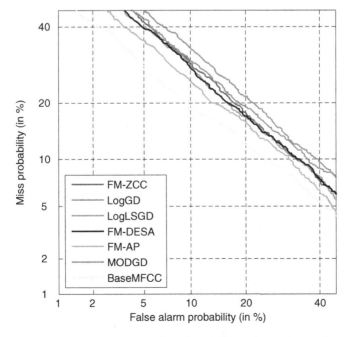

Fig. 3.9.   Comparison of DET curves for selected feature extraction configurations.

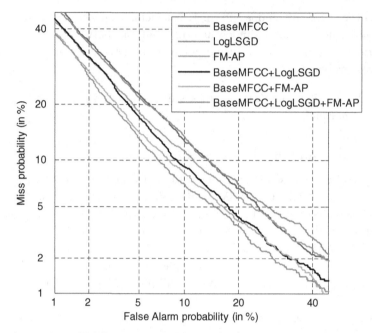

Fig. 3.10. Comparison of DET curves for common feature extraction configurations, combining various conventional system components (GMM–SVM back-end).

Fig. 3.10 where a GMM–SVM back-end is used. Least squares regularization provided a significant improvement over the modified group delay and log MODGD features. The FM-AP method outperformed the DESA-based FM feature extraction, although the faster FM-ZCC approach did not match the error rate of FM-DESA, in contrast with the findings of Thiruvaran et al. (2009).

3.3.4 Comparison of recent features for speaker recognition

In this experiment, a mel cepstral-based front-end was compared with the current state-of-the-art group delay-based features (LogLSGD) and the current state-of-the-art FM features (FM-AP) for a more contemporary speaker-recognition system incorporating mixture adaptation, channel compensation, SVM classification, and score normalization. Contemporary speaker-recognition systems often comprise fused subsystems, as explained in Chapter 1. The fusion of the MFCC, LogLSGD, and FM-AP systems, conducted at the score level, is of interest, for two reasons:

(1) when systems based on two different features are fused and are found to provide a large performance improvement over either individual system, this suggests that the features provide somewhat complementary information; and

(2) Understanding the complementary characteristics of different features is one means of improving both our understanding of how speaker-specific information is characterized and the performance of practical systems.

As seen in Fig. 3.10, results show that group delay and frequency modulation features, extracted using suitable methods, each contain significant complementary information to MFCC-based features. The FM-AP method does not always outperform MFCC-based features as seen above, however in all research to date, fused subsystems based on FM-AP and MFCC features always provide a significant performance improvement over MFCC-based systems (Thiruvaran *et al.*, 2008).

3.4 Summary

In this chapter, the origins and motivations for a number of features have been discussed. Although a variety of different features were compared empirically, the practical performance of speaker-recognition front-ends has been shown to be strongly dependent in the first instance on effective voice activity detection, representation of dynamic feature information, and suitable feature normalization.

Emerging features, based on frequency modulation information and group delay, were also discussed, and for these features a common thread is the need for effective regularization: for FM features, this means averaging is needed during the FM extraction process, while for group delay, this refers to the need to mitigate numerical instability.

Given the limitations of any single feature for speaker-recognition systems, there has recently been considerable interest in fusing systems that are complementary in one or more respects, including the front-end. Overall system performance can be improved in this manner, but it is generally assumed that this holds only if the features of the fused systems contain different and complementary information. The evaluations of cepstral-, FM-, and group delay-based features in this chapter therefore suggest that these features are to some extent complementary, and each contains speaker-discriminant information not contained in the others. The notion of a single feature that could capture the information contained in all the three features remains an open research problem. Alternatively, the performance gains from fusing complementary features may suggest that there is no single ideal feature, supporting the hypothesis that multiple sources of speaker-specific information are required (Lavner *et al.*, 2000).

The fact that there are no known features that are exclusively speaker-specific essentially pushes the problem of determining the variations in feature values due to different speakers into the modeling domain. A typical contemporary example is the use of Gaussian mixture models to represent broad acoustic classes. In the MAP-adapted universal background model approach to speaker modeling, the universal background model essentially acts as a kind of phonetic classifier, while the adaptation process captures the deviations in feature values due to speaker identity. Speaker modeling is discussed in depth in Chapter 1; however, the prospect of either a feature that contains solely speaker-specific information, or a joint feature extraction and speaker modeling framework that isolates the phonetic and speaker-specific characteristics of speech remains in the domain of open research questions.

Acknowledgements

The authors gratefully acknowledge experimental work conducted by Tharmarajah Thiruvaran, with assistance from Jia Min Karen Kua and Mohaddeseh Nosratighods.

References

Atal, B. S. Effectiveness of linear prediction characteristics of the speech wave for automatic speaker identification and verification, *JASA* **55**, 1304–1312, 1974.

Atal, B. S. and Hanauer, S. Speech analysis and synthesis by linear prediction of the speech wave, *JASA* **50**, 2, 637–655, 1971.

Atal, B. S. and Rabiner, L. R. A pattern recognition approach to voiced-unvoiced-silence classification with applications to speech recognition, *IEEE Trans. Acoust., Sp. and Sig. Proc.* **24**, 23, 201–212, 1976.

Benyassine, A., Shlomot, E., Su, H.-Y., Massaloux, D., Lamblin, C., and Petit, J.-P. ITU-T Recommendation G.729 Annex B: A silence compression scheme for use with G.729 optimized for v.70 digital simultaneous voice and data applications, *IEEE Communications Magazine* **35**, 9, 64–73, 1997.

Campbell, J. P. Speaker recognition: a tutorial, *Proc. IEEE* **85**, 9, 1437–1462, 1997.

Davis, S. B. and Mermelstein, P. Comparison of parametric representations for monosyllabic word recognition in continuously spoken sentences, *IEEE Trans. Acoust., Speech and Signal Processing* **28**, 357–366, 1980.

Doddington, G. R. Speaker recognition — identifying people by their voices, *Proc. IEEE* **73**, 11, 1651–1664, 1985.

Fant, G. *Acoustic Theory of Speech Production* (Mouton & Co, Gravenhage, The Netherlands), 1960.

Hermansky, H., Morgan, N., Bayya, A., and Kohn, P. Rasta-plp speech analysis technique, in *Proc. IEEE ICASSP*, pp. 1:121–124, 1992.

Kitamura, T., Honda, K., and Takemoto, H. Individual variation of the hypopharyngeal cavities and its acoustic effects, *Acoust. Sci. Tech.* **26**, 1, 16–26, 2005.

Kua, J. M. K., Epps, J., and Ambikairajah, E. LS regularization of group delay features for speaker recognition, in *Proc. INTERSPEECH* (Brighton, UK), pp. –, 2009.

Lavner, Y., Gath, A. and Rosenhouse, A. The effects of acoustic modifications on the identification of familiar voices speaking isolated vowels, *Speech Communication* **30**, 9–26, 2000.

Lu, X. and Dang, J. An investigation of dependencies between frequency components and speaker characteristics for text-independent speaker identification, *Speech Communication* **50**, 4, 312–322, 2008.

Maragos, P., Kaiser, J. F., and Quatieri, T. F. Energy separation in signal modulations with application to speech analysis, *IEEE Trans. Signal Processing* **41**, 10, 3024–3051, 1993.

Morrison, G. S. Likelihood-ratio-based forensic speaker comparison using parametric representations of vowel formant trajectories, *JASA* **125**, 2387–2397, 2009.

Murthy, H. A. and Gadde, V. The modified group delay function and its application to phoneme recognition, in *Proc. IEEE ICASSP*, pp. 1:68–71, 2003.

Oppenheim, A. and Schafer, R. Homomorphic analysis of speech, *IEEE Trans Audio and Electroacoustics* **16**, 2, 221–226, 1968.

Reynolds, D., Andrews, W., Campbell, J., Navratil, J., Peskin, B., Adami, A., Jin, Q., Klusacek, D., Abramson, J., Mihaescu, R., Godfrey, J., Jones, D., and Xiang, B. The SuperSID project: Exploiting high-level information for high-accuracy speaker recognition, in *Proc. IEEE ICASSP*, pp. 4:784–787, 2003.

Reynolds, D. A. and Rose, R. C. Robust text-independent speaker identification using gaussian mixture models, *IEEE Trans. Acoust., Speech and Signal Processing* **3**, 1, 72–83, 1995.

Rose, P. *Forensic Speaker Identification* (Taylor and Francis, New York), 2002.

Rosenburg, A. E. Automatic speaker verification: a review, *Proc. IEEE* **64**, 4, 475–487, 1976.

Segura, J. C., Benitez, M. C., Torre, A., and Rubio, A. J. Feature extraction combining spectral noise reduction and cepstral histogram equalization for robust ASR, in *Proc. Int. Conf. Spoken Lang. Process*, pp. 1:225–228, 2002.

Sönmez, K., Shriberg, E., Heck, L., and Weintraub, M. Modeling dynamic prosodic variation for speaker verification, in *Proc. Int. Conf. on Spoken Lang. Process.*, 3189–3192, 1998.

Thiruvaran, T., Ambikairajah, E., and Epps, J. Group delay features for speaker recognition, in *Proc. IEEE Int. Conf. Inf. Comm. Sig. Proc.* (Singapore), pp. 1–5, 2007.

Thiruvaran, T., Ambikairajah, E., and Epps, J. Extraction of FM components from speech signals using an all-pole model, *IET Electronics Letters* **44**, 6, 449–450, 2008.

Thiruvaran, T., Nosratighods, M., Ambikairajah, E., and Epps, J. Computationally efficient frame-averaged FM feature extraction for speaker recognition, *IET Electronics Letters* **45**, 6, 335–337, 2009.

Toledano, D. T., Fombella, C., Rodriguez, J. G., and Gomez, L. H. On the relationship between phonetic modeling precision and phonetic speaker recognition accuracy, in *Proc. INTERSPEECH*, pp. 1993–1996, 2005.

Torres-Carrasquillo, P. A., Singer, E., Kohler, M. A., Greene, R. J., Reynolds, D. A., and Deller, J. R. Approaches to language identification using Gaussian mixture models and shifted delta cepstral features, in *Proc. Int. Conf. Spoken Lang. Proc.*, pp. 89–92, 2002.

Part II

Face

Chapter 4

FUNDAMENTALS OF EDGE-BASED FACE RECOGNITION

Yongsheng Gao

*School of Engineering, Griffith University,
QLD 4111, Australia*

†*Queensland Research Lab, National ICT Australia,
QLD 4067, Australia*
yongsheng.gao@griffith.edu.au
†*yongsheng.gao@nicta.com.au*

4.1 Introduction

Edge information is a useful object representation feature that is insensitive to illumination changes to certain extent. This chapter summarizes our researches in face recognition that particularly uses edge information, and consolidates individual approaches at different feature representation levels into a single face recognition concept: edge-based face recognition. This concept may be considered as one of the categories of face recognition techniques.

Centered at using edge information, the chapter covers all three (low, intermediate, and high) levels of pattern recognition methodologies that make use of information from spatial to structural and syntactic representations. The investigation covers face recognition under (1) controlled/ideal condition, (2) pose variation, (3) varying lighting condition, and (4) varying facial expression. Figure 4.1 gives the conceptual organization of this chapter.

4.2 Face Recognition Using Line Edge Map

Psychological studies (Biederman and Gu, 1988; Bruce, 1982) indicated that human recognizes line drawings as quickly and almost as accurately as gray level pictures. These results imply that edge images of faces could be used for face recognition and achieve similar accuracy as gray level face images.

4.2.1 *Line edge map*

Based on the above psychological studies, we proposed a conceptually novel face recognition approach to harness the structural and spatial information of a face

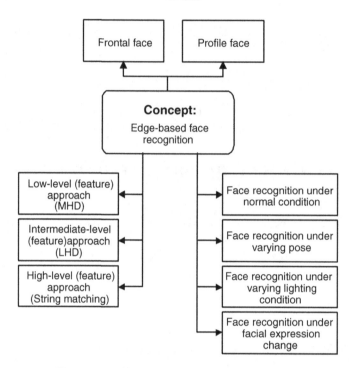

Fig. 4.1. Conceptual organization of the chapter.

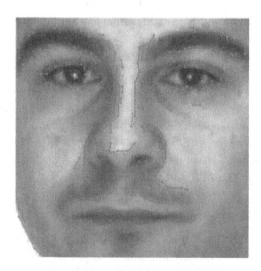

Fig. 4.2. An illustration of the LEM of a face.

edge map. Edge images have the advantage of less demand on storage space and they are less sensitive to illumination changes (Takács, 1998). After thinning of the edge map, a polygonal line fitting process (Leung and Yang, 1990) is applied to generate the line edge map (LEM) of a face. An example of frontal face LEM is illustrated in Fig. 4.2. The LEM representation, using dominant points (i.e., endpoints of line segments) on the curves, further reduces the storage requirement. Efficient coding of faces is a very important aspect in a face recognition system. The LEM is also expected to be insensitive to illumination changes due to the fact that it is an intermediate-level image representation derived from low-level edge map representation. The basic unit of LEM is the line segment grouped from pixels of the edge map. We explored the information of LEM and investigated the feasibility and efficiency of human face recognition using LEM. The line segment Hausdorff distance (LHD) measure was proposed by the authors (Gao and Leung, 1999, 2002a) to match faces. Compared to conventional applications of Hausdorff distance, LHD has better discriminative power because it can make use of the additional attributes of line orientation and line-point association, i.e., it is not encouraged to match two lines with large orientation difference, and all the points on one line have to match to points on another line only.

4.2.2 *Line segment hausdorff distance*

An object in an image can be represented by its edges, and each edge curve can be approximated by a chain of line segments determined by dominant points. However, many factors, such as lighting condition, noise, segmentation error, and object affine deformation, can affect the consistency and accuracy of dominant point detection. These will give rise to adding, missing and shifting of feature points that can cause problems in the object matching phase. These problems can be overcome by (1) choosing a reliable dominant point detection algorithm, and (2) building in some error correction mechanisms in LHD. In this study, the dominant point detection method (Leung and Yang, 1990) is used. The error correction mechanisms are described below in the design of LHD.

Given two finite line segment sets $M^l = \{m_1^l, m_2^l, \ldots, m_p^l\}$ (representing a model in the database) and $T^l = t_1^l, t_2^l, \ldots, t_q^l$ (representing a test image), LHD is built on the vector $\vec{d}(m_i^l, t_j^l)$ that represents the distance between two line segments m_i^l (in the model) and t_j^l (in the test image). The vector is defined as

$$\vec{d}(m_i^l, t_j^l) = \begin{bmatrix} d_\theta(m_i^l, t_j^l) \\ d_{//}(m_i^l, t_j^l) \\ d_\perp(m_i^l, t_j^l) \end{bmatrix}$$

where $d_\theta(m_i^l, t_j^l)$, $d_{//}(m_i^l, t_j^l)$, and $d_\perp(m_i^l, t_j^l)$ are the *angle distance, parallel distance,* and *perpendicular distance,* respectively. All these three entries are independent and are defined as

$$d_\theta(m_i^l, t_j^l) = f(\theta(m_i^l, t_j^l)) \tag{4.1}$$

$$d_{//}(m_i^l, t_j^l) = \min(l_{//1}, l_{//2}) \tag{4.2}$$

$$d_\perp(m_i^l, t_j^l) = l_\perp \tag{4.3}$$

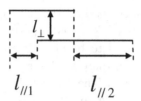

Fig. 4.3.   Line displacement measures.

$\theta(m_i^l, t_j^l)$ computes the smallest angle between the lines m_i^l and t_j^l. $f()$ is a non-linear penalty function to map the angle to a scalar. It is desirable to ignore small angle variation but penalize heavily on large deviation. In this study, the tangent function is used. The design of the parallel and perpendicular displacements can be illustrated with a simplified example of two parallel lines, m_i^l and t_j^l, as shown in Fig. 4.3. $d_{//}(m_i^l, t_j^l)$ is defined as the minimum displacement to align either the left endpoints or the right endpoints of the lines. $d_\perp(m_i^l, t_j^l)$ is simply the vertical distance between the lines. In general, m_i^l and t_j^l would not be parallel but one can rotate the shorter line with its midpoint as rotation center to the desirable orientation before computing $d_{//}(m_i^l, t_j^l)$ and $d_\perp(m_i^l, t_j^l)$. The shorter line is selected to rotate because this would cause less distortion to the original line pair as illustrated in Fig. 4.4. In order to cater for the effect of broken lines caused by segmentation error, and alleviate the effect of adding, missing and shifting of feature points (i.e., endpoints of line segments) caused by inconsistency of feature point detection, the parallel shifts $l_{//1}$ and $l_{//2}$ are reset to zero if one line is within the range of the other as shown in Fig. 4.5. Finally, the distance between two line segments m_i^l and t_j^l is defined as

$$d(m_i^l, t_j^l) = \sqrt{(W_a d_\theta(m_i^l, t_j^l))^2 + d_{//}^2(m_i^l, t_j^l) + d_\perp^2(m_i^l, t_j^l)} \qquad (4.4)$$

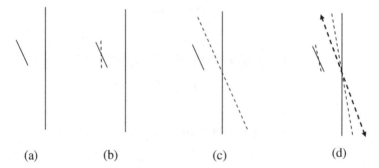

(a)   (b)   (c)   (d)

Fig. 4.4.   (a) Two lines to be measured, (b) Rotate the shorter line, (c) Rotate the longer line, and (d) Rotate both lines half of their angle difference in opposite direction. Solid lines represent lines before rotation. Dashed lines represent lines after rotation. The line with arrows shows the angle difference of the two lines.

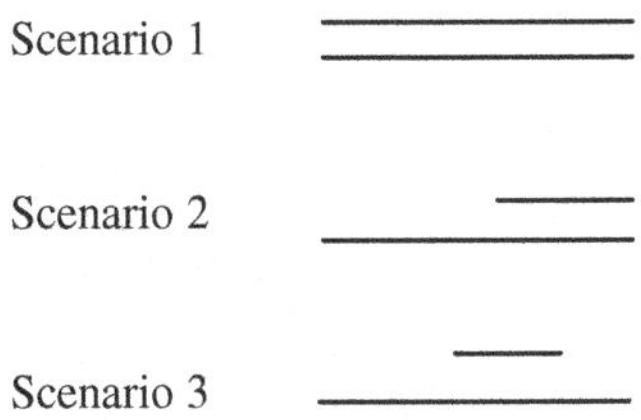

Scenario 1 ═══════════

Scenario 2 ─────────

Scenario 3 ──────

Fig. 4.5. All scenarios with $d_{//}(m, t) = 0$.

where W_a is the weight for the *angle distance* to be discussed later. The directed and undirected LHDs are defined in Eqs. (4.5) and (4.6), as

$$h_l(M^l, T^l) = \frac{1}{\sum_{m_i^l \in M^l} l_{m_i^l}} \sum_{m_i^l \in M^l} l_{m_i^l} \cdot \min_{t_j^l \in T^l} d(m_i^l, t_j^l) \tag{4.5}$$

$$H_l(M^l, T^l) = \max(h_l(M^l, T^l), h_l(T^l, M^l)) \tag{4.6}$$

where $l_{m_i^l}$ is the length of line segment m_i^l.

In the definition of LHD, we can find that the displacement distance (Fig. 4.3) depends on the smaller distance between the left/right endpoints of the two segments to be matched, which means LHD only reflects the smallest shift of the two segment endpoints. If one of the segment's endpoints (dominant points) is consistently detected and the other one shifts, the displacement distance is almost zero no matter how far the other endpoint shifts. This helps to alleviate the problem of shifting feature points. The Hausdorff distance measure is advantageous over other shape similarity measures (Takács and Wechsler, 1998) due to its tolerance to local, non-rigid distortions and noise, exception to establish point-to-point correspondence, and efficient computation.

The proposed LHD has the following additional advantages over Hausdorff distance measure: (1) Sensitive to edge orientations, thus it is more distinctive to dense edge images, (2) Tolerant to broken lines caused by edge detection and lighting condition, and (3) Less storage requirement and computational time.

On the other hand, the above discussion on LHD is based on the feature points (endpoints of segments) on the curves. It relies, to a certain extent, on the consistency of feature point detection.

W_a is the weight to balance the contribution of the angle distance $d_\theta(m_i^l, t_j^l)$ and the displacement distance $\sqrt{d_{//}^2(m_i^l, t_j^l) + d_\perp^2(m_i^l, t_j^l)}$ in Eq. (4.4). The following discussion on computing the value of W_a is based on the assumption that both distances contribute equally. The idea can be illustrated in Fig. 4.6 where $\vec{d}^{\text{cor}}$ is the average distance vector of the correct matches while $\vec{d}^{\text{all}}$ is the average distance vector of all matches. Note that the y-axis (orientation distance) has been scaled by W_a as $[W_a \cdot d_\theta(m_i^l, t_j^l)]$. It is expected that $|\vec{d}^{\text{cor}}|$ would be less than $|\vec{d}^{\text{all}}|$. Since each can be seen as composed of two orthogonal distance components, one can

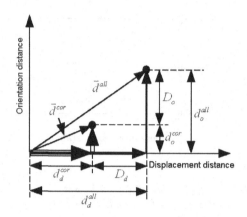

Fig. 4.6.   Illustration of average LHD compositions.

decompose the distance along these two directions to get $d_{\mathrm{d}}^{\mathrm{cor}}$, $d_{\mathrm{o}}^{\mathrm{cor}}$, $d_{\mathrm{d}}^{\mathrm{all}}$, and $d_{\mathrm{o}}^{\mathrm{all}}$ as shown in Fig. 4.6. The capability of LHD to find the correct match is reflected in the disparity $D_{\mathrm{d}}(= d_{\mathrm{d}}^{\mathrm{all}} - d_{\mathrm{d}}^{\mathrm{cor}})$ and $D_{\mathrm{o}}(= d_{\mathrm{o}}^{\mathrm{all}} - d_{\mathrm{o}}^{\mathrm{cor}})$. In order to place equal weights on both measures, one can select appropriate value for W_{a} based on

$$D_o = D_d \tag{4.7}$$

Another method to determine W_{a} is to choose a value that gives the best recognition rate experimentally. The W_{a} determined by either of the two methods should not have too much difference. This is supported by the experimental results later in which W_{a} was assigned the value of 20.

4.2.3 *LHD with number disparity*

Suppose T is the LEM of a test image to be matched and t_i is a line segment in T, M_c is the corresponding identical model of T in the database. M_n is a non-identical model of T in the database. If the corresponding line of t_i in M_c is missing because of segmentation error, LHD will take the nearest line, $m_{cn} \in M_c$, as the corresponding line of t_i. In addition, $d(m_{cn}, t_i) = \min d(m_c, t_i)$ is used in the calculation of LHD. Similarly, the nearest line ($m_{nn} \in M_{ni}$) of t_i in M_n is considered as the correspondent line of t_i, though M_n and T are different objects. It is possible to have $d(m_{cn}, t_i) \gg d(m_{nn}, t_i)$ for the matching of complicated and similar objects such as faces. This kind of missing lines can cause larger disparity between T and M_c than that between T and M_n, though both m_{cn} and m_{nn} are actually not the corresponding line segment of t_i and both $d(m_{cn}, t_i)$ and $d(m_{nn}, t_i)$ are relatively large. This may cause mismatch.

The number of corresponding lines between the input and the model is another measure of similarity. The number of corresponding lines between two identical images should be larger than that between two images of different objects.

Hence, the problem mentioned above can be alleviated by introducing this number information into LHD measure.

Assume that for each line t_j in the test LEM T, the corresponding line m_i in model M of the identical object should be located within a range of t_j in position because the test image and the model have been aligned and scale normalized by preprocessing before matching. Therefore a position neighborhood N_p and an angle neighborhood N_a are introduced. *Similarity neighborhood* N_s is a combination of N_p and N_a as $N_s = N_p \cap N_a$.

If at least one line in model M is located within the similarity neighborhood of a line t_j in test LEM T (i.e., locates in a given position neighborhood of t_j, and their angle difference is also within the given angle neighborhood), it is highly possible to find a correct corresponding line of t_j among those lines inside similarity neighborhood. This line (t_j) is named as a *high confident line*. A *high confident line ratio* (R) of an image is defined as the ratio of the number of high confident line (N_{hc}) to the total line number (N_{total}) in the LEM:

$$R = \frac{N_{hc}}{N_{total}} \tag{4.8}$$

Hence, an enhanced version of LHD integrated with number disparity (LHD_n) is defined by taking the effect of similarity neighborhood into account:

$$H_{l\_n}(M,T) = \sqrt{H_l^2(M,T) + (W_n D_n)^2} \tag{4.9}$$

where $H_l(M,T)$ is the LHD defined in Eq. (4.6) and W_n is the weight of number disparity D_n.

Number disparity is defined as a measure indicating the average ratio of the number of lines located outside the similarity neighborhood to the total line number of the two LEMs to be compared:

$$D_n = 1 - \frac{R_M + R_T}{2} = \frac{(1 - R_M) + (1 - R_T)}{2} \tag{4.10}$$

where R_M and R_T are the high confident line ratio of the model and the test LEMs, respectively. Further, LHD_n had shown better performance over LHD according to the experiments with appropriate values of position neighborhood, angle neighborhood, and W_n obtained by an off-line training process using simulated annealing.

One way of determining the parameters (W_n, N_n, N_a) in a LHD_n face recognition system is to select the values with the smallest error rate of face matching using a typical database. We use simulated annealing (Van Laarhoven and Aarts, 1987; Otten and van Ginneken, 1989) to perform global minimization of the error rate of face identification. Simulated annealing is a well-known stochastic optimization technique where during the initial stages of the search procedure, moves can be accepted which increase the objective function. The purpose is to

do enough exploration of the search space before resorting to greedy moves in order
to avoid local minima. Candidate moves are accepted according to probability p as

$$p = e^{-\frac{\Delta \text{Err}}{t}} \tag{4.11}$$

where Err is the error rate of face identification and t is the temperature parameter,
which is adjusted according to a certain cooling schedule. Exponential cooling
schedule (Kirkpatrick et $al.$, 1993) is adopted in this work.

Since the parameter selection process is conducted off-line, it is worth spending
a substantial effort to design the best LHD_n format (in the sense of minimizing
error rate). This can result in optimal performance of the proposed LHD_n face
recognition system.

4.2.4 *Experimental results*

The proposed LHD approach was investigated and compared to MHD approach
(Takács, 1998; Gao and Leung, 2002c) in the following experiments to evaluate
their performance on human frontal and profile face matching. The face database
from the University of Bern (Ber, 1990) was used to test the system performances
on (1) frontal faces, (2) profile faces, (3) profile outlines, and (4) misaligned profile
faces. The AR face database (Purdue University) of Purdue University was used
to investigate the LHD and LHD_n performances on larger frontal face dataset. In
all experiments, LHD (LHD_n) performed satisfactorily and consistently superior
to MHD. The effect of W_a from Eq. (4.4) on LHD and adaptive weight are also
investigated experimentally and discussed in this section.

In this study, the MHD approach on edge map is used as a benchmark of
LHD on LEM as LEM is an intermediate representation generated from low-level
edge map representation. The superiorities of LHD over MHD on accuracy, speed,
and economic storage space are the major consideration in the system design. The
well-known eigenface approach is the most widely used baseline for human face
recognition. The proposed LHD technique is also compared with this baseline with
respect to normal condition, varying lighting condition, and facial expression.

4.2.4.1 *Face recognition on the face database of Bern university*

A face database (Ber, 1990) of 30 persons with 2 profiles and 2 frontal images per
person from the University of Bern was used to test the capability of the proposed
LHD approach. Each image has the size of 512×342 pixels with 256 gray levels and
variations of the head position, size, and contrast. The lighting conditions during
image acquisition were carefully controlled. One profile and one frontal face images
of each person were used as models while the other was used as input in the frontal
and profile face recognitions, respectively. Though there are only 30 pairs of models
and inputs, one can have 60 matching experiments if the roles of model and input
are interchanged. Sample pairs of the frontal and profile face LEMs (models and

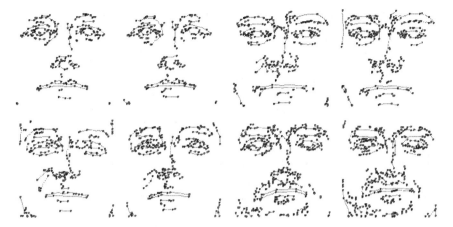

Fig. 4.7. Sample pairs of frontal face LEMs.

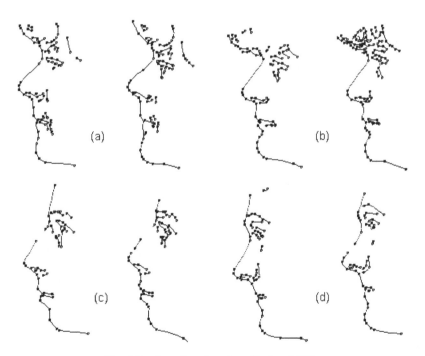

Fig. 4.8. Sample pairs of profile face LEMs.

test images) are shown in Figs. 4.7 and 4.8 Note that there are instances of broken lines, dense edges, and adding/missing/shifting of feature points from one image to its match.

The recognition results on faces are summarized in Table 4.1 while the legends of symbols are displayed in Table 4.2. Four types of data were tested. They were the frontal faces, profile faces, profile outlines (Fig. 4.9), and misaligned profile faces

Table 4.1:   Face recognition results of MHD and LHD with $W_a = 20$

Data method	Frontal faces		Profiles		Profile outlines		Misaligned profiles	
	MHD	LHD	MHD	LHD	MHD	LHD	MHD	LHD
R	96.7%	100%	96.7%	96.7%	93.3%	96.7%	87.5%	95%
$|\vec{D}|$	2.85	4.00	4.66	6.06	4.09	4.80	3.98	5.35
D_d	2.85	2.78	4.66	4.37	4.09	3.50	3.98	3.72
D_o	NA	2.88	NA	4.20	NA	3.28	NA	3.84
$|\vec{d}^{\,\text{all}}|$	4.72	8.59	6.82	10.99	5.30	7.93	6.70	10.80
$|\vec{d}^{\,\text{cor}}|$	1.87	4.68	2.16	5.05	1.29	3.20	2.72	5.50

R: Recognition rate; $|\vec{D}|$: Disparity ($|\vec{d}^{\,\text{all}} - \vec{d}^{\,\text{cor}}|$); D_d: Displacement disparity ($\vec{d}_d^{\,\text{all}} - \vec{d}_d^{\,\text{cor}}$); D_o: Orientation disparity ($\vec{d}_o^{\,\text{all}} - \vec{d}_o^{\,\text{cor}}$); $|\vec{d}^{\,\text{all}}|$: Average distance of all matches; and $|\vec{d}^{\,\text{cor}}|$: Average distance of the correct matches. NA: Not available.

Table 4.2:   Recognition results using LHD and LHD_n

	Frontal faces (in %)	Profiles (in %)	Profile outlines (in %)	Misaligned profiles (in %)
LHD	100	96.7	96.7	95.0
LHD_n	100	98.3	100	95.0

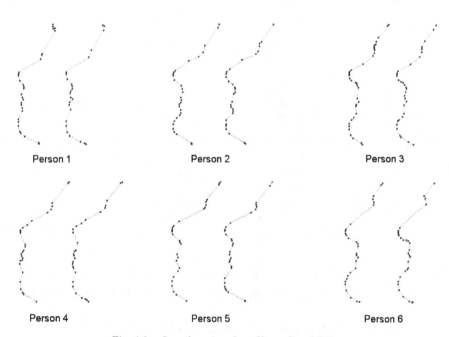

Fig. 4.9.   Sample pairs of profile outline LEMs.

Fig. 4.10.   An example of misaligned model and input faces.

(Fig. 4.10). The misalignments were simulated by shifting the normalized nose tip and chin point of L independently by a few pixels. As many as 20 people with 2 profiles per person in the database were used to examine the effect of misalignment. It is found that LHD scores equally well or better in all experiments (Table 4.1 row 3).

LHD achieved 100% recognition rate on frontal faces while MHD could only correctly identify 96.7% of the inputs. For the profile faces, LHD achieved a recognition rate of 96.7%. The only case of mismatch happened to the person whose hair area showed great difference from the input to the model (Fig. 4.8(b)). They matched best to a person with similar hairstyle (Fig. 4.8(a)). Similar to the well-known eigenface method and template-matching methods, the performance of recognition by using distance measure depends on how well the images are normalized and aligned. The tolerance of LHD to misaligned images created by shifting the two reference points (nose tip and chin point) a few pixels was also evaluated. Figure 4.10 shows one example of the misaligned image in the experiment. For the misaligned profiles, the recognition rate of LHD was remarkably higher than MHD by 7.5%. This demonstrates that the added structural information makes LHD robust to image-alignment errors.

The disparity vector, $\overrightarrow{D} = \vec{d}^{\text{all}} - \vec{d}^{\text{cor}}$, which is the difference of $\vec{d}^{\text{all}}$ and $\vec{d}^{\text{cor}}$ (Fig. 4.6), are displayed on row 4 by its scalar value, $|\overrightarrow{D}|$. It can be used as another measure to compare system-recognition capability. It can be seen that LHD has a much higher value in all the four experiments. The projections of $\overrightarrow{D}$ along the directions of displacement and orientation are shown in rows 5 and 6. It is observed that LHD and MHD share similar values on row 5. This suggests that the proposed LHD displacement computation, D_{d}, is comparable to the $|\overrightarrow{D}|$ (equal to D_{d}) of MHD. Note that with $W_{\text{a}} = 20$, the LHD values of D_{d} and D_{o} are approximately the same as specified in Eq. (4.7). The increase of the disparity, $|\overrightarrow{D}|$, for LHD with respect to MHD is due to the contribution of the new attribute of orientation distance, D_{o}, which is orthogonal/independent to the displacement distance D_{d}.

As the D_d of LHD is comparable to the disparity ($|\vec{D}|$) of MHD, the 3D disparity $|\vec{D}|$ of LHD should indicate a greater discriminating power than the 2D disparity of MHD. This is indeed reflected in row 4 in Table 4.1 and serves to demonstrate that LHD is a more discriminative measure than MHD.

4.2.4.2 *The effect of W_a*

The effect of W_a in Eq. (4.4) was investigated using profile faces (Fig. 4.10). The recognition rate is plotted against the normalized W_a (i.e., W_a/L where L is the distance between the nose tip and the chin point after normalization) in Fig. 4.11. It is found that LHD without the orientation information (i.e., $W_a = 0$) performed worse than MHD. It improved quickly with $W_a/L = 0.1$ and reached the optimal value when W_a/L ranged from 0.1 to 0.3. For all the other experiments in this study, W_a/L was set as 0.2 (i.e., $W_a = 20$). With this setting, it has been shown in Table 4.1 that D_d and D_o have complied with Eq. (4.7) in all the four experiments.

4.2.4.3 *Performance of LHD_n*

Outliers between images to be matched can be considered as either noise line segments caused by segmentation error or distinctive features of that particular individual, such as dimples, moles, and so on. Since distinctive features behave like noise line segments for matching between images of different people, one can hardly distinguish an outlier is a noise line segment or a distinctive feature. The system using LHD achieved a recognition rate of 96.7% on profiles. The only 2 cases of mismatch happened to the same person whose hair area showed great difference from the input to the model. This shows that even though LHD with average definition can average out some effect of outliers, the outliers still have negative effects on achieving very high recognition rate.

The proposed *similarity neighborhood* and *number disparity* can further alleviate the effect of noise by taking advantage of the segment number in *similarity neighborhood*. It is because the number disparity between the images of the same

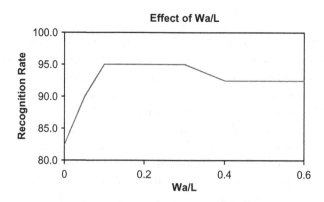

Fig. 4.11. The effect of W_a on recognition.

person is smaller than that between the images of different people. The result in Table 4.2, as we expected, indicated that line segment Hausdorff distance with number disparity (LHD_n) performs better than (or equally well as) LHD. The experimental results in the later sections demonstrate that LHD_n performs consistently superior to LHD.

Adaptive W_a

Since a longer line segment has less orientation perturbation caused by feature point shifting than a shorter one, the contributions of long line segments (whose angle distances are more reliable) should be enhanced while the effects of short line segments (whose angle distances are more unreliable) should be penalized. Therefore, an adaptive factor was introduced into the calculation of the weight W_a as

$$W_a = k \min(l_{m_i}, l_{t_j}) \tag{4.12}$$

where k is a scalar, l_{m_i} and l_{t_j} are the lengths of line segment m_i in model M and line segment t_j in the test LEM T, respectively. However, this was found not appropriate experimentally. It was found that LHD with adaptive weight could only achieve 90% correct identification on the misaligned profile data. This result is worse than the performance (95%) of standard LHD, which contradicts to what we expected. The explanation can be given with an example illustrated in Fig. 4.12. Suppose line segment 1 belongs to the test image, and line segments 2 and 3 are from the model image, it is obvious to human observers that line segment 2 is the corresponding line segment of 1. Since the adaptive weight of angle distance, W_a, for matching between line segments 3 and 1 is much smaller than that between line segments 2 and 1 according to Eq. (4.12), the system would prefer matching line segment 1 to 3. This shows that this adaptive weight idea is not appropriate for the current LHD measure.

4.2.4.4 Face recognition on AR face database

The AR face database (Purdue University) from Purdue University was also used to evaluate the performances of LHD and LHD_n. The database contains color images corresponding to 126 people's faces (70 men and 56 women). However, some images were found lost or corrupted. As many as 112 sets of images (61 men and 51 women)

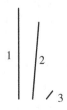

Fig. 4.12.   Illustration of line segment correspondence.

were found complete and appropriate for our experiments though some images still have impaired areas (e.g., on eyebrows in image# m-036-2 and eyelids image# m-073-18). No restrictions on wear (clothes, glasses, etc.), make-up, hairstyle etc. were imposed to the participants. Note that the test images were taken 2 weeks later after the model images were taken. Figure 4.13 illustrates an example pair of test and model face images in the AR face database.

The experimental results are summarized in Fig. 4.14 with three classification conditions (top1, top3, and top5). In the top1 classification, the correct match is only counted when the best matched face from models is the identical face (of the same person) of the input. In the top3 or top5 classification, the correct match is counted when the identical face (of the same person) of the input is among the best 3 or 5 matched faces from models, respectively. It was found that for the top 1 match, LHD performed better than MHD by 5.36%, and LHD_n could further improve the performance of LHD by 2.68%, i.e., it correctly identified 96.43% of the input faces. Both LHD and LHD_n can correctly identify 100% of the input faces with respect to top 5 match.

Fig. 4.13. An example pair of faces from the AR face database (Purdue University). The two faces were taken with 2 weeks time difference.

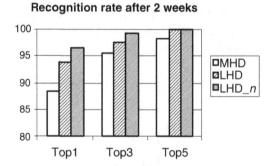

Fig. 4.14. Recognition results on the AR face database.

4.2.4.5 *Storage requirement and computational complexity*

The storage requirement of LEM is analyzed and compared with edge map based on the two profile and frontal face databases from Bern University (Ber, 1990). The data sizes in the experiments are listed in Table 4.3. On average, a profile face can be represented by an LEM with 78 feature points and a frontal face can be coded with 293 feature points. Compared with the edge map, LEM requires only 27.3% and 28.5% storage space for the profile and frontal face representations, respectively. This is an important improvement of edge map matching especially for large database identification application.

The computational complexities of LHD and MHD are of the order $O(k_l m_l t_l)$ and $O(k_p m_p t_p)$, respectively. m_l and t_l are the line segment numbers of model and test LEMs while m_p and t_p are pixel numbers of model and test edge maps, respectively. k_l and k_p are the time to compute $d(m_i^l, t_j^l)$ in LHD and the Euclidean norm $\|m_i^p - t_j^p\|$ in MHD. Table 4.4 shows the average real computation time of MHD and LHD on profile and frontal faces of (Ber, 1990). The experiments were conducted on a SGI Octane workstation with 300 MHz CPU and 512 MB RAM. The computational time for LHD is less than 50% of MHD. LHD took 0.051 seconds for one profile match and 0.502 seconds for one frontal face match. Since the calculation of $d(m_i^l, t_j^l)$ takes much more time than a simple Euclidean distance calculation in MHD (that is k_l is larger than k_p), $\frac{O(k_l m_l t_l)}{k_p m_p t_p} > \frac{O(m_l t_l)}{O(m_p t_p)}$. With some acceleration techniques (such as hardware acceleration, look-up table), the LHD computational time can be further reduced by minimizing k_l. When $k_l = k_p$, the LHD computational time could be reduced to only about 10% of MHD ($\frac{m_l}{m_p} \frac{t_l}{t_p} = (28.5\%)^2 < 10\%$). This is the ideal upper bound of computational time decrement for LHD with respect to MHD.

Table 4.3: Storage requirement of profile and frontal faces in the experiments

	Mean	Range
Pixel number per profile edge map	287	183–563
Feature point number per profile LEM	78	46–155
Line segment number per profile LEM	62	37–119
Pixel number per frontal face edge map	1027	616–1423
Feature point number per frontal face LEM	293	173–435
Line segment number per frontal face LEM	219	130–322

Table 4.4: Average computational time of MHD and LHD on (Bern University)

	MHD	LHD
Profile	0.109 s	0.051 s
Frontal face	1.146 s	0.502 s

Table 4.5:   Performance comparison on the frontal face
database of Bern University

LHD (in %)	LHD_n (in %)	Eigenface (20 eigenvectors) (in %)
100	100	100

Table 4.6:   Performance comparison on the AR database

Methods	Recognition rate (in %)
LHD	93.75
LHD_n	96.43
Eigenface (20-eigenvectors)	55.36
Eigenface (30-eigenvectors)	61.61
Eigenface (60-eigenvectors)	71.43
Eigenface (112-eigenvectors)	78.57

4.2.4.6 *Comparison with eigenface approach*

Eigenface approach based on principal component analysis (PCA) is a well-known face recognition method (Kirby and Sirovich, 1990; Turk and Pentland, 1991; Chellappa *et al.*, 1995; Swets and Weng, 1996). It is usually used as baseline of comparisons. The above two frontal face databases were also experimented by eigenface face recognition system. Their results together with the proposed LHD (LHD_n) are tabulated in Tables 4.5 and 4.6. Both the LHD (LHD_n) and eigenface achieved 100% accuracy for identifying faces in the database of Bern University (Table 4.5). However, LHD and LHD_n significantly outperformed eigenface on the AR face database (Table 4.6).

The performance of PCA depends on the number of eigenvectors, m. If this number is too low, important information about the identity is likely to be lost. If it is too high, the weights corresponding to small eigenvalues might be noisy. The number of eigenvectors, m, is limited by the rank of the training set matrix. The upper bound of m is 112 in the experiment of the AR database and thus 78.57% may be the best performance that PCA can achieve here.

One way to interpret this is that the eigenface approach will work well as long as the test image is "similar" to the ensemble of images used in the calculation of eigenface (Chellappa *et al.*, 1995). In addition, the training set should include a number of images for each person with some variations (Turk and Pentland, 1991) to obtain a better performance. Here, only one image per person was used for training and the other is used for testing.

Another reason is the differences between two identical faces are larger in the AR database than that in the database of Bern University. In particular, the illumination of the input and the model is different. This might be the major negative impact to the eigenface approach as compared with LHD (on LEM) since LEM is relatively insensitive to illumination changes.

The storage requirement for the eigenface approach is $Nm + dm$ where N is number of faces, m is the number of eigenvectors, and d is the dimensionality of the image. The storage demand of LEM is Nn where n is the average number of feature points. n is content based whereas m is fixed. Usually, LEM demands more storage space than the eigenface approach for large N as n is larger than m (not always) but LEM does not need to store any vector of size d, whereas the eigenface approach must store the projection matrix (m vectors of dimension d). d is $160 \times 160 = 25600$ in this experiment.

The computational complexity includes three aspects, i.e., matching time, training time, and updating time. The matching time is the most important one for large database searching. LHD requires more matching time than the eigenface approach as $n > m$. However, the eigenface approach demands a substantial amount of training time in the order of $O(N^3 + N^2d)$ to obtain a satisfactory projection matrix, which is not required in LHD. When a new individual is added into the database, the projection matrix needs to be recomputed. This incremental update retraining of $O(N^3 + N^2d)$ is another expensive operation that LHD does not need too. This retraining can be avoided by assuming that the new images do not have a significant impact on the eigenfaces, this is, just calculating the weights for the new images using the old projection matrix. This is only valid if the system was initially "ideally" trained.

4.2.5 *Face recognition under varying poses*

This section investigates the effect of pose variation on the proposed face recognition techniques. The face database from the University of Bern was used to test the effectiveness of the proposed approach. The database contains frontal views of 30 people. Each person has 10 gray-level images with different head pose variations (Two fronto-parallel pose, two looking to the right, two looking to the left, two looking downwards, and two looking upwards). An example set of the poses are shown in Fig. 4.15.

Two different clipfaces, which are the facial area used for face recognition, are generated using four different normalization methods. In the first normalization, the faces were scale- and orientation normalized by aligning the locations of the two eyes. The scales in the horizontal and vertical directions were set equal. In the second normalization, the faces were scale- and orientation normalized by aligning the locations of the two eyes and the distance between the eyes and the mouth. The scales in the horizontal and vertical directions were independent and determined by the interpupil distance and the distance from the mouth to the line connecting the eyes. We attempt to investigate the ability of this method to compensate for the pose variations of looking upwards and downwards.

In order to perform the experiment on face images of different pose, one fronto-parallel clipface per person was used as the model. The system was tested using the 8 poses looking to the right, left, up, and down for each person. There were

Fig. 4.15.   An example set of different poses.

Table 4.7:   Recognition results on face images of different poses

	MHD			LHD			LHD_n		
	%	$|\vec{d}^{\,\text{cor}}|$	$|\vec{d}^{\,\text{all}}|$	%	$|\vec{d}^{\,\text{cor}}|$	$|\vec{d}^{\,\text{all}}|$	%	$|\vec{d}^{\,\text{cor}}|$	$|\vec{d}^{\,\text{all}}|$
Left/Right (top1)	50.00	3.79	5.43	54.17	7.05	9.27	74.17	10.18	14.37
Up (top1)	65.00	3.37	5.25	65.00	6.72	9.13	70.00	10.51	14.37
Down (top1)	67.67	3.56	5.51	68.33	6.89	9.38	70.00	10.56	14.89
Left/Right (top3)	67.50	–	–	74.17	–	–	85.83	–	–
Up (top3)	78.33	–	–	81.67	–	–	85.00	–	–
Down (top3)	83.33	–	–	81.67	–	–	85.00	–	–
Left/Right (top5)	79.17	–	–	85.83	–	–	92.50	–	–
Up (top5)	86.67	–	–	86.67	–	–	88.33	–	–
Down (top5)	85.00	–	–	88.33	–	–	95.00	–	–

240 test images in total. The recognition results are summarized in Table 4.7. It can be observed that pose variations degrade the recognition rate of all the three investigated methods (MHD, LHD, and LHD_n), but LHD and LHD_n are more robust to pose variation than MHD. Note that the recognition rate using LHD_n for faces looking to the left and right is 14.17% higher than MHD.

The effectiveness of vertical scale normalization was examined with experiments, see examples in row 2 in Fig. 4.16. The results were summarized in Table 4.8. The results were surprising at first glance. With this normalization, the recognition rates of all poses including faces looking up and down decreased. It was assumed that the vertical scale normalization is able to recover the looking up/down pose variations to some extent. If we further analyze the data as illustrated in Tables 4.9–4.12, it can be found that the disparity ($\vec{D}$) in the experimental result of each pose reduced after vertical scale normalization. This implies that the system discriminative power is reduced by the process. The average distance between the correct matches would not always decrease as expected. Figure 4.16 is an example

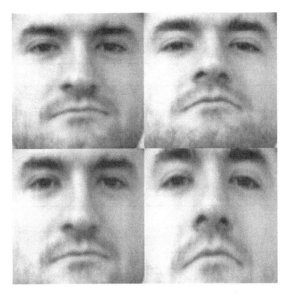

Fig. 4.16.   Examples without (row 1) and with (row 2) vertical scale normalization.

Table 4.8: Recognition results with vertical scale normalization. The value in the bracket is the result without vertical scale normalization

	MHD			LHD		
	%	$|\vec{d}^{\text{cor}}|$	$|\vec{d}^{\text{all}}|$	%	$|\vec{d}^{\text{cor}}|$	$|\vec{d}^{\text{all}}|$
Frontal	93.33	1.92	4.62	93.33	4.72	8.26
	(96.67)	(2.00)	(4.88)	(100)	(4.79)	(8.53)
Left/Right	42.50	3.68	5.19	50.83	6.90	9.05
Up	45.00	3.41	5.12	61.67	6.82	9.16
Down	60.00	3.37	5.32	71.67	6.66	9.17

Table 4.9: The effects on disparity by vertical scale normalization

	Fronto-parallel pose		
	$\vec{D}$	$|\vec{d}^{\text{cor}}|$	$|\vec{d}^{\text{all}}|$
Before normalization	2.88	2.00	4.88
After normalization	2.70	1.92	4.62
Difference	−0.18	−0.08	−0.26
Relative difference	−6.25%	−4.00%	−5.33%

to illustrate the distortion caused by vertical scale normalization. The images on the first row are the original faces of fronto-parallel and looking up poses. The images on the second row are the images after vertical scale normalization. The most important side effect is that the distinctive difference between two different people

Table 4.10:   The effects on disparity by vertical scale
normalization

	Looking left/right poses		
	$\vec{D}$	$|\vec{d}^{\text{cor}}|$	$|\vec{d}^{\text{all}}|$
Before normalization	1.64	3.79	5.43
After normalization	1.51	3.68	5.19
Difference	−0.13	−0.11	−0.24
Relative difference	−7.93%	−2.90%	−4.42%

Table 4.11:   The effects on disparity by vertical scale
normalization

	Looking up pose		
	$\vec{D}$	$|\vec{d}^{\text{cor}}|$	$|\vec{d}^{\text{all}}|$
Before normalization	1.88	3.37	5.25
After normalization	1.71	3.41	5.12
Difference	−0.17	−0.04	−0.13
Relative difference	−9.04%	−1.19%	−2.48%

Table 4.12:   The effects on disparity by vertical scale
normalization

	Looking down pose		
	$\vec{D}$	$|\vec{d}^{\text{cor}}|$	$|\vec{d}^{\text{all}}|$
Before normalization	1.96	3.55	5.51
After normalization	1.95	3.37	5.32
Difference	−0.01	−0.18	−0.19
Relative difference	−0.51%	−5.07%	−3.45%

would be decreased by aligning the positions of eyes and mouth. Thus the vertical
scale normalization, which aligns facial components, is found not advantageous for
upwards and downwards pose compensation.

The difficulty to recover poses looking up and down from a single 2D view is
that we cannot find any information related to head rotation in this direction. As
an alternative, we investigated the possibility to compensate, to some extent, the
variations of up and down poses for recognition applications instead of recovering
them exactly. The vertical scale normalization, which we attempted to employ to
compensate the pose variations of looking upwards and downwards, was proved
useless experimentally. An analysis of this issue is necessary to overcome problems
using similar idea. Vertical scale normalization is expected to reduce the disparity
within class (Here, the class denotes a set of face images from the same person.).
However, the disparity between classes would decrease since the longitudinal
differences among faces of different individuals would decrease. Obviously, the

effectiveness of this method relies on the assumption that the decrease of within-class disparity should be larger than that of between-class disparity. Experimental results show that the effect of between-class disparity is larger than that of within-class disparity and within-class disparity does not always decrease after vertical scale normalization. This is because the human head is not a planar object. In short, poses looking upwards or downwards will cause non-linear distortions of its 2D projections. This could increase the dissimilarity between the fronto-parallel image and the compensated pose image. It is worthwhile, though very difficult, to investigate the pose recovery or compensation method with respect to longitudinal pose variations in future research.

4.2.6 *System performance on varying lighting condition and facial expression*

In this section, the sensitivity to lighting condition and facial expression variations are evaluated. The results indicate that the proposed LHD (on LEM) face matching approach is relatively more robust to lighting condition and expression changes compared to the eigenface and MHD (on edge map) approaches.

The approaches to deal with image variations that are due to illumination changes can be roughly classified into three categories (Adini *et al.*, 1997). The first approach employs the gray-level information to extract 3D shape of the object (Brooks and Horn, 1989; Georghiades *et al.*, 2001). The next approach is based on representations of the faces that are relatively insensitive to lighting condition changes. The edge map of the image (Davis, 1975; Haralick, 1984; Canny, 1986; Torre and Poggio, 1986; Deriche, 1987) is often considered as the basic object representation, which is insensitive to illumination changes to a large extent. It was also used for human face representation (Kanade, 1977; Govindaraju *et al.*, 1989; Wong *et al.*, 1989; Bruneli and Poggio, 1991; Takács, 1998; Gao and Qi, 2005). The line edge map (LEM) (Gao and Leung, 1999, 2002a), which is derived from the edge map with more efficient representation, was proposed for face recognition. It is also expected to be insensitive to illumination changes due to the fact that LEM is an intermediate-level image representation derived from low-level edge map representation. The basic unit of LEM is the line segment grouped from pixels of the edge map. The robustness of LEM to lighting variability and expression changes will be evaluated with respect to the edge map and other face-recognition methods as well. Note that lighting variability includes not only intensity, but also direction and number of light sources. The third approach to handle illumination variations is to use view-based recognition/matching scheme, which employs several images of the same face taken under different lighting conditions as models of the person.

Ideally, an object representation employed for recognition should be invariant to lighting variations. It has been shown theoretically that, for the general case, a function invariant to illumination does not exist (Moses and Ullman, 1992). Edge maps can serve as robust representations to illumination changes for some classes of objects with sharp edges, such as computers, tables, etc. However, for other objects, such as faces, part of the edges can not be obtained consistently. It can be shown theoretically that edges on a smooth surface are not stable with changes in the lighting direction (Moses, 1993). It remains an open question whether LEM, edge maps, and other possible representations provide an illumination-insensitive representation for face recognition.

The issue addressed in this section is whether the LEM representation is sufficient or how well it performs for recognizing faces under varying lighting condition and expression. To answer this question, an empirical study was performed to evaluate the sensitivity of LEM, edge map representation, and eigenface approach to these appearance changes through the performance of face-recognition system.

Two face databases were used in this investigation. The face database from Purdue University was used to evaluate the system performance on lighting condition and expression variations. Figure 4.17 shows 7 sample images of one subject. The image on the first row is in neutral expression with background illumination. The images on the second row are the faces with different facial expressions, i.e., smiling, angry, and screaming. The last row lists the faces under different lighting conditions with left light on, right light on and both lights on.

In order to make an explicit comparison of our proposed methods with the performance of existing approaches in (Belhumeur *et al.*, 1997), the Yale face database (Yale University) was used in the view-based identification experiment.

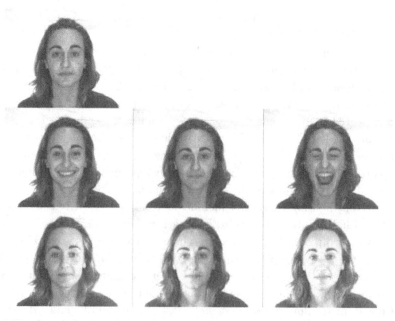

Fig. 4.17.   Sample images of one subject with expression and lighting condition variations.

4.2.6.1 *System evaluation on lighting condition changes*

To evaluate the system performance to lighting condition variations, an experiment was designed using face images taken under different lighting conditions from Purdue University. The faces in neutral expression with background illumination were used as single models of the subjects. The images under three different lighting conditions were used as test images. There are a total of 112 models (representing 112 individuals) and 336 test images. The 112 images in neutral expression with background illumination taken after 14 days were also used to generate a performance benchmark without lighting condition changes. Note that the experiment was based on a single model view. The experimental results with three different lighting conditions are illustrated in Fig. 4.18.

These experiments reveal a number of interesting points:

(1) In all the four experiments, the LHD consistently performed better than MHD with an improvement of 5–7% in recognition rate. The LHD_n further improved the recognition ability over LHD with an additional increment of 3–14%.

(2) The variations of lighting condition did affect the system performance. Nevertheless, the recognition rates were still high and acceptable for real applications. Note that the recognition rate of LHD_n, when only one light was on, stayed higher than 90% (92.86% and 91.07%, respectively). The large number of subjects, compared with the database used in Adini *et al.* (1997) and Belhumeur *et al.* (1997), made it especially interesting. It had also been noted that the rates of correct identification within the top 5 matches were all higher than 92% for LHD_n with all three lighting conditions. The 99.11% and 98.21% for left and right light on were surprisingly high. These results indicate that the proposed LEM and LHD (LHD_n) is insensitive to varying lighting condition to some extent.

(3) It was found that the recognition rates with left light on were always higher than that with right light on. This could imply that the illumination on faces from the right light was actually stronger than that from the left light, though we can not observe these kinds of intensity differences from the images.

(4) When both lights were on, the error rates became much higher than that of only one light on. This evidence shows that the LEM (and edge map) would

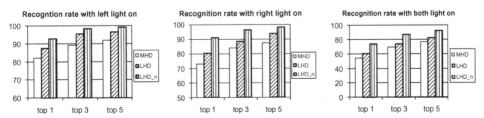

Fig. 4.18. Left: Recognition results with the left light on; Middle: Recognition results with the right light on; Right: Recognition results with both lights on.

still be affected by extreme lighting condition variations, such as over-illumination, though it is insensitive to some extent. The over-illumination would cause strong specular reflection on the face skin. Therefore the shape information on faces would have been suppressed or lost, which would result in the increase of the error rate of classification.

4.2.6.2 *System evaluation on facial expression changes*

Similar experiments were conducted to evaluate the effects of different facial expressions (smile, anger, and scream) on the system performance. The face images of different facial expressions from Purdue University (Purdue University) were used in the experiments. The faces in neutral expression were used as single models of the subjects. There were totally 112 models (representing 112 individuals) and 336 test images.

The experimental results on faces with smile, anger and scream expressions were summarized in Fig. 4.19, respectively. The smile expression caused recognition rate to drop from 17.86% to 35.71% as compared to neutral expression. On the other hand, the anger expression caused only 3.57% to 7.14% drop of the rate. This was not unexpected because the anger expression had produced less physical variation from neutral expression than the expression of smile. The scream expression could be the extreme case of deformation among various human facial expressions, i.e., most facial features had been distorted. The variations between images of the same face were larger than variations due to different face identities. The experimental result on this extreme facial expression was very interesting. Instead of a total failure, LHD and LHD_n could still identify 24.11% and 31.25% of the inputs.

4.2.6.3 *View-based identification experiment and comparison*
with existing approaches

Belhumeur *et al.* (1997) designed tests to determine how different face-recognition methods compared under a different range of conditions and presented the error rates of 5 different face-recognition approaches (eigenfaces, eigenfaces without the three most significant principal components, correlation, linear subspace, and

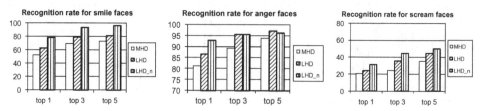

Fig. 4.19.   Left: Recognition result on smile expression; Middle: Recognition result on anger expression; Right: Recognition result on scream expression.

fisherface) using the Yale face database (Yale University). The database, constructed at the Yale Centre for Computational Vision and Control, is composed of 165 images of 15 subjects. The images demonstrate variations in lighting condition (left-light, center-light, right-light), facial expression (normal, happy, sad, sleepy, surprised, and wink) and with/without glasses. A nearest-neighbor classifier operating in various spaces was used. Experiments were performed using a "leaving-one-out" strategy: the models were constructed with all images of a subject except one image that was used as input.

The same strategy and database were adopted here in order to compare LHD (LHD_n) and MHD approaches to methods studied in Belhumeur *et al.* (1997). For comparison purposes, the images were similarly processed as stated by Belhumeur *et al.* to generate closely cropped images that included the internal structures such as the eyebrows, eyes, nose, and mouth, but did not extend to the face contour. The result can not be compared exactly because the cropped face used by Belhumeur *et al.* are not available and our cropped face may be slightly different from theirs. Here we tried our best to clip the same cropped faces as Belhumeur *et al.* did, and intentionally excluded the chins from the cropped faces though they were included in the closely cropped faces by Belhumeur *et al.* Thus, the image condition imposed on our system is stricter (contain less facial area) than that in Belhumeur *et al.* (1997).

The experimental results together with the results conducted by Belhumeur *et al.* were summarized in Table 4.13. A rough comparison of the experimental results shows that LHD_n is superior to all methods except the Fisherface method (Table 4.13). It is worth highlighting that though the performance of MHD is the worst among all the methods in Table 4.13, LHD and LHD_n have greatly improved the system performance to ranks 5 and 2. Note that LHD (LHD_n) uses a more compact (less storage requirement) LEM representation than edge map that MHD uses. The results indicate that LHD (LHD_n) performed slightly better than the eigenface (Eigenface w/o 1st 3) method. Fisherface is specifically designed and only valid for applications of multiple models per person. By complicated computation, it maximizes the difference of between-person variation and the within-person

Table 4.13: "Leave-one-out" test of Yale face database

Method	Error rate (in %)
MHD	**26.06**
Eigenface*	24.40
Correlation*	23.90
LHD	**21.82**
Linear Subspace*	21.60
Eigenface w/o 1st 3*	15.30
LHD_n	**14.55**
Fisherface*	7.30

*Values are from Belhumeur *et al.* (1997).

variation. The test and database (leave-one-out test on 15 individuals and 11 images/person) are extremely "ideal" for Fisherface, whereas all the other 7 methods that can be applied on single-model recognition do not get any favor.

4.3 Face Profile Silhouette Matching Using Strings

Face profile matching is another important aspect of human-face recognition. A face profile provides a complementary structure of the face that is not seen in the frontal view. The combination of the matching results of both frontal and profile faces can improve the false acceptance rate. In addition, the system would be more foolproof because it is difficult to forge the profile face identification by a mask. Profile analysis has also been used to assess the profile changes due to surgical correction (Campos *et al.*, 1993) and to create 3D facial models (Akimoto *et al.*, 1990).

Most traditional methods on profile recognition depend on the correct detection of fiducial points. Unfortunately, some features, such as concave nose, protrude lips, flat chin etc., make detection of such points difficult and unreliable. The human face profile is a highly structured geometric curve. From the viewpoint of representation, the set of fiducial points is a "sparse" representation of the underlying structures while the outline curve is a "dense" but honest representation of the shape. A high-level curve matching approach is therefore more appropriate and robust than point-matching methods. A novel syntactic technique using attributed strings was proposed by the authors (Gao and Leung, 2002b) to recognize a chain of profile line segments rather than a set of inconsistent fiducial points. It highlights the favor of curve matching by suppressing the edit operations of "insert" and "delete". The major operations are the "merge" and "change" of string primitives. A quadratic penalty function is employed to prohibit large angle changes and overmerging. This technique provides strong discriminative power into the string matching method for similar shape classification and is found to be more accurate to distinguish one face from the other.

4.3.1 *Merge dominant string match*

The proposed string representation is based on the line segments generated from polygonal line fitting (Leung and Yang, 1990) on face-profile outlines. Line segments are 2D entities with attributes of orientation, length, and the structural information of relative location to each other. The shape of an object can be described as a set of ordered line segments using appropriate string representation.

4.3.1.1 *Attributes determination*

In order to enhance the representation power of attributes in (Tsai and Yu, 1985) for similar shape matching, the relative locations of line segments from each other should be included. This can be achieved with the line primitive representation as

$P(l, \theta, x, y)$ where l, θ, x, and y are the length, orientation, and midpoint location of the line, respectively. The line orientation θ is defined as the minimum angle formed between the line segment and the reference line. The line between the nose tip and chin point is used as the reference line in this study.

4.3.1.2 *String edit operations*

The sequence of line segments from a face profile can be obtained through polygonal approximation or dominant points detection techniques. However, some objects, such as the face profiles lack sharp turning curvatures. This causes the adding, missing, and shifting of feature points. Conventional string-matching methods (Tsai and Yu, 1985) that use three types of edit operations (i.e., change, insertion, and deletion) to transform one string into another would behave badly under such circumstance. A merge dominant string matching method that suppresses insertion and deletion but encourage merging is proposed here to tackle this inconsistency problem.

Let A and B be two strings of line segment primitives, $A\langle i \rangle$ and $B\langle j \rangle$ be the ith and jth primitives in A and B with attributes $(l_i, \theta_i, x_i, y_i)$ and $(l_j, \theta_j, x_j, y_j)$, respectively. Define $A\langle i : j \rangle$ to be the substring from the ith to the jth primitives of A, and $A(i)$, $B(j)$ to be $A\langle 1 : i \rangle$, $B\langle 1 : j \rangle$. The cost function for a change operation from $A\langle i \rangle$ to $B\langle j \rangle$, denoted as $A\langle i \rangle \rightarrow B\langle j \rangle$, is defined as

$$C(A\langle i \rangle \rightarrow B\langle j \rangle) = |l_i - l_j| + \sqrt{(x_i - x_j)^2 + (y_i - y_j)^2} + f(\Delta(\theta_i, \theta_j)) \qquad (4.13)$$

where

$$\Delta(\theta_i, \theta_j) = \begin{cases} |\theta_i - \theta_j|, & \text{if } |\theta_i - \theta_j| \leq 90° \\ 180° - |\theta_i - \theta_j|, & \text{if } 90° < |\theta_i - \theta_j| \leq 180° \\ |\theta_i - \theta_j| - 180°, & \text{if } 180° < |\theta_i - \theta_j| \leq 270° \\ 360° - |\theta_i - \theta_j|, & \text{if } 270° < |\theta_i - \theta_j| \leq 360° \end{cases} \qquad (4.14)$$

$f()$ is a non-linear penalty function to map an angle to a scalar. It is desirable to ignore small angle variation but penalize heavily on large deviation. In this study, the function

$$f(x) = x^2/W \qquad (4.15)$$

is used where W is the weight to be determined experimentally.

A merge operation (Tsai and Yu, 1985) with modified merge cost is used to tackle the problem of adding, missing, and shifting of feature points. Let $A\langle i - k + 1 : i \rangle = P_{i-k+1} P_{i-k+2} \cdots P_i$ be a sequence of k primitives on a boundary to be merged, and $A^k \langle i \rangle$ be the merged primitive of these k primitives. One example is illustrated in Fig. 4.20 with $k = 4$. The merge operation is, therefore, denoted as $A\langle i - k + 1 : j \rangle \rightarrow A^k \langle i \rangle$. For $k = 1$, it becomes $A\langle i - k + 1 : i \rangle = A\langle i : i \rangle$, which is the case without any merge operation. The cost function in merging k primitives

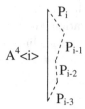

Fig. 4.20.   An example of the merge operation.

is defined as

$$C(A\langle i - k + 1 : i\rangle \rightarrow A^k\langle i\rangle) = f\left(\frac{k-1}{l^k} \sum_{n=i-k+1}^{i} \Delta(\theta^k, \theta_n) \times l_n\right) \quad (4.16)$$

where l^k and θ^k respectively are the length and line orientation of the merged primitive $(A^k\langle i\rangle)$, l_n and θ_n are the length and line orientation of primitive P_n before merging. Every $\Delta(\theta^k, \theta_n)$ is weighted by the line segment's length l_n because the contribution of angle difference of a primitive is assumed to be proportional to its length. The number of merge operations, $k-1$, is also taken into the consideration of the cost.

The cost function of a change operation after merge can be rewritten as

$$C(A^k\langle i\rangle \rightarrow B^l\langle j\rangle) = |l^k - l^l| + \sqrt{(x^k - x^l)^2 + (y^k - y^l)^2} + f(\Delta(\theta^k, \theta^l)) \quad (4.17)$$

Equation (4.13) is the special case of Eq. (4.17) with $k = l = 1$, which is the case without merge operation.

4.3.1.3 *Merge dominant mechanism*

For the costs of insert and delete operations, a null primitive Λ with zero length and indefinite angle and location is used. Suppose strings A and B are two profile strings from the same person. Intuitively, the new strings A' and B' after merging would have the same number of primitives with minimal merge costs. In addition, each corresponding primitive from A' and B' would resemble each other with little change cost. This would change completely with much higher costs if A and B are from different people. Thus, the matching process can be accomplished with just the merge and change operations. The insert and delete operations would only be useful if there are missing parts of the profile curve. Based on the above assumption, a merge dominant method is applied to encourage merge operation but penalize heavily the insert and delete operations by increasing the costs of these two operations as

$$C(A\langle i\rangle \rightarrow \Lambda) = f(K_\theta) + l_i + K_{\text{loc}} \quad (4.18)$$

$$C(\Lambda \rightarrow B\langle j\rangle) = f(K_\theta) + l_j + K_{\text{loc}} \quad (4.19)$$

where l_i and l_j are the lengths of the ith and jth primitives in strings A and B, while K_θ and K_{loc} are constants to represent the indefinite orientation and location of the line segment. For the purpose of penalization, the maximum angle difference, $90°$, is assigned to K_θ, and the maximum location difference, the diagonal distance of the input image, is assigned to K_{loc}. String matching is conducted according to Algorithm 1 where *merg_limitA* and *merg_limitB* are the controlled upper limit of merged primitives in strings A and B, respectively. More details of these numbers can be found in the next section. $D(i, j)$ is the edit distance or the minimum cost to match substring $A(i)$ to substring $B(j)$. Figure 4.21 illustrates two examples in applying the technique to handle adding, missing, and shifting feature points.

4.3.1.4 *Merge number limit*

The proposed dynamic programming technique is computationally expensive with time complexity as $O(m^2 \times n^2)$ for strings of lengths m and n (Fig. 4.22). In order to cut down the computation time, an upper limit on the number (*merge_limit =*

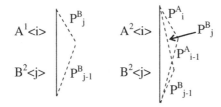

Fig. 4.21.   Examples of match pairs with the merge dominant string matching.

```
D(0,0):=0
for i:=1 to m do  D(i,0):=D(i-1,0)+C( A<i>→∧ )
for i:=1 to n do  D(0,j):=D(0,j-1)+C( ∧→B<j> )
for i:=1 to m do
    for j:=1 to n do
        begin
            m1:=D(i,j-1)+ C(∧→B<j>);
            m2:=D(i-1,j)+ C(A<i>→∧);
            for k:=1 to min(i, merge_limitA)
                for l:=1 to min(j, merge_limitB)
                    mm3(k,l):=D(i-k,j-l)
                                 + C(A<i-k+1:i>→ A^k<i>)
                                 + C(B<j-l+1:j>→ B^l<j>)
                                 + C(A^k<i>→ B^l<j>);
            m3:=        min        mm3(k,l);
                1≤k≤min(i,merge_limit A)
                1≤l≤min(j,merge_limit B)
            D(i,j):=min(m1,m2,m3);
        end
```

Fig. 4.22.   Algorithm 1: Merge dominant string matching. m and n are the line segment numbers of strings A and B.

$merge\_limitA = merge\_limitB$) of merged primitives to form a new one is imposed in this work. The computation complexity can then be reduced to $O(m \times n \times merge\_limit^2)$. In this study, $merge\_limit$ is found suitable to take a value ≥ 3 for human face profile recognition (see next section).

4.3.2 Experimental results

A face database of 30 persons with 2 profiles images per person from the University of Bern was used to test the capability of the proposed approach. Each image has the size of 512×342 pixels with very high contrast. The two profile images of each person were used as model and input, respectively. There are 60 matching experiments in total if the roles of model and input are interchanged. The nose tip and chin point for each profile face were detected automatically in the pre-processing stage. The line, L, between these two points was used to normalize image size, align face position, and crop facial area to avoid processing subject's hair. The face-profile images were segmented by binarization, edge detection, and thinning process to obtain 1-pixel-wide outline curves and the feature point detection algorithm (Leung and Yang, 1990) was used to approximate the curves with line segments. Thus, every face-profile outline was represented by a set of segment endpoints. Note that some pairs are so similar that even human observers can hardly distinguish them. In addition, there are instances of adding, missing, and shifting of feature points from one profile to its match.

To evaluate the overall recognition performance and analyze parameter sensitivity, two experiments were conducted with W and $merge\_limit$ as variables. W was found to be easily tuned since the recognition rate remained higher than 96% when W ranged from 30 to 100 (Fig. 4.23). Note that the recognition rate was as high as 100% when W ranged from 40 to 50 with $merge\_limit = 3$.

It is found that the system without merging (i.e., $merge\_limit = 1$, which means only one line is merged into a line) could only correctly recognize 10% of the faces (Fig. 4.24). It improved quickly with merge operations and reached the optimal value of 100% when $merge\_limit$ was 3. The system performance then degraded

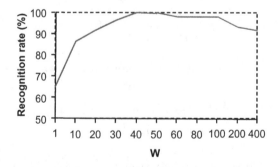

Fig. 4.23.   The effect of W on the recognition rate ($merge\_limit = 3$).

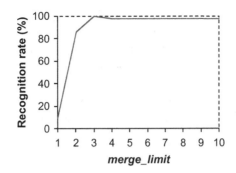

Fig. 4.24. The effect of merge_limit on the recognition rate ($W = 50$).

Table 4.14: Performance comparison of 3 different level approaches

Method	MHD (point-to-point matching) (in %)	LHD (line-to-line matching) (in %)	MDSM (curve-to-curve matching) (in %)
Recognition rate	93.3	96.7	$98.33 \sim 100$

MDSM: merge dominant string matching.

slightly to 98.33% and kept unchanged even when *merge_limit* approached infinitive. This result demonstrates that the system design is correct with excellent and stable performance.

It is interesting to compare the proposed method with other techniques as shown in Table 4.14. MHD is the modified Hausdorff distance (Takács, 1998) to match one template to the other in a point-to-point matching manner while LHD is the line segment Hausdorff distance (Gao and Leung, 1999, 2002a) to match in a line-to-line fashion. The current method proposes a curve-to-curve matching approach. From Table 4.14, it is obvious that the results improve (become more accurate) from the point-to-point approach to the curve-to-curve technique. On the other hand, the former is more flexible while the proposed might be restricted to well-segmented curves. This is a reasonable trade-off between flexibility and accuracy.

4.3.3 *Summary*

This section presents a new curve-matching method for human face profile recognition. The technique relies mainly on the merge and change operations of string to tackle the inconsistent problem of feature-point detection. Hence, the proposed approach suppresses the string edit operations of insert and delete. A quadratic penalty function is used to prohibit large angle changes and overmerging. This makes the proposed technique robust to the errors from previous low-level processing that are usually inevitable in practice. The method produces very encouraging results and is found to be suitable for similar shape classification.

Compared with previous human face profile recognition methods, our method employs line segments derived objectively from the outlines instead of fiducial marks that were based on heuristic rules and may be invalid for unusual faces. Moreover, line segments are more reliable and accurate than fiducial marks to represent the distinctive details of an object. The experimental results also indicate that merge dominant string matching approach provides a new way to enhance the discriminative capability of string matching for the application of similar object classification.

4.4 Conclusion

The automatic recognition of human faces presents a significant challenge to the pattern recognition research community. Typically, human faces are very similar in structure with minor differences from person to person. They are actually within one class of "human face." Furthermore, the appearances vary depending on the circumstances. Pose variations, lighting condition changes, and facial expressions further complicate the face-recognition task as one of the difficult problems in pattern analysis.

This research demonstrated that faces can be recognized using edges. A compact face feature, LEM, is extracted for face coding and recognition. A complete investigation on the proposed concept is conducted according to two independent organization schemes. The first scheme covers all three (low, intermediate, and high) level pattern recognition approaches on face recognition. They are:

(1) Low-level (representation) approach: The pixel-wise modified hausdorff distance (MHD) face-recognition approach using spatial information of a face edge map.
(2) Intermediate-level (representation) approach: The proposed LHD (LHD_n) face-recognition approach using both spatial and local structural information of a face LEM.
(3) High-level (representation) approach: The proposed syntactic face representation and matching approach using structural and string representation of faces.

The second scheme covers all major aspects on human face recognition. They are:

(1) Face recognition under controlled condition.
(2) Face recognition under varying pose.
(3) Face recognition under varying lighting condition.
(4) Face recognition under varying facial expression.

The system performances are also compared with the eigenface method and reported experiment results of other methods. The results demonstrate that edges on human faces provide sufficient information for face recognition. LHD (LHD_n) and LEM provide a effective way for face coding and recognition.

References

Bern university face database, ftp://iamftp.unibe.ch/pub/Images/FaceImages/, 1990.

Adini, Y., Moses, Y., and Ullman, S. Face recognition: the problem of compensation for changes in illumination direction, *IEEE Trans. PAMI* **19**, 721–732, 1997.

Akimoto, T. A., Wallace, R., and Suenaga, Y. Feature extraction from front and side views of faces for 3d model creation, in *Proc. of IAPR Workshop on Machine Vision and Application* (Tokyo), pp. 291–294, 1990.

Belhumeur, P. N., Hespanha, J. P., and Kriegman, D. J. Eigenfaces vs. fisherfaces: recognition using class specific linear projection, *IEEE Trans. PAMI* **19**, 711–720, 1997.

Biederman, I. and Gu, J. Surface versus edge-based determinants of visual recognition, *Cognitive Psychology* **20**, 38–64, 1988.

Brooks, M. J. and Horn, B. K. *Shape from Shading* (MIT Press, Cambridge), 1989.

Bruce, V. Changing faces: Visual and non-visual coding processes in face recognition, *Br. J. Psychol.* **73**, 105–116, 1982.

Bruneli, R. and Poggio, T. Hyperbf networks for real object recognition, in *Proceedings IJCAI*, 1278–1284, 1991.

Campos, J. C., Linney, A. D., and Moss, J. P. The analysis of facial profiles using scale space techniques, *Pattern Recognition* **26**, 819–824, 1993.

Canny, J. A computational approach to edge detection, *IEEE Trans. Pattern Anal. Machine Intelligence* **8**, 679–698, 1986.

Chellappa, R., Wilson, C. L., and Sirohey, S. Human and machine recognition of faces: a survey, *Proc. IEEE* **83**, 705–740, 1995.

Davis, L. S. A survey of edge detection techniques, *Computer Graphics Image Processing* **4**, 248–270, 1975.

Deriche, R. Optimal edge detection using recursive filtering, in *Proc. IEEE Int. Conf. Comput. Vision*, 501–504, 1987.

Gao, Y. and Leung, M. K. Human face recognition using line edge maps, in *Proc. IEEE Second Workshop on Automatic Identification Advanced Technologies* (New Jersey), pp. 173–176, 1999.

Gao, Y. and Leung, M. K. Face recognition using line edge map, *IEEE Trans. PAMI* **24**, 6, 764–779, 2002a.

Gao, Y. and Leung, M. K. Human face profile recognition using attributed string, *Pattern Recognition* **35**, 2, 353–360, 2002b.

Gao, Y. and Leung, M. K. Line segment hausdorff distance on face matching, *Pattern Recognition* **35**, 2, 361–371, 2002c.

Gao, Y. and Qi, Y. Robust visual similarity retrieval in single model face databases, *Pattern Recognition* **38**, 1009–1020, 2005.

Georghiades, A. S., Belhumeur, P. N., and Kriegman, D. J. From few to many: illumination cone models for face recognition under variable lighting and pose, *IEEE Trans. PAMI* **23**, 6, 643–660, 2001.

Govindaraju, V., Sher, D. B., Srihari, R., and Srihari, S. N. Locating human faces in newspaper photographs, in *Proc. IEEE Int. Conf. Comput. Vision Pattern Recognition*, 549–554, 1989.

Haralick, R. M. Digital step edges from zero crossing of second directional derivatives, *IEEE Trans. Pattern Anal. Machine Intelligence* **6**, 58–68, 1984.

Kanade, T. *Computer Recognition of Human Faces* (Basel and Stuttgart, Birkhauser Verlag), 1977.

Kirby, M. and Sirovich, L. Application of the karhunen-loève procedure for the characterisation of human faces, *IEEE Trans. Pattern Analysis Machine Intelligence* **12**, 831–835, 1990.

Kirkpatrick, S., Gelatt, J. C. and Vecchi, M. P. Optimization by simulated annealing, *Science* **220**, 671–680, 1993.

Leung, M. K. and Yang, Y. H. Dynamic two-strip algorithm in curve fitting, *Pattern Recognition* **23**, 69–79, 1990.

Moses, Y. *Face Recognition: Generalization to Novel Images*, Ph.D. thesis, Weizman Institute of Science, 1993.

Moses, Y. and Ullman, S. Limitation of non-model-based recognition schemes, in *Proc. ECCV*, 820–828, 1992.

Otten, R. H. J. M. and van Ginneken, L. P. P. P. *The Annealing Algorithm* (Kluwer Academic Publishers), 1989.

Swets, D. L. and Weng, J. Using discriminant eigenfeatures for image retrieval, *IEEE Trans. Pattern Anal. Machine Intelligence* **18**, 831–836, 1996.

Takács, B. Comparing face images using the modified hausdorff distance, *Pattern Recognition* **31**, 1873–1881, 1998.

Takács, B. and Wechsler, H. Face recognition using binary image metrics, in *Proc. Second Face and Gesture Recognition*, 294–299, 1998.

Torre, V. and Poggio, T. On edge detection, *IEEE Trans. Pattern Anal. Machine Intelligence* **8**, 147–163, 1986.

Tsai, W. H. and Yu, S. S. Attributed string matching with merging for shape recognition, *IEEE Trans. Pattern Anal. Machine Intelligence* **7**, 453–462, 1985.

Turk, M. A. and Pentland, A. P. Eigenfaces for recognition, *J. Cognitive Neurosci.* **3**, 71–86, 1991.

van Laarhoven, P. J. and Aarts, E. H. *Simulated Annealing: Theory and Applications* (Kluwer Academic Publishers), 1987.

Wong, K., Law, H., and Tsang, P. A system for recognising human faces, in *Proc. ICASSP*, 1638–1642, 1989.

Chapter 5

ENHANCING THE PERFORMANCE OF LOCAL BINARY PATTERNS FOR FACE RECOGNITION BY SPECTRAL REGRESSION

Bailing Zhang

Department of Computer Science and Software Engineering
Xi'an Jiaotong-Liverpool University, Suzhou, China
bailing.zhang@xjtlu.edu.cn

Yanchun Zhang

Centre for Applied Informatics Research
School of Engineering and Science, Victoria University, Australia

5.1 Introduction

Face recognition has remained to be one of the most challenging research topics in computer vision over the past two decades. It is also considered as an important field in biometrics. Mug-shot database matching, identity authentication for credit card or drivers license, access control, and video surveillance are the typical examples of potential applications. Motivated by the demands from security, finance, law enforcement, and military, face recognition has received substantial attention from both research communities and the industry in recent years. Many influential methods, such as eigenface, Fisherface (Belhumeur *et al.*, 1997), and elastic graph matching (Wiskott *et al.*, 1997), have been proposed in the past. Recent years have also seen considerable progress made on other related problems such as facial expression recognition, face tracking and detection. Despite the substantial effort and some success, the face-recognition problem remains one of the most challenging computer vision problem for real-time applications. One of difficulties arises from the fact that "the variations between the images of the same face due to illumination and viewing direction are almost always larger than image variations due to change in face identity" (Moses *et al.*, 1994). These variations are made even greater by additional wide range of real-world conditions such as partial occlusion, facial expression, perspiration, hair styles, cosmetics, and even changes due to aging. How to create a face-recognition system which is robust to these variations is still an open problem calling for sustained efforts.

Face recognition is a typical pattern classification problem: Given a set of face images labeled with the person's identity (the gallery set), a face-recognition system should identify a specific subject by a query face image and the objective of face recognition is to decide in which class a query facial image belongs to. The general methodology in face recognition adopts the multiclass classification paradigm, with a range of different classification methods having been attempted, for example, the nearest neighbor (NN) classifier and multilayer perceptron (MLP). One of the fundamental issues in designing a face-recognition system is finding efficient and discriminative facial features, which will be used by the classifier. Ideal facial features should be able to counteract large variations in illumination, pose, facial expression, aging, partial occlusions, and other changes. In recent years, facial feature description based on extracting and pooling local structural information ("micro-patterns") from images has been considered as one of the most successful methods. Among them, the local binary pattern (LBP) has become influential for facial representation recently (Ahonen et al., 2006; Marcel et al., 2007). As an efficient non-parametric method summarizing the local structure of an image, LBP descriptor has important properties of their tolerance against monotonic illumination changes and their computational simplicity.

In the existing LBP-based facial representation, face images are first equally divided into non-overlapping blocks to extract the LBP histograms within each block, which are then concatenated into a single, spatially enhanced feature histogram. The LBP histograms extracted from local facial blocks are the region-level description. However, not all bins in the LBP histogram contain useful discriminant information for facial recognition. Due to the existence of variations on occlusions, pose, or illumination in face images, some of the raw LBP features may even degrade the system performance. Naturally, selecting useful information from the original LBP features is an important step prior to classification, which is usually implemented by dimension reduction. Principal component analysis (PCA) and linear discriminant analysis (LDA) have been two of the most commonly used linear dimension reduction methods in face-recognition. The PCA provides an optimal linear transformation from the original image space to an orthogonal eigenspace with reduced dimensionality in the sense of the least mean square reconstruction error. In LDA, a dimension reducing linear transformation that preserves the clustered structure of the original space is sought after. The class separability can be optimized by maximizing the scatter between classes and minimizing the scatter within classes. However, both the PCA and LDA have their deficiencies. The PCA optimizes for reconstruction rather than discrimination, and LDA is constrained both by its Gaussian with equal-covariance construction and by its inability to handle degenerate class covariance.

In recent years, manifold learning for non-linear dimensionality reduction has been extensively studied. Some techniques are based on local neighborhood relationships such as isomap (Tenenbaum et al., 2000), Locally linear embedding (Roweis and Saul, 2000), and Laplacian eigenmaps (Belkin and Niyogi, 2001).

But these approaches are essentially descriptive methods not discriminative ones. In fact, as initially defined, they handle only training data. In other words, they do not generally provide a functional mapping between the high- and low-dimensional spaces that are valid both on and off the training data (Cai *et al.*, 2007). Cai accordingly proposed a novel dimensionality reduction algorithm, called spectral regression (SR), which is based on regression- and spectral-graph analysis. An affinity graph over the labeled points is first constructed to represent each vertex of a graph as a low-dimensional vector that preserves similarities between the vertex pairs, where similarity is measured by the edge weight. The intrinsic discriminant structure in the data can then be discovered and used to learn responses for labeled points. Once the responses are obtained, the ordinary regression is applied for learning the embedding function. In this paper, we propose to improve the LBP performance for face recognition by applying the non-linear dimension reduction SR. With dimension-reduced LBP histogram features, face recognition is implemented in a multiclass classification framework, with some well-known classifiers compared including k-NN, Naive Bayes, Fisher discriminant analysis, MLP, and support vector machine.

The chapter is organized as follows. In Sec. 1.2, we first briefly review the local binary pattern and its application in face recogntion, followed by the introduction of the non-linear dimension reduction SR in Sec. 5.3. Section 5.4 describes the experiments with a number of different benchmarking face datasets and several different classification techniques. Conclusions are summarized in Sec. 5.5.

5.2 Local Binary Patterns

Local binary pattern (LBP) operator was introduced as a texture descriptor for summarizing local gray-level structure (Ojala *et al.*, 2000). The LBP labels pixels of an image by taking a local neighborhood around each pixel, thresholding the pixels of the neighborhood at the value of the central pixel and using the resulting binary-valued image patch as a local image descriptor. In other words, the operator assigns a binary code of 0 and 1 to each neighbor of the neighborhoods. The binary code of each pixel in the case of 3×3 neighborhoods would be a binary code of 8 bits and by a single scan through the image for each pixel the LBP codes of the entire image can be calculated. Figure 5.1 shows an example of an LPB operator utilizing 3×3 neighborhoods.

Formally, the LBP operator takes the form

$$\mathrm{LBP}(x_c, y_c) = \sum_{n=0}^{8} 2^n s(i_n - i_c) \tag{5.1}$$

where in this case n runs over the 8 neighbors of the central pixel c, i_c and i_n are the gray-level values at c and n, and $s(u)$ is 1 if $u \geq 0$ and 0 otherwise.

An useful extension to the original LBP operator is the so-called uniform patterns (Ojala *et al.*, 2002). An LBP is "uniform" if it contains at most two bitwise

B. Zhang and Y. Zhang

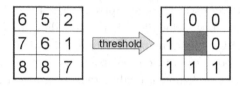

Binary code = **11110001**
LBP = 1 + 16 +32 + 64 + 128 = **241**

Fig. 5.1.   Illustration of the basic LBP operator.

transitions from 0 to 1 or vice versa when the binary string is considered circular. For example, 11100001 (with 2 transitions) is a uniform pattern, whereas 11110101 (with 4 transitions) is a non-uniform pattern. The uniform LBP describes those structures, which contain at most two bitwise (0 to 1 or 1 to 0) transitions. Uniformity is an important concept in the LBP methodology, representing important structural features such as edges, spots, and corners. Ojala *et al.* observed that although only 58 of the 256 8-bit patterns are uniform, nearly 90% of all observed image neighborhoods are uniform (Ojala *et al.*, 2002). We use the notation $\text{LBP}_{P,R}^{u}$ for the uniform LBP operator. $\text{LBP}_{P,R}^{u}$ means using the LBP operator in a neighborhood of P sampling points on a circle of radius R. The superscript u stands for using uniform patterns and labeling all remaining patterns with a single label. The number of labels for a neighborhood of 8 pixels is 256 for standard LBP and 59 for $\text{LBP}_{8,1}^{u}$.

A common practice to apply the LBP coding over the image is by using the histogram of the labels, where a 256-bin histogram represents the texture description of the image and each bin can be regarded as a micropattern. Local primitives, which are coded by these bins include different types of curved edges, spots, flat areas, etc. The distribution of these patterns represents the whole structure of the texture. The number of patterns in an LBP histogram can be reduced by only using uniform patterns without losing much information. There are totally 58 different uniform patterns at 8-bit LBP representation and the remaining patterns can be assigned in one non-uniform binary number, thus representing the texture structure with a 59-bin histogram instead of using 256 bins.

LBP-based face representation scheme as introduced in Ahonen *et al.* (2006) for face recognition can be outlined as follows. First, face images are divided into M small non-overlapping rectangular blocks $R_0, R_1, \ldots, R_{M-1}$. On each block, the histogram of local binary patterns is calculated. The procedure can be illustrated by Fig. 5.2. The LBP histograms extracted from each image block $f_l(x, y)$ are then concatenated into a single, spatially enhanced feature histogram defined as

$$H_{ij} = \sum_{x,y} I(f_l(x,y) = i), \quad I(x,y) \in R_j \tag{5.2}$$

where $i = 0, \ldots, L - 1, j = 0, \ldots, M - 1$. The extracted feature histogram describes the local texture and global shape of face images. The same face representation has also been proved effective for facial expression recognition (Shan *et al.*, 2005).

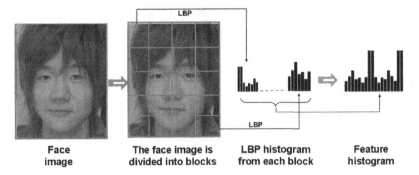

| Face image | The face image is divided into blocks | LBP histogram from each block | Feature histogram |

Fig. 5.2.   Feature extraction diagram for face recognition with local binary patterns.

LBP has been proved to be a good texture descriptor that is easy to compute and has high extraclass variance (i.e., between different persons in the case of face recognition) and low intraclass variance, which means that the descriptor is robust with respect to aging of the subjects, alternating illumination, and other factors. Recently, a number of variants of LBP have been proposed. For example, Adaboost later was adopted to learn the most discriminative subregions (in term of LBP histogram) from a large pool of subregions generated by shifting and scaling a subwindow over face images (Zhang *et al.*, 2004). The LBP approach has also inspired many other algorithms on face recognition. In Zhang *et al.* (2005), LBP is performed on Gabor-filtered images and the obtained representation is used for face recognition the same way as in Ahonen *et al.* (2006).

5.3 Dimension Reduction with SR

The LBP histogram method introduced above often results in very high dimensional feature vectors that are obtained by concatenating the local LBP histograms. Not all of the histogram bins contain useful discriminant information for facial recognition. Due to the existence of variations on occlusion, pose, or illumination in face images, some of the LBP bins may even degrade the system performance. The recognition performance can be improved by applying appropriate dimensionality reduction, which extracts a smaller number of intrinsic features.

The goal of dimensionality-reduction techniques is to map high-dimensional data samples to a lower-dimensional space such that certain properties are preserved. A unified view for understanding and explaining many popular dimensionality-reduction algorithms is the graph-embedding framework, which has attracted much research interest over the past few years. The graph-embedding framework typically relies on some graph to capture the salient geometric relations of the data in the high-dimensional space. This graph is usually called an affinity graph, since its edge set conveys some information about the proximity of the data in the input space. The eigenvectors of the corresponding affinity (i.e., item–item similarity) matrix can reveal low-dimensional structure in high-dimensional data.

Among the new developments, a novel dimensionality-reduction method, called SR, was proposed in Cai *et al.* (2007), which casts the problem of learning an embedding function into a regression framework without the eigen decomposition of dense matrices.

Given m samples $\{\mathbf{x}_i\}_{i=1}^m \subset R^n$, we wish to produce a set $\{\mathbf{a}_i\}_{i=1}^m \subset R^d$, which is an accurate representation of $\{\mathbf{x}_i\}$, but whose dimension d is much less than the original dimension n. We can use a graph with m vertices to model the geometry inherent in the data, with each vertex representing a data point. For classification purpose, the class labels can be used to build the graph, with edge weights assigned in order to determine how each sample is influenced by its neighbors.

To be more specific, Graph Laplacian starts with the construction of a similarity matrix $m \times m$ matrix W by finding the k-NN points using the Euclidean norm in R^n and weights are assigned as follows: $W_{ij} = 1$ if two points $\mathbf{x}_i$ and $\mathbf{x}_j$ are neighbors and $W_{ij} = 0$, otherwise. Alternatively, weights can be assigned by using the heat kernel, $W_{ij} = \exp(-(\|\mathbf{x}_i - \mathbf{x}_j\|^2)/t)$ (Niyogi, 2003). The weight assignment can be supervised if the class labels for these points are also given. Therefore, a symmetric $m \times m$ matrix W is defined with W_{ij} having the weight of the edge-joining vertices i and j if and only if x_i and x_j belong to the same class. In this chapter, the supervised method is used to calculate W.

With the similarity matrix W defined above, graph embedding can be elaborated as in the following. Let $\mathbf{y} = [y_1, y_2, \ldots, y_m]^T$ be the map from the graph to the real line. The optimal y tries to minimize the following graph-preserving criterion:

$$\mathbf{y} = \arg \min_{\mathbf{y}^T D \mathbf{y} = 1} \sum_{ij} (y_i - y_j)^2 W_{ij} = \arg \min_{\mathbf{y}} \mathbf{y}^T L \mathbf{y} \tag{5.3}$$

where $L = D - W$ is is called Laplacian matrix (Belkin and Niyogi, 2001) and D is a diagonal matrix whose entries are column (or row, since W is symmetric) sums of W, $D_{ii} = \sum_j W_{ji}$. In the above optimization, a high penalty will exert on the similar vertices $\mathbf{x}_i$ and $\mathbf{x}_j$ when they are mapped far apart. Therefore, it tries to preserve the neighborhood structure of the original data points in the low-dimension embedding. The optimization problem can be solved efficiently by calculating the eigenvectors of the generalized eigenproblem $W\mathbf{y} = \lambda D\mathbf{y}$. The solution can be expressed as

$$\mathbf{y}^* = \arg \max_{\mathbf{y}} \frac{\mathbf{y}^T W \mathbf{y}}{\mathbf{y}^T D \mathbf{y}} \tag{5.4}$$

The solution y can be obtained by solving the generalized eigenproblem corresponding to the maximum eigenvalue

$$W\mathbf{y} = \lambda D\mathbf{y} \tag{5.5}$$

Graph Laplacian provides one of the most common and useful tools for dimensionality reduction and can be combined with regression technique for classification. For classification purpose, a mapping for all samples, including new test samples, is required. If we choose a linear function, i.e., $y_i = f(\mathbf{x}_i) = \mathbf{a}^T\mathbf{x}_i$, the following regularized least squares problem need to be solved to find $c - 1$ vectors $\mathbf{a}_1, \mathbf{a}_2, \ldots, \mathbf{a}_{c-1} \in R^n$:

$$\mathbf{a}_k = \arg\min_{\mathbf{a}} \left\{ \sum_{i=1}^{m} (\mathbf{a}^T\mathbf{x}_i - y_i^k)^2 + \alpha||\mathbf{a}||^2 \right\} \tag{5.6}$$

where y_i^k is the ith element of $\mathbf{y}_k$. The regularization term guarantees that the least squares problem is well posed and has a unique solution. It is easy to check that $\mathbf{a}_k$ is the solution of the linear equations system:

$$(XX^T + \alpha I)\mathbf{a}_k = X\mathbf{y}_k \tag{5.7}$$

where I is a $n \times n$ identity matrix.

This technique is called SR since it performs spectral analysis on the Laplacian graph followed by least squares regression. Once the relationship is learned from training data, it can be extended to out-of-sample data. The essence of SR introduced above is the linearization of graph embedding. Many linear subspace learning methods such as the PCA, LDA, locality preserving projections (LPPs) (He and Niyogi, 2003) etc. can all be elaborated in such a framework by defining different similarity matrix W. For example, for LDA, the similarity matrix W can be defined as follows

$$W_{ij} = \begin{cases} 1/m_t & \text{if } \mathbf{x}_i \text{ and } \mathbf{x}_j \text{ belong to the } t\text{th class} \\ 0 & \text{otherwise} \end{cases} \tag{5.8}$$

where m_t is the number of samples in the tth classes.

In summary, the linear embedding functions can be acquired through the following two steps (Cai *et al.*, 2007)

(1) Solve the eigenproblem $W\mathbf{y} = \lambda D\mathbf{y}$ from Eq. (5.4) to get y.
(2) Find $\mathbf{a}$ from Eq. (5.6).

5.4 Experiments

In this section, we evaluate face-recognition performance from applying LBP with the non-linear dimension-reduction SR, by conducting a number of experiments using different scenarios and several publically available datasets. In all the experiments, we consider only the rank 1 recognition rate percentage results, where rank actually shows among how many top matches is the correct answer. We address the issue of evaluating face-recognition algorithm using descriptive statistics by repetitively and randomly dividing the dataset in probe and gallery sets. For all the datasets, we do not employ any kind of preprocessing or normalization such as detecting and fixing eye location or eye distance, which have been adopted for most of the previous face-recognition researches, particularly for face images across pose which suffers from typical misalignments.

As most of the texture information is contained in the uniform patterns (Ojala *et al.*, 2002), a 59-label $\text{LBP}_{8,1}^u$ operator as introduced in Sec. 5.2 is used throughout our experiments, i.e., $\text{LBP}_{8,1}^u$ operator is applied to non-overlapping image subregions to form a concatenated histogram. We directly use the plain LBP for all images without weighting over different subregions as proposed in Ahonen *et al.* (2006). As noted in Ahonen *et al.* (2006), the subregions do not need to be of the same size and do not necessarily have to cover the whole image. It was also pointed out in the same paper that the LBP representation is quite robust with respect to the selection of parameters when looking for the optimal window size. Changes in the parameters may cause big differences in the length of the feature vector, but the overall performance is not necessarily affected significantly. Therefore, in all the experiments we fixed a subregion (window) size for a given dataset.

For each dataset, we randomly split it into training and testing sets, each time with 20% of each subject's images reserved for testing while the rest for training. In all the experiments, the number of subjects in the training set was equal to the number of subjects in the test set. The classification accuracy results reported are the average accuracies of 100 runs, such that each run used a random split of the data to training and testing sets. This is different with most of the previous face-recognition experiments where researchers tested their methods using restricted databases or some special subset of a given dataset.

We compare the recognition performance from five classification methods, with more details described as follows.

(1) Linear discriminant analysis. With the PCA or SR subspace projection as a first step in processing the LBP features, the Fisher linear discriminants are then defined in the resulted d dimensional subspace. A mathematical representation of the Fisher linear discriminant is a set of discriminant functions, $g_i(\mathbf{x}), i = 11, \ldots, c$ where c is the number of classes. The discriminant functions classify a pattern $\mathbf{x}$ by assigning $\mathbf{x}$ to class ω_i if $g_i(\mathbf{x}) \geq g_j(\mathbf{x})$ for all $j \neq i$. Under the assumption that the distribution of the feature vectors $\mathbf{x}$ within the ith class is multivariate Gaussian with mean μ_i and covariance matrix Σ_i and that the covariance matrices for all the classes are identical, the resulting decision function attains a linear form, and the classifier is referred to as linear discriminant analysis.

(2) Naive Bayes classifier. A naive Bayes classifier models a joint distribution over a label Y and a set of features, $f_1, f_2, \ldots, f_n$, using the assumption that the full joint distribution can be factored as follows

$$P(f_1, f_2, \ldots, f_n, Y) = P(Y) \prod_i P(f_i | Y) \qquad (5.9)$$

To classify a datum, we can find the most probable class given the feature values:

$$\arg\max_y P(y|f_1,\ldots,f_m) = \arg\max_y P(y) \prod_{i=1}^{m} P(f_i|y) \qquad (5.10)$$

where $P(Y)$ can be estimated directly from the training data $P(\hat{Y}) = c(y)/n$ with $c(y)$ being the number of training instances with label y and n the total number of training instances.

(3) k-NN. It simply stores the training examples and when a new query instance is presented to be classified, its relationship to the previously stored examples is examined in order to assign a target function value. In other words, the k-NN rule classifies an unlabeled sample based on its similarity with samples in the training set. For a given unlabeled sample x, the k-NN rule finds the k-nearest labeled samples in the training dataset based on some distance metric. The NNs of an instance are normally defined in terms of the standard Euclidean distance. For k-NN classifier, we have chosen $k = 1$.

(4) Artificial neural networks (ANNs). We apply the most popular ANN model MLP with the commonly used learning algorithm backpropagation, which uses gradient descent to minimize the squared error between the network output values and the target values and learns the weights for a multilayer network, given a network with a fixed set of units and interconnections.

(5) The support vector machine (SVM). This technique utilizes the minimal structural risk principle and generally performs effectively on pattern-classification problems without incorporating domain knowledge (Shawe-Taylor and Cristianini, 2004). The SVM in our experiments comes from LibSVM (Chang and Lin, 2001), which is based on the sequential minimal optimization (SMO) scheme (Hsu and Lin, 2002), with values of the regularization parameter $C = 100$ and sigma parameter ($\sigma = 1$) by using the radial basis function kernel.

The non-linear dimension-reduction SR derives ($\#class - 1$) meaningful eigenvectors. This subspace will be then used for recognition in the same way as PCA subspace. In other words, after all the subspaces have been derived, all images' LBP histogram from datasets were projected onto the subspace and recognition using the above classifiers was conducted. To compare the performance of SR dimension reduction, we also apply the conventional linear dimension reduction method PCA, which derives a new set of features that are uncorrelated linear combinations of the original variables.

5.4.1 *Experiment with the AR faces*

The AR database has been often used as a benchmarking data for robust face-recognition algorithms, which consists of over 3200 frontal face images of

126 subjects (Martinez and Benavente, 1998). For each subject, these images were recorded in two different sessions separated by 2 weeks, each session consisting of 13 images. For each session, the first one is of neutral expression, the second to the fourth are of facial-expression variations, the fifth to the seventh of illumination variations, the eighth to the tenth wearing glasses, and the eleventh to the thirteenth wearing scarf.

In the first experiment, we have chosen 120 people from AR data, each one with 26 images (low resolution, 104×85). Each image is divided into $3 \times 3 = 9$ small non-overlapping regions, with each region of 32×28 pixels, thus giving a concatenated LBP histogram of dimensionality $9 \times 59 = 531$. Each training set of LBP features is then subject to SR dimension reduction, yielding new feature vectors for each image with length 119. When classifying a given unknown sample, it is first projected by the obtained SR projection matrix, and then classified to a subject by applying the classifiers above. Due to singularity problem, LDA and Naive Bayes are not applied with original LBP features. As a comparison, the PCA-based dimension reduction is also carried out with the same dimensionality as from SR. The five different classifiers are compared simultaneously, with the averaged accuracies illustrated in Table 5.1. It is obvious that among the five classifiers compared, LBP-SR yields better performance than both of LBP and LBP–PCA, and the best is 99.3% from k-NN. We can also find that with kNN, MLP, and SVM, PCA projection does not bring any improvement. On the contrary, their recognition rates decrease. The boxplots of the recorded accuracies from 100 runs are illustrated in Fig. 5.3, corresponding to LBP–PCA and LBP-SR. Box plots are an excellent tool for summarizing distributions of data to allow visual comparisons of centers and spread.

We also experimented the robustness of the proposed algorithm for occluded face recognitions. We used the original high-resolution images (576×768) of 120 subjects from the AR data. In our experiment, the non-occluded images from both sessions were used for the training (12 face images per person) and the remaining occluded images by sunglasses and scarf were used for testing (6 for sunglass occlusion and 6 for scarf occlusion, respectively). The first row of Fig. 5.4 gives examples of training images of the third subject from the AR database, while the second row of Fig. 5.4 contains the test images for the same subject. For LBP descriptions, each image is divided into $7 \times 9 = 63$ small non-overlapping blocks, with each block of 85×80 pixels, thus giving a concatenated

Table 5.1:   Average accuracy for AR faces from holdout experiment by LBP

	LDA (in %)	Naive Bayes (in %)	k-NN (in %)	MLP (in %)	SVM (in %)
LBP	NA	NA	88.9	97.2	97.6
LBP–PCA	96.1	92.3	88.0	95.0	96.7
LBP-SR	97.5	97.1	99.3	95.6	98.7

NA: Not available.

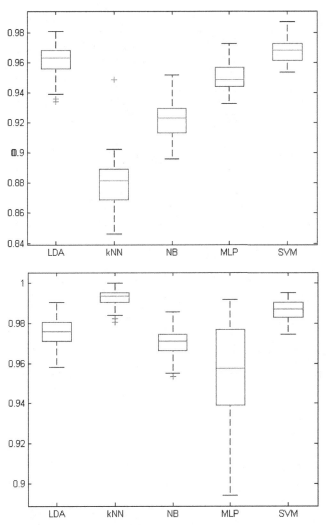

Fig. 5.3. Boxplots of the recorded accuracies from 100 runs, corresponding to LBP–PCA (upper), and LBP-SR (lower).

LBP histogram of dimensionality $63 \times 59 = 3717$. Each training set of LBP features is then subject to SR dimension reduction, yielding new feature vector for each image with length 119. The experiment results are given in Tables 5.2 and 5.3. For sunglass-occluded faces, a perfect accuracy of 100% is obtained with LBP-SR from several classifiers, including LDA, k-NN, and SVM. While the result from LPB–PCA is also close to 100% for LDA, the accuracies from Naive Bayes, k-NN, and SVM are all much less than those from LBP-SR. Similar results could also be found from the experiment with scarf-occluded face images, with best performance 76% offered by LDA approach in combination with LBP-SR. The

B. Zhang and Y. Zhang

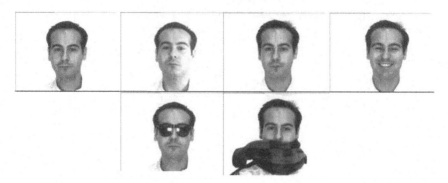

Fig. 5.4. Sample images from the AR database. First row: training images. Second row: test images with occlusion by sunglasses/scarf, and with screaming expression.

Table 5.2: Recognition accuracy for AR faces with sunglass occlusion

	LDA (in %)	Naive Bayes (in %)	k-NN (in %)	MLP (in %)	SVM (in %)
LBP–PCA	99.4	96.0	93.2	96.3	96.5
LBP-SR	100	98.5	100	97.8	99.9

Table 5.3: Recognition accuracy for AR faces with scarf occlusion

	LDA (in %)	Naive Bayes (in %)	k-NN (in %)	MLP (in %)	SVM (in %)
LBP–PCA	55.8	18.4	29.2	20.0	40.4
LBP-SR	76.0	49.0	70.0	38.0	71.3

results also show that the occlusion of the mouth area may lower the recognition performance.

Recently, occlusion robust face recognition has attracted much attention and many algorithms have been published. In Oh *et al.* (2008) a Selective local non-negative matrix factorization (S-LNMF) technique was proposed, which includes occlusion detection step and the selective LNMF-based recognition step. A so-called *locally salient ICA* method was proposed in Kim *et al.* (2005) and a *face-ARG matching* scheme was proposed in Park *et al.* (2005) in which a line feature based on face-ARG model is used to describe face images. Based on robust estimation, (Fidler *et al.*, 2006) propounded a classification method that combines reconstructive and discriminative models. For brief, we term it as reconstructive and discriminative subspace model (RDS for brief). These published recognition performances on the AR face are compared in Table 5.4, which shows that our proposed LBP-SR is the best for sunglass-occluded faces recognition. It is worthy to note that the experimental settings from these publications are not the same as ours except the RDS in Fidler *et al.* (2006). Therefore the comparison can only give an intuitive meaning.

Table 5.4:   Comparison with some published recognition accuracies for the AR-occluded faces

	RDS (in %)	LS-ICA (in %)	S-LNMF (in %)	Face-ARG (in %)	**LBP-SR** (in %)
Sunglasses	84	65	66.3	80.7	**100**
Scarf	93	NA	77	85.2	**76**

NA: Not available.

Note: The result from S-LNMF is from the average of Table 12 in Oh *et al.* (2008).

5.4.2 *Experiments with FERET datasets*

The proposed methods have also been tested using a subset of the FERET face database (Jonathon *et al.*, 1998). FERET2, the second release of the FERET, consists of 14,051 8-bit gray-scale images of human heads with views ranging from frontal to left and right profile, and the database design took into account of a number of factors including different expressions, different eyewear/hairstyles, and varied illuminations. Our experimental data consists of a subset of FERET images with 100 persons and 1779 images, with more than 5 images for each subject. Figure 5.5 shows some sample images for a subject from the FERET dataset.

For LBP features, each image with size 384×256 is divided into $6 \times 4 = 24$ small blocks, with each block of 64×64 pixels, thus giving a concatenated LBP histogram of dimensionality $24 \times 59 = 1416$. Each training set of LBP features is then subject to SR dimension reduction, yielding new feature vector for each image with length 99. The experimental results from comparing three different kind of features (original LBP histogram, LBP followed by PCA, and LBP followed by SR) and five different classifiers are proceeded in the similar way as for AR faces, with the results summarized in Table 5.5. The boxplot of the recorded classification

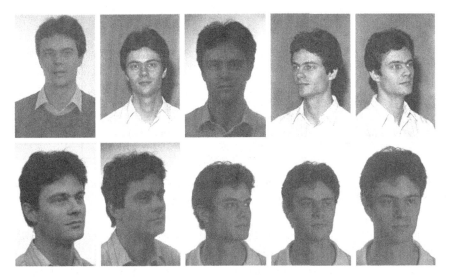

Fig. 5.5.   Samples from the FERET dataset.

Table 5.5:   Average accuracy for FERET faces from holdout experiment by LBP

	LDA (in %)	Naive Bayes (in %)	k-NN (in %)	MLP (in %)	SVM (in %)
LBP	NA	NA	65.7	89	89.3
LBP–PCA	86	74.4	63.7	84.6	82.5
LBP-SR	93.3	90	95.5	93.4	94.5

NA: Not available.

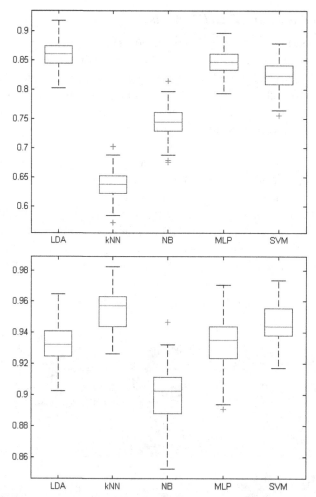

Fig. 5.6.   Boxplot of the recorded classification accuracies with FERET faces. Upper: result from LBP–PCA. Lower: result from LBP-SR.

accuracies is illustrated in Fig. 5.6. The performance enhancement from LBP-SR is remarkable for FERET faces as compared with the AR faces. This is because FERET faces included pose variations in terms of pixel appearance, which is highly nonlinear in 2D, but linear in 3D.

View-independent face recognition is a great challenge in computer vision because the variations between the images of the same face due to viewing direction are almost always larger than image variations due to change in face identity (Huang *et al.*, 2000). A face-recognition system robust to pose variances, should be able to recognize the person even though the test image and the database images have quite different poses. Our experiments reveal that LBP-SR provide a good solution toward view-independent recognition.

5.4.3 *Experiment with the CAS-PEAL pose variant face dataset*

CAS-PEAL (Gao *et al.*, 2004) is a large-scale face database for multiview face recognition. It currently contains 14,384 pose images of 1040 individuals. There are 9 different poses including looking up pose, looking middle pose, and looking down pose with 0 degree, 15 degree, and 30 degree, respectively. Some of the examples from a given subject is illustrated in Fig. 5.7.

We use $LBP_{8,1}^u$ and the 260×220 pixels image is divided into 4×4 blocks, each with size 64×55. The LBP histograms of blocks are extracted and concatenated into a single, spatially enhanced feature histogram with length $16 \times 59 = 944$. The experimental results summed up in Table 5.6 shows that the correct recognition rates of LBP-SR method are obviously higher than LBP and LBP–PCA, with a highest correct rate 82.1% from k-NN. More specifically, on all of the datasets, the LBP–PCA method gives poor performance with a low accuracy around 50%

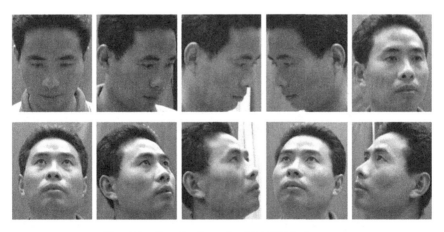

Fig. 5.7.   Samples from the CAS-PEAL dataset.

Table 5.6:   Average accuracy for CAS-PEAL faces from holdout experiment

	LDA (in %)	Naive Bayes (in %)	k-NN (in %)	MLP (in %)	SVM (in %)
LBP	NA	NA	30.1	76.3	65.1
LBP–PCA	50.1	37.6	17.5	54.6	38.7
LBP-SR	73	72.7	82.1	73.3	76

NA: Not available.

with LDA and MLP and less than 50% for other classifiers, while LBP-SR method dramatically increases the correct recognition rates on these corresponding datasets, with a highest improvement of 82.1% from k-NN.

For pose-invariant face recognition, most of the research is based on either using different views of the person for training, or by generating a 3D model by which more views can be synthesized. The method proposed in Huang *et al.* (2000) is a typical example that build a view-specific eigenspace and train a corresponding neural network for classification. Generally, the issue of recognizing faces from different poses is largely unresolved. Experimental results on the CAS-PEAL multiposes faces show that our proposed method can achieve high recognition accuracy even if the poses undergo very large changes (Fig. 5.8).

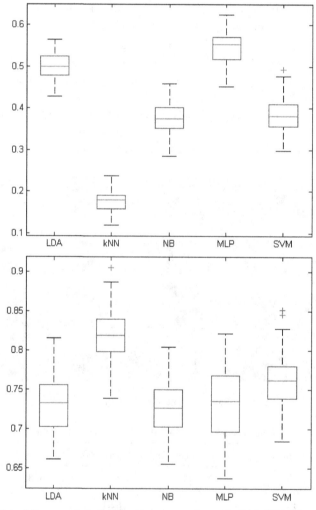

Fig. 5.8.   Boxplot of the recorded classification accuracies with CAS-PEAL faces. Upper: result from LBP–PCA. Lower: result from LBP-SR.

5.4.4 *Experiment with the Yale-B illumination variant face dataset*

Illumination is the next most significant factor affecting the appearance of faces (Gross *et al.*, 2004). Research has shown that for a face image, the variability caused by illumination changes even exceeds the variability caused by identity changes (Moses *et al.*, 1994). In the following the Yale B Face Database (Georghiades *et al.*, 2001) was used to evaluate the proposed method, which contains face images of 10 subjects (each with 64 images) seen under 576 viewing conditions (9 poses and 64 illumination conditions). Figure 5.9 shows some sample images of the same subject under different illuminations from Yale Face Database B. Such illuminations largely influence the performance of most of the face-recognition algorithms.

The LBP operator is applied to the Yale B face images of size 340×270 via 4×4 blocks, each block with size 83×66. The LBP histograms extracted from each block are then concatenated into an overall feature histogram, which is of length $16 \times 59 = 944$. As with all the experiments above, for each subject, the extracted features are randomly partitioned into subsets with 80% retained for training, and 20% for testing. The random partition process is carried out 100 rounds for each subject. The performances of the five different classification methods are compared, as shown in Table 5.7. The corresponding performance distribution is illustrated in the boxplot in Fig. 5.10. It can be seen that for all the subjects in the dataset, the LBP-SR method consistently achieves the best performance which is close to 100%

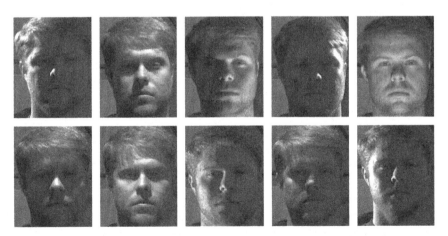

Fig. 5.9.   Samples from the Yale B dataset.

Table 5.7:   Average accuracy for Yale-B faces from holdout experiment by LBP

	LDA (in %)	Naive Bayes (in %)	k-NN (in %)	MLP (in %)	SVM (in %)
LBP	NA	NA	93	99	99.4
LBP–PCA	72.4	68.1	79.7	86.3	82.5
LBP-SR	99.8	99.8	99.8	99.7	99.8

NA: Not available.

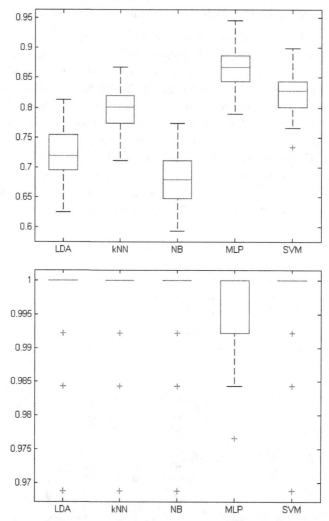

Fig. 5.10. Boxplot of the recorded classification accuracies with Yale B faces. Upper: result from LBP–PCA. Lower: result from LBP-SR.

for all of the classifiers. Again, PCA dimension reduction dramatically downgrades the recognition accuracies.

Since dealing with illumination variation is a central topic in computer vision, numerous approaches for illumination-invariant face recognition have been proposed. For example, in Lee *et al.* (2005), the authors proposed a method for acquiring linear subspaces in case of variable lighting. Various face recognition methodologies based on fitting 3D morphable model (Blanz and Vetter, 2003) and by fusing thermal infrared and visible imagery (Bebis *et al.*, 2006) have been proposed. Many works have attempted to find illumination insensitive image representations, including edge maps, 2D Gabor-like filters, first and second derivatives of the gray-level image, and the logarithmic transformations of the intensity image along with these representations. However, none of these image representations is found to be sufficient by itself to overcome variations due to illumination changes. A different recent line of research tries to extract the object's surface reflectance as an illumination invariant description of the object. It is beyond the scope of this chapter to thoroughly compare the available works. Our experimental work on the Yale B data confirm that the LBP features is robust to illumination variability and LBP-SR could further enhance the performance for a wide choice of classification methods.

5.5 Discussions and Conclusions

The LBPs have already shown to provide robust face representation in terms of having less sensitivity against variations that may occur on the facial appearance due to illumination, pose, etc. In addition to that, the computational simplicity has also added to its merits for the general acceptance in face recognition. In this chapter, we have proposed an improvement for the LBP approach for face recognition based on a recently developed graph embedding dimension reduction method called SR. Through SR dimension reduction, the LBP's original invariance on several factors including occlusion, pose, and illumination were enhanced. We have presented empirical studies using several popular benchmarking face datasets comparing the new method with previous LBP and LBP followed by PCA. Several different classifiers have also been simultaneously compared. Our studies revealed that dimension-reduced LBP features are more effective and efficient for facial recognition, as evidenced by the promising performances.

References

Ahonen, T., Hadid, A., and Pietikainen, M. Face description with local binary patterns: application to face recognition, *IEEE Trans. Pattern Anal. Machine Intelligence* **28**, 12, 2037–2041, 2006.

Bebis, G., Gyaourova, A., Singh, S., and Pavlidis, I. Face recognition by fusing thermal infrared and visible imagery, *Image Vision Comput.* **24**, 727–742, 2006.

Belhumeur, P., Hespanha, J., and Kriegman, D. Eigenfaces vs fisherfaces: recognition using class specific linear projection, *IEEE Trans. Pattern Anal. Machine Intelligence* **19**, 7, 711–720, 1997.

Belkin, M. and Niyogi, P. Laplacian eigenmaps and spectral techniques for embedding and clustering, *Advances in Neural Information Processing Systems*, Vol. 14 (MIT Press, Cambridge, MA), pp. 585–591, 2001.

Blanz, V. and Vetter, T. Face recognition based on fitting a 3d morphable model, *IEEE Trans. Pattern Anal. Machine Intelligence* **25**, 3, 1–12, 2003.

Cai, D., He, X., and Han, J. Spectral regression for dimensionality reduction, Technical Report UIUCDCS-R-2007-2856, UIUC, 2007.

Chang, C.-C. and Lin, C.-J. Libsvm: a library for support vector machines, 2001. http://www.csie.ntu.edu.tw/~cjlin/libsvm

Fidler, S., Skocaj, D., and Leonardis, A. Combining reconstructive and discriminative subspace methods for robust classification and regression by subsampling, *IEEE Trans. Pattern Anal. Machine Intelligence* **28**, 337–350, 2006.

Gao, W., Cao, B., and Shan, S. G. The CAS-PEAL large-scale chinese face database and baseline evaluations, Technical report of JDL, 2004. http://www.jdl. ac.cn/~peal/peal tr.pdf.

Georghiades, A., Belhumeur, P., and Kriegman, D. From few to many: illumination cone models for face recognition under variable lighting and pose, *IEEE Trans. Pattern Anal. Machine Intelligence* **23**, 6, 643–660, 2001.

Gross, R., Baker, S., Matthews, I., and Kanade, T. Face recognition across pose and illumination, in S. Z. Li and A. K. Jain (eds.), *Handbook of Face Recognition* (Springer, New York), 2004.

He, Z. and Niyogi, P. *Locality Preserving Projections*, Vol. 16 (MIT Press), 2003.

Hsu, C.-W. and Lin, C.-J. A comparison of methods for multi-class support vector machines, *IEEE Trans. Neural Networks* **13**, 2, 415–425, 2002.

Huang, F., Chen, T., Zhou, Z., and Zhang, H. Pose invariant face recognition, in *Proc. IEEE Intl Conf. Automatic Face and Gesture Recognition*, pp. 245–250, 2000.

Jonathon, P., Wechsler, H., Huang, J., and Rauss, P. The feret database and evaluation procedure for face-recognition algorithms, *Image Vision Comput.* **16**, 5, 295–306, 1998. http://www.itl. nist.gov/iad/humanid/feret/.

Kim, J., Choi, J., Yi, J., and Turk, M. Effective representation using ica for face recognition robust to local distortion and partial occlusion, *IEEE Trans. Pattern Anal. Machine Intelligence* **27**, 12, 1977–1981, 2005.

Lee, K., Ho, J., and Kriegman, D. Acquiring linear subspaces for face recognition under variable lighting, *IEEE Trans. Pattern Anal. Machine Intelligence* **27**, 5, 684–698, 2005.

Marcel, S., Rodriguez, Y., and Heusch, G. On the recent use of local binary patterns for face authentication, *Int. J. Image Video Processing, Special Issue on Facial Image Processing* 2007.

Martinez, M. and Benavente, R. The AR face database, CVC Technical Report 24, 1998.

Moses, Y., Adini, Y., and Ullman, S. Face recognition: the problem of compensating for changes in illumination direction, in *Proc. European Conf. Comp. Vision*, pp. 286–296, 1994.

Niyogi, P. Laplacian eigenmaps for dimensionality reduction and data representation, *Neural Computation* **15**, 6, 1373–1396, 2003.

Oh, H., Lee, K., and Lee, S. Occlusion invariant face recognition using selective local non-negative matrix factorization basis images, *Image Vision Comput.* **26**, 11, 1515–1523, 2008.

Ojala, T., Pietikainen, M., and Maenpaa, M. Multiresolution gray-scale and rotation invariant texture classification with local binary patterns, *IEEE Trans. Pattern Anal. Machine Intelligence* **24**, 7, 971–987, 2002.

Ojala, T., Pietikainen, M., and Maenpaa, T. Gray scale and rotation invariant texture classification with local binary patterns, in *Proc. European Conference on Computer Vision*, pp. 1:404–420, 2000.

Park, B., Lee, K., and Lee, S. Face recognition using face-ARG matching, *IEEE Trans. Pattern Anal. Machine Intelligence* **27**, 1982–1988, 2005.

Roweis, S. and Saul, L. Nonlinear dimensionality reduction by locally linear embedding, *Science* **290**, 5500, 2323–2326, 2000.

Shan, C., Gong, S., and McOwan, P. Conditional mutual information based boosting for facial expression recognition, in *Proc. British Machine Vision Conference (BMVC)*, pp. 1:399–408, 2005.

Shawe-Taylor, J. and Cristianini, N. *Kernel Methods for Pattern Analysis* (Cambridge University Press), 2004.

Tenenbaum, J., Silva, V., and Langford, J. A global geometric framework for nonlinear dimensionality reduction, *Science* **290**, 5500, 2319–2323, 2000.

Wiskott, L., Fellous, M., Kruger, N., and Malsburg, C. Face recognition by elastic bunch graph matching, *IEEE Trans. Pattern Anal. Machine Intelligence* **19**, 7, 775–779, 1997.

Zhang, G., Huang, X., Li, S., Wang, Y., and Wu, X. Boosting local binary pattern (lbp)-based face recognition, in *Proc. Chinese Conference on Biometric Recognition*, pp. 179–186, 2004.

Zhang, W., Shan, S., Gao, W., and Zhang, H. Local gabor binary pattern histogram sequence (lgbphs): a novel non-statistical model for face representation and recognition, in *Proc. IEEE Int. Conf. on Computer Vision (ICCV)*, pp. 786–791, 2005.

Chapter 6

FUNDAMENTALS IN KERNEL DISCRIMINANT ANALYSIS AND FEATURE SELECTION FOR FACE RECOGNITION

Qingshan Liu[*,†], Hanqing Lu[†], and Dimitris N. Metaxas[*]

[*]*Department of Computer Science, Rutgers University*
Piscataway, New Jersey, 08904 USA
qsliu@cs.rutgers.edu
dnm@cs.rutgers.edu

[†]*National Laboratory of Pattern Recognition*
Chinese Academy of Sciences, Beijing, China, 100080
qsliu@nlpr.ia.ac.cn
luhq@nlpr.ia.ac.cn

6.1 Introduction

Principal component analysis (PCA) and linear discriminate analysis (LDA) are two popular feature representation methods. The PCA generates a set of orthonormal basis vectors aiming at maximizing the variance over all the samples. A new face image can be represented by a linear combination of these basis vectors, i.e., eigenfaces (Turk and Pentland, 1991). It is optimal for reconstruction, but it is not optimal for discrimination. For better discrimination, LDA tries to find a linear projection to maximize the between-class scatter S_B and minimize the within-class scatter S_W, which can be obtained by maximizing the Fisher discriminant function, $J(W) = \frac{w^T S_B w}{w^T S_W w}$ (Zhao *et al.*, 1999; Belhumeur *et al.*, 1997). Mathematically, it is equivalent to solving leading eigenvectors of $S_W^{-1} S_B$.

However, there exist two key problems for face recognition using LDA. One is that LDA is that as a linear representation method it cannot well describe complex non-linear variations of images with illumination, pose, and facial expression changes. Another is that S_W tends to be singular, since face recognition often has a small training sample size. This gives rise to a problem of unstable numerical computation. Several techniques have been developed to alleviate this problem. For example, the well-known Fisherface employs PCA at first for dimension reduction, and then LDA is performed (Zhao *et al.*, 1999; Belhumeur *et al.*, 1997). Belhumeur *et al.* (1997) and Zhao *et al.* (1999) showed that Fisherface gave a much higher recognition performance than eigenface. Liu *et al.* (Liu and Wechsler, 1998) proposed simultaneous diagonalization of the within- and between-class scatter matrices to improve LDA. Direct LDA proposed by Yu and Yang (2001) actually depends on between-class scatter, while the null-space methods use information in the null space of within-class scatter only (Chen *et al.*, 2000; Huang *et al.*, 2003). To deal with the first problem, Mika *et al.* (1999) and Baudat *et al.* (Baudat and Anouar, 2000) proposed a kernel-based non-linear discriminant analysis, which combines the kernel trick with LDA, i.e., kernel discriminant analysis (KDA). However, the within-class scatter in the KDA feature space is often singular too due to small training sample size. Similarly, several techniques have been proposed to handle the problem of numerical computation (Liu *et al.*, 2002a; Yang, 2002; Liu *et al.*, 2004a; Lu *et al.*, 2003; Liu *et al.*, 2004c).

In this chapter, we focus on the kernel discriminating features for face recognition. We first introduce the idea of KDA (Mika *et al.*, 1999; Baudat and Anouar, 2000), and feature vector selection scheme for reducing the computational cost in KDA implementation. Then, we propose a kernel scatter-difference-based discriminant analysis (KSDA) method to overcome both the matrix singularity problem and the non-linear problem existing in LDA for face recognition (Liu *et al.*, 2004b, 2006). The kernel trick is first employed to construct an implicit feature space F, and then a new scatter-difference-based discriminant rule is defined to analyze the data in F and produce non-linear discriminating features. The scatter-difference-based discriminant rule is consistent with the principle of maximizing between-class scatter and minimizing within-class scatter. It can also avoid the matrix singularity problem. The proposed method approximates the null-space method (Huang *et al.*, 2003; Chen *et al.*, 2000) in F when the balance factor $M \rightarrow \infty$. The maximum margin criterion proposed in Li *et al.* (2003) can also be regarded as a special case of the method at $M = 1$.

In a sense, the kernel function can be regarded as a non-linear similarity measurement. The traditional kernel method often considers the dot product of two images as a global single similarity, and the dot products between the image and all the training samples can be regarded as its kernel feature vector. From the view of human vision system, we often compare two objects from different cues, such as color, shape, and texture. In this chapter, we also extend the tradition single similarity kernel features into the multiple similarity kernel features (Liu *et al.*, 2008; Yan *et al.*, 2006) for object recognition.

6.2 Kernel-based Discriminant Analysis and Feature Vector Selection

In this section, we present two parts: one is the basic theory of KDA, and another is a feature vector selection scheme for reducing the computational cost of KDA, which is especially useful for a large training sample set.

6.2.1 *Kernel-based discriminant analysis*

Since the non-linear kernel trick achieved a great success in support vector machine (SVM) (Osuna *et al.*, 1997), it has attracted much attention in the community of pattern recognition. The idea of KDA is to yield a non-linear discriminating features in the input space through combining the kernel trick with LDA. First, the input data is projected into an implicit feature space F by a non-linear mapping, $\phi : x \in R^N \rightarrow \phi(x) \in F$, then KDA seeks to find a linear transformation in F which can maximize the between-class scatter and minimize the within-class scatter in F. In implementation, it is unnecessary to compute ϕ explicitly but compute the inner product of two vectors in F with an inner product kernel function:

$$k(x_i, x_j) = (\phi(x_i) \cdot \phi(x_j)) \tag{6.1}$$

For the following analysis, we define some symbols first. $X = \{x_1, x_2, \dots, x_N\}$ is the training set with N images of C. Each class has N_c samples, and X_c represents the sample set of the cth class. Define the dot product matrix $K = [K_1, K_2, \dots, K_N]$, where the column vector K_i is composed of the dot products between x_i and all the training images, i.e., $K_i = (k(x_i, x_1), k(x_i, x_2), \dots, k(x_i, x_N))^T$, so K is a symmetrical matrix. m represents the mean of all the K_i, and μ is the mean of all the $\phi(x_i)$, i.e., $m = \frac{1}{N} \sum_{i=1}^{N} K_i$, and $\mu = \frac{1}{N} \sum_{i=1}^{N} \phi(x_i)$. For simplicity, $\phi(x_i) \in F_c$ means $x_i \in X_c$, and $K_i \in F_c$ means $x_i \in X_c$. m_c represents the mean of all the K_is with $K_i \in F_c$, and μ_c is the mean of all the $\phi(x_i)$s with $x_i \in X_c$. Define between-class scatter matrix S_b^ϕ and within-class matrix S_w^ϕ in the feature space F as

$$S_W^\phi = \sum_{l=1}^{C} \sum_{\phi(x_j) \in F_l} (\phi(x_j) - \mu_l)(\phi(x_j) - \mu_l)^T \tag{6.2}$$

$$S_B^\phi = \sum_{l=1}^{C} N_i (\mu_l - \mu)(\mu_l - \mu)^T \tag{6.3}$$

KDA is equivalent to find a linear transformation w^ϕ in F to maximize S_B^ϕ and minimize S_W^ϕ, i.e., maximizing the following Fisher object function

$$J(w^\phi) = \frac{(w^\phi)^T S_B^\phi w^\phi}{(w^\phi)^T S_W^\phi w^\phi} \tag{6.4}$$

Because w_ϕ is a linear transformation in F, any solution w^ϕ can be represented by a combination of all the $\phi(x_i)$s

$$w^\phi = \sum_{i=1}^{N} \alpha_i \phi(x_i) = \Phi(X)\alpha \tag{6.5}$$

where $\alpha = (\alpha_1, \alpha_2, \dots, \alpha_N)^T$ is the coefficient vector, and $\Phi(X) = [\phi(x_1), \phi(x_2), \dots, \phi(x_N)]$. Projecting x_i and μ_l onto w^ϕ are respectively as following

(6.6) and (6.7)

$$w^T x_i = \alpha^T (k(x_1, x_i), k(x_2, x_i), \ldots, k(x_N, x_i))^T = \alpha^T K_i \qquad (6.6)$$

$$w^T \mu_l = \alpha^T \begin{pmatrix} \frac{1}{N_l} \sum_{j=1}^{n_l} k(x_1, x_j) \\ \frac{1}{N_l} \sum_{j=1}^{n_l} k(x_2, x_j) \\ \ldots \ldots \\ \frac{1}{N_l} \sum_{j=1}^{n_l} k(x_N, x_j) \end{pmatrix} = \alpha^T m_l, \quad x_j \in X_l \qquad (6.7)$$

Thus, maximizing Eq. (6.4) is converted to maximize

$$J(\alpha) = \frac{\alpha^T K_B \alpha}{\alpha^T K_W \alpha} \qquad (6.8)$$

where

$$K_B = \sum_{i=1}^{C} N_i (m_i - m)(m_i - m)^T \qquad (6.9)$$

$$K_W = \sum_{i=1}^{C} \sum_{K_j \in X_i} (K_j - m_i)(K_j - m_i)^T \qquad (6.10)$$

Similar to LDA, this problem can be solved by finding the leading eigenvectors of $K_W^{-1} K_B$, and the projection of a new point z onto w^ϕ in F is given by

$$y = ((w^\phi)^T \phi(z)) = \alpha^T K_z \qquad (6.11)$$

where $K_z = (k(z, x_1), k(x, x_2), \ldots, k(x, x_N))^T$.

6.2.2 Feature vector selection

From the above description, KDA needs to compute the dot-product matrix K. Its computation is directly based on the number of training samples, and its dimension is $N \times N$. When the training sample set becomes very large, the computational cost of K is very high. In the following, we address how to handle this issue by a feature vector selection scheme.

In Eq. (6.5), all the training samples in F, $\phi(x_i)$, are used to represent w^ϕ. In practice, the dimensionality of the subspace spanned by $\phi(x_i)$ is just equal to the rank of the matrix K, and the rank of K is often less than N, rank$(K) < N$, especially when the training data set is very large, rank$(K) << N$, (Baudat and Anouar, 2001; Wu et al., 2001). If a basis of the feature vectors, $\phi(x_{bi})$,

$bi = 1, 2, \ldots, \mathrm{rank}(K)$, is known, we can rewrite Eq. (6.5) as follows

$$w^\phi = \sum_{bi=1}^{\mathrm{rank}(K)} \alpha_{bi} \phi(x_{bi}) \tag{6.12}$$

This dimensionality reduction will largely improve the computational efficiency.

In this chapter, we adopt a scheme based on a geometrical consideration (Baudat and Anouar, 2001) to select such a basis of the feature vectors in F (Liu *et al.*, 2002b). The idea is to look for a subset of the samples whose mappings in F are sufficient to express all the data in F as a linear combination of them.

Assume $S = \{x_{S_1}, x_{S_2}, \ldots, x_{S_L}\}$ is a selected sample set, where L is the number of selected vectors. The estimation of the mapping of any vector x_i is regarded as a linear combination of S in F, given by

$$\hat{\phi}(x_i) = \Phi_S \cdot \alpha_i \tag{6.13}$$

where $\Phi_S = (\phi(x_{S_1}), \phi(x_{S_2}), \ldots, \phi(x_{S_L}))$ is the mapping matrix of the selected samples in F and $\beta_i = (\beta_i^1, \beta_i^2, \ldots, \beta_i^L)$ is the coefficient vectors.

Now, we aim to find the coefficients β_i so as to make the estimated mapping $\hat{\phi}(x_i)$ as close to the real mapping $\phi(x_i)$ as possible. It can be achieved by minimizing the following criterion

$$\min \delta_i = \frac{\|\phi(x_i) - \hat{\phi}(x_i)\|^2}{\|\phi(x_i)\|^2} \tag{6.14}$$

Substituting the derivatives with respect to β_i to zero, i.e., $\frac{\partial \delta_i}{\partial \beta_i} = 0$, and rewriting it in matrix form

$$\min \delta_i = 1 - \frac{K_{Si}^T K_{SS}^{-1} K_{Si}}{k_{ii}} \tag{6.15}$$

where K_{SS} is a square matrix of dot products of the selected vectors: $K_{SS} = (k_{s_p, s_q})_{1 \leq p, q \leq L}$, and $K_{Si} = (k_{s_p, i})_{1 \leq p \leq L}$ is the vectors of dot product between x_i and the selected set S.

The final goal is to let Eq. (6.13) satisfy all the samples, i.e.

$$\max_S J_S = \frac{1}{N} \sum_{x_i \in X} \left(\frac{K_{Si}^T K_{SS}^{-1} K_{Si}}{k_{ii}} \right) \tag{6.16}$$

The problem of solution can be implemented by an iterative process, and the process stops when K_{SS} is no longer invertible (Baudat and Anouar, 2001). The algorithm is outlined in Algorithm 1.1:

Algorithm 1.1. Feature vector selection algorithm

1: **Input** the training samples X and the kernel function and its parameters
2: **Initialize** $S = \Phi$, $L = 0$

3: **First iteration** select a sample that maximizes J_S and add it to S; Let $L = 1$.

4: **while** K_{SS} is invertible **do**

5:   Combining with previous L samples, select a sample from the remaining samples

6:   **if** K_{SS} is invertible **then**

7:     Append the sample that can maximize J_S to S

8:     Let $L = L + 1$

9:   **end if**

10: **end while**

11: **Output** S.

6.3 Scatter Difference-based Kernel Discriminating Features for Face Recognition

Though KDA can produce non-linear discriminating features, the problem of numerical computation for face recognition still exists, i.e., the matrix K_W cannot be guaranteed to be nonsingular. There are some similar techniques to deal with this problem in KDA as in LDA. For example, we used $K_W + \mu I$ to replace K_W (Liu *et al.*, 2002a, 2004a) in our previous work, where μ is a very small constant and I is the identity matrix (we call it KFDA for convenience in the following); Yang (2002) made K_W nonsingular by performing PCA in the feature space first (we call this method KEDA); Lu *et al.* (2003) adopted the idea of direct LDA to develop the KDDA method, and in Liu *et al.* (2004c), the idea of null space was used to develop the KNDA method.

6.3.1 *Kernel scatter difference-based discriminant analysis*

Here, we propose a new kernel scatter-difference-based discriminant analysis (KSDA) for face recognition, in which non-linear discriminating features are extracted without the numerical computation problem (Liu *et al.*, 2004b, 2006). First, the kernel trick is performed to construct an implicit feature space F. A scatter-difference-based discrimination rule is then defined in F to produce non-linear discriminating features as follows

$$J_M(w^\phi) = (w^\phi)^T (S_B^\phi - M \cdot S_W^\phi) w^\phi \qquad (6.17)$$

where M is a non-negative constant to balance S_B^ϕ and S_W^ϕ. In a sense, maximizing $J_M(W)$ is also equivalent to maximizing S_B^ϕ and minimizing S_W^ϕ, so it is consistent with the Fisher discriminant rule. Moreover, the scatter-difference-based discriminant rule can be regarded as a generalization of the techniques in Chen *et al.* (2000), Huang *et al.* (2003), Yu and Yang (2001), and Li *et al.* (2003). When $M = 0$, it means to use the between-class scatter only, and it approximates the null-space methods at $M \to \infty$. The maximum margin criterion proposed in Li *et al.* (2003) is also a special case with $M = 1$. Similarly, since w^ϕ can be represented by a linear combination of all the $\phi(x_i)$s, i.e., $w^\phi = \Phi(X)\alpha$, we can rewrite Eq. (6.9) as

$$J_M(\alpha) = \alpha^T(K_B - M \cdot K_W)\alpha \tag{6.18}$$

Assuming $\|\alpha\| = 1$, the maximization problem of is equivalent to solving the maximum of the Lagrange function

$$L(\alpha, \lambda) = J_M(\alpha) - \lambda(\|\alpha\| - 1) \tag{6.19}$$

Let $\frac{\partial L(\alpha, \lambda)}{\partial \alpha} = 0$, we can have

$$(K_B - M \cdot K_W)\alpha = \lambda\alpha \tag{6.20}$$

Thus, the problem of KSDA is translated into finding the leading eigenvectors of $K_B - M \cdot K_W$. Since no matrix inverse needs to be computed, KSDA successfully avoids any numerical computation problem.

The factor M is used to balance the matrix K_B and K_W, and its value depends on the training data. Practically M can be regarded as balancing the energy variations of K_B and K_W. Assuming the energy variation ratio between the matrix K_B and K_W is β, we can use the product of β and a non-negative constant D to approximate M, i.e., $M = D\beta$, where D is independent of the matrix K_B and K_W. Then, Eq. (6.4) is converted into

$$(K_B - D \cdot \beta \cdot K_W)\alpha = \lambda\alpha \tag{6.21}$$

Given a database, K_B, K_W, and β are known, so the optimal discriminating features are only related to the independent factor D. Therefore, we can use a good D value estimated from a database as an empirical estimation of D for other databases. Certainly, how to define and evaluate the energy variation ratio β is not trivial. For simplicity, we use the largest eigenvalues of K_B and K_W to approximate their energy variations in the experiments, noted as $\lambda_{\max}(K_B)$ and $\lambda_{\max}(K_W)$, i.e., $\beta = \lambda_{\max}(K_B)/\lambda_{\max}(K_W)$. The following experiments show that such a simplification is suitable.

6.3.2 *Experiments*

We conduct experiments on two databases, i.e., the ORL and the YALE databases as in Liu *et al.* (2002a), and Yang (2002), and the "leave one out" statistical testing strategy is adopted. The proposed method is compared with KFDA (Liu *et al.*, 2002a), KEDA (Yang, 2002), KDDA (Lu *et al.*, 2003), KNDA (Liu *et al.*, 2004c), and two well-known linear methods, i.e., Fisherface (Zhao *et al.*, 1999) and eigenface (Turk and Pentland, 1991). In our experiments, the polynomial kernel is chosen, $k(x, y) = (\phi(x) \cdot \phi(y)) = (a(x \cdot y) + b)^d$, as in Liu *et al.* (2002a), (Yang, 2002), and Liu *et al.* (2004c). Its parameters are set as, $a = 0.001, b = 0$, and $d = 2$ as in Liu *et al.* (2002a). In Liu *et al.* (2002a), K_W is replaced by $K_W + \mu I$ to deal with the problem of numerical computation. As in Liu *et al.* (2002a), we set $\mu = 10^{-4}$ in the experiments.

There are 40 persons in the ORL database with 10 different images for each person, including variations in pose, facial expression and with or without glasses, but there is little illumination variation. The YALE database contains 11 subjects, and each subject has 11 different front view images that include variations in facial expression (normal, happy, sad, sleepy, surprised, and wink), illumination (left-light, center-light, right-light) and with or without glasses. We down-sample the image size to to reduce computational complexity. No other pre-processing except histogram equalization is performed. Some samples are shown in Figs. 6.1 and 6.2, respectively.

We first compare the proposed method to the other six methods under $D = 8$. Two popular distance measures are computed to test the performance of the proposed method, i.e., the Euclidean distance, $d = \|x - y\|$, and the cosine distance, $d = 1 - \frac{x \cdot y}{\|x\| \|y\|}$. We set $\beta = 4$ and $\beta = 1$ for the ORL and the YALE databases respectively, for their $\lambda_{\max}(K_B)/\lambda_{\max}(K_W)$s approximate to 4 and 1, respectively. Tables 6.1 and 6.2 report the comparison results. We can see that KSDA gives a better performance than the other six methods with both the Euclidean and cosine distances. In the case of the Euclidean distance, KSDA gives a recognition error rate of 1.0% that means only 4 samples are incorrectly recognized among 400 samples. On the YALE database, KSDA has an error rate of 2.42% that represents 161

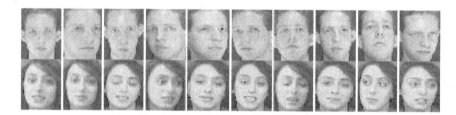

Fig. 6.1.   Samples from the ORL database.

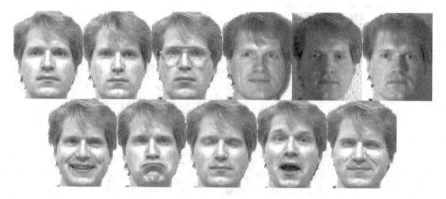

Fig. 6.2.   Samples from the YALE database.

Table 6.1:   The error rates (%) on the ORL database

Method	KSDA	KFDA	KEDA	KNDA	KDDA	Fisherface	Eigenface
Euclidean	1.0	2.0	2.5	2.0	2.75	2.5	3.0
Cosine	1.25	1.75	2.5	1.75	2.5	2.5	2.75
Feature numbers	39	39	39	39	39	39	80

Table 6.2:   The error rates (%) on the YALE database

Method	KSDA	KFDA	KEDA	KNDA	KDDA	Fisherface	Eigenface
Euclidean	2.42	4.24	3.64	6.06	21.21	7.27	20.61
Cosine	2.42	4.24	3.64	6.67	21.21	4.84	21.21
Feature numbers	14	14	14	14	14	14	75

images of 165 images are recognized correctly. The error rate of KDDA is very high on the YALE database, because the YALE database only has 15 classes, and KDDA discards the null space of K_B firstly, i.e., the dimensions of K_B and K_W are first reduced to $ClassNum - 1 = 14$, thus too much discriminating information is lost. In addition, each database embodies different variations in our experiments. The ORL database has pose and facial expression variations. The variations in the Yale database are illumination and facial expression.

We also investigate the performance of KSDA with different D values on these two databases. Tables 6.3 and 6.4 illustrate the experimental results on the two databases, respectively. On the ORL database, KSDA gives a better performance in the range of $D = 4$ to 12, i.e., M is from 24 to 48. On the YALE database, KSDA performs well for the range of $D = 6$ to 10, i.e., M is from 6 to 10. We can see that their good D values are similar, while their good M values are different. We can also see that the result of maximum margin criterion (Li *et al.*, 2003), i.e., $M = 1$, is not good.

Table 6.3:   The error rates (%) with different D values on the ORL database

D values	$M = 1$	$D = 1$	$D = 2$	$D = 4$	$D = 6$	$D = 8$	$D = 10$	$D = 12$	$D = 20$	$D = 40$
Euclidean	13.33	13.33	5.45	3.03	2.42	2.42	2.42	3.03	3.64	3.64
Cosine	10.30	10.30	5.45	2.42	2.42	2.42	2.42	3.03	3.64	4.24

Table 6.4:   The error rates (%) with different D values on the YALE database

D values	$M = 1$	$D = 1$	$D = 2$	$D = 4$	$D = 6$	$D = 8$	$D = 10$	$D = 12$	$D = 20$	$D = 40$
Euclidean	2.5	1.50	1.25	1.00	1.00	1.00	1.00	1.0	1.25	1.75
Cosine	2.5	2.25	1.25	1.25	1.25	1.25	1.25	1.5	1.50	1.75

6.4 Multiple Similarities Kernel Discriminating Features for Face Recognition

From the description in Sec. 6.2, we see that KDA is based on finding the leading eigenvectors of $K_W^{-1} K_B$, where K_W and K_B are the within class scatter and the between class scatter based on the all the K_is, respectively. Actually the K_i can be considered the kernel feature of x_i, which is composed of the dot products between x_i and all the training samples, and KDA is equivalent to performing LDA on the kernel features K_is in implementation.

Actually the dot-product kernel is a non-linear similarity measure. The traditional kernel methods often consider the global representations of the images in the form of vectors, and compute the dot products between an image and all the training images to form its kernel feature vector, i.e., single similarity kernel features. Thus, they ignore detailed visual information except global information, and they cannot provide refined visual representation. Many studies show that global representations are sensitive to environment noise (Vasconcelos *et al.*, 2004; Heisele *et al.*, 2001). From the view of human vision system, we often compare two object from different cues, such as, color, shape, and texture. In the following, we extend the single similarity kernel features to the multiple similarity kernel features for image classification including face recognition.

6.4.1 *Multiple similarities kernel discriminant analysis*

It is known that, to better capture the complex structure and appearance of the objects, we should represent the images with different cues. Here, we propose to perform the dot product kernels on different cues respectively, and the kernel feature vector is extended to a kernel feature matrix. This extension considers different information respectively, so it should be more accurate for describing the images than the traditional one only considering the global information.

Assuming that the images are represented by p cues, we use dot-product kernels on p cues, respectively. Then, the kernel feature vector K_i of the image x_i becomes a feature matrix $\tilde{K}_i$ as

$$\tilde{K}_i = \begin{bmatrix} k_1(x_i^1, x_1^1) & k_2(x_i^2, x_1^2) & \cdots & k_p(x_i^p, x_1^p) \\ k_1(x_i^1, x_2^1) & k_2(x_i^2, x_2^2) & \cdots & k_p(x_i^p, x_2^p) \\ \vdots & \vdots & \vdots & \vdots \\ k_1(x_i^1, x_N^1) & k_2(x_i^2, x_N^2) & \cdots & k_p(x_i^p, x_N^p) \end{bmatrix} \tag{6.22}$$

where k_p is the dot production kernel function for the pth cue. We also call it multiple similarities-based kernel features. This extension is different from Couple KDA (CKDA) in Yan *et al.* (2005). The former is based on an explicit kernel matrix feature, while CKDA is still based on implicit feature space. Moreover, our work aims to consider multiple visual cues respectively, but CKDA uses multiple kernels for a single image cue. However, because the kernel mapping of each kernel is implicit, simply putting them together and regarding them as a matrix are practically unreasonable. The proposed method gives an explicit interpretation for the kernel matrix feature.

This extended kernel feature embodies more information, but it brings with a problem of numerical computation, for the popular data analysis methods are all based on the vector-based data. The intuitive idea is to reshape $\tilde{K}_i$ as a vector with $N \times p$ elements. However, this reshaping loses coupled information existed in rows and columns of $\tilde{K}_i$, which is very useful for recognition. We can see that the rows of $\tilde{K}_i$ are multiple similarities information between two images, and the columns of $\tilde{K}_i$ represent the kernel features based on each cue. Moreover, the reshaping leads to expensive computation due to dimension increasing with p times. For example, if there are 1000 training samples and 10 different cues, then the number of dimension becomes 10^4. With subspace learning, performing eigen-decomposition in such a high-dimensional space may cause instability of numerical computation. In order to efficiently deal with these problems, we develop a multiple similarity kernel discriminant analysis (MKDA) algorithm to learning non-linear discriminating features in the following.

Similar to the traditional KDA, based on the extended kernel features, $\tilde{K}_i$s, MKDA also employs the Fisher criterion that maximizes the between-class scatter and minimizes the within-class scatter, but it extends the vector-based norm into the Frobenius norm as in Yan *et al.* (2005), and Ye *et al.* (2004). With the kernel features $\tilde{K}_i$, $n = 1, 2, \ldots, n$, the between-class scatter $\tilde{S}_\mathrm{b}$ and the within-class scatter $\tilde{S}_\mathrm{w}$ measured by the Frobenius norm are

$$\tilde{S}_\mathrm{B}^\phi = \sum_{i=1}^{C} N_i \|M_i - \bar{M}\|_F^2 \tag{6.23}$$

$$\tilde{S}_\mathrm{W}^\phi = \sum_{i=1}^{C} \sum_{\tilde{K}_j \in X_i} \|\tilde{K}_j - M_i\|_F^2 \tag{6.24}$$

where $\bar{M}$ is the mean matrix of all the $\tilde{K}_i$, and M_i represents the mean matrix of the ith class, and $\tilde{K}_j \in X_i$ means that $\tilde{K}_i$ belongs to the ith class.

The goal is to find the optimal projection matrices $L \in \Re^{N \times d_L}$ and $R \in \Re^{p \times d_R}$, which maximize $\tilde{S}_\mathrm{B}^\phi$ and $\tilde{S}_\mathrm{W}^\phi$ in the low-dimensional subspace of $L \otimes R$, i.e., minimizing

$$\hat{S}_\mathrm{W}^\phi = \sum_{i=1}^{C} \sum_{\tilde{K}_j \in X_i} \|L^T (\tilde{K}_j - M_i) R\|_F^2$$

and maximizing

$$\hat{S}_\mathrm{B}^\phi = \sum_{i=1}^{C} N_i \|L^T (M_i - \bar{M}) R\|_F^2$$

at the same time.

Because of $\|X\|_F^2 = \text{trace}(XX^T)$, $\hat{S}_B^\phi$ and $\hat{S}_W^\phi$ can be written as

$$\hat{S}_B^\phi = \text{trace}(L^T D_B^R L)$$

$$\tilde{S}_W^\phi = \text{trace}(L^T D_W^R L)$$

where

$$D_B^R = \sum_{i=1}^{C} N_i (M_i - \bar{M}) RR^T (M_i - \bar{M})^T \tag{6.25}$$

$$D_W^R = \sum_{i=1}^{C} \sum_{\tilde{K}_j \in X_i} (\tilde{K}_j - M_i) RR^T (\tilde{K}_j - M_i)^T \tag{6.26}$$

Then, we can get the optimal projection L by maximizing

$$\text{trace}((L^T D_W^R L)^{-1} (L^T D_B^R L))$$

i.e., computing the eigenvectors of $(D_W^R)^{-1} D_B^R$.

Similarly, if L is fixed, we can rewrite $\hat{S}_B^\phi$ and $\hat{S}_W^\phi$ as

$$\hat{S}_B^\phi = \text{trace}(R^T D_B^L R)$$

$$\hat{S}_W^\phi = \text{trace}(R^T D_W^L R)$$

because of $\text{trace}(AB) = \text{trace}(BA)$, where

$$D_B^L = \sum_{i=1}^{C} N_i (M_i - \bar{M})^T LL^T (M_i - \bar{M}) \tag{6.27}$$

$$D_W^L = \sum_{i=1}^{C} \sum_{\tilde{K}_j \in X_i} (\tilde{K}_j - M_i)^T LL^T (\tilde{K}_j - M_i) \tag{6.28}$$

Then, the optimal projection R can be obtained by maximizing

$$\text{trace}\left((R^T D_W^L R)^{-1} (R^T D_B^L R)\right)$$

i.e., solving the eigenvectors of $(D_W^L)^{-1} D_B^L$.

Thus, the final optimal solution can be computed by an iterative procedure as in Algorithm 1.2.

Algorithm 1.2. The MKDA algorithm

1: **Input** $\tilde{K}_1, \tilde{K}_2, \ldots, \tilde{K}_N$
2: **Initialize** Set $R_0 \leftarrow (I_{d_R}, 0)^T$, and compute all the class mean M_is and the global mean $\bar{M}$
3: **for** $t = 1$ to T **do**

4:   For a given R_{t-1}, compute D_{W}^R and D_{B}^R using Eqs. 6.25 and 6.26, and get the optimal L_t by solving the first d_L leading eigenvectors of $(D_{\mathrm{W}}^R)^{-1}D_{\mathrm{B}}^R$;

5:   Based on L_t, compute D_{W}^L and D_{B}^L using Eqs. 6.27 and 6.28, and get the optimal R_t by solving the first d_R leading eigenvectors of $(D_{\mathrm{W}}^L)^{-1}D_{\mathrm{B}}^L$;

6:   **if** $\|L_t - L_{t-1}\| < \varepsilon$ and $\|R_t - R_{t-1}\| < \varepsilon$ **then**

7:      break;

8:   **else**

9:      continue.

10:   **end if**

11: **end for**

12: **Output** $L = L_t$ and $R = R_t$.

It can be found that the MKDA algorithm not only avoids the eigen-decomposition in the $N \times p$ dimensional space, but also it well preserves the geometric relations of row and column of $\tilde{K}_i$. In addition, in the traditional KDA, the available dimension has the upper bound $C - 1$, while the MKDA algorithm has no such constraint.

For a new pattern , its projection is

$$Y_i = L^T \tilde{K}_z R \qquad (6.29)$$

where $\tilde{K}_z$ is the kernel feature matrix of the image z, $\tilde{K}_z = \{A_{i,j} = \{k_i(z^i, x_j^i)\}\}$, and $i = 1, 2, \ldots, p$ and $j = 1, 2, \ldots, N$.

6.4.2 *Experiments*

The experimental data include the FA and FB sets, and 1000 front view face images selected from training CD of the FERET database (Phillips *et al.*, 2000), which is widely used to evaluate the face-recognition methods. There are 1196 images in the FA set and 1195 images in the FB set, and all of the subjects have only one image in the FA and FB sets, respectively. Same as the FERET test protocol, we use 1000 images from the training CD as the training set. The FA images are used for the gallery images, and the FB images are taken as the probe images. All the images are cropped by fixing two eye locations at $(12, 14)$ and $(36, 14)$. The variations include illumination, expression, and tiny pose changes. Figure 6.3 shows some samples.

We use Gabor representations of the image as different cues, for Gabor-based face recognition has achieved great success (Shen and Bai, 2004; Liu and Wechsler, 2002) due to the good properties of Gabor filters, such as spatial localization, spatial frequency characteristic, and orientation selectivity. Same as previous studies, 40 Gabor filters are adopted, i.e., five scales and eight orientations, and then 40 Gabor images are obtained for each image. In previous work, such as LDA (Liu and Wechsler, 2002) and KDA (Shen and Bai, 2004), they often consider 40 Gabor images together and reshape them into a vector. To reduce the computation complexity, the popular technique is to down sample the Gabor images. Actually

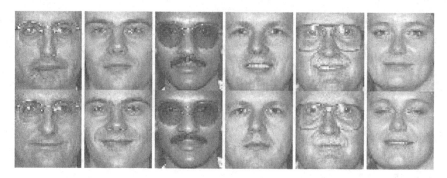

Fig. 6.3.   Samples from the FERET database.

40 Gabor images correspond to different scales and orientations respectively, so they should have different response characteristics. Here, we take them as 40 different cues of the face image in MKDA.

We compare MKDA with KDA (Shen and Bai, 2004), LDA (Liu and Wechsler, 2002), and the method that reshaping the kernel feature matrix as a vector (we denote it as VKDA for simplicity). The Gaussian kernel, $k(x, y) = \exp\left(-\gamma \left\|\frac{x-y}{\sigma}\right\|^2\right)$, is employed for all the k_p in MKDA, VKDA, and KDA. As for the parameter γ, we set it as $\gamma = \beta/s$, where s is the dimension of x and y, and β is an adjustable constant. It seems that β is better for KDA among $[0.1\ 1]$ in the three databases. For comparison and simplicity, we simply set $\beta = 0.5$ in the experiments for all the kernel functions. Similar to Liu and Wechsler (2002) and Shen and Bai (2004), we down sample the Gabor images with sampling factor $\rho = 4$ and reshaped them as a vector to test the LDA and KDA methods. The Euclidean distance-based nearest neighbor classifier is used for classification.

Table 6.5 reports the best recognition rates of four methods. The MKDA gives a higher recognition rate than LDA, KDA, and VKDA. The performance of MKDA is also comparable with the result reported in the latest literature (Shan et al., 2005). Further MKDA gets the recognition rate of 97.57%, while the best recognition rate of the state of arts (Shan et al., 2005) is 97.2%. We also investigate the recognition performance with variation of feature numbers shown in Fig. 6.4(a), where we fix the feature numbers in the right matrix R, and test the performance of MKDA with the variation of left matrix L. We can observe the superiority of MKDA. Figure 6.4(b) shows the performance of MKDA with variation of d_L and d_R. We can observe that the performance of MKDA stabilizes near the best result when $d_R \geq 10$ and d_L between 100 and 600. Comparing with the original dimension of kernel features, $10^3 \times 40$, MKDA can give a good performance with a small number of dimensions.

We also test the proposed method on the COIL-100 object database and WANG's nature image database. The COIL-100 (Murase and Nayar, 1995) database has 100 different objects, and each object has 72 color images at pose intervals of 5 degrees. The image size is 128×128. Figure 6.5 shows some samples. In our experiments, we convert the images into gray images, and evaluate the robustness

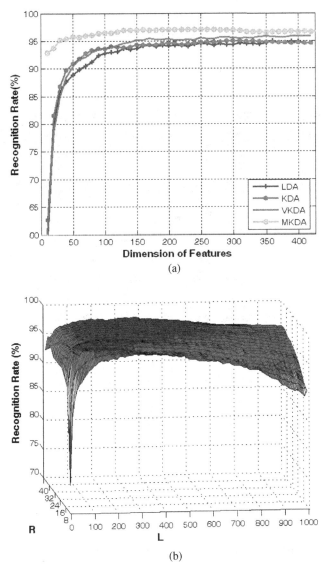

Fig. 6.4. Results on the FERET database. (a) Recognition rates with different dimensions. (b) The performance of MKDA with different dimensions.

to such view changes for general objects. Similar to Matas and Obdrazalek (2004) and Maree *et al.* (2005), we select 18 views of each of the 100 objects as the training samples, starting with the pose at 0° and continuing at intervals of 20°, and the rest images for testing. For simplicity, we divide the images into 16 patches with size of 32×32, and take these patches as local components of the object to test MKDA. Thus, the dimension of a kernel feature matrix is 1800×16. The best recognition rates of the four methods are reported in Table 6.6, where MKDA keeps $d_R = 8$

Table 6.5: The best recognition rates (%) on the FERET database

Method	LDA	KDA	VKDA	MKDA
Recognition rate	94.98	95.07	95.99	97.57

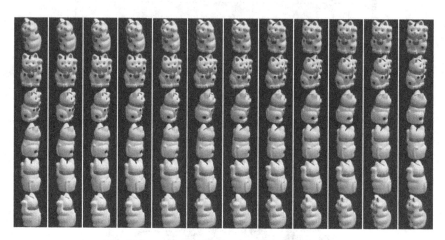

Fig. 6.5.   Samples from the COIL-100 database.

Table 6.6: The best recognition rates (%) on the COIL-100 database

Method	LDA	KDA	VKDA	MKDA
Recognition rate	84.59	95.65	94.29	99.22

and $d_L = 70$. The recognition rate of MKDA is also comparable with the reported results in Matas and Obdrazalek (2004) and Maree *et al.* (2005). Figure 6.6 gives the recognition performances of four methods with the variation of feature numbers. The results are similar to those on the FERET database, where MKDA gives the best performance than the other three methods. Using the same testing protocol, methods in the literature report the recognition rate from 87.5% to 99.9%. We just simple divide the image into 16 patches on the average, and take them as local components in the experiments. Perhaps the performance of MKDA can be further improved, if we automatically detect local components according to object structure.

Wang's database consists of 1000 nature images of 10 categories, each represented by 100 images, illustrating the following themes (Chen and Wang, 2004; Maree *et al.*, 2005): African people and villages, beach, buildings, buses, dinosaurs, elephants, flowers, horses, mountain and glaciers, and food. Such common categories exhibit high intraclass variability. The images are of size 384×256. Some samples are shown in Fig. 6.7. Similar to Chen and Wang (2004), and Maree *et al.* (2005),

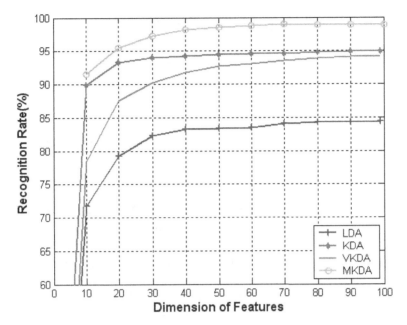

Fig. 6.6.   Comparison with different dimensions on the COIL-100 database.

Fig. 6.7.   Samples from the Wang's database.

the leave-one-out testing protocol is adopted to test the proposed method for image classification.

Four kinds of visual features are used to represent the images (Wu *et al.*, 2003; Yan *et al.*, 2006): color histogram, color moments, wavelet based texture, and directionality. Color histogram is taken in HSV space with quantization of $8 \times 4 = 32$ bins on H and S channels; the first three moments from each of the three color channels are used for color moment; a 24-dimensional PWT-based wavelet texture features and an 8-dimensional directionality features are contained to construct a 73-dimensional feature vector for each image. For MKDA, these four kinds of visual features are considered, respectively. Thus, the dimension of the kernel feature matrix is 999×4. Table 6.7 reports the error rates of four methods, where MKDA shows $d_L = 100$ and $d_R = 3$. Similar to the above experiments, MKDA has a better classification performance than the three related methods. The error rate of MKDA

Table 6.7: The classification error rates (%) on WANG's database

Method	LDA	KDA	VKDA	MKDA
Error rate	12	10.9	13.5	10.4

is 10.4%. This result is also better than the published results. Error rates in the literature vary from 62.5% to 15.9% (Chen and Wang, 2004; Maree *et al.*, 2005).

6.5 Conclusion

In order to deal with two problems existing in LDA for face recognition, this chapter presented kernel scatter difference-based non-linear discriminating features for face recognition. The kernel trick is first used to map the input data into an implicit feature space, and then a scatter difference-based discriminant rule is performed to avoid the numerical problem in KDA. Because the traditional kernel features only consider a single similarity between images, we further extended the kernel features into multiple similarity kernel features, and designed the MKDA algorithm to extract the non-linear discriminating features.

Acknowledgment

This work is partially supported by NSFC 60675003 and NSFC 60835002.

References

Baudat, G. and Anouar, F. Generalized discrimant analysis using a kernel approach, *Neural Comput.* **12**, 10, 2385–2404, 2000.

Baudat, G. and Anouar, F. Kernel-based methods and function approximation, in *Proc. of Intl Conf. Neural Networks*, pp. 2:1244–2:1249, 2001.

Belhumeur, P. N., Hespanha, J. P., and Kriegman, D. J. Eigenfaces vs. fisherfaces: recognition using class specific linear projection, *IEEE Trans. Pattern Anal. Machine Intelligence* **19**, 7, 711–720, 1997.

Chen, L. F., Liao, H. M., Lin, J. C., Ko, M. T., and Yu, G. J. A new lda-based face recognition system which can solve the small sample size problem, *Pattern Recognition* **22**, 10, 1713–1726, 2000.

Chen, Y. and Wang, J. Z. Image categorization by learning and reasoning with regions, *J. Machine Learning Res.* **5**, 913–939, 2004.

Heisele, B., Ho, P., and Poggio, T. Face recognition with support vector machines: global verus component based approach, in *Proc. of Intl Conf. Comput. Vision*, pp. 688–694, 2001.

Huang, R., Liu, Q. S., Lu, H. Q., and Ma, S. D. Sovling the small smaple size problem, in *Proc. of Intl Conf. Pattern Recognition*, pp. 3:29–3:32, 2003.

Li, H. F., Jiang, T., and Zhang, K. S. Efficient and robust feature extraction by maximum margin criterion, in *Advances in Neural Information Processing Systems*, pp. 157–165, 2003.

Liu, C. J. and Wechsler, H. Enhanced fisher linear discriminant models for face recognition, in *Proc. of Intl Conf. Pattern Recogntion*, pp. 2:1368–2:1371, 1998.

Liu, C. J. and Wechsler, H. Gabor feature-based classification using the enhanced fisher linear discriminant model for face recognition, *IEEE Trans. Image Processing* **11**, 4, 467–476, 2002.

Liu, Q. S., Huang, R., Lu, H. Q., and Ma, S. D. Face recognition using kernel-based fisher discriminant analysis, in *Proc. of Intl Conf. Automatic Face and Gesture Recognition*, pp. 187–191, 2002a.

Liu, Q. S., Huang, R., Lu, H. Q., and Ma, S. D. Kernel-based optimized feature vectors selection and discriminant analysis for face recognition, in *Proc. of Intl Conf. Pattern Recognition*, pp. 2:362–2:365, 2002b.

Liu, Q. S., Lu, H. Q., and Ma, S. D. Improving kernel fisher discriminant analysis for face recognition, *IEEE Trans. Circuits Syst. Video Technol.* **14**, 1, 42–49, 2004a.

Liu, Q. S., Tang, X., Lu, H. Q., and Ma, S. D. Kernel scatter-difference based discriminant analysis for face recognition, in *Proc. of Intl Conf. Pattern Recognition*, 2:419–2:422, 2004b.

Liu, W., Wang, Y. H., Li, S. Z., and Tan, T. N. Null space based kernel fisher discriminant analysis for face recognition, in *Proc. of Intl Conf. Automatic Face and Gesture Recognition*, pp. 369–374, 2004c.

Liu, Q. S., Tang, X., Lu, H. Q., and Ma, S. D. Face recognition using kernel scatter-difference-based discriminant analysis, *IEEE Trans. Neural Networks* **17**, 4, 1081–1085, 2006.

Liu, Q. S., Jin, H. L., Tang, X., Lu, H. Q., and Ma, S. D. A new extension of kernel feature and its application for visual recognition, *NeuroComputing* **71**, 10–12, 1850–1856, 2008.

Lu, J., Plataniotis, K. N., and Venetsanopoulos, A. N. Face recognition using kernel direct discriminant analysis algorithms, *IEEE Trans. Neural Networks* **14**, 1, 117–126, 2003.

Maree, R., Geurts, P., Piater, J., and Wehenkel, L. Random subwindows for robust image classification, in *Proc. of Intl Conf. Computer Vision and Pattern Recognition*, pp. 1:34–1:40, 2005.

Matas, J. and Obdrazalek, S. Object recognition methods based on transformation covariant features, in *Proc. of European Conf. Signal Processing*, pp. 2310–2317, 2004.

Mika, S., Ratsch, G., and Weston, J. Fisher discriminant analysis with kernels, in *Proc. of Neural Networks for Signal Processing Workshop*, pp. 41–48, 1999.

Murase, H. and Nayar, S. K. Visual learning and recognition of 3d objects from appearance, *Int. J. Computer Vision* **14**, 1, 5–24, 1995.

Osuna, E., Freund, R., and Girosi, F. Support vector machines: training and applications, Technical report, AI Lab, MIT, 1997.

Phillips, P. J., Moon, H., Rizvi, S., and Rauss, P. The feret evaluation methodology for face-recognition algorithms, *IEEE Trans. Pattern Anal. Machine Intelligence* **22**, 10, 1090–1104, 2000.

Shan, S. G., Yang, P., Chen, X. L., and Gao, W. Adaboost gabor fisher classifier for face recognition, in *Proc. of Intl Workshop on Analysis and Modeling of Face and Gestures, joint with ICCV*, pp. 279–292, 2005.

Shen, L. and Bai, L. Gabor feature-based face recognition using kernel methods, in *Proc. of Intl Conf. Automatic Face and Gesture Recognition*, pp. 170–176, 2004.

Turk, M. and Pentland, A. Eigenfaces for recognition, *J. Neuroscience* **3**, 1, 72–86, 1991.

Vasconcelos, N., Ho, P., and Moreno, P. The kullback-leibler kernel as a framework for discriminant and localized representations for visual recognition, in *Proc. of European Conf. Comput. Vision*, pp. 430–431, 2004.

Wu, H., Lu, H. Q., and Ma, S. D. A practical svm-based algorithm for ordinal regression in image retrieval, in *Proc. of ACM Multimedia*, 612–621, 2003.

Wu, Y., Huang, T. S., and Toyama, K. Self-supervised learning for object based on kernel discriminant-em algorithm, in *Proc. of Int. Conf. Comput. Vision*, pp. 1:275–1:280, 2001.

Yan, S., Xu, D., Zhang, L., Zhang, B., and Zhang, H. Coupled kernel-based subspace learning, in *Proc. of Intl Conf. Comput. Vision and Pattern Recognition*, pp. 1:645–1:650, 2005.

Yan, W., Liu, Q. S., Lu, H. Q., and Ma, S. D. Multiple similarities-based kernel subspace learning for image classification, in *Proc. of Asian Conf. Computer Vision*, pp. 244–253, 2006.

Yang, M. H. Kernel eigenfaces vs. kernel fisherfaces: face recognition using kernel methods, in *Proc. of Intl Conf. Automatic Face and Gesture Recognition*, pp. 215–210, 2002.

Ye, J. P., Janardan, R., and Li, Q. Two dimensional linear discriminant analysis, in *Advances in Neural Information Processing Systems*, pp. 1569–1576, 2004.

Yu, H. and Yang, J. A direct lda algorithm for high-dimensional data—with application to face recognition, *Pattern Recognition* **34**, 10, 2067–2070, 2001.

Zhao, W., Chellappa, R., and Phillips, P. J. Subspace linear discriminant analysis for face recognition, Technical Report CAR-TR-914, University of Maryland, 1999.

Part III

Fingerprint

Chapter 7

ROBUST REFERENCE POINT DETECTION AND FEATURE EXTRACTION ALGORITHM IN FINGERPRINT VERIFICATION SYSTEM

Junbum Park[*,‡], David K. Han[†,§] and Hanseok Ko[*,¶]

School of Electrical Engineering, Korea University, Seoul, Korea

†*Office Naval Research, Washington D.C. USA*

‡*jbpark@ispl.korea.ac.kr*

§*david.k.han@navy.mil*

¶*hsko@korea.ac.kr*

7.1 Introduction

Reference point detection is an important component of fingerprint verification. In this chapter, a reference point detection method using relative entropy for directional components is introduced. This method can capture the ridge and valley information of fingerprint texture. The detection of the reference point is accomplished by finding the point at which the relative entropy is the minimum among all pixels in the global region. The reference point is obtained using relative entropy representing the texture's directional feature to determine the core point itself or those of similar points that can be used to establish a rigid reference from which to map the features for verification. The advantages of this method include the reduction in pre-processing time and consistency of locating the same point as reference even when processing the arch type and tented arch type fingerprints. Moreover, this chapter introduces a fingerprint verification algorithm, which comprises of a reference point correction technique and a feature extraction method. The method begins with the Poincare-index algorithm to determine the reference point of a test fingerprint image. The reference correction algorithm then adjusts the acquired reference point using cross correlation between the acquired point and the reference point of a reference fingerprint image. From the adjusted reference point, this algorithm extracts approximated multiscale features by Gabor filter using image data obtained by wavelet transform in eight orientations.

The experimental results using the NIST Special Database 4 demonstrate the superiority of the proposed scheme in terms of accuracy for reference point detection and feature extraction under various noisy environments.

7.2 Reliable Reference Point Detection using Relative Entropy

The most important procedure is reliable reference point detection in the implementation of a fingerprint verification system. A reference point to be used as the basis for texture features of fingerprints should be a point in the texture field that can be reproducible. The features for verification are then extracted with respect to the position of the reference point. Along with the unique features, the location of the reference point is the discerning element that distinguishes one person from another. In most cases of fingerprint texture, either the core point or reference point satisfies the reproducibility requirement, given that they exist. Among various methods, Method of Orientation Field Estimation (MOFE) (Jain *et al.*, 2000) is the most widely used for reference point detection. Essentially, it searches for the point of high gradient component in the texture field. Thus, while it is reliable for detecting the reference point in fingerprints of right loop type, left loop type, and whole type, it is somewhat limited in arch type and tented arch type having low gradient variation (Liu *et al.*, 2005, 2006; Jiang *et al.*, 2004). Moreover, it is insensitive to the variation of gradient components when the discontinuity of the fingerprint ridge induced by exterior blemishes on the finger surface exists. As a result, it becomes sensitive to the image quality and thus complicated signal processing procedure is required. To improve from these deficiencies, the proposed algorithm calculates the directional probability density at each pixel located at the region whose four principal directions are most evenly distributed. This region of uniform directionality can be indicated by locating the highest intensity points over the single image obtained by superimposing the four principal directional images. The directional probability density is used to determine the relative entropy at each pixel. This method then searches for the point whose relative entropy is the minimum among its neighboring pixels in the candidate region of uniform directionality. Moreover, this method defines this point as the reference point. By finding the reference point, the method achieves excellent verification performance whereby it becomes less sensitive to image quality than MOFE in various fingerprint types including arch type and tented arch type.

This part is organized as follows. Section 7.2.1 elaborates the problem of the previous reference point detection algorithm and addresses the issues described above. Moreover, the reference point detection algorithm is detailed. Section 7.2.2 illustrates the reliable point detection algorithm using relative entropy.

7.2.1 *Problem formulation*

For a reliable fingerprint recognition system, establishing a consistent reference point is important. The fingerprint features of an individual need to be based on some reference point that does not change over time such that the same person's features can be well traced by locating the same reference point. As a result, the reliability of fingerprint verification is heavily dependent on successfully establishing a rigid reference point. MOFE, which essentially searches for the point of large gradient as a reference, is frequently used in a fingerprint recognition system. However, this method alone cannot produce reliable reference point detection, due to the following reasons. First, this method requires a detailed pre-processing procedure because it uses a variation of gradient components, which are sensitive to the quality of the initial image captured. Second, although the method shows that the reference point can be reasonably well detected in the captured images with large gradient variation in ridges, it performs poorly in those with relatively small gradient variations such as the arch type and tented arch type of fingerprints. Figure 7.1 gives some examples of fingerprints well suited for MOFE and Fig. 7.2 shows some examples of fingerprints not well suited for MOFE.

The main steps of MOFE can be summarized as follows.

(1) Divide input image into blocks of size $W \times W$ (16×16).
(2) Compute the gradients $G_x(i,j)$ and $G_y(i,j)$ at each pixel. Depending on the computational requirement, the gradient operator may vary from the simple Sobel operator

$$\text{Sobel operator: } H_v = \begin{bmatrix} 1 & 0 & -1 \\ 2 & 0 & -2 \\ 1 & 0 & -1 \end{bmatrix}, \quad H_h = \begin{bmatrix} 1 & 0 & 1 \\ 0 & 0 & 0 \\ -1 & -2 & -1 \end{bmatrix}$$

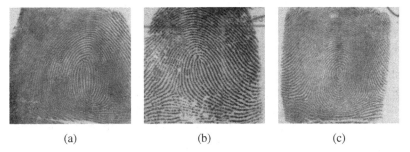

(a)   (b)   (c)

Fig. 7.1. Examples of fingerprint texture well suited for MOFE. (a) Double loop type, (b) Loop type, and (c) Whole type.

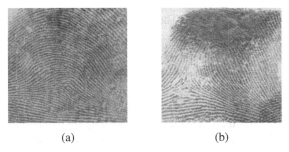

(a)   (b)

Fig. 7.2. Examples of fingerprint texture not well suited for MOFE. (a) Arch type with small gradient variation in ridges. (b) Scar in reference point neighborhood.

(3) Estimate the local orientation of each block centered at pixel (i, j) using the following formula

$$G'_x(i, j) = \sum_{u=-W/2}^{W/2} \sum_{v=-W/2}^{W/2} 2G_x(i + u, j + v)G_y(i + u, j + v), \qquad (7.1)$$

$$G'_y(i, j) = \sum_{u=-W/2}^{W/2} \sum_{v=-W/2}^{W/2} G_x^2(i + u, j + v) - G_y^2(i + u, j + v) \qquad (7.2)$$

$$\theta(i, j) = \frac{1}{2} \tan^{-1} \left(\frac{G'_y(i, j)}{G'_x(i, j)} \right) \qquad (7.3)$$

where $\theta(i, j)$ is the orientation field at coordinates (i, j), $G_x = H_h * I$ and $G_y = H_v * I$ are the gradient magnitudes in x and y directions, respectively, "$*$" denotes the convolution operator while "I" represents the input image.

(4) Orientation fields, found by step 3, are smoothened by a low-pass filter

$$O'(i, j) = \tan^{-1} \left(\frac{\sum_{i=-W/2}^{W/2} \sum_{j=-W/2}^{W/2} \sin(\theta(i, j))}{\sum_{i=-W/2}^{W/2} \sum_{j=-W/2}^{W/2} \cos(\theta(i, j))} \right) \qquad (7.4)$$

$$\theta'(i, j) = \frac{1}{2} \tan^{-1}(O'(i, j)) \qquad (7.5)$$

where $O'(x, y)$ denotes smoothened orientation fields and $\theta'(i, j)$ denotes the final local ridge orientation at coordinate (i, j).

As shown in Fig. 7.2, arch type fingerprints have very small gradient component variation in ridges (Fig. 7.2(a)). Therefore, the existing MOFE, which searches for a point of large gradient component variation as a reference point, is not effective for arch type and tented arch type. Moreover, if a scar exists in the reference point neighborhood as shown in Fig. 7.2(b), further processing is required to improve the detection reliability.

7.2.2 *Reliable reference point detection*

To address the weakness of the method against arch type and tented arch type fingerprints, an alternative method that utilizes the relative entropy for the curvature texture to establish the reference point is presented in this section. Directional component is extracted to calculate relative entropy. The directional component can be obtained by convolution operation between directional filter (0°, 45°, 90°, 135°) and original fingerprint image. This algorithm searches for global region using the directional component. The method then calculates probability for extracted directional component using Parzen window of fixed size. From global region, it searches for the one point where the directional probability distribution is flattest (uniform density) for its reliability. This means that relative entropy is

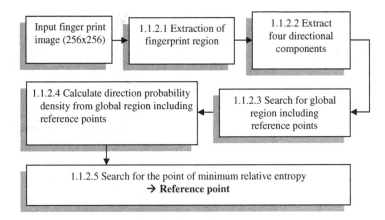

Fig. 7.3.   Reference point detection algorithm.

minimum at the point. Such a point can certainly be used as a desirable reference point because of its consistency and the reproducibility of finding it. In addition, because the method uses probability density for directional component, no detailed preprocessing is required. However, the MOFE requires detailed preprocessing such as connecting ridge when ridges are cut by scar or dryness. The procedure of the proposed reference point detection algorithm is shown in Fig. 7.3.

7.2.2.1 *Extraction of fingerprint region*

Before the directional component of a fingerprint is calculated, this method extracts the fingerprint region to reduce searching area, by transforming the gray image into a binary image, which distinguishes ridges from valleys. To obtain the binary image B, the method takes low-pass filtered image LF of the fingerprint by convolving a unit circle filter U of 21×21 size to the input image I. Then, the binary image is obtained by applying a local threshold to the low-pass filtered image as shown in Fig. 7.4(c). Morphological masking operations MM then follow to generate the fingerprint region R. The following equations denote extraction of the fingerprint region:

$$B(i, j) = \begin{cases} 1, & \text{if } I(i, j) \geq LF(i, j) \\ 0, & \text{otherwise} \end{cases} \tag{7.6}$$

$$LF(i, j) = \sum_{u=0}^{q-1} \sum_{v=0}^{q-1} I(i + c - u, j + c - v)U(u, v) \tag{7.7}$$

$$U(i, j) = \begin{cases} 1, & \text{if } (i - x)^2 + (j - y)^2 \leq r^2 \\ 0, & \text{otherwise} \end{cases} \tag{7.8}$$

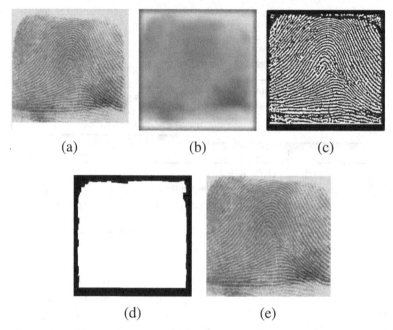

Fig. 7.4.   Extraction of fingerprint region. (a) Input image, (b) low-pass filtered image, (c) binary image, (d) fingerprint region obtained by morphology operation, and (e) result image of fingerprint region.

$$R(i,j) = \sum_{u=0}^{q-1} \sum_{v=0}^{q-1} B(i + c - u, j + c - v) MM(u,v)$$

$$0 \le i < M, \ 0 \le j < N, \ c = (q-1)/2 \qquad (7.9)$$

where (i, j) denotes image coordinate, M and N represent image size, q is the size of image filter, (u, v) is coordinate of image filter, (x, y) denotes the center coordinate of the unit circle filter, and r is the radius of the circle.

7.2.2.2 Extraction of four directional components

This method extracts four directional components ($0°$, $45°$, $90°$, and $135°$) for reference point detection. If this algorithm extracts four directional binary images by convolution operation between general filter and binary image as in Fig. 7.4(c), it is difficult to obtain directional components that can distinguish ridges from valleys because ridges of the binary image are rather thick. Thus, more detailed directional component images are required. In addition, ridge components are squashed as shown in Fig. 7.5.

Thus, this algorithm makes use of four new directional filters as in Fig. 7.6, to slenderize ridges. Here, each filter is defined as F_0, F_{45}, F_{90}, and F_{135}. Images in Fig. 7.7 are the normalized forms after convolution operation between the new

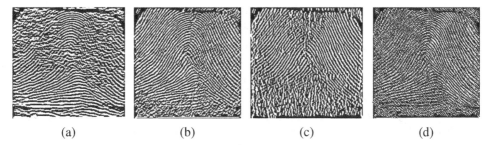

Fig. 7.5.   Examples of hard to distinguish directional component. (a) 0° directional binary image, (b) 45° directional binary image, (c) 90° directional binary image, and (d) 135° directional binary image.

-1.6	-1.6	-1.6	-1.6	-1.6
0.4	0.4	0.4	0.4	0.4
2.4	2.4	2.4	2.4	2.4
0.4	0.4	0.4	0.4	0.4
-1.6	-1.6	-1.6	-1.6	-1.6

-2.6	-1.6	-0.6	0.4	2.4
-1.6	-0.6	0.4	2.4	0.4
-0.6	0.4	2.4	0.4	-0.6
0.4	2.4	0.4	-0.6	-1.6
2.4	0.4	-0.6	-1.6	-2.6

2.4	0.4	-0.6	-1.6	-2.6
0.4	2.4	0.4	-0.6	-1.6
-0.6	0.4	2.4	0.4	-0.6
-1.6	-0.6	0.4	2.4	0.4
-2.6	-1.6	-0.6	0.4	2.4

-1.6	0.4	2.4	0.4	-1.6
-1.6	0.4	2.4	0.4	-1.6
-1.6	0.4	2.4	0.4	-1.6
-1.6	0.4	2.4	0.4	-1.6
-1.6	0.4	2.4	0.4	-1.6

Fig. 7.6.   Direction filters of 5 × 5 size. (a) 0° directional filter (F_0), (b) 45° directional filter (F_{45}), (c) 135° directional filter (F_{135}), and (d) 90° directional filter (F_{90}).

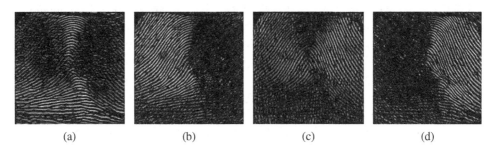

Fig. 7.7.   Directional components extracted by direction filters. (a) 0° directional image (ND_0), (b) 45° directional image (ND_{45}), (c) 90° directional image (ND_{90}), and (d) 135° directional image (ND_{135}).

directional filters of Fig. 7.6 and the binary image of Fig. 7.4(c). This is denoted in Eqs. (7.10) and (7.11):

$$D_k(i,j) = \sum_{u=0}^{q-1} \sum_{v=0}^{q-1} B(i + c - u, j + c - v) F(u, v),$$

$$k = 0, 45, 90, 135 \tag{7.10}$$

$$ND_k(i,j) = D_k(i,j) / \arg[\max_{k'}(D_{k'}(i,j))] \tag{7.11}$$

where D denotes directional components obtained by convolution operation between binary image and newly constructed filters F, ND denotes each normalized image obtained by D as shown in Fig. 7.7 and max is the largest value in directional component D. Moreover, the size of the direction filter is set at a 5×5 masking window. In Fig. 7.7, the result shows that a more detailed directional component is detected in the fingerprint region and we label each directional component image as ND_0, ND_{45}, ND_{90}, and ND_{135}, respectively.

After extracting the normalized images, we obtain 4 directional binary images CB for the detailed images shown in Fig. 7.7, as denoted in the following expression:

$$CB_k(i,j) = \begin{cases} 1, & \text{if } ND_k(i,j) \geq m - \beta \times \sigma \\ 0, & \text{otherwise} \end{cases} \tag{7.12}$$

where k denotes $0°$, $45°$, $90°$, and $135°$, m is the global average of image ND, σ is the standard deviation, and β is obtained by experiment. The detailed binary image is shown in Fig. 7.8.

7.2.2.3 *Search for global region including reference points*

In Fig. 7.8, the point at which all directional distributions are equal is not identifiable yet because these images only include the ridge component. Thus, instead of finding a reference point, we first search for the global region, which includes possible reference point candidates. It is worthy to note that the reference point may exist in more than two locations in one fingerprint. To search the global region, we first search for each directional region DR through convolution operation between the binary image CB as in Fig. 7.8 and a normalized circle filter NF defined as Eq. (7.13). Here, we do not use the unit circle filter as Eq. (7.8). If we perform convolution operation between binary image CB and unit circle filter U, even the dark part would appear bright, resulting in eliminating the directional

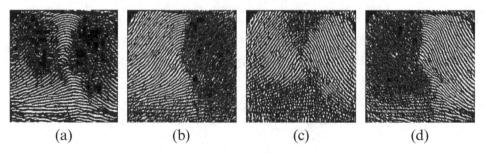

| (a) | (b) | (c) | (d) |

Fig. 7.8. The detailed 4 directional binary images. (a) $0°$ directional binary image (CB_0), (b) $45°$ directional binary image (CB_{45}), (c) $90°$ directional binary image (CB_{90}), and (d) $135°$ directional binary image (CB_{135}).

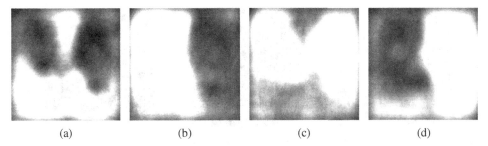

| (a) | (b) | (c) | (d) |

Fig. 7.9. Region for each directional component: (a) 0° directional region (DR_0), (b) 45° directional region (DR_{45}), (c) 90° directional region (DR_{90}), and (d) 135° directional region (DR_{135}).

information acquired in Fig. 7.8. Therefore, we use a normalized circle filter defined as follows

$$NF(i,j) = U(i,j)/\sum_{u=0}^{q-1}\sum_{v=0}^{q-1}U(i+c-u, j+c-v) \tag{7.13}$$

$$DR_k(i,j) = \sum_{u=0}^{q-1}\sum_{v=0}^{q-1}ND_k(i+c-u, j+c-v)NF_k(u,v) \tag{7.14}$$

where $k = 0, 45, 90, 135$. In Fig. 7.9, we define each directional region as DR_0, DR_{45}, DR_{90}, and DR_{135}. In the figure, the bright part includes each directional component while the dark part does not. Moreover, the intensity value is between 1 and 2, and between 0 and 1, for the bright part and dark part, respectively.

In Fig. 7.9, we use distance (difference) for the combination of each DR image. Namely, if the distance between two DR images at all coordinates is small, it means that two directional components at each coordinate will be included. On the contrary, if distance is large, the coordinate should not include two directional components. Figure 7.10 shows the inverse image G for distance images d between directional region images. Therefore, we conclude that the coordinate with 4 directional components has a uniformly low-value. We accentuate the low-value regions (in white) through inverse image G, obtained by subtracting the image pixels' values from 1 as described in Eq. (7.15). Moreover, the intensity of these images is between a negative value and positive value. We define each image of Fig. 7.10 as G_{0_45}, G_{0_90}, G_{0_135}, G_{45_90}, G_{45_135}, G_{90_135}.

$$G_{n\_m}(d_{nm}(i,j)) = \arg[ones(i,j)] - d_{nm}(i,j) \tag{7.15}$$

$$d_{nm}(i,j) = |DR_n(i,j) - DR_m(i,j)|,$$

$$n = 0, 45, 90; \; m = 45, 90, 135; \; n < m \tag{7.16}$$

where *ones* denotes an image whose intensity value is uniformly equal to 1.

Finally, we stack up all inverse images one-by-one by aligning identical pixel coordinates. We then add these stacked up inverse images to extract the global

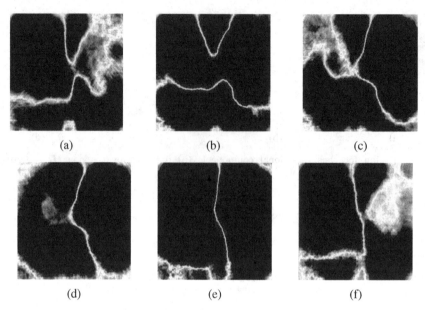

Fig. 7.10.   Inverse images showing the difference between two adjacent DR images. (a) inverse image (G_{0_45}) between DR_0 and DR_{45}, (b) inverse image (G_{0_90}) between DR_0 and DR_{90}, (c) inverse image (G_{0_135}) between DR_0 and DR_{135}, (d) inverse image (G_{45_90}) between DR_{45} and DR_{90}, (e) inverse image (G_{45_135}) between DR_{45} and DR_{135}, and (f) inverse image (G_{90_135}) between DR_{90} and DR_{135}.

reference points. In the combined image, the bright region indicates that the region includes various directional components. Thus, we search for these regions:

$$K(i,j) = \sum_n \sum_m G_{n\_m}(i,j), \ 0 \le i < X, \ 0 \le j < Y$$

$$n = 0, 45, 90; \ m = 45, 90, 135; \ n < m \qquad (7.17)$$

where K denotes global regions that include the reference points and (X, Y) is the size of inverse image G. Figure 7.11(a) shows the global regions that include the reference points obtained after convolution operation between Gaussian filter and this image. Figure 7.11(b) is obtained through postprocessing by taking a convolution with a Gaussian filter. In this figure, we can find that the white parts representing various directional components and thus reference point(s) exists in each of the regions. Moreover, Fig. 7.11(c) and (d) show the detected global region including reference points for each (a) and (b) using a mesh function. In the figure, the red peak indicates a high value.

7.2.2.4 *Calculation of directional probability density from global regions including reference points*

In Sec. 7.2.2.3, we already found two regions that include each reference point. However, the fingerprint has to have only one reference point for recognition. Thus,

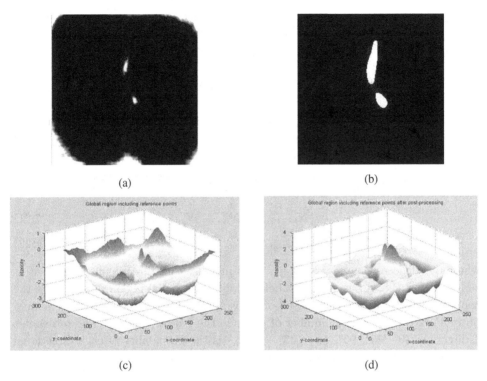

(a)   (b)

(c)   (d)

Fig. 7.11.   The detected global regions including reference points. (a),(b) Global region including reference points before and after postprocessing. (c),(d) Mesh function for each (a) and (b).

we need to select one global reference point in one region. For selection of reliable reference point, the probability of each directional component at all coordinates of each region is computed. Note that the selected reference point should be at the location where probability distribution is the most uniform. To compute the probability for all coordinates of each region, the Parzen window is used. The point having uniform distribution can be extracted by counting the numbers of each directional component in a fixed Parzen window. The Parzen window PW is a good approach that can easily compute the probability distribution for each directional component in the window. It can be described by the following procedure.

(1) Set Parzen window of fixed size (50×50).
(2) Calculate the probability for four directional components using Parzen window at all coordinates of global regions.

In step (1), the Parzen window contains 2005 pixels among 2500 pixels because this window is a circle that has a value of 1 in a fixed region. In step (2), the probability (Babich and Camps, 1996; Erdogmus *et al.*, 2004) can be written as

$$p(x) = \frac{q/n}{V(x)} \Rightarrow p(x)V(x) = \frac{q}{n} \tag{7.18}$$

where $p(x)$ is the probability density function (PDF), $V(x)$ is the size of the Parzen window, n is the number of pixels in the Parzen window, and q denotes the number of samples. Then, we can derive Eq. (7.19) from Eq. (7.18)

$$P(\theta_m(i,j)|K(i,j)) \Rightarrow \sum_m P(\theta_m(i,j)|K(i,j)) = 1 \qquad (7.19)$$

where K denotes the detected global region, (i,j) is the coordinate in global region, θ_m denotes directional components, and m denotes 4 directions ($0°$, $45°$, $90°$, and $135°$). The probability obtained by Eq. (7.19) is represented by Eqs. 1.11:

$$P(\theta_m(K_L)) = \frac{\arg[\text{count}\{CB_m(K_L)PW(K_L) == 1\}]}{S} \qquad (7.20)$$

$$K_L = \{N_1, N_2, \ldots, N_i, \ldots, N_M\} \qquad (7.21)$$

$$N_i = \{\bar{b}_{i1}, \bar{b}_{i2}, \ldots, \bar{b}_{ij}, \ldots, \bar{b}_{ij}\}, \quad \bar{b}_{ij} \in L^2 \qquad (7.22)$$

where CB denotes the binary image, which includes each directional component as shown in Fig. 7.8, K_L is a set of labeled blob N for global region image, $\bar{b}_{ij}$ is the coordinate vector of pixel composed of blobs N in the region image K, S is an area of the Parzen window (the number of pixels in the Parzen window), and m denotes 4 directions ($0°$, $45°$, $90°$, and $135°$). $P(\theta_m)$ is the probability of each directional component at all coordinates of global regions.

7.2.2.5 Search for the point of minimum relative entropy

After the probabilities for all pixels in global regions are computed, we select the point having the most uniform probability in all directions. We use the relative entropy, Kullback-Leibler distance (Erdogmus et al., 2002), to find the point with the most uniform probability. If A and B are distributions, a relative entropy (H) is defined by

$$H(A(\alpha), B(\alpha)) = \sum_\theta a_\theta(\alpha) \log \frac{a_\theta(\alpha)}{b_\theta(\alpha)}, \quad \alpha = K_L, \quad \theta = 0°, 45°, 90°, 135° \qquad (7.23)$$

where H is entropy between PMF computed by the Parzen window and desired PMF, $[O_x, O_y]$ is the optimal coordinate of a reliable reference point and α denotes all coordinates of labeled blob in global regions.

Figure 7.12 shows a reliable reference point detected by relative entropy. In Fig. 7.12, (a) shows the point where the relative entropy has the minimum value in each global region and (b) shows the final reference point having the minimum value.

7.3 Reliable Point Correction using Cross Correlation and Robust Fingerprint Verification by Gabor-Wavelet Feature Extraction

One of the key features in fingerprint recognition is the algorithm's ability to consistently select the same reference point even when different fingerprint images

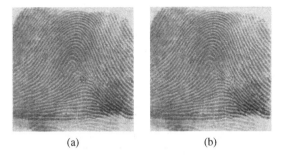

(a)   (b)

Fig. 7.12. Reliable reference point detected by entropy. (a) Point detection where relative entropy is the minimum value for each global region as in (b). (b) Final reference point having the minimum value for relative entropy.

of the same source were presented. The method should be robust enough against rotation, translation, and scale variation, so that in each recognition process an identical reference point should be detected from different images of an identical finger. Moreover, an ideal fingerprint recognition system should extract only the minimally required amount of individually unique features from fingerprints so that small quantity of feature data is sufficient for representing an individual. Existing algorithm such as Gabor feature-based filter bank matching (Jain *et al.*, 2000) and Gabor feature-based descriptor matching (Patil *et al.*, 2005) are shown to be robust in dealing the problem of rotation and translation variation of fingerprint image. They are, however, observed to be sensitive to the detected reference point position because these methods use fingercode for Gabor feature. Image-based matching using phase (Ito *et al.*, 2005) has been shown to be effective in handling rotational variations of fingerprint images. Nevertheless, the method has shown some recognition performance degradation when test images had some scale variations. Statistic-based minutiae matching algorithms (Espinosa-Duro, 2001; Jain *et al.*, 2007) have shown robust performance for low-quality images, but the methods require some levels of preprocessing such as ridge segmentation, or thinning. Moreover, wavelet feature-based matching algorithm (Tico *et al.*, 2001) has to use the limited features because the method cannot extract various directional features such as Gabor filter while the method can recognize using only small quantity of feature data. Thus, we propose a method of reference point correction which consistently delivers an identical reference point from several fingerprint images of a single source, and a robust feature extraction method which can provide high recognition performance while using only small quantity of feature data. As discussed earlier, existing fingerprint recognition algorithms are sensitive to location of the detected reference point. To overcome this shortcoming, we use detailed wavelet features of fingerprint images. From the extracted wavelet features, we correct the initially acquired reference point using cross correlation-based local matching. For high recognition performance, most of the existing algorithms require a large feature dataset. To alleviate this problem, we extract Gabor-wavelet features

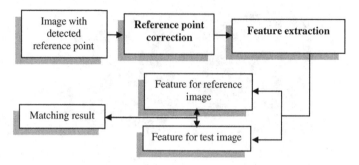

Fig. 7.13.   Typical fingerprint recognition procedure.

using wavelet transform, thus requiring only one-eighth or one-sixteenth of the original data.

In the following parts of this section, we present the details of our fingerprint recognition algorithm as summarized in Fig. 7.13. In Sec. 7.3.1, we introduce the reference point correction algorithm. The feature extraction algorithm is discussed in Sec. 7.3.2.

7.3.1 *Reference point correction*

An ideal fingerprint recognition system should deliver robust and consistent results regardless of rotation, translation, and scale variation of fingerprint images. One crucial step here is the process of consistently selecting identical location of a reference point in the image. To insure that the reference point is selected consistently, we added a reference point correction algorithm in addition to using the Poreincare-index method for selecting an initial reference point. The procedure of the proposed reference point correction algorithm is shown in Fig. 7.14.

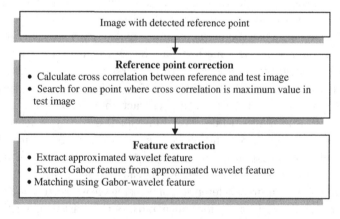

Fig. 7.14.   Reference point correction algorithm.

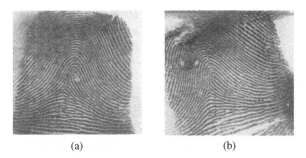

(a)   (b)

Fig. 7.15.   Reference point position detected by Poincare-index method in reference image(a) and test image(b).

7.3.1.1 *Calculating cross correlation between reference image and test image*

We use the Poincare-index algorithm to detect reference points in a reference image and a test image. Figure 7.15 shows reference point positions detected by the Poreincare-index method in the reference image and the test image.

Once reference point is detected in the reference image, we extract wavelet features as horizontal, vertical, diagonal, and approximation components. Equation (7.24) denotes the 1D continuous wavelet transform (Hwang *et al.*, 2005; De Wouwer *et al.*, 1999) using the base function of the Haar wavelet:

$$CWT(a,b) = \frac{1}{\sqrt{a}} \int_{-\infty}^{\infty} s(t)\Psi_{a,b}(t)dt \tag{7.24}$$

$$\Psi_{a,b} = \frac{1}{\sqrt{a}} \Psi\left(\frac{t-b}{a}\right) \tag{7.25}$$

where CWT is the wavelet-transformed result, $s(t)$ is signal, a is a scaling factor, b is a translation factor, and Ψ is the wavelet. Equation (7.24) can be extended to 2D discrete wavelet transform as Eq. (7.26).

$$f_{k,l}^{j}(t) = \sum_{n=1}^{N} \sum_{m=1}^{M} h_{m-2k,n-2l} f_{m,n}^{j+1} + \sum_{n=1}^{N} \sum_{m=1}^{M} g_{m-2k,n-2l}^{(s)} f_{m,n}^{j+1} \tag{7.26}$$

$$h = \left[\frac{1}{\sqrt{2}}, \frac{1}{\sqrt{2}}\right], \quad g = \left[\frac{1}{\sqrt{2}}, -\frac{1}{\sqrt{2}}\right] \tag{7.27}$$

where f is the wavelet-transformed image, h and g denote Harr wavelet for approximation and detailed components, respectively. Moreover, j is the level of wavelet transform, s is the detailed vertical, horizontal, and diagonal components, respectively. Figure 7.16(b) shows the approximated values of the features from the 2D discrete wavelet transform (Eq. (7.26)) applied to a constant region shown in Fig. 7.16(a). Figures 7.16(c)–(e) show normalized images of vertical, horizontal, and diagonal wavelet features of the same region. The image size of the wavelet transform is 128×128 and the size of selected feature images is 45×45. Features of

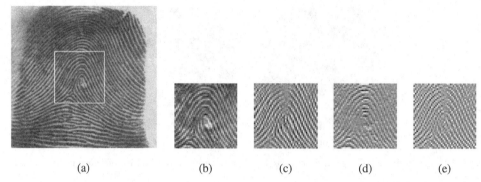

(a)	(b)	(c)	(d)	(e)

Fig. 7.16. Wavelet features extracted from a reference point of a reference image. (a) constant region selected from reference point, (b) approximated wavelet feature (ra_i), (c) detailed vertical wavelet feature (rd_i^1), (d) detailed horizontal wavelet feature (rd_i^2), and (e) detailed diagonal wavelet feature (rd_i^3).

the wavelet transform in reference image are denoted as $ra_i, rd_i^1, rd_i^2, rd_i^3$. Therefore, the wavelet feature set can be defined as

$$Wf_r = \{ra_i, rd_i^1, rd_i^2, rd_i^3\}, \quad i = 1, \dots, I \tag{7.28}$$

where Wf_r is the feature set by wavelet transform in reference image, ra_i is an approximated feature, and rd_i^1, rd_i^2, rd_i^3 denote detailed vertical, horizontal, and diagonal features, respectively. i denotes levels of wavelet transform, which is set at 1.

Similarly, detailed features of the test images were extracted using the wavelet transform. Figure 7.17 shows these feature images of a test image. In Fig. 7.17, size of the fixed region is 70×70 and each feature of the wavelet transform in the test image is denoted as $ta_i, td_i^1, td_i^2, td_i^3$. These features then form a set

$$Wf_t = \{ta_i, td_i^1, td_i^2, td_i^3\}, \quad i = 1, \dots, I \tag{7.29}$$

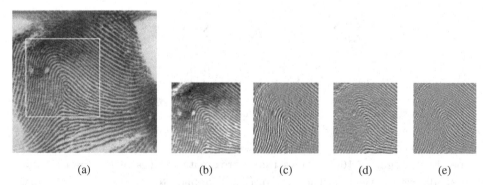

(a)	(b)	(c)	(d)	(e)

Fig. 7.17. Wavelet features extracted from a reference point of the test image. (a) constant region selected from reference point, (b) approximated wavelet feature (ta_i), (c) detailed vertical wavelet feature (td_i^1), (d) detailed horizontal wavelet feature (td_i^2), and (e) detailed diagonal wavelet feature (td_i^3).

where Wf_t is the wavelet feature set of the test image, ta_i is the approximated feature, and td_i^1, td_i^2, and td_i^3 denote detailed vertical, horizontal, and diagonal wavelet features, respectively.

To insure that the cross correlation between the two images can be conducted with the coincidental image area, the size of the test image is set at 70×70 so that the reference image would be a subset of the test image. We extract each representative feature by calculating the average of each detailed feature in Wf_r and Wf_t. In calculating the average, only the directional components, namely the vertical, horizontal, and the diagonal features, were used since these values are more relevant in locating the reference point. The representative feature is obtained by Eqs. (7.30) and (7.31) and its result is shown as Fig. 7.18.

$$Rf_r(i,j) = \frac{1}{K} \sum_{k=1}^{K} rd_1^k(i,j), \quad 0 \le i < M, 0 \le j < N, N = M = 45 \quad (7.30)$$

$$Rf_t(i,j) = \frac{1}{K} \sum_{k=1}^{K} td_1^k(i,j), \quad 0 \le i < M, 0 \le j < N, N = M = 70 \quad (7.31)$$

where Rf_r and Rf_t are representative features of the reference image and the test image, $K = 3$ is the number of detailed feature images. Moreover, N and M are the size of the detailed feature image in reference image and test image. We now proceed to calculate cross correlation to find an identical reference point position between a reference and a test images. As a first step for computing the cross correlation between Rf_r and Rf_t, rotation and scaling operation for Rf_r is accomplished. The rotated and scaled features for Rf_r are obtained by Eqs. (7.32)–(7.34) and Eq. (7.35), respectively.

$$R(\theta) = \begin{bmatrix} \cos\theta & \sin\theta & 0 \\ -\sin\theta & \cos\theta & 0 \\ 0 & 0 & 1 \end{bmatrix}, \quad -60° \le \theta \le 60° \quad (7.32)$$

 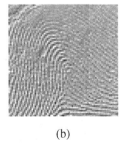

(a)   (b)

Fig. 7.18. Representative features for each reference image and test image. (a) Representative features have a size of 45×45 in the reference image (Rf_r). (b) Representative features have a size of 70×70 in the test image (Rf_t).

$$S(s_x, s_y) = \begin{bmatrix} s_x & 0 & 0 \\ 0 & s_y & 0 \\ 0 & 0 & 1 \end{bmatrix}, \quad -0.6 \le s_x, s_y \le 1.6, s_x = s_y \qquad (7.33)$$

$$V = \begin{bmatrix} X \\ Y \\ 1 \end{bmatrix}, \quad v = \begin{bmatrix} x \\ y \\ 1 \end{bmatrix} \qquad (7.34)$$

where V is the column vector for the transformed coordinate, v is the column vector for the original coordinate, s_x and s_y are magnification, and θ denotes rotational angle. Here, the magnification is at 0.2 intervals and the angle is at 10 degrees. The angular range was selected under the assumption that, for most fingerprint acquisition devices, the rotation of the image from the vertical direction would be no more than 60 degrees. R is the rotation matrix and S is the scale matrix. We can obtain the transformed Rf_r by applying Eqs. (7.32)–(7.34) to Eq. (7.35):

$$T\_Rf_{(\theta, s_x, s_y)}(V) = R(\theta)S(s_x, s_y)v \qquad (7.35)$$

where T_Rf denotes the transformed Rf_r and Fig. 7.19 shows example of T_Rf.

We then calculate the cross correlation R between each T_Rf and Rf_t through Eq. (7.40). Let $\overline{m_r}$ and $\overline{m_t}$ denote the average value of each T_Rf and Rf_t, respectively:

$$\overline{m_r} = \frac{1}{NM} \sum_{i=1}^{N} \sum_{j=1}^{M} T\_Rf_{(\theta, s_x, s_y)}(i, j) \qquad (7.36)$$

$$\overline{m_t} = \frac{1}{NM} \sum_{i=1}^{N} \sum_{j=1}^{M} Rf_t(i, j) \qquad (7.37)$$

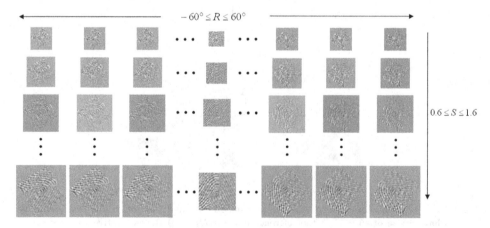

Fig. 7.19.   Examples of T_Rf. Scale S is at 0.2 intervals and rotation R is at 10 degrees.

The variations of values at each pixel to the mean values in T_Rf and Rf_t can be defined as

$$\Delta_r(i,j) = T\_Rf_{(\theta,s_x,s_y)}(i,j) - \overline{m_r} \qquad (7.38)$$

$$\Delta_t(i,j) = Rf_t(i,j) - \overline{m_t} \qquad (7.39)$$

Then, the cross correlation R can be computed as

$$R_{(\theta,s_x,s_y)}(i,j) = \frac{\sum_{u=1}^{N} \sum_{v=1}^{M} \Delta_r(u,v)\Delta_t(i+u,j+v)}{\sqrt{\sum_{u=1}^{N} \sum_{v=1}^{M} (\Delta_r(u,v))^2} \sqrt{\sum_{u=1}^{N} \sum_{v=1}^{M} (\Delta_t(i+u,j+v))^2}} \qquad (7.40)$$

where $-60° \le \theta \le 60°$ and $0.6 \le s_x, s_y \le 1.6$ for $s_x = s_y$.

7.3.1.2 *Search for the maximum cross correlation point in test image*

We then use Eq. (7.41) to correct the reference point position of Fig. 7.15(b) to the position where cross correlation is the maximum value:

$$(C_i, C_j) = \arg\left[\max_{k,l} \left(R_{(\theta,s_x,s_y)}(k,l)\right)\right] \qquad (7.41)$$

where (C_i, C_j) denotes the corrected reference point position and Fig. 7.20 shows the position where the cross correlation is the maximum value using mesh. Figure 7.21 shows the corrected reference point position where the cross correlation is the maximum.

7.3.2 *Feature extraction*

Once a reference point is corrected, the next step is to extract the unique and characterizing features from the image. A feature extraction algorithm for efficient memory usage of hardware is presented here.

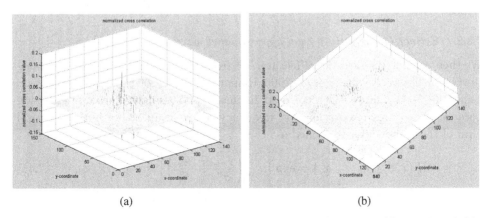

(a) (b)

Fig. 7.20.   Normalized cross correlation value at all coordinate using 3D mesh (a) and 2D mesh (b).

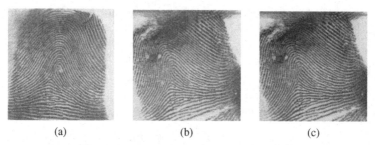

(a)   (b)   (c)

Fig. 7.21. Corrected reference point position. (a) detected reference point position using the Poincare index method in the reference image, (b) detected reference point position using the Poincare index method in the test image, and (c) corrected reference point position from (b).

7.3.2.1 *Extract approximated wavelet feature*

From the corrected reference point, a region in the size of 128×128 is selected from the image. The selected region is decomposed into four wavelet features using wavelet transform as shown in Figs. 7.16 and 7.17. These features form the sets for the reference image, R_f_r, and the test image, R_f_t, as

$$R\_f_r = \{f\_ra_i, f\_rd_i^1, f\_rd_i^2, f\_rd_i^3\}, \quad i = 2 \tag{7.42}$$

$$R\_f_t = \{f\_ta_i, f\_td_i^1, f\_td_i^2, f\_td_i^3\}, \quad i = 2 \tag{7.43}$$

In the above equations, f_ra and f_ta are the approximated features extracted by wavelet transform from a selected region of the reference image and the test image. Similarly, f_rd and f_td represent detailed features from the selected region of each image. i, set at 2, denotes the level of wavelet transform used. The detailed wavelet feature is used in the reference point correction process described in the previous section. For actual recognition process, however, we use only the approximated features rather than the detailed features to minimize the size of the feature data set. Figure 7.22 shows approximated features obtained by wavelet transform from a selected region of each image. Figures 7.22(c) and (f) is defined as f_ra and f_ta, respectively.

7.3.2.2 *Extract Gabor feature from approximated wavelet feature*

We then extract the directional feature DF from the approximated features using the Gabor-filter GF (Zhang *et al.*, 2006; Hamamoto *et al.*, 2004). Feature extraction using the Gabor filter is widely used in image processing and computer vision because it captures orientation and frequency information of the image. General form of the Gabor filter is defined as

$$GF(x, y, f, \theta_k, \sigma_x, \sigma_y) = \exp\left[-\frac{1}{2}\left(\frac{x_{\theta_k}^2}{\sigma_x^2} + \frac{y_{\theta_k}^2}{\sigma_y^2}\right)\right] \times \exp(i2\pi f x_{\theta_k}) \tag{7.44}$$

$$x_{\theta_k} = x \sin\theta_k + y \cos\theta_k \tag{7.45}$$

$$y_{\theta_k} = x \cos\theta_k - y \sin\theta_k \tag{7.46}$$

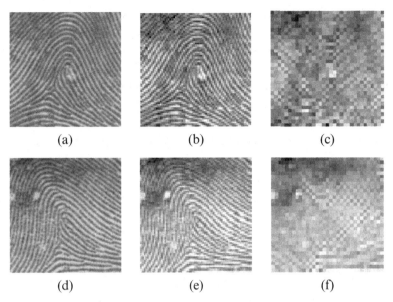

Fig. 7.22.   Approximated features for each levels of wavelet transform. (a),(d) Selected constant region from reference point in reference image and test image (128 × 128). (b),(e) Approximated features in one level of wavelet transform (64 × 64). (c),(f) Approximated features in two levels of wavelet transform (32 × 32).

In the equations, f denotes the frequency of the sinusoidal plane wave corresponding to the number of pixels between ridges, and θ_k is the orientation of the Gabor-filter GF. σ_x and σ_y are the standard deviations of the Gaussian envelope along the x and y axes, respectively. The Gabor filter from Eq. (7.44) can be represented in complex form as

$$GF(\cdot) = GF_{\text{even}}(\cdot) + jGF_{\text{odd}}(\cdot) \tag{7.47}$$

$$GF_{\text{even}}(x, y, f, \theta_k, \sigma_x, \sigma_y) = \exp\left[-\frac{1}{2}\left(\frac{x_{\theta_k}^2}{\sigma_x^2} + \frac{y_{\theta_k}^2}{\sigma_y^2}\right)\right] \cos(2\pi f x_{\theta_k}) \tag{7.48}$$

$$GF_{\text{odd}}(x, y, f, \theta_k, \sigma_x, \sigma_y) = \exp\left[-\frac{1}{2}\left(\frac{x_{\theta_k}^2}{\sigma_x^2} + \frac{y_{\theta_k}^2}{\sigma_y^2}\right)\right] \sin(2\pi f x_{\theta_k}) \tag{7.49}$$

We extract eight directional features, fr_DF and ft_DF, by convolution operation between GF and each approximated feature f_ra and $f_t a$ as follows

$$fr\_DF_{\theta_k}(i, j) = \sum_{n=1}^{N} \sum_{m=1}^{M} GF_{\theta_k}(n, m) f\_ra\left(i + \frac{N}{2} - n\right)\left(j + \frac{M}{2} - m\right), \tag{7.50}$$

$$ft\_DF_{\theta_k}(i, j) = \sum_{n=1}^{N} \sum_{m=1}^{M} GF_{\theta_k}(n, m) f\_ta\left(i + \frac{N}{2} - n\right)\left(j + \frac{M}{2} - m\right),$$

$$\theta_k = 0°, 22.5°, 45°, \ldots, 157.5° \tag{7.51}$$

Figure 7.23 depicts graphical representations of the Gabor filter in the eight orientations, and Fig. 7.24 shows an example of the eight directional features fr_DF extracted by Eq. (7.47). Here, we define eight directional features of the reference image as $fr\_DF_{\theta_0}$, $fr\_DF_{\theta_{22.5}}$, $fr\_DF_{\theta_{45}}, \ldots, fr\_DF_{\theta_{157.5}}$. Similarly from the test image, each directional feature ft_DF extracted by Eqs. (7.50) and (7.51) is also defined as $ft\_DF_{\theta_0}$, $ft\_DF_{\theta_{22.5}}$, $ft\_DF_{\theta_{45}}, \ldots, ft\_DF_{\theta_{157.5}}$.

7.3.2.3 *Matching using Gabor-wavelet feature*

The fingerprint recognition process using the Gabor-wavelet features is performed as follows. We employ the filter-bank method (Xu and Zhang, 2005; Jain *et al.*, 1999) with fingercode for the recognition process. Steps of the filter-bank method used here are as follows:

(1) Construct a filter bank composed of 5 bands and 16 sectors using the corrected reference point location as the center as shown in Fig. 7.25. Thus, the number of sectors is 80 per one directional feature.
(2) Apply this filter bank to eight directional features $fr\_DF_{\theta_k}$ and $ft\_DF_{\theta_k}$.
(3) Calculate the average for each sectors of $fr\_DF_{\theta_k}$ and $ft\_DF_{\theta_k}$ using equation below. Sector for $fr\_DF_{\theta_k}$ and $ft\_DF_{\theta_k}$ is defined as $fr\_DF_{\theta_k}\_S$ and $ft\_DF_{\theta_k}\_S$, respectively:

$$Sr\_m_{\theta_k}(r) = \frac{1}{NM} \sum_{i=1}^{N} \sum_{j=1}^{M} (fr\_DF_{\theta_k}\_S(i,j)) \tag{7.52}$$

$$St\_m_{\theta_k}(r) = \frac{1}{NM} \sum_{i=1}^{N} \sum_{j=1}^{M} (ft\_DF_{\theta_k}\_S(i,j)) \tag{7.53}$$

where $r = 1, 2, 3, \ldots, 80$ and $\theta_k = 0°, 22.5°, 45°, \ldots, 157.5°$. Sr_m and St_m denote the average values of each sector for fr_DF_S and $ft\_DF\S$. Moreover, r is the number of sectors. Figure 7.26 shows examples for each $fr\_DF_{\theta_k}\_S$ and $ft\_DF_{\theta_k}\_S$.
(4) Measure similarity by calculating the AAD average absolute deviation (AAD) between each sector for $Sr\_m_{\theta_k}(r)$ and $St\_m_{\theta_k}(r)$ as follows

$$D = \frac{1}{n} \left(\sum_{\theta_k} \sum_{r} |Sr\_m_{\theta_k}(r) - St\_m_{\theta_k}(r)| \right), \quad r = 1, 2, 3, \ldots, 80 \tag{7.54}$$

where n is the total number of sectors for each of the eight directional features. Since r ranges to 80, n is 640. D denotes the distance between Sr_m and St_m.

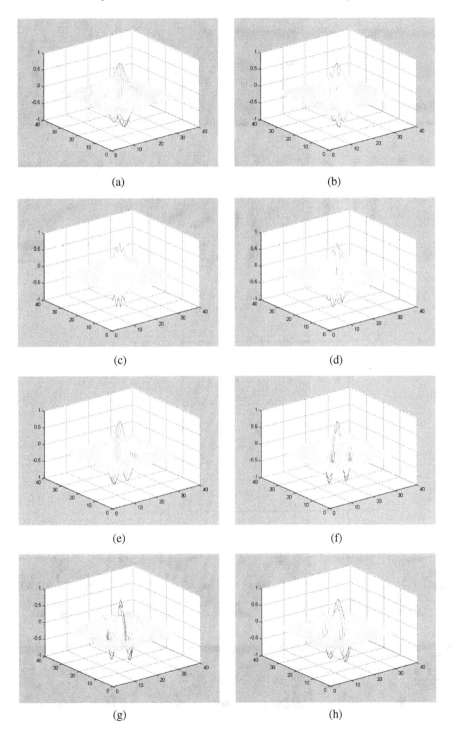

Fig. 7.23.   Forms of Gabor filter with orientation $\theta_k = 0°, 22.5°, 45°, \ldots, 157.5°$ from (a) to (h).

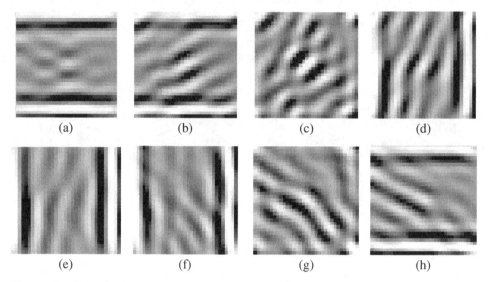

Fig. 7.24. Example for eight directional features $(fr\_DF_{\theta_0}, \ fr\_DF_{\theta_{22.5}}, \ fr\_DF_{\theta_{45}}, \ldots, \\ fr\_DF_{\theta_{157.5}})$ of approximated feature f_ra extracted by Eqs. (7.50) and (7.51).

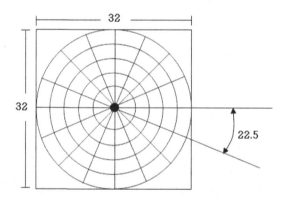

Fig. 7.25. Filter-bank composed of 5 bands and 16 sectors.

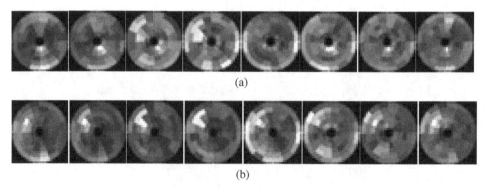

Fig. 7.26. Example of the filter bank for each direction. (a),(b) Filter banks for each $fr\_DF_{\theta_k}\_S$ and $ft\_DF_{\theta_k}\_S$ at 22.5 degree intervals.

7.4 Conclusions

In this chapter, a reference point correction algorithm for more accurate feature extraction and a novel feature extraction algorithm which can recognize fingerprints using feature data of a small quantity obtained by the Gabor-wavelet transform are proposed. From the experimental results, it was shown that the method using the proposed reference point correction algorithm in addition to the Poincare-index method yielded improved performance of 6.39% in error equal rate (EER) compared to the Poincare-index method alone. It was also shown that the proposed feature extraction algorithm using Gabor-wavelet requires significantly less feature data, typically requiring one-sixteenth of the data, for equivalent verification performance compared to the existing feature extraction methods such as the Gabor filter-based approach.

References

Babich, G. A. and Camps, O. I. Weighted parzen windows for pattern classification, *IEEE Trans. Pattern Anal. Machine Intelligence* **18**, 567–700, 1996.

de Wouwer, G., Scheunders, P., Livens, S., and Dyck, D. V. Wavelet correlation signatures for color texture characterization, *Pattern Recognition* **32**, 443–451, 1999.

Erdogmus, D., Hild, K. E., and Principe, J. C. The centroid of the symmetry kullback-leibler distance, *IEEE Trans. Inf. Theory* **48**, 96–99, 2002.

Erdogmus, D., Hild, K. E., and Principe, J. C. Adaptive blind deconvolution of linear channels using renyi's entropy with parzen window estimation, *IEEE Trans. Signal Processing* **52**, 6, 2004.

Espinosa-Duro, V. Minutiae detection algorithm for fingerprint recognition, in *Proc. Intl Carnahan Conf. Security Technology*, pp. 264–266, 2001.

Hamamoto, Y., Uchimura, S., Watanabe, M., Yasuda, T., Mitani, Y., and Tomita, S. A gabor filter based fingerprint enhancement algorithm in wavelet domain, in *Proc. IEEE India Annual Conference*, pp. 256–261, 2004.

Hwang, H., Choi, H., Kang, B., Yoon, H., Kim, H., Kim, S., and Choi, H. Classification of breast tissue images based on wavelet transform using discriminant analysis, neural network and svm, in *Proc. Intl Workshop Enterprise Networking and Computing in Healthcare Industry*, pp. 345–349, 2005.

Ito, K., Morita, A., Higuchi, T., Nakajima, H., and Kobayashi, K. A fingerprint recognition algorithm using phase-based image matching for low-quality fingerprints, in *Proc. Intl Conf. Image Processing(ICIP2005)*, pp. 2:11–14, 2005.

Jain, A. K., Prabhakar, S., and Pankanti, S. A filterbank-based representation for classification and matching of fingerprints, in *Proc. Int. Joint Conf. on Neural Networks*, pp. 5:3284–3285, 1999.

Jain, A. K., Parbhakar, S., Hong, L., and Pankanti, S. Filterbank-based fingerprint matching, *IEEE Trans. Image Processing* **9**, 5, 2000.

Jain, A. K., Chen, Y., and Demirkus, M. Pores and ridges: high-resolution fingerprint matching using level 3 features, *IEEE Trans. Pattern Anal. Machine Intelligence* **29**, 1, 15–27, 2007.

Jiang, X., Liu, M., and Kot, A. C. Reference point detection for fingerprint recognition, in *Proc. Intl Conf. Pattern Recognition*, pp. 1:540–543, 2004.

Liu, T., Hao, P., and Zhang, C. Fingerprint singular point detection and direction estimation with a "t" shape model, in *Proc. Audio and Video-Based Biometric Person Authentication*, pp. 201–207, 2005.

Liu, T., Zhang, C., and Hao, P. Fingerprint reference point detection based on local axial symmetry, in *Proc. Intl Conf. Pattern Recognition*, pp. 1:1050–1053, 2006.

Patil, P. M., Suralkar, S. R., and Abhyankar, H. K. Fingerprint verification based on fixed length finger code, in *Proc. IEEE Intl Conf. Tools with Artificial Intelligence(ICTAI'05)*, pp. 14–16, 2005.

Tico, M., Immonen, E., Kuosmanen, P. R. P., and Saarinen, J. Fingerprint recognition using wavelet features, in *Proc. IEEE Int. Symposium on Circuits and System*, pp. 2:21–24, 2001.

Xu, Y. and Zhang, X. Gabor filterbank and its application in the fingerprint texture analysis, in *Proc. Int. Conf. on Parallel and Distributed Computing, Applications and Technologies*, pp. 829–831, 2005.

Zhang, B., Leung, C., and Gao, Y. Face recognition by combining kernel associative memory and gabor transforms, in *Proc. Int. Conf. Pattern Recognition(ICPR2006)*, pp. 3:465–468, 2006.

Chapter 8

CONSTRAINED NON-LINEAR PHASE PORTRAIT MODEL OF FINGERPRINT ORIENTATION AND ITS APPLICATION TO FINGERPRINT CLASSIFICATION

Jun Li* and Wei-Yun Yau†

Institute for Infocomm Research
1 Fusionopolis Way, #21-01 Connexis (South Tower)
Singapore, 138632
*jli@i2r.a-star.edu.sg
†wyyau@i2r.a-star.edu.sg

8.1 Introduction

Fingerprint biometrics are increasingly being used in the commercial, civilian, and financial domains. The demand varies across a wide range of applications from law enforcement, banking, physical access control, time-and-attendance to consumer products. These result in a large volume of fingerprints being collected and stored in the database. For example, there are more than 81 million fingerprints currently in the FBI Fingerprint database, and every day approximately 7000 new individual records are added to the files.* To perform fingerprint recognition, both recognition accuracy and processing time are critical performance issues. In order to achieve an efficient identification, fingerprints in the database are usually classified into a number of subgroups sharing similar properties. Therefore, we only need to compare a given query fingerprint with those in one single subgroup. This will reduce the processing time significantly. The most popular scheme of fingerprints classification is to classify fingerprints into 5 classes, namely, plain arch (A), tented arch (T), left loop (L), right loop (R), and whorl (W) as shown in Fig. 8.1.

Fingerprint classification research has been active in recent decades. Many fingerprint classification algorithms have been proposed (Candela *et al.*, 1995; Karu and Jain, 1996; Ratha *et al.*, 1996; Shah and Sastry, 2004; Nyongesa *et al.*, 2004; Zhang and Yan, 2004; Jain *et al.*, 1999; Yao *et al.*, 2003; Cappelli *et al.*, 1999a). As the most popular features for fingerprints classification, both SPs

---

*http://www.fbi.gov/hq/cjisd/ident.pdf

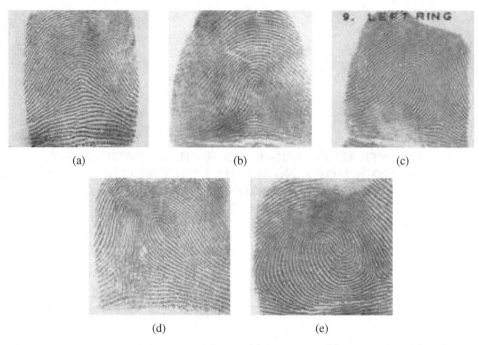

Fig. 8.1.   The examples of five classes scheme. (a) plain arch, (b) tented arch, (c) left loop, (d) right loop, and (e) whorl.

and OIs are effective for fingerprint classification. However, it is not usual for researchers to adopt the combination of both features to improve the classification accuracy.

Since both features are commonly used, many algorithms have been proposed to compute them. The general methods to detect SPs are Poincare-based method (Kawagoe and Tojo, 1984), Intersection-based method (Ramo et al., 2001), or filter-based method (Nilsson and Bigun, 2003). In all these methods, SPs are extracted from the OI. Therefore in SPs extraction, the OI is considered trustworthy. If OI is wrongly obtained or corrupted by noise, SPs detection may fail. Consequently, it becomes important how to correctly estimate the OI. The gradient-based approaches is generally adopted to estimate the OI. In order to obtain the robust features, a low-pass filter is deployed to reduce the noise from the OI. Such filtering operation can reduce the noise but risk smoothing the orientation of SP regions. Hence, the orientation patterns of SPs may disappear. Furthermore, such filtering only deals with a local region. Thus if there exists a large patch of noise, the local filtering will fail, which results in fake detection of SPs too.

Filtering-based methods can be viewed as the local constraint methods. In recent years, model-based methods are proposed to make use of the global orientation pattern to reconstruct the OI. For each grid of OI, all other grids of OI will involve in estimation of its value. In this way, the model-based methods are able to overcome the local filtering shortcomings. Furthermore, considering that fingerprint OI is quite smooth except for the SP regions and there are limited SPs, some authors put an effort to investigate the mathematical modeling of fingerprint OI and the relationship between OI and SPs. From the positions of all SPs in a fingerprint image, the orientation trend is able to be estimated (Sherlock and Monro, 1993).

From the above analysis, it will improve the performance of SPs detection and fingerprint classification if a robust reconstruction of the OI can be obtained.

In this work, we developed a new unified OI model, which is based on the constrained non-linear phase portrait model. In this model, we proposed a descriptor for the local orientation behaviors near SPs using the first-order phase portrait model. In order to globally describe the whole OI, a non-linear phase portrait model with the first-order phase portrait as the constraints was proposed to reconstruct the global and local OI simultaneously.

Moreover, this unified model can be used to mutually validate SPs and OI. Since from the unified model, it could be understood how the SPs' behaviors affect the OI. Thus, SPs were extracted from the original OI. If SPs were wrongly detected, the wrong orientation patterns will be brought into the reconstructed orientation patterns. Comparing the reconstructed OI and the reliable original one, if they deviated from each other too much, the wrongly detected SPs could be found out. Such a procedure was called "the mutual validation." The best results for both SPs and OI were selected to form the final feature vectors for classification. In order to reduce the dimensionality of the features used, the coefficients of the orientation model are used to represent the orientation image. We postulate that the coefficients of the orientation model contain information as rich as the orientation image as it can be used to correctly reconstruct the orientation image.

The rest of this chapter is organized as follows. Section 8.2 introduces constrained non-linear phase portrait model (CNPPM) with a prediction model. In Sec. 8.3, we describe the implementation detail of the proposed classification method, including mutual validation of SPs and OI. This is followed by Sec. 8.4, which describes the experimental results obtained using the NIST database 4. Section 8.5 then concludes the chapter.

8.2 Constrained Non-linear Phase Portrait Model with Prediction

8.2.1 *Literature review on fingerprint modeling*

Fingerprint images consist of oriented texture. Therefore, the orientation information plays a very important role in fingerprint processing. Moreover, the orientation of the fingerprint follows a certain structure that is not random. Such oriented structure provides a possibility to recover the OI in fingerprints corrupted by noise, even for a large noise patch which cannot be solved by the traditional gradient-based methods.

Several model-based methods have been proposed in the literature. We coarsely divide the model-based method into three categories: Zero-Pole model-based method, phase portrait model-based methods, and the topological model.

8.2.1.1 *Zero-pole model-based methods*

In 1993, Sherlock *et al.* presented an approach to model the fingerprint orientation topology (Sherlock and Monro, 1993). The basic mathematical description of this model was given in Eq. (8.1):

$$O_m(z) = O_0 + \frac{1}{2}\Sigma_{l=1}^L \arg(z - z_{c_l}) - \Sigma_{k=1}^K \arg(z - z_{d_k}) \tag{8.1}$$

where z_{c_l} and z_{d_k} are the core point positions, and delta point positions, respectively; z is the position of an arbitrary point; O_0 is an initial or background orientation; O_m is the orientation at z; K and L are the numbers of delta points and core points, respectively. The zero-pole model provided not a quantitative but a qualitative analysis of the fingerprint orientation as it cannot differentiate two OIs with the same SPs. It also cannot model the fingerprint OI without any SPs.

In 1996, Vizcaya *et al.* revised the zero-pole model to a non-linear orientation model (Vizcaya and Gerhardt, 1996). Equation (8.2) describe this model in a mathematical form:

$$O_m(z) = O_0 + \frac{1}{2}\Sigma_{l=1}^L g_{c_l}(\arg(z - z_{c_l})) - \Sigma_{k=1}^K g_{d_k}(\arg(z - z_{d_k})) \tag{8.2}$$

The difference between Eqs. (8.1) and (8.2) was the addition of the non-linear function g. g was some family of non-linear functions that preserve the singularity at the given point. In this non-linear model, the orientation at any point was determined from the location of the SPs plus an additional correction term obtained for each orientation matrix. Essentially, g was decided by the mean-square orientation error between the actual OI estimated from the fingerprint images and the OI provided by the zero-pole model.

Zhou and Gu (2004) presented another complex model as shown in Eq. (8.3) in 2004, which was also based on the zero-pole model while the high-order rational function $f(z)$ was used as the non-linear correction instead:

$$O_m = \frac{1}{2}\arg\left[f(z)\frac{\prod_{l=1}^L(z - z_{c_l})}{\prod_{k=1}^K(z - z_{d_k})}\right] \tag{8.3}$$

Zero-pole based methods have capability to recover the fingerprint OI. While these methods encounter a problem in actual usage that they require all the SPs appearing in the image. This is not always true as the sensors size becomes smaller and smaller for the commercial purpose.

8.2.1.2 *Phase portrait model-based methods*

Zero-pole model-based methods focused on obtaining the local orientation patterns near the SPs' regions followed by a series of linear/non-linear functions to correct the global patterns. Unlike these methods, phase portrait model-based methods focused on obtaining the global orientation patterns first. A correction would be given to compensate the local errors near SPs if necessary. Thus, the model would not depend on the existence of SPs.

Zhou *et al.* (2004) proposed a combination model, which consisted of a polynomial model[**] as in Eq. (8.4) and a point charge model as in Eq. (8.5). The phase portrait model was used to approximate the global OI and the point charge model to correct the OI formed by the phase portrait model near SPs. This combination model gave better estimation of the orientation compared to the other previous models:

$$\cos(2\theta') = \Sigma_{i=0}^{n}\Sigma_{j=0}^{i}a_{(i-j)j}x^{i-j}y^{j} \tag{8.4a}$$

$$\sin(2\theta') = \Sigma_{i=0}^{n}\Sigma_{j=0}^{i}b_{(i-j)j}x^{i-j}y^{j} \tag{8.4b}$$

$$PC_c = \begin{cases} \dfrac{y-y_s}{r}Q - i\dfrac{x-x_s}{r}Q & r \leq R \\ 0 & r > R \end{cases},$$

$$PC_d = \begin{cases} -\dfrac{y-y_s}{r}Q - i\dfrac{x-x_s}{r}Q & r \leq R \\ 0 & r > R \end{cases} \tag{8.5}$$

where Q represents the strength of SPs and R denotes the radius of the region, which the point charge model can affect; a_{ij}, b_{ij} represent the coefficients of high-order phase portrait models; (x_s, y_s) indicate the position of an SP; (x, y) are the ordinates of the OI; n is the order of the phase portrait model.

The combination model empirically determined r, which depended on the difference between the original OI and the phase portrait model reconstructed OI. Furthermore, because the combination model represented the global and local OI separately, it was hard to directly understand how SPs affect the OI.

Unlike using two separated models, Li *et al.* proposed another phase portrait-based model where a high-order phase portrait model was used to describe the global OI with a low-order phase portrait model as a constraint of OI near each SP. This constrained model comprised both global information and local information. Therefore, it was able to represent the OI with a unified representation and concise coefficients. In addition, it is able to perform fingerprint classification based on these coefficients as they carry all the coarse-level orientation information.

[**]In their paper, two polynomial models are used. Here, we call two polynomial models as phase portrait according to the convention in ordinary differential equations.

In addition to the above-mentioned methods, there are several other variations of phase portrait model-based methods. Wang *et al.* (2007) used 2D Fourier Expansion (FOMFE) to replace the general Taylor expansion basis for phase portrait models. Equation (8.6) show its mathematical format:

$$f(x,y) = \sum_{m=0}^{k} \sum_{n=0}^{k} \Psi(m\nu x, n\omega y; \beta_{mn}) + \varepsilon(x,y) \tag{8.6}$$

where $m, n \in N$; the fundamental frequencies $\nu = \pi/l$ and $\omega = \pi/h$ are on the orthogonal x and y axes, respectively; and

$$\begin{aligned} \Psi(m\nu x, n\omega y; \beta_{mn}) = \lambda_{mn} [&a_{mn} \cos(m\nu x) \cos(n\omega y) + b_{mn} \sin(m\nu x) \cos(n\omega y) \\ &+ c_{mn} \cos(m\nu x) \sin(n\omega y) + d_{mn} \sin(m\nu x) \sin(n\omega y)] \end{aligned} \tag{8.7}$$

where λ_{mn} is a constant scalar that can be expressed as

$$\lambda_{mn} = \begin{cases} 1/4 & m = n = 0 \\ 1/2 & m = 0, n > 0 \quad \text{or} \quad n = 0, m > 0 \\ 1 & m > 0, n > 0 \end{cases} \tag{8.8}$$

The authors reported good performance of constructed orientation field and its application to fingerprint indexing. The most attractive characteristic of FOMFE model is that FOMFE model does not require singular points information. Since the authors did not provide any mathematical proof, it is still unclear how to guarantee accurate representation of the singular point pattern by FOMFE model. Recent research (Ram *et al.*, 2010) shows that the singular points' position could be displaced from the original position when adopting FOMFE model to rebuild an ideal core type OI.

Based on this observation, Ram *et al.* (2010) proposed a new phase portrait model based on Legendre polynomial-based phase portrait.

Each univariate Legendre polynomial can be expressed as Eq. (8.9):

$$\phi_n(x) = \frac{1}{2^n n!} \frac{d^n}{dx^n} [(x^2 - 1)^n] \tag{8.9}$$

Then, one can compute the set of basis functions for the kth order Legendre polynomial expansions as follows

$$\phi_{nm}(x,y) = \phi_{n-m}(x)\phi_n(y) \tag{8.10}$$

where $n = 0, 1, \ldots, k$ and $m = 0, 1, \ldots, n$.

These polynomials are orthogonal in the interval $[-1, 1]$, a necessary property which improves the stability of the optimization process by creating good conditioned linear equation systems.

The method consists of two steps to obtain the accurate modeling: first, a Legendre polynomial model was used to model the global OI; second, in order to compensate errors around the singular point regions, a cost function was defined to minimize such errors by Levenberg-Marquard-algorithm (LMA) iteratively. However, the computation time needs to be improved for practical use which requires 2 seconds to process a 388×374 size image. In addition, as LMA addresses the local minimum, it may cause overfitting problem.

8.2.1.3 *OI topological modeling*

In 2008, Hou *et al.* proposed another interesting approach to reconstruct fingerprint OI by topological modeling (Hou and Li, 2008). The approach is quite different with the previous methods as it addresses the OI model by analyzing its topological structure.

In their paper, the topological structure was generated by quantizing the original OI into different OI bins. To analyze this topological structure, two assumptions were made: (1) regional coherence assumption: the orientation structure between neighboring geometric objects is coherent and (2) convexity assumption: the geometric object in a naturally acquired fingerprint image will be convex.

The purpose of regional coherence assumption is to ensure that the global orientation flows smoothly. Note that in regions near the singular point, the local orientation does not preserve the coherence in nature; however, in the more global level, the regional coherence assumption remains valid among these regions. This is because the continuity in orientation between neighboring geometrical objects is not affected in good-quality fingerprints.

Though the convexity assumption is not always held due to severe distortion in fingerprint images, it still can help to identify the potentially erratic orientation patches which intrude the coherence region of fingerprint OI, especially for identifying the structure irregularities.

In summary, zero-pole-based methods require all singular points information. However, it is not always true in real applications. The topological model is a new research direction on fingerprint OI modeling as it does not require prior knowledge of SPs. As a potential method, several questions need to be answered before it can be applied in a real fingerprint identification system. For example, how to reconstruct OI when the structure irregularities were identified.

Phase portrait-based models were mostly addressed in recent works. The most difficult problem is how to robustly compensate the local pattern near SPs and at the same time to keep robustness against the noise. For this purpose, we introduce a constraint phase portrait model which integrated the local SPs' patterns into the global pattern in a concise and unified form.

We start from an analysis of OI near SPs in the following section.

8.2.2 Orientation behavior near singular points

Since SPs bring the discontinuity into the fingerprint OI, it is important to investigate the orientation patterns around SPs before modeling the whole fingerprint OI.

There are two kinds of SPs in fingerprints: core and delta. Bazen and Gerez (2002) reported a reference model to describe the double orientation behaviors of the SPs as shown by Eqs. (8.11) (a–d):

$$DX_{\text{core,ref}} = \frac{-(y - y_s)}{\sqrt{(x - x_s)^+(y - y_s)^2}} \tag{8.11a}$$

$$DY_{\text{core,ref}} = \frac{(x - x_s)}{\sqrt{(x - x_s)^+(y - y_s)^2}} \tag{8.11b}$$

$$DX_{\text{delta,ref}} = \frac{-(y - y_s)}{\sqrt{(x - x_s)^+(y - y_s)^2}} \tag{8.11c}$$

$$DY_{\text{delta,ref}} = \frac{-(x - x_s)}{\sqrt{(x - x_s)^+(y - y_s)^2}} \tag{8.11d}$$

where (x_s, y_s) are the coordinates of an SP. $DX_{\text{core,ref}}, DY_{\text{core,ref}}$ are the x and y components of the reference core; and $DX_{\text{delta,ref}}, DY_{\text{delta,ref}}$ are the x and y components of the reference delta.

The reference model described only the constant form of the core and delta behaviors regardless of the local patterns around them. In other words, this reference model assumes that all the core (or delta) regions have the same behavior and therefore unable to model the local variations in the SP region (Fig. 8.2).

In fact, different SPs have their own distinct behaviors. In the following sections, we introduce a new model based on the first-order phase portrait model to describe the behaviors of the SPs.

In order to get the various behaviors of the SPs, we rewrite Eq. (8.11)(a–d) as Eq. (8.12):

$$\begin{bmatrix} dx \\ dy \end{bmatrix} = \begin{bmatrix} c & d \\ a & b \end{bmatrix} \begin{bmatrix} x \\ y \end{bmatrix} + \begin{bmatrix} f \\ e \end{bmatrix} = \mathbf{A}\mathbf{x} + \mathbf{B} \tag{8.12}$$

where dx and dy are the x, y components of the OI; (x, y) are the coordinates; and $[a-f]$ are the coefficients of the phase portrait model. The eigenvalues of the matrix $\mathbf{A}$ determine the type of SPs and $\mathbf{B}$ allows the translation of the SPs (Shu and Jain, 1994; Ford et al., 1994). Hence, the reference models of the SPs are regarded as special cases of the first-order phase portrait model. For example, when

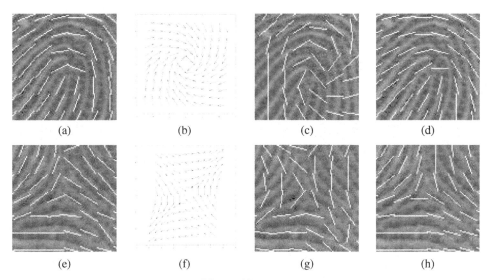

(a)	(b)	(c)	(d)

(e)	(f)	(g)	(h)

Fig. 8.2. Behaviors of singular points: (a) and (e) show the original orientation near the core and delta; (b) and (f) show the behaviors of the spiral and saddle type phase portraits; (c) and (g) show the double orientation of the core and delta; (d) and (f) show the reconstructed orientation by the first-order phase portrait.

$\{c = 0; d = 1; a = -1; b = 0\}$ are satisfied, Eq. (8.12) represents the same behavior as Eqs. (8.11a) and (8.11b) and when $\{c = 0; d = -1; a = -1; b = 0\}$ are satisfied, Eq. (8.12) represents the same behavior as Eqs. (8.11c) and (8.11d). Thus, the double orientation image of the SPs can be modeled by the first-order phase portrait. The coefficients [a–d] can be obtained using the least square algorithm (Shu and Jain, 1994).

8.2.3 *Prediction model*

Behaviors of SPs can be described by the first-order phase portrait. Noted that the OI of a fingerprint image is flat beyond SPs regions, it is possible to reconstruct the OI if all SPs have been located. Based on this assumption, we developed a prediction model for fingerprint orientation. The first-order phase portrait model was used to describe the behavior of its SPs, which was then combined in a piecewise manner to represent the global fingerprint orientation. The parameters of this model could be obtained using just the regions near SPs. Complementing it with the regularity of the fingerprint orientation patterns, we are able to reconstruct the orientation beyond the known region. Therefore, this model has prediction capability.

The following rules are formulated to effectively form the whole model of a fingerprint OI:

(1) If there is no delta point in the fingerprint impression, the image will be divided into 2 sections by a horizontal line through its reference point. Then in each part,

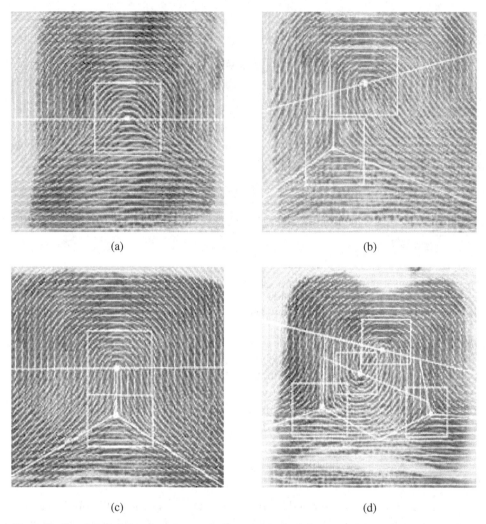

(a)

(b)

(c)

(d)

Fig. 8.3. Examples of the piecewise prediction model; the behaviors of SPs can be delivered by the orientations in the white rectangle; beyond white rectangle region, the orientation can be predicted. (a) predicted orientations of plain arch, (b) predicted orientations of loop, (c) predicted orientations of tented arch, and (d) predicted orientations of plain whorl.

we can view its orientation pattern as one type of phase portrait and reconstruct the orientation by its corresponding first-order phase portrait. Figure 8.3(a) illustrates this case. However, if there is no SP, the reference point can be a point with maximum curvature. This can be viewed as a part of the first-order phase portrait where the SP is located outside the image. The orientation estimated will not be as accurate as when the orientation is reconstructed using a valid core point. The less abrupt the orientation is at the reference region, the less reliable is the estimated orientation.

(2) If there is one delta point in the fingerprint image, the range influenced by the core and delta is divided into two subregions as shown by the white line in Figs. 8.3(b) and 8.3(c). In each subregion, the OI will be reconstructed by the corresponding SPs as stated in Sec. 8.2.2.

(3) If there are two delta points and two core points, the asymptotes are used to partition the lower region as shown in Fig. 8.3(d). Then in each part, the orientations will be reconstructed by the behaviors of its nearest SPs.

8.2.4 *Constrained non-linear phase portrait model*

In the previous section, we proposed to represent the behaviors of SPs using the first-order phase portrait model. This model gives accurate local description near an SP but has limited capability to globally describe the OIs of all the fingerprints. The first-order phase portrait model can only deal with the OI in which there exists at most one SP and will fail for loop and whorl where there are more than two SPs.

On the other hand, the non-linear polynomial phase portrait model has been verified to be able to effectively reconstruct the global OI of fingerprints in Zhou *et al.* (2004). But in the SP region, the reconstructed orientation may be wrong.

In order to examine the SP behavior in the non-linear phase portrait model, we rewrite Eqs. (8.4) (a and b):

$$dx = m * x + n * y + O_1(x, y) \tag{8.13a}$$

$$dy = c * x + d * y + O_2(x, y) \tag{8.13b}$$

where $O_i(x,y)/r \to 0$ as $r = (x^2 + y^2)^{1/2} \to 0, i = 1, 2, (c, d, m, n)$ are the first-order coefficients.

The linear system

$$dx = m * x + n * y \tag{8.14a}$$

$$dy = c * x + d * y \tag{8.14b}$$

is said to be the linearization (or linearized system) of Eqs. (8.13) (a and b) at the origin. The components of the linear vector field in Eqs. (8.14) (a and b) are said to form the linear part of the high-order phase portrait model.

According to the linearization theorem stated in Arnold (1973): "*Let the non-linear system has a simple SP at $\vec{x} = 0$. Then in a neighborhood of the origin the phase portraits of the system and its linearization are qualitatively equivalent. Here a SP at the origin of a non-linear system is said to be simple if its linearized system is simple*", since the SP in fingerprints has its own complete behavior and can be considered as the simple SP, the non-linear phase portrait model can be linearized at the SP.

By shifting the origin in Eqs. (8.4) (a and b) to the SP (x_s, y_s) (replace (x, y) as $(x - x_s, y - y_s)$) and expanding it, we obtain Eqs. (8.15) (a and b):

$$\cos(2\theta') = \sum_{i=0}^{n} \sum_{j=0}^{i} a_{(i-j)j}(x - x_s)^{i-j}(y - y_s)^{j}$$

$$= \sum_{i=0}^{n} \sum_{j=0}^{i} a_{(i-j)j}(-x_s)^{i-j}(-y_s)^{j} + \sum_{i=0}^{n} \sum_{j=0}^{i} a_{(i-j)j}(i - j)(-y_s)^{j}x$$

$$+ \sum_{i=0}^{n} \sum_{j=0}^{i} a_{(i-j)j}j(-x_s)^{i-j}y + O_1(x^p y^q) \quad p + q \geq 2 \tag{8.15a}$$

$$\sin(2\theta') = \sum_{i=0}^{n} \sum_{j=0}^{i} b_{(i-j)j}(x - x_s)^{i-j}(y - y_s)^{j}$$

$$= \sum_{i=0}^{n} \sum_{j=0}^{i} b_{(i-j)j}(-x_s)^{i-j}(-y_s)^{j} + \sum_{i=0}^{n} \sum_{j=0}^{i} b_{(i-j)j}(i - j)(-y_s)^{j}x$$

$$+ \sum_{i=0}^{n} \sum_{j=0}^{i} b_{(i-j)j}j(-x_s)^{i-j}y + O_2(x^p y^q) \quad p + q \geq 2 \tag{8.15b}$$

where $O_i(x^p, y^q)$ are the high-order terms.

Neglecting the high-order terms, Eqs. (8.15) (a and b) should have the similar orientation pattern as in Eqs. (8.14) (a and b). Comparing Eq. (8.15) (a) with Eq. (8.13) (a) gives the set of constraints for estimating coefficients $\{a_{ij}\}$ using the pre-computed low-order coefficients (m, n) for a particular SP as shown in Eq. (8.16) (a):

$$\begin{cases} \displaystyle\sum_{i=0}^{n} \sum_{j=0}^{i} a_{(i-j)j}(i - j)(-y_s)^{j} = m \\ \displaystyle\sum_{i=0}^{n} \sum_{j=0}^{i} a_{(i-j)j}j(-x_s)^{i-j} = n \end{cases} \tag{8.16}$$

and $\{b_{ij}\}$ using (c, d) with constraints in Eq. (8.17):

$$\begin{cases} \displaystyle\sum_{i=0}^{n} \sum_{j=0}^{i} b_{(i-j)j}(i - j)(-y_s)^{j} = c \\ \displaystyle\sum_{i=0}^{n} \sum_{j=0}^{i} b_{(i-j)j}j(-x_s)^{i-j} = d \end{cases} \tag{8.17}$$

Equations (8.16) and (8.17) are the pattern constraints, which guarantee orientation pattern near the SPs is similar to core or delta pattern. In order to make the point a SP, singularity constraints should be added as Eq. (8.18) state.

$$
\begin{cases}
\displaystyle\sum_{i=0}^{n}\sum_{j=0}^{i} b_{(i-j)j}(-x_s)^{i-j}(-y_s)^j = 0 \\
\displaystyle\sum_{i=0}^{n}\sum_{j=0}^{i} a_{(i-j)j}(-x_s)^{i-j}(-y_s)^j = 0
\end{cases} \tag{8.18}
$$

Incorporating the constraints of the first-order phase portrait with local descriptions of the high-order phase portrait gives the constrained high-order phase portrait model. Thus, the proposed model incorporates the best of both the local and global descriptions, which can describe the global orientation image but still preserves an accurate local description near the SPs.

8.2.5 *Solution of coefficients and perturbation analysis*

The solution of the coefficients $\{a_{ij}\}$ and $\{b_{ij}\}$ are obtained from the x and y components separately. Thus, the perturbation analysis is also done on each component separately. To understand the stability of the solution for either $\{a_{ij}\}$ or $\{b_{ij}\}$, the following analysis takes the $\{a_{ij}\}$ as the example of perturbation analysis. The x component can be represented by its corresponding coefficients $\{a_{(n-m)m}\}$ as shown in Eq. (8.19):

$$
dx(x_i, y_j) = \sum_{n=0}^{N}\sum_{m=0}^{n} a_{(n-m)m} x_i^{n-m} y_j^m \tag{8.19}
$$

where N represents its order.

We rewrite it in a matrix form as follows

$$
\mathbf{DX} = \mathbf{XY} \cdot \mathbf{A} \tag{8.20}
$$

where $\mathbf{A} = \begin{bmatrix} a_{00} & a_{10} & a_{01} & \cdots & a_{(n-m)m} & \cdots & a_{0N} \end{bmatrix}^T$

$$
\mathbf{DX} = \begin{bmatrix} \cos(2\theta(x_1,y_1)) \\ \cos(2\theta(x_1,y_2)) \\ \vdots \\ \cos(2\theta(x_I,y_J)) \end{bmatrix}
\quad \text{and} \quad
\mathbf{XY} = \begin{bmatrix} 1 & x_1 & y_1 & \cdots & x_1^{n-m}y_1^m & \cdots & y_1^N \\ 1 & x_1 & y_2 & \cdots & x_1^{n-m}y_2^m & \cdots & y_2^N \\ \vdots & \vdots & \vdots & \vdots & & \ddots & \vdots \\ 1 & x_I & y_J & \cdots & x_I^{n-m}y_J^m & \cdots & y_J^N \end{bmatrix}
$$

The existence of noise in a fingerprint image causes the OI to deviate from its accurate value. Instead of not considering the information on the noisy region, a looser weight is associated with this region.

Let $\mathbf{W} = \text{diag}(\omega(x_1,y_1), \omega(x_1,y_2), \ldots, \omega(x_I,y_J))$ be a diagonal matrix; $\omega(x_i, y_j)$ denotes the weight in (x_i, y_j). Multiply $\mathbf{W}$ a both sides of Eq. (8.20)

$$
\mathbf{W} \cdot \mathbf{DX} = \mathbf{W} \cdot \mathbf{XY} \cdot \mathbf{A} \tag{8.21}
$$

The weights can be obtained using the coherence value of the orientation as described in Eq. (8.32).

The constraints in Eqs. (8.16)–(8.18) have its matrix form as shown in Eq. (8.22):

$$\mathbf{L} \cdot \mathbf{A} = \mathbf{H} \tag{8.22}$$

where $\mathbf{H} = \begin{bmatrix} 0 & m & n \end{bmatrix}^T$ and

$$\mathbf{L} = \begin{bmatrix} 1 & \dots & (-x_s)^{i-j}(-y_s^j) & \dots & (-y_s)^n \\ 1 & \dots & (i-j)(-y_s)^j & \dots & 0 \\ 0 & \dots & j(-x_s)^{i-j} & \dots & n \end{bmatrix} \tag{8.23}$$

Hence the CNPPM can be viewed as the weighted linear least square problem with linear equality constraints, as stated in Eq. (8.24):

$$\min_{A \in B} \|\mathbf{W}(\mathbf{XY} \cdot \mathbf{A} - \mathbf{DX})\|_2, \quad B = \{\mathbf{A} | \mathbf{L} \cdot \mathbf{A} = \mathbf{H}\} \tag{8.24}$$

where $\| \cdot \|_2$ is the norm.

If the constrained matrix $\mathbf{L}$ has full row rank: $\mathrm{rank}(\mathbf{L}) = p$, the least square problem has the unique solution, which has been proofed by Eldèn (1980) (The following Eqs. (8.25)–(8.30) are based on the perturbation analysis in the work of Eldèn (1980):

$$\mathbf{A} = \mathbf{L}_{I \cdot W \cdot XY^+} \cdot \mathbf{H} + (\mathbf{W} \cdot \mathbf{XY} \cdot \mathbf{P_0})^+ \cdot \mathbf{W} \cdot \mathbf{DX} \tag{8.25}$$

where $(\cdot)^+$ represents the pseudoinverse of a matrix, $\mathbf{L}^+_{I \cdot W \cdot XY} = (\mathbf{I} - (\mathbf{W} \cdot \mathbf{XY} \cdot \mathbf{P_0})^+ \cdot \mathbf{W} \cdot \mathbf{XY}) \cdot \mathbf{L}^+$, and $\mathbf{P_0} = \mathbf{I} - \mathbf{L}^+ \cdot \mathbf{L}$.

Now, let us consider the perturbation problem defined in Eq. (8.26):

$$\min_{A \in \tilde{B}} \|\tilde{\mathbf{W}} \cdot \tilde{\mathbf{XY}} \cdot \mathbf{A} - \tilde{\mathbf{W}} \cdot \tilde{\mathbf{DX}}\|, \quad \tilde{B} = \{\mathbf{A} | \tilde{\mathbf{L}} \cdot \mathbf{A} = \tilde{\mathbf{H}}\} \tag{8.26}$$

where

$$\tilde{\mathbf{XY}} = \mathbf{XY} + \Delta XY \mathbf{E}_{XY}$$

$$\tilde{\mathbf{DX}} = \mathbf{DX} + \Delta DX \mathbf{E}_{DX}$$

$$\tilde{\mathbf{L}} = \mathbf{L} + \Delta L \mathbf{E}_L$$

$$\tilde{\mathbf{H}} = \mathbf{H} + \Delta H \mathbf{E}_H$$

$$\tilde{\mathbf{W}} = \mathbf{W} + \Delta W \mathbf{E}_W \tag{8.27}$$

and $\|\mathbf{E}_{XY}\| = \|\mathbf{E}_{DX}\| = \|\mathbf{E}_L\| = \|\mathbf{E}_H\| = \|\mathbf{E}_W\| = 1$,

$$\Delta XY, \Delta L, \Delta DX, \Delta H, \Delta W >= 0.$$

In this study, the matrices $\mathbf{XY}$ and $\mathbf{L}$ are combination of the coordinates of the points (x, y); so, we have $\Delta XY = 0$ and $\Delta L = 0$.

According to the perturbation theory for the least square problem with linear equality constraints developed by Eldèn (1980), the estimation errors $\Delta \mathbf{A} = \tilde{\mathbf{A}} - \mathbf{A}$ can be expressed as Eq. (8.28):

$$\|\Delta \mathbf{A}\| \leq \|(\mathbf{XY} \cdot \mathbf{P_0})^+\| \|\mathbf{W}^+\| \|\mathbf{DX} - \mathbf{XY} \cdot \mathbf{A}\| \Delta \mathbf{W}$$
$$+ \|(\mathbf{XY} \cdot \mathbf{P_0})^+\| \Delta DX + \|\mathbf{L}_{I,XY}\| \Delta H \tag{8.28}$$

The relative error can be estimated using Eq. (8.29):

$$\frac{\Delta \mathbf{A}}{\mathbf{A}} \leq \frac{\Delta \mathbf{DX}}{\mathbf{DX}} \cdot \kappa_L(\mathbf{XY}) \frac{\|\mathbf{DX}\|}{\|\mathbf{XY}\| \|\mathbf{A}\|} + \frac{\Delta \mathbf{H}}{\mathbf{H}} \cdot \kappa^{XY}(\mathbf{L}) \frac{\|\mathbf{H}\|}{\|\mathbf{L}\| \|\mathbf{A}\|}$$
$$+ \frac{\Delta \mathbf{W}}{\mathbf{W}} \kappa_W \kappa_L(\mathbf{XY}) \frac{\Delta \mathbf{DX}}{\mathbf{DX}} \tag{8.29}$$

where

$$\kappa_L(\mathbf{XY}) = \|\mathbf{XY}\| \cdot \|(\mathbf{XY} \cdot \mathbf{P_0})^+\| \tag{8.30a}$$

$$\kappa^{XY}(\mathbf{L}) = \|\mathbf{L}\| \cdot \|\mathbf{L}^+_{\mathbf{I} \cdot \mathbf{XY}}\| \tag{8.30b}$$

$$\kappa_W = \|\mathbf{W}\| \|\mathbf{W}^+\| \tag{8.30c}$$

We may justify the stability of estimation of the coefficients $\mathbf{A}$ according to the constrained condition numbers $\kappa_L(\mathbf{XY})$, $\kappa^{XY}(\mathbf{L})$, and κ_W defined in Eqs. (8.30)(a–c) and its relative error bound according to $(\Delta \mathbf{A})/(\mathbf{A})$ defined in Eq. (8.29).

From Eq. (8.29), the estimation error of coefficients comes from two cases: the original orientation and constraints. If the perturbation of the original orientation is large, which is always indicated by the small coherence value, this will cause large κ_W, ΔDX, and ΔW. Therefore, the estimated error of coefficients $\mathbf{A}$ will be large as well. On the other hand, if the constrained matrix $\mathbf{L}$ is ill-conditioned, which means that the $\mathbf{L}$ tends to be singular, it will result in a large $\kappa^{XY}(\mathbf{L})$. Therefore, in this case, the estimated error of the coefficients $\mathbf{A}$ may be large also.

In the following two parts, we discuss the solution for these two cases.

8.2.5.1 *Robustness in case of a large patch of noise*

If the most orientations in the fingerprint image are spoiled by noise, we do not expect to reconstruct such orientation. In this section, we try to reconstruct the orientation in a fingerprint image where there exists a large patch of noise that affects an enclosed region while out of this region we can still obtain the trustworthy orientation.

In order to solve this problem, we proposed to combine the prediction model with the constrained non-linear phase portrait model. Generally, there are several approaches to compute the quality of a region in an image (Hong *et al.*, 1998). In this work, a simple method to segment the good-quality image from the noisy region is to use the coherence value. When the coherence value of a block in an image is below a certain threshold, we regard it as an untrustworthy region. So, we replace the original orientation with the predicted one. However, the coherence value assigned to these predicted orientations is small, leading to a small weight value. This is to reduce the impact of the predicted orientation on the original trustworthy orientations.

8.2.5.2 *Robustness in cases where SPs are close to one another*

In this section, we discuss the second case where there are large perturbation of the constraints.

The constraints that will be added to the non-linear phase portrait shall abide by the linearization theorem. Therefore, in fingerprints the two SPs should be well separated so that each SP exhibits a simple behavior that can be described by the first-order phase portrait.

The computation of the orientation uses the pixel values in a block of size $h \times w$. Thus, the OI has a smaller size. In some loop (or tented arch) cases, the core point and the delta point are close to each other in the OI. Therefore, the SP regions will interact with each other such that the first-order phase portrait description fail near these regions. Consequently, the perturbation ΔH of $\mathbf{H}$ computed from the first-order phase portrait is quite large. Moreover, it will cause a smaller (x_s, y_s). Let us consider the constraints matrix in Eq. (8.22). If (x_s, y_s) is small, the elements in the first row will be smaller than the elements in the other rows. This will cause the condition number $\kappa^{XY}(\mathbf{L})$ large, which means the $\mathbf{L}$ tends to be singular. With large $\kappa^{XY}(\mathbf{L})$ and ΔH, the estimated error of the coefficients $\mathbf{A}$ will be large. In Fig. 8.4 (a), we show a fingerprint with two close SPs. Its reconstructed OI using the first-order phase portrait as constraints near SPs is shown in Fig. 8.4 (b). In Fig. 8.4 (c), we also show the reconstructed OI using the phase portrait model without any constraints. They all fail to precisely reconstruct the orientation at the SP region.

In order to model the OI in these cases, we add the loose constraints where only singularity constraints are applied while pattern constraints are ignored. This is reasonable as the orientation patterns of two close SPs interact with each other and no more simple SP behaviors are exhibited. But the discontinuity (singularity constraints) at SPs regions are still kept.

In Fig. 8.4 (d), we show an example of the reconstructed OI using only the singularity constraints in Eq. (8.18).

More examples are shown in Fig. 8.5.

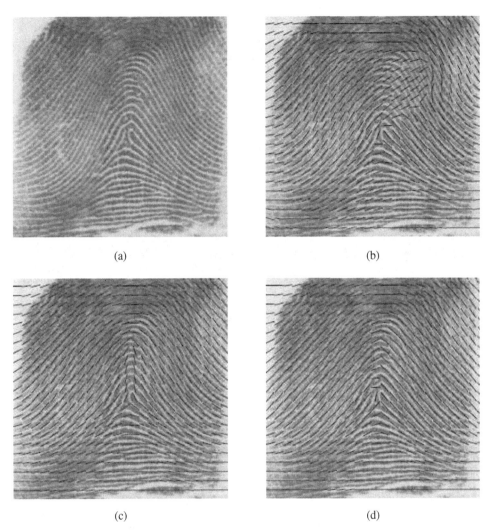

(a)   (b)

(c)   (d)

Fig. 8.4. Examples of fingerprint with two close singular points. (a) An original image; (b) Reconstructed orientation by the first-order phase portrait constraints; (c) Reconstructed orientation by the polynomial model without any constraint; and (d) Reconstructed orientation by the model proposed in this section.

8.2.6 *Implementation of the constrained non-linear phase portrait model*

In this section, we describe in detail the proposed algorithm.

(1) Compute the original OI θ_{orig} and its coherence Coherence$_{\text{orig}}$, respectively using Eqs. (8.31) and (8.32);

$$\theta_{\text{orig}}(x_i, y_i) = \frac{1}{2}\arctan\left(\frac{\sum 2G_x G_y}{\sum(G_x^2 - G_y^2)}\right) + \frac{\pi}{2} \qquad (8.31)$$

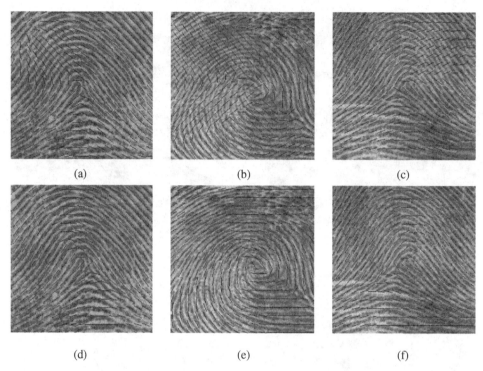

Fig. 8.5. Comparisons of reconstructed OI of fingerprint with two close SPs. The first row shows the reconstructed orientation by the constrained non-linear phase portrait model; and the second row by the proposed method.

$$\text{Coherence}_{\text{orig}}(x_i, y_i) = \frac{(\sum(G_x^2 - G_y^2))^2 + 4(\sum G_x G_y)^2}{(\sum(G_x^2 + G_y^2))^2} \qquad (8.32)$$

where G_x and G_y are the gradient vectors along the x and y components, respectively computed in the window region centered at (x_i, y_i).

(2) Compute the predicted orientation using the proposed prediction model described in Sec. 8.2.3:

   (a) For each located SP, the first-order phase portrait described in Sec. 8.2.3 is used to reconstruct its orientation.

   (b) In terms of the number and the position of SPs, the rules in Sec. 8.2.3 are adopted to form the predicted orientations θ_{pred} for the whole image.

(3) Form the training data θ_{trn} by combining the original orientation θ_{orig} and the predicted orientation θ_{pred} according to the following criteria:

$$\theta_{\text{trn}} = \begin{cases} \theta_{\text{pred}} & \text{if Coherence}_{\text{orig}} < 0.5 \\ \theta_{\text{orig}} & \text{if Coherence}_{\text{orig}} \geq 0.5 \end{cases}$$

and

$$\text{Coherence}_{\text{trn}} = \begin{cases} 0.3 & \text{if Coherence}_{\text{orig}} < 0.5 \\ \text{Coherence}_{\text{orig}} & \text{if Coherence}_{\text{orig}} \geq 0.5 \end{cases} \tag{8.33}$$

Note that once the original orientation is replaced with the predicted orientation, the coherence should also be changed to a value $0 < \text{Coherence}_{\text{trn}} < 0.5$. We use a value of 0.3 which we found suitable through trial and error.

(4) Compute the orientation model using the CNPPM.

(a) Compute the first-order phase portrait at each SP region as the constraints using Eq. (8.12);

(b) Prepare the training data obtained in step 3 along the x and y components, respectively:

$$dx = \cos(2 * \theta_{trn}(x, y))$$
$$dy = \sin(2 * \theta_{trn}(x, y)) \tag{8.34}$$

(c) Compute all the coefficients of the CNPPM a_{ij} and b_{ij}.

For each SPs, three constraints will be given by Eq. (8.16), Eq. (8.17), and Eq. (8.18) for a_{ij} and b_{ij}, respectively. Thus, a total of $3n$ (where n is the number of the SPs) coefficients will be reduced from Eq. (8.15). Weighted least square algorithm is used to compute the coefficients a_{ij} and b_{ij} so that the least square errors between training data θ_{trn} and the phase portrait model is minimized. Coherence matrix will act as the weighting factor when determining the overall orientation value from the actual, predicted, and the computed value of the model.

Figure 8.6(a–f) show the resultant images obtained in each step.

8.3 Fingerprint Classification Based on the Mutual Validated Information

Fingerprint OI is crucial for SPs detection and classification. In the previous section, a CNPPM was developed to precisely reconstruct the OI. A piecewise first-order phase portrait prediction model is introduced to make the CNPPM robust to the large patch of noise. Besides the capability of precise reconstruction of OI, another unique advantage to the other model-based methods is that CNPPM has the unified form. It implies that existence of SPs would influence the OI computation. Therefore, if SPs are wrongly detected, the wrong orientation patterns will be brought into the reconstructed OI. This will help us validate SPs and OI in a mutual way.

In most existing computation of SPs and OI, there is no consideration of such mutual validation. The reasons that there is no such mutual validation considered are that: (1) in zero-pole model-based methods, the core–delta pair needs to appear at the same time while this is not always true; (2) in phase portrait model-based

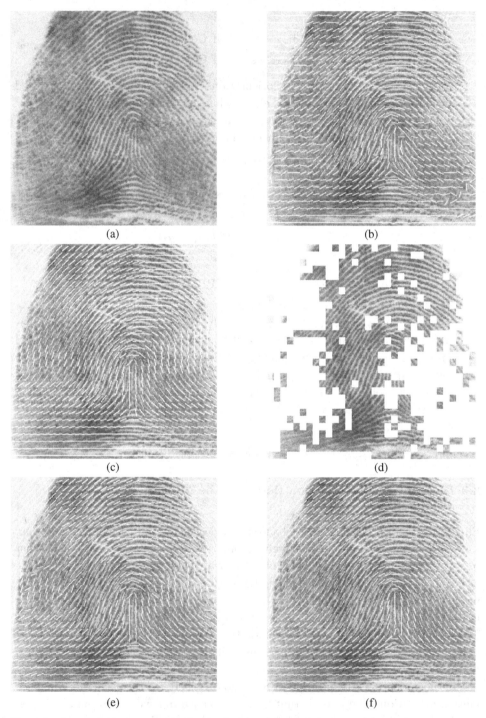

(a)

(b)

(c)

(d)

(e)

(f)

Fig. 8.6.   Resultant images obtained in each step. (a) original image; (b) original orientation image; (c) predicted orientation image; (d) segmentation by coherence; (e) training data using original and predicted data; and (f) reconstructed orientation image.

methods, the models consider the global and local OIs separately. It implies that SPs' information has its effect only in a local OI.

Since the CNPPM brings all the OI information and it could be used to validate the SP information, a new algorithm combining the mutual validated information of CNPPM coefficients and SPs' information is developed to perform the fingerprints classification. In the following parts, we address fingerprints classification problem using the new algorithm.

8.3.1 *Literature review on fingerprint classification*

In the last 30 years, although fingerprint classification has been extensively investigated and many different methods had been proposed, limited features and classifiers were used to perform the classification. An overview of fingerprint classification according to the features are given:

Singularities

There are two kinds of SPs in the fingerprint, core point and delta point. A core point is the turning point of an innermost ridge and a delta point is a place where two ridges running side-by-side diverge (Federal Bureau of Investigation, 1984). According to the position and number of SPs, a fingerprint can be classified into classes as stated in Table 8.1.

The algorithms based on singularities included Kawagoe and Tojo (1984), Karu and Jain (1996), and in Ballan *et al.* (1997), Hong and Jain (1999a), Cho *et al.* (2000), Zhang and Yan (2004), Klimanee and Nguyen (2004), Mohamed and Nyongesa (2002), Nyongesa *et al.* (2004), Wang and Dai (2007), Li *et al.* (2008), Hong *et al.* (2008), Liu (2009).

In all these papers, the common approach for classification task is rule based. However, it is worth paying attention to the paper by Liu (2009). In this paper, the author extracted as many as singular points and its relative information (positions and orientations) to form feature vectors in multiple scales. The Ada-boost learning algorithm was applied to select the suitable feature vectors to perform classification.

Orientation image

OI can be interpreted as the direction of the ridge flow. The following algorithms are based on the OI of the fingerprints.

Table 8.1: Classification based on singularities

Classes	Cores	Deltas	Core's position to delta's
Whorl	2	2	—
Right loop	1	1	Left
Left loop	1	1	Right
Tented arch	1	1	Beneath
Plain arch	0	0	—

- Moayer and Fu in 1975 (Moayer and Fu, 1975) and 1976 (Moayer and Fu, 1976). The features were extracted from the OIs. Through the analysis of the orientation, the OI can be encoded into 12-bit binary number, called "containment code C". Thereafter, a syntactic approach was used to perform the classification.
- Candela et al. (Candela et al., 1995; Wilson et al., 1994). In their method, 1690 orientations in the OI were reduced to 64 principal components by KL transformation. A neural network was then employed as classifier using these 64 features. Similar algorithms could be found in Halici and Ongun (1996), Kamei and Mizoguchi (1998), Kamijo (1993), and Bernard et al. (2001).
- Cappelli et al. (Cappelli et al., 2002, 2003). The authors represented a fingerprint pattern as a combination of several subspaces. For each subspace, KL transform were applied to extract the features from the OI. Multiple KL features were then formed for classification.
- Cappelli et al. (Cappelli et al., 1999b, 2002) and Maio and Maltoni (Maio and Maltoni, 1996). In these papers, the authors proposed a method to partition the OI by grouping the "homogeneous" OI regions using dynamic masks. This could be viewed as a compact representation of the orientation image. The relational graphs, with each node from a homogeneous region, were then formed as the features.

Ridge information

Ridge information is another common feature used for fingerprints classification. The following lists the methods that utilize ridge information.

- Kawagoe and Tojo (Kawagoe and Tojo, 1984) in 1984. After a coarse classification by singularities, the different features were extracted using the ridge flow tracing to further classify whorls into double loop and whorl, loops into left loop, right loop, and pocket and tented arch.
- Candela et al. (Candela et al., 1995; Wilson et al., 1994) in 1994 and 1995. A pseudoridge tracing was used to improve the accurate classification of the whorl type.
- Chong et al. (Chong et al., 1997) in 1997. They represented the ridges with B-spline function. Then, the similarities between two features were computed to perform the classification.
- Senior (Senior, 1999) in 2001. In this method, a fingerprint was first thinned into one pixel width. Thereafter, two feature vectors were formed. The first feature was generated by the intersection points of fiducial lines and the thinned ridges. The other feature consisted of key points of a thinned ridge. HMM and decision trees were adopted as the classifiers for these two features.
- Jain and Minut (Jain and Minut, 2002) in 2002. The pseudoridge tracing was used to extract features which was being compared with the pre-defined kernels to decide its attribute class.

- Chang and Fan (Chang and Fan, 2002) in 2002. A series of ridge patterns were defined in this approach. Then, a query fingerprint was described according to the existence and position of these ridge patterns. The sequences of these ridge patterns then determined which class the fingerprint belonged to.
- Shah and Sastry (Shah and Sastry, 2004) in 2003. In this method, they first obtained a thinned ridge with which multiple oriented points would be preserved. Then, the thinned ridge plane was divided into several sections. In each section, the two major orientations were extracted as features. The features were then verified with support vector machine, neural networks, and the k-nearest neighbor (NN) classifiers.
- Zhang and Yan (Zhang and Yan, 2004) in 2004. They performed fingerprint classification in terms of singularities first, thereafter a pseudoridge tracing was used to improve the classification results. This was a rule-based classification.
- Dass and Jain (Dass and Jain, 2004) in 2004. In this approach, the salient features were exploited after ridge tracing. The salient features were the number and locations of the sign-change point as well as the number and locations of local maximums and minimums.
- Xu et al. (Xu et al., 2005) in 2005. Here, ridge tracing was applied to extract the points with the maximum curvature as feature points.

The classifiers used for ridge information include: syntactic approach (Chang and Fan, 2002), rule-based approaches (Zhang and Yan, 2004; Jain and Minut, 2002; Kawagoe and Tojo, 1984; Chong et al., 1997; Dass and Jain, 2004; Xu et al., 2005), neural network based approaches (Dass and Jain, 2004; Candela et al., 1995; Wilson et al., 1994), structural approaches (Senior, 1999; Neuhaus and Bunke, 2005), and statistical approaches (Shah and Sastry, 2004).

Gabor filter responses

In 1999, Jain et al. (Jain et al., 1999) proposed a novel method based on Gabor filters. The Gabor filters were described as follows

$$G(x, y; f, \theta) = \exp\left\{\frac{-1}{2}\left[\frac{x_1^2}{\delta_x^2} + \frac{y_1^2}{\delta_y^2}\right]\right\} \cos(2\pi f x_1)$$

where $x_1 = x \sin\theta + y \cos\theta$, $y_1 = x \cos\theta - y \sin\theta$. f is the frequency of the sinusoidal plane wave along the direction θ from the x-axis, and δ_x and δ_y specify the Gaussian envelope along the x and y axes, respectively.

For a given query image, Gabor filters were first applied around the core point. The fingerprints were then separated into 48 sections. In each section with the 4 different θ values, the standard deviation was computed as feature vectors, called "FingerCode". Then, it was fed into a k-NN classifier and a neural network classifier.

In 2008, Hong et al. used "FingerCode" as the input of Naive Bayes classifiers and SVM classifiers.

8.3.2 Feature extraction based on the mutual validation

Both SPs and OI are effective for fingerprint classification. However, it is not usual for researchers to adopt the combination of both features to improve the classification accuracy.

The difficulties of singularities-based methods are due to the following reasons: (1) SPs may not appear in the query image; and (2) The noise in the fingerprint images makes the SP extraction unpredictable (missing or wrong detection). On the other hand, the difficulties of OI-based methods are due to the following two reasons: (1) there are small interclass variabilities of orientation pattern (which make their orientation pattern similar); and (2) large intraclass variabilities of orientation patterns (which make the similarity measurement big). Under such circumstances, the singularities would be more useful for the classification process. Similarly, for some cases where SPs cannot be commonly detected in the query image, the OI still exhibits certain information that is useful for classification. Therefore the advantages of both features complement each other to produce an improved classification accuracy compared to the approach that relies on a single feature.

In order to mutually validate SPs and OI, a gradient-based method was adopted to compute the original OI (Bazen and Gerez, 2002). This original OI is used to extract the SP candidate and it will be refined by CNPPM.

The simplest way to compute SPs is based on the Poincaré Index method. In this work, we adopted the complex filter-based method proposed by Bigun, and Bigun and Nilsson (Nilsson and Bigun, 2003), where two types of filters were defined by $h = (x + iy)^m g(x, y)$, where $g(x, y) = \exp\{-(x^2 + y^2)/(2\sigma^2)\}$ and (x, y) are the coordinates. Compared with the Poincaré Index method, complex symmetrical filters-based method has at least three advantages:

(1) The filter-based method indicates not only the existence of the SP but also the orientation of the SP. Thus, the alignment of the SP can be done with respect to the position and the orientation of the SP.
(2) There is potential to speed up the detection process due to the separable property of the complex symmetrical filters from one 2D filter into two 1D filters.
(3) The magnitude of complex symmetrical filter provides a numerical measurement of how similar the SP is to the symmetrical pattern, whereas the Poincare Index-based method can only give "Yes" or "No" answer to the existence of the SP.

Figures 8.7(a) and 8.7(b) show the patterns with the local description of $z = \exp\{i\phi\}$, $z = \exp\{-i\phi\}$, respectively. Correspondingly, there are two kinds of orientation patterns in the fingerprint images, called "core pattern" and "delta pattern" as shown in Figs. 8.7(c) and 8.7(d), respectively.

In their work, a fix threshold is set empirically, which can make the tradeoff between missed detection and false detection. Therefore, a high threshold could

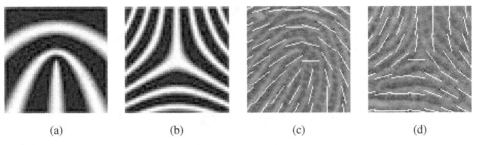

(a)   (b)   (c)   (d)

Fig. 8.7. Patterns with local orientation description of $z = \{im\phi\}$, $m = 1, -1$ respectively and orientation patterns in fingerprints. (a) pattern with local orientation description of $z = \exp\{i\phi\}$, (b) pattern with local orientation description of $z = \exp\{-i\phi\}$, (c) core's orientation pattern, and (d) delta's orientation pattern.

result in the misdetection of SPs in noisy regions. In fact, the filters' response provides a continuous measurement of the orientation patterns. At the local regions around SPs, the filters responses always take the local maximum values.

In this work, the use of complex symmetrical filters is to extract, as much as possible, all the candidate SPs which yields the local maximum magnitudes even if these SPs lie at the boundary of the OI or are partially corrupted by noise. Using the local maximum criteria, more than 2 cores or deltas can be extracted. However, we are faced with a new dilemma of choosing the true SPs from the list of candidate SPs. To solve this problem, a mutual validation approach using candidates of SPs and CNPPM is proposed.

The basic idea of the mutual validation approach is that we use the SPs information detected by the complex filters to obtain the CNPPM and reconstruct the whole OI. On the other side, we use the CNPPM and the original OI to help select the true SPs.

For a specific candidate SP, we define 4 features to select the true one.

$$D = \frac{1}{N} \sum_{i,j} (\sin(\theta_{\text{orig}}(i,j) - \theta_{\text{model}}(i,j))^2 * (1 - \text{Coh}(i,j))) \qquad (8.35)$$

(1) The magnitude of the complex symmetrical filters' response; the different types of the local orientation structures have the different filters' response. The true SP has generally a large response to the corresponding type of filter.

(2) The error (or difference) D between the reconstructed OI and the original OI (defined in Eq. 8.35); This feature is based on the fact that for a real SP, the difference should be small.

(3) The mean orientation coherence; this value is used to indicate the quality of images and the candidate SP will be rejected if the value is low.

(4) The consistency of the type of the candidate singular points. The coefficients $[m, n, c, d]$ of the first phase portrait model can provide the type of the SP. This type should be as the same as the type decided by the complex filters for a real SP. Otherwise, the SP is regarded as spurious.

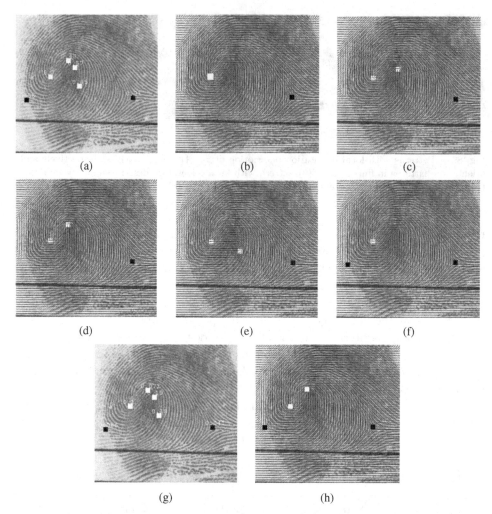

Fig. 8.8. An example for the mutual validation of the SPs and OI. (a) all the possible candidates of the SPs obtained using the complex filter approach; (b–f) the reconstructed OIs using different combinations of the candidate SPs; (g) the orientation error, D, of all the candidates SPs; and (h) the final reconstructed orientations using four SPs. The core candidates are marked as the white rectangles; the delta candidatures are marked as the black rectangles.

In Fig. 8.8, an example is given to show the process of mutual validation of SPs and OI. In this example, a complex filter-based method is used to extract all the possible candidate SPs. A threshold, T_s is set to limit the number of candidates to a reasonable range (in this work, a value of 0.45 is used). There are 4 core candidates and 2 delta candidates having filters' response magnitudes greater than the preset threshold T_s.

Figure 8.8 (a) shows these candidate SPs with their corresponding response marked on the image, (b–f) show the reconstructed OIs using different combination of the candidate SPs; (g) shows the orientation error, D, between the reconstructed

OIs and the original OIs for all the candidate SPs. Two of the core candidates have the value D greater than 0.15 and are thus regarded as spurious SPs and subsequently rejected.

The final reconstructed OIs and the core points (marked as white rectangles) and the delta points (marked as black rectangles) are shown in Fig. 8.8 (h).

8.3.3 *Implementation of the proposed method*

Based on the orientation and singularity information, fingerprint classification can be performed. The overall approach can be divided into 7 stages. This section describes the overall approach in detail.

Stage 1: Compute the original OI and the coherence matrix

Stage 2: Extract the candidate SPs with the local maximum filters response by the complex filter-based method

To keep the number of candidate SPs to a reasonable number, the local maximum magnitude of filter response should be larger than a pre-determined threshold. Otherwise, the points will be removed from the candidate SPs. Note that the threshold value is not restrictive as it merely determines the processing time needed for stage 3.

Stage 3: Verification of the candidate SPs

With the different combination of the candidate SPs, we can get the different CNPPMs. According to the mutual validation of coefficients of these CNPPMs and the candidate SPs described in the previous section, the true SPs and the best CNPPM are decided.

Stage 4: Alignment of the OI

To achieve translation and rotation invariance, it is necessary to align and crop all the fingerprint images to a canonical size and orientation. From the response of the core-type filter, the position and orientation of the primary core (corresponding to the maximum certainty of the core-type filter response) can be obtained. Taking the primary core as the origin, the image is rotated by (90-core_orientation) degrees to align the core orientation into vertical orientation. Figures 8.9(a) and 8.9(b) show an example of a fingerprint image before and after alignment. The alignment ensures that all the images used for the orientation modeling have consistent translation and orientation. For the whorl type fingerprint images, there are two core points and two delta points. The primary core will be defined as the core with the smaller distance with the deltas.

The fingerprint images acquired from the sensor will usually contain noise in the background region. If the entire image is used, the orientation model generated will be affected by the noise and background region. However, care must be taken such that the cropped image will contain critical information necessary for the classification and at the same time, removing as much background region as possible.

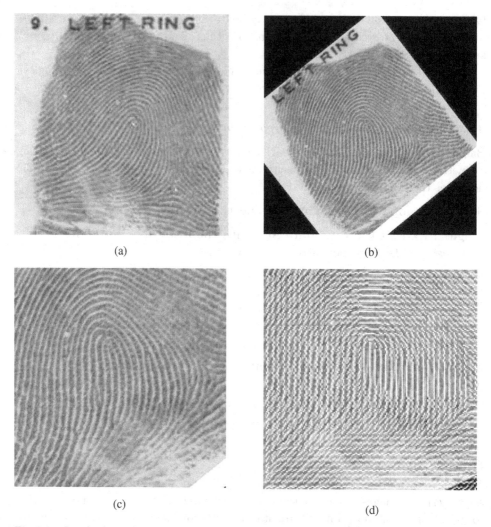

(a)   (b)

(c)   (d)

Fig. 8.9.   Results for each step in the pre-processing stage. (a) original fingerprint image with the detected SPs marked; (b) fingerprint image after alignment; (c) fingerprint image after cropping; and (d) reconstructed orientation overlaid on the cropped fingerprint image.

For example, a whorl type fingerprint might possess SPs that are separated far apart. In this case, the cropping process should preserve all SPs as much as possible. After an extensive study, we found that a cropped image of size 320 by 320 pixels is reasonable for fingerprint images obtained using sensor with 500 dpi resolution. Cropping is done with respect to the primary core point after the alignment process. The ratio of the top portion to the bottom portion is around 1:3 as the lower portion contains more information that is useful for classification. Figure 8.9(c) shows a sample fingerprint image obtained after the cropping process.

Stage 5: Modeling of the orientation fields

Here again, we use the determined SPs in the normalized image to reconstruct the whole OI. The coefficients will be used to perform the classification.

An example of the reconstructed orientation is shown in Fig. 8.9(d).

Stage 6: Form the feature vectors

In this work, the feature vectors consist of two parts — the coefficients of CNPPM and the SPs' information. The dimension of the coefficients of the CNPPM is $(N + 1) \times (N + 2) - 2$, where N indicates the order of the phase portrait. Singularities information includes:

(1) the number of SPs present in the original OI $\times$ the maximum magnitude of complex filters;
(2) the angles between the primary core point and the delta points; since the number of the deltas is varied and maximum number is 2 we adopt a 2D vector to represent the angles between the primary core point and each delta point. When there is no delta detected, the vector is set to $[0, 0]$ and when there is only one delta detected, the vector is set to $[R, 0]$, where R is the real angle between the primary core point and the detected delta point. In addition, the vector $[R, R]$ represents the angles when two delta points are detected. Such an operation can keep the fixed length of the feature vectors.

The reason for using the first information instead of the number of SPs is that magnitudes of complex symmetrical filters provide a continuous way to measure the strength of SPs which is a more robust information compared to the number of SPs. The second information provides the relative difference in the core and delta points that cannot be determined from the orientation model (which only provides the orientation information). An illustration is shown in Fig. 8.10.

Fig. 8.10. Fingerprint type left loop, tented arch, right loop (from left to right). The solid lines show the orientation of the core points and dashed lines show the connection between core point and the delta point. The angle between these two lines is used to separate these three types of fingerprints.

Stage 7: Perform fingerprint classification using Support Vector Machine

The feature vectors are then used as input to a classifier to perform the fingerprint classification. Based on our study, support vector machine (SVM) (Gunn, 1998) is found to be the superior classifier and is adopted. In order to get the best parameters for the SVM classifier, a training set is needed and cross validation technique is used in the training process.

8.4 Experimental Results

In this part, we conduct 2 sets of experiments: the first one is to evaluate the CNPPM; and the second one is for fingerprint classification.

8.4.1 *Experiments for orientation modeling*

In this part, three experiments are conducted. Experiment I aims to test the performance of the prediction model quantitatively. Experiment II is used to evaluate the constrained non-linear phase portrait model quantitatively, while experiment III is designed to show the effectiveness of the algorithm qualitatively in the region that does not contain full ridge information.

In order to evaluate the effectiveness of the proposed orientation algorithm quantitatively, we compute the original orientation image using a Gabor filter bank (64 filters). Then, the mean absolute error (MAE)[‡] between the predicted orientation and the original orientation is computed as follows

$$MAE = \frac{1}{N} \sum_{(x,y)\in\Omega} d(\theta_{\text{pred}}(x,y) - \theta_{\text{gabor}}(x,y)) \tag{8.36}$$

where Ω is the region of comparison, which contains a total of N points. (x,y) is the coordinate of a point in Ω, θ_{pred}, and θ_{gabor} denote the predicted orientation using the proposed algorithm and the orientation image computed using the Gabor filter bank, respectively. Since the orientation is in $[-pi/2, pi/2)$, the function $d(\cdot)$ is defined as

$$d(\theta) = \begin{cases} |\theta|, & |\theta| < \pi/2 \\ \pi - |\theta|, & \text{otherwise} \end{cases} \tag{8.37}$$

The experiments are conducted on the first 500 images (f0001-f0250 and s0001-s0250) of the NIST special Database 4 where the fingerprint image size is relatively large (512×480 pixels). Here, the orientations are computed using an 8×8 pixel block.

[‡]The method is also adopted by other researchers (Zhou *et al.*, 2004).

Experiment I: Quantitative analysis of prediction model

In experiments I and II, the data used to predict the orientation is obtained using a 8×8 window centered at the SPs. In addition, we artificially removed the orientation with a size 10×10 blocks near the pattern area. The average MAE obtained is $14.2043°$ with a standard deviation of $5.0465°$. The main reason why the MAE is not close to zero is that the first-order phase portrait has limited capability to describe the oriented pattern. Some of the examples are shown in Fig. 8.11.

The low MAE with the low standard deviation of the prediction model shows the accuracy of the predicted orientation. Thus, once the orientations are corrupted by noise and are not reliable, these predicted orientations will give good estimation

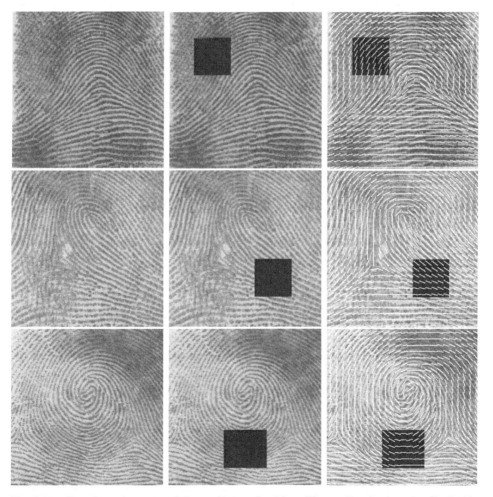

Fig. 8.11. Sample performance of the prediction algorithm. The predicted orientation lies inside the dark area. The images in the last column show the coarse predicted orientation using phase portrait. The images in each row are the same. Images in the first row belong to the plain arch; the second row to tented arch; and the last row to whorl.

of the true orientations. It is also the experimental explanation that before we get the CNPPM a prediction model is applied to replace the unreliable orientation if applicable.

Experiment II: Quantitative analysis of CNPPM

In experiment II, we evaluate our proposed CNPPM algorithm on the same images as those used in experiment I (500 NIST DB4 images). We set the order of non-linear phase portrait to 8 as a trade-off between accuracy and conciseness of the model. The *MAE* of the model is 9.4025° with a standard deviation (std) of 5.8084°.

As the comparisons, we list the *MAE* with the corresponding std using the proposed CNPPM, our earlier prediction model and the reported approaches of zero-pole model, linear piecewise zero-pole model, and combination model. In our experiment, the most accurate method is the CNPPM, which is followed by combination model, linear piecewise zero-pole model, prediction model, and the zero-pole model in the descending order. This order is reasonable. The zero-pole model only considers the positions of SPs. Thus, it can only give constant description of the orientation as long as the positions of SPs are known. The prediction model and the linear piecewise zero-pole model improve the estimation of the orientation by certain linear rectification. However, they cannot represent the non-linear changes of the orientation images. Compared with the combination model, the CNPPM integrates the description of SPs into the high-order phase portrait model. Therefore, the CNPPM is able to describe both the local OI near SPs and the global OI. By incorporating the prediction model to remove the unreliable orientation in the noisy regions, the CNPPM is more robust to the large patch of noise than the combination model.

Experiment III: Qualitative analysis of CNPPM

For fingerprint images that do not contain full ridge information, it is difficult to evaluate the effectiveness of the algorithm quantitatively. Here, we give some resultant images with its reconstructed orientation using the proposed model to show the effectiveness of our algorithm qualitatively. In Fig. 8.12, we give four examples, each belonging to a different fingerprint type: plain arch, tented arch, loop, and whorl, respectively. In these examples, the orientation images are given in the region where there is clear ridge information, as well as in the region without clear ridge information, such as in the peripheral areas.

Experimental results for cases of fingerprints containing a large noise patch

Since the predicted orientation images are computed using only partial data (around SPs), our proposed method can be used to replace the orientation with weak coherence value, especially at areas with large noisy patch. In Fig. 8.13, a

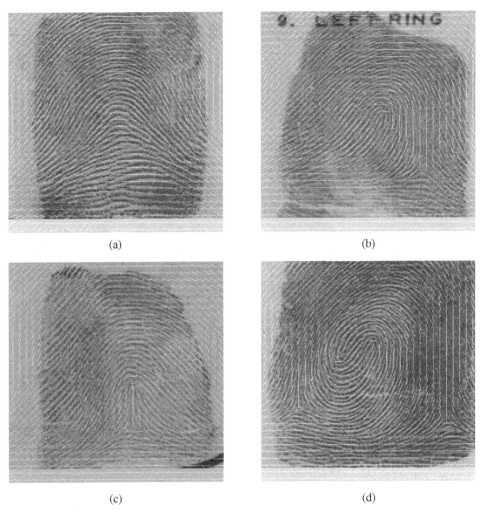

Fig. 8.12.   Examples of reconstructed orientation. (a) plain arch; (b) loop; (c) tented arch; and (d) whorl.

comparative result is given between the proposed model and the combination model, which is chosen as it is the most accurate approaches in the prior art as shown in Table 8.2. Figure 8.13 (a) shows an original fingerprint image with a large noisy patch at the left-bottom section of the image. Figure 8.13 (b) shows its original orientation image computed. Figure 8.13 (d) shows the reconstructed orientation using the combination model approach. The combination model cannot provide a correct solution for the large noisy area as it only uses the weights as the constraints when estimating the coefficients. Thus when the noisy area is large, the error will be large as well. Our proposed model considers the prior knowledge and uses the global constraints to predict the orientation with weak coherence value. This can

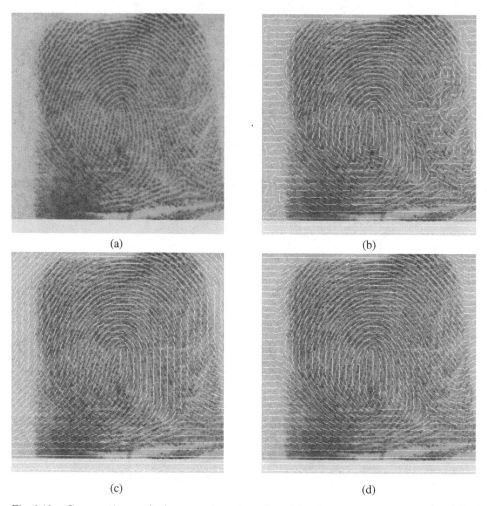

(a)　　　　　　　　　　　　　　　(b)

(c)　　　　　　　　　　　　　　　(d)

Fig. 8.13.　Comparative results between the proposed model and the combination model. (a) the original image; (b) the original orientation image; (c) reconstructed orientation using the proposed model; and (d) reconstructed orientation using the combination model.

correct the orientation in a large noisy area. The result shown in Fig. 8.13 (c) is the reconstructed orientation using our proposed model, which is qualitatively better than the result in Fig. 8.13 (d).

Two more examples for reconstructed orientation from poor-quality fingerprint images with a large patch of noise are illustrated in Fig. 8.14 (a–d). Though the middle part of Fig. 8.14 (a) and the left upper part of Fig. 8.14 are damaged by a large noise patch, our proposed method can still correctly reconstruct their orientation.

We test our algorithm on the first 500 images of the NIST database 4 ($f0001$–$f0250$ and $s0001$–$s0250$). For most of the images, our method can correctly model

Table 8.2: Comparison results of the different orientation models

	Zero-pole model	Piecewise non-linear model	Combination model	Prediction model	Constrained non-linear model
MAE^a	21.5556	15.2376	11.7357	16.2043	9.4025
std^b	8.3821	6.8435	4.2698	7.7401	5.8084

[a]MAE: mean absolute error.
[b]std: standard deviation.

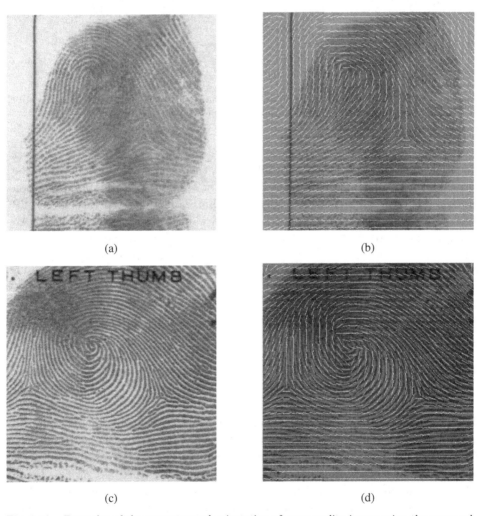

(a)　　　　　　　　　　　　　　　(b)

(c)　　　　　　　　　　　　　　　(d)

Fig. 8.14. Examples of the reconstructed orientation of poor-quality image using the proposed model. (a) a loop image with a large noisy patch; (b) reconstructed orientation of (a) using the proposed method; (c) a whorl image with a large noisy patch; and (d) reconstructed orientation of (c) using the proposed method.

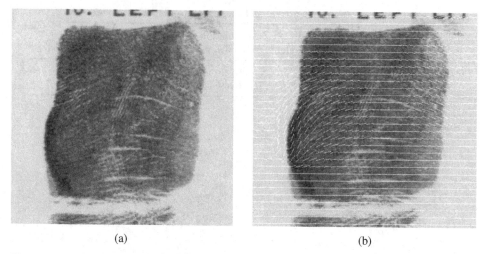

(a)   (b)

Fig. 8.15. Example of a poor-quality image where the reconstruction fails. (a) a poor quality image; and (b) reconstructed orientation using the proposed model.

the orientation images. However, for 30 images, the reconstructed model cannot be formed properly. These images do not have sufficient good orientation information around the SP regions and thus the algorithm cannot extract the correct SP behavior. In such cases, the prediction model cannot be obtained properly. An example of an error image is shown in Fig. 8.15. If we fail to extract the singular point in the image due to poor quality, the proposed model will fail; similarly for the combination model.

8.4.2 *Experimental results for fingerprint classification*

Dataset

The NIST Special Database 4 (DB4), which contains 2000 pairs of fingerprint image (two instances, f and s, for each entity), is used to evaluate the proposed fingerprint classification algorithm. Each image in DB4 has 8-bit gray level with a size of 512 × 480 pixels. The five classes: arch (A), left loop (L), right loop (R), tented arch (T), and whorl (W), are uniformly distributed in the database. The images are numbered from $f0001$ to $f2000$ and from $s0001$ to $s2000$. In DB4, there exist about 17% ambiguous fingerprints that have additional "secondary" class assigned to them. Therefore, in our experiment, output that corresponds to either the primary class or secondary class is taken as a correct classification. This consideration is also adopted by other researchers (Marcialis *et al.*, 2001; Zhang and Yan, 2004; Jain *et al.*, 1999; Yao *et al.*, 2003; Karu and Jain, 1996). Figure 8.16 below shows a fingerprint image that has 2 classes, its primary class is tented arch (T), and its secondary class is left loop (L).

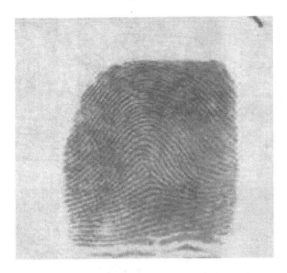

Fig. 8.16.   An example of an ambiguous fingerprint class.

8.4.3 *Performance measurement*

The performance of the fingerprint classification system is measured in terms of error rate or accuracy. The error rate is computed as the ratio between the number of misclassified fingerprints and the total number of samples in the test set. The accuracy is thus the percentage of correctly classified fingerprints.

$$\text{error rate} = \frac{\text{number of misclassified fingerprints}}{\text{total number of fingerprints}} \times 100\% \qquad (8.38)$$

$$\text{accuracy} = 100\% - \text{error rate} \qquad (8.39)$$

In our experiment, all images are being used regardless of its quality. The images in the database are divided into the training set and the testing set. The training set includes 2000 images of the first 1000 pairs for both "f" and "s" instances. The rest of the images are used as the testing set.

8.4.4 *Coefficients used for classification*

The order of constrained non-linear orientation model is a tradeoff between the accuracy of the reconstructed orientation and the conciseness of the model. Based on our extensive experiment, the order of the CNPPM is set to 6 as it can model the orientation well while only requiring a total of 54 coefficients.

In these 54 coefficients, the first-order coefficients $\{a_{01}, a_{10}, b_{01}, b_{10}\}$ exhibit the behavior of the primary core point while the higher-order coefficients act as the correction terms. With higher-order coefficients, the correction terms will affect larger areas of the fingerprint. Figure 8.17 shows the examples of reconstructed orientation with different number of coefficients as the correction

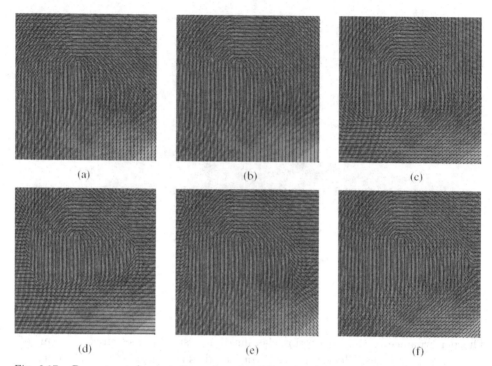

Fig. 8.17. Reconstructed orientation using the different order coefficients. (a) reconstructed orientation using the coefficients of the first 1 order; (b) reconstructed orientation using the coefficients of the first 2 order; (c) reconstructed orientation using the coefficients of the first 3 order; (d) reconstructed orientation using the coefficients of the first 4 order; (e) reconstructed orientation using the coefficients of the first 5 order; and (f) reconstructed orientations using the full coefficients.

terms. Figure 8.17(f) shows the orientation obtained when all the coefficients are used to reconstruct the orientation while Figs. 8.17(a)–(e) show the orientation obtained when only coefficients up to order 1, 2, 3, 4, and 5, respectively of the 6-order model are used to reconstruct the orientation. As expected, Fig. 8.17 shows that as the order of the coefficient used increases, the size of the region with correctly reconstructed orientation increases. Using coefficients up to order 6, the orientation of the entire cropped image can be correctly reconstructed. Since the important pattern of a fingerprint is mainly characterized by the orientation near the primary core point region, we hypothesized that using the first k-order coefficients, here $4 \leq k \leq 6$, is sufficient to perform fingerprint classification with reasonable accuracy. To validate this hypothesis, we feed the coefficients up to order 4, 5, and 6, respectively from the 6-order constrained non-linear model as the input to the classifier, respectively. Table 8.3 shows the classification accuracy achieved.

From Table 8.3, the accuracy of the classification achieved using the number of coefficient up to order 4 and with the full 6 order is quite similar. However, with order 4, the number of input elements to the classifier is reduced significantly,

Table 8.3:   Classification results with different amounts of coefficients

	Up to order 4 (in %)	Up to order 5 (in %)	full 6 order (in %)
Classification accuracy	87.4	87.6	87.9

thus simplifying the structure of the classifier. Therefore, we have opted to use only coefficients up to order 4, which results in only 28 elements for the orientation component.

8.4.5 *Classification results using orientation model*

The publicly available OSU SVM Classier Matlab Toolbox version 3.00 (Ma *et al.*, 2002) is used as the classifier. The RBF kernel is selected. The kernel parameters are selected using the cross-validation and grid-search technique proposed by the developers. First, the training data is separated into v folds, then one subset is tested for each parameter pairs $C = 2^{-5}, 2^{-3}, \ldots, 2^{15}, \gamma = 2^{-15}, 2^{-13}, \ldots, 2^3$ using the classifier trained on the remaining $v - 1$ subset until the best cross-validation accuracy is attained.

In our experiments, the best parameters for g and c are set to $c = 2^8; g = 2^{-7}$. The accuracy rate is 93.5%. There are 468 support vectors in this experiments. If no secondary classes are considered right, the performance reduces to 88.9%.

The confusion matrix is shown in Table 8.4.

8.4.6 *Analysis of the results*

The final result 93.5% is better than the result 87.4% obtained only using the coefficients of the orientation model. In Table 8.5, we listed the performance comparisons using the coefficients, singularity information and their combination.

By analysis, the main errors happen due to the fol lowing reasons:

(1) Missing the information during the normalization. Because the coefficients are extracted from the normalized image, the coefficients cannot be used to

Table 8.4:   Confusion matrix

True class	Hypothesized class					Total
	L	**R**	**W**	**T**	**A**	
L	390	1	4	10	18	423
R	6	408	1	6	12	433
W	11	19	370	0	0	400
T	3	3	0	247	25	278
A	4	4	0	3	455	466
Grand total						2000

L = Left loop; **R** = Right loop; **W** = Whorl; **T** = Tented arch; **A** = Plain arch.

Table 8.5: Performance comparisons using single features and the combinational feature

	Coefficients (in %)	Singular points (in %)	Combination (in %)
Classification accuracy	87.4	88.3	93.5

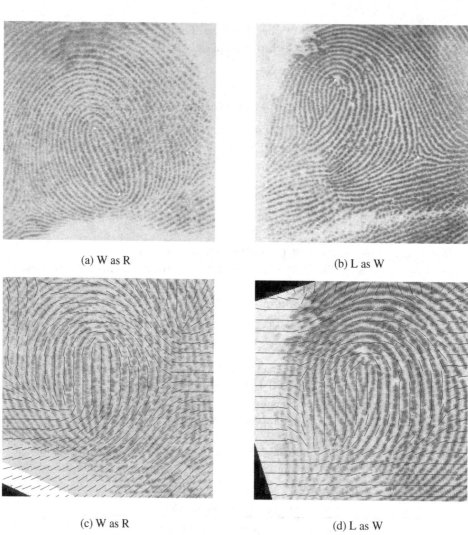

(a) W as R   (b) L as W

(c) W as R   (d) L as W

Fig. 8.18. Examples for the errors related to the whorl type. The images in the same column belong to the same finger. The first row comprises the original images; and the second row comprised the normalized images.

reconstruct the orientation beyond the normalized region. Consequently, some information will be lost for classification. In this experiment, most of such errors happen to the whorl when the two cores are separated too far. Figures 8.18(c) and (d) show the examples. The orientation reconstructed using the constrained non-linear phase portrait model is similar to the loop type image in Fig. 8.18(d). These two images are both misclassified.

(2) Ambiguous information. For loops, when the core and the delta are not separated well (close to each other), there is a small deviation of the loops from the plain arch. Because there is no enough orientations exhibited for the local patterns, the coefficients more likely represent the global patterns. In such case, some plain arches with sharp curvature may be confused as tented arch (examples in Fig. 8.19(b)) or loops and some tented arches or loops with a flat curvature may be misclassified as the plain arch (examples in Fig. 8.19(a)). In Fig. 8.18 (c), the classification fails because one core and one delta are close to each other and are hard to detect.

(3) Misalignment and noise. The alignment is not perfect especially for the arch type because there is no typical core type or delta type existing in the arch type fingerprint. The misalignment will cause the normalization fail, then affect the consistency of the arch type representative using the coefficients. There are some images with the bad quality due to the noise. These images are hard to classify. The examples of misalignment and noise are shown in Fig. 8.20.

(4) Others errors. There are some other errors in Fig. 8.21. Figure 8.21(c) is defined as "T" while its orientation pattern is quite similar to "A." Figure 8.21(a) is

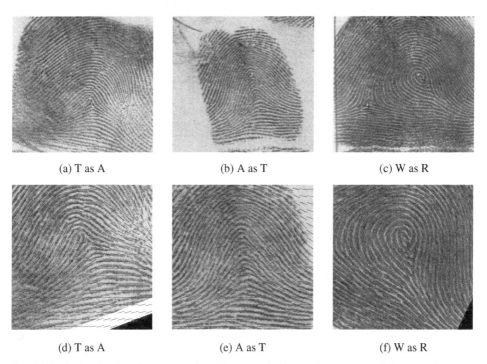

| (a) T as A | (b) A as T | (c) W as R |
| (d) T as A | (e) A as T | (f) W as R |

Fig. 8.19. Examples for the errors related to non-whorl type images. The images in the same column belong to the same finger. The first row comprises the original images; and the second row comprised the normalized images.

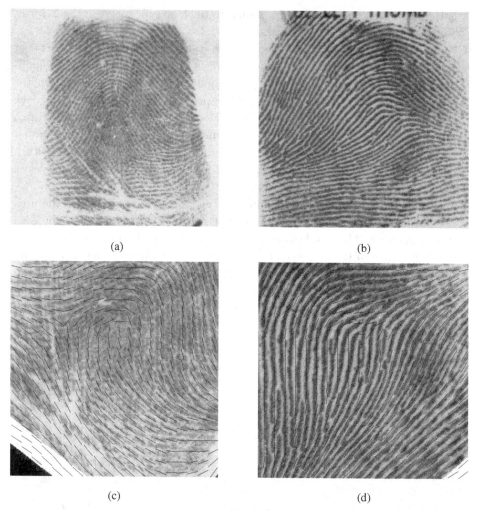

Fig. 8.20. Examples for the noise, misalignment. (a) misalignment and noise (the original image); (b) misalignment (the original image); (c) misalignment and noise (the normalized image of (a)); and (d) misalignment (the normalized image of (a)).

defined as "T" while its orientation pattern is quite similar to "L." Though SPs are correctly detected, its normalized orientation pattern is similar to the "L". The similar situation happens to Fig. 8.19(b), where the image belongs to "L" while its normalized orientation pattern behaves as "T."

Combining the SP information, the accuracy rate is improved to 93.5%. This is due to the complementary of the SP information and the OI model in the following aspects.

(1) For the missing information during the normalization of the whorl, SPs can provide the useful information to amend the wrong classification due to this kind of error. Figure 8.18 can be rectified by the SP information.

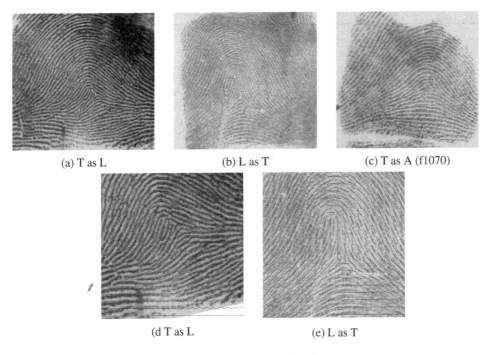

(a) T as L   (b) L as T   (c) T as A (f1070)

(d T as L   (e) L as T

Fig. 8.21.   Examples for the others.

(2) For the ambiguous information of the loops, the SP information is more useful feature to perform classification because the global orientation patterns of loops, tented arch, and the plain arch have small difference when the delta is close to the core as shown in Figs. 8.19(a) and (b).

(3) Misalignment. Misalignment is brought by the complex filter for the arch type. This will cause confusion of the classification. While the complex filter also provides another feature: the magnitude of the complex filter on the SP. This value should be small for the plain arch all the times and it is independent of the alignment. Therefore, we use it as the singularities information to improve the classification performance of the usage of coefficients. Figures 8.20(b) and (d) show an example with the false classification due to the misalignment (true P as L) by orientation model. The examples are correctly classified after combining the SPs information.

8.4.7 *Comparisons*

As a comparison, we list the results reported by other researchers in Table 8.6 together with the result of our proposed approach. These results are reported on the same database NIST DB4.

In Table 8.6, the method proposed by Cappelli *et al.* (2003) has the best performance in both 5- and 4-class problems. Though the feature they used is the orientation image only, they have two different classifiers: the MKL-based

Table 8.6: Literature reviews of the fingerprint classification

Algorithms	Features	Classifier	DB4 results 5 classes (in %)	4 classes (in %)	Comments
Wilson *et al.* (1994)	OI	NN	90.2	—	64 features and 10% rejection
Karu and Jain (1996)	SP	Rule-based	85.4	91.1	—
Jain *et al.* (1999)	GF	k-NN and NN	90	95.8	1.8% rejects, 192 features
Cappelli *et al.* (1999b)	OI	The minimum cost	87.1	—	MKL features from OI
Cappelli *et al.* (2002)	OI	k-NN and minimum cost	92.2	—	PCA features from OI
Chang and Fan (2002)	RI	Rule-based	94.8	—	5.1% rejects; 93.4% for 7 classes
Cappelli *et al.* (2003)	OI	Minimum cost and quadratic DF	95.2	96.3	—
Yao *et al.* (2003)	OI and GF	SVM, RNN	90.0	94.7	1.8% rejects
Nyongesa *et al.* (2004)	SP	RBF, MLP, and FNN	93.75	—	—
Zhang and Yan (2004)	SP and RI	Rule-based	84.3	92.7	—
Park and Park (2005)	FT	Nonlinear-DA	90.7	94.0	—
Neuhaus and Bunke (2005)	OI variance	NN	86.01	—	—
Wang and Dai (2007)	SP	Rule	88.6	—	a close pair of core–delta was defined as a new type SP.
Hong *et al.* (2008)	SP and RI and Fingercode	OVA, SVM and, Naive NN	90.8	94.9	1.8% rejects
Liu (2009)	SP	Decision tree	94.1	95.7	AdaBoosting methods to select feature; multiscale processing.
Our method	OI and SP	SVM	93.5	95	Modeling of OI as features

SP = Singular point; RI = Ridge information; OI = Orientation image; FT = Fourier transformation; GF = Gabor filters; DF = Discriminant function;
NN = Neural networks; k-NN = k-Nearest neighbor; HMM = Hidden markov model; SOM = Self-organizing mapping; and SVM = Supported vector machine;

classifier and the subspace-based pattern discrimination (SPD) classifier. These two classifiers extract the more subtle subclass orientation pattern. In addition, a two-stage strategy is used to transfer the more complex 5-class problem (using the MKL-based classifier in the first stage) into ten 2-class problems (using the SPD classifier in the second stage). In our proposed method, the coefficients extracted using the constrained non-linear phase portrait represents the macroorientation image information, which is not as good as the subclass features using the MKL-based classifier and the SPD classifier. Therefore, subclass feature extraction and a two-stage strategy using two classifiers make their method better than our method where the feature extraction is at the macrolevel. The subclass feature extraction will improve the classification performance, which is not used in this chapter as we use the combinational features of the orientation image information and SPs information to conduct the fingerprint classification. More efforts will be made to extract the subclass features by further analysis of the coefficients.

For the 4-classes problem, Jain *et al.* (1999) also got better performance than our proposed method and used only the single feature. However, it should be noted that in their experiments there are 1.8% rejection of the data. Moreover, our method has a better performance for the 5-class problem than their method. This implies that our method is more suitable for fingerprints classification. In addition, our method takes 32-dimensional feature vector, which is less than 192-dimensional feature vector used by Jain *et al.*

There are also other works to perform the fingerprint classification using the combinational features. In Kawagoe's work (Kawagoe and Tojo, 1984), the authors used a two-stage classification scheme where SPs information was used to classify the fingerprint into 4 groups: whorl, loops, twin loop, and arch. In the second stage, the authors used ridge tracing to further classify the fingerprint into 7 classes. Their method is tested on 92 images. In such small database, it is hard to evaluate the performance.

Yan *et al.* (Zhang and Yan, 2004), Hong and Jain (1999b), and Jain *et al.* (2001) proposed similar methods which was based on the singularities with the pseudoridges as the supplement. In their methods, the SPs were extracted first. Then, the pseudoridges were used to improve the performance. Compared with their methods, our method has the following 3 specified features:

(1) We use the magnitude of the filters' response to represent the singularities information. The magnitude is continuous, so it provides the more representatives of the feature spaces than the Poincare Index-based method where only "0" (nonexisting) and "1" (existing) are used.

(2) The orientation model is trying to provide both the global information beyond the singular regions and the local information near the singular region. Consequently, it provides more information than the pseudoridges tracing.

(3) The interactive mechanism allows to verify the SPs when the orientation is trustworthy and vice versa. This will help improve the orientation reconstruction and the SP detection.

(4) In this work, the orientation model and the singular information can complement each other by the above analysis, which make the performance improve by 5%.

The CNPPM aims to robustly reconstruct the orientation image. Unlike the other OI-based methods, no further analysis of more subtle subclass structure is taken on these coefficients in this work. While using these coefficients together with SPs information, our experimental results take advantage over most of the results reported currently. It implies that the orientation information extracted using the CNPPM and SPs information can be complementary to each other as well. Such combination is found to be helpful to improve the performance of fingerprint classification.

8.5 Conclusion

In this chapter, orientation and singularity information are combined as input features for fingerprint classification. The orientation information is obtained from the orientation model computed using the CNPPM approach while the singularity information is obtained from the response of the complex symmetrical filters. As the computation of the orientation model and SPs are interdependent, a mutual validation approach is suggested whereby potential candidate SPs are detected and then verified using the difference in the orientation model at the SP region with the original orientation. This improves both the accuracy of the SP detection and the orientation model.

The combined orientation and singularity features are used to classify fingerprints using an SVM classifier. The classification accuracy on NIST database 4 reached is shown to be good, achieving a rate of 93.5%.

In this study, all images are used to perform fingerprint classification regardless of their quality. However, some of the orientation image cannot be reconstructed well due to the noise. Thus, the usage of such features will affect the parameter selection during the training and decrease the classification accuracy during the testing. In future, two-stage training will be considered with the initial stage training not considering the poor quality fingerprint images. Furthermore, since more subtle orientation image description in the subclass spaces could result in better classification accuracy, using the CNPPM to discriminate such subclass feature will be further investigated.

References

Arnold, V. I. *An Introduction to Analysis(2nd ed.)* (MIT Press), 1973.

Ballan, M., Sakarya, F. A., and Evans, B. L. A fingerprint classification technique using directional images, in *Proc. IEEE Asilomar Conference on Signals, Systems, and Computers*, pp. 1:101–1:104, 1997.

Bazen, A. and Gerez, S. Systematic methods for the computation of the directional fields and singular points of fingerprints, *IEEE Trans. Pattern Anal. Machine Intelligence* **24**, 7, 905–919, 2002.

Bernard, S., Boujemaa, N., Vitale, D., and Bricot, C. Fingerprint classification using kohonen topologic map, in *Proc. International Conference on Image Processing*, pp. 3:230–233, 2001.

Candela, G., Grother, P., Watson, C., Wilkinson, R., and Wilson, C. Pcasys: a pattern-level classification automation system for fingerprints, National institute of standards and technology technical report, 1995.

Cappelli, R., Lumini, A., Maio, D., and Maltoni, D. Fingerprint classification by directional image partitioning, *IEEE Trans. Pattern Anal. Machine Intelligence* **21**, 5, 402–421, 1999a.

Cappelli, R., Maio, D., and Maltoni, D. Fingerprint classification based on multi-space kl, in *Proc. Workshop on Automatic Identification Advances Technologies*, pp. 117–120, 1999b.

Cappelli, R., Maio, D., and Maltoni, D. A multi-classifier approach to fingerprint classification, *Pattern Anal. Appl.* **5**, 2, 136–144, 2002.

Cappelli, R., Maio, D., Maltoni, D., and Nanni, L. A two-stage fingerprint classification system, in *Proc. ACM SIGMM workshop on Biometrics methods and applications*, pp. 95–99, 2003.

Chang, J. and Fan, K. A new model for fingerprint classification by ridge distribution sequences, *Pattern Recognition* **35**, 6, 1209–1223, 2002.

Cho, B.-H., Kim, J.-S., Bae, J.-H., Bae, I.-G., and Yoo, K.-Y. Fingerprint image classification by core analysis, in *Proc. 5th International Conference on Signal Processing*, pp. 3:1534–3:1537, 2000.

Chong, M., Ngee, T., Jun, L., and Gay, R. Geometric framework for fingerprint image classification, *Pattern Recognition* **30**, 9, 1475–1488, 1997.

Dass, S. C. and Jain, A. K. Fingerprint classification using orientation field flow curves, in *Proc. 4th Indian Conference on Computer Vision, Graphics and Image Processing*, 2004.

Eldèn, L. Perturbation theory for the least squares problem with linear equality constraints, *SIAM J. Num. Anal.* **17**, 3, 338–350, 1980.

Federal Bureau of Investigation, *The Science of Fingerprints: Classification and Uses* (U.S. Department of Justice), 1984.

Ford, R., Strickland, R., and Thomas, B. A. Image models for 2-d flow visualization and compression, *CVGIP: Graphical Models Image Process.* **56**, 1, 75–93, 1994.

Gunn R. S. *Support Vector Machines for Classification and Regression* (Univerity of Sounthampton), 1998.

Halici, U. and Ongun, G. Fingerprint classification through self-organizing features maps modified to treat uncertainties, *Processings of the IEEE* **84**, 10, 1497–1512, 1996.

Hong, L. and Jain, A. Classification of fingerprint images, in *Proc. 11th Scandinavian Conference on Image Analysis*, 1999a.

Hong, L. and Jain, A. Classification of images, in *Proc. 11th Scandinavian Conference on Image Analysis*, 1999b.

Hong, L., Wan, Y., and Jain, A. Fingerprint image enhancement: algorithm and performance evaluation, *IEEE Trans. Pattern Anal. Machine Intelligence* **20**, 8, 777–789, 1998.

Hong, J.-H., Min, J.-K., Cho, U.-K., and Cho, S.-B. Fingerprint classification using one-vs-all support vector machines dynamically ordered with naive bayes classifiers, *Pattern Recognition* **41**, 2, 662–671, 2008.

Hou, Z. and Li, J. Fingerprint orientation analysis with topological modeling, in *Proc. Intl. Conf. Pattern Recognition*, pp. 1–4, 2008.

Jain, A. and Minut, S. Hierarchical kernel fitting for fingerprint classification and alignment, in *Proc. Int. Conf. Pattern Recognition*, pp. 2:469–473, 2002.

Jain, A. K., Prabhakar, S., and Lin, H. A multichannel approach to fingerprint classification, *IEEE Trans. Pattern Anal. Machine Intelligence* **21**, 4, 348–359, 1999.

Jain, A., Prabhakar, S., and Pankanti, S. Matching and classification: a case study in fingerprint domain, in *Proc. Indian National Science Academy*, **67**, 67–85, 2001.

Kamei, T. and Mizoguchi, M. Fingerprint preselection using eigenfeatures, in *Proc. IEEE Conf. Comput. Vision Pattern Recognition*, pp. 918–923, 1998.

Kamijo, M. Classifying fingerprint images using neural network: deriving the classification state, in *Proc. the Third International Conference On Neural Network*, pp. 1932–1937, 1993.

Karu, K. and Jain, A. K. Fingerprint classification, *Pattern Recognition* **29**, 3, 389–404, 1996.

Kawagoe, M. and Tojo, A. Fingerprint pattern classification, *Pattern Recognition* **17**, 3, 295–303, 1984.

Klimanee, C. and Nguyen, D. T. Classification of fingerprints using singular points and their principal axes, in *Proc. International Conference on Image Processing*, pp. 849–852, 2004.

Li, J., Yau, W.-Y., and Wang, H. Combining singular points and orientation image information for fingerprint classification, *Pattern Recognition* **41**, 1, 353–366, 2008.

Liu, M. Fingerprint classification based on adaboost learning from singularity features, *Pattern Recognition* **42**, 2009.

Ma, J., Zhao, Y., and Ahalt, S. *OSU SVM Classier Matlab Toolbox (ver 3.00)*, http://eewww.eng.ohiostate.edu/maj/osusvm/, 2002.

Maio, D. and Maltoni, D. A structural approach to fingerprint classification, in *Proc. Int. Conf. Pattern Recognition*, pp. 3:578–585, 1996.

Marcialis, G., Roli, F., and Frasconi, P. Fingerprint classification by combination of flat and structural approaches, in *Proc. Int. Conf. Audio- and Video-Based Biometric Person Authentication*, pp. 241–246, 2001.

Moayer, B. and Fu, K. S. A syntactic approach to fingerprint pattern recognition, *Pattern Recognition* **7**, 1-2, 1–23, 1975.

Moayer, B. and Fu, K. S. An application of stochastic languages to fingerprint pattern recognition, *Pattern Recognition* **8**, 3, 173–179, 1976.

Mohamed, S. and Nyongesa, H. Automatic fingerprint classification system using fuzzy neural techniques, in *Proc. International Conference on Fuzzy Systems*, pp. 1:358–1:362, 2002.

Neuhaus, M. and Bunke, H. A graph matching-based approach to fingerprint classification using directional variance, in *Proc. 5th Audio- and Video-Based Biometric Person Authentication*, pp. 191–200, 2005.

Nilsson, K. and Bigun, J. Localization of corresponding points in fingerprints by complex filtering, *Pattern Recognition Lett.* **24**, 3, 2135–2144, 2003.

Nyongesa, H. O., Al-Khayatt, S., Mohamed, S. M., and Mahmoud, M. Fast robust fingerprint feature extraction and classification, *J. Intelligent Robotic Syst.* **40**, 1, 103–112, 2004.

Park, C. and Park, H. Fingerprint classification using fast fourier transform and nonlinear discriminant analysis, *Pattern Recognition* **38**, 4, 495–503, 2005.

Ram, S., Bischof, H., and Birchbauer, J. Modelling fingerprint ridge orientation using legendre polynomials, *Pattern Recognition* **43**, 1, 342–357, 2010.

Ramo, P., Tico, M., Onnia, V., and Saarinen, J. Optimized singular point detection algorithm for fingerprint images, in *Proc. Intl. Conf. Image Processing*, pp. 242–245, 2001.

Ratha, N. K., Karu, K., Chen, S., and Jain, A. K. A real-time matching system for large fingerprint databases, *IEEE Trans. Pattern Anal. Machine Intelligence* **18**, 8, 799–813, 1996.

Senior, A. A combination fingerprint classifier, *IEEE Trans. Pattern Anal. Machine Intelligence* **21**, 5, 402–421, 1999.

Shah, S. and Sastry, P. Fingerprint classification using a feedback-based line detector, *IEEE Transactions on Systems, Man, and Cybernetics-Part B: Cybernettics* **34**, 1, 85–94, 2004.

Sherlock, B. and Monro, D. A model for interpreting fingerprint topology, *Pattern Recognition* **26**, 7, 1047–1055, 1993.

Shen, C. and Jain, R. Vector field analysis for oriented patterns, *IEEE Trans. Pattern Anal. Machine Intelligence* **16**, 9, 946–950, 1994.

Vizcaya, P. and Gerhardt, L. A nonlinear orientation model for global description of fingerprints, *Pattern Recognition* **29**, 7, 1221–1231, 1996.

Wang, L. and Dai, M. Application of a new type of singular points in fingerprint classification, *Pattern Recognition Lett.* **28**, 13, 1640–1650, 2007.

Wang, Y., Hu, J., and Phillips, D. A fingerprint orientation model based on 2d fourier expansion (fomfe) and its application to singular point detection and fingerprint indexing, *IEEE Trans. Pattern Anal. Machine Intelligence* **29**, 4, 573–585, 2007.

Wilson, C., Candela, G., and Watson, C. Neural network fingerprint classification, *J. Artifical Neural Networks* **1**, 2, 203–228, 1994.

Xu, Y., Yang, S. X., He, G., and Zhang, X. Macroscopic curvature-based fingerprint feature extraction and analysis, in *Proc. DCDIS 4th International Conference on Engineering Applications and Computational Algorithms*, pp. 584–589, 2005.

Yao, Y., Marcialis, G., Pontil, M., Frasconi, P., and Roli, F. Combining flat and structured representations for fingerprint classification with recursive neural networks and support vector machines, *Pattern Recognition* **36**, 2, 397–406, 2003.

Zhang, Q. and Yan, H. Fingerprint classification based on extraction and analysis of singularities and pseudo ridges, *Pattern Recognition* **37**, 11, 2233–2243, 2004.

Zhou, J. and Gu, J. Modeling orientation fields of fingerprints with rational complex functions, *Pattern Recognition* **37**, 2, 389–391, 2004.

Zhou, J., Gu, J., and Zhang, D. A combination model for orientation field of fingerprints, *Pattern Recognition* **37**, 3, 543–553, 2004.

Part IV

Gait

Chapter 9

HUMAN IDENTIFICATION BY FUSION
OF MULTIPLE GAIT REPRESENTATIONS

Euntai Kim*, Sungjun Hong, and Heesung Lee

School of Electrical & Electronic Engineering
Yonsei University, Korea
* etkim@yonsei.ac.kr

9.1 Introduction

Biometrics is a technology that observes the physiological and behavioral characteristics of humans and authenticates humans based on these characteristics (Gavrila, 1999). Recently, biometrics has received much attention from scientists and engineers due to increasing demands for automatic authentication and access control systems at airports, banks, and other locations that requires a high level of security.

Gait is a biometric, which aims to recognize people from their manner of walking. Unlike other biometrics, gait measurement is unobtrusive and can be captured at a distance. Moreover, it can be detected and measured at low resolution (Boulgouris *et al.*, 2005). In contrast, most other biometrics such as fingerprint (Jain *et al.*, 1999), face (Turk and Pentland, 1991), iris (Daugaman, 1993), signature (Qi and Hunt, 1995), and voice (Rabiner and Juang, 1993) are restricted to controlled environments. They can be captured only by physical contact or at a close distance from the probe. Even face and iris requires a high-resolution probe. Gait can thus be alternatively used in situations where other biometrics might not be applicable. Therefore, there has been an increase in research related to gait recognition over recent years.

Gait analysis can mainly be classified under two major approaches: model-based approach and model-free approach (Boulgouris *et al.*, 2005; Han and Bhanu, 2006). The model-based approach adopts a human model and maps those extracted image features onto the components of the human model. Unfortunately, the model-based approaches require high-quality gait sequences and high computational cost to recover related human parameters in order to achieve good recognition performance. Furthermore, many approaches are limited by the imperfect foreground segmentation and the high computational cost incurred. Cunado *et al.* (1997) extracted a gait signature by fitting the movement of the thighs to an articulated pendulum-like motion model. Johnson and Bobick (2001) proposed a multiview gait recognition method using the static body parameters such as the height, the distance between head and pelvis, and the distance between the feet, which are measurements taken from static gait frames. Lee and Grimson (2002) described a moment-based representation of gait appearance and applied it to identification. In their work, a silhouette of a walking person was divided into seven regions and ellipses were fit to each region, forming a gait-feature vector composing of averages of the centroid and the aspect ratio, etc. Wagg and Nixon (2004) proposed a more detailed model using ellipse for the torso and the head, line segments for the legs, and a rectangle for each foot.

In contrast, the model-free approach acts directly on a video sequence and characterize the walking pattern by signal analysis. Unlike the model-based approach, the model-free approach does not assume any specific human model, thereby saving much computational resources. Han and Bhanu (2006) proposed a model-free gait representation, called gait energy image (GEI), and derived both real- and synthetic templates for subsequent gait matching. A fusion of synthetic- and real templates was adopted to obtain the final recognition results. Yang *et al.* (2008) obtained a dynamic region in GEI which reflects the walking manner of an individual, called an enhanced GEI. Li *et al.* (2008) decomposed a silhouette into seven components and performed human gait recognition based on each of the seven individual components or by combining the seven components. Wang *et al.* (2003) used the outer contour directly instead of the entire silhouette and unwrapped it into a distance signal to recognize a person. Among other things, the width and projection of silhouette are among the best features in gait since they reflect the direct change of gait pattern. Kale *et al.* (2003) proposed a gait representation called the width vector profile. The width of the outer contour of a silhouette image is used as a gait feature in their works. Hong *et al.* (2009) used multiple gait representations called the multibipolarized contour vector and combined them to identify the walking individuals. These gait representations are described in detail in the next section. Liu *et al.* (2002) used the horizontal and vertical projections of silhouettes as a gait representation. Ekinci (2006) developed automatic gait recognition system based on analyzing the multiple projections to silhouette. The horizontal projection representation looks similar to the width of silhouette but it is more robust to silhouette errors and can be computed in real time (Boulgouris *et al.*, 2005).

In this chapter, multiple 1D templates based on the width representation and the projection representation are presented. This chapter is an extended version of the Hong's previous work (Hong *et al.*, 2009). The templates based on the width of a silhouette image are modified from multibipolarized contour vectors (MBCVs) in Hong *et al.* (2009). In addition to the previous work, the templates based on the projection representation are also considered and extensive experiments are conducted. As in Hong's previous work (Hong *et al.*, 2009), gait representations are obtained from silhouette images not only in the vertical direction but also in the horizontal direction. Furthermore, the templates are fused at a feature level and a score level and extensive experiments are conducted to test the effectiveness of the independent templates and their combinations. In the experiments, a variety of fusion rules that combine the match scores are adopted.

9.2 Gait Representation

9.2.1 *Template based on the width of a silhouette image*

The gait of different subjects varies in period, width, and distribution due to the diversity in individuals' geometrical configurations, Kale *et al.* (2003) used the width of the outer contour of the silhouette as a gait feature in their research.

In this section, a 1D gait representation called the width vector is presented. This vector is motivated by Kale's works. Unlike Kale's work in which the whole width of the contour was considered as a single-feature vector, here, the width contour is decomposed into two halves along the horizontal and vertical directions and a total of four width vectors are considered as independent feature vectors in this chapter. In other words, the contour is decomposed into the left- and right halves along the vertical direction and into the upper- and lower halves along the horizontal direction.

From these considerations, the four templates for a silhouette image with the size of $H \times W$ at time t are defined as follows:

Left width vector

$$W_L(t) = [w_L^1(t), w_L^2(t), \ldots, w_L^y(t), \ldots, w_L^H(t)] \in \mathbf{R}^H \tag{9.1}$$

$$\text{with } w_L^y(t) = |x_L^y(t) - W/2| \tag{9.2}$$

where $x_L^y(t)$ represents the x-coordinate values of the leftmost boundary pixel along a given row y at time t and H and W are the height and width of a silhouette image, respectively.

Right width vector

$$W_R(t) = [w_R^1(t), w_R^2(t), \ldots, w_R^y(t), \ldots, w_R^H(t)] \in \mathbf{R}^H \tag{9.3}$$

$$\text{with } w_R^y(t) = |x_R^y(t) - W/2| \tag{9.4}$$

where $x_R^y(t)$ represents the x-coordinate values of the rightmost boundary pixel along a given row y at time t and H and W are the height and width of a silhouette image, respectively.

Up width vector

$$W_U(t) = [w_U^1(t), w_U^2(t), \ldots, w_U^x(t), \ldots, w_U^W(t)] \in \mathbf{R}^W \tag{9.5}$$

$$\text{with } w_U^x(t) = |y_U^x(t) - H/2| \tag{9.6}$$

where $y_U^x(t)$ represents the y-coordinate values of the uppermost boundary pixel along a given column x at time t and H and W are the height and width of a silhouette image, respectively.

Down width vector

$$W_D(t) = [w_D^1(t), w_D^2(t), \ldots, w_D^x(t), \ldots, w_D^W(t)] \in \mathbf{R}^W \tag{9.7}$$

$$\text{with } w_D^x(t) = |y_D^x(t) - H/2| \tag{9.8}$$

where $y_D^x(t)$ represents the x-coordinate values of the lowermost boundary pixel along a given column x at time t and H and W are the height and width of a silhouette image, respectively.

These templates are similar to the multibipolarized contour vectors of Hong *et al.* (2009) except for using the arithmetic absolute values of differences as a measurement. Figure 9.1 shows the geometrical descriptions for the above proposed gait representation and Fig. 9.2 depicts some examples of width vectors for a gait cycle.

9.2.2 *Template based on the projection of a silhouette image*

Liu *et al.* (2002) used the projection of a silhouette image as a gait-feature vector. In their work, the vertical projection vector is defined as a count of the number of

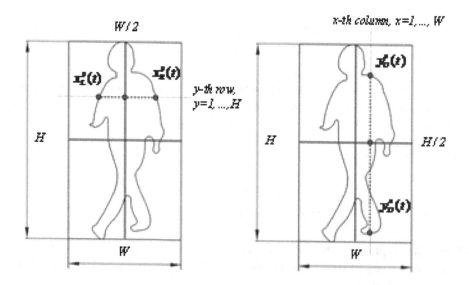

Fig. 9.1.   Geometrical descriptions for four kinds of the width vector.

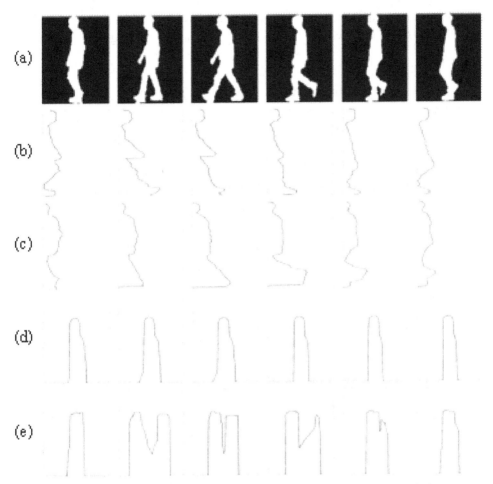

Fig. 9.2. Examples of (a) normalized silhouette image for a walking subject and their corresponding (b) left, (c) right, (d) up, and (e) down width vectors.

non-zero pixels in row of a silhouette image. It is actually *a frieze pattern* in the literature of mathematics and geometry. As for the width vector, four templates are considered in the projection vector of a silhouette image: *left, right, up, and down projection vectors*. When $I_{xy}(t) \in \{0,1\}$ denotes a binarized silhouette image with the size of $H \times W$ at time t, the templates in the projection of a silhouette image $I_{xy}(t)$ are defined as follows:

Left projection vector

$$P_L(t) = [p_L^1(t), p_L^2(t), \ldots, p_L^y(t), \ldots, p_L^H(t)] \in \mathbf{R}^H \qquad (9.9)$$

$$\text{with } p_L^y(t) = \sum_{x=1}^{W/2} I_{xy}(t) \qquad (9.10)$$

along a given row y at time t where x and y being indices in the 2D image coordinate, and W and H being the width and the height of a silhouette image, respectively.

Right projection vector

$$P_R(t) = [p_R^1(t), p_R^2(t), \ldots, p_R^y(t), \ldots, p_R^H(t)] \in \mathbf{R}^H \qquad (9.11)$$

$$\text{with } p_R^y(t) = \sum_{x=W/2}^{W} I_{xy}(t) \qquad (9.12)$$

along a given row y at time t where x and y being indices in the 2D image coordinate, and W and H being the width and the height of a silhouette image, respectively.

Up projection vector

$$P_U(t) = [p_U^1(t), p_U^2(t), \ldots, p_U^x(t), \ldots, p_U^W(t)] \in \mathbf{R}^W \qquad (9.13)$$

$$\text{with } p_U^x(t) = \sum_{y=1}^{H/2} I_{xy}(t) \qquad (9.14)$$

along a given column x at time t where x and y being indices in the 2D image coordinate, and W and H being the width and the height of a silhouette image, respectively.

Down projection vector

$$P_D(t) = [p_D^1(t), p_D^2(t), \ldots, p_D^x(t), \ldots, p_D^W(t)] \in \mathbf{R}^W \qquad (9.15)$$

$$\text{with } p_D^x(t) = \sum_{y=H/2}^{H} I_{xy}(t) \qquad (9.16)$$

along a given column x at time t where x and y being indices in the 2D image coordinate, and W and H being the width and the height of a silhouette image, respectively.

Some examples of the projection vectors are shown in Fig. 9.3.

9.3 Gait Recognition

9.3.1 *Individual features without fusion*

In this section, single templates are used to identify subjects without adopting any fusion methodology. Let T_i and R_j denote the templates corresponding to the ith subject in the test database and the jth subject in the reference database, respectively. The match score to measure their dissimilarity is defined as

$$d(T_i, R_j) = \|T_i - R_j\|_2 = \left\| \frac{1}{N_i} \sum_{m=1}^{N_i} t_i(m) - \frac{1}{N_j} \sum_{n=1}^{N_j} r_j(n) \right\|_2 \qquad (9.17)$$

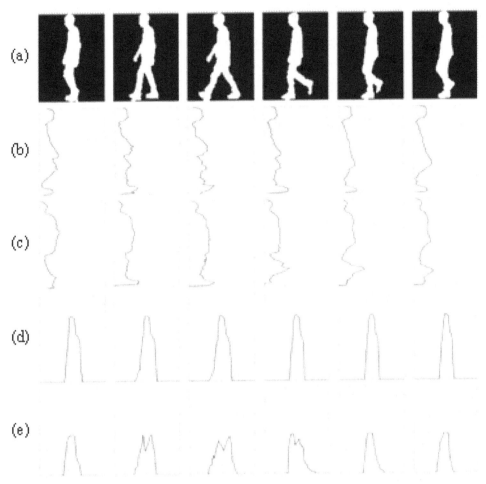

Fig. 9.3. Examples of (a) normalized silhouette image for a walking subject and their corresponding (b) left, (c) right, (d) up, and (e) down projection vectors.

where $\|\cdot\|$ is the ℓ^2-norm and $t_i(m)$ and $r_j(n)$ denote one of the proposed templates (introduced in Sec. 9.2) belonging to the ith subject in the test database and the jth subject in the reference database, respectively. N_i and N_j are the total number of feature vectors extracted from a gait sequence, and m and n are the frame indices (or time indices), respectively. Here, a smaller match score means a closer match between the templates. Thus, the class label of a test template is predicted by

$$\mathrm{cls}(T_i) = \arg\min_j\{d(T_i, R_j)\}, \quad j = 1, 2, \ldots, C \qquad (9.18)$$

9.3.2 *Feature-level fusion*

To improve the recognition performance, we combine some of the proposed templates into a new template at a feature level. The combined templates based on the width representation are given by

$$W_V(t) = [W_L(t), W_R(t)] \in \mathbf{R}^{2H}$$

$$W_H(t) = [W_U(t), W_D(t)] \in \mathbf{R}^{2W}$$

$$W_{\text{ALL}}(t) = [W_L(t), W_R(t), W_U(t), W_D(t)] \in \mathbf{R}^{2(H+W)} \qquad (9.19)$$

Here, $W_V(t)$, $W_H(t)$, and $W_{\text{ALL}}(t)$ are the combined templates of vertical templates, horizontal templates, and all templates based on the width representation, respectively. Similarly, the combined templates based on the projection representation are given by

$$P_V(t) = [P_L(t), P_R(t)] \in \mathbf{R}^{2H}$$

$$P_H(t) = [P_U(t), P_D(t)] \in \mathbf{R}^{2W}$$

$$P_{\text{ALL}}(t) = [P_L(t), P_R(t), P_U(t), P_D(t)] \in \mathbf{R}^{2(H+W)} \qquad (9.20)$$

where $P_V(t)$, $P_H(t)$, and $P_{\text{ALL}}(t)$ are combined templates of the vertical templates, the horizontal templates, and all the templates based on the width representation, respectively.

9.3.3 *Score-level fusion*

Instead of using a single distance for the evaluation of similarity between the ith and the jth subjects, we use multiple distances and fuse them at a score level. Several individual templates are applied and different distances associated with each of the templates are combined by min, max, median, product, simple sum (Kittler *et al.*, 1998), and weighted sum (Huang and Boulgouris, 2008) of the distances. Let $d_k(T_i, R_j)$ denote the match score of the ith subject in the test database and the jth subject in the reference database based on the kth template. Then, the combined match score using the min rule is given by

$$D(T_i, R_j) = \min_k \{d_k(T_i, R_j)\}, \quad k = 1, 2, \ldots, K, \qquad (9.21)$$

where K is the total number of different templates. Similarly, the match scores of different templates can be easily combined using the max rule or the median rule. Another possible total match score is a product of distances given by

$$D(T_i, R_j) = \prod_{k=1}^{K} d_k(T_i, R_j) \qquad (9.22)$$

Analogously, the total match score, which is equal to simple sum of distances is given by

$$D(T_i, R_j) = \sum_{k=1}^{K} d_k(T_i, R_j) \qquad (9.23)$$

Furthermore, Huang and Boulgouris (2008) proposed a fusion methodology based on the weighted sum rule at a score level. In their works, the weight is determined to yield a small total distance when $i = j$, and a large total distance when $i \neq j$. The combined total distance is given by

$$D(T_i, R_j) = \sum_{k=1}^{K} w_k d_k(T_i, R_j) \tag{9.24}$$

where w_k is the weight of each distance between two subjects and K is the total number of different templates. The weights are calculated using statistical processing based on the importance of each template. Let d_{bk}, $k = 1, 2, \ldots, K$ be the within class distance between a test subject and its corresponding reference subjects and d_{fk}, $k = 1, 2, \ldots, K$ be the between class distance between a test subject and a reference subject other than its corresponding subject. Then, the optimal weight of each template is given by

$$w_k = \frac{m_{d_{bk}} - m_{d_{fk}}}{\sigma_{d_{bk}}^2 + \sigma_{d_{fk}}^2} \tag{9.25}$$

where $m_{d_{bk}}$ and $m_{d_{fk}}$ are the means of d_{bk} and d_{fk}, and $\sigma_{d_{bk}}$ and $\sigma_{d_{fk}}$ are the standard deviations of d_{bk} and d_{fk}, respectively (Huang and Boulgouris, 2008).

9.4 Experiments

9.4.1 *Gait database*

To demonstrate the validity of the suggested gait-recognition method, we use the NLPR database (Wang *et al.*, 2003) in our experimentation. The NLPR database is a concurrent gait database available in the public domain and is also called CASIA gait dataset A. The database includes 20 subjects. All subjects walk along a straight-line path at free cadences in three different views with respect to the image plane, namely, canonical $(0°)$, oblique $(45°)$, and frontal $(90°)$ views. Each subject has four sequences for each viewing angle: two sequences from left to right and two sequences in the reverse direction. Thus, the database includes a total of 240 gait sequences. In this experiment, only 80 gait sequences captured at a canonical view are considered. The length of each image sequence is about 90 frames but differs, depending on the pace of the walker. These sequence images are 24-bit full color, captured at a rate of 25 frames per second, and have a resolution of 352×240 pixels.

9.4.2 *Preprocessing*

In preprocessing, the background should be subtracted from the original visual image to extract a binarized foreground image involving human movements and the extracted foreground image should be normalized. In the experiments, since the NLPR gait database provides foreground images, the background subtraction is skipped here.

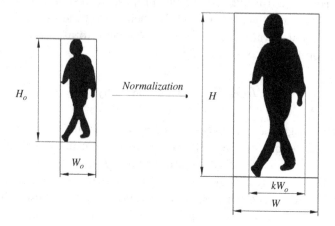

Fig. 9.4.   Silhouette normalization based on height.

The foreground images are normalized to reduce the effect of changes in silhouette size in walking. Let us denote the size of original silhouette by $H_o \times W_o$, and the size of the normalized silhouette image by $H \times W$. We normalize the size of the silhouette image based on height. In other words, we resize the width of silhouettes in the horizontal direction with a scale factor of $k = H/H_o$, so that the width of the normalized silhouette is kW_o. Finally, as shown in Fig. 9.4, we align the normalized silhouette by shifting its horizontal center of mass to the horizontal center of frame, $W/2$. In this experiment, all the silhouette images are normalized into the size of 150×120 pixels.

9.4.3 *Performance evaluation criterion*

The correct classification rate (CCR) is adopted as the performance measure in the experiments. The CCR is the ratio of correctly classified number of subjects to the total number of subjects in the test database defined by

$$CCR = \frac{\text{Number of correctly classified subjects}}{\text{Total number of subjects in the test database}} \qquad (9.26)$$

and the leave-one-out cross validation is performed for all experimental results concerned.

Further, the cumulative match score (CMS) is also considered. In identification problem, the question is not always "Is the top match correct?" but "Is the correct answer in the top n matches?" This gives the information about the number of samples needed in order to get a desired level of performance (Phillips *et al.*, 2000). For example, rank 5 results report the ratio of test subjects whose actual match in the reference database was in the top 5 matches. In particular, rank 1 is equal to

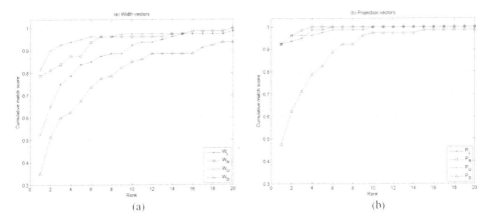

Fig. 9.5.   CMSs for (a) the width vectors and (b) the projection vectors.

Table 9.1:   The CCRs of the width vectors and the projection vectors

Template	Rank 1	Rank 5
Left width W_L	0.8125	0.9500
Right width W_R	0.7875	0.8750
Up width W_U	0.5250	0.8375
Down width W_D	0.3500	0.6750
Left projection P_L	0.9250	0.9750
Right projection P_R	0.9250	1.0000
Up projection P_U	0.9250	0.9875
Down projection P_D	0.4750	0.8250

the CCR. In this experiment, we consider the CMS at rank 1 and rank 5 to compare the performance of gait recognition for human identification.

9.4.4 *Results (i): individual features without fusion*

The CMSs and the CCRs are shown in Fig. 9.5 and Table 9.1 for individual templates. It can be observed that the projection vectors outperform the width vectors. Further, left and right vectors exhibit better performance than up and down vectors except the up projection vector. This means that the left and right vectors capture most of the gait information of the walking subjects and are among the most discriminate vectors.

9.4.5 *Results (ii): feature-level fusion*

Shown in Fig. 9.6 and Table 9.2 are the CMSs and the CCR for the combination of width vectors or the projection vectors at a feature level. Compared to the results in Sec. 9.4.4, the fused feature vectors show better performance than the individual

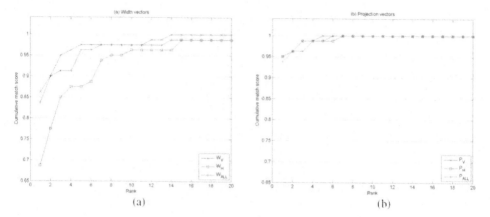

Fig. 9.6.   CMSs for (a) the combined width vectors and (b) the combined projection vectors.

Table 9.2:   The CCRs of the combined width vectors and the combined projection vectors

Template	Rank 1	Rank 5
Vertical width W_V	0.8625	0.9750
Horizontal width W_H	0.6875	0.8750
All width W_{ALL}	0.8375	0.9625
Vertical projection P_V	0.9375	1.000
Horizontal projection P_H	0.9500	0.9875
All projection P_{ALL}	0.9500	0.9875

ones. In particular, the combination of the left and right vertical width vectors exhibits a substantial improvement from the individual templates.

9.4.6 *Results (iii): score-level fusion*

The match scores between the left, the right, the up, and the down vectors based on the width and the projection of a silhouette image are combined by several combination rules. Here, K, the number of different templates, is 4 (see Sec. 9.3.3). Among all the combination rules, the combination of the width vectors by the product and the weighted sum rules and the combination of the projection vectors by the simple sum and the weighted sum rules exhibit the relatively good performances as shown in Fig. 9.7 and Table 9.3. Since the weighted sum rule works well for both the projection and width vectors, it can be concluded that the weighted sum rule is the most attractive score-level fusion method in our gait-recognition experiments.

Further, it can be noted from Fig. 9.8 that the fusion at a score-level demonstrates the significant improvement from not only the individual recognition but also the feature-level fusion. In particular, the fusion of all the width vectors at a

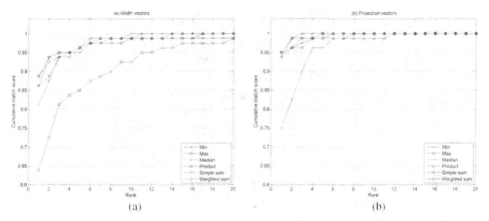

Fig. 9.7. CMSs for (a) the width vectors and (b) the projection vectors adopting score-level fusion with various combination rules.

Table 9.3: CCRs of (a) the width vectors and (b) the projection vectors adopting score-level fusion with various combination rules

	Width vector		Projection vector	
Score-fusion rule	Rank 1	Rank 5	Rank 1	Rank 5
Min	0.8125	0.9625	0.7500	0.9625
Max	0.6375	0.8500	0.9500	0.9875
Median	0.8625	0.9500	0.9375	0.9875
Product	0.8875	0.9625	0.9375	1.0000
Simple sum	0.8625	0.9625	0.9500	1.0000
Weighted sum	0.8875	0.9625	0.9500	1.0000

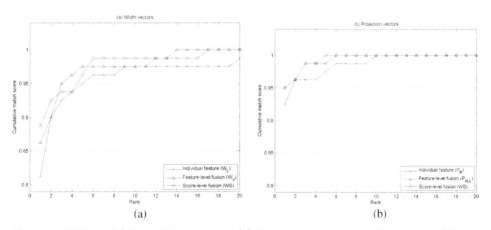

Fig. 9.8. CMSs for (a) the width vectors and (b) the projection vectors with respect to different fusion methodologies.

Fig. 9.9. Gait sequence involving the binary silhouette images corrupted by the imperfect foreground segmentation.

score level using the weighted sum rule outperforms the all the possible combinations of the templates at feature level in terms of the CMSs at rank 1. Therefore, it can be concluded that the score-level fusion is more reliable than the feature-level fusion when all the templates are used.

Shown in Fig. 9.9 is the example of a gait sequence that only the score-level fusion correctly classifies but the feature-level fusion and the individual recognition misclassify. From the example, it can be noted that the score-level fusion outperforms the other two methods when the binarized silhouette image includes quite a few corrupted pixels due to the imperfect foreground segmentation.

Besides, the fusion at a score level demonstrates the improvement from the fusion at a feature level as well as of the individual templates. Particularly, the fusion of multiple distances associated with all the features at a score level outperforms the combination of all the templates at feature level in terms of the CMSs. Thus, we can conclude that the score-level fusion shows more reliability than the feature-level fusion when all the templates are used for human identification.

9.5 Conclusion

In this work, a multiple number of gait representations were proposed to measure the dissimilarity among walking subjects. All the representations are based on the width and the projection of a silhouette image. The first experiment on the NLPR gait database showed that each template has unequal discrimination power and insufficient recognition performance for human identification. To improve the performance, we adopted a combination of templates at feature- and at match-score level. By adopting the fusion methodology, significant improvement in terms of recognition accuracy was achieved comparing with those results obtained from individual templates.

References

Boulgouris, N., Hatzinakos, D., and Plataniotis, K. Gait recognition: a challenging signal processing technology for biometric identification, *IEEE Signal Processing Magazine* **22**, 6, 78–90, 2005.

Cunado, D., Nash, J. M., Nixon, M. S., and Carter, J. N. Gait extraction and description by evidence-gathering, in *Proc. Int. Conf. Audio- and Video-Based Biometric Person Authentication*, pp. 43–48, 1999.

Daugaman, J. High confidence visual recognition of persons by a test of statistical independence, *IEEE Trans. Pattern Anal. Machine Intelligence* **15**, 11, 1148–1161, 1993.

Ekinci, M. Automatic gait recognition by multi-projection analysis, in *Proc. Int. Conf. Automatic Face and Gesture Recognition*, pp. 517–522, 2006.

Gavrila, D. The visual analysis of human movement: a survey, *Comput. Vision Image Understanding* **73**, 1, 82–98, 1999.

Han, J. and Bhanu, B. Individual recognition using gait energy image, *IEEE Trans. Pattern Anal. Machine Intelligence* **28**, 2, 316–322, 2006.

Hong, S., Lee, H., Toh, K.-A., and Kim, E. Gait recognition using multi-bipolarized contour vector, *Int. J. Control, Automation, Syst.* **7**, 5, 799–808, 2009.

Huang, X. and Boulgouris, N. Human gait recognition based on multiview gait sequences, *Eurasip J. Adv. Signal Processing* **8**, 2008.

Jain, A., Hong, L., Pankanti, S., and Bolle, R. An identity verification system using fingerprints, *Proc. IEEE* **85**, 9, 1365–1388, 1999.

Johnson, A. Y. and Bobick, A. F. A multi-view method for gait recognition using static body parameters, in *Proc. Int. Conf. on Audio- and Video-Based Biometric Person Authentication*, pp. 301–311, 2001.

Kale, A., Cuntoor, N., Yegnanarayana, B., Rajagopalan, A. N., and Chellappa, R. Gait analysis for human identification, in *Proc. 4th Int. Conf. Audio- and Video-Based Biometric Person Authentication*, pp. 706–714, 2003.

Kittler, J., Hatef, M., Duin, R., and Matas, J. On combining classifiers, *IEEE Trans. Pattern Anal. Machine Intelligence* **20**, 3, 226–239, 1998.

Lee, L. and Grimson, W. E. L. Gait analysis for recognition and classification, in *Proc. IEEE Int. Conf. Automatic Face and Gesture Recognition*, pp. 155–162, 2002.

Li, X. L., Maybank, S. J., Yan, S., Tao, D., and Xu, D. Gait components and their application to gender recognition, *IEEE Transactions on Systems Man and Cybernetics Part C-Applications and Reviews* **38**, 2, 145–155, 2008.

Liu, Y. X., Collins, R., and Tsin, Y. H. Gait sequence analysis using frieze patterns, in *Proc. Eur. Conf. Comput. Vision*, pp. 657–671, 2002.

Phillips, P., Moon, H., Rizvi, S., and Rauss, P. The feret evaluation methodology for face-recognition algorithms, *IEEE Trans. Pattern Anal. Machine Intelligence* **22**, 10, 1090–1104, 2000.

Qi, Y. and Hunt, B. A multiresolution approach to computer verification of handwritten signatures, *IEEE Trans. Image Processing* **4**, 6, 870–874, 1995.

Rabiner, L. and Juang, B. *Fundamentals of Speech Recognition* (Prentice-Hall, Englewood Cliffs, NJ), 1993.

Turk, M. and Pentland, A. Face recognition using eigenfaces, in *Proc. IEEE Conf. Comput. Vision Pattern Recognition*, pp. 586–591, 1991.

Wagg, D. K. and Nixon, M. S. On automated model-based extraction and analysis of gait, in *Proc. IEEE Int. Conf. Automatic Face and Gesture Recognition*, pp. 11–16, 2004.

Wang, L., Tan, T., Ning, H. Z., and Hu, W. M. Silhouette analysis-based gait recognition for human identification, *IEEE Trans. Pattern Anal. Machine Intelligence* **25**, 12, 1505–1518, 2003.

Yang, X. C., Zhou, Y., Zhang, T. H., Shu, G., and Yang, J. Gait recognition based on dynamic region analysis, *Signal Processing* **88**, 9, 2350–2356, 2008.

Part V

Hand Geometry

Chapter 10

PERSONAL VERIFICATION FROM THE GEOMETRY OF HUMAN HANDS

Vivek Kanhangad and Ajay Kumar
Department of Computing
The Hong Kong Polytechnic University
Hung Hom, Kowloon, Hong Kong
csvivek@comp.polyu.edu.hk
csajaykr@comp.polyu.edu.hk

10.1 Introduction

Biometrics offers natural and scientific solution to key aspects of security management problems. Due to the increased security concerns in the past decade, biometrics has seen enormous growth and has found widespread applications in our everyday life. Widely researched biometric traits include face, iris, fingerprint, hand geometry, palmprint, voice, and signature. Of these, face and hand geometry biometric traits enjoy high user acceptance as these characteristics can be measured in a non-intrusive manner, causing very little inconvenience to the user.

Hand geometry, along with the fingerprint and palmprint, is one of the hand-based biometric modalities. Hand geometry-based biometric systems exploit various features extracted from hand images to perform personal authentication. Due to limited discriminatory power of these features, hand geometry systems are rarely employed for applications that require performing identity recognition from a large-scale database or applications where the highest level of security is desired. Nevertheless, these systems have gained immense popularity and public acceptance as evident from their extensive deployment for applications in access control, time and attendance applications, and several other verification tasks. Major advantages of hand geometry systems include simple imaging requirements (features can be extracted from low-resolution hand images), ability to operate under harsh environmental conditions (immune to dirt on the hand and other external factors), and low data storage requirements. In addition, hand geometry acquisition and verification is extremely fast. These distinct advantages over other biometrics helped the hand geometry systems capture a niche market.

History of hand geometry biometric technology/systems dates back over three decades. The hand geometry system *Identimat*, developed by *Identimation* in the 1970s, was one of the earliest reported implementations of a biometric system for commercial applications. Since then, the hand geometry biometric systems have found applications in a wide variety of fields ranging from airports to nuclear power plants (Sidlauskas and Tamer, 2008). The hand geometry systems have traditionally enjoyed a market share of about 10% and have been quite popular for medium-size verification applications. The *Recognition Systems*[a] offers a range of time and attendance, and access control solutions based on hand geometry biometrics. Their access control solution named *HandKey* extracts over 90 measurements from the user's hand image and stores the information into a 9-byte template. *VeryFast* access control terminal, manufactured by *BioMet* partners,[b] captures the image of user's two fingers. Features extracted by processing this image are encrypted and stored as a 20-byte template. *Accu-Time Systems*[c] also manufactures a similar access control device based on user's finger geometry. Several units of the above-mentioned systems have been installed at various places around the world. The *INSPASS* is the first and the largest biometric verification program undertaken by the US government. The *HandKey* scanners were installed at certain airports in the United States to accelerate the process of immigration for frequent fliers. Another large scale deployment was at the 1996 Olympics Games, where hand geometry scanners were installed to restrict access to the Olympic Village.

Despite the commercial development and success of the hand geometry technology, there was not much literature available in the public domain until the late 1990s. However, since as early as 1970, several US patents have been issued for personal identification devices based on hand/finger geometry measurements (Sidlauskas, 1988; Miller, 1971; Ernst, 1971; Jacoby et al., 1972). Table 10.1 summarizes the inventions described in these patents. Most of the early work in the hand geometry literature was based on 2D images (intensity and color) of the human hand. However, with advancements in range image acquisition technology, a few researchers have also explored the utility of features extracted from range images of the hand. In the following sections, we describe in detail various methodologies proposed in the literature for 2D as well as 3D hand geometry biometrics.

10.2 2D Hand Geometry

2D hand geometry technology is based on the features extracted from 2D image of the human hand. Major processing modules in a 2D hand geometry system are: image acquisition system, preprocessing and feature extraction, feature matching,

---

[a]http://www.handreader.com/transition/index.htm
[b]http://www.biomet.ch
[c]http://www.accu-time.com

Table 10.1:   Summary of inventions on hand/finger geometry identification systems

Patent	Invention
Ernst (1971)	Mechanical device (using bars and springs) to measure length and width measurements of the hand, placed palm down on a flat surface.
Miller (1971)	Mechanical contact members are employed to measure outer dimension of fingers, while photoelectrical sensing devices compare the measurements with these stored in an identity card.
Jacoby *et al.* (1972)	Optical scanning device to measure finger lengths of four fingers (thumb not considered). Optical sensors are embedded on the flat surface to sense measurements, with a light source on top.
Sidlauskas (1988)	Device captures virtual 3D image of the hand using a mirror to reflect the side view. Flat surface has four pegs with an illumination source on top. Various measurements including finger lengths/widths, hand thickness, surface area, and perimeter are computed.

and decision making. The following sections provide a detailed discussion on various approaches available for these processing tasks.

10.2.1 *Imaging techniques*

A typical imaging set up for a 2D hand geometry system would involve the following components: a CCD camera, illumination source, and a flat surface. CCD camera employed is usually low-to-medium resolution as the hand geometry features can be extracted from binary images of the hand. Joshi *et al.* (1998) are one of the earliest researchers to build a prototype hand-based biometric system. Their system mainly comprised a CCD camera for imaging finger creases and a fluorescent tube for illumination. In order to minimize variations in imaging and subsequent performance deterioration, the placement of the fingers was constrained using a metal strip and a microswitch, which also activates the frame grabber to capture images of the fingers. Another prototype hand geometry system developed by Jain *et al.* (1999) employs image-acquisition module that includes a camera, an illumination source, and a flat surface with five pegs (similar to the one in patent of Sidlauskas (1988). A mirror was employed to project the lateral view of the hand on to the CCD. This enables the system to acquire top and lateral view of the user's hand in a single image of 640×480 resolution. The hand geometry system developed by Sanchez-Reillo *et al.* (2000) employs an image-acquisition module similar to the one in Jain and Duta (1999). Pegs in their system, however, are equipped with pressure sensors to trigger the camera when a hand is detected on the platform.

Most of the early works in the literature employ pegs (on the flat surface where the user is required to place his/her hand) to restrict the position and movement of the hand during image acquisition. Though use of such constraints helps avoid registration/alignment of hand images before feature extraction, such systems cause inconvenience to the user and therefore are less user friendly. For example, elderly or people with arthritis and other conditions that limit dexterity may have difficulty placing their hand on a surface guided by pegs. Hence, a lot of researchers have focused their efforts to eliminate the use of pegs. Kumar *et al.* (2003) employed a peg-free imaging set up to acquire hand images. Users were requested to place their hand on the imaging table, with a digital camera mounted on top. They did not employ any special illumination, as the images were acquired in a well-lit indoor environment. Authors in Amayeh *et al.* (2006) employed an image-acquisition system that includes a flat surface (for hand placement) with a VGA resolution CCD camera mounted on top. A uniform illumination is provided underneath the flat surface. Such an arrangement helps to acquire high-contrast hand images which can be binarized by simple thresholding. A few researchers (Yrk *et al.*, 2006; Wong and Shi, 2002) have even used low-resolution digital scanners to acquired hand images in a peg-free manner. Though the above approaches do not use pegs to constrain hand placement, they require the user to place his/her hand on a flat surface. Such contact may give rise to security as well as hygiene concerns among users. Fingerprint or palm-print impressions left on the surface by the user may actually be picked up and used to fabricate fake biometric samples to gain unauthorized access. Zheng *et al.* (2007) have investigated this problem by exploring a non-contact, peg-free imaging set up that allows users the freedom of presenting their hands at any orientation, as long as the major part of the hand is captured. They employed a digital color camera to acquire hand images for authentication. However, the reliability of results in Zheng *et al.* (2007) is very low as the experimental results are presented on very small database of 20 subjects. Kumar (2008) has also recently investigated the contact-free hand identification and illustrated promising results on the publicly available contact-free database from 234 subjects.

10.2.2 *Preprocessing and feature extraction*

Prior to feature extraction, acquired hand images are usually processed to obtain a binary image of the hand or sometimes, a hand contour. In most cases, a simple thresholding scheme followed by morphological operations can be used to segment the hand from the background. Figure 10.1 shows the typical hand geometry features extracted from the silhouette of the hand. Finger length is computed as the distance from the finger tip to its base along the orientation of the finger. Finger-width measurements are made at a number of evenly spaced points along the finger length. Finger perimeter refers to the number of pixels on the finger contour. All the measurements shown in Fig. 10.1 are usually made in terms of pixels. Please note that measurements from thumb have been found to be unreliable and therefore, in most cases hand geometry features are extracted only from the remaining four fingers. This is especially true in the case of peg-free image acquisition systems where the variations in measurements of the thumb are extremely large.

Hand geometry system described in Jain *et al.* (1999) measures features such as finger length, finger width, and thickness of the hand along 16 different axes. Finger thickness features are computed from the lateral view of the hand. Authors propose

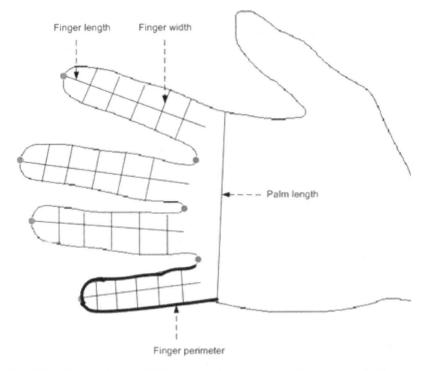

Fig. 10.1. Commonly used 2D hand geometric features marked on a hand silhouette.

to model the gray-level profile along the measurement axis for feature extraction. Instead of explicitly measuring geometry features on the hand, Jain and Duta (1999) and Xiong *et al.* (2005) propose to align finger shapes (contours) from a pair of hand images. In order to deal with the deformation of the hand shape (contour) caused by the movement of fingers, authors individually align respective pairs of fingers from the hand images. Sanchez-Reillo *et al.* (2000) extracted an extended set of geometry features from the contour of the hand. In addition to the length and width features from the fingers, various angles and deviations at specific points on the fingers are extracted. A feature-selection scheme, based on the discriminatory power of the features, is used to reduce the dimension of the feature vector.

Hand geometry systems that do not employ pegs to register/align hand images usually locate key points (commonly finger tips and valleys) in the hand image (Fig. 10.1). This information can be used to align hand images prior to feature extraction. An alternate approach would be to extract features that are invariant to translation and rotation of the hand in the image plane. Oden *et al.* (2003) explored one such method by modeling finger contours using implicit polynomials and computing algebraic invariants (features) from polynomial coefficients. The approach proposed in Amayeh *et al.* (2006) represents hand shapes using Zernike moments that are invariant to transformation and scale. The resulting high-dimensional feature vector undergoes a dimensionality-reduction technique, PCA.

Yrk *et al.* (2006) applied dimensionality-reduction techniques on the binary images of the hand that are prealigned using orientations of the fingers. Zheng *et al.* (2007) proposed hand geometry technique using projective invariant hand features. Feature points detected on the fingers creases are used to compute the projective invariant hand features. Kumar *et al.* (Kumar and Zhang, 2007) demonstrated that discretization of the hand geometry features leads to significant improvement in performance. Various hand geometry features such as finger lengths/widths, palm length/width, hand length, and perimeter are extracted and discretized before matching.

10.2.3 *Feature matching*

Feature matching process computes the similarity (or dissimilarity) between the user's feature vector and the one stored during the enrolment. Various matching metrics proposed in the literature include Euclidean distance (Sanchez-Reillo *et al.*, 2000; Jain *et al.*, 1999; Zheng *et al.*, 2007; Amayeh *et al.*, 2006) absolute distance (Jain *et al.*, 1999), hamming distance (Sanchez-Reillo *et al.*, 2000), normalized correlation (Kumar *et al.*, 2003), cosine similarity (Yrk *et al.*, 2006) and Mahalanobis distance (Oden *et al.*, 2003). In addition to these simple matching metrics various trainable classifiers such as radial basis function (RBF) (Sanchez-Reillo *et al.*, 2000), support vector machine (SVM) (Kumar and Zhang, 2007), and Gaussian mixture model (GMM) (Sanchez-Reillo *et al.*, 2000) have also been used to classify the user's feature vector into genuine or impostor class. Approaches based on alignment of hand contours use metrics such as mean alignment error (Jain and Duta, 1999), goodness of alignment (Xiong *et al.*, 2005) (based on finger-width measurements) to compare a pair of hand shapes.

Match score generated from feature matching process is used to make a decision as to whether the user is a genuine or an impostor. This decision is usually made based on whether the match score is above or below a given threshold.

10.3 3D Hand Geometry

Most of the hand geometry systems/techniques proposed in the literature is based on user's 2D hand images. These approaches extract various features from the binarized version of the acquired hand image. Unique information in such binary images is very limited, leading to low discriminatory power for hand geometry biometric systems and thus they are suitable only for small-scale applications. With the advances in 3D image-acquisition technology, 2- and 3D images of the hand can be acquired simultaneously. Features from these images can be combined to significantly improve the performance. The following sections provide a detailed discussion on different processing modules and approaches for 3D hand geometry systems.

10.3.1 *Imaging techniques*

Image-acquisition module in a 3D hand geometry system captures a range image of the user's hand. Active 3D scanners are usually preferred as they can effectively capture dense and accurate 3D data. Woodard *et al.* (Woodard and Flynn, 2005) are perhaps the first researchers to work on the range images of the hand for biometric recognition/verification. Their approach (Woodard and Flynn, 2005) uses laser-based vivid 910 3D scanner (Konica Minolta, 2008) to simultaneously acquire color and registered range images of the hand. In order to simplify the hand-segmentation process, users were requested to place their right hand against a wall covered with black cloth. In another system developed by Malassiotis *et al.* (2006), users were asked to hold their hand in front their face while an in-house developed low-cost 3D sensor was used to capture color and range images of the back surface of the hand. The 3D sensor employed in their system consisted of a color camera and a standard video projector.

10.3.2 *Preprocessing and feature extraction*

Segmentation of the hand in the acquired range images can be made simple by making use of the simultaneously captured (and registered) color or intensity image. Woodard *et al.* (Woodard and Flynn, 2005) worked on a combination of edge and skin detection algorithms to segment hand from the uniform background. Convex hull of the hand contour was used to locate finger valleys and to extract index, middle, and ring fingers from the range image of the hand. Malassiotis *et al.* (2006) employed a more complex approach to segment the hand from other parts of the body appearing in the image. Working solely on range images, the authors used mixture of Gaussians to model and to subsequently segment hand.

Various features have been proposed for 3D hand/finger geometry biometric. The approach proposed in Lay (2000) investigates the pattern distorted by the shape (or curvature) of the hand. The distorted pattern captured by a CCD camera is coded by quad-tree to extract 1D binary features. Though this approach does not extract 3D features from the range image of the hand, it essentially utilizes the 3D surface features in an indirect manner. Woodard *et al.* (Woodard and Flynn, 2005) computed shape index, defined in terms of principal curvatures, at every pixel in the range images of fingers and stored as feature templates for matching. The approach in Malassiotis *et al.* (2006) extracts two signature functions, namely, 3D width and mean curvature at a number of cross-finger sectional segments. Features computed for four fingers are concatenated to form a feature vector.

10.3.3 *Feature matching*

Similar to the 2D hand geometry matchers, simple distance metrics can be used to match hand geometry features extracted from range images. In the literature, normalized correlation (Woodard and Flynn, 2005) and L_1 distance metric (Malassiotis et al., 2006) are employed for 3D feature matching.

10.4 Performance

Hand geometry biometry systems based on 2D as well as 3D features have been shown to offer sufficiently high accuracy to reliably authenticate individuals. Researchers have been exploring various approaches to improve the performance of the existing systems. Table 10.2 provides a comparative summary of various hand geometry approaches discussed in this chapter.

10.5 An Example: Hand Geometry System Based on 3D Features

In this section, we illustrate an authentication system based on 3D hand geometry features. The system utilizes a laser-based 3D digitizer (Konica Minolta, 2008) to acquire registered color and range images of the presented hands in a completely contact-free manner, without using any hand position restricting mechanism. The block diagram of the system is shown in Fig. 10.2. Major processing modules include image normalization (in the pre-processing stage), feature extraction, and feature matching. Details of these processing steps are provided in the following sections.

10.5.1 *Preprocessing and finger extraction*

The first major step is to locate finger tips and finger valleys in the acquired image. These reference points are then used to determine the orientation of each finger and to extract them from the input hand image. Since there is a pixel-to-pixel correspondence between the intensity and range image, the acquired color image can be utilized to determine key points and orientation. The steps involved in the process of extracting fingers are illustrated in Figs. 10.3 and 10.4. To start with, the 2D image is binarized using Otsu's threshold (Otsu, 1979). Resulting binary image is further processed using morphological operators to remove small regions that are not part of the hand. Boundary pixels of the hand in the processed binary image are then identified using the 8-connected contour tracing algorithm. Plotting the distance from the reference point R (Fig. 10.3(b)) to every point on the extracted hand contour, we obtain a curve as shown in Fig. 10.4(a). Local minima and local maxima on this plot correspond to finger tips and finger valleys, which can be easily located. In order to estimate the orientation of each finger, four points on the finger contour (two points each on both sides of the fingertip) at fixed distances from the finger tip are identified. Two middle points are computed for corresponding points on both sides and are joined to obtain the finger orientation. Having determined the finger orientation and finger tip/valley points, it is a straightforward task to extract a rectangular region of interest for fingers.

Table 10.2:   Comparative summary of some of the approaches for hand geometry authentication

Reference	Methodology	Imaging Modality	Pegs	Database size (Users)	Performance (EER %)
Jain *et al.* (1999)	Measurements are made along 16 different axes, and matched using weighted Euclidean distance	2D	Yes	50	6[a]
Jain and Duta (1999)	Individual finger shapes are aligned and a shape distance (mean alignment error) is computed as match score	2D	Yes	53	2.5–3[a]
Sanchez-Reillo *et al.* (2000)	Feature vector comprises several width, height, and angle measurements. GMM is used for matching.	2D	Yes	20	6[a]
Kumar *et al.* (2003)	Feature vectors comprising 16 geometry measurements are matched using normalized correlation	2D	No	100	8.5
Xiong *et al.* (2005)	Fusion of invariants from implicit polynomials and geometric features	2D	No	28	1
Konica Minolta (2008)	Individual finger shapes are aligned using a elliptical model and finger tip/valley information	2D	No	108	2.4
Woodard ande Flynn (2005)	Shape index image is extracted from range images of fingers and is matched using normalized correlation coefficient	3D	No	177 (probe) 132 (gallery)	5.5
Malassiotis *et al.* (2006)	Feature vectors comprising 96 curvature and 3D finger width measurements are matched using L1 distance	3D	No[b]	73	3.6
Lay (2000)	Independent component analysis (ICA) on binary images of the hand. Feature vectors are matched using cosine similarity measure.	2D	No	458	2
Amayeh *et al.* (2006)	Principal component analysis (PCA) on extracted higher-order Zernike moment features. Reduced feature vectors are matched using Euclidean distance.	2D	No	40	2
Kumar and Zhang (2007)	Discretization of hand geometry features to improve the performance	2D	No	100	1.9
Zheng *et al.* (2007)	Feature points on finger creases are detected and used to compute projective invariant features. Feature vectors are matched using normalized Euclidean distance.	2D	No[b]	23	0

[a]Equal error rate has been approximated from the ROC plot reported in the paper.
[b]System acquires hand images in a completely contact free manner.

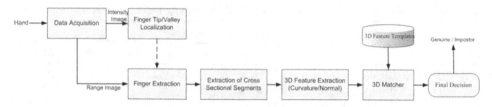

Fig. 10.2.   Block diagram of the biometric system utilizing 3D hand geometric features.

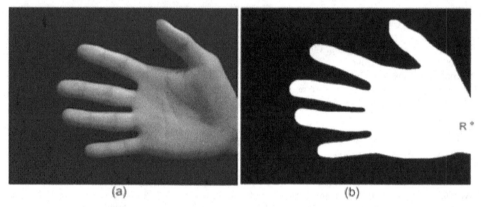

Fig. 10.3.   Pre-processing stages: (a) acquired intensity image, and (b) binary hand image after thresholding and morphological operations.

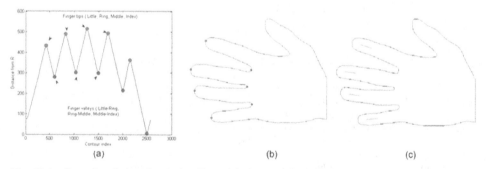

Fig. 10.4.   Locating finger tips and valleys. (a) distance from the reference R to points on the contour; (b) finger tips and valleys located; and (c) estimated finger orientations.

The process of finger extraction discussed above can handle rotation and translation of the hand in the image plane, which are inevitable in a peg-free data acquisition set up.

10.5.2 *3D finger feature extraction*

Based on the finger-localization algorithm discussed in the previous section, individual fingers can be located and extracted from the acquired range image.

Each of the four finger range images is further processed for feature extraction. For each finger, a number of cross-sectional segments are extracted at uniformly spaced distances along the finger length. The next step in the feature extraction process is to compute two representations, namely, mean curvature and unit normal vector, for every data point on the extracted segments. Before computing these features, a 2D polynomial is used to model the data point and its neighbors. The mean curvature and normal vector features can then be computed for the fitted 2D polynomial by estimating numerical partial derivates of the polynomial at each data point. A 2D polynomial $f(x, y)$ has the following form

$$f(x, y) = c_{00} + c_{10}x + c_{01}y + c_{11}xy + c_{20}x^2 + c_{02}y^2 \qquad (10.1)$$

where x and y are the 2D coordinates of a data point. The expression for mean curvature of a 2D polynomial in terms of its coefficients is given by

$$\kappa_{2D} = \frac{\left(1 + c_{10}^2\right)c_{02} + \left(1 + c_{01}^2\right)c_{20} - c_{10}c_{01}c_{11}}{\left(1 + c_{10}^2 + c_{01}^2\right)^{3/2}} \qquad (10.2)$$

Mean curvature in Eq. (10.2) is computed for every data point on the cross-sectional segments and stored as feature templates in the database. Figure 10.5(a) shows a cross-sectional finger segment extracted from the 3D finger and the corresponding mean curvature plot (Fig. 10.5(b)). In addition to the curvature feature, surface normal vector can be computed at every data point on the segment.

10.5.3 *3D feature matching*

In the matching stage, features extracted from each of the four fingers are matched individually and then combined to obtain a final matching score. Assume we have extracted features for a number of cross-sectional segments from template and probe (query) fingers represented by T_i and Q_i respectively, where the subscript i represents the index for fingers and takes values from 1 to 4 for little, ring, middle,

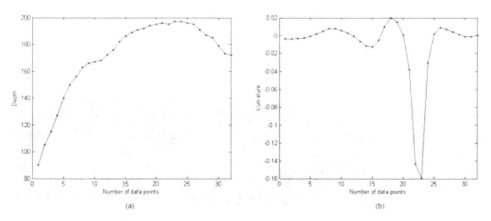

Fig. 10.5. (a) A cross-sectional finger segment and (b) its computed curvature features.

and index fingers. Matching of curvature features from a corresponding pair of fingers (denoted as s_i^c) is based on the cosine similarity metric and the match score is computed as

$$s_i^c = \frac{1}{N_s} \sum_{j=1}^{N_s} \phi_i^j \tag{10.3}$$

where

$$\phi_i^j = \begin{cases} \dfrac{T_i^j Q_i^j(1:l_T^j)}{|T_i^j||Q_i^j(1:l_T^j)|}, & \text{if } l_T^j < l_Q^j \\[3mm] \dfrac{T_i^j(1:l_Q^j)Q_i^j}{|T_i^j(1:l_Q^j)||Q_i^j|}, & \text{otherwise} \end{cases} \tag{10.4}$$

where l_T^j and l_Q^j are the number of feature points on the jth cross-sectional segment of the template (T_i^j) and query (Q_i^j) fingers, respectively. $S_{\text{curv}}(= \frac{1}{4} \sum_{i=1}^{4} s_i^c)$ is the final score generated from curvature feature matching as illustrated above.

10.5.4 *Performance evaluation*

This section provides a discussion on the performance evaluation of the system on a database of 3540 right-hand images. For image acquisition, each user holds his/her right hand in front of the scanner at a distance of about 0.7 m. No constraints were employed to confine the position of the hand nor were the users instructed to remove any jewelry that they were wearing. Users were only asked to hold their hand with their palm approximately parallel to the image plane of the scanner and inside the imaging area. Figure 10.6 shows a picture of the data-acquisition set up as well as sample hand images (range as well as color) acquired using this imaging set up. Figure 10.7 depicts the overall 3D hand geometry performance resulting from the combination of curvature and normal features. As shown in Fig. 10.8, the combination of the 3D hand geometry features achieves an equal error rate (EER) of 3.8%. This result clearly demonstrates that features extracted from 3D hand images carry significant discriminatory information to authenticate individuals.

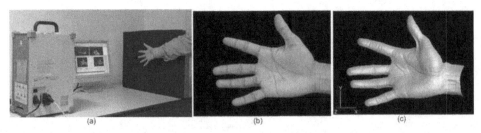

Fig. 10.6.   (a) Image acquisition set up and (b) an example of the acquired color and range images.

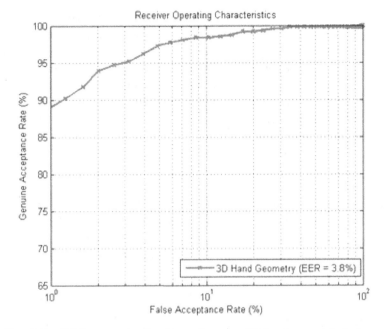

Fig. 10.7. ROC curves showing the performance 3D hand geometric features.

10.6 Summary

This chapter provided a discussion on various methodologies/techniques available for the hand geometry biometrics. A detailed description of the design of a biometric system using 3D hand geometry features is also presented. While the history of commercial hand geometry systems dates back over three decades, academic research addressing critical issues lagged behind and appears to have begun only in the late 1990s. However, literature currently available in the public domain clearly shows that the research has now caught up with and has in fact transcended the commercially available systems. Majority of the early systems employed pegs to restrict hand placement in order to simplify the subsequent processing steps. This, however, caused inconvenience to the users. Several researchers have addressed this problem by proposing approaches to do away with pegs and thus contributed to the increase in user friendliness of the hand geometry systems. Recently, a few researchers have gone even further and came up with techniques that allow users to simply hold their hand in front of the camera, in a completely unconstrained manner, in order to get authenticated. These promising attempts will certainly help to make the hand geometry as acceptable and popular as face biometrics. However, these systems need to be rigorously evaluated on larger databases before they can be deployed for real-world applications. In addition, only a few researchers have explored the use of 3D hand geometric features. 3D hand features can be simultaneously extracted and combined to significantly improve the performance of the system. Therefore, there is tremendous scope for further research in this direction. Finally, there is a pressing need to develop anti spoofing measures for hand geometry systems, especially in view of the ease with which researchers have been able to circumvent a commercially available hand geometry system (Chen *et al.*, 2005). Antispoofing measures proposed in the literature (Reddy *et al.*, 2008) to detect fake fingerprints based on liveness detection can very well be employed in hand geometry systems. However, further research and development efforts are required to adapt these techniques and design hand geometry systems that can thwart attacks based on fake hands.

References

Amayeh, G., Bebis, G., Erol, A., and Nicolescu, M. Peg-free hand shape verification using high order zernike moments, in *Proc. of the CVPR* (New York, USA), 2006.

Chen, H., Valizadegan, H., Jackson, C., Soltysiak, S., and Jain, A. Fake hands: spoofing hand geometry systems, in *Proc. Biometric Consortium* (Washington DC), 2005.

Ernst, R. H. Hand id system, U.S. patent No. 3576537, 1971.

Jacoby, I., Giordano, A. J., and Fioretti, W. H. Personnel identification apparatus, U.S. patent No. 3648240, 1972.

Jain, A., and Duta, N. Deformable matching of hand shapes for verification, in *Proc. Int. Conf. Image Processing*, pp. 857–861, 1999.

Jain, A. K., Ross, A., and Pankanti, S. A prototype hand geometry-based verification system, in *Proc. AVBPA* (Washington DC), pp. 166–171, 1999.

Joshi, D. G., Rao, Y. V., Kar, S., and Kumar, V. Computer vision-based approach to personal identification using finger crease pattern, *Pattern Recognition* **31**, 1, 15–22, 1998.

Konica Minolta Minolta vivid 910 noncontact 3d digitizer, http://www.konicami nolta.com/instruments/products/3d/non-contact/vivid910/index.html 2008.

Kumar, A. Incorporating cohort information for reliable palmprint authentication, in *Proc. ICVGIP* (Bhubaneshwar, India), pp. 583–590, 2008.

Kumar, A., and Zhang, D. Hand geometry recognition using entropy-based discretization, *IEEE Trans. Inf. Forensics Security* **2**, 2, 181–187, 2007.

Kumar, A., Wong, D., Shen, H., and Jain, A. Personal verification using palmprint and hand geometry biometric, in *Proc. AVBPA* (Guildford, UK), pp. 668–675, 2003.

Lay, Y. Hand shape recognition, *Opt. Laser Technol.* **32**, 1, 1–5, 2000.

Malassiotis, S., Aifanti, N., and Strintzis, M. G. Personal authentication using 3-d finger geometry, *IEEE Trans. Info. Forensics Security* **1**, 1, 12–21, 2006.

Miller, R. P. Finger dimension comparison identification system, U.S. patent No. 3576538, 1971.

Oden, C., Ercil, A., and Buke, B. Hand recognition using implicit polynomials and geometric features, *Pattern Recognition Lett.* **24**, 13, pp. 2145–2152, 2003.

Otsu, N. A threshold selection method from gray-level histograms, *IEEE Trans. Syst, Man Cybernetics* **9**, 1, 62–66, 1979.

Reddy, P. V., Kumar, A., Rahman, S. M. K., and Mundra, T. S. A new method of antispoofing for biometric devices, *IEEE Trans. Biomed. Circuits Syst.* **2**, 4, 328–337, 2008.

Sanchez-Reillo, R., Sanchez-Avila, C., and Gonzalez-Macros, A. Biometric identification through hand geometry measurements, *IEEE Trans. Pattern Anal. Machine Intelligence* **22**, 10, 1168–1171, 2000.

Sidlauskas, D. P. 3d hand profile identification apparatus, U.S. patent No. 4736203, 1988.

Sidlauskas, D. P. and Tamer, S. Hand geometry recognition, in A. K. Jain, P. Flynn, and A. Ross (eds.), *Handbook of Biometrics* (Springer), 2008.

Wong, L. and Shi, P. Peg-free hand geometry recognition using hierarchical geometry and shape matching, in *Proc. IAPR Workshop on Machine Vision Applications* (Nara, Japan), pp. 281–284, 2002.

Woodard, D. L., and Flynn, P. J. Finger surface as a biometric identifier, *Comput. Vis. Image Understanding* **100**, 3, 357–384, 2005.

Xiong, W., Toh, K., Yau, W., and Jiang, X. Model-guided deformable hand shape recognition without positioning aids, *Pattern Recognition* **38**, 10, 1651–1664, 2005.

Yrk, E., Konukoglu, E., Sankur, B., and Darbon, J. Shape-based hand recognition, *IEEE Trans. Image Processing* **15**, 7, 1803–1815, 2006.

Zheng, G., Wang, C. J., and Boult, T. E. Application of projective invariants in hand geometry biometrics, *IEEE Trans. Inf. Forensics Security* **2**, 4, 758–768, 2007.

Part VI

Handwriting

Chapter 11

WRITER IDENTIFICATION WITH HYBRID EDGE DIRECTIONAL FEATURES AND NONLINEAR DIMENSION REDUCTION

Bailing Zhang
Department of Computer Science and Software Engineering
Xi'an Jiaotong-Liverpool University, Suzhou, China
bailing.zhang@xjtlu.edu.cn

Yanchun Zhang
Centre for Applied Informatics Research
School of Engineering and Science, Victoria University, Australia

11.1 Introduction

Writer identification from handwriting is an important behavioral biometric research area with many applications where one needs to decide the identity of writer for a handwritten document. For example, in the criminal justice system, a forensic handwriting analysis is often required for identification of handwritten documents without signature such as a threatening letter (Franke *et al.*, 2003; Pervouchine and Leedham, 2007). Paleographic analysis is another interesting application of writer identification where the authorship of historical manuscript is to be determined (Bulacu and Schomaker, 2007a; Bar-Yosef *et al.*, 2007). A writer identification system aims to determine the writer of the handwritten text by comparing the handwritten text with those stored in the reference database and the research is based on the assumption that handwriting is as unique to each individual as is their fingerprints. Scientists have found evidence regarding the constancy of individual writing habits, which means that the relation of character, shape, and the styles of writing is characteristic to a specific person (Srihari *et al.*, 2002). In recent years, writer identification has received renewed interest (Schomaker, 2007; Srihari and Ball, 2008; Bensefia *et al.*, 2005a; Schlapbach and Bunke, 2007).

There are two broad categories of writer identification methods (Schomaker, 2007): text-dependent vs. text-independent methods. The signature verification is a special type of text-dependent approach for which the same content of text for each writer must be considered each time. Text-independent approach for identification is based on some features extracted from the image of a text block, without regard to the contents of the handwritten text. Text-independent methods have acquired more attention in recent years due to a number of advantages in applications, for example, the difficulty for the imposter to imitate. Some significant methods for text-independent cases have been proposed, such as using connected-component contours and edge-based features (Schomaker and Bulacu, 2004), using dynamic features on strokes (Yu *et al.*, 2004) or on hinge angles (Bulacu and Schomaker, 2007b).

The main pursuit in writer identification research is to define features that reflect the large variability between handwriting from different writers while remaining constant over samples produced by the same writer. In other words, extracting appropriate feature representation of the written images that characterize the difference between handwritings of different individuals is a decisive step in developing writer identification system. In the past, a number of feature representations have been attempted, which can be roughly classified as global or local features (Schomaker, 2007). Global features describe an entire image as a whole. Examples include using the histogram of the wavelet coefficients (He *et al.*, 2008) and multichannel Gabor filtering and gray-scale co-occurrence matrix techniques (Said *et al.*, 2000). Local features are confined to a limited portion (e.g., a grid) of the handwriting samples for describing a particular geometrical and topological characteristic of local segments. For example, Bensefia used local features based on graphemes that are produced by a segmentation algorithm based on the analysis of the minima of the upper contour and writer identification is then carried out by a textual-based information retrieval model (Bensefia *et al.*, 2005b). The edge-based directional probability distributions have been used as features in Bulacu *et al.* (2003). Combination of different types of features has been discussed in Siddiqi and Vincent (2008).

Though much progress have been made in the writer identification recently, there are still a number of open problems that pose challenges. First of all, all the existed identification systems are much inferior when compared to human capability. Our work is concerned with more reliable feature extraction techniques for writer identification. The feature information is based on some recently proposed edge-directional features, including the histogram of oriented gradients (HOGs) (Dalal and Triggs, 2005) and a curve fragment feature (Tamrakar and Kimia, 2007), which can be termed as histogram of edge direction (HED). HOG has been successfully applied to a number of different object detection tasks such as human detection. The representation of a shape descriptor can consist of concatenation of these HOG histograms in a single vector, which is referred to as pyramid histogram of oriented gradients (PHOGs) (Bosch *et al.*, 2007). HED is based on a new edge detection and edge-linking algorithms, which robustly extract well-localized subpixel edges and stably links these into curve fragments. An evidence of the plausibility of directional features comes from physiology that the cells in the visual cortex of animals are selective to the orientation of perceived objects (Hubel and Wiesel, 1977). Edge directional features have been extensively applied in various object detection problems in computer vision. This chapter shows that the similar effectiveness can be reached for writer identification. Compared with many previously proposed feature-extraction approaches, PHOG can extract discriminating features from handwritten text images in a general way that may include global, structural, geometric, or statistical information. A hybrid feature from the combination of PHOG and HED can give further improved identification accuracy.

Although the edge-directional features like PHOG or HED are sufficiently discriminative to enable writers classification based on their handwritten text images, the large number of features are not equally necessary for predicting the class labels. The identification performance can be enhanced by applying appropriate dimensionality reduction for extracting a smaller number of good features. One of the best known dimensionality-reduction techniques is PCA which projects the original n-dimensional data onto a $d(\ll n)$-dimensional linear subspace spanned by the leading eigenvectors of the data's covariance matrix. In many real-world problems, however, the data is not sampled from a linear subspace as PCA implicitly assumes. In the last few years, many manifold learning techniques have been developed for non-linear dimensionality reduction (Tenenbaum *et al.*, 2000; Roweis and Saul, 2000; Belkin and Niyogi, 2001), which reduce the dimensionality of a fixed training set in a way that maximally preserve certain interpoint relationships. But the manifold learning methods have a major limitation that there is no functional mapping between the high- and low-dimensional spaces that are valid for both of the training and testing data. A novel dimensionality-reduction algorithm called spectral regression (SR) was proposed in Cai *et al.* (2007), which is based on regression and spectral graph analysis. More specifically, an affinity graph over labeled points is constructed to discover the intrinsic discriminant structure in the data and the graph is then used to learn responses for the labeled points. Once the responses are obtained, the ordinary regression is applied for learning the embedding function.

In this chapter, we propose to enhance the writer identification performance by applying the non-linear dimension reduction SR to the edge-directional features extracted by PHOG and HED. With dimension reduced hybrid edge directional features, writer identification is implemented as a multiclass classification issue. Using a benchmarking writer identification database IAM (Marti and Bunke, 1999), experimental results have supported the effectiveness of our scheme.

11.2 Edge Directional Feature Extraction

Among the various feature extraction techniques for writer identification, geometrical features based on the edge content of handwriting text have been well known. As the elements of characters in different language, strokes consist of oriented lines, curves or polygons and the orientation or direction of strokes is important in sufficiently discriminating various characters. In character recognition, for example, stroke orientation or direction has been used for a long time (Cheriet et al., 2007). The local stroke orientation/direction of a character can be determined in different ways: skeleton orientation, stroke segment, contour chaincode, gradient direction, and so on (Cheriet et al., 2007). In writer identification, edge-based directional probability distributions has been proposed as features in Bulacu et al. (2003). Though much progress has been made from these efforts, most of the edge-related feature extraction techniques fall short of general significance, if not being ad hoc.

Our interests in further exploring edge-conveyed geometrical information of a handwritten text image is motivated by the increasingly popular descriptors of local features in computer vision, particularly the edge direction histogram, which describe objects in a redundant way and have been proven to be powerful in accomplishing object detection and recognition purposes. In recent years, there has been much progress in the efficient extraction of various edge-directional features from images. Edge-direction histogram is a representative example, which can be described as a weighted histogram wherein each histogram bin collects votes from gradients near particular locations and particular orientations. Examples include Lowe's SIFT (Lowe, 2004), Malik's shape context (Belongie et al., 2002), and Dalal and Triggs's HoG (Dalal and Triggs, 2005). Among them, the HOG has been applied to a number of different object detection tasks such as human detection with excellent results reported.

In the following, we briefly introduce two kind of edge-directional features that are applied in writer identification.

11.2.1 Pyramid histogram of oriented gradients

The local geometrical shape within a text image can be characterized by the distribution of edge directions, which can be represented by the local shape descriptor HOG. HOG describes the local shape by the distribution of intensity gradient. By taking the partial derivatives of image intensity at each pixel in Cartesian coordinates, gradient vectors can be conveniently calculated for the representation of edge orientation. For any given subwindow of the image, a HOG accumulates, over each edge point, the angles of the gradients that fall into a particular range. The contribution of an edge point to the HOG is weighted by the gradient magnitude at that point. The basic procedure for calculating HOG feature can be illustrated in Fig. 11.1.

We follow the construction in Bosch et al. (2007) to define a dense representation of an image at a particular resolution. Specifically, an image is first divided into non-overlapping pixel regions, called cells. For each cell, a 1D histogram of edge orientations over pixels is accumulated. The most common method is to apply 1D centered point discrete derivative mask in both the horizontal and vertical directions. Specifically, a grayscale image I is filtered with the following

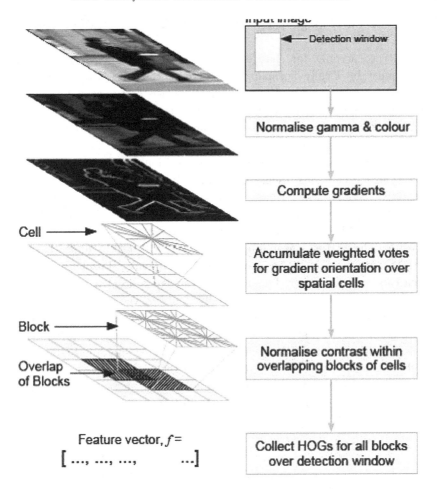

Fig. 11.1. A schematic illustration of HOG (Dalal and Trigg, 2005).

filter kernels

$$D_X = [-101] \quad \text{and} \quad D_Y = [-101]^T \tag{11.1}$$

Then, the horizontal and vertical derivatives are obtained using convolution operations $I_X = I * D_X$ and $I_Y = I * D_Y$. The magnitude of the gradient is

$$|G| = \sqrt{I_X^2 + I_Y^2} \tag{11.2}$$

and the orientation of the gradient is given by

$$\theta = \arctan \frac{I_Y}{I_X} \tag{11.3}$$

The edge orientations at each pixel is discretized into one of nine orientation bins for an angular range of $[0, 180]$. Each pixel within a cell casts a weighted vote for the orientation of its gradient, with a strength that depends on the gradient magnitude.

In order to account for changes in illumination and contrast, the gradient strengths must be locally normalized with respect to the gradient energy in a neighborhood around it. The HOG descriptor consists of concatenation of these histograms in a single vector. HOG bears some important advantages over other descriptor methods, for example, it is invariant to small deformations, and robust in terms of outliers and noise.

The HOG feature encodes the gradient orientation of one image patch without consideration of where this orientation is from in this patch. Therefore, it is not discriminative enough when there is crucial spatial property of the underlying structure of the image patch. The objective of the PHOGs is to take the spatial property of the local shape into account while representing an image by HOG (Bosch *et al.*, 2007). The spatial information is recorded by tiling the image into regions at multiple resolutions, based on spatial pyramid matching (Lazebnik *et al.*, 2006). The idea can be explained by Fig. 11.2. Each image is divided into a sequence of increasingly finer spatial grids by repeatedly doubling the number of divisions in each axis direction. The number of points in each grid cell is then recorded. The number of points in a cell at one level is simply the sum over those contained in the four cells it is divided into at the next level, thus forming a pyramid representation. The cell counts at each level of resolution are the bin counts for the histogram representing that level. The soft correspondence between the two point sets can then be computed as a weighted sum over the histogram intersections at each level.

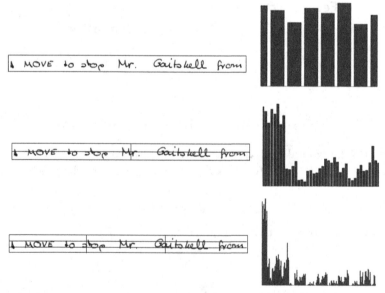

Fig. 11.2.   A schematic illustration of PHOG. The descriptor consists of a histogram of orientation gradients over each image subregion at each resolution level.

More specifically, for each grid cell at each pyramid resolution level, a HOG vector is computed. The final PHOG descriptor for the image is then a concatenation of all the HOG vectors. In the implementation, we follow the practice in Bosch *et al.* (2007) by limiting the number of levels to $L = 3$ to prevent overfitting. The final PHOG vector is then normalized to sum to unity.

11.2.2 *Histogram of edge direction*

The gradient-based methods above have some limitations. Since the gradients of image intensity are usually computed on pixel level, the related methods are quite sensitive to noise even after the averaging/smoothing process. On the other hand, as the core component of HOG descriptor, the gradient orientation is computed using a derivative operation on the location of the edge. As being pointed out in a recent publication (Tamrakar and Kimia, 2007), any orientation measurement should involve operators one order of derivative higher than those used in measuring its location. Edges are typically localized by finding peaks in response to some first-order derivative (gradient) operator, which implies a second-order operation. However, the gradient direction, a first-order operator, is assigned as the orientation of the edge. In other words, the edge-directional features from such gradient-based orientation definition is not very reliable. Tamrakar accordingly proposed an edge orientation as tangent of a localized curve based on third-order derivatives, which can be briefly explained as follows.

The traditional approach for edge detection using image derivatives localizes edge at the maxima of the gradient magnitude $|\nabla I|$ in the direction of the gradient $\frac{\nabla I}{|\nabla I|}$, which gives

$$\nabla |\nabla I| \cdot \frac{\nabla I}{|\nabla I|} = 0 \tag{11.4}$$

An equivalent expression of it in Cartesian coordinates can be written as

$$I_x^2 I_{xx} + 2I_x I_y I_{xy} + I_y^2 I_{yy} = 0 \tag{11.5}$$

The orientation of this edge can be obtained by the normal to the edge $\vec{N}$, which can be obtained by differentiation with the following components

$$
\begin{aligned}
N_x = {} & 2I_x I_{xx}^2 + 2I_x I_{xy}^2 + 2I_y I_{xx} I_{xy} + 2I_y I_{yy} I_{xy} \\
& + 2I_x I_y I_{xxy} + 2I_y^2 I_{xyy} + I_x^2 I_{xxx} \\
N_y = {} & 2I_y I_{yy}^2 + 2I_y I_{xy}^2 + 2I_x I_{xx} I_{xy} + 2I_x I_{yy} I_{xy} \\
& + 2I_x I_y I_{xyy} + 2I_x^2 I_{xxy} + I_y^2 I_{yyy}
\end{aligned}
\tag{11.6}
$$

A robust numerical technique using "interpolating operator" for the computation of the above third-order derivatives was developed in Tamrakar *et al.* (2007).

The edge directions in the image can then be measured based on the above third-order operator. It has long been known from handwriting recognition research that the distribution of directions in handwritten traces, as a polar plot, yields useful information for writer identification or coarse-style classification (Cheriet et al., 2007). An off-line, edge-based version of the edge-directional distribution was developed in Schomaker and Bulacu (2004). Computation of this feature starts with conventional edge detection: convolution with two orthogonal differential kernels (Sobels), followed by thresholding. We calculated the edge-direction histogram (EDH) in a very simple way. The edge-direction distribution is extracted by considering the orientation of the line joining two consecutive edge points. The angle that the line segment makes with the horizontal is computed using

$$\phi = \arctan\left(\frac{y_{k+1} - y_k}{x_{k+1} - x_k}\right) \tag{11.7}$$

As the algorithm runs over the edge map, the histogram of angles is built. For example, edge directions can be quantized at 1.8-degree intervals from 0 to 180. Thus, 100 bins are used to represent the edge directions. This angle histogram is then normalized to a probability distribution, which gives the probability of finding in the handwritten text image a contour fragment oriented with each ϕ. A schematic illustration of EDH is given in Fig. 11.3.

As expected, the more information the feature vectors used to construct the recognition system the better the results would be. Therefore, we propose to combine the features extracted by PHOG and EDH into a hybrid one.

11.3 Dimension Reduction by SR

Although the edge-directional features like PHOG or HED are sufficiently discriminative to enable writers classification based on their handwritten text images, the large number of features are not in equal importance in predicting the class labels and some of the "features" are actually irrelevant, noisy, or redundant, which have been proved to be the detrimental elements leading to the inaccuracies in classification performance. Moreover, as the number of features used for classification increases, the number of training samples required for statistical modeling and/or learning systems grows exponentially (Duda et al., 2001). Principal component analysis (PCA) is a simple method that is often used to reduce the dimension of features. PCA carries out linear transformation of data and projects it to a lower dimensional subspace in such a way that most of the information is retained while discarding the noisy component of data. However, PCA is limited in many applications as data could live on a non-linear manifold and then variance may not capture important structure.

Recently, some entirely new approaches have been devised to address the non-linear dimension reduction, for example, the spectral methods have been proved a powerful tool (Saul et al., 2006). The methods use information contained in the

SOME 17 years ago, in the early summer of 1934,

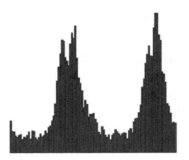

To observe the colour rise in her cheek

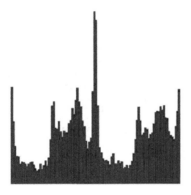

Fig. 11.3. A schematic illustration of EDH.

eigenvectors of a data affinity (i.e., item-item similarity) matrix to reveal low-dimensional structure in high-dimensional data. Among the new developments, a novel dimensionality-reduction method, called SR, was proposed in (Cai *et al.*, 2007), which casts the problem of learning an embedding function into a regression framework without the eigen-decomposition of dense matrices.

Given m samples $\{\mathbf{x}_i\}_{i=1}^m \subset R^n$, dimensionality reduction aims at finding $\{\mathbf{a}_i\}_{i=1}^m \subset R^d, d \ll n$, where $\mathbf{a}_i$ can represent $\mathbf{x}_i$. In the graph-embedding framework, a graph G with m vertices is defined, with each vertex representing a data point. Let W be a symmetric $m \times m$ matrix with W_{ij} having the weight of the edge-joining vertices i and j. The G and W can be defined to characterize certain statistical or geometric properties of the dataset. The purpose of graph embedding is to represent each vertex of a graph as a low-dimensional vector that preserves similarities between the vertex pairs, where similarity is measured by the edge weight.

Let $\mathbf{y} = [y_1, y_2, \ldots, y_m]^T$ be the 1D projection of $X = [\mathbf{x}_1, \mathbf{x}_2, \ldots, \mathbf{x}_m]$. The optimal $\mathbf{y}$ tries to minimize the following objective with constraint $\mathbf{y}^T D \mathbf{y} = 1$:

$$\sum_{ij} (y_i - y_j)^2 W_{ij} = 2\mathbf{y}^T L \mathbf{y} \tag{11.8}$$

where $L = D - W$ is the graph Laplacian (Belkin and Niyogi, 2001) and D is a diagonal matrix whose entries are column (or row, since W is symmetric) sums of W, $D_{ii} = \sum_j W_{ji}$. The objective function encourages neighboring vertices i and j be mapped closer in the embedding space.

The minimization problem reduces to find

$$\mathbf{y}^* = \arg\min_{\mathbf{y}^T D \mathbf{y} = 1} \mathbf{y}^T L \mathbf{y} = \arg\max_{\mathbf{y}} \frac{\mathbf{y}^T W \mathbf{y}}{\mathbf{y}^T D \mathbf{y}} \tag{11.9}$$

The optimal $\mathbf{y}$ can be obtained by solving the maximum eigen-problem:

$$W\mathbf{y} = \lambda D\mathbf{y} \tag{11.10}$$

For classification purpose, a mapping for all samples, including new test samples, is required. If we choose a linear function, i.e., $y_i = f(\mathbf{x}_i) = \mathbf{a}^T \mathbf{x}_i$, Eq. (11.9) can be rewritten as

$$\mathbf{a}^* = \arg\max_{\mathbf{a}} \frac{\mathbf{a}^T X W X^T \mathbf{a}}{\mathbf{a}^T X D X^T \mathbf{a}} \tag{11.11}$$

The optimal $\mathbf{a}$ are the eigenvectors corresponding to the minimum eigenvalue of eigen-problem:

$$X W X^T \mathbf{a} = \lambda X D X^T \mathbf{a} \tag{11.12}$$

With different choices of W, the above framework leads to different subspace learning methods. A common problem of these methods is the high computational cost from the eigen-decomposition of dense matrices. To address this problem, Cai (Cai *et al.*, 2007, 2008) introduced spectral regression discriminant analysis (SRDA) which instead of solving the eigen-problem in Eq. (11.10) or Eq. (11.12), derives the linear functions via the following two steps:

Many different subspace learning methods can be described within the above framework with different choices of W. For example, linear discriminant analysis (LDA) can be considered as a special case where the weight matrix W is constructed by incorporating the label information. If there are c classes in the dataset and m_t samples in the tth class, i.e., $m_1 + m_2 + \cdots + m_c = m$, then W is defined as

$$W_{ij} = \begin{cases} 1/m_t & \text{if } \mathbf{x}_i \text{ and } \mathbf{x}_i \text{ belong to the } t\text{th class} \\ 0 & \text{otherwise} \end{cases} \tag{11.13}$$

Many of them share the same problem of heavy computational cost from the eigen-decomposition of dense matrices. Cai (Cai *et al.*, 2008) proved that instead of solving the eigen-problem Eq. (11.10) or Eq. (11.12), the linear embedding functions can be acquired through the following two steps:

(1) Solve the eigen-problem $W\mathbf{y} = \lambda D\mathbf{y}$ from Eq. (11.10) to get $\mathbf{y}$.
(2) Find $\mathbf{a}$ which satisfies $\mathbf{X}^T\mathbf{a} = \mathbf{y}$. In reality, such $\mathbf{a}$ might not exist. A possible way is to find $\mathbf{a}$, which can best fit the equation in the least squares sense:

$$\mathbf{a}^* = \arg\min_{\mathbf{a}} \sum_{i=1}^{m} (\mathbf{a}^T\mathbf{x}_i - y_i)^2 \tag{11.14}$$

where y_i is the ith element of $\mathbf{y}$.

The minimization of Eq. (11.14) is often ill-posed. The SRDA in Cai *et al.* (2008) proposed to apply the regularization technique to obtain the regularized estimator

$$\hat{\mathbf{a}}^* = (XX^T + \alpha I)^{-1}X\mathbf{y} \tag{11.15}$$

where $\alpha(\geq 0)$ is the regularization parameter to control the smoothness of the estimator $\hat{\mathbf{a}}^*$.

11.4 Classification Methods

With appropriate image features, writer identification can be systematically studied in the general multiclass classification framework. In machine learning, there are a number of well-known classification methods, for example, the k-nearest neighbor (k-NN) classifier, Fisher linear discriminant, Naive Bayes, artificial neural networks (e.g., multilayer perceptrons), and support vector machine. In the following, we briefly summarize a few of the most commonly used methods for comparison purpose. For more details, the readers can refer to Duda *et al.* (2001).

11.4.1 *Linear discriminant analysis*

In linear discriminant analysis (LDA), each class is modeled by a multivariate Gaussian, where each class is assumed to have the same covariance matrix. Specifically, LDA finds Gaussian distributions of the data by maximum likelihood estimations for several parameters: the prior probability of class k; the mean of class k; and the common covariance matrix. A test sample can be classified to the class of the nearest mean vector according to Mahalanobis distance, or by a likelihood ratio test, which reduces to a particularly simple form: $\mathbf{x} \cdot \mathbf{w} > t$, where t is a decision threshold, $\mathbf{w}$ is a parameter vector computed from the Gaussian parameters.

11.4.2 *Naive Bayes*

The Naive Bayes classifier is based on the Bayesian theorem and assumes that the effect of a variable value on a given class is independent of the values of other variable. As we can compute the 1D class-conditional density for each feature individually, the class-conditional independence assumption tremendously simplifies

the training step. While the class-conditional independence between features is
not true in general, research shows that this optimistic assumption works well in
practice. Naive Bayes classifier classifies data in two steps:

(1) Training step: using the training samples, the method estimates the parameters
    of a probability distribution, assuming features are conditionally independent
    given the class.
(2) Classification step: for a test sample, the method computes the posterior
    probability of that sample belonging to each class. It then classifies the test
    sample according to the largest posterior probability.

11.4.2.1 *k-NN classifier*

k-NN classifier is a prototype-based classifier among the oldest types of classification
methods. It is based on a distance function, for example, the Euclidean distance,
for comparing pairs of data samples. It classifies a test sample by first finding the
k-closest samples in the training set, and then predicting the class label by majority
voting. In other words, the class that is most common among those k-neighbors is
chosen as the predicted label. Obviously, the k-NN classifier needs to access all the
training data every time when a new test case is to be classified.

11.4.2.2 *Multilayer perceptron*

The multilayer perceptrons (MLPs) is a common type of neural network classifier,
which is often trained by the error back-propagation algorithm. MLP usually
consists of a layer of input nodes, each linked by weighted connections to every
one of a layer of hidden nodes, each of which is linked, in turn, to a set of output
nodes. It has been shown that the MLPs can virtually approximate any function
with any desired accuracy, provided that enough hidden units and enough data are
given. Therefore, it can also implement a discrimination function that separates
input data into classes. Such an ability of an MLP to learn from data makes
it a practical classifier for many classification tasks. Though successful for many
applications, however, MLP classifier has several limitations and training an MLP
network involves a considerable degree of empiricism. In addition, the performance
often depends on the nature and quality of the data on which it is trained. For
example, the classification accuracies may be sensitive for different class frequencies
in the training set.

11.4.3 *Support vector machine*

For binary pattern classification, SVM tries to find the optimal separating
hyperplane that separates the positive and negative examples with a maximal
margin. The optimal separating hyperplane is determined by giving the
largest margin of separation between different classes, following structural risk

minimization principle (Shawe-Taylor and Cristianini, 2004). The following constrained minimization then needs to be satisfied

$$\text{Minimize:} \quad \frac{1}{2}\mathbf{w}^T\mathbf{w},$$

$$\text{Subject to:} \quad y_i(\mathbf{w}\cdot\mathbf{x}_i + b) \geq 1, i = 1, \ldots, l \qquad (11.16)$$

The obtained SVM classifier involves the inner product $\mathbf{x}_i^T\mathbf{x}$, where $i \subset S$, the set of support vectors. However, it is not necessary to use the explicit input data to form the classifier. Instead, all that is needed is to use these inner products between the support vectors and vectors of the feature space. That is, by defining the kernel

$$k(\mathbf{x}_i, \mathbf{x}) = \mathbf{x}_i^T\mathbf{x} \qquad (11.17)$$

a non-linear classifier can then be formulated as

$$f(x) = \text{sign}\{\alpha_0 y_i K(\mathbf{x}_i, \mathbf{x}) + b_0\} \qquad (11.18)$$

The commonly applied Gaussian kernel is

$$k(\mathbf{x}, \mathbf{y}) = \exp\left(-\frac{||\mathbf{x}-\mathbf{y}||^2}{2\sigma^2}\right) \qquad (11.19)$$

where the parameter σ controls the support region of the kernel.

The aforementioned SVM were primarily designed for binary classification problems. Based on the relationship between binary classification and multiclass classification, many methods have been proposed in the literature for solving multiclass problem (Hsu and Lin, 2002; Franc and Hlavac, 2002). In our study, we use the scheme *One-against-all*, by which an SVM is constructed for each class by discriminating that class against the remaining $(k-1)$ classes.

11.5 Experiments

Experiments have been performed with the IAM Handwriting Database (Marti and Bunke, 1999) that is publicly available and has been used by many research groups. It contains forms of handwritten English text which can be used to carry out handwritten text recognition and to perform writer identification and verification experiments. The unconstrained handwritten text were scanned at a resolution of 300 dpi and saved as PNG images with 256 gray levels. A sample of the IAM form and the corresponding two lines of the segmented text are illustrated in Fig. 11.4. From IAM-database sets of 4307 text lines from 100 different writers, we used 39 sets (i.e., from 39 different writers). Samples of the segmeted text lines from two different authors are shown in Fig. 11.5.

We proceeded identification experiments in a general multiclass classification framework, with three different features applied. As described in Sec. 11.2, the PHOG algorithm is applied to all the text images, with three levels of pyramids and 16 Sbins in each level. In forming the pyramid, the grid at level l has 2^l cells along

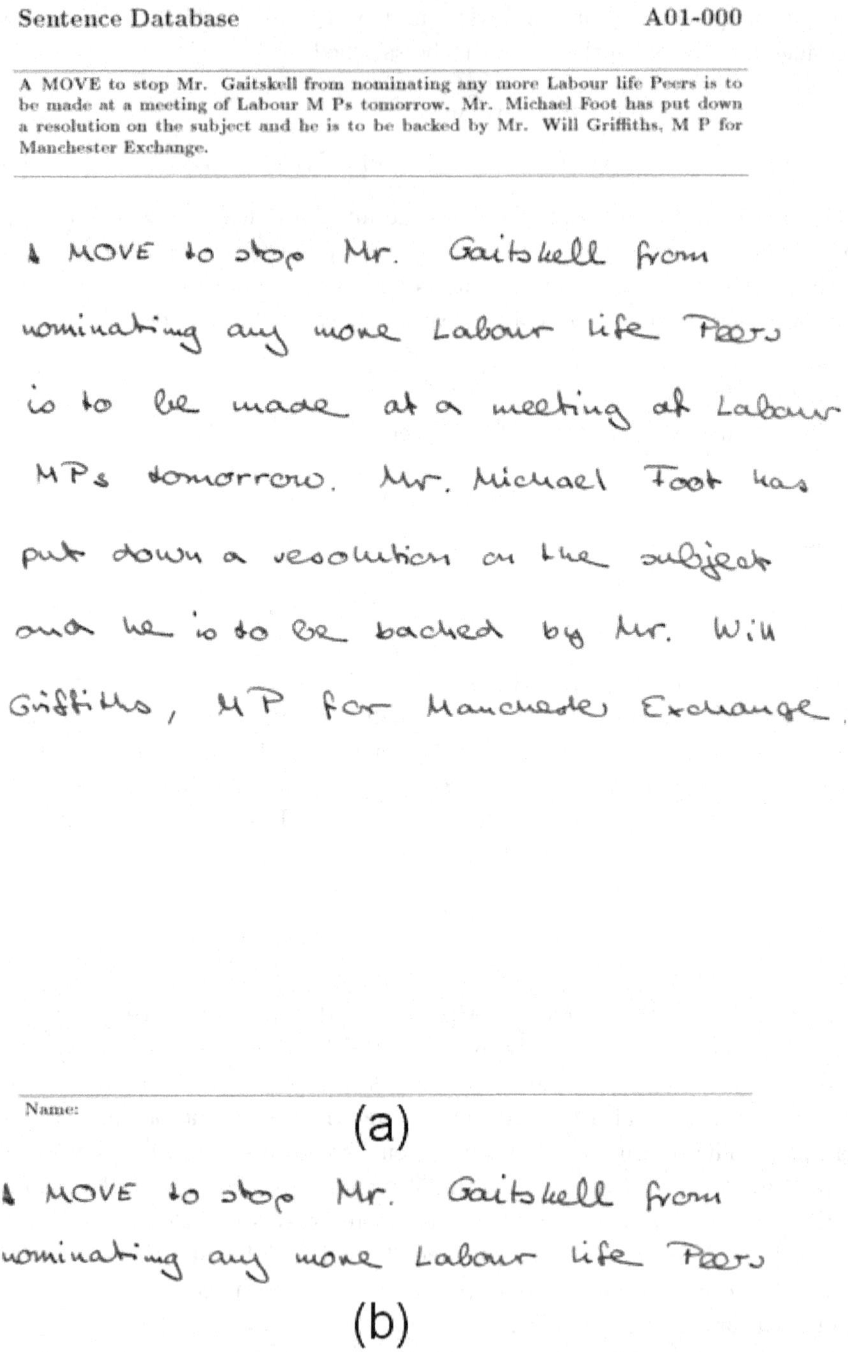

Sentence Database A01-000

A MOVE to stop Mr. Gaitskell from nominating any more Labour life Peers is to be made at a meeting of Labour M Ps tomorrow. Mr. Michael Foot has put down a resolution on the subject and he is to be backed by Mr. Will Griffiths, M P for Manchester Exchange.

Name:

(a)

(b)

Fig. 11.4. Samples from the IAM Handwriting Database. (a) forms from the database, and (b) segmented text lines.

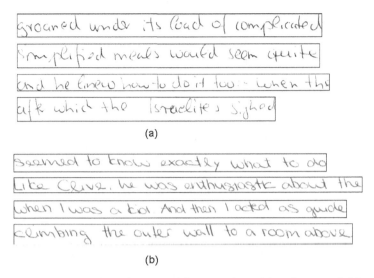

(a)

(b)

Fig. 11.5. Segmented text lines from two different authors: (a) author 1, and (b) author 2.

each dimension. Consequently, level 0 is represented by a 16-vector corresponding to the 16 bins of the histogram, level 1 by a 4×16-vector *et al.* Therefore, the three-level PHOG descriptor of an image is a vector with dimensionality $16 \sum_{l=0}^{2} 4^l = 336$. The HED features were extracted globally for each image, with 128 bins for the angle discretization. The two features are then simply concatenated together to form a hybrid feature.

We compared five classification methods, i.e., LDA, k-NN, Naive Bayes, MLP, and SVM as outlined in the previous section. The experimental settings for all the classifiers are summarized as follows. For MLP, we experimented with a three-layer network with the following structure. The number of inputs is the same as the number of features (i.e., 336 for PHOG histogram, 128 for HED, and 464 for the hybrid features), one hidden layer with 50 units and 39 output units, where each output unit designates one of the 39 writers. During training, the output units are clamped to 0.0, except for the unit corresponding to the desired class, which is clamped at 1.0. During classification, a new value is assigned to the class whose output unit has the highest activation. This is called the *one-per-class* approach. It is our experience that varying the number of hidden units in such an MLP usually does not significantly change the performance. The MLP was trained during 5000 iterations using a learning rate equal to 0.01.

The SVM applied is based on the sequential minimal optimization (SMO) scheme (Hsu and Lin, 2002), with values of the regularization parameter $C = 100$ and sigma parameter ($\sigma = 1$) by using the radial basis function kernel. The values are from the so-called grid search (Hsu and Lin, 2002). We experimented with multiclass SVM method *one-against-all*. For k-NN classifier, we chosen $k = 1$ after testing a range of different values of k with the similar results.

Table 11.1: Average accuracy from holdout experiment by using PHOG, HED, and hybrid features

	PHOG (in%)	HED (in%)	Hybrid (in%)
LDA	93.1	90.6	94.1
Naive Bayes	87.9	83.6	89.2
k-NN ($k = 1$)	88.4	86.0	91.1
MLP	89.9	90.1	93.6
SVM	89.9	83.9	92.8

There are many standard procedures to test the performance of a general pattern classification scheme. The commonly used ones include *holdout* and *k-fold cross-validation* methods. In the first experiment, random splitting the data into training/testing was repeated 100 times, each time with 20% of each writer's text line images reserved for testing while the rest for training. The performances from the five classifiers are recorded simultaneously. The averaged accuracies from the experiment were illustrated in Table 11.1. The box plot of the recorded performances is given in Fig. 11.6 (a), which conveys the location and variation information in the classification accuracies. It is obvious that among the five classifiers compared, LDA is the best. The advantage of combining the two edge-directional features is evidenced by the improved identification accuracies.

We then attempted to increase the identification performance by applying appropriate dimensionality reduction, which could extract a smaller number of "good" features. The first candidate is PCA, by which the number of principal component is chosen as the number of classes (39). The performance from PCA-based dimension reduction, however, does not indicate improvement for most of the classifiers: for LDA, the classification results are almost the same as with original features. The better accuracies with Naive Bayes classifier is from the independent variables after PCA transform. For other classifiers, results from applying PCA transform become poorer compared with the classifiers with original features. This confirms the general discussion that PCA is not effective for some practical data.

The second candidate for dimension reduction is the graph embedding based spectral regression as introduced in Sec. 11.3. The number of new dimension from SR is the number of class-1 (Cai *et al.*, 2007). Being similar to PCA, every training set is subject to the optimization procedure as given in Eq. (11.9), yielding transformation **a** which will then apply to all the testing set. Obviously the classification accuracies from all of the classifiers improved, as indicated in Table 11.3. The best performance 96% is from the dimension-reduced hybrid features using LDA classifier. The box plots corresponding to Tables 11.2 and 11.3 are given in Figs. 11.6 (b) and (c).

Recently, the IAM handwriting database has been used by a number of researchers for writer identification with many different algorithms published. In Schlapbach and Bunke (2007), Hidden Markov Model-based recognizers are designed for text line recognition, with features extracted from a text line and used to train the recognizers. The average identification rate from the different

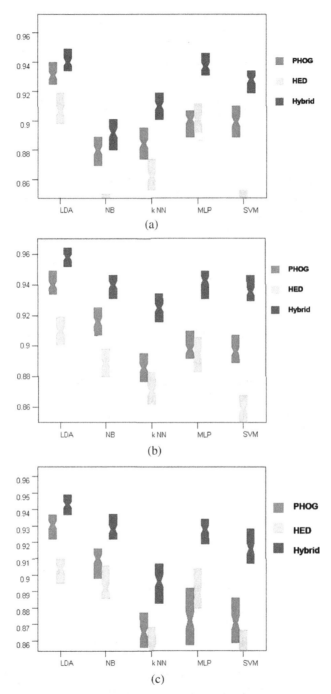

Fig. 11.6.   Box plots of the writer classification accuracies from holdout experiments: (a) applying edge-directional feature extracted by PHOG, HED, and the bybrid, (b) applying edge-directional features extracted by PHOG, HED, and the bybrid, followed by PCA projection, and (c) applying edge-directional feature extracted by PHOG, HED, and bybrid, followed by spectral regression-based dimension reduction. The results were from the average of 100 repeats.

Table 11.2:   Average accuracy from holdout experiment by using
PHOG, HED, and hybrid features followed by PCA projection

	PHOG (in%)	HED (in%)	Hybrid (in%)
LDA	92.9	90.2	94.2
Naive Bayes	90.8	83.4	92.9
k-NN ($k = 1$)	86.6	85.5	89.5
MLP	89	87.2	92.8
SVM	87.2	85.1	91.7

Table 11.3:   Average accuracy from holdout experiment by
using PHOG, HED, and hybrid features together with the
dimension-reduction method SR

	PHOG (in%)	HED (in%)	Hybrid (in%)
LDA	94.1	90.9	96
Naive Bayes	91.5	88.9	94
k-NN ($k = 1$)	88.4	87.1	92.5
MLP	90.0	89.4	94.1
SVM	89.7	85.9	93.7

experiments is around 90.6%. In Bensefia *et al.* (2005b), local features such as graphemes are extracted from the segmentation of cursive handwriting and a textual-based information retrieval model is used for the writer identification stage. As mush as 86% correct identification was obtained on the IAM data. In Schlapbach and Bunke (2007) feature selection by genetic algorithm is experimented with correct identification rate 94.2% achieved for the IAM data. The experimental settings from these publications are different from each other and not the same as ours. Therefore, the comparison can only give an intuitive meaning. Nevertheless, we can conclude that on the IAM data the identification rate from our method is very promising. A more detailed description about our experiment results can be illustrated by confusion matrix, which gives the number/proportion of examples from one class classified into another (or same) class. Figure 11.7 shows the confusion matrix from the LDA classifier with dimension reduced hybrid features.

The k-fold crossvalidation is another established technique for estimating the accuracy of a classifier. In general, all of the examples are partitioned into k-subsamples, of which the kth subsample is retained for testing the model while the remaining $k - 1$ subsamples are used as training data. Crossvalidation is then repeated k-times, with all of the k-subsamples used exactly once as the validation data. The cross-validation estimation of accuracy is the overall number of correct classifications, divided by the number of instances in the dataset. The popular holdout experiment can be considered as a special kind of crossvalidation with 2 folds, i.e., with the dataset being separated into training set and testing set of equal size.

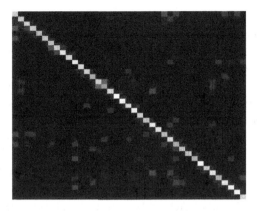

Fig. 11.7.   Confusion matrix from the LDA classifier with dimension-reduced hybrid features.

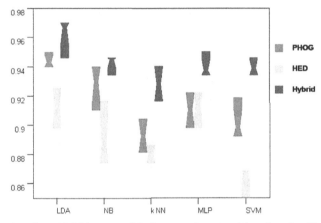

Fig. 11.8.   Box plots from 10-fold cross-validation experiments with writer classification accuracies from applying the edge-directional feature extracted by PHOG, HED, and the hybrid, followed by dimension-reduction spectral regression. The results were from the average of 10 iterations.

We conducted experiment with 10-fold crossvalidation for the five classifiers. This process of randomly generated partitions is repeated 10 times, with randomly chosen training and testing sets giving up 100 unbiased estimates of discriminant ability. As the test samples are independent of the training data, the results derived from this 10-fold crossvalidation are reliable. The experiment results of classification accuracies as shown in Fig. 11.8 demonstrated that, with the same PHOG features, LDA is the best which gives classification accuracy of 96.2%. This is completely consistent with the holdout experiment.

11.6 Conclusion

Writer identification and verification have been extensively researched over the past years aiming to add new discoveries to the field especially in terms of features that can uniquely identify writers and classification techniques that keep the phase simple yet achieve high accuracy. The research would continue as the demand for such applications is increasing along with the technology advances and problems that occur in the field that need to be solved. In this chapter, writer identification was studied and a new feature extraction method is proposed based on the hybrid edge-directional features, which is text independent and easy to compute. We assumed handwriting as text image and after a pre-processing stage, a set of features which are based on the HOG and HED, were extracted from the image of the documents. Our works show that local descriptors which have been increasingly used for object detection and recognition tasks also offer good alternative tools for writer recognition systems. The recently developed graph embedding-based dimension reduction demonstrate further improvement over the identification of the system performance. Experimental results show that hybrid feature perform much better than both of the HOG and HED methods. Ongoing works include the integration of more distinct features and decision fusion from different classifiers.

References

Bar-Yosef, I., Beckman, I., Kedem, K., and Dinstein, I. Binarization, character extraction, and writer identification of historical hebrew calligraphy documents, *Int. J. Document Anal. Recognition* **9**(2), 89–99, 2007.

Belkin, M., and Niyogi, P. Laplacian eigenmaps and spectral techniques for embedding and clustering, in *Advances in Neural Information Processing Systems*, Vol. 14 (MIT Press, Cambridge, MA), pp. 585–591, 2001.

Belongie, S., Malik, J., and Puzicha, J. Shape matching and object recognition using shape contexts, *IEEE Trans. Pattern Anal. Machine Intelligence* **24**(4), 509–522, 2002.

Bensefia, A., Paquet, T., and Heutte, L. Handwritten document analysis for automatic writer recognition, *Electronic Lett. Comput. Vision Image Anal.* **5**(2), 72–86, 2002.

Bensefia, A., Paquet, T., and Heutte, L. A writer identification and verification system, *Pattern Recognition Lett.* **26**(13), 2080–2092, 2005.

Bosch, A., Zisserman, A., and Munoz, X. Representing shape with a spatial pyramid kernel, in *Proc. ACM Int. Conf. Image Video Retrieval*, pp. 401–408, 2007.

Bulacu, M., and Schomaker, L. Automatic handwriting identification on medieval documents, in *Proc. Int. Conf. Image Anal. Processing (ICIAP 2007)*, pp. 279–284, 2007a.

Bulacu, M., and Schomaker, L. Text-independent writer identification and verification using textural and allographic features, *IEEE Trans. Pattern Anal. Machine Intelligence* **29**(4), 701–717, 2007b.

Bulacu, M., Schomaker, L., and Vuurpijl, L. Writer identification using edge-based directional features, in *Proc. Int. Conf. Document Anal. Recognition (ICDAR 2003)*, pp. 2:937–941, 2003.

Cai, D., He, X., and Han, J. Spectral regression for dimensionality reduction, Technical Report UIUCDCS-R-2007-2856, UIUC, 2007.

Cai, D., He, X., and Han, J. SRDA: An efficient algorithm for large scale discriminant analysis, *IEEE Trans. Knowledge Data Eng.* **20**(1), 1–12, 2008.

Cheriet, M., Kharma, N., Liu, L., and Suen, C. *Character Recognition Systems: A Guide for Students and Practitioners* (Wiley-Interscience), 2007.

Dalal, N., and Triggs, B. Histograms of oriented gradients for human detection, in *Proc. IEEE Conf. Comput. Vision Pattern Recognition (CVPR 2005)*, pp. 886–893, 2005.

Duda, R., Hart, P., and Stork, D. *Pattern Classification*, 2nd edn. (John Wiley and Sons, New York), 2001.

Franc, V., and Hlavac, V. Multi-class support vector machine, in *Proc. Int. Conf. Pattern Recognition (ICPR'02)*, pp. 236–239, 2002.

Franke, K., Schomaker, L., Veenhuis, C., Taubenheim, C., Guyon, I., Vuurpijl, L., Erp, M. V., and Zwarts, G. WANDA: a generic framework applied in forensic handwriting analysis and writer identification, in *Proc. Int. Conf. Hybrid Intelligent Syst. (HIS03)*, pp. 927–938, 2003.

He, Z., You, X., and Yan, Y. Writer identification using global wavelet-based features, *Neurocomputing* **71**(10–12), 1832–1841, 2008.

Hsu, C., and Lin, C. A comparison on methods for multi-class support vector machines, *IEEE Trans. Neural Networks* **13**(2), 415–425, 2002.

Hubel, D., and Wiesel, T. Functional architecture of macaque monkey visual cortex, *Proc. Royal Soc. London B* **198**, 1–59, 1977.

Lazebnik, S., Schmid, C., and Ponce, J. Beyond bags of features: spatial pyramid matching for recognizing natural scene categories, in *Proc. IEEE Int. Conf. Comput. Vision Pattern Recognition (CVPR'06)*, pp. 2169–2178, 2006.

Lowe, D. Distinctive image features from scale-invariant keypoints, *Int. J. Comput. Vision* **60**(2), 91–110, 2004.

Marti, U., and Bunke, H. A full english sentence database for off-line handwriting recognition, in *Proc. Int. Conf. Document Anal. Recognition*, pp. 705–708, 1999.

Pervouchine, V., and Leedham, G. Extraction and analysis of forensic document examiner features used for writer identification, *Pattern Recognition* **40**(3), 1004–1013, 2007.

Roweis, S., and Saul, L. Nonlinear dimensionality reduction by locally linear embedding, *Science* **290**(5500), 2323–2326, 2000.

Said, H., Tan, T., and Baker, K. Personal identification based on handwriting, *Pattern Recognition* **33**(1), 149–160, 2000.

Saul, L., Weinberger, K., Ham, J., Sha, F., and Lee, D. Spectral methods for dimensionality reduction, in O. Chapelle, B. Schoelkopf and A. Zien (eds.), *Semisupervised Learning* (MIT Press, Cambridge, MA), 2006.

Schlapbach, A., and Bunke, H. A writer identification and verification system using HMM based recognizers, *Pattern Anal. Applications* **10**(1), 33–43, 2007.

Schomaker, L., and Bulacu, M. Automatic writer identification using connected-component contours and edge-based features of uppercase western script, *IEEE Trans. Pattern Anal. Machine Intelligence* **26**(6), 787–798, 2004.

Schomaker, L. Advances in writer identification and verification, in *Proc. Int. Conf. Document Anal. Recognition(ICDAR 2007)*, pp. 1268–1273, 2007.

Shawe-Taylor, J., and Cristianini, N. *Kernel Methods for Pattern Analysis* (Cambridge University Press), 2004.

Siddiqi, I., and Vincent, N. Combining global and local features for writer identification, in *Proc. Int. Conf. Frontiers Handwriting Recognition (ICFHR 2008)*, pp. 48–53, 2008.

Srihari, S., and Ball, G. Writer verification of arabic handwriting, in *Proc. Int. Workshop Document Anal. Syst.*, pp. 28–34, 2008.

Srihari, S., Cha, S., Arora, H. and S., L. Individuality of handwriting, *J. Forensic Sci.* **47**(4), 1–17, 2002.

Tamrakar, A., and Kimia, B. No grouping left behind: from edges to curve fragments, in *Proc. IEEE Int. Conf. Comput. Vision (ICCV'07)*, pp. 1–8, 2007.

Tenenbaum, J., Silva, V., and Langford, J. A global geometric framework for nonlinear dimensionality reduction, *Science* **290**(5500), 2319–2323, 2000.

Yu, K., Wang, Y., and Tan, T. Writer identification using dynamic features, in *Proc. Int. Conference Biometric Authentication (ICBA 2004)*, pp. 1–8, 2004.

Part VII

Human Behavior Analysis

Chapter 12

HUMAN GROUP ACTIVITIES: DATABASE AND ALGORITHMS

Bingbing Ni*, Shuicheng Yan†, and Ashraf Kassim‡

Department of Electrical and Computer Engineering
National University of Singapore, Singapore, 117576
* g0501096@nus.edu.sg
† eleyans@nus.edu.sg
‡ eleashra@nus.edu.sg

12.1 Introduction

Video-based human action and activity analysis has attracted much interest in computer vision research community throughout the decades. A bunch of applications ranging from smart video surveillance for security purpose to advanced human computer interaction have drastically driven the development of video-based human activity analysis methods towards the application frontend. We begin this chapter with a comprehensive review on previous works on human activity analysis with categorizations. A quick summary is shown in Table 12.1.

Video-based human activity analysis was first studied in the setting of single human action recognition. Blank *et al.* (2005) introduced a 3D spatial-temporal volumetric modeling method to recognize single human's action, given that the background is known as a prior. Bobick and Davis (2001) proposed to use *temporal template* to represent human movement and they performed the action recognition by comparing the temporal template against stored instances of known actions, however, this method is not invariant to viewpoint changes since the temporal templates are a set of images taken as certain motion status at a fixed viewpoint. Madabhushi and Aggarwal (1999) proposed a Bayesian framework to classify a set of human actions such as standing, sitting, bending, getting up, and walking based on the detection of the human head region. Yacoob and Black (1998) presented a parameterized motion exemplar modeling method to represent and recognize human actions based on the principal components. Bobick and Davis (2001) proposed an appearance-based representation using motion energy images (MEI) to model actions. Ben-Arie (Ben-Arie *et al.*, 2002) developed an activity recognition method based on multidimensional hash table indexing from each detected body parts'

Table 12.1: A summary on the previous works on human activity analysis. Four categories of problems are defined as solo activity, pair activity, human-object interaction, and abnormal event. We also list the related feature representations and methods.

Category	Related works	Feature representation	Method
Solo activity	Blank *et al.* (2005), Bobick and Davis (2001), Madabhushi and Aggarwal (1999), Yacoob and Black (1998), Bobick and Davis (2001), Ben-Arie *et al.* (2002), Dollar *et al.* (2005), Ali *et al.* (2007), Parameswaran and Chellappa(2006)	Temporal template, spatio-temporal shape, head region, motion energy image, motion exemplar, detected body parts, trajectories of interest points	Database indexing, Bayesian method, principal component analysis, hash table, chaotic system
Human-object interaction	Bauckhage *et al.* (2004), Moore *et al.* (1999), Wu *et al.* (2007), Laxton *et al.* (2007)	Object region, body parts region, RFID, low-level visual feature	HMM, DBN, visual learning, contextual modeling, probabilistic reasoning
Pair activity	Park and Aggarwal (2002), Park and Aggarwal (2004), Zhou *et al.* (2008)	Body parts, motion trajectories	DBN, causality analysis
Abnormal event	Andrade *et al.* (2006a), Wu *et al.* (2005), Xu and Anjulan (2008), Zhong *et al.* (2004)	Optical flows, image regions of interest	Principal component analysis, HMM, prototype-segment matching, SVM

movements. Dollar *et al.* (2005) proposed a human behavior recognition method based on the usage of sparse spatial-temporal features. Ali *et al.* (2007) introduced an action recognition framework that uses concepts from the theory of chaotic systems to model and analyze non-linear dynamics of human actions based on the trajectories of reference points. Parameswaran and Chellapa (2006) presented a viewpoint-invariant action approach by exploiting the view-invariant canonical body poses and trajectories in 2D invariance space.

Motivated by the applications such as smart office surveillance system, video conferences, advanced human computer interfaces, etc. the interpretations of the interactions between human and the surrounding objects become very important in the human behavior understanding. Bauckhage *et al.* (2004) presented a system for object and action recognition in an office environment, which fuses the results from attention mechanisms, visual learning, and contextual as well as probabilistic reasoning. Moore *et al.* (1999) exploited human motion and object context to perform action recognition and object classification by measuring image, object, and action-based information from video. Hidden Markov Models (HMMs) and a Bayesian classifier are adopted to perform the action classification. Wu *et al.* (2007) used the cues of object use to detect and analyze the video sequence in the domains such as cooking. Besides the video input, their system also leverages the sparse and noisy readings from RFID tagged objects. Laxton *et al.* (2007) proposed a dynamic Bayesian network (DBN)-based approach by integrating temporal, contextual, and ordering constraints with output from low-level visual detectors to recognize complex, long-term human activities.

Many works consider the interpretation and recognition of the interactions of two persons. Park and Aggarwal (2002) presented a system to segment and track multiple body parts of interacting humans in the presence of mutual occlusion and shadow. They also proposed an approach for the recognition of two-person interactions using a hierarchical Bayesian network (BN) (Park and Aggarwal, 2004). The system is capable of recognizing interactions such as hugging, shaking hands, or fighting. Recently, Zhou *et al.* (2008) proposed a method for pair-activity recognition by analyzing the causality features (Sims, 1972) between the two simultaneously tracked motion trajectories. Pair activities such as chasing, following, walking independently, meeting could be interpreted.

However, the interactions among a group of persons (e.g., crowded people in public areas; a group of people in the meeting room; in football and basketball games, the players actually interact with each other), namely human group activities, occur much more often in real scenarios, and the study of these human group activities based on visual cues has great potentials for many applications such as smart video surveillance and human–computer interfaces. Many studies on the abnormal event detection in crowded places such as railway stations, shopping malls have been proposed such as Andrade *et al.* (2006a), Wu *et al.* (2005), Xu and Anjulan (2008). Further, some works have been reported on sports videos (Ekin *et al.*, 2003; Liu *et al.*, 2006), however, these works do not focus on the group interactions of the players. Providing limited information (e.g., normal or abnormal), these applications could not tell the detailed higher-level information about the activities, e.g., what are the people actually doing?

Little research work devoted to the problem of recognizing human group activities has been reported. This is probably due to two factors, i.e., the difficulties caused by the varying number of participants as well as mutual occlusions and the lack of usable benchmark databases. In literature, different visual features, e.g., trajectories of the human body/body parts (Medioni *et al.*, 2001; Nascimento *et al.*, 2005; Prati *et al.*, 2008; Ribeiro and Victor, 2005; Stauffer and Grimson, 2000), optical flows (Andrade *et al.*, 2006b), and detected moving image regions (Blank *et al.*, 2005; Brand *et al.*, 1997; Moore *et al.*, 1999; Park and Aggarwal, 2002, 2004; Turaga *et al.*, 2007; Wu *et al.*, 2007; Zhong *et al.*, 2004), have been proposed for human activity representation. However, these features are limited in their use for recognizing human group activities, since (1) these features do not explicitly encode the information on the *interactions* among a group of persons,

(2) it is difficult or even infeasible to robustly track a long trajectory of a person in crowded scenarios with occlusions, and (3) the segmentation of human body/body parts in crowded scenes itself is a very challenging problem. Corresponding to the state-of-the-art of research on this topic, most currently available databases mainly include the activities of a single person (possibly including interactions with surrounding objects) or between two persons, e.g., the CAVIAR database (Fisher *et al.*, 2005) and recent UIUC pair-activity database (Zhou *et al.*, 2008), or collected for abnormal event detection in crowded scenes (Andrade *et al.*, 2006b). The BEHAVE (Fisher *et al.*, 2007) database was recently released for human group activity analysis, but the very limited number of annotated video samples makes it unsuitable for statistically sufficient studies of this problem.

In this chapter, we first investigate how to develop an effective representation method for modeling human group activities. Note that a preliminary version on theoretical development and results was published in (Ni *et al.*, 2009) and this chapter gives a more comprehensive introduction and recent advances in experimental results. On the one hand, the number and identities of persons involved in a group activity video clip are changing from time to time; therefore, the high-level visual information which models individual subjects is not applicable in the scenario of characterizing human group activities. On the other hand, low-level visual information, e.g., color patches or optical flow patterns, is however not descriptive enough to describe the interactions among a group of persons. We therefore find that it is more critical to use the middle-level visual cues for representing human group activities, e.g., the motion trajectories of the participants and their interactions. More specifically, we propose to represent the human group activities with three types of localized causality features, i.e., self-causalities, pair causalities, and group causalities, which can be utilized to encode the causal properties for individual trajectories, trajectory pairs, and trajectory groups, respectively. Each type of causality could be regarded as a digital filter, whose frequency responses then constitute the feature space for human group activity representation. Since the mutual occlusions as well as the inherent limitations of the tracking algorithms always exist, the trajectory of a moving person within a video clip is often broken into several segments. To deal with this issue, we propose to extract causality features locally based on the short segments, instead of the entire motion trajectory. As a consequence, these localized causalities can describe the spatially local and temporally short-term behaviors of a human group. Due to the fact that a sequence of human group activities are always composed of a set of such local behaviors, we can then treat each group activity sample as a bag of orderless localized causalities/filters for efficient representation.

We have collected a human group activity video database, which contains six types of popular group activities including: *walk-in-group*, *run-ingroup*, *stand-andtalk*, *gathering*, *fighting*, and *ignoring* (i.e., the subjects walk independently). We show some sample frames of the activity videos in Fig. 12.1. We capture the video database under five different sessions in a school car park environment, where the

| Walk-in-group | Run-in-group | Stand-and-talk | Gathering | Fighting | Ignoring |

Fig. 12.1. An illustration of the image frames (stacked together) for six types of human group activities. Note that the camera view angle may be different in different sessions, which brings greater difficulties in recognizing human group activities.

number of participants and the capture time are varying from session to session. After we get the raw video, we manually segment the videos into small video clips which contain a single activity and finally we get about 80 video clips for each category of group activity in average. This database is then used to evaluate the effectiveness of our proposed localized causality features for recognizing human group activities.

12.2 Representation by Localized Causalities

We consider the problem of recognizing human group activities in this section. To begin with, we assume that each sample of certain human group activity is instantiated as a set (or bag) of short segments of the human motion trajectories, which are extracted by some object tracking algorithm. Afterwards, we introduce the methodology we use to design the causality features within, between, and among these segments. We introduce our notations in the following. The motion segments within an video clip instance is denoted as $S = \{s^1, s^2, \dots, \}$, where $s^k(t) = [s_x^k(t), s_y^k(t)]^T$ is the center position of the human body in 2D image plane. A set of training samples are given as $\mathfrak{S} = \{S_1, S_2, \dots, S_N\}$, where N is the number of training samples, and their human activity labels are denoted as $\{c_1, c_2, \dots, c_N\}$, where $c_i \in \{1, 2, \dots, N_c\}$ with N_c as the number of human group activity categories. Then, we formulate the task of recognizing human group activities as to learn an activity discriminative function from the labeled training samples and the activity labels of the novel samples could be properly predicted. A justification of our motivation is given prior to the detailed introduction to our method.

12.2.1 *Motivations*

On the one hand, tracking of the human body/body parts for accurate human interaction modeling is always infeasible under the video surveillance scenarios, provided that the size of human body is often very small. On the other hand, only segments of the motion trajectories are obtainable with the state-of-the-art tracking algorithms. Regarding these two points, our motivation to utilize the localized causality features for human group activity representation is explained as follows:

Why use causalities for group activity representation? The human group activities are mainly characterized by the dynamic interaction properties among a set of persons (generally >2), and conventional features for solo-activity analysis often ignore this important information on interactions. From a causality point of view, the interactions between human subjects are essentially embodied as the affection, or mathematically stated as causality and feedback, between two persons or among multiple persons. Thus, the representation of group activities finally ends at how to model the causalities among a group of persons. These causalities can be further divided into three types: (1) *self-causality*, which describes the affection of the past status history to the current status of a person and mainly characterizes the behavior properties of a single person; (2) *pair causality*, which measures the interactions between two persons, e.g., meeting, chasing; and (3) *group causality*, which shows the affect of other persons' behaviors to the behavior of the concerned person, and is unique for group activity modeling.

Why use localized causality features? We propose to perform localized causality analysis instead of computing the causality features by fitting a global model using the complete motion trajectories throughout a video clip. More specifically, we first decompose the whole motion trajectory into short overlapped segments and the causality features are calculated based on these segments. This is due to the following two main reasons. First, the dynamic interaction property of a human group activity instance within a video clip may vary throughout frames, e.g., for the activity *fighting*, the identity of the person to interact with a certain person may change frequently or in the case of *ignoring*, the subjects' motion status is unstable and random. Therefore, the localized interactions are more repeatable for different samples. Second, self-occlusions, mutual occlusions, shadows, image noises all make the tracking of the entire motion trajectories difficult, and on the contrary, tracking a short segment of motion trajectory is always tractable. Thus, it is more feasible and practical under real scenarios to calculate the causalities in a spatially and temporally local way.

Therefore, we introduce three types of localized causality features, namely self-causalities, pair causalities, and group causalities introduced in the following for the purpose of modeling the dynamic interaction properties of different human group activities. In particular, we formulate each style of causality as the frequency responses of a specific digital filter, by taking the trajectory segments as input and output signals, respectively. The frequency responses are uniformly sampled in the frequency domain the sampled coefficients are further used to build the *visual word dictionary* by K-means clustering. Eventually, the histogram vector based on these visual words is used as final feature representation for recognizing human group activities.

12.2.2 *Self-causality analysis*

We refer the concept of self-causality to the effect of the past status history of a person to his/her current status. Namely, what is the mechanism that the previous motion trajectory positions of a person affect her/his current position. Image that

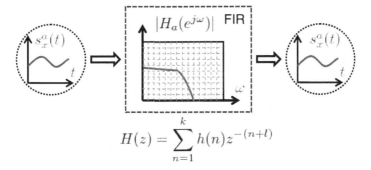

$$H(z) = \sum_{n=1}^{k} h(n) z^{-(n+l)}$$

Fig. 12.2.   Digital filter representation for self-causality analysis of the human motion segment.

a human trajectory segment denoted as s can be regarded as a digital signal. Then, this self-causality is modeled as a digital filter as shown in Fig. 12.2 with the input and output signals as the same digital signal s. A mathematical form for this filter, which represents the self-causality could be denoted as a finite impulse response (FIR) digital filter i.e.,

$$s(t) = \sum_{n=1}^{k} h(n) s(t - n - l) + \epsilon(t) \qquad (12.1)$$

where $h(n)$ is the impulse response of the FIR digital filter, k is the order of FIR filter, $\epsilon(t)$ is a stationary Gaussian noise with the variance as σ^2, and l is a manually set time lag which may avoid the overfitting issue in estimating the model parameters for the FIR filter. Note that in Eq. (12.1), the signal s is a 2D vector which contains both x and y coordinates, i.e., $s(t) = (x(t), y(t))^T$.

To recover the impulse response $h(n)$ and σ^2, we use all the frames in the motion trajectory segment s and calculate based on the least square errors (LSE) method to fit the $h(n)$ by minimizing the variance σ^2 of the noise term. Note that to obtain a solution for $h(n)$ at least k-linear equations are required. Thus, the length of each motion trajectory segment should be at least $2k + l$.

The obtained FIR digital filter then encodes the self-causality property of a human motion trajectory segment. To avoid the possible instability caused by the value of k, instead of directly using the $h(n)$'s as the self-causality features, we transform $h(n)$ into its frequency domain by z-transform to obtain the frequency responses for feature extraction. More specifically, the z-transform of $h(n)$ is calculated as

$$H(z) = \sum_{n=1}^{k} h(n) z^{-(n+l)} \qquad (12.2)$$

Generally, the frequency domain is more robust than the time domain for feature representation, and thus the self-causality property conveyed by the motion trajectory segment s can be represented as five evenly sampled frequency responses (magnitudes and phases):

$$f_1(s) = [|H(e^{j0})|, |H(e^{j\frac{\pi}{4}})|, \ldots, |H(e^{j\pi})|, \quad \angle H(e^{j\frac{\pi}{4}}), \ldots, \angle H(e^{j\frac{3\pi}{4}})]^T \quad (12.3)$$

which is a 8D vector. Note that for $z = e^{j0}$ and $z = e^{j\pi}$, we do not calculate their phases since they are always equal to zeros. Our offline experiments show that five frequencies are generally enough to achieve near-optimal recognition performance; therefore, we do not sample more frequencies to constitute longer-length $f_1(s)$.

Intuitively, different category of human motion trajectory segment may have an FIR digital filter with distinctive impulse response $h(n)$. For example, the $h(n)$'s for static, constant-speed, constant-acceleration motion trajectory segments could be expressed as $s(t) = s(t-1), s(t) = 2s(t-1) - s(t-2)$, and $s(t) = s(t-1) - 3s(t-2) + s(t-3)$, respectively.

12.2.3 *Pair-causality analysis*

Similarly, we use pair causality to describe the interaction properties of two persons, which is presented as follows. The pair-causality information is composed of two parts. The first part is the *strength* of one person's affect on another one, and the second part is *how* one person affects another one. Zhou *et al.* (2008) used the Granger causality test (GCT) (Sims, 1972) to obtain two quantities, causality ratio and feedback ratio, for measuring the causality and feedback strength between two persons based on their tracked concurrent motion trajectories.

More specifically, for a concurrent human motion trajectory pair of $s_a = [s_a(1), s_a(2), \ldots, s_a(t), \ldots]$ and $s_b = [s_b(1), s_b(2), \ldots, s_b(t), \ldots]$, we assume that the interaction between two trajectories is a stationary process, i.e., the prediction functions $P(s_a(t)|s_a(1:t-l), s_b(1:t-l))$ and $P(s_b(t)|s_a(1:t-l), s_b(1:t-l))$ do not change within a short time period, where $s_a(1:t-l) = [s_a(t-l), s_a(t-l-1), \ldots, s_a(1)]$ and so for $s_b(1:t-l)$.

To model $P(s_a(t)|s_a(1:t-l), s_b(1:t-l))$, we can use kth order linear predictor, namely

$$s_a(t) = \sum_{n=1}^{k} \beta(n)s_a(t-n-l) + \gamma(n)s_b(t-n-l) + \epsilon_a(t) \quad (12.4)$$

where $\beta(n)$'s and $\gamma(n)$'s are the regression coefficients, and $\epsilon_a(t)$ is the Gaussian noise with standard deviation $\sigma(s_a(t)|s_a(1:t-l), s_b(1:t-l))$. These model parameters can be derived based on the concurrent human motion trajectory segment pair of s_a and s_b. Similarly, we use the linear predictor to model $P(s_a(t)|s_a(1:t-l))$ as in Eq. (12.1), and the standard deviation of the noise signal is denoted as $\sigma(s_a(t)|s_a(1:t-l))$.

According to the GCT theory (Sims, 1972) and pair-trajectory analysis in Zhou *et al.* (2008), we could obtain two measurements on the causality strength, namely:

(1) **Causality ratio**:

$$r_c = \frac{\sigma(s_a(t)|s_a(1:t-l))}{\sigma(s_a(t)|s_a(1:t-l), s_b(1:t-l))}$$

which measures the relative strength of the causality.

(2) **Feedback ratio**:

$$r_f = \frac{\sigma(s_b(t)|s_b(1:t-l))}{\sigma(s_b(t)|s_a(1:t-l), s_b(1:t-l))}$$

which measures the relative strength of the feedback.

The causality ratio and feedback ratio can characterize how strong one person affects the motion of another one; however, it cannot tell us the underlying mechanism that drives the motions of these two persons. In other words, the causality ratio and feedback ratio only tell the *strength* of the model, by leveraging the information from the noise terms, namely the standard deviations. However, it cannot essentially describe the model structure (how one person affects another one), which is reflected by the information characterized by $\beta(n)$ and $\gamma(n)$

We thus seek a representation method to reflect the mechanism of the pair-interaction relationship. If we regard this relationship in Eq. (12.4) as a digital filter with the input signal as $s_b(t)$ and the output signal as $s_a(t)$, as illustrated in Fig. 12.3, we can calculate the z-transforms for both sides, and then we obtain the following equation by ignoring the noise term:

$$X_a(z) = \sum_{n=1}^{k} \beta(n)X_a(z)z^{-n-l} + \gamma(n)X_b(z)z^{-n-l} \tag{12.5}$$

where $X_a(z)$ and $X_b(z)$ are the z-transforms for the output and input signals, respectively. Denoting the impulse response of this digital filter as $H_{ba}(z)$, and

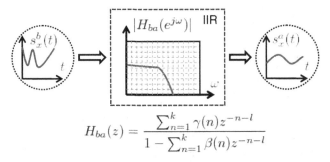

$$H_{ba}(z) = \frac{\sum_{n=1}^{k} \gamma(n)z^{-n-l}}{1 - \sum_{n=1}^{k} \beta(n)z^{-n-l}}$$

Fig. 12.3.   Digital filter representation for pair-causality analysis of the human motion trajectory segment pair.

based on the relation of $H_{ba}(z) = \frac{X_a(z)}{X_b(z)}$, we have

$$H_{ba}(z) = \frac{\sum_{n=1}^{k} \gamma(n) z^{-n-l}}{1 - \sum_{n=1}^{k} \beta(n) z^{-n-l}} \tag{12.6}$$

from which we can observe that this digital filter is an infinite impulse response (IIR) digital filter.

Similar to self-causality analysis, the magnitudes and the phases of the z-transform function at a set of evenly sampled frequencies are used to describe the digital filter (i.e., the style of the pair causality). More specifically, we use the magnitudes of the frequency responses at 0, $\pi/4$, $\pi/2$, $3\pi/4$, π and the phases of the frequency responses at $\pi/4$, $\pi/2$, $3\pi/4$ (constant values for frequency 0 and π), namely

$$f_{ba} = [|H_{ba}(e^{j0})|, |H_{ba}(e^{j\frac{\pi}{4}})|, \ldots, |H_{ba}(e^{j\pi})|, \quad \angle H_{ba}(e^{j\frac{\pi}{4}}), \ldots, \angle H_{ba}(e^{j\frac{3\pi}{4}})] \tag{12.7}$$

Similarly we can define the feature vector f_{ab} by considering s_a as the input signal and s_b as the output signal for an IIR digital filter which characterizes how the person in the trajectory segment s_a affects the motion of the person in the trajectory segment s_b.

In this way, the extracted frequency response features f_{ab} and f_{ba} convey how one person affects another one, while the causality ratio and feedback ratio characterize the strength of one person's affect on another one. These two aspects have complementary natures, and hence we combine them to form the description vector for pair-causality representation. We also add the relative distance Δd_{ba} and relative speed Δv_{ba} of two interacting persons for the final representation vector since they have shown to be very useful for discriminating activities such as *walk-in-group* and *gathering*,

$$f_2(s_a, s_b) = (f_{ab}, f_{ba}, r_c, r_f, \Delta d_{ba}, \Delta v_{ba})^T \tag{12.8}$$

which is a 20D feature vector with 5×2 magnitude values, 3×2 phase values, the causality and feedback ratio values, as well as the relative distance and speed.

12.2.4 *Group-causality analysis*

Human group activities characterize the behaviors of a group of persons, and the information conveyed may be beyond the self-causality and pair-causality features. For example, the group activity *gathering* generally involves three or more persons walking towards the same point. Therefore, we need features which can describe the interaction properties among multiple persons. In this section, we present the prediction model to describe the affects of all other persons to a certain person, namely

$$s^m(t) = \sum_{o \neq m, o \in \Omega_m} \sum_{n=1}^{k} h^o(n) s^o(t - n - l) + \xi^m(t) \qquad (12.9)$$

where Ω_m is the index set for all concurrent motion trajectory segments with s^m within a video clip, $h^o(n)$'s are the regression parameters, and $\xi^m(t)$ is the Gaussian noise term. Here, the trajectory $s^m(t)$ is predicted by utilizing all the other trajectories, and the model parameters could be estimated using LSE approach based on all the motion trajectory segments concurrent with s^m.

From the perspective of digital filters, the whole system can be regarded as the integration of a set of FIR digital filters. Among the filter set, each filter describes the causality relation as

$$\hat{s}^o(t) = \sum_{n=1}^{k} h^o(n) s^o(t - n - l), \quad o \neq m, \qquad (12.10)$$

where $\hat{s}^o(t)$ is unknown beforehand. Its z-transform function is then

$$H_{om}(z) = \sum_{n=1}^{k} h^o(n) z^{-n-l}, \quad o \neq m. \qquad (12.11)$$

Finally the outputs from all these FIR digital filters are summed to output the signal $s^m(t)$ along with the noise signal $\xi^m(t)$, namely

$$s^m(t) = \sum_{o \neq m, o \in \Omega_m} \hat{s}^o(t) + \xi^m(t) \qquad (12.12)$$

Figure 12.4 shows the whole system.

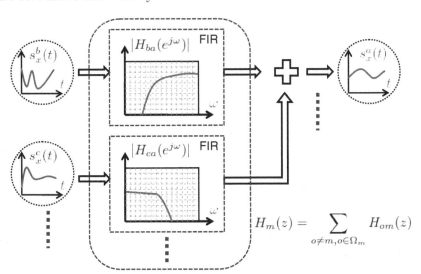

Fig. 12.4.   Digital filter representation for group-causality analysis of a group of human motion trajectory segments.

The number of input signals does not convey information for characterizing
the human group activity, and hence for group causality, we use the sum of the
frequency responses from all the FIR digital filters as the feature space for group-
causality representation. Denote

$$H_m(z) = \sum_{o \neq m, o \in \Omega_m} H_{om}(z) \tag{12.13}$$

and the group-causality features related with human motion trajectory segment s^m
are finally represented as

$$f_3(s^m) = [|H_m(e^{j0})|, |H_m(e^{j\frac{\pi}{4}})|, \dots, |H_m(e^{j\pi})|, \quad \angle H_m(e^{j\frac{\pi}{4}}), \dots, \angle H_m(e^{j\frac{3\pi}{4}})]^T \tag{12.14}$$

12.3 Other Trajectory-Related Features

Besides the localized causality features, some trajectory-related features are also
useful for encoding group activities partially. Similar to Zhou et al. (2008), we
define a set of features based on the relative distance and relative speed between
two moving subjects. Different from Zhou et al. (2008), we also use the covariances
of the relative distance and speed from many pair moving subjects, due to the
nature group activity problem. For example, relative distance with its covariance
are very helpful in discriminating walking/running together from gathering since in
walking/running together, the relative distances between subjects throughout the
frames have little variation; while for the activity gathering, the relative distances
between subjects are changing. More specifically, we calculate the relative distances
and speeds from all possible pair trajectories as well as the covariances for these
relative distances and speeds. These calculations result in a set of 2D vectors
for the relative speeds and distances and a set of 4D vectors for the covariance
features.

12.4 Classification with Localized Causalities

In this work, for the tracked long motion trajectories, we extract the short trajectory
segments (about $4k$ frames) by applying a temporal sliding window on the long
trajectories. Then, a group activity video clip can consist of a large number of short
human motion trajectory segments. From the previous section, we can extract a
8D feature vector for each segment to represent the self-causality. In a similar
way, we can extract a 20D feature vector for a concurrent segment pair, and a 8D
feature vector for each group of segments, to represent pair- and group-causality,
respectively. Further, we have a set of relative distance, speed, and covariance
features for each video clip. As the number of trajectory segments and the number
of concurrent trajectory segment pairs may be different in different video clips,
we use the bag-of-words approach to construct four visual word dictionaries based

on three types of causality features as well as the non-causality features. Then, each video clip is represented as four histogram vectors based on these four visual word dictionaries. The feature extraction as well as the formulation of the bag-of-words representation procedure is illustrated in Fig. 12.5. Finally, direct classifiers like nearest neighbor (NN) and other machine learning algorithms such as support

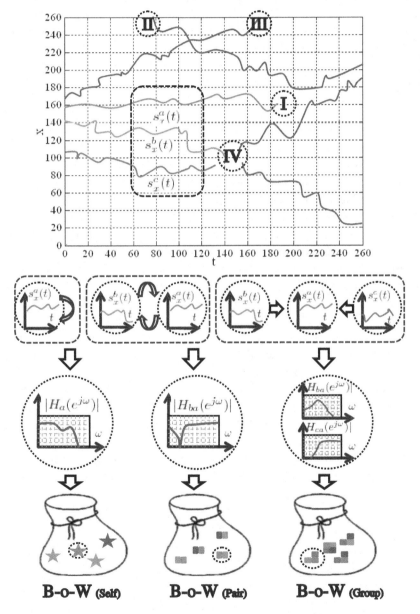

Fig. 12.5.   An example illustration of the process to extract localized causality features.

vector machine (SVM) (Chang and Lin, 2001) are used for human group activity classification.

12.5 Experiments

In this section, we first introduce the details of the group activity database we collected, demonstrate the effectiveness of the proposed three types of localized causality features as well as the combined features with relative distance, speed, and their covariance. Then, we further compare these features with the low-level visual features extracted at the space–time interest points (Laptev *et al.*, 2008) and the hierarchical spatio-temporal context-based features (Sun *et al.*, 2009), which have been verified effective in many applications.

12.5.1 *Group activity database construction*

The human group activity database was collected in an outdoor scene (an university car park) environment. We used a Panasonic-NV-DX100EN video camera with frame rate of 25 fps and image size of 720×576 pixels. The video camera was mounted about 6 meters higher over the ground and we adjusted the camera settings so that the captured persons are in proper scale for ease of human tracking and detection. We conducted 5 sessions of video collection. Each session is performed by different actors or different number of actors and there is some background changing from session to session. In each session, six categories of group activities were staged by the actors and each activity contains 10–20 instances with 4–8 actors, and each session spans several minutes. For each video sequence, we manually segment the entire video into small video clips, each of which contains a human activity instance of 8–15 seconds and has a corresponding activity label, e.g., *walk-in-group*, *fighting*, etc. The whole database includes 476 labeled video samples in total. A summary of the segmented video samples is given in Table 12.2.

We track the human motion trajectory by taking each human actor as a 2D blob. By this simplification, we can utilize many state-of-the-arts tracking algorithms, e.g., the *CONDENSATION* (Isardl and Blake, 1998) algorithm to perform our tracking task. In our implementation, we used a particle filter (with about 100 particles) to track each person for the tradeoff of accuracy and computational cost. The initialization is done manually by asking the users to provide bounding rectangles

Table 12.2: A summary on the collected human group activity database

Category	W	R	S	G	F	I	Total
No. of sessions	5	5	5	5	5	5	5
No. of segments	94	65	88	86	74	69	476

For simplicity, we denote W (walk-in-group), R (run-in-group), S (stand-and-talk), G (gather), F (fight), and I (ignore).

for the first frame. The tracking fails easily due to the mutual occlusions and manual reinitializations are used for simplicity. Note that some motion segmentation algorithms can be developed for automatic reinitializations (Haritaoglu *et al.*, 2000; Wren *et al.*, 1997). Finally, for each video clip, a set of short human motion trajectory segments are obtained, and we downsample the frame rate by a factor of 2 for further process.

12.5.2 *Localized causality feature visualization*

Figure 12.5 shows an example of the tracked human trajectory. A sliding window is used to obtain overlapped short motion segments. We can observe that there exist several scenarios that a trajectory breaks into two, e.g., tracker's failure (marked by I), subject entering the view (marked as II), and out of the view (marked as III), and the manual reinitialization after occlusion (marked as IV). Therefore, it is intractable to extract the complete trajectory throughout the whole video clip. In Fig. 12.6, we further illustrate the examples of the extracted human motion trajectories, the three types of filter responses from the localized causality analysis, as well as the three histogram representations based on the bag-of-words models. Each of the subfigures on the right of the sampled video frames shows the tracked trajectories of the human group activities. Note that there exist distinctive patterns associated with different categories of group activities. For *walk-in-group* and *run-in-group* activities, all the trajectories are nearly parallel; for *stand-and-talk* and *fighting* activities, the trajectories are more random, and for *fighting* activity, there exist lager variations among trajectories; for *gathering* activity, all the trajectories converge to a common point; and for *ignoring* activity, each trajectory points to a different direction. The subfigures below show examples of the filter responses in terms of magnitude (2nd row) and phase (third row) for self-causality (left), pair-causality (middle), and group-causality (right) features. The last row shows the histogram representations for three types of causality features based on the bag-of-words models. As there are two examples shown for each activity class, it is easily verified that activities from distinctive classes exhibit large difference in the bag-of-words representation (i.e., the last row of each subfigure); however, both the samples from the same class have similar representations. This observation further demonstrates the validity of our proposed feature representation methods.

12.5.3 *Classification with localized causalities*

We use the leave-one-session-out strategy for group activity classification tasks. For the parameter l, k, and the sizes of four visual word dictionaries, we evaluate all the proper combinations of these parameters and set them to be optima in the experiments, and finally $l = 4$, $k = 4$, and the dictionary size is set to be 20 for each type of causality feature. For the NN classifier, we use the well-known χ^2 distance

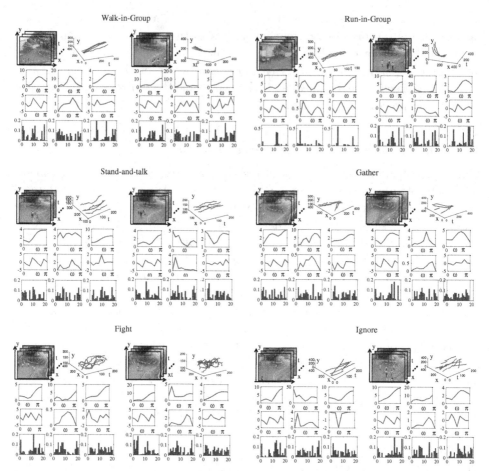

Fig. 12.6.   An illustration of the captured video sequences (left 1st row), tracked motion trajectory segments (right 1st row), examples of the filter responses for both magnitudes (2nd row) and phases (3rd row), and bag-of-words representations (4th row) for different types of group activities. Note that for the 2–4th rows, from left to right, the subfigures correspond to self-, pair-, and group-causality features, respectively. Totally, 2 examples are shown for each activity category.

for dissimilarity measure

$$d(x, y) = \frac{1}{2} \sum_i \frac{(x_i - y_i)^2}{x_i + y_i} \qquad (12.15)$$

where x and y are the concatenated vector from the three histogram vectors based on three types of localized causality features. For SVM, we use the following kernel based on the χ^2 distance

$$k(x, y) = \exp\left\{ -\frac{1}{\gamma} d(x, y) \right\} \qquad (12.16)$$

where the kernel parameter γ is tuned to be optimal. We use the non-linear multi-class SVM toolbox LIBSVM in Chang and Lin (2001) for model training and final classification.

Figure 12.7 lists the classification accuracies in terms of confusion matrices by using different types of causality features, as well as their combination, based on both NN and SVM classifiers. From Fig. 12.7 (self-causality NN-41.4%) and Fig. 12.7 (Pair causality NN-69.1%), we can observe that, on the one hand, self-causality features carry limited information for discriminating the activities *walk-in-group*, *ignoring*, or *gathering* from each other since when specific to a person, his/her motion trajectory segment may be similar for these three activities, however, they could be easily differentiated by the pair-causality features. On the other hand, the pair-causality features cannot effectively discriminate the activity *walk-in-group* from *run-in-group* since the pair interaction properties of these two activities are similar; however, the self-causality features can properly deal with this case since the motion models of walking and running for a single person are different. When these three types of localized causality features are combined, the classification performance could be further boosted (Fig. 12.7 (combination NN-72.3%)).

We also show the effectiveness of relative distance (with its covariance) and relative speed (with its covariance) features. The classification performance using the relative distance and relative speed feature as well as their combination with the localized causality features are shown in Fig. 12.8 in terms of class confusion matrix (by NN and SVM). Note that we set the codebook size as 20 for both relative distance and speed features. While these features are combined with localized causality features, the recognition accuracy is significantly boosted.

We further compare the localized causality features with the state-of-the-art low level visual features, i.e., the features extracted at the space-time interest points (STIP) (Laptev *et al.*, 2008) and the hierarchical spatio-temporal feature proposed in Sun *et al.* (2009). The first method extracts the histograms of oriented gradients (HOG) and histograms of optical flow (HOF) features computed within a 3D video patch around each detected STIP. The patch is partitioned into a grid with $3 \times 3 \times 2$ spatio-temporal blocks, and the 4-bin HOG descriptors and 5-bin HOF descriptors are then computed for all blocks and are concatenated into a 72-element and 90-element descriptors, respectively. Finally they are concatenated into a 162D description vector. We model the video clips based on the bag-of-words method by first clustering all the description vectors from the training set using K-means method. We vary the dictionary size from 10 to 2000 and compare with our proposed features also in a leave-one-session-out strategy. For SVM classifier, the kernel used is the same as in Eq. (12.16). From the comparison results shown in Fig. 12.9, it is observed that STIP-based low-level features yield very low performance compared with our proposed localized causality features, since no interaction information among a group of persons is explicitly exploited for the features extracted at the space–time interest points.

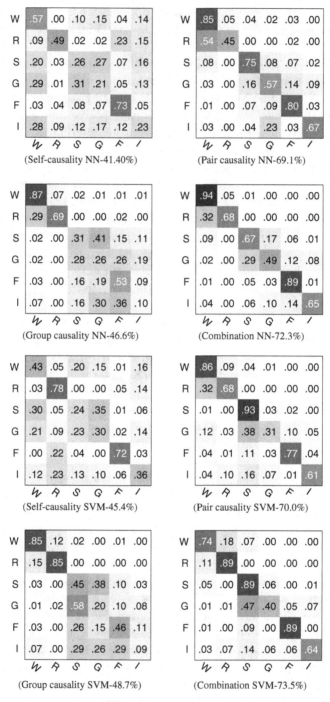

Fig. 12.7.   The confusion matrices of the human group activity classification results with different features and classifiers. For ease of display, each activity is denoted by its first character, i.e., "W" for walk-in-group, "R" for run-in-group, "S" for stand-and-talk, "G" for gathering, "F" for fighting, and "I" for ignoring. For better viewing, please see the pdf file.

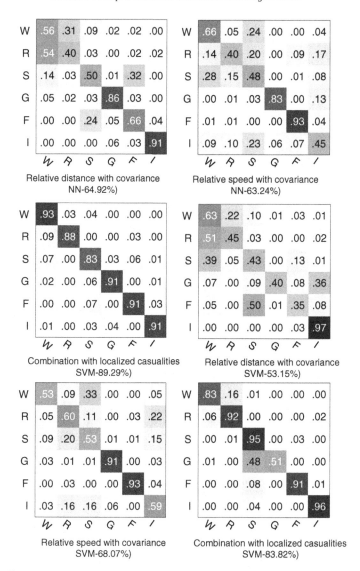

Fig. 12.8.   The confusion matrices of the human group activity classification results with relative distance and relative speed (with their covariances) feature and the combination of these features with our proposed localized causality features.

The second method first extracted SIFT (Lowe, 2004) features from each frame of the videos and then match these SIFT feature points to form a set of SIFT point trajectories for each video clip. Three types of descriptors, namely, average SIFT descriptor (SIFT), trajectory transition descriptor (TTD), and trajectory proximity descriptor (TPD) are developed to represent the intra- and interrelationship between the tracked trajectories. K-means clustering is also used to form the visual dictionary for these three types of features. We vary the size

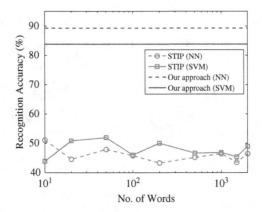

Fig. 12.9. Classification comparison between our proposed localized causality features and the local features exacted at the STIPs.

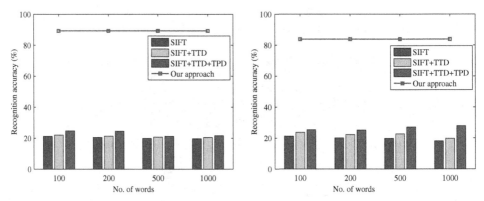

Fig. 12.10. Classification comparison between our proposed localized causality features and the spatio-temporal feature (SIFT+TTD+TPD).

of the codebook and report the leave-one-session-out classification performance using both NN and SVM to compare with our proposed feature representation method, i.e., localized causality features. The results are illustrated in Fig. 12.10. From Fig. 12.10, we can see that the TPD feature improves the performance of SIFT and TTD due to its capability of modeling interactions, which is consistent with the experimental results from (Sun *et al.*, 2009). However, the overall discriminative performance of the SIFT+TTD+TPD feature is still much lower than our proposed method.

12.6 Future Research Directions

Although some preliminary results have been obtained in our current work, we think the current setting of the problem is still simplified and to achieve applications for real scenarios, there is still a long way to go. In this section, we list the limitations of our current work and also propose the future research directions.

(1) The current approach relies on the correct track of the short motion trajectories; however, for real applications, robust and efficient tracking is not trivial. An alternative is to use salient point-based trajectories, e.g., SIFT trajectories (Sun *et al.*, 2009). Detecting salient point is straightforward and can avoid the requirement of manual initializations in human tracking process. For modeling human group activities, we can calculate the solo-, pair-, and group-causality for SIFT trajectories in a similar way of the approach used in the current work.
(2) The current human group activity database is acted out by our group members. Therefore, the video quality is very good without any disturbance from other pedestrians. However, in a real scenario, the context of the video is often very complicated with crowded people, significant occlusions, disturbance from vehicles etc. In the future work, we plan to extend the current group activity video database to add different levels of background clutters, noises, occlusions, disturbances for simulating the real cases. In the same time, the database size (currently 476 samples) should be greatly enlarged.
(3) The current work only focus on feature extraction and classification for human group activities, however, for a realistic application, several related tasks are also essential and worth investigating. First, a raw video sequence is often very long and composed of a set of activity instances in temporal order, and sometimes overlapped. For further processing, e.g., recognition, we must segment the long video sequence into several small clips according to some consistent measurement. The segmented video clips are expected to have atomic group activities which has consistent semantic meaning. Another task is, given some query, e.g., activity labels, to localize or detect the related context in the video sequence. This task is a key component in event detection. In general, segmentation and localization in the context of human group activity is more challenging compared with single human activity video, due to the complexity of group activity and the overlapping of different activities. We plan to investigate the group activity-related video segmentation and group activity localization in our future work.

12.7 Conclusion

In this chapter, we introduced the video database collected for the rarely studied problem of recognizing human group activities in surveillance videos. Three types of causality features, characterizing the dynamic interaction properties within, between, and among human motion trajectory segments, were proposed to obtain a fixed-length representation for video clip with variable length and number of persons. To the best of our knowledge, the group activity database introduced in this work is the first one available for extensively studying the human group activities, and also it is the first work to extensively study the human group activity classification problem.

Acknowledgment

This work is supported by the NRF/IDM Program, under research grant NRF2008IDM-IDM004-029.

References

Ali, S., Basharat, A., and Shah, M. Chaotic invariants for human action recognition, in *Proc. IEEE Int. Conf. Comput. Vision (ICCV'07)*, pp. 1619–1926, 2007.

Andrade, E. L., Blunsden, O. J., and Fisher, R. B. Hidden markov models for optical flow analysis in crowds, in *Proc. Int. Conf. Pattern Recognition*, pp. 1:460–463, 2006a.

Andrade, E. L., Blunsden, O. J., and Fisher, R. B. Modelling crowd scenes for event detection, in *Proc. Int. Conf. Pattern Recognition*, pp. 1:175–178, 2006b.

Bauckhage, C., Hanheide, M., Wrede, S., and Sagerer, G. A cognitive vision system for action recognition in office environments, in *Proc. IEEE Int. Conf. Comput. Vision Pattern Recognition (CVPR'04)*, pp. 2:827–833, 2004.

Ben-Arie, J., Wang, Z., Pandit, P., and Rajaram, S. Human activity recognition using multidimensional indexing, *IEEE Trans. Pattern Anal. Machine Intelligence* **24**, 8, 1091–1104, 2002.

Blank, M., Gorelick, L., Shechtman, E., Irani, M., and Basri, R. Actions as space-time shapes, in *Proc. IEEE Int. Conf. Comput. Vision (ICCV'05)*, pp. 2:1395–1402, 2005.

Bobick, A. F. and Davis, J. W. The recognition of human movement using temporal templates, *IEEE Trans. Pattern Anal. Machine Intelligence* **23**, 3, 257–267, 2001.

Brand, M., Oliver, N., and Pentland, A. Coupled hidden markov models for complex action recognition, in *Proc. IEEE Int. Conf. Comput. Vision Pattern Recognition*, pp. 994–999, 1997.

Chang, C. and Lin, C. LIBSVM: A library for support vector machines, http://www.csie.ntu.edu.tw/~cjlin/libsvm, 2001.

Dollar, P., Rabaud, V., Cottrell, G., and Belongie, S. Behavior recognition via sparse spatio-temporal features, in *Proceedings of the International Workshop on Visual Surveillance and Performance Evaluation of Tracking and Surveillance*, pp. 65–72, 2005.

Ekin, A., Tekalp, A., and Mehrotra, R. Automatic soccer video analysis and summarization, in *Proc. IEEE Int. Conf. Image Processing*, pp. 796–807, 2003.

Fisher, R., Blunsden, S., and Andrade, E. BEHAVE, http://homepages.inf.ed.ac.uk/rbf/BEHAVE/, 2007.

Fisher, R., Santos-Victor, J., and Crowley, J. CAVIAR, http://homepages.inf. ed.ac.uk/rbf/CAVIAR/, 2005.

Haritaoglu, I., Harwood, D., and Davis, L. W4: real-time surveillance of people and their activities, *IEEE Trans. Pattern Anal. Machine Intelligence* **22**, 8, 809–830, 2000.

Isardl, M. and Blake, A. CONDENSATION — conditional density propagation for visual tracking, *Int. J. Comput. Vision* **29**, 5–28, 1998.

Laptev, I., Marszatek, M., Schmid, C., and Rozenfeld, B. Learning human actions from movies, in *Proc. IEEE Int. Conf. Comput. Vision Pattern Recognition (CVPR'08)*, pp. 1–8, 2008.

Laxton, B., Lim, J., and Kriegman, D. Leveraging temporal, contextual and ordering constraints for recognizing complex activities in video,in *Proc. IEEE Int. Conf. Comput. Vision Pattern Recognition (CVPR'07)*, pp. 876–883, 2007.

Liu, S., Xu, M., Yi, H., Chia, L. T., and Rajan, D. Multimodal semantic analysis and annotation for basketball video, *EURASIP J. Appl. Signal Processing* **2006**, 182–194, 2006.

Lowe, D. Distinctive image features from scale-invariant keypoints, *Int. J. Comput. Vision* **60**, 2, 91–110, 2004.

Madabhushi, A. and Aggarwal, J. K. A bayesian approach to human activity recognition, in *Proc. IEEE Workshop Visual Suerveillance*, pp. 25–32, 1999.

Medioni, G., Cohen, I., Bremond, F., Hongeng, S., and Nevatia, R. Event detection and analysis from video streams, *IEEE Trans. Pattern Anal. Machine Intelligence* **23**, 8, 873–889, 2001.

Moore, D., Essa, I., and Haye, M. Exploiting human actions and object context for recognition tasks, in *Proc. IEEE Int. Conf. Comput. Vision (ICCV'99)*, pp. 1:80–86, 1999.

Nascimento, J., Figueiredo, M., and Marques, J. Segmentation and classification of human activities, in *Proc. Int. Workshop Human Activity Recognition Modelling*, pp. –, 2005.

Ni, B., Yan, S., and Kassim, A. Recognizing human group activities with localized causalities, in *Proc. IEEE Int. Conf. Comput. Vision Pattern Recognition (CVPR'09)*, pp. 1470–1477, 2009.

Parameswaran, V. and Chellappa, R. View invariance for human action recognition, *Int. J. Comput. Vision* **66**, 1, 83–101, 2006.

Park, S. and Aggarwal, J. Segmentation and tracking of interacting human body parts under occlusion and shadowing, in *Proc. IEEE Workshop Motion Video Computing*, pp. 105–111, 2002.

Park, S. and Aggarwal, J. A hierarchical bayesian network for event recognition of human actions and interactions, *Multimedia Syst.* **10**, 2, 164–179, 2004.

Prati, A., Calderara, S., and Cucchiara, R. Using circular statistics for trajectory shape analysis, in *Proc. IEEE Int. Conf. Comput. Vision Pattern Recognition (CVPR'08)*, pp. 1–8, 2008.

Ribeiro, P. and Victor, J. Human activity recognition from video: modeling, feature selection and classification architecture, in *Proc. Int. Workshop Human Activity Recognition and Modelling*, pp. –, 2005.

Sims, C. Money, income, and causality, *Ame. Economic Rev.*, pp. –, 1972.

Stauffer, C. and Grimson, W. Learning patterns of activity using realtime tracking, *IEEE Trans. Pattern Anal. Machine Intelligence* **22**, 8, 747–757, 2000.

Sun, J., Wu, X., Yan, S., Cheong, L. F., Chua, T. S., and Li, J. Hierarchical spatio-temporal context modeling for action recognition, in *Proc. IEEE Int. Conf. Comput. Vision Pattern Recognition (CVPR'09)*, pp. 1–8, 2009.

Turaga, P., Veeraraghavan, A., and Chellappa, R. From videos to verbs: mining videos for activities using a cascade of dynamical systems, in *Proc. IEEE Int. Conf. Comput. Vision Pattern Recognition (CVPR'07)*, pp. 1–8, 2007.

Wren, C., Azarbayejani, A., Darrell, T., and Pentland, A. Pfinder: realtime tracking of the human body, *IEEE Trans. Pattern Anal. Machine Intelligence* **19**, 7, 780–785, 1997.

Wu, X., Ou, Y., Qian, H., and Xu, Y. A detection system for human abnormal behavior, in *Proc. Int. Conf. Int. Robots Syst.*, pp. 1204–1208, 2005.

Wu, J., Osuntogun, A., Choudhury, T., Philipose, M., and Rehg, J. A scalable approach to activity recognition based on object use, in *Proc. IEEE Int. Conf. Comput. Vision (ICCV'07)*, pp. 206–213, 2007.

Xu, L. and Anjulan, A. Crowd behaviours analysis in dynamic visual scenes of complex environment, in *Proc. Int. Conf. Image Processing*, pp. 9–12, 2008.

Yacoob, Y. and Black, M. J. Parameterized modeling and recognition of activities, in *Proc. IEEE Int. Conf. Comput. Vision (ICCV'98)*, pp. 120–127, 1998.

Zhong, H., Shi, J., and Visontai, M. Detecting unusual activity in video, in *Proc. IEEE Int. Conf. Comput. Vision Pattern Recognition (CVPR'04)*, pp. 2:819–826, 2004.

Zhou, Y., Yan, S., and Huang, T. S. Pair-activity classification by bitrajectory analysis, in *Proc. IEEE Int. Conf. Comput. Vision Pattern Recognition (CVPR'08)*, pp. 1–8, 2008.

Chapter 13

SWIMMER BEHAVIOR ANALYSIS AND EARLY DROWNING DETECTION AT POOL

How-Lung Eng
Institute for Infocomm Research
1 Fusionopolis Way, #21 01 Connexis Tower
Singapore 138632
hleng@i2r.a-star.edu.sg

13.1 Introduction

Human behavior analysis from videos has become one of the most interesting topics in vision understanding (Gavrila, 1999; Hu *et al.*, 2004). This research investigates into using vision-based human behavior analysis for swimmer behavior monitoring and early drowning detection at pool. A visual surveillance system typically involves complex tasks like (Collins *et al.*, 2000; Regazzoni *et al.*, 2001; Ohya *et al.*, 2002): detection of targets under varying ambient conditions, simultaneous detection and tracking of multiple targets, and recognition of complex behaviors which vary each time they are performed. These challenging tasks have traditionally led to research based on captured footages (Friedman and Rusell, 1997) or simulations done in lab environment (Wren *et al.*, 1997; Koller *et al.*, 1994) with the objective to yield a fundamental understanding of different vision components. While varied degrees of success have been reported in these early studies, directly deploying these methods to real-world problems remains insufficient, particularly, the robustness to address long-hour operation and technical complexity involved. Hence, this observation has motivated several recent works looking into live systems under *different real-world environments* and their *societal importances* (Haritaoglu *et al.*, 2000; Boult *et al.*, 2001; Stauffer and Grimson, 1999, 2000; Pavlidis *et al.*, 2001; Cucchiara *et al.*, 2000; Foresti, 1998).

In this chapter, we address the problem of developing a *live* surveillance system at *pool* environment. It involves a new branch of visual surveillance study which is in *aquatic* environment. The objectives here are to recognize different swimming activities and to provide constant monitoring to watch out for occurrence of any early drowning incidents. Thus, we have named the proposed system as drowning early warning system, or DEWS in short. The intended application of the proposed

DEWS system is to provide an additional level of safety on top of watchful eyes of lifeguards.

In our problem, water disturbance of aquatic background that exhibits random and continual movement poses new technical challenges. This has led to difficulties to distinguish between foreground or background movements and to recognize different swimming behaviors. In this chapter, we focus the discussion on two basic aspects: *foreground silhouette extraction* and *behavioral recognition*. We begin this work by describing a statistical method that models background in terms of homogeneous blob movements. To detect different swimming activities, a framework for recognizing each activity trait is developed. The aim here is to recognize different types of swimming behaviors, in particular, early drowning events in a real environment setup.

In addition, we explore in this work solutions to address: removal of highlights for operation at night time and separating contiguous blob of a few foreground targets into separate entities in order to handle a moderate level of crowd.

This chapter gives a summary based on papers we have published earlier (Eng *et al.*, 2003, 2004, 2005, 2006, 2008). The outline of this chapter comprises the following: Section 13.2 presents a detailed study of our problem and a review of relevant works. Section 13.3 describes a proposed foreground silhouette extraction module. In Sec. 13.4, details of a proposed water crisis inference scheme are explained. Following that, Sec. 13.5 describes a blob-splitting mechanism to handle moderate level of crowd. Lastly, in Secs. 13.6 and 13.7, experimental results and concluding remarks are reported.

13.2 Our Work in Perspective

13.2.1 *Proposed DEWS system*

Building a vision-based surveillance system for pool environment has attracted some attention recently. Relevant work can be referred to Menoud (1999), Meniere (2000), Guichard *et al.*(2001) and Lavest *et al.* (2002), which proposed a system that utilizes *underwater* cameras to detect drowning event at its *later* stage, where the victim has sunk to the bottom of a pool. The primary concept of this system is to detect motionless drowned victims.

From the point to yield a more stringent safety, detecting drowning event at its *early* stage while the victim is struggling at water surface sounds an attractive alternative. This motivates the exploration of using *overhead* cameras as shown in Fig. 13.1. The proposed system consists of overhead cameras mounted surrounding the pool. In the setup, each camera monitors a local region and there is overlapping between the views of two adjacent cameras. The combined view of all the cameras then provides a full coverage of the pool.

The use of *overhead cameras* as proposed may do away and complement a few practical concerns that a system of using underwater cameras may have. For the setup of using underwater cameras, blocking of camera views by standing swimmers

Fig. 13.1.   The proposed DEWS system installed at an outdoor public swimming pool.

will become an issue when it is deployed at a shallow pool. This issue is of particular
concern in our consideration since shallow pools are more commonly found in our
region. Second, the use of underwater cameras may incur additional requirement of
water proof feature, which may lead to higher installation and maintenance cost. On
the other hand, the ability to monitor different swimming activities and detection
of early drowning incidents based on overhead views can potentially contribute to
a faster drowning detection.

13.2.2 *Technical challenges and reviews*

Before proceeding further, we first analyze the technical challenges of our problem
and its key differences compared with other state-of-the-art problems. This shall
put our problem in perspective.

Figure 13.2 presents a study of background movements at four arbitrary selected
points on each image on the left by analyzing the intensity distributions of these
pixels. The horizontal axis of subfigures on the right represents gray level of pixel.
Each row in the vertical axis represents intensity histogram of a selected pixel's
values over 200 frames. Thus, the figure shows intensity distributions at the four
selected points over 40,000 frames. When comparing with the problem of detecting
human on the ground (Boult *et al.*, 2001), wider distributions are observed in our
problem. This is due to continual and random movement of aquatic background
which will contribute to greater level of noise to the steps of foreground subtraction
and features extraction.

For behavioral recognition, one major challenge faced is the need to identify
different complex behaviors from segmented targets which are typically of moderate
size. This is due to the constraint where only a limited number of cameras
can possibly be installed. Figure 13.3 shows silhouettes of segmented targets
demonstrating different types of swimming behaviors. Foreground features extracted
from these silhouette maps are expected to be noisy with distributions of different
behavioral classes may overlap. A number of early works have shown the merits

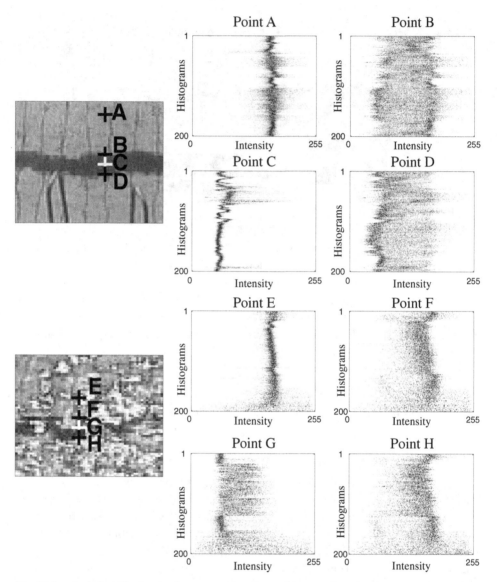

Fig. 13.2.   A study of background movements at four arbitrary selected points on each image on the left, labeled as points A to D and points E to H. Widely distributed intensity histograms are observed due to continual and random movement of the aquatic background.

of using geometrical model (Ohya *et al.*, 2002). However, the need to have a high resolution foreground target makes this approach generally less applicable in visual surveillance context. Instead, our problem requires a robust scheme that can address the overlapping of different feature classes for accurate pattern classification.

In the following, we present reviews in the fields of background subtraction and behavior and activity recognition.

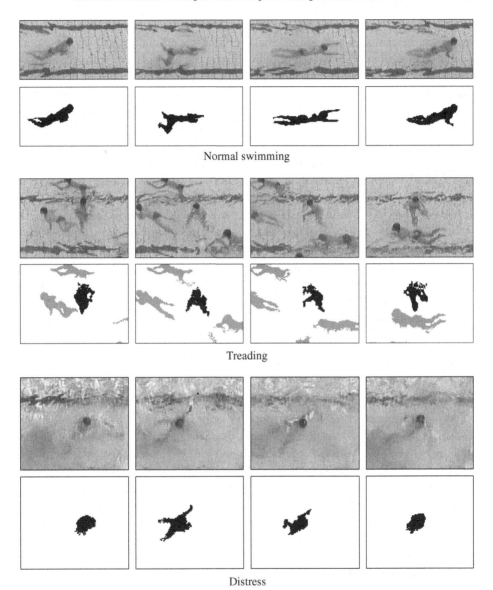

Fig. 13.3.   Segmented silhouettes of foreground targets demonstrate: normal swimming, treading, and distress. Foreground targets are marked in black color. (Odd rows show frames captured. Even rows show silhouette maps of segmented foreground.)

13.2.2.1 *Relevant works on background subtraction*

Existing methods of background modeling can be broadly classified into: (1) pixel-based method and (2) block-based method. One example of pixel-based method is Pfinder system by Wren *et al.* (1997), which demonstrated good results to perform real-time tracking by constructing each background pixel as a single Gaussian distribution in YUV color space. When addressing outdoor surveillance (on the ground), recent efforts Friedman and Rusell (1997), Stauffer and Grimson (1999, 2000) proposed mixture of Gaussians for background modeling. Besides, non-parametric modeling is also found popular among the works Haritaoglu *et al.* (2000) and Elgammal *et al.* (2002). One common limitation of these mentioned pixel-based techniques is that they are generally not meant for the purpose to address situation with significant background movements. Thus, these methods are generally more confined to environment with less background movements, e.g., within controlled indoor and outdoor environments.

Examples of block-based method can, meanwhile, be referred to the works by Hsu *et al.* (1984) and Matsuyama *et al.* (2000). The need of using image block is one limitation of these methods, which has constrained the detection to be in block-based unit. As a result, these methods are limited to coarse detection.

In view of the aquatic background that exhibits random homogeneous blob movements, we propose in this work a modeling of background based on a set of block-derived homogeneous region units. By matching a pixel of a current frame to models of homogeneous regions within a search window, this can produce good performance of detecting foreground while reducing false detection due to background movement.

13.2.2.2 *Relevant works on recognition of behaviors and events in visual surveillance context*

Among those works on surveillance and human behavior recognition, it is noted that rule-based method has been a popular approach, owing to its simplicity to establish a knowledge-based framework. A good example of rule-based approach can be referred to the work by Cucchiara *et al.* (2000), which comprises a high-level module that operates on symbolic data and some heuristic rules. One advantage of rule-based approach is that it provides the flexibility of having a reasoning module which could be progressively improved by adding new rules. This provides a simple yet convenient syntax for interfacing with expert knowledge. However, one limitation is its simplicity at each decision level which often relies on simple conditional rules. Thereby, information is not being efficiently utilized.

In contrast to rule-based technique, probabilistic graph models such as Hidden Markov models (HMMs) have also been receiving enormous attention for modeling state transition process in temporal domain (Yamato *et al.*, 1992; Wilson and Bobick, 1995, 1999; Oliver *et al.*, 2000). For example, in a work by Oliver *et al.* (2000), Coupled-HMMs were exploited to model patterns of human activities. However, one common limitation of the mentioned HMM-based methods is that these methods provide little semantic information about behaviors being modeled; instead, semantic information is learnt indirectly through low-level features extracted from training sequences.

In our problem, it is noticed that drowning research has a long history among lifeguarding community (Pia, 1974, 1994). A drowning incident can be understood as a constellation of nervous response due to suffocation in water, which then triggers external and internal movements known to be *instinctive drowning response*. Therefore, we aim to develop a framework that can classify different behaviors based on the traits of each behavioral class. Visual indicators used by lifeguards for drowning detection are important prior knowledge in our case. In the proposed framework, expert knowledge with semantic meanings are incorporated through a set of defined foreground descriptors. Data fusion and HMMs modeling are applied to learn the state transition of different behaviors, while addressing overlapping of feature classes from different behaviors. Through this framework, we hope to combine the advantages of rule-based approach–that yields a simple and efficient syntax for incorporating semantic meanings, and HMM approach–that yields a probabilistic framework.

13.3 Scene Modeling and Foreground Detection in Aquatic Background

The first processing block of the proposed system comprises: (1) a background modeling module, (2) a foreground detection module, and (3) a specular reflection removal module for detection of foreground at day time and night time.

13.3.1 *Region-based background modeling and subtraction*

Our proposed approach is to model background as a composition of dynamic region-based processes. This is to account for aquatic background, which constitutes homogeneous patches that exhibit random movements in space as well as variations in illumination and color.

Consider a sequence of $N_1 \times N_2$ background frames, and each background frame is divided into $n_1 \times n_2$ non-overlapping square blocks of size $w \times w$ each, i.e., $n_1 = (N_1/w)$ and $n_2 = (N_2/w)$. Denote $\boldsymbol{X}_{u,v}$ as a set of color vectors collected from square blocks-(u, v), where $1 \leq u \leq n_1$ and $1 \leq v \leq n_2$. And, $\boldsymbol{X}_{u,v}$ is to be decomposed into c number of homogeneous regions $\{\boldsymbol{R}_{u,v}^1, \ldots, \boldsymbol{R}_{u,v}^c\}$. The proposed modeling of background is defined as a composition of the statistical models of $\{\boldsymbol{R}_{u,v}^k\}$, $\forall u, v, k$.

Figure 13.4 illustrates a study of luminance histogram of pixels collected from different square blocks as marked at the images on the left. Multiple peaks are observed when there are more than one background elements within the same block. For example, two distinct peaks are observed for the cases of blocks B and D that contain both elements of water and lane divider. Composition of a few single multivariate Gaussians (in the 3D color space) forms a mixture of Gaussian-like distribution for each block as shown. The clustering step produces the effect of breaking down complicated signals of a block into homogeneous region processes, where each could be reasonably modeled using one single multivariate Gaussian distribution.

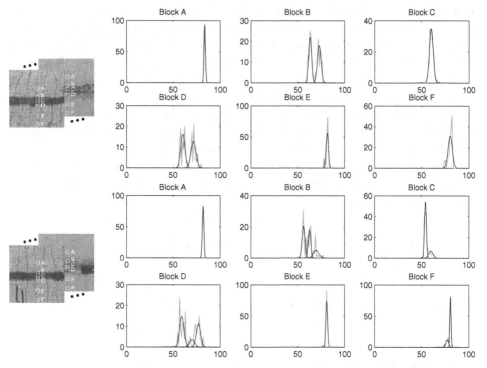

Fig. 13.4.　Luminance histograms of pixel intensities extracted from blocks A to F as marked at two typical example images on the left, showing multiple peaks when more than one objects projected onto the block over time. Modeling each homogeneous region as one single-Gaussian distribution demonstrates good approximation of the original signal.

Background models. Let $\mu_{R_{u,v}^k} = \{\mu_{R_{u,v}^k}^1, \ldots, \mu_{R_{u,v}^k}^d\}$ and $\Sigma_{R_{u,v}^k}$ be the mean and covariance matrices of color vectors of $R_{u,v}^k$, and $d = 3$ is the dimension of the color space. By modeling color distribution of each $R_{u,v}^k$ as a single multivariate Gaussian distribution, the probability of a pixel at (i, j) belonging to $R_{u,v}^k$ can be computed based on similarity in color:

$$P(\boldsymbol{x}_{i,j} | \boldsymbol{\mu}_{R_{u,v}^k}, \Sigma_{R_{u,v}^k}) = \frac{1}{(2\pi)^{d/2} |\Sigma_{R_{u,v}^k}|^{1/2}}$$

$$\times \exp\left\{ -\frac{1}{2}(\boldsymbol{x}_{i,j} - \boldsymbol{\mu}_{R_{u,v}^k}) \Sigma_{R_{u,v}^k}^{-1} (\boldsymbol{x}_{i,j} - \boldsymbol{\mu}_{R_{u,v}^k})^T \right\} \quad (13.1)$$

where $\boldsymbol{x}_{i,j} = \{x_{i,j}^1, \ldots, x_{i,j}^d\}$ denotes color vectors. Without compromising much of the accuracy, we further assume that each color dimension is independent. This gives simplification of Eq. (13.1) to be

$$P(\boldsymbol{x}_{i,j} | \boldsymbol{\mu}_{R_{u,v}^k}, \boldsymbol{\sigma}_{R_{u,v}^k}) = \prod_{m=1}^{d} \frac{1}{\sqrt{2\pi}\sigma_{R_{u,v}^k}^m} \exp\left\{ -\frac{(x_{i,j}^m - \mu_{R_{u,v}^k}^m)^2}{2(\sigma_{R_{u,v}^k}^m)^2} \right\} \quad (13.2)$$

where $\boldsymbol{\sigma}_{\boldsymbol{R}_{u,v}^k} = \{\sigma_{\boldsymbol{R}_{u,v}^k}^1, \ldots, \sigma_{\boldsymbol{R}_{u,v}^k}^d\}$ is the standard deviations matrix of $\boldsymbol{R}_{u,v}^k$.

Therefore, the color similarity between a pixel and a homogeneous region can be computed based on

$$D(\boldsymbol{x}_{i,j} | \boldsymbol{\mu}_{\boldsymbol{R}_{u,v}^k}, \boldsymbol{\sigma}_{\boldsymbol{R}_{u,v}^k}) = \sqrt{\sum_{m=1}^{d} \frac{(x_{i,j}^m - \mu_{\boldsymbol{R}_{u,v}^k}^m)^2}{(\sigma_{\boldsymbol{R}_{u,v}^k}^m)^2}} \tag{13.3}$$

Through continually updating $\boldsymbol{\mu}_{\boldsymbol{R}_{u,v}^k}$ and $\boldsymbol{\sigma}_{\boldsymbol{R}_{u,v}^k}$, a temporal adaptation to background change can be further achieved.

The steps for the above background modeling scheme are listed below.

Step 1: Generating background frames. During initialization, recorded frames are likely to contain both foreground and background. To address the problem, we explore a temporal vector median filter to generate a sequence of background frames.

Let $\boldsymbol{X}_{i,j}^\tau$ be an array of color vectors collected over τ number of frames, i.e., $\boldsymbol{X}_{i,j}^\tau = \{\boldsymbol{x}_{i,j}^t \mid t = 1, \ldots, \tau\}$, where $\boldsymbol{x}_{i,j}^t$ is the color vector of tth image at position-(i,j). A "clean" background frame is generated by applying a vector median filter on $\boldsymbol{X}_{i,j}^\tau$, $\forall\, i, j$ that gives

$$\boldsymbol{B}^1 = \{\boldsymbol{z}_{i,j} \mid i = 1, \ldots, N_1 \quad \text{and} \quad j = 1, \ldots, N_2\} \tag{13.4}$$

where $\boldsymbol{z}_{i,j}$ is computed based on

$$\boldsymbol{z}_{i,j} = \left\{ \boldsymbol{x}_{i,j}^q \in \boldsymbol{X}_{i,j}^\tau \mid \min_{\boldsymbol{x}_{i,j}^q} \sum_{r=1}^{\tau} |\boldsymbol{x}_{i,j}^r - \boldsymbol{x}_{i,j}^q| \right\} \tag{13.5}$$

In the process, duration to be taken and efficiency to remove swimmer pixels are two determining factors deciding the sampling rate between two $\boldsymbol{x}_{i,j}^t$, which has been determined empirically in this work.

To prepare for step 2 below, background frames $\{\boldsymbol{B}^l \mid l = 2, \ldots, \kappa\}$ are then generated by applying Eq. (13.5) using a sliding window of $\{\boldsymbol{x}_{i,j}^t \mid t = l, \ldots, \tau + l\}$ $\forall i, j$.

Step 2: Generating initial background models. After obtaining $\{\boldsymbol{B}^l \mid l = 1, \ldots, \kappa\}$, the region-based background modeling are implemented by:

(1) Dividing each $\boldsymbol{B}^l$ into $n_1 \times n_2$ non-overlapping $w \times w$ square blocks, and
(2) Applying a hierarchical k-means (Duda *et al.*, 2001) on each $\boldsymbol{X}_{u,v}$ to obtain cluster centers $\boldsymbol{\mu}_{\boldsymbol{R}_{u,v}^k}$ and standard deviations $\boldsymbol{\sigma}_{\boldsymbol{R}_{u,v}^k}$ of homogeneous regions $\boldsymbol{R}_{u,v}^k, \forall k$.

The clustering process starts by initiating one dominant data cluster. In the subsequent iterations, smaller and more compact data clusters are formed through splitting. The process of splitting is terminated when the distance of any two closest cluster centers reaches a pre-determined value or the number of cluster centers is greater than 5, whichever is achieved first. Therefore, this forms c-number of homogeneous regions $R_{u,v}^k$ that gives the initial background models $C_{u,v}$ to be

$$C_{u,v} = [\boldsymbol{\mu}_{R_{u,v}^k}\ \boldsymbol{\sigma}_{R_{u,v}^k}], \quad \text{where } k = 1,\ldots,c \tag{13.6}$$

Typically, the value of c ranges from 2 to 5.

Step 3: Updating background models. To adapt to changes in an outdoor environment, we adopt a recursive linear interpolation scheme for continual updating which shares certain degrees of similarity as the scheme used in (Stauffer and Grimson, 1999, 2000). In the updating step, parameters $\boldsymbol{\sigma}_{R_{u,v}^k}$ and $\boldsymbol{\mu}_{R_{u,v}^k}$ at time t are updated according to

$$\boldsymbol{\mu}_{R_{u,v}^k}^t \leftarrow (1-\rho)\boldsymbol{\mu}_{R_{u,v}^k}^{t-1} + \rho\boldsymbol{\mu}_{R_{u,v}^k}^t \tag{13.7}$$

$$\boldsymbol{\sigma}_{R_{u,v}^k}^t \leftarrow (1-\rho)\boldsymbol{\sigma}_{R_{u,v}^k}^{t-1} + \rho\boldsymbol{\sigma}_{R_{u,v}^k}^t \tag{13.8}$$

where $\rho = 1/\kappa$ is the learning factor for adapting current changes. Parameter κ is defined previously in step 1, which is the number of "clean" background frames generated. Equivalently, we can interpret Eqs. (13.7) and (13.8) as the averages of all $\boldsymbol{\mu}_{R_{u,v}^k}^t$ and $\boldsymbol{\sigma}_{R_{u,v}^k}^t$ of $R_{u,v}^k$ over a sliding window of length κ. In practice, the updating process is performed by considering only pixels within a threshold distance from the mean. This is to ensure that each Gaussian background model is being adopted slowly while avoiding corruption by outliers. In order to maintain a dynamic background modeling, the ability to create and destroy unnecessary distributions is implemented by assigning a lifespan of κ to each distribution.

13.3.2 *Foreground swimmer detection and modeling*

To account for aquatic background, we explore a foreground detection scheme that incorporates active background movements and an enhanced thresholding. Let $\boldsymbol{x}_{i,j}$ be the color vector of pixel at location-(i,j) in the square block-(u,v). Using Eq. (13.3) and considering movements of pixel within a local window, color discrepancy of a pixel and background models is computed to be

$$D_{i,j}^{\min} = \min\{D(\boldsymbol{x}_{i,j}|\boldsymbol{\mu}_{R_{u+q,v+r}^k}, \boldsymbol{\sigma}_{R_{u+q,v+r}^k})\} \tag{13.9}$$

where q and r determine a local window in square-block unit. As observed in experiments, the consideration of neighboring blocks in Eq. (13.9) has contributed to reduction of misclassification errors at regions, such as areas around lane dividers.

Figure 13.5 illustrates the thresholding module we have implemented. The module involves first applying a low-threshold value to yield a good segmentation of foreground targets. To suppress noise, a high-threshold map and a parent map are formed. Parent map is a low-resolution version of the high-threshold map, where its each element corresponds to a 4×4 non-overlapping block in the high-threshold map. An element of the parent map is labeled as "1" when more than 50% pixels of

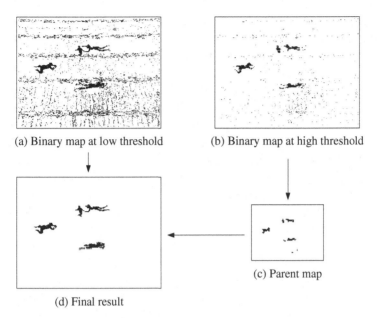

(a) Binary map at low threshold   (b) Binary map at high threshold

(c) Parent map

(d) Final result

Fig. 13.5. The thresholding step that combines principles of thresholding-with-hysteresis, denoising, and connected component grouping.

its corresponding 4×4 block in the high-threshold map are of $D_{i,j}^{\min}$ greater than the high threshold. The final detection map is last formed, which comprises connected blobs of low-threshold map that also gives smaller connected blobs in the parent map. This yields an enhanced detection performance with a lower number of false positive as shown in Fig. 13.5 (d).

Updating swimmer models. In the same way as forming the background model, region-based swimmer models are computed and updated every frame once a swimmer is detected. During the online processing phase, color discrepancy measures between pixel's color and neighboring foreground models, denoted by $D_{i,j}^{f\,\min}$, are computed. Pixels with $D_{i,j}^{f\,\min} < D_{i,j}^{\min}$ will be classified as the highest confident swimmer pixels.

13.3.3 *Swimmer detection with filtering scheme for night time*

Operation at night in aquatic environment faces additional challenges posed by glare and reflection from artificial lighting. In this section, we first describe the study of using polarizer in our problem. Then, we introduce the suggested filtering method for reflection removal.

13.3.3.1 *The use of polarizer for reflection removal*

The use of polarizer has been a well-known photographic technique to suppress virtual layer and reflection (Shurcliff and Ballard, 1964). As discovered in several works, if the position and orientation of camera as well as the reflecting surface are known, the use of polarizer could be a simple yet efficient method in removing reflection by setting camera at the Brewster (Schechner and Shamir, 2000). In Schechner and Shamir (2000), the work demonstrated demonstrated the success of separating transmitted and reflected images off a semireflecting medium (e.g., a glass window). This was achieved through accurately estimating the inclination angle. In Fujikake *et al.* (1998), an electrically controllable polarizing filter filter was developed, which could automatically reduce undesirable reflected light by estimating the polarization state of incident light. The method did away the need to manually rotate polarizer while claiming the capability of removing 80% of the reflected light for some experiments.

A study of using polarizer in our problem has been performed as demonstrated in Fig. 13.6. The figure shows comparison of different sample images captured with and without polarizer at different inclination angles of camera and polarization orientations. As evident from the figure, the use of polarizer does not bring perfect solution to our problem, where roughly equal amount of reflection is still observed. Referring to the second row of the figure, there is still significant amount of reflection observed when the camera is positioned roughly at the Brewster angle, which is approximately 40° looking down from the horizon.

We believe that polarizer could be useful in many aspects. However, we face difficulty to achieve good results in our system. Due to the inaccessibility of camera which is mounted high at building structure, we also face additional difficulty to adjust the polarizer. Therefore, we have resorted to filtering approach for reflection removal.

13.3.3.2 *Filtering approach for reflection removal*

Instead, we resort to a simple filtering approach to address the issue. The main idea here is first to have a pixel classification step. Subsequently, appropriate filtering actions are applied accordingly for different classes of pixel. Statistical study in temporal domain suggests that the rate of pixel's color or intensity fluctuation in temporal domain is a useful feature in our problem for the classification step. Denote $I_{i,j}^{t-\xi}, I_{i,j}^{t-\xi+1}, \ldots, I_{i,j}^{t}$ as the intensity values of a pixel at spatial location (i, j) for $\xi + 1$ consecutive frames. A heuristic *fluctuation count* is defined to be

$$\varpi_{i,j}^t = \frac{1}{FR} \sum_{u=0}^{\xi} \Xi_{i,j}^u, \quad \Xi_{i,j}^u = \begin{cases} 1, & \text{if } |I_{i,j}^t - I_{i,j}^{t-\xi+u}| > \Upsilon \\ 0, & \text{otherwise} \end{cases} \tag{13.10}$$

where FR is the frame rate of video. Condition $|\cdot| > \Upsilon$ provides the measure of significant change in intensity.

With the computation of $\varpi_{i,j}^t$, we classify each pixel into one of the three pre-identified classes using two empirical thresholds η_1 and η_2, where η_1 and η_2 are empirically set to be one-third and two-third of ξ/FR in our context. Typically, pixels with $\varpi_{i,j}^t > \eta_2$ are fast moving part of foreground. A spatial mean filter with

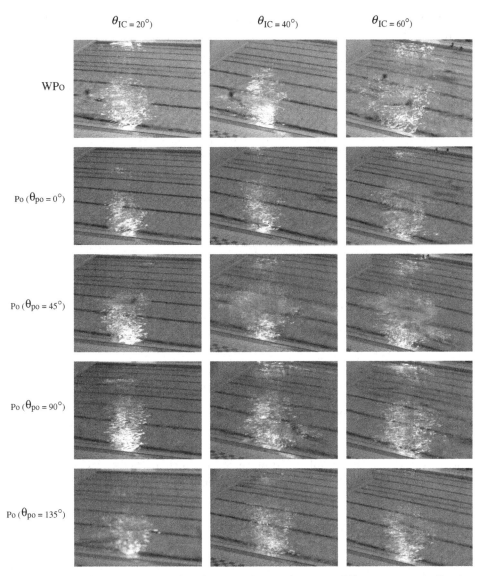

Fig. 13.6. Sample images captured with and without polarizer at different camera inclination angles and polarization orientations. Looking from top to bottom shows camera inclination angle with respect to the horizon approximately at $20°$, $40°$, and $60°$. Looking from left to right, it starts with images captured without polarizer, and followed by orientation of polarizer approximately at $0°$, $45°$, $90°$, $135°$. (Legends: WPo denotes "without polarizer", Po denotes "with polarizer", θ_{Po} denotes "orientation of polarizer", and θ_{IC} denotes "inclination angle of camera looking down from the horizon".)

window dimension of 3×3 is employed by only considering pixels within the window with the same $(\varpi > \eta_2)$ condition. The mean filtering operation serves the purpose to remove any sensor and digitization noise. On the other hand, there is no filtering if $\varpi^t_{i,j} \leq \eta_1$, which avoids unnecessary blurring on background.

For the class of $\eta_1 < \varpi_{i,j}^t \leq \eta_2$, it contains mostly corrupted foreground pixels due to specular reflection and glare. In this step, we aim to generate a "pseudocolor" based on spatio-temporal filtering operation. This is done by first computing a set of mean filtered pixels W by applying a 3×3 spatial mean filter centers at (i, j) to the current and a number of successive previous frames. Only pixels with the same $(\eta_1 < \varpi \leq \eta_2)$ condition are considered here. Compensated pixel value is then computed to be the median of W. Thus, the overall process provides color estimation based on dominant color of pixels from the class of $\eta_1 < \varpi_{i,j}^t \leq \eta_2$ over current and a number of successive previous frames.

13.4 Swimming and Water Crises Behaviors Modeling

This section describes the details, which comprises: (1) a hierarchical representation of swimmer descriptors that incorporates expert knowledge, (2) a data fusion module, and (3) a hidden markov modeling for describing state transition process of behaviors. One technical challenge addressed here is the issue of high correlation between different classes of behaviors due to behavioral variability and inconsistency in the results of foreground silhouette.

13.4.1 *Swimmer descriptors extraction*

13.4.1.1 *Drowning research by lifeguarding community*

In the drowning behavioral studies (Pia, 1974, 1994), two possible types of water crisis incidents have been identified: distress and drowning. A distress incident involves victim exhibiting involuntary movements such as active struggling or waving. A drowning incident meanwhile can be understood as suffocation in water that triggers external and unlearned movements, which are known to be instinctive drowning response. Both *distress* and *early drowning* victims exhibit the following common visual indicators:

(1) There will be instinctive response with repetitive arm movements of extending out and pressing down.
(2) The body will be perpendicular (vertical up) in water with small movements in horizontal and diagonal directions.
(3) The period of struggling on water surface is on average within the range of 20 to 60 seconds (Pia, 1994).

In this work, both distress and drowning cases are considered under the same event class where alert is to be triggered.

13.4.1.2 *Definition of swimmer descriptors*

After studying footages of swimmers demonstrating normal swimming, treading, and simulation of actual water crisis incidents (distress and drowning scenarios), we define the following set of descriptors to characterize the unique trait of each behavior.

(1) *Movement range*, f_{MR}. It is noted that activity of normal swimming typically has a larger spatial displacement range over a period of time comparing with the cases of distress, drowning, and treading. Hence, this motivates the computation of a movement range parameter, f_{MR}, which is defined to be the maximum displacement of any two centroids recorded over a given period.

(2) *Speed product*, f_{sp}. To describe the pattern of movement, velocity is a natural choice. A target's velocity at an instance can be computed since its centroid positions in current and previous frames have been recorded. Let v^t and v^{t-1} be the velocity vectors at the current and previous instances, respectively, and δ be the angle between v^t and v^{t-1}. We compute a speed product parameter to be $|v^{t-1}||v^t|\cos(\delta/2)$, where $|\cdot|$ denotes the magnitude of the velocity vector. The cosine term is to impose penalty to chaotic movement, which is observed in the cases of distress and drowning. The division by two in the cosine term confines the angle to be in the range between $0°$ and $180°$.

(3) *Posture variation*, f_{pos}. The angle between the principle axis of computed best-fit-ellipse and the horizontal axis gives the orientation of a swimmer. Since a drowning victim typically shows repetitive arm and leg movements, it corresponds to a continual change in the swimmer's posture. Let θ_{min} and θ_{max} be the minimum and maximum values of the orientation angles computed over a given period. We hence measure the posture variation to be $(\theta_{max} - \theta_{min})$. A high-value f_{pos} is expected when there is a struggling event.

(4) *Activity variation*, f_{act}. Arm and leg movements of extending out and contracting in during distress and early drowning incidents typically lead to a change in numerical value of the ratio between area of best-fit-ellipse and size of foreground silhouette. We hence compute f_{act} to be the difference between maximum and minimum values of these ratios over a temporal window.

(5) *Size variation*, f_s. We also compute $f_s = (A_{max} - A_{min})/A_{mean}$, where A_{max}, A_{min} and A_{mean} denote maximum, minimum and average of foreground silhouette's sizes recorded over a temporal window. A high value of this measure is typically observed for distress and drowning cases, due to less consistency in foreground size resulted by water surface disturbance.

(6) Submersion index, f_{sub}. This measure is defined to infer the position of a swimmer to be below or above water surface. A sinking swimmer more commonly exhibits a higher color saturation, which adds a blanket of bluishness to skin appearance. The submersion index is computed to be the difference between a swimmer's mean color saturation and minimum saturation value of the swimmer since it is being tracked.

Figures 13.7 (b)–(g) show plots of the above descriptors in temporal domain when target is in different stages. Figure 13.7 (h) shows the likelihood plots when

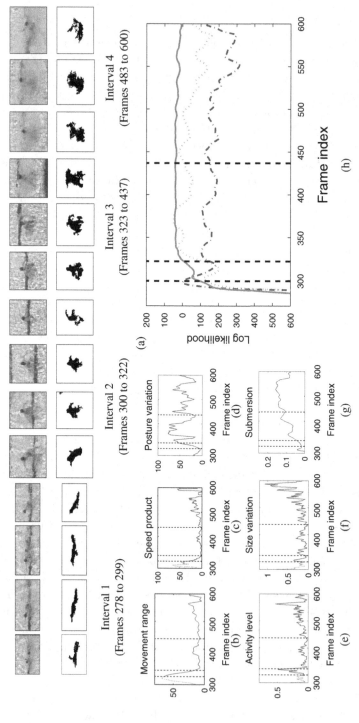

Fig. 13.7. A simulation of a realistic water-crisis incident involves stages: swimming → slowing down → gentle struggling → distress. (b) to (g) show the corresponding plots of the defined descriptors in temporal domain. (h) shows the likelihood plots when classifying the target to be in swimming mode (denoted by dash-dotted line "–·–"), treading mode (denoted by dotted line "···") and alert mode for possible detection of a water-crisis incident (denoted by solid line "——"). The vertical lines divide the plot into the four corresponding intervals given in (a).

classifying the target to be in swimming mode, in treading mode as well as in alert mode. The following two sections shall explain the details to compute these likelihood plots.

13.4.2 *Data fusion*

Figure 13.8 shows scatter plots of defined swimmer descriptors for events of swimming, treading, and water crises (distress and drowning scenarios). It shows high correlation among these events where swimmer descriptors of one type overlaps with that of others. To ensure a more accurate decision based on these descriptors, the problem demands more than just a simple linear decision hypersurface. Thus, we explore data fusion technique in this section to yield better information fusion.

Several high performance data fusion techniques are considered for best achievable results. Reduced model (RM) (Toh *et al.*, 2004) is a relatively new classifier proposed recently by our team in the application of biometrics, which has shown potential due to its fast single step computation without compromising

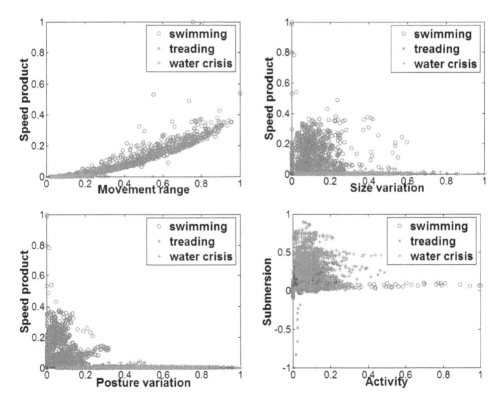

Fig. 13.8. Scatter plots of defined swimmer descriptors. Data is collected from videos comprising swimmers demonstrate: normal swimming, treading, and water crisis (distress and drowning). We consider distress and drowning to be under one class where alert is to be triggered. (Legends: "o" refers to normal swimming, "×" refers to treading, and "+" refers to water crisis (distress and drowning).)

much of the accuracy performance. Hence, this motivates us to extend our study of this algorithm in this problem.

Denote $\Phi = [\phi_1, \ldots, \phi_6]^T$ be a set of swimmer descriptors in vector form extracted from silhouette of a foreground with label, i.e., $\phi_1 \equiv f_{\mathrm{MR}}; \ldots; \phi_6 \equiv f_{\mathrm{sub}}$. The RM classifier is expressed as

$$g_{\mathrm{RM}}(\boldsymbol{\alpha}, \Phi) = \alpha_0 + \sum_{k=1}^{r}\sum_{j=1}^{l} \alpha_{k,j}\phi_j^k + \sum_{k=1}^{r} \alpha_k \left(\sum_{j=1}^{l}\phi_j\right)^k$$

$$+ \sum_{n=2}^{r}\left(\sum_{i=1}^{l}\alpha_{n,i}\phi_i\right)\left(\sum_{j=1}^{l}\phi_j\right)^{k-1} \tag{13.11}$$

where $\phi_j, j = 1, \ldots, l$ are the polynomial inputs, $\boldsymbol{\alpha} = [\alpha_0, \alpha_{k,j}, \alpha_k, \alpha_{n,i}]$ are the weighting coefficients to be estimated. Parameters l and r correspond to input dimension and order of the RM classifier, respectively. As can be seen from Eq. (13.11), the basic component of this polynomial model boils down to construction of new pattern features which are sums of the original features, and combination of these new and original features using power and product terms.

By adopting the least squares error (LSE) objective for computation of $\boldsymbol{\alpha}$, a simple single-step computation has been derived. Given m number of training data points and using a regularized LSE minimization objective

$$R(\boldsymbol{\alpha}) = \sum_{i=1}^{m}[y_i - g(\boldsymbol{\alpha}, \Phi_i)]^2 + \varrho\|\boldsymbol{\alpha}\|_2^2 \tag{13.12}$$

the parameter vector $\boldsymbol{\alpha}$ for a 2-class problem (single output target vector $\mathbf{y} = [y_1 \ y_2 \ \cdots \ y_m]$ containing "m" elements of either "0" or "1" to represent each class) can be estimated from a single step as

$$\boldsymbol{\alpha} = (Q^T Q + \varrho\Lambda)^{-1}Q^T\mathbf{y} \tag{13.13}$$

where $Q \in \Re^{m \times K}$ denotes the Jacobian matrix of $g_{\mathrm{RM}}(\boldsymbol{\alpha}, \Phi)$, Λ is an identity matrix, and ϱ is a small regularization constant.

For a problem with multiple classes as what is being considered, Φ_i is classified to be one of the event classes which is three here. Denote the true events of water crisis (distress and drowning), treading and normal swimming incidents as $\mathbf{y}^T \in \{[1\ 0\ 0], [0\ 1\ 0], [0\ 0\ 1]\}$, respectively. Let the target training vectors packed as

$$Y = [\mathbf{y}_1 \ \mathbf{y}_2 \ \cdots \ \mathbf{y}_m]^T \tag{13.14}$$

where each sample row of $Y \in \Re^{m \times 3}$ contains only a "1" for the corresponding class and "0" otherwise. Having learned

$$\Theta = (Q^T Q + \varrho\Lambda)^{-1}Q^T Y \tag{13.15}$$

in a single step, the multiclass model outputs for test can be computed as

$$\hat{Y}_{\mathrm{test}} = Q_{\mathrm{test}}\,\Theta \tag{13.16}$$

using Q_{test} generated from test set. For each test data sample (each row of $\hat{Y}_{\text{test}}$), the largest row element shall determine the output pattern class.

13.4.3 *State transition modeling*

Data fusion step in the previous section provides classification at every instance. Temporal information, which is another important aspect of behavior analysis, has been missing in our consideration so far. To proceed, we formulate the problem to identify the most likely state-transition process of a behavior within a local temporal window.

HMM modeling. The problem is formulated by considering three discrete states of HMM (Yamato *et al.*, 1992; Wilson and Bobick, 1995, 1999; Oliver *et al.*, 2000; Rabiner, 1989), corresponding to the output of the RM classifier. A state variable at time t is given by $s^t \in \{S1, S2, S3\}$. Denote the state transition probabilities as $A = \{a_{u,v}\}$, the observation probabilities as $B = \{b_v\}$, and the initial probabilities being in the respective state as $\pi = \{\pi_u\}$. With the definition of HMM model $\lambda = (A, B, \pi)$, the problem is formulated to identify a state sequence $S = s^1, s^2, \ldots, s^T$ from a sequence of observations $O = o^1, o^2, \ldots, o^T$ so that $P(O, S|\lambda)$ is maximized:

$$S = \underset{\{s^t\}_{t=1}^T}{\operatorname{argmax}} P(O, s^1, \ldots, s^T|\lambda) \tag{13.17}$$

Fully connected HMMs are considered in our context. By referring to Fig. 13.8, we model the distribution of $\{\hat{y}_i\}$ for each analyzed behavior using one single multivariate distribution. Therefore, the observation probabilities $B = \{b_v\}$ could be statistically defined with each b_v as follows

$$b_v = \frac{1}{(2\pi)^{d/2}|\Sigma_v|^{1/2}} \times \exp\left\{-\frac{1}{2}(\hat{y}_i - \mu_v)^T \Sigma_v^{-1}(\hat{y}_i - \mu_v)\right\} \tag{13.18}$$

where Σ_v and μ_v are the covariance and mean of $\{\hat{y}_i\}$, respectively for each behavior class. The transition probabilities are determined through learning training sequences of normal swimming, treading, and water crisis (distress and drowning) (Fig. 13.9). Once the HMMs are specified, the state sequence that gives $\operatorname{argmax}\{P(O, S|\lambda)\}$ could be obtained by using Viterbi algortihm (Forney Jr., 1973).

We have performed a 10-fold validation to decide on parameters used for the above data fusion and HMM modeling schemes. The experiment of this validation process is detailed in Sec. 13.6.3.

13.5 Water Crisis Detection in a Crowded Scenario

When addressing a crowded scenario, a higher level of complexity is involved due to *occlusion*. In an occlusion event, silhouette mask of close foreground targets may overlap. This hence results formation of large contiguous blob with foreground

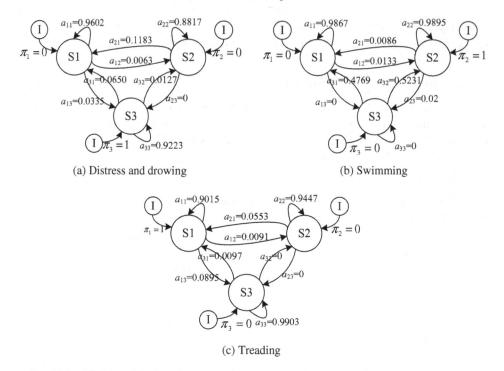

(a) Distress and drowing

(b) Swimming

(c) Treading

Fig. 13.9.   HMM models describe state transition process of the considered behavior classes.

targets becoming inseparable. In order to extend our drowning detection engine to moderate level of crowded scenario, we describe in this section a blob-splitting mechanism developed.

In the problem formulation, we view silhouette map of a foreground target as a cluster of labeled foreground pixels where clustering and modelfitting concepts are deployed. To simplify the discussion, the following discusses the splitting step for one detected large contiguous blob. When processing a frame, such process will be repeated for any detection of contiguous blob. Denote a contiguous blob in frame t as $\boldsymbol{M}^t$, which is the union of silhouette maps belonging to a group of close foreground targets. Let also γ_i^t be the parameter vector characterizing an ellipse-shaped model for foreground i. The problem involves a process to identify a set of $\Gamma = \{\gamma_i^t\}$ such that this splits a contiguous blob into smaller ellipses. Equivalently, as reported in some relevant earlier works such as Zhao and Nevatia (2003), this can be formulated to maximize a posteriori given by

$$\Gamma^{t*} = \operatorname*{argmax}_{\Gamma^t} P(\Gamma^t | \Gamma^{t-1}, \boldsymbol{M}^t)$$

$$= \operatorname*{argmax}_{\Gamma^t} P(\boldsymbol{M}^t | \Gamma^t) P(\Gamma^t | \Gamma^{t-1}) \tag{13.19}$$

To measure the goodness of fitting $\{\gamma_i^t\}$ to $\boldsymbol{M}^t$, the aim here is to find a solution such that $\{\gamma_i^t\}$ in the image lattice space to give: (1) a good coverage that includes as many considered foreground pixels but fewer background pixels and (2) there should be minimum overlapping between any two ellipse-shaped models to ensure the visibility of each ellipse. With the stated objectives, we propose a blob-splitting mechanism comprising the following steps:

Step 1: Initialization of splitting M^t into k smaller blobs

(i) The process starts by performing hierarchical k-means clustering on a data matrix, which comprises coordinates of foreground pixels. Let the number of cluster centers be k. Since the clustering step involves minimizing a function of spatial distances between cluster centers and foreground pixels, this yields cluster centers converging to the respective centroid of k-targets. Equivalently, this fits k-number ellipses centered at obtained cluster centers. Since Euclidean distance is used in this initialization step, this gives an initial fitting with round-shape models as presented in Fig. 13.10 (a).

(ii) With the obtained initial cluster centers from (i), foreground pixels are classified and labeled to the respective nearest cluster center. The ellipse-models fitting is then improved by using criteria: Mahalanobis distance of a pixel to its nearest cluster center is less than a threshold. An empirical value of 1.8 has been applied that gives consistent fitting results as shown in Figs. 13.10(b)–(d).

Step 2: Selection of the best combination of ellipses. This step involves a recursive process where parameters of ellipses $\{\gamma_i\}$, $i = 1, \ldots, k$ are perturbed to provide different likely hypotheses. A validity score defined based on the likelihood

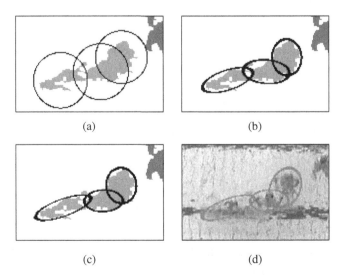

(a)   (b)

(c)   (d)

Fig. 13.10. Steps taken in blob-splitting process. (a) Clustering based on Euclidean distance that gives round-shape fitting; (b) Improved fitting by computing Mahalanobis distance and computing ellipse parameters $\{\gamma_i\}$; (c) Parameters of ellipses $\{\gamma_i\}$ are perturbed to give better fitting; and (d) Final result of the blob-splitting process.

and prior components of Eq. (13.19) is then computed for each hypothesis to allow selection of the best solution.

(i) The perturbation starts by considering an ellipse j, $j \in i$. Pixels in the overlapping area between ellipse j and other ellipses are reassigned based on nearest distance criteria of these pixels to other cluster centers. This allows ellipse j to shrink while other ellipses to expand, generating new solution to the fitting. Likelihood and prior measures are then computed using Eqs. (13.20) and (13.21) defined below

$$P(\boldsymbol{M}^t|\Gamma^t) \propto \sum_{i=1}^{k} \frac{A_{\gamma_i}^{\text{bg}} + A_{\gamma_i}^{\text{ov}}}{A_{\gamma_i}^{\text{fg}}} \qquad (13.20)$$

where $A_{\gamma_i}^{\text{bg}}$ and $A_{\gamma_i}^{\text{fg}}$ give background and foreground pixel counts, respectively within the area defined by γ_i^t, and $A_{\gamma_i}^{\text{ov}}$ gives foreground pixel count within the overlapping area of ellipse i and other ellipses. In addition

$$P(\Gamma^t|\Gamma^{t-1}, \boldsymbol{M}^t) \propto \varphi \,|\, k^t - k^{t-1}\,| \qquad (13.21)$$

where k^t denotes the current number of targets and k^{t-1} denotes the number of targets formed in the previous frame associated to $\boldsymbol{M}^t$ in the current frame. Parameter φ serves as an empirical weight. Therefore, a validity score is computed as the product of Eqs. (13.20) and (13.21).

(ii) The above step (i) is then repeated by selecting another value for j and the corresponding validity score is recorded. An intermediate solution of $\{\gamma_i\}$ is obtained, which gives a minimum value for these computed validity scores.

The above (i) and (ii) of step 2 are then repeated to continuously improve the fitting. Since the process is aimed to achieve a solution that gives a minimum value of the validity score, the process is terminated when the next validity score is greater than the current validity score. This produces the end results as given in (c) and (d) of Fig. 13.10.

Step 3: Selection of best k. In order to select the best k, the above steps 1 and 2 are repeated for a range of k values, where corresponding validity score for each k is recorded. The best k value is decided to be the one which gives the minimum validity score.

13.6 Experimental Results

Below is the summaries of different aspects of analysis performed in the experiment, which comprise:

- qualitative and quantitative evaluations of foreground detection on a whole day sequence given in Sec. 13.6.1;
- evaluation of foreground detection in challenging situations and its comparison to state-of-the-art background subtraction methods given in Sec. 13.6.2;
- accuracy of water crisis and swimming activities detection given in Sec. 13.6.3;

- accuracy of water crisis detection in moderate level of crowded situation given in Sec. 13.6.4; and
- false alarm cases of an on-site trial given in Sec. 13.6.5.

In the system setup, eight overhead cameras have been installed to divide the pool equally into eight zones. Since cross cameras tracking is not a focus of this work, we have ensured that there is overlapping between the views of any two adjacent cameras. This is to account for the case where an event of interest may happen on the boundary between two cameras' views. The proposed system runs at 4 frames/second under different ambient variations and at different levels of crowd density and activity.

13.6.1 *Foreground detection on a whole day video*

Qualitative evaluation

Figure 13.11 presents results of continuous running on a whole day sequence from 8 am to 9 pm. As our system operates at 4 frames/second, the figure shows snap shots of different interesting events from the processed 129,600 (=9 × 3600 × 4) frames. In (a), images arranged from top to bottom, left to right depict: (i) a less crowded scene in morning; (ii) a high-activity scene during a training lesson on afternoon; and (iii) a scene with specular reflection at night. In (b), it meanwhile shows images captured by a side camera at a shallower zone. It is noted that

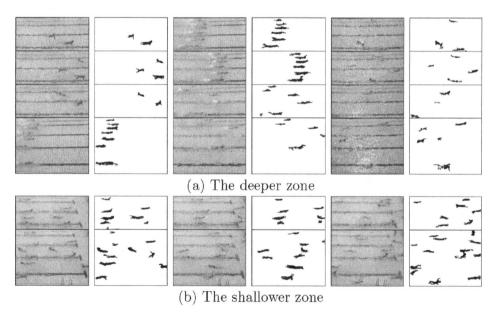

(a) The deeper zone

(b) The shallower zone

Fig. 13.11. (Top to bottom, left to right) Detection of swimmers for frames: (a) recorded by a camera at a deeper zone from 8 am to 9 pm, demonstrating different activities in the pool, (b) recorded by a camera at a shallower zone. (Odd columns: Frames recorded at different time intervals; Even columns: Silhouette maps of segmented foreground.)

visibility of swimmers in these presented images is generally weak attributed by noisy background.

In the figure, obtained foreground silhouette maps are presented side by side comparing with the corresponding original frames. From these results, most foreground targets have been correctly segmented, and consistent performance has been observed over different periods of time.

Quantitative evaluation
In Table 13.1, we meanwhile report quantitative results in terms of true positive, false negative, and false positive rates for four video sequences, corresponding to the different time intervals and cameras shown in Fig. 13.11. Each of these sequences is selected to be of length 2000 frames. The ground truth was obtained by manual checking of these 8000 frames.

(1) The study of morning sequence shows a detection rate of ≈98%. The ≈2% miss detection has been mainly due to low contrast between swimmers and background. In addition, there are swimmers of smaller size, which has made the detection a difficult task. A low false positive rate (i.e., ≈0%) shows the robustness of the proposed algorithm to address dynamic aquatic background.

(2) The afternoon sequence comprises frames captured during a swimming lesson. A more dynamic background is involved here. In this study, water splashes caused by greater swimming movement is one main factor contributing to the slightly higher false positive rate (wrongly detecting movement of some background patches as foreground).

(3) We observe deterioration of the performance at night time due to strong specular reflection, which has led to a noisier environment. The higher false positive rate observed has been mostly attributed by cases of wrongly detecting background as foreground in reflective region.

(4) The fourth video sequence shows a study at a shallower zone, corresponding to scenario given in Fig. 13.11 (b). Equally good performance of foreground detection has been obtained. This shows the developed algorithm can directly be applied at different zones of the pool.

Table 13.1: Quantitative evaluation on video sequences in Fig. 13.11. In this evaluation, manual inspection was performed to derive the ground truth (Legends: TP represents true positive; FN represents false negative; FP represents false positive.)

		TP (%)	FN (%)	FP (%)
	Morning	≈98	≈2	≈0
Deep zone	Day time	≈99	≈1	≈1
	Night time	≈95	≈5	≈10
Shallow zone	Day time	≈99	≈1	≈1

13.6.2 *Challenging scenarios and performance comparison*

We shall highlight in this section the performance yielded corresponding to a few challenging scenarios faced and its performance comparison against a few state-of-the-art methods for performance benchmarking.

Case 1: Night time sequence with specular reflection

Figure 13.12 (a) presents challenge due to specular reflection at night time scene. The 3rd row of the figure shows results obtained after incorporating the developed filtering scheme. Improved performance with greater noise immunity and higher detection accuracy is observed. We would like to highlight that there are constraints to use polarizer in an efficient manner in our system setup. Thus, the developed image filtering technique by exploiting momentary characteristic of pixel signal in temporal domain shows an attractive alternative approach.

Case 2: Sequence with swimmers playing, generating background disturbance

Figure 13.12 (b) depicts a scenario with significant water disturbance. As shown, lane dividers disappear after swimmers jump into the pool. Such water movement will likely be misinterpreted as foreground when applying conventional approaches. The devised spatial matching mechanism has played a key role here to efficiently recognize such water movement. Promising results have also been observed after the lane dividers reappear again given in 3rd and 4th rows.

Case 3: Performance comparison

Figure 13.12 (c) shows performance comparison to state-of-the-art methods. When implementing W4 (Haritaoglu *et al.*, 2000) and mixture of Gaussian (MoG) (Stauffer and Grimson, 1999, 2000) methods, we have carefully tuned these methods to obtain the best results in our context. These results show that our algorithm has yielded a higher efficiency in detecting small and poorly visible swimmer while maintaining a low false positive error. It is understandable that this may not be a fair comparison. However, it reveals that the current state-of-the-art algorithms may not be straightforwardly extended to such new problem, and naturally there is a need for further research.

Case 4: Comments on other scenarios

We observed that images obtained from rainy sequence have a calmer background. This has made the foreground detection task less difficult. In addition, from the operational aspect, accurate foreground detection is less required as swimming is generally not permitted during rainy period.

Due to constraints such as permission of accessing a pool and costs needed, in this chapter, we have yet to set up and evaluate the proposed DEWS system at

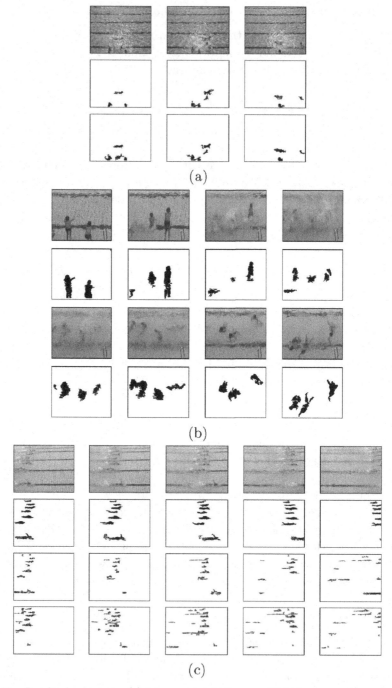

Fig. 13.12.   Results demonstrate: (a) foreground detection on night time scenes for cases without (2nd row) and with (3rd row) the proposed spatio-temporal filtering scheme, (b) a scenario with swimmers playing causes significant background disturbances, (c) performance comparison: our algorithm in 2nd row W_4 (Haritaoglu *et al.*, 2000) in 3rd row, and mixture of Gaussian (Stauffer and Grimson, 1999, 2000) in 4th row.

other pool with unusual geometry dimension. However, based on the results from the above experiments, we believe that the proposed system can be extended to such a pool with proper number of cameras to avoid any blind spots and to ensure good monitoring views.

13.6.3 *Off-line evaluation of water crisis detection*

To perform the experiment, 20 sequences comprising events of *swimming*, *treading*, and simulations of actual *water crisis* (distress and drowning) are collected. These sequences have been collected from different cameras with each sequence may contain a series of activities as given in Fig. 13.7. We have manually segmented these sequences to collect approximately 2000, 6000, and 6000 sets of swimmer descriptors for each respective class. This is equivalent to a continuous sequence of approximately an hour in our context.

In this experiment, a 10-fold validation study is carried out: i.e., 90% of each class is selected as training dataset while the remaining as testing dataset. This process is repeated 10 times with different combinations of training and testing data sets. In the experiment, the ground truth is manually annotated by assigning the three events {water crisis, treading, normal swimming} to be $\{[1\ 0\ 0], [0\ 1\ 0], [0\ 0\ 1]\}$, respectively. For the SVM method (Burges, 1998), RBF kernel is used, where we have explored different combinations of gamma values in the range of $\{0.1, \ldots, 0.9, 1, \ldots, 9, 10, \ldots, 400\}$ and parameter C values in the range of $\{0.01, 0.1, 1, 10, 100\}$.

Table 13.2 tabulates average error rates of the 10-fold validation performed. Two sets of results (run 1 and run 2), which give best training and best testing errors are listed in the table. Since OWM (Ueda, 2000) is a simple method where a set of optimum weights can be uniquely computed during training, there is only a set of average error rate given in the table.

Table 13.2:   Average error rates of the respective classifiers based on a 10-fold validation process. For FNN, SVM, and RM methods, two sets of results (run 1 and run 2) from parameter settings that give best training and best testing errors are presented. OWM method is a simple method where a set of optimum weights are uniquely computed.

	%Error$_\text{train}$	%Error$_\text{test}$
OWM	≈17.59	≈18.78
FNN-run 1 (best training)	≈17.64	≈21.53
FNN-run 2 (best testing)	≈19.08	≈19.08
SVM-run 1 (best training)	≈7.18	≈21.71
SVM-run 2 (best testing)	≈11.87	≈15.15
RM-run 1 (best training)	≈12.64	≈15.70
RM-run 2 (best testing)	≈12.67	≈15.57
RM+HMM($T = 16$)	≈8.88	≈12.28

Table 13.2 shows better performance attained by the developed RM with smaller error rates for both the training and testing data sets, comparing with *optimal weighting method* (OWM) (Ueda, 2000) and *feedforward neural network* (FNN) (Schurmann, 1996; Hornik *et al.*, 1989). The reason that FNN has a larger classification error is due to its convergence to local error solution. The developed RM has also achieved a comparable performance as what achieved by the well-known SVM (Burges, 1998). One technical merit of developed RM is its fast single computation step while without compromising much the performance accuracy. The incorporation of HMM module which exploits temporal information has further contributed to additional performance improvement. A reduction of about 4% in the error rates is recorded as tabulated.

From the training result that has given the minimum testing error, the order of the RM classifier in Eq. (13.11) and regularization constant in Eq. (13.13) are obtained to be $r = 3$ and $\varrho = 1e - 2$. Meanwhile, HMM models that describe state transition of the analyzed activities are given in Fig. 13.9.

Figures 13.13 and 13.14 show analysis in time domain. The first two scenarios in Figs. 13.13 (a) and (b) give simulations of *distress* event, where the victims demonstrate attributes having large arm movements to keep body afloat and small lateral movements with body perpendicular to water surface. The details of these experiments are further tabulated in Table 13.3. Parameters L_{wc}, L_{tread}, and L_{swim} denote likelihood scores for water crisis, treading, or swimming events. The experiment in Fig. 13.13 (a) starts by having treading activity for frames 320–326 and follows by a realistic distress simulation for frames 327–400. The result shows a larger L_{wc} ($L_{wc} > L_{tread}$ and $L_{wc} > L_{swim}$) obtained for frames 340–400, in which an alert has been successfully triggered.

The alarm-triggering step involves checking a cumulative score, which is increased by "1" when L_{wc} is the largest compared with L_{tread} and L_{swim}; otherwise, decreased by "1" until reaching "0." A swimmer will be labeled the stage of "yellow," if the cummulative score is more than a value equivalent to three seconds. If such observation is maintained with the cumulative score exceeds a value equivalent to 6 seconds, the status of the victim will be turned to "red." Thus, an alert will be automatically triggered. After factoring in the lag due to the temporal window used in the HMM step, time taken to trigger the alarm for this experiment is approximately 9.25 seconds.

Likewise for the case study given in Fig. 13.13 (b), a larger L_{wc} is observed for frames 1481–1515, in which an alarm has been triggered. It is noted that L_{tread} value is close to L_{wc} for frame 1500 onwards. One reason contributed to this observation is less accurate foreground silhouette being generated.

In Figs. 13.13 (c) and (d), we meanwhile show two simulations of *drowning* event. More specifically, these are simulations of unconscious drowning. The main differences of these two simulations from the previous described distress simulations are that there is less arm movement and the event happens with the victim sinks to the bottom of the pool with little struggling. In these two case studies, the

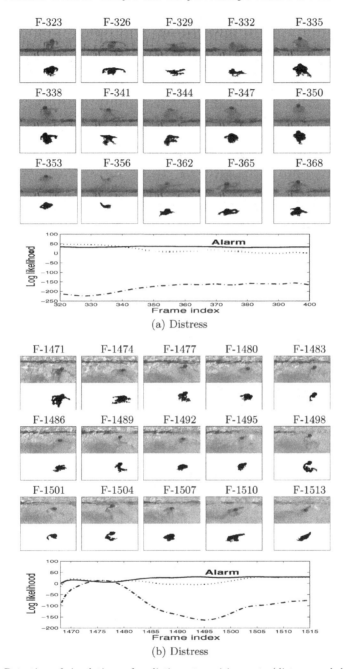

Fig. 13.13. Detection of simulations of realistic water-crisis events (distress and drowning). For simulations of distress in (a) and (b), the victim demonstrates large arm movements but small lateral body movements. Meanwhile, for simulations of drowning in (c) and (d), the victim sinks beneath water surface without much arm movements. Result shows higher water crisis likelihood yielded when the target is exhibiting distress for (a) and (b) and drowning for (c) and (d). (Legends: solid line "—" denotes water crisis likelihood, dotted line "···" denotes treading likelihood, and dash-dotted line "-·-" denotes swimming likelihood.)

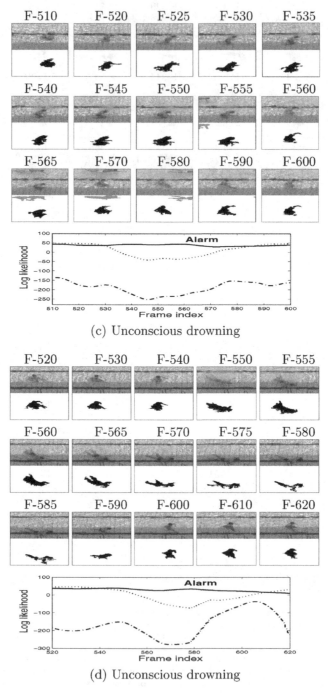

(c) Unconscious drowning

(d) Unconscious drowning

Fig. 13.13.   (Continued)

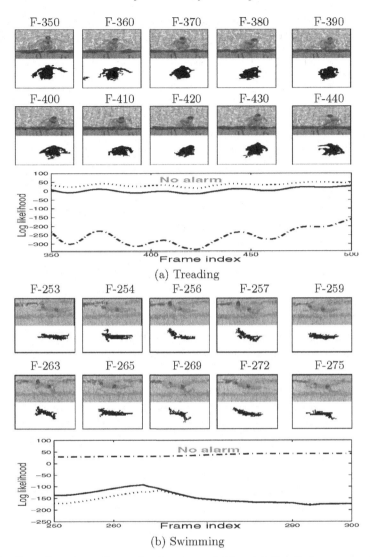

Fig. 13.14. Detection of treading and swimming activities. (a) Result shows correct detection of the treading activity, demonstrating a higher treading likelihood curve. Knowing the margin between treading likelihood and water crisis likelihood can allow an incorporation of a bias for better water crisis detection while balancing the false alarm. (b) Result shows that swimming likelihood curve is far above treading and distress likelihood curves. (Legends: solid line "—" denotes distress likelihood, dotted line "···" denotes treading likelihood, and dash-dotted line "-··-" denotes swimming likelihood.)

victims demonstrate treading in the beginning, and then followed by sinking to the bottom of the pool. The figure shows good recognition of these swimmers' activities, which matches well to the actual actions. It reports a higher treading likelihood in the beginning of the experiment, and followed by a higher distress likelihood observed in between frames 530–585 for (c) and frames 541–610 for (d),

Table 13.3: The different stages of activities for video segments given in Fig. 13.13, and the different event classes {normal swimming, treading, water crisis} which have the highest likelihood scores at different intervals. Time taken to trigger alarm from the onset of water crisis is given in the last column. (Legends: L_{wc} and L_{tread} denote likelihood scores for water crisis and treading classes, respectively.)

	Activities at different intervals	Largest likelihood	Time taken (alarm triggered)
Fig. 13.13 (a)	F-320 → F-326 (treading)	F-320 → F-340 (L_{tread} is the largest)	
	F-327 → F-400 (distress)	F-341 → F-400 (L_{wc} is the largest)	9.25 s
Fig. 13.13 (b)	F-1468 → F-1473 (treading)	F-1470 → F-1480 (L_{tread} is the largest)	
	F-1475 → F-1515 (distress)	F-1481 → F-1515 (L_{wc} is the largest)	7.5 s
Fig. 13.13 (c)	F-510 → F-519 (treading)	F-510 → F-539 (L_{tread} is the largest)	
	F-520 → F-570 (drowning)	F-530 → F-585 (L_{wc} is the largest)	8.5 s
	F-571 → F-600 (treading)	F-586 → F-600 (L_{tread} is the largest)	
Fig. 13.13 (d)	F-520 → F-537 (treading)	F-520 → F-540 (L_{tread} is the largest)	
	F-538 → F-594 (drowning)	F-541 → F-610 (L_{wc} is the largest)	6.75 s
	F-595 → F-620 (treading)	F-611 → F-620 (L_{tread} is the largest)	

respectively. A higher treading likelihood at the end is observed for both cases is due to the simulations are completed with a treading activity. Meantime, swimming action to move to water surface has led to a rise in L_{swim} towards the end of the sequence.

Among activities in pool, it is identified that *treading* activity shares similarity as distress. Figure 13.14 (a) presents a study of treading event, showing a higher treading likelihood curve. The observed margin between the treading and distress likelihood curves is useful to incorporate an additional bias to enhance the detection of distress while balancing between false detection in the practical implementation.

Figure 13.14 (b) demonstrates a study of normal swimming event. The figure shows swimming likelihood curve is far above treading and distress curves. This infers that it is less likely of wrongly detecting a normal swimming activity as distress.

13.6.4 *On-site testing: water crisis detection in a crowded scenario*

Figure 13.15 reports results obtained when evaluating the trained system in a life-saving lesson. This is a challenging scenario as it involves a close group of swimmers demonstrating realistic water crisis scenario in water. Occlusion happened has caused formation of large silhouette blob, leading to issues like change in target's label and destroy of the past cumulated record.

The odd rows of Fig. 13.15 present sample frames from the sequence. Red circles overlaid on these frames show fitting a k number of ellipses by the developed blob-splitting mechanism. The figure shows reasonably good separation obtained where

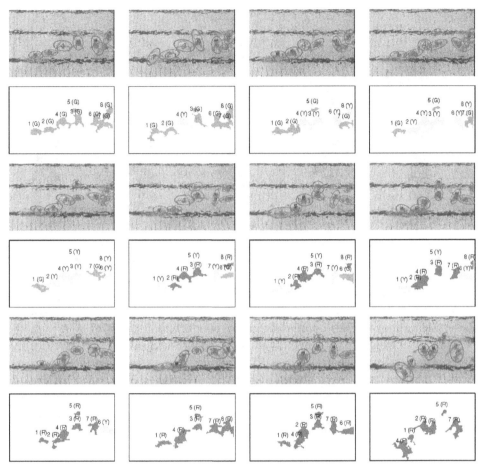

Fig. 13.15. Sequence images from a life-saving lesson. In the lesson, swimmers demonstrate distress in water. Occlusion happened causes silhouette masks of nearby swimmers overlap, forming a contiguous blob. The above results show the implemented blob-splitting mechanism can do reasonably well in separating a contiguous blob into the respective swimmers.

contiguous blobs have been segregated into individual entities. Since tracking is not a key focus of this work, we have adopted a linear tracking scheme where centroids of detected swimmers from previous frame are linearly projected onto current frame, and the association is done by pairing up centroids in current frame to the projected centroids from previous frame based on shortest distance. In this study, the blob-splitting mechanism has contributed to the improvement of cumulating evidence for the event detection step.

In the even rows, individual target's label and its status (i.e., in either "green", "yellow", or "red") are presented. Statuses of all the swimmers are in "green" in the beginning, showing no water crisis event. As the struggling action progresses, statuses of swimmer turn into yellow and then "red" eventually, as shown.

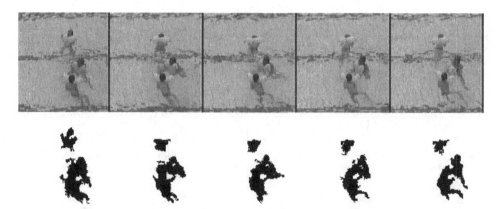

Fig. 13.16.   Detection of a scenario which looks similar to a distress case during the on-site trial.

13.6.5 *On-site trial: false alarm cases*

In the current implementation, we ensure the developed system should response to cases which is similar to behaviors/scenarios as have been collected in the training phase. Meantime, the false alarm rate is at about 1 to 5 cases for each camera in a day. We would like to note that these results are subject to activities in the pool and the sensitivity of detecting genuine cases as required by end users. Figure 13.16 shows an example that have triggered the alarm, which involves a group of new learners practising their swimming skill. Based on feedbacks from end users (lifeguards), triggering alarm for such scenario is desirable as which shall draw their attention to higher risk area.

13.7 Conclusions and Future Works

We have presented in this chapter a vision system based on innovative human behavior analysis approaches for early drowning detection at an outdoor swimming pool. Based on identified technical challenges, a set of methods which are new variations in the fields of background subtraction, denoising, data fusion, and blob-splitting technique are proposed. In particular, we have addressed fundamental problems like: (1) the issue of devising a good modeling scheme for dynamic aquatic background, (2) the issue of recognizing behaviors and activities in swimming pool context, and (3) the issue of addressing moderate level of crowded scenario. Promising results yielded in the experiments demonstrate that our proposed DEWS system is beyond the stage of proof-of-concept. Currently, we are working towards delivering a set of operation specifications with inputs from the end user (lifeguard).

It is also realized that a number of issues remain unexplored in this work, and thus shall be considered in our future works. One issue is a drowning incident may happen in a form which can be different from the learned instinctive drowning response model. Therefore, this poses the challenge on how our system will react to an event, which the system is not trained to. On the other hand, it is also desirable to recognize group activity to complement the current approach which is primarily relying on analysis of activity for every single target.

Acknowledgment

This work is supported by the Enterprise Challenge Unit, Singapore's Prime Minister's Office, and the Singapore Sports Council.

References

Boult, T. E., Micheals, R. J., and Gao, X. Into the woods: visual surveillance of noncooperative and camouflaged targets in complex outdoor settings, *Proc. IEEE* **89**, 10, 1382–1402, 2001.

Burges, C. J. C. A tutorial on support vector machines for pattern recognition, *Data Mining Knowledge Discovery* **2**, 2, 121–167, 1998.

Collins, R. T., Lipton, A. J., and Kanade, T. Introduction to the special section on video surveillance, *IEEE Trans. Pattern Anal. Machine Intelligence* **22**, 8, 745–746, 2000.

Cucchiara, R., Piccardi, M., and Mello, P. Image analysis and rule-based reasoning for a traffic monitoring system, *IEEE Trans. Intelligent Transportation Syst.* **1**, 2, 119–130, 2000.

Duda, R. O., Hart, P. E., and Stork, D. G. *Pattern Classification* (John Wiley & Sons), 2001.

Elgammal, A., Duraiswami, R., Harwood, D., and Davis, L. S. Background and foreground modeling using nonparametric kernel density estimation for visual surveillance, *Proc. IEEE* **90**, 7, 1151–1163, 2002.

Eng, H.-L., Toh, K.-A., Kam, A.-H., Wang, J., and Yau, W.-Y. An automatic drowning detection surveillance system for challenging outdoor pool environments, in *Proc. IEEE Int. Conf. Comput. Vision (ICCV'03)*, pp. 532–539, 2003.

Eng, H.-L., Wang, J., Kam, A. H., and Yau, W.-Y. Novel region-based modeling for human detection within highly dynamic aquatic environment, in *Proc. IEEE Int. Conf. Comput. Vision Pattern Recognition (CVPR'04)*, pp. 2:390–397, 2004.

Eng, H.-L., Toh, K.-A., Yau, W.-Y., and Chiew, T.-K. Recognition of complex human behaviors in pool environment using foreground silhouette using foreground silhouette, in *Proc. Int. Symp. Visual Computing*, pp. 371–379, 2005.

Eng, H.-L., Wang, J., Kam, A. H., and Yau, W.-Y. Robust human detection within a highly dynamic aquatic environment in real time, *IEEE Trans. Image Processing* **15**, 6, 1583–1600, 2006.

Eng, H.-L., Toh, K.-A., Yau, W.-Y., and Wang, J. Dews: a live visual surveillance system for early drowning detection at pool, *IEEE Trans. Circuit Syst. Video Technol.* **18**, 2, 187–196, 2008.

Foresti, G. L. A real-time system for video surveillance of unattended outdoor environments, *IEEE Trans. Circuits Syst. Video Tech.* **8**, 6, 697–704, 1998.

Forney Jr., G. D. The viterbi algorithm, *Proc. IEEE* **61**, 3, 263–278, 1973.

Friedman, N. and Rusell, S. Image segmentation in video sequences: a probabilistic approach, in *Proc. Int. Conf. Uncertainty Artificial Intelligence*, pp. 175–181, 1997.

Fujikake, H., Takizawa, K., Aida, T., Negishi, T., and Kobayashi, M. Video camera system using liquid-crystal polarizing filter to reduce reflected light, *IEEE Trans. Broadcasting* **44**, 4, 419–426, 1998.

Gavrila, D. M. The visual analysis of human movement: a survey, *Computer Vision Image Understanding* **73**, 1, 82–92, 1999.

Guichard, F., Lavest, J., Liege, B., and Meniere, J. Poseidon technologies: the world's first and only computer-aided drowning detection system, in *Proc. IEEE Int. Conf. Comput. Vision Pattern Recognition (CVPR'01)*, pp. –, 2001.

Haritaoglu, I., Harwood, D., and Davis, L. S. W4: real-time surveillance of people and their activities, *IEEE Trans. Pattern Anal. Machine Intelligence* **22**, 8, 809–830, 2000.

Hornik, K., Stinchcombe, M., and White, H. Multi-layer feedforward networks are universal approximators, *Neural Networks* **2**, 5, 359–366, 1989.

Hsu, Y.-H., Nagel, H. H., and Rekers, G. New likelihood test methods for change detection in image sequences, *Comput. Vision, Graphics, Image Processing* **26**, 73–106, 1984.

Hu, W., Tan, T., Wang, L., and Maybank, S. A survey of visual surveillance of object motion and behaviors, *IEEE Trans. Syst., Man, Cybernetics — Part C: Appl. Rev.* **34**, 3, 334–352, 2004.

Koller, D., Weber, J., Huang, T., Malik, J., Ogasaware, G., Rao, B., and Russell, S. Towards robust automatic traffic scene analysis in real-time, in *Proc. Int. Conf. Pattern Recognition*, pp. 126–131, 1994.

Lavest, J. M., Guichard, F., and Rousseau, C. Multi-view reconstruction combining underwater and air sensors, in *Proc. IEEE Int. Conf. Image Processing*, pp. 3:24–28, 2002.

Matsuyama, T., Ohya, T., and Habe, H. Background subtraction for non-stationary scenes, in *Proc. Asian Conf. Comput. Vision*, pp. 662–667, 2000.

Meniere, J. System for monitoring a swimming pool to prevent drowning accidents, US. Patent No. 6,133,838, 2000.

Menoud, E. Alarm and monitoring device for the presumption of bodies in danger in a swimming pool, US. Patent No. 5,886,630, 1999.

Ohya, J., Utsumi, A., and Yamato, J. *Analyzing Video Sequences of Multiple Humans Tracking, Posture Estimation and Behavior Recognition, The International Series in Video Computing*, **3** (Springer), 2002.

Oliver, N., Rosario, B., and Pentland, A. A bayesian computer vision system for modeling human interactions, *IEEE Trans. Pattern Anal. Machine Intelligence* **22**, 8, 844–851, 2000.

Pavlidis, I., Morellas, V., Tsiamyrtzis, P., and Harp, S. Urban surveillance systems: from the laboratory to the commercial world, *Proc. IEEE* **89**, 10, 1478–1497, 2001.

Pia, F. Observation on the drowning of nonswimmers, *J. Physic. Edu.*, pp. 164–167, 1974.

Pia, F. Reflections on lifeguarding surveilance programs, in *Proc. Reflections Lifeguarding Conf.*, pp. –, 1994.

Rabiner, L. R. A tutorial on hidden markov models and selected applications in speech recognition, *Proc. IEEE* **77**, 2, 257–288, 1989.

Regazzoni, C., Ramesh, V., and Foresti, G. L. Scanning the issue/technology: special issue on video communications, processing and understanding for third generation surveillance system, *Proc. IEEE* **89**, 10, 1355–1367, 2001.

Schechner, Y. Y. and Shamir, J. Polarization and statistical analysis of scenes containing a semireflector, *J. Opt. Soc. Am. A* **17**, 2, 276–284, 2000.

Schurmann, J. *Pattern Classification: A Unified View of Statistical and Neural Approaches* (Wiley, New York), 1996.

Shurcliff, W. A. and Ballard, S. S. *Polarized Light* (Van Nos-trand, Princeton, N.J.), 1964.

Stauffer, C. and Grimson, W. E. L. Adaptive background mixture models for real-time tracking, in *Proc. IEEE Int. Conf. Comput. Vision Pattern Recognition (CVPR'99)*, pp. 2:246–252, 1999.

Stauffer, C. and Grimson, W. E. L. Learning patterns of activity using real-time tracking, *IEEE Trans. Pattern Anal. Machine Intelligence* **22**, 8, 747–757, 2000.

Toh, K.-A., Tran, Q.-L., and Srinivasan, D. Benchmarking a reduced multivariate polynomial pattern classifier, *IEEE Trans. Pattern Anal. Machine Intelligence* **26**, 6, 740–755, 2004.

Ueda, N. Optimal linear combination of neural networks for improving classification performance, *IEEE Trans. Pattern Anal. Machine Intelligence* **22**, 207–215, 2000.

Wilson, A. D. and Bobick, A. F. Learning visual behavior for gesture analysis, in *Proc. Int. Symp. Comput. Vision*, pp. 229–234, 1995.

Wilson, A. D. and Bobick, A. F. Parametric hidden markov models for gesture recognition, *IEEE Trans. Pattern Anal. Machine Intelligence* **21**, 9, 884–900, 1999.

Wren, C. R., Azarbayehani, A., Darrell, T., and Pentland, A. P. Pfinder: real-time tracking of the human body, *IEEE Trans. Pattern Anal. Machine Intelligence* **19**, 7, 780–785, 1997.

Yamato, J., Ohya, J., and Ishii, K. Recognizing human action in time-sequential images using hidden markov model, in *Proc. IEEE Int. Conf. Comput. Vision Pattern Recognition (CVPR'92)*, pp. 379–385, 1992.

Zhao, T. and Nevatia, R. Bayesian human segmentation in crowded situations, in *Proc. IEEE Int. Conf. Comput. Vision Pattern Recognition*, pp. 2:459–466, 2003.

Chapter 14

HUMAN METRIC CONSTRAINED HUMAN DETECTION

Liyuan Li

Institute for Infocomm Research
1 Fusionopolis Way, #21-01 Connexis (South Tower)
Singapore, 138632
lyli@i2r.a-star.edu.sg

14.1 Introduction

Detection of human objects in images and videos of natural scenes is among the most interesting topics in computer vision and applications. For decades, this problem has caught the attention of researchers from both the academia and the industry. The potential applications include content-based image/video analysis, human robot interaction, security and surveillance, intelligent vehicles, and interactive entertainment. Many interesting approaches for human detection have been proposed (Pentland, 2000; Gavrila, 1999), particularly with the recent combination of powerful learning-based classifiers, great progress has been achieved and many encouraging detectors have been developed (Dalal and Triggs, 2005; Leibe *et al.*, 2005; Viola *et al.*, 2005; Tuzel *et al.*, 2007; Gavrila, 2007).

The most common approach to human detection is to slide a window across the image, and then classify each local window as one which contains either a human object or background according to the spatial arrangement of local visual features (Gavrila and Munder, 2007). The sliding window approach shifts detection windows of all possible scales at all locations over the image while performing feature extraction and pattern classification. This brute-force approach is too computationally intensive for real-time applications. The appearance of a human object in an image, e.g., the position, size, and body orientation, is determined by the human metrics, e.g., the height, width, and depth of the standing body in the 3D real-world scene and the scene perspective to the camera. Hence, it is possible to perform efficient human detection by exploiting those cues based on human metrics and scene perspective from the image of interest.

Under the Bayesian framework, the problem of human detection based on an image can be described as follows. Given an image I, the detection of a human at position $\mathbf{x}$ is to compute the likelihood $P(I, \mathbf{x}|H)$, where H denotes a human model. Without any knowledge of the human appearance in the image, the likelihood should be evaluated over all possible scales, orientations, and viewing angles, i.e.,

$$P(I, \mathbf{x}|H) = \arg \max_{\{a,s,o\}} P(I, \mathbf{x}|A(a, s, o)) \qquad (14.1)$$

where $A(a, s, o)$ indicates a human appearance model constrained by the corresponding viewing angle, scale, and body orientation. The likelihood probability Eq. (14.1) is not easy to compute directly because the search space is too large under this optimization framework. Another potential drawback for simply using Eq. (14.1) is that too many false positives may be generated due to the complexity of natural backgrounds.

In most application scenarios particularly the public scenes, humans often stand or walk on the ground surface. Let A_a represent the human appearance observed from a tilt angle a of the camera to the scene, (14.1) can be written as

$$P(I, \mathbf{x}|H) = \arg \max_{\{s,o\}} P(I, \mathbf{x}|A_a(s, o)) \qquad (14.2)$$

According to Bayesian law and with appropriate assumptions of constant priors, we have

$$P(I, \mathbf{x}|A_a(s, o)) \propto P(I|A_a(s, o), \mathbf{x}) P(A_a(s, o)|\mathbf{x}) \qquad (14.3)$$

Once the pose of the camera is fixed, the perspective of the scene to the camera is determined. The scale and orientation of a human object in an image are determined by his/her distance to the camera and the position $(\mathbf{x})$ in the image. Such relationships can be described as mappings $s(\mathbf{x})$ and $o(\mathbf{x})$ constrained by human metrics and scene perspective. Hence, it can be assumed that

$$P(A_a(s(\mathbf{u}), o(\mathbf{u}))|\mathbf{x}) = \begin{cases} 1, & \text{if } \mathbf{u} = \mathbf{x}; \\ 0, & \text{otherwise.} \end{cases} \qquad (14.4)$$

Combining Eq. (14.1) with (14.4), the likelihood probability of observing a human object at position $\mathbf{x}$ in an image becomes

$$P(I, \mathbf{x}|H) \propto P(I|A_a(s(\mathbf{x}), o(\mathbf{x})), \mathbf{x}) \qquad (14.5)$$

This means that, with the human metric constrained mappings of scale and orientation from image-related local measurements, there is no need to compute the likelihood over multiple scales, orientations, and appearances at each position. This will improve not only the efficiency but also the accuracy of human detection.

In the remaining body of this chapter, two methods of human metric constrained human detection are presented. In Sec. 14.2, a method which estimates the mappings $s(\mathbf{x})$ and $o(\mathbf{x})$ from local measures of potential human body for human detection from disparity images is described. In Sec. 14.3, another method, which estimates the mapping $s(\mathbf{x})$ and $o(\mathbf{x})$ from the human perspective context (HPC) for human detection in surveillance applications is presented. Finally, the conclusion and discussion are given in Sec. 14.4.

14.2 Human Detection from Stereo Images

The disparity image from a stereo camera provides a 2.5D information of the observed objects within the field of view. It provides a measurement to separate human objects from the backgrounds without the need of background subtraction. It is particularly useful to detect humans from a mobile platform, e.g., a robot head for human robot interaction (HRI). Most existing methods are based on the bottom-up depth segmentation of human bodies for human detection (e.g., Zhao and Thorpe 2000). As the disparity data on human bodies are often incomplete and/or inaccurate, and even merged together under cluttered or crowded scenes, these methods are unreliable under real-world scenarios (Shashua *et al.*, 2004). In this chapter, a new top-down method is proposed for stereo-based human detection and segmentation exploiting the human metric constraint. The basic idea behind the method is that, if we know the distance between the person and the camera, we can estimate the scale of the person in the image and then apply a detector with the most suitable scale to evaluate the likelihood of human presence at the position.

14.2.1 *Human detection*

In the applications for HRI, the camera is usually installed at the top of a robot and looks forward horizontally. Human objects are assumed standing or walking in front of the robot. In this case, the viewing tilt angle of the camera can be assumed to be fixed at zero degree, and the orientations of humans in the image are parallel to the vertical axis of the image. Therefore, the human appearance model $A_a(s(\mathbf{x}), o(\mathbf{x}))$ can be simplified as $A(s(\mathbf{x}))$.

To estimate the human scale from his/her distance to the camera, we have to first build the relationship between the distance (z) and disparity (d). Theoretically, the relation between the depth distance and the disparity is described as $z = bf/d = K_1/d$, where b is the baseline, f is the focal length, and $K_1 = bf$. In practice, K_1 is not a constant, and decreases when d decreases, or z increases as shown in Fig. 14.1. By examining the curves of K_1 with respect to d from several stereo cameras, we propose the use of the logarithm model for describing the K_1 coefficient, i.e.,

$$z = K_1(d)/d, \quad \text{with } K_1(d) = K_d \log d + B_d \qquad (14.6)$$

where K_d and B_d are the model parameters. For each stereo camera, the model can be obtained from offline calibration. The new model can extend the effective range of z-d relation more than 2 times compared to that of a simple inverse proportion model adopting a constant K_1.

In a disparity image, the disparity data cloud from a standing person in the scene can be described by an ellipsoid characterized by human metrics. Suppose

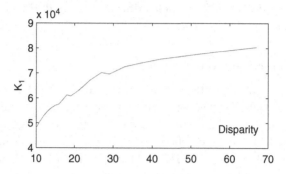

Fig. 14.1.   The curve of K_1-disparity relationship from a STOC stereo head.

the image position $\mathbf{x}_0 = (x_0, y_0)$ is the center of a person in the image and its disparity value is d_0. The disparity data cloud from the person can be represented by a Gaussian-like kernel function as

$$A(s(\mathbf{x}_0)) = \frac{1}{C_{\mathbf{x}_0}} \exp\left[-\left(\frac{(x-x_0)^2}{\sigma_{x_0}^2} + \frac{(y-y_0)^2}{\sigma_{y_0}^2} + \frac{(d-d_0)^2}{\sigma_{d_0}^2}\right)\right] \qquad (14.7)$$

where $C_{\mathbf{x}_0}$ is a constant for normalization, and the scale parameters $\sigma_{x_0}, \sigma_{y_0}$, and σ_{d_0} are determined by human metrics of height, width, and depth measurements. In this formulation, the mappings $s(\mathbf{x}_0)$ can be represented by $\sigma_{x_0} = s_x(d_0)$, $\sigma_{y_0} = s_y(d_0)$, and $\sigma_{d_0} = s_d(d_0)$, respectively.

From the perspective transformation of imaging, the mappings can be evaluated as follows. Let H_b, W_b, and D_b be the average height, width, and depth of a standing human body in 3D real-world environment. According to the perspective triangularity, the height and width of the person in the image can be expressed as

$$h_b = K_2(d_0)H_b d_0, \quad \text{and} \quad w_b = K_2(d_0)W_b d_0 \qquad (14.8)$$

where $K_2(d) = f/K_1(d)$ and f is the focal length of the lens. Then, the mappings to estimate the spatial scales of the person in the image can be defined as

$$\sigma_{x_0} = s_x(d_0) = k_s w_b = k_s K_2(d_0)W_b d_0 \qquad (14.9)$$

$$\sigma_{y_0} = s_y(d_0) = k_s h_b = k_s K_2(d_0)H_b d_0 \qquad (14.10)$$

Due to the non-linear relationship between z and d, the distributions of disparity data on both sides of d_0 are asymmetric. The margins of the disparity measures on both sides of the center d_0 can be estimated as

$$d_\pm = \frac{K_1(d_0)}{z_0 \mp D_b/2} = \frac{K_1(d_0)d_0}{K_1(d_0) \mp D_b d_0/2} \qquad (14.11)$$

where $d_- < d_0$ and $d_+ > d_0$. Now, the mapping to estimate the depth scale of the person in the image can be defined as

$$\sigma_{d_{0+}} = s_{d+}(d_0) = k_d(d_+ - d_0), \quad \text{for } d \geq d_0 \tag{14.12}$$

$$\sigma_{d_{0-}} = s_{d-}(d_0) = k_d(d_0 - d_-), \quad \text{for } d < d_0 \tag{14.13}$$

With the human metric constrained mappings for the 3D scales of a potential human object at position $\mathbf{x}_0$ in the image from the local measurement d_0 from the body as described by Eq. (14.9), Eq. (14.10), Eq. (14.12), and Eq. (14.13), as well as the ellipsoid model of the 3D human body as described by Eq. (14.7), the likelihood of observing a standing person centered at position $\mathbf{x}_0$ in the disparity image can be calculated as

$$P(I|A(s(\mathbf{x}_0)), \mathbf{x}_0) = \frac{\sum_{\mathbf{x} \in B} \exp\left[-\left(\frac{(x-x_0)^2}{\sigma_{x_0}^2} + \frac{(y-y_0)^2}{\sigma_{y_0}^2} + \frac{(d-d_0)^2}{\sigma_{d_0}^2}\right)\right]}{\sum_{\mathbf{x} \in B} \exp\left[-\left(\frac{(x-x_0)^2}{\sigma_{x_0}^2} + \frac{(y-y_0)^2}{\sigma_{y_0}^2}\right)\right]} \tag{14.14}$$

where B is the 3D bounding box of $h_b \times w_b \times d_b$ centered at $\mathbf{x}_0$ with $d_b = d_+ - d_-$, and the denominator in the RHS is a factor for normalization. In practice, the term within the summation in the numerator can be written as $\exp[-((x - x_0)^2/\sigma_{x_0}^2 + (y - y_0)^2/\sigma_{y_0}^2)] \exp(-(d - d_0)^2/\sigma_{d_0}^2)$, in which the former can be considered as the weight of Gaussian-like spatial kernel and the later as the evidence from the disparity measurements. The local maxima of the likelihood probabilities in the image indicate the possible presence of human objects in the view.

14.2.2 *Human segmentation*

From the detected human candidate and the estimated 3D scales, a top-down segmentation process can be performed to extracted the human body from the image. The model described by Eq. (14.7) gives a general representation of a standing human body. It ignores the variations of human shapes and poses. To achieve an accurate segmentation in crowded scenarios, it is better to first obtain a distinctive distribution model of the disparity data cloud for the detected person. In this chapter, we propose to perform human segmentation under the maximum-likelihood (ML) framework from learned distinctive model for each human candidate.

Suppose the ith detected person is located within a 3D box B_i of size $h_b \times w_b \times d_b$ centered at $(\mathbf{x}_i, d_i)$. Then, a 3D Gaussian distribution $\mathcal{N}(\mathbf{v}_i, \Sigma_i)$ can be obtained from the disparity data within the bounding box B_i, where $\mathbf{v}_i = (\bar{x}_i, \bar{y}_i, \bar{d}_i)$ is the mean vector and Σ_i is the covariance matrix with non-zero correlation coefficients. This online learned distinctive model is much more accurate than the general model (Eq. (14.7)) since it characterizes not only the size but also the shape and pose information of the detected person. In segmentation, for a pixel $\mathbf{x} = (x, y)$ in the disparity image with the feature vector $\mathbf{v} = (x, y, d(x, y))$, it is assigned to a human region according to the ML probability

$$l_\mathbf{v} = \arg\max_i P_i(\mathbf{v}) \quad \text{and} \quad P_i(\mathbf{v}) > T_1 \tag{14.15}$$

where $P_i(\mathbf{v}) = (2\pi)^{-1}|\Sigma_i|^{-\frac{1}{2}} \exp\left(-\frac{1}{2}(\mathbf{v} - \mathbf{v}_i)\Sigma_i^{-1}(\mathbf{v} - \mathbf{v}_i)^T\right)$. Equation (14.15) indicates a top-down model-driven human segmentation process. Hence, it is very robust to noise, missing data, and complex situations.

14.2.3 The algorithm

Now, the algorithm of human metric constrained human detection from a disparity image can be described as follows. As formulated by Eq. (14.5), we also scan the image to perform human detection, but at each position only the detector of one suitable scale is applied. Normally, humans are quite large objects in the images. Hence, there is no need to detect humans pixel-by-pixel in an image. In the proposed method, we detect humans at the positions of a sparse grid on the image. Suppose $d_{\min}$ is the smallest disparity value for the humans can be reliably detected from the disparity image and $w_{\min} = K_2(d_{\min})W_b d_{\min}$ is the corresponding body width of the humans in the image. The offset between grid points in both horizontal and vertical directions can be determined as the half of the minimum body width, i.e., $w_{\min}/2$. At a grid position $\mathbf{x}_{g_i}$, the local disparity value d_{g_i} is calculated as the average of the valid disparity values within a box of $w_{\min} \times w_{\min}$ size centered at $\mathbf{x}_{g_i}$. If the d_{g_i} is smaller than $d_{\min}$, no detection has to be performed at the position and the likelihood probability $P(I|A(s(\mathbf{x}_{g_i})), \mathbf{x}_{g_i})$ is set to 0. The steps of the algorithm for human detection and segmentation are listed below.

(1) Human detection: scan the image at grid positions and compute the likelihood probabilities using Eq. (14.14).
(2) Searching: locate valid detections one-by-one.

    (a) Find the ML probability value. If the value is too small, i.e., less than a threshold T_{hd}, terminate the searching and go to (3).

    (b) Estimate the distinctive distribution $\mathcal{N}(\mathbf{v}_i, \Sigma_i)$ and perform the pixel-level labelling of the human body using Eq. (14.15). If the body size is too small, drop the detection, set the likelihood value at the grid position as 0, and go to (a).

    (c) Set the likelihood probability values as 0 for the grid points covered by the labelled region to suppress duplicate detections and go to (a).

(3) Human segmentation: extract human body regions in a global ML-framework from the disparity image using Eq. (14.15) for all the valid detections.

The detected humans are finally verified according to the edge evidence from the color image along the head-shoulder contour as described in Li *et al.* (2004c).

14.2.4 *The results*

We have tested and evaluated the proposed method for human detection on images captured by stereo cameras from both static and mobile platforms. In the testing, the STOC cameras from Videre Design were employed. The effect depth range of the disparity measurements depends on the focal length of the lens. STOC cameras of 2.5 mm or 2.8 mm lens and 9 cm baseline were used.

The algorithm has been tested on various scenarios of varying complexities, including multiple persons gathering, humans moving in cluttered backgrounds, and various degrees of occlusions. In this section, we first present some examples of human detection for complicated situations, and then report the quantitative evaluation on three sequences containing one person, two persons, and four persons moving around in the view from static and mobile cameras.

Visual examination

Some examples of detecting two persons, three persons, and four persons under different scenarios are shown in Figs. 14.2–14.4, respectively. In each figure, the images are arranged as follows. The first row are the original color images and the second row are the disparity images from the stereo camera, and the third row are the human detection results from the corresponding input images displayed above. For the detection results, each segmented human object is displayed with a distinctive color. The white bounding boxes of the head and body overlapping on the segmented region indicate a confirmed detection according to the edge evidence of the head-shoulder contour from the color image.

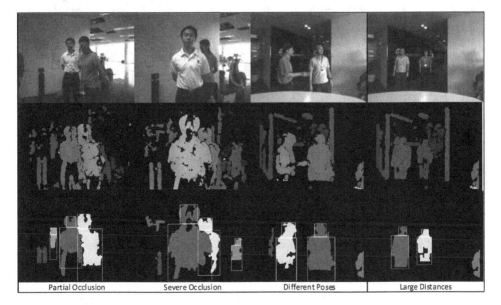

Fig. 14.2. The examples of human detection in images containing two persons.

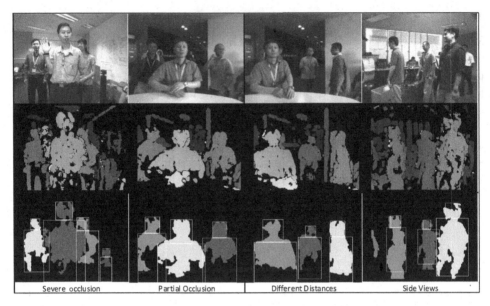

Fig. 14.3. The examples of human detection in images containing three persons.

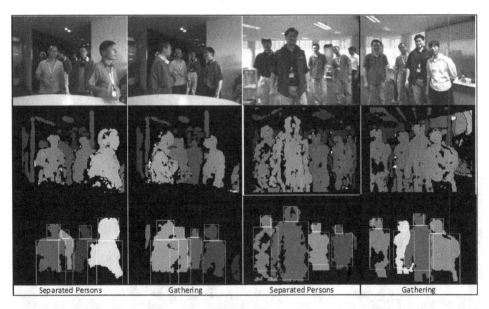

Fig. 14.4. The examples of human detection in images containing four persons.

Figure 14.2 shows four examples of human detection from images containing two persons in the view. These examples show the performance of human detection and segmentation under the scenarios of partial occlusion, severe occlusion, various human poses (e.g., front view and side view body poses), and distant humans to the camera.

In Fig. 14.3, four examples of three persons in the view are displayed. The examples come from the scenarios of three persons gathering with severe occlusion, three persons at various distances to the camera with partial occlusion and different body poses, and three persons walking laterally in front of a moving robot.

Finally, in Fig. 14.4, four examples of much more complicated scenarios involving four persons in the view are presented. They are under the scenario of four persons wandering or gathering in front of a moving robot.

In Li *et al.* (2004c), we have previously proposed a top-down stereo-based human detection approach from the disparity images. Assuming humans standing on the ground plane and the stereo camera looking forward horizontally on the top of a robot, we projected the disparity measures vertically on the $X - Z$ plane which is parallel to the ground plane. Then, a scale-adaptive filtering is applied to the 2D histogram to aggregate the evidence of human presences. The peaks in the filtered 2D histogram indicate the positions of potential persons standing on the ground surface. By locating and extracting the peaks, a heuristic process is designed to segment human objects from close to distance in the disparity image. Obviously, the 3D distribution model according to human metrics proposed here is more accurate than the 2D distributions of the peaks on the filtered histogram, especially in the crowded scenarios where the disparity clouds from closed persons may merge together. A few examples to show the comparison between the two methods are displayed in Fig. 14.5. The examples are shown row-by-row in the figure. In each row, the images displayed from the left to the right are: the input color image, the input disparity image, the result of human segmentation and detection by Li *et al.* (2004c) , and the result of the proposed method. Significant improvements in human segmentation and detection can be found. However, the proposed method is slower than the previous method.

From these examples, one can find that the 3D ellipsoid model of a suitable scale is able to well locate the human positions in the disparity images and the person-adapted distinctive model is able to well segment human individuals from the uncompleted disparity measurements and merged data clouds when multiple people gathering.

Quantitative evaluation

We also performed quantitative evaluation of the proposed method on three test sequences. The sequences of color and disparity images were recorded at about 10 fps from a STOC stereo camera installed on the head of a mobile robot. The first sequence (Seq1) provides a test scenario of following a person moving around along a long corridor in an office environment. The sequence contains 1200 frames. The second sequence (Seq2) captures the scenarios of two persons moving in an office environment, with changes of body poses and distances to the robot. The third sequence (Seq3) contains four persons moving and gathering in front of the robot. The detection results are compared with ground truth in every 10 frames. The summary of the performance are listed in Table 14.1,where "Frames" indicates

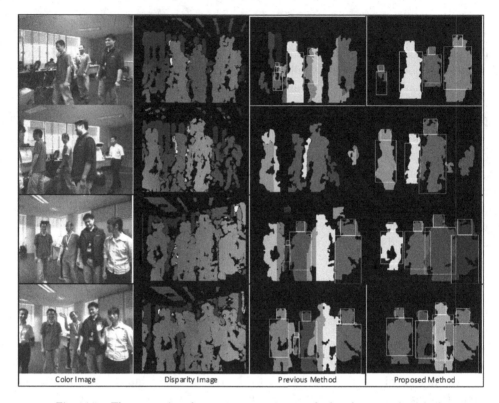

Fig. 14.5.　The comparison between our previous method and proposed method.

Table 14.1:　The quantitative evaluation of proposed stereo-based human detection

	Frames	GT	DP	DR	FP	FPPF
Seq1	120	111	101	91.0%	105	0.875
Seq2	30	45	41	91.1%	0	0
Seq3	30	95	85	89.5%	0	0
All	180	251	227	90.4%	105	0.583

the number of the sampled frame for evaluation, "GT" is the ground truth persons in the sampled frames, "DP" is the detected persons from the sampled frames, "DR" is the detection rate, "FP" is the false positive detections from the sampled frames, and "FPPF" is the false positive per frame. From the table, it can be seen that whether the sequence is captured from static or mobile platform or sequence contains one or multiple persons in the view, the detection rate is stable at about 90%. However, the false positive rate is scene dependent. If the scene contains many cluttered background objects close to the camera, many false positive detections will be generated since there are rich edge features. More accurate models, such as Dalal and Triggs (2005), can be used to suppress the false detections.

It is observed that, if the disparity measurements are poor, especially lack of valid disparity measures for the body center part of a person due to less texture features or poor lighting conditions, the proposed method will fail. It is because no valid disparity measures around the center of human region can be used to estimate the scale of the person.

14.3 Human Detection from Surveillance Video

The human appearance features in an image can also be inferred from the human metrics relative to the scene background. Such information belongs to scene contextual information. Recent researches have shown that the contextual information is much helpful for object detection (Torralba, 2003), including pedestrian detection (Hoiem *et al.*, 2008). In this section, we present a general method to learn and apply the human metric constraints from the scene context for efficient and accurate human detection for video surveillance applications. The conference version of the work can be found in Li and Leung (2008).

14.3.1 *Definition of human perspective context*

In video surveillance applications, a scene is usually monitored with a stationary camera from a higher position with an oblique angle to the ground plane. The human objects either stand or move around on the ground surface. The human metrics, his/her position on the ground plane, and the perspective projection transformation determine the appearance of the human object in the image, as illustrated by Fig. 14.6. The human shape image with respect to the corresponding

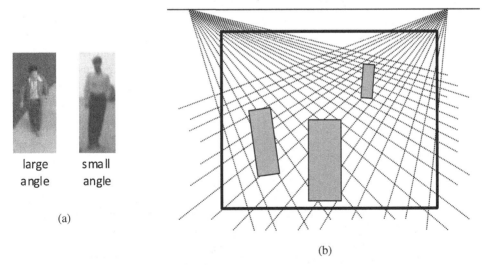

large   small
angle   angle

(a)

(b)

Fig. 14.6. Illustration of human perspective context. (a) human appearances observed from large and small angles with respect to the ground plane and (b) the mappings of human scale and orientation from the foot positions.

camera viewing angle is determined by the camera tilt angle to the ground surface. For the images of human objects observed from the high position with a large tilt angle and from the low position with a small tilt angle, the shape aspect ratios and the shapes of the upper and lower body parts are significantly different, as shown in the left panel in Fig. 14.6. The scale and body orientation of a human object in the image is determined by his foot position on the ground plane, as shown in the right of Fig. 14.6. Hence, to perform human metric constrained human detection under the scenario of video surveillance, we have to estimate the camera tilt angle with respect to the ground plane to determine which model of human appearance (i.e., $A_a(\cdot, \cdot)$) should be used, and the mappings for human scale and orientation from his foot position in the image, (i.e., $s(\mathbf{x}_f)$ and $o(\mathbf{x}_f)$). In this chapter, we define the camera tilt angle and the mappings for the body scale and orientation from the foot position as the human perspective context (HPC) of a scene.

Camera tilt angle categorization

Estimation of the exact camera tilt angle from the image features is a difficult problem unless some landmark objects in the image with the real-world measurements are known. Fortunately, for the purpose of selecting a proper appearance model for human detection, we may not need to obtain the exact camera tilt angle. Considering that the appearance variations of a person observed from a certain range of viewing angles may be comparable to the appearance variations of different persons with various sizes and poses when observed from a fixed camera viewing angle, a few categories of the camera tilt angles may be accurate enough for selecting a proper statistic appearance model for human detection. According to this observation, in this work, the camera tilt angles are classified into three categories, i.e., *large, small,* and *zero* angles, as depicted in Fig. 14.7. The angular ranges are set empirically as $[50°, 25°)$, $[25°, 8°)$, and $[8°, 0°]$, respectively for these three categories. In practice, the human appearances observed from the angles of small and zero categories are very similar. We use one statistical appearance model for these two categories. We separate the small and zero categories for the learning of the mappings for scale and orientation, as described later in this section.

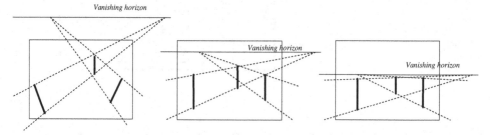

Fig. 14.7. The pictures from left to right illustrate the cases for large, small, and nearly zero tilt angles of the camera to the scene.

Mappings for body scale and orientation

In principle, the perspective projection determines the transformation from the real-world coordinate system to the image coordinate system. Using homogeneous coordinates, let $\tilde{\mathbf{X}} = (X, Y, Z, 1)^\tau$ be a point in a real-world coordinate system. The projection transformation is described as $\tilde{\mathbf{x}} = H\tilde{\mathbf{X}}$, where $\tilde{\mathbf{x}} = (\tilde{x}, \tilde{y}, z)^\tau$ and H is the projection matrix or camera matrix (Forsyth and Ponce, 2003; Hartley and Zisserman, 2003). The image position is obtained as $x = \tilde{x}/z$ and $y = \tilde{y}/z$.

Let the XY plane be the ground surface. The foot position of a person can be denoted as $\mathbf{X}_f = (X, Y, 0)^\tau$. Since $Z = 0$, one can remove the 3rd column in H. The perspective projection becomes $\tilde{\mathbf{x}}_f = H_f\tilde{\mathbf{X}}_f$ with $\tilde{\mathbf{X}}_f = (X, Y, 1)^\tau$. Similar, if the XY plane is translated upwards to the head plane, there is $\tilde{\mathbf{x}}_h = H_h\tilde{\mathbf{X}}_h$. Both H_f and H_h are 3×3 matrices. For a standing person, the foot location on the ground plane corresponds to exactly one location in the head plane, hence we have $\tilde{\mathbf{X}}_f - \tilde{\mathbf{X}}_h$ and

$$\tilde{\mathbf{x}}_h = H_{hf}\tilde{\mathbf{x}}_f \quad \text{and} \quad \tilde{\mathbf{x}}_f = H_{fh}\tilde{\mathbf{x}}_h \qquad (14.16)$$

where $H_{hf} = H_h H_f^{-1}$ and $H_{fh} = H_f H_h^{-1}$. They are 3×3 matrices and $H_{hf}H_{fh} = H_{fh}H_{hf} = I$. The linear mapping H_{hf} or H_{fh} is called the homology between two parallel planes in real world (Semple and Kneebone, 1998; Hartley and Zisserman, 2003). The homology can also be derived from the plane vanishing horizon, the vertical vanishing point, and the physical distance between the two planes in the scene (Criminisi *et al.*, 2000).

In principle, the foot $\rightleftharpoons$ head homologies exist except when the camera is placed at the height of head plane. In this case, the head plane is projected into the vanishing horizon so that H_h becomes singular. Since both H_{hf} and H_{fh} involve H_h, the foot $\rightleftharpoons$ head homologies become invalid. In practice, when the tilt angle is close to $0°$, it is difficult to obtain a valid homology from noisy data since it is nearly singular. Unfortunately, this case happens frequently when a camera is installed almost horizontally in order to have a large depth coverage. In this case, a simple linear model of scale-position mapping can be used instead. When the camera tilt angle is close to $0°$ (e.g., below $10°$), the principal axis of a standing human in 3D space is nearly parallel to the image plane. According to the relations for similar triangles, one can obtain $y_f = k_s s + y_0$, where s is the scale (height) and y_f is the corresponding vertical foot position in the image (Li and Leung, 2008). The scale $\rightleftharpoons$ position mappings can be expressed as

$$s = \mathbf{m}_{sf}\tilde{\mathbf{y}}_f \quad \text{and} \quad y_f = \mathbf{m}_{fs}\tilde{\mathbf{s}} \qquad (14.17)$$

where $\tilde{\mathbf{s}} = (s, 1)^\tau$, $\tilde{\mathbf{y}}_f = (y_f, 1)^\tau$, $\mathbf{m}_{fs} = (k_s, y_0)$, and $\mathbf{m}_{sf} = (\frac{1}{k_s}, -\frac{y_0}{k_s})$.

For the case of one camera tilt angle category, the model, i.e., foot $\rightleftharpoons$ head homologies Eq. (14.16) or scale $\rightleftharpoons$ position mappings Eq. (14.17), is the sought mappings for scale and orientation from the foot position.

14.3.2 *Estimation of camera tilt angle*

Two visual clues are exploited for estimating the camera tilt angle. The first is the shape feature of the observed human individuals, and the second is based on the vertical distributions of head and foot positions of humans in images. Fuzzy reasoning is employed to fuse these two clues.

Visual clues from human shapes

When observed from different camera tilt angles, the silhouettes of a standing and walking person are different, especially in aspect ratios. On the other hand, when observed from a fixed camera tilt angle, the human silhouettes may vary due to the view angles to the body (e.g., front view or side view). To estimate the camera tilt angle from the silhouettes of the observed humans, the shape feature needs to differentiate human shape variations caused by the change of the camera tilt angle from those caused by the variations of human poses to the camera.

In this work, three shape features are employed. First, the moment-based descriptor can capture the shape features of standing and walking persons (Sonka *et al.*, 1999). The head-shoulder width ratio can then be used to distinguish side view from front view. From the front view, the head-shoulder width ratio is small ($\approx 1/3$), but it becomes larger (≈ 1) for a side view image. Lastly, the aspect ratio of an observed human can reflect the camera tilt angle also.

The 2nd-order moments, which are invariant to translation and scaling (Li *et al.*, 2004a), are employed to describe the shapes of isolated standing and walking persons. Given a silhouette region R, a set of central moments are computed as

$$\mu_{jk} = \sum_{(x,y)\in R} (x - \bar{x})^j (y - \bar{y})^k \tag{14.18}$$

where $(\bar{x}, \bar{y}) = \sum_{(x,y)\in R}(x, y)/|R|$ is the gravity center of the shape with $|R|$ being the size of the region. Using Eq. (14.18), the normalized 2nd-order central moments are defined as

$$\phi_1 = \sqrt{|\mu_{11}|}/|R|, \quad \phi_2 = \sqrt{\mu_{20}}/|R|, \quad \phi_3 = \sqrt{\mu_{02}}/|R| \tag{14.19}$$

The aspect ratio and head-shoulder width ratio are obtained from the horizontal and vertical projections of the human silhouette. From the projection of R on the horizontal axis, we can obtain the left and right ends x_l and x_r, and from the projection on the vertical axis, we can get the top and bottom ends y_t and y_b. To be robust to noise and shape details, the tails on both sides of a projection (i.e., histogram) are cut at 10% of the peak height (Li *et al.*, 2004a). The aspect ratio of the 2D shape is computed as $r_a = (x_r - x_l)/(y_u - y_l)$. For a standing person, the neck position is usually at 81% location of the height from the foot (Elgammal and Davis, 2001). The average widths of head and shoulder (w_h and w_s) can be computed from the silhouette parts over and below the neck position. Then the head-shoulder width ratio is obtained as $r_{\mathrm{hs}} = w_{\mathrm{h}}/w_{\mathrm{s}}$. The feature vector from an individual shape is defined as $\mathbf{v} = (r_{\mathrm{a}}, r_{\mathrm{hs}}, \phi_1, \phi_2, \phi_3)^{\tau}$.

In this investigation, it is found that the shape features are similar for humans observed from small camera tilt angles of categories 2 and 3. The measurements from category 1, however, are significantly different. Hence, human shapes are first categorized into two classes corresponding to *large* and *small* (including *zero*) camera tilt angles divided at about 25°. A multivariate Gaussian is used for each class. The multivariate Gaussian models (i.e., $\mathcal{N}_i(\bar{\mathbf{v}}_i, \Sigma_i), i = 1, 2$) can be obtained from offline training, where $\bar{\mathbf{v}}_i$ is the mean vector and Σ_i is the covariance matrix. They are then used for online tasks. For a human silhouette R represented by feature vector $\mathbf{v}$, the likelihood of R being observed from a camera tilt angle of the ith class is

$$P_i(\mathbf{v}) \propto \frac{1}{|\Sigma_i|^{1/2}} \exp\left[-\frac{1}{2}(\mathbf{v} - \bar{\mathbf{v}}_i)^{\tau}\Sigma_i^{-1}(\mathbf{v} - \bar{\mathbf{v}}_i)\right] \qquad (14.20)$$

The shape features may be affected by camera aspect ratio. Evaluation on sequences from different cameras shows that, with a high threshold value for $P_i(\mathbf{v})$, the rates of correct classifications are over 73% and the rates of misclassifications are below 19% for both models. This result is good enough for the classification based on majority voting from a large number of samples.

Visual clues from head/foot positions

As illustrated in Fig. 14.7, in a scene observed from a large camera tilt angle, the vertical positions of both head and foot vary greatly in the images when a person moves from close to faraway positions. However, when the camera tilt angle decreases with the drop of camera position, the vertical range of head positions shrinks quickly. The comparison between vertical ranges of head and foot positions from a large number of observed humans provides a global-level clue about the camera tilt angle.

When a large number of isolated humans around the scene have been observed, the 1D histograms of vertical head and foot positions can be generated. Truncating the 10% tails of a histogram on both sides, the vertical ranges of the head and foot positions can be obtained as d_h and d_f, respectively. The ratio of them is $r_{hf} = d_h/d_f$. In this chapter, the linear fuzzy membership is employed to describe the likelihood of camera tilt angle from the ratio value r_{hf}. The membership functions for the three tilt angle categories, i.e., $Q_i, i = 1, 2, 3$ for *large*, *small*, and *zero* camera tilt angles, are depicted in the left image of Fig. 14.8, where the parameters are determined empirically.

Fuzzy integration

Fusing the visual clues from human shapes and head/foot positions, the camera tilt angle can be inferred online. When a surveillance camera is installed, the moving foreground objects can be detected continually from the stream of incoming images

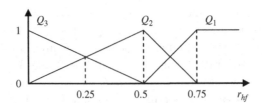

Fig. 14.8. Fuzzy membership functions for the likelihoods of camera tilt angle categories with respect to the ratio r_{hf} from head/foot positions.

using background subtraction. Employing the human shape model, we can select samples of isolated standing and walking persons from these foreground objects. Let $R_t^j(\mathbf{x})$ be the jth foreground object detected at time t and $\mathbf{v}_j$ be its shape feature vector. If it is recognized as a standing or walking person for one of the two categories of camera tilt angles, i.e., $\exists i, P_i(\mathbf{v}_j) \geq T_p$, it is selected as one sample of human objects. A large threshold T_p can be used to get good samples since abundant samples are available from a scene.

When enough number (e.g., M) of human samples have been collected, the likelihood for the jth category of camera tilt angles from visual clue of human shapes is calculated as $L_j = \frac{1}{M} \sum_m P_j(\mathbf{v}_m)$, where $j = 1, 2, 3$ and $P_3() = P_2()$. The likelihood for the jth category of camera tilt angles from visual clue of head/foot positions of the M samples can be obtained as Q_j. Then, the category of the camera tilt angle is estimated as

$$a = \arg \max_{j \in [1,2,3]} \{L_j + Q_j\} \tag{14.21}$$

With the estimated camera tilt angle, these M samples are further refined, i.e., only the samples with $P_a(\mathbf{v}_j) \geq T_p$ are retained and used to learn mappings for scale and orientation from the foot position.

14.3.3 *Learning mappings from position to scale and orientation*

An online system has to learn the model of foot $\rightleftharpoons$ head homologies Eq. (14.16) or scale $\rightleftharpoons$ position mappings Eq. (14.17) from automatically selected samples. Due to the inaccuracy and uncertainty of sample data, a robust learning method is required. In this work, we propose a new robust method (i.e., ME-DT algorithm) to estimate the model of a scene.

ME-DT algorithm

The proposed approach is an iterative process comprising two steps in each iteration: model estimation (ME) and data tuning (DT). The first step estimates the linear model from the updated sample data by using the least-square estimation (LSE) method, while the second step predicts and updates the sample data according to the obtained model. When the iterative process converges, we obtain the mapping model from the predicted virtual ideal sample data, or predicted noise-free sample data.

Let (μ, ν) be a pair of observed data. For the foot $\rightleftharpoons$ head homologies, (μ, ν) is $(\mathbf{x}_f, \mathbf{x}_h)$, and for the scale $\rightleftharpoons$ position mappings, (μ, ν) is (y_f, s). Furthermore, let the pair of the mappings between the observed data be $\mathcal{H}_1$ and $\mathcal{H}_2$, i.e., $\nu = \mathcal{H}_1 \mu$ and $\mu = \mathcal{H}_2 \nu$. For foot $\rightleftharpoons$ head homologies, we have $\mathcal{H}_1 = H_{hf}$ and $\mathcal{H}_2 = H_{fh}$, and for scale $\rightleftharpoons$ position mappings, we have $\mathcal{H}_1 = \mathbf{m}_{sf}$ and $\mathcal{H}_2 = \mathbf{m}_{fs}$. Suppose the sample dataset is $\{(\mu_i, \nu_i)\}_{i=1}^N$. For initialization, let the dataset be $\{(\mu_i^j, \nu_i^j)\}_{i=1}^N$ with $j = 0$ (i.e., the first iteration). A weight w_0 is used to control the data tuning. Then, the following two steps can be performed iteratively:

(1) Model estimation (ME): The linear transformations $\hat{\mathcal{H}}_1^j$ and $\hat{\mathcal{H}}_2^j$ are generated from the dataset $\{(\mu_i^j, \nu_i^j)\}_{i=1}^N$ by using the LSE method.
(2) Data tuning (DT): From the new models of transformation, the real data can be predicted as $\dot{\nu}_i^j = \hat{\mathcal{H}}_1^j \mu_i^j$ and $\dot{\mu}_i^j = \hat{\mathcal{H}}_2^j \nu_i^j$. Combining the original and predicted data, the data tuning is performed as

$$\mu_i^{j+1} = (1 - w_j)\hat{\mu}_i^j + w_j \mu_i^0 \tag{14.22}$$

$$\nu_i^{j+1} = (1 - w_j)\hat{\nu}_i^j + w_j \nu_i^0 \tag{14.23}$$

In Eqs. (14.22) and (14.23), the original observation (μ_i^0, ν_i^0) is used as a dock to prevent the data moving too far away from the original positions when the transformations have not become stable. The difference between the estimated data of the latest two iterations is defined as

$$D_j = \frac{1}{N} \sum_{i=1}^N \left[(\hat{\mu}_i^j - \hat{\mu}_i^{j-1})^2 + (\hat{\nu}_i^j - \hat{\nu}_i^{j-1})^2 \right] \tag{14.24}$$

This difference measure will drop significantly after a few iterations. Once it becomes stable, the best estimation is considered to be reached. Here, the condition for the iteration termination is defined as $D_{j+1} \geq D_j$ or $j > 5$, where the former condition would be applied in case the iteration procedure turns to divergence. If the difference is still dropping, the weight is updated as $w_{j+1} = \gamma w_j$ with $\gamma < 1$, and j is set as $j+1$ for the next iteration. In this work, w_0 and γ are set as 0.5 and 0.7, respectively. When ME-DT terminates, the refined samples would be close to the noise-free positions (i.e., $\{(\mu_i^*, \nu_i^*)\} \approx \{(\mu_i^j, \nu_i^j)\}$). The linear transformations obtained from the tuned data become the perspective model for humans in the scene (i.e., $\mathcal{H}_1^* \approx \hat{\mathcal{H}}_1^j$ and $\mathcal{H}_2^* \approx \hat{\mathcal{H}}_2^j$).

Estimate the mappings using ME-DT algorithm

Considering various errors in the automatically sampled data from different camera tilt angles, slightly different implementations of the ME-DT algorithm are applied to the three camera tilt angle categories.

For a scene observed from a *large* camera tilt angle, the head, and foot positions of human samples can be directly used to estimate the foot $\rightleftharpoons$ head homologies. Let $\mathbf{x}_h = (x_h, y_h)$ and $\mathbf{x}_f = (x_f, y_f)$ be the head and foot points of a sample located along the principal axis of the silhouette, and $H_{hf} = [a_{mn}]_{3 \times 3}$ be the foot $\rightarrow$ head homology. Since H_{hf} is a mapping between homogeneous coordinates, we can assume $a_{33} = 1$. Then, the left equation in Eq. (14.16) can be rewritten as

$$
\begin{bmatrix} x_f & y_f & 1 & 0 & 0 & 0 & -x_f x_h - y_f x_h \\ 0 & 0 & 0 & x_f & y_f & 1 & -x_f y_h - y_f y_h \end{bmatrix} \mathbf{a} = \begin{bmatrix} x_h \\ y_h \end{bmatrix} \tag{14.25}
$$

where $\mathbf{a} = (a_{11}\ a_{12}\ a_{13}\ a_{21}\ a_{22}\ a_{23}\ a_{31}\ a_{32})^{\tau}$ are the rest elements of H_{hf}. From Eq. (14.25), the LSE $\hat{H}_{hf}$ can be obtained from a set of N samples $\{\mathbf{x}_{hi}, \mathbf{x}_{fi}\}_{i=1}^{N}$. Similarly, $\hat{H}_{fh}$ can be obtained. Using such LSEs in the ME step in the ME-DT algorithm, a robust estimation of the foot $\rightleftharpoons$ head homologies can be obtained.

For a scene observed from a *small* camera tilt angle, the foot $\rightleftharpoons$ head homologies are still used to describe the human perspective context, but there are two differences in the implementation of ME-DT algorithm to estimate the homologies. First, the x-position of the center is used for both the foot and the head, i.e., $x_f = x_h = x_c$. This is because for a small tilt angle, the principal axis of an upright human anywhere in an image is close to a vertical line. The biases of the head's and foot's x-positions to the center point are caused by the variations of poses and segmentation errors. They often causes the failure in homology estimation. Second, only the foot $\rightarrow$ head homology estimate $\hat{H}_{hf}^{j}$ is generated from the sample data using the least-square fitting. Since in vertical direction, the head $\rightarrow$ foot homology is a linear mapping from a narrow range to a wide range. It is easy to lead to large divergence from the true model when noisy and inaccurate sample data is used. The head $\rightarrow$ foot homology is obtained as $\hat{H}_{fh}^{j} = (\hat{H}_{hf}^{j})^{-1}$.

In the case of *zero* camera tilt angle, the scale $\rightleftharpoons$ position mappings in Eq. (14.17) are used to describe mapping from position to scale. Each sample data is a pair of foot position and the height of the body, i.e., $(\mu_i, \nu_i) = (y_{fi}, h_i)$. In the ME step, the standard least-square fitting is used to estimate $\hat{\mathbf{m}}_{fs}^{j}$ and $\hat{\mathbf{m}}_{sf}^{j}$.

14.3.4 *Human metric constrained human detection*

In this work, the histogram of oriented gradients (HOG) human detector (Dalal and Triggs, 2005) is employed. First, two HOG human detectors for *large* and *small* camera tilt angles are trained offline, i.e., $A_a(\cdot, \cdot), a = 1, 2$, for the human appearances as shown in Fig. 14.6 (a) as samples. For a specific scene, once the camera tilt angle is recognized online, the corresponding HOG detector $A_a(\cdot, \cdot)$ will be applied. To adapt to large-scale variations of humans in some scenes, the detection window is divided into 4×8 cells, whereas the size of the cells varies from 4×4 to 20×20 pixels. Therefore, we have detection windows of 17 scale levels from 16×32 to 80×160 pixels. Each detection window consists of 3×7 blocks formed by

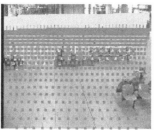

Fig. 14.9. Examples of scene-adaptive grids for *large, small,* and *zero* camera tilt angles.

2×2 cells in a sliding fashion. In Dalal and Triggs (2005), detection window of 8×16 cells with 8×8 pixel cells were used. We use the detection window of fewer cells to detect humans as small as possible in low-resolution images from surveillance cameras of real-world CCTV systems.

Using learned mappings, a scene-adaptive grid on the floor which determines the scale and orientation of a human in a position in the image can be generated as shown in Fig. 14.9. The grid is generated row by row from the bottom of the image. The horizontal distance between two adjacent grid points in the same row is the half of human width. The vertical distance between two adjacent rows is set so that there is just $\beta\%$ (e.g., 70%–90%) vertical overlap of human heights in the two rows. In detail, the offsets between the grid points are determined as follows. Let $\mathbf{x}_f^i$ be the middle grid point of the ith row, so that the estimated height of humans standing at the point in the image is $|y_f^i - y_h^i|$. The width of a front view human object is about one-third of his/her height according to average human metrics. Hence, the horizontal offset of the grid points in the ith row is set as $\frac{1}{6}|y_f^i - y_h^i|$. Let $\mathbf{x}_f^{i+1}$ be the middle point of the next row. Since the $(i+1)$th row is over the ith row, the overlapping vertical segment of human heights between the two rows is $[y_f^{i+1}, y_h^i]$. Therefore, the vertical offset between the ith and the $(i+1)$th rows is determined according to $|y_f^{i+1} - y_h^i|/|y_f^i - y_h^i| = \beta\%$. The algorithm to generate the grid is described in the following.

Initialization: set $y_{f(r,c)} = 0$, $x_{f(r,c)} = x_V$, $\mathbf{x}_{f(r,c)} = (x_{f(r,c)}, y_{f(r,c)})$, $r = 0$ and $c = 0$, where x_V is the horizontal position of the vertical vanishing point (VVP).

(1) Local scale estimation: calculate the vertical scale of human objects standing at $\mathbf{x}_f^r = \mathbf{x}_{f(r,c)}$. Using corresponding perspective model, we can compute the head position $\mathbf{x}_h^r$ from $\mathbf{x}_f^r$.
(2) Horizontal extension: extend the grid points horizontally to both sides in the horizontal offset till reaching the image boundary.
(3) Moving up to next row: moves up from $\mathbf{x}_f^r$ to y_f^{r+1}. Then set $\mathbf{x}_{g(r+1,0)} = (x_V, y_f^{r+1})$, $r \leftarrow r + 1$ and go to step (1). The algorithm is terminated when $h^{r+1} \leq h_{\min}$ or y_h^r reaches the upper boundary of the image. The $h_{\min}$ is the minimum height of human objects, which can be detected in the image.

In step (3), the grid row moves up along the vertical vanishing line. For small camera tilt angles, the vertical vanishing line can be assumed passing through the image center since the VVP is far away below the image. However, for large camera tilt angles, this would not be true. Due to the effect of perspective, the orientation variation of human bodies in different locations in the image is significant. In this case, it is possible to find the VVP from the samples. In this work, a batch algorithm is used to find the VVP in a sense of minimizing the global errors for all the samples. First, for each sample silhouette, the center point, the principal axis, and the top and bottom points along the principal axis are computed. Let $\mathbf{x}_c^i = (x_c^i, y_c^i)$, $\mathbf{x}_t^i = (x_t^i, y_t^i)$, and $\mathbf{x}_b^i = (x_b^i, y_b^i)$ be the center, top, and bottom points of the ith sample. Suppose the VVP for the scene is $\mathbf{x}_V = (x_V, y_V)$. The line connecting $\mathbf{x}_V$ and $\mathbf{x}_c^i$ can be written as

$$(y_c^i - y_V)x - (x_c^i - x_V)y - (y_c^i x_V - x_c^i y_V) = 0 \tag{14.26}$$

The distances from the top and bottom points to the line become

$$d_t^i = (y_c^i - y_V)x_t^i - (x_c^i - x_V)y_t^i - (y_c^i x_V - x_c^i y_V)$$
$$d_b^i = (y_c^i - y_V)x_b^i - (x_c^i - x_V)y_b^i - (y_c^i x_V - x_c^i y_V) \tag{14.27}$$

In ideal case, there should be $d_t^i = 0$ and $d_b^i = 0$. The sum of the squared distances for all the samples can be defined as

$$S = \sum_i [(d_t^i)^2 + (d_b^i)^2] \tag{14.28}$$

Obviously, the VVP is the point which minimizes S. It can be obtained from $\frac{\partial S}{\partial x_V} = 0$ and $\frac{\partial S}{\partial y_V} = 0$. From Eq. (14.28), the partial derivatives of S to x_V and y_V are

$$\frac{\partial S}{\partial x_V} = \sum_i \left(2d_t^i \frac{\partial d_t^i}{\partial x_V} + 2d_b^i \frac{\partial d_b^i}{\partial x_V} \right) \quad \text{and} \quad \frac{\partial S}{\partial y_V} = \sum_i \left(2d_t^i \frac{\partial d_t^i}{\partial y_V} + 2d_b^i \frac{\partial d_b^i}{\partial y_V} \right) \tag{14.29}$$

where

$$\frac{\partial d_t^i}{\partial x_V} = y_t^i - y_c^i, \quad \frac{\partial d_b^i}{\partial x_V} = y_b^i - y_c^i \quad \text{and} \quad \frac{\partial d_t^i}{\partial y_V} = -(x_t^i - x_c^i), \quad \frac{\partial d_b^i}{\partial y_V} = -(x_b^i - x_c^i) \tag{14.30}$$

Combining Eqs. (14.27)–(14.30), the equations for VVP can be derived as

$$\begin{cases} ax_V - by_V + c = 0 \\ bx_V - dy_V + e = 0 \end{cases} \tag{14.31}$$

where

$$
\begin{cases}
a = \sum_i [(y_t^i - y_c^i)^2 + (y_b^i - y_c^i)^2] \\
b = \sum_i [(y_t^i - y_c^i)(x_t^i - x_c^i) + (y_b^i - y_c^i)(x_b^i - x_c^i)] \\
c = \sum_i [(y_t^i - y_c^i)(x_t^i y_c^i - x_c^i y_t^i) + (y_b^i - y_c^i)(x_b^i y_c^i - x_c^i y_b^i)] \\
d = \sum_i [(x_t^i - x_c^i)^2 + (x_b^i - x_c^i)^2] \\
e = \sum_i [(x_t^i - x_c^i)(x_t^i y_c^i - x_c^i y_t^i) + (x_b^i - x_c^i)(x_b^i y_c^i - x_c^i y_b^i)]
\end{cases} \tag{14.32}
$$

From Eq. (14.31), the x_V can be obtained as

$$
x_V = \frac{bc}{ad - b^2} \frac{dc}{} \tag{14.33}
$$

Since the grid density is determined by the related human scales, the number of the grid points, or detection windows, is not much related to the image size if the relative sizes of the smallest detection windows are similar. However, if the smallest detection window is fixed as 16×32 pixels, the number of detection windows for the high-resolution images is larger than that for low-resolution images.

For a new incoming image, human detection is performed one-by-one at each grid point. Let a grid point be the foot position of a possible person and denoted as $\mathbf{x}_f$. The corresponding head position $\mathbf{x}_h$ can then be estimated using the learned mapping. The height $\|\mathbf{x}_f - \mathbf{x}_h\|$ determines the scale of the detection window. To include enough margin space surrounding the human object (Dalal and Triggs, 2005), we set the cell size as $(\|\mathbf{x}_f - \mathbf{x}_h\|)/6$. When a detection window of 4×8 cells is generated, it contains a one-cell size margin space around the human object. The orientation of the window is $\theta = \tan^{-1}\left(\frac{x_h - x_f}{y_h - y_f}\right)$. The subregion within the window is rotated to the upright position around the point $\mathbf{x}_f$ and the HOG feature vector from the window can be obtained. The feature vector is then fed to the SVM model for classification. The output of the SVM classifier can be considered as the likelihood probability $P(I|A_a(s(\mathbf{x}_f), o(\mathbf{x}_f)), \mathbf{x}_f)$ in Eq. (14.5).

14.3.5 *Experiments*

The proposed method has been tested on dozens of sequences from a variety of public and private scenes. To obtain a quantitative result, we evaluated the method on 15 test sequences from several well-known benchmark datasets (e.g., PETS 2001 [PETS (2001)], PETS 2006 [PETS (2006)], VSSN06 [VSSN (2006)], and ETISEO [ETISEO (2006)] and real CCTV systems. These 15 sequences contain 32771 frames in total. The evaluation includes two parts: ME-DT-based learning and human metric constrained human detection, and their performances are evaluated separately.

The performance of ME-DT-based learning

Once a camera is set up, an adaptive background subtraction (e.g., Li *et al.* (2004b) is performed. Foreground regions are extracted and shadows are suppressed (Horprasert *et al.*, 1999). Samples of moving persons are automatically selected according to the human shape model described in Sec. 14.3.2 for learning the HPC mappings Eq. (14.16) or Eq. (14.17). To evaluate the robustness of ME-DT-based learning, four approaches are compared: (1) single model (foot ⇌ head homology) and LSE learning; (2) multiple models (foot ⇌ head homology and scale ⇌ position mapping) and LSE learning; (3) multiple model and RANSAC learning; and (4) multiple model and ME-DT learning. The error rate of the estimation is defined as

$$ER = \frac{1}{N} \sum_{i=1}^{N} \frac{|\mathbf{x}_{fi}^* - \hat{\mathbf{x}}_{fi}| + |\mathbf{x}_{hi}^* - \hat{\mathbf{x}}_{hi}|}{2|\mathbf{x}_{fi}^* - \mathbf{x}_{hi}^*|} \qquad (14.34)$$

where $(\mathbf{x}_{fi}^*, \mathbf{x}_{hi}^*)$ is the ith ground truth position and $(\hat{\mathbf{x}}_{fi}, \hat{\mathbf{x}}_{hi})$ is the corresponding estimation. Totally 1278 ground truth samples are manually annotated in 707 frames evenly selected from the 15 sequences. The average error rates of 4 approaches on the 15 scenes are listed in Table 14.2, where the average rate of RANSAC is obtained from 14 sequences since it failed to generate the HPC mapping model for one sequence from a shopping mall. The performance of ME-DT is the best. The average error rate is 5.0% when manually annotated ground truths are used to learn the HPC mapping models by using LSE algorithm. The error rate of 5.0% (i.e., deviation of ground truths) is caused by variations of human heights and poses. The comparison of HPC mapping models learned by ME-DT and RANSAC from the automatically selected samples as well as learned by LSE from ground truth samples on each of the 15 sequences is depicted in Fig. 14.9, where red bars represent the error rates of RANSAC approach, blue bars represent the error rates of ME-DT approach, and green bars represent the error rates when the HPC mapping model learned from the ground truth data is used. The last error rate (green bar) indicates the deviation of the manually marked ground truth data. It can be seen that the error rates of ME-DT approach are close to the deviations of the ground truth samples (Fig. 14.10).

Table 14.2:   The comparison of error-rates on learning the HPC mappings

Method	Large (in %)	Small (in %)	Zero (in %)	Average (in %)
1 model	14.9	343.2	144.9	105.6
2 models	14.9	18.7	8.8	14.4
RANSAC	10.8	10.8	4.8	9.5
ME-DT	7.4	7.2	4.0	6.7

Here, the results of ME-DT are slightly different with Li and Leung (2008) since more data are used.

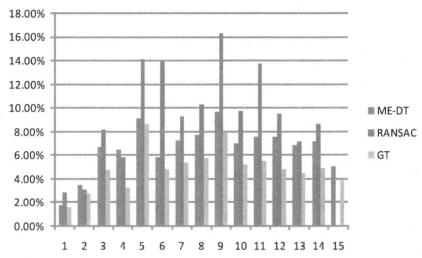

Fig. 14.10. The comparison of error rates of ME-DT approach, RANSAC approach, and ground truth (GT) deviation on the 15 test sequences.

The performance of human detection

One benefit of human metric constrained human detection is the significant reduction of window number for each image. With no knowledge on human appearance in the scene, we have to scan the image with multiscale detection windows, e.g., for an image of 320×240 pixels, over 200,000 windows of 5 scales are used in (Viola *et al.*, 2005; Wu and Yu, 2006). The average and maximum numbers of detection windows from the 15 scenes are 810 and 1826. This means that, comparing with the conventional methods, less than 1% detection windows are required for an image.

Another benefit of human metric constrained human detection is the improvement in human detection accuracy. This can be seen from the comparison with conventional method on some examples as displayed in Fig. 14.11, where the postprocessing of clustering is not performed. In the figure, one sample image frame from each of the 15 sequences with detected humans is displayed. For each scene, the upper image shows human detection without human metric constraint and the lower image shows the result with human metric constraint. From the comparison, several improvements can be observed. First, human-like objects but much larger, smaller or taller, such as the trees and the pillars in the three examples from sequences PETS2001-Camera1, VSSN06-OSAC-Cam2, and NUS-Campus-SlopeRoad, would not be detected. Second, when the camera tilt angle is large, the leaning of body orientation for humans on both sides of the scene is significant. Extracting HOG features from the rotated detection window according to the HPC mapping can improve the human detection performance, as shown in the example from VSSN06-OSAC-Cam2. Third, the proposed method can also be used for the scenes where the ground surfaces are not parallel to the horizontal sea plane. One example from

Fig. 14.11.   The examples of human detection with and without human metric constraint from the 15 test sequences.

NUS-Campus-SlopeRoad is shown in the 4th column of the 1st row. Fourth, since HPC helps to avoid some impossibly false positives, we can use a low threshold for human detection. In this case, the partial occluded humans can be detected with a HOG detector trained with no occlusion samples. As shown in the two examples from sequences ETISEO-VS2-RD-6-C7 and PETS2006-S1-T1-C4, the persons partially occluded by car door or other person can be detected. In addition, human detection under the human metric constraint also provides clues about 3D spatial correlations of humans in the group, as shown in the examples from ShoppingCenter1, PETS2006-S1-T1-C4, and JP-ShoppingCenter.

A systematic evaluation of human metric constrained human detection was also performed. We sampled the detection results every 50 frames evenly from the 15 test sequences. In the evaluation, a person with more than 30% area being visible is counted as a valid person. Persons of extremely small scales (e.g., height < 20

Table 14.3: The evaluation results of human metric constrained human detection on the 15 test sequences

Sequence name	DW	CTA	VP	DP	DR	FPPF
I2R-KR-Office-5l	244	Zero	48	48	100%	1.35
NTU-Auditorium	363	Zero	120	112	93.3%	1.44
ISS-Carpark	511	Zero	57	51	89.5%	1.68
NUS-Campus-SlopeRoad	1088	Small	57	50	87.7%	1.27
ShoppingCenter1	938	Small	231	208	90.0%	8.62
Hall1	828	Small	139	122	87.8%	4.21
Hall2	489	Small	106	94	88.7%	0.88
ETISEO-VS2-RD-6-C7	1546	Large	48	43	89.6%	2.58
VSSN06-OSAC-Cam1	707	Large	79	75	94.9%	1.5
VSSN06-OSAC-Cam2	774	Large	100	97	97.0%	1.67
PETS2001-Camera1	1826	Large	58	51	87.9%	0.21
PETS2006-S1-T1-C3	732	Large	67	59	88.1%	2.52
PETS2006-S1-T1-C4	1285	Large	141	132	93.6%	0.33
I2R-KR-Hall	356	Large	51	47	92.2%	1.21
JP-ShoppingCenter	513	Large	308	269	87.3%	1.33
Average	810				91.4%	2.05

DW: detection windows; CTA: camera tilt angle; VP: valid persons; DP: detected persons; DR: detection rate; FPPF: false positive per-frame.

pixels) are not counted. For a valid person, if the overlap of the body and a detected window is over 50%, it is accepted as being detected. If less than 30% coverage of a detected window is related to a valid person, it is labelled as a false positive. Cluster of overlapped detections over the same background object is counted as one false positive since no postprocessing is performed. The final results of the statistics on the 15 scenes can be found in Table 14.3. On average, our method achieved 91.4% detection rate with 2.05 false positives per frame (FPPF). State-of-the-art human detection methods can achieve 80–90% detection rate at 10^{-4} false positives per window (FPPW) which corresponds to 2–3 false positives per image (Viola *et al.*, 2005; Wu and Yu, 2006; Dalal and Triggs, 2005; Zhu *et al.*, 2006). In Zhang *et al.* (2007), it has been shown that when tested on surveillance scenarios, both Edgelet and HOG detectors achieve a detection rate of about 80% with 2.5 FPPF, which are similar to the results in Dalal and Triggs (2005) and Wu and Nevatia (2005). However, our result is obtained with HOG detectors trained by less than 200 samples (positive and negative samples together) and we counted small and partially occluded persons in the evaluation. The majority of false positives are detected with small windows for humans of heights between 20 to 40 pixels, which are too small to be detected by existing methods.

14.4 Conclusion

Based on the Bayesian framework, we show that there is an efficient way to perform ML based human detection under some constraints of human metrics and scene perspective. The proposed method requires an online estimation of view angle and mappings from local measurements to scale and orientation measurements for a potential person in the image. Two human metric constrained human detection methods are presented. The first method detects humans in a disparity image from a stereo camera for intelligent human robot interaction. The human metric information, i.e., the scale parameters in 3D space, is estimated from local disparity measures. A novel scale-adaptive 3D ellipsoid model is proposed for human detection and a person-adapted distribution model is proposed for adaptive human segmentation. Good performance in both human detection and segmentation has been achieved under various complicated scenarios, particularly under crowded scenarios when people gather closely. The second method detects humans based on surveillance videos. The human metric information has been learned from the scene geometric information of human head and foot positions in the scene from historic data. In the online learning phase, human shape and head/foot positions are analyzed from foreground regions generated by adaptive background subtraction. A new ME-DT algorithm is proposed to estimate the mappings from foot position to human scale and orientation from noisy and uncertain data. The learned HPC is then applied to perform human metric constrained human detection. Significant improvements on both efficiency and accuracy of human detection have been achieved on real-world surveillance videos.

References

Criminisi, A., Reid, I., and Zisserman, A. Single view metrology, *IJCV* **40**, 2, 123–148, 2000.

Dalal, N. and Triggs, B. Histograms of oriented gradients for human detection, in *Proc. IEEE Int. Conf. Comput. Vision Pattern Recognition (CVPR'05)*, vol. 1, pp. 893, 2005.

Elgammal, A. and Davis, L. Probabilistic framework for segmenting people under occlusion, in *Proc. IEEE Int. Conf. Comput. Vision (ICCV'01)*, pp. II–145–II–152, 2001.

ETISEO http://www-sop.inria.fr/orion/ETISEO/download.htm\#video_data, 2006.

Forsyth, D. and Ponce, J. *Computer Vision: a Modern Approach* (Prentice Hall, Inc.), 2003.

Gavrila, D. M. The visual analysis of human movement: a survey, *CVIU* **73**, 1, 82–98, 1999.

Gavrila, D. M. A bayesian, exemplar-based approach to hierarchical shape matching, *IEEE Trans. PAMI* **29**, 8, 1408–1421, 2007.

Gavrila, D. M. and Munder, S. Multi-cue pedestrian detection and tracking from a moving vehicle, *IJCV* **73**, 1, 41–59, 2007.

Hartley, R. and Zisserman, A. *Multiple View Geometry in Computer Vision* (Cambridge University Press), 2003.

Hoiem, D., Efros, A., and Hebert, M. Putting objects in perspective, *IJCV* **80**, 1, 3–15, 2008.

Horprasert, T., Harwood, D., and Davis, L. A statistical approach for real-time robust background subtraction and shadow detection, in *Proc. IEEE ICCV FRAME-RATE Workshop*, 1999.

Leibe, B., Seemann, E., and Schiele, B. Pedestrian detection in crowded scenes, in *Proc. IEEE Int. Conf. Comput. Vision Pattern Recognition (CVPR'05)*, vol. 1, pp. 885, 2005.

Li, L. and Leung, M. Unsupervised learning of human perspective context using me-dt for efficient human detection in surveillance, in *Proc. IEEE Int. Conf. Comput. Vision Pattern Recognition (CVPR'08)*, 2008.

Li, L., Gu, I., Leung, M., and Tian, Q. Adaptive background subtraction based on feedback from fuzzy classification, *OE* **43**, 10, 2381–2394, 2004a.

Li, L., Huang, W., Gu, I., and Tian, Q. Statistical modeling of complex background for foreground object detection, *IEEE Trans. IP* **13**, 11, 1459–1472, 2004b.

Li, L., Koh, Y., Ge, S., and Huang, W. Stereo-based human detection for mobile service robots, in *Proc. ICARCV*, vol. 1, pp. 79, 2004c.

Pentland, A. Looking at people: sensing for ubiquitous and wearable computing, *IEEE Trans. PAMI* **22**, 1, 107–119, 2000.

PETS http://www.cvg.cs.rdg.ac.uk/PETS2001/pets2001-dataset.html, 2001.

PETS http://www.cvg.rdg.ac.uk/PETS2006/data.html, 2006.

Semple, J. and Kneebone, G. *Algebraic Peojection Geometry* (Oxford Classic Texts in the Physical Sciences. Clarendon Press, Oxford, UK), 1998.

Shashua, A., Gdalyahu, Y., and Hayun, G. Pedestrian detection for driver assistance systems: Single-frame classification and system level performance, in *Proc. IEEE Intelligent Vehicle Symposium*, 2004.

Sonka, M., Hlavac, V., and Boyle, R. *Image Processing, Analysis, and Machine Vision* (PWS Publishing), 1999.

Torralba, A. Contextual priming for object detection, *IJCV* **53**, 2, 153–167, 2003.

Tuzel, O., Poriki, F., and Meer, P. Human detection via classification on riemannian manifolds, in *Proc. IEEE Int. Conf. Comput. Vision Pattern Recognition (CVPR'07)*, 2007.

Viola, P., Jones, M., and Snow, D. Detecting pedestrians using patterns of motion and appearance, *IJCV* **63**, 2, 153–161, 2005.

VSSN http://mmc36.informatik.uni-augsburg.de/VSSN06_OSAC/, 2006.

Wu, B. and Nevatia, R. Detection of multiple, partially occluded humans in a single image by bayesian combination of edgelet part detectors, in *Proc. IEEE Int. Conf. Comput. Vision (ICCV'05)*, pp. 97, 2005.

Wu, Y. and Yu, T. A field model for human detection and tracking, *IEEE Trans. PAMI* **28**, 5, 753–765, 2006.

Zhang, L., Wu, B., and Nevatia, R. Pedestrian detection in infrared images based on local shape features, in *Proc. IEEE CVPR OTCBVS Workshop*, 2007.

Zhao, L. and Thorpe, C. Stereo- and neural network-based pedestrian detection, *IEEE Trans. ITS* **1**, 3, 148–154, 2000.

Zhu, Q., Avidan, S., Yeh, M., and Cheng, K. Fast human detection using a cascade of histograms of oriented gradients, in *Proc. IEEE Int. Conf. Comput. Vision Pattern Recognition (CVPR'06)*, vol. 2, pp. 1498, 2006.

Part VIII

Multibiometrics

Chapter 15

MULTIMODAL BIOMETRICS: AN OVERVIEW AND SOME RECENT DEVELOPMENTS

Kar-Ann Toh

Biometrics Engineering Research Center
School of Electrical & Electronic Engineering
Yonsei University, Seoul, Korea
katoh@yonsei.ac.kr

15.1 Introduction

15.1.1 *Background*

Due to external manufacturing constraints in sensing technologies as well as inherent limitations within each biometric, no single biometric method to date can warrant a 100% authentication accuracy and usage by itself. For example, even the most advanced iris- or fingerprint-recognition system has yet to be shown foolproof and can be applied to all users. The situation can nevertheless be improved or alleviated through a combination of multiple biometric sources and methods. This combination of multiple biometric methods or modalities is commonly referred to as multimodal biometrics fusion and such a system is often called a multibiometric system (Ross *et al.*, 2006; Toh *et al.*, 2004a).

15.1.2 *Fusion information and common terminologies*

According to Ross *et al.* (2006) and Ross and Jain (2003), the information sources adopted for combination can be categorized into the following types:

(1) Multisensor systems: In these systems, different types of sensors are used for the acquisition of biometric data from a single modality, in the hope that diversity of information can be achieved from various sensors. For example, both the optical and the CMOS sensors can be adopted to image a fingerprint where possibly different variations of signal and noise sources can be captured for an enhanced inference.

(2) Multi-instance systems: Here, the same biometric modality or trait are recorded in terms of multiple instances or parts. For example, fingerprints from the index

and the middle fingers can be used in a fusion system to obtain a higher level of security. Another example is the left and the right iris or retinal, which can be used in multiinstance fusion.

(3) Multisample systems: Using the same sensor and the same biometric trait, a multiple number of samples can be acquired and this constitutes a multisample system. Similar to the multisensor system, the multiple sample system can account for the variations that can occur in the biometric trait.

(4) Multialgorithm systems: Using the same biometric data, different processing and feature extraction methods can yield different outcomes and this may form the desired source of information variation. For example, in face recognition, the global feature extraction methods (such as PCA) are usually fused with the local feature extraction methods (such as geometrical sizes of eye, nose, mouth, etc.) to yield an improved system over that based on a single method.

(5) Multimodal systems: In these systems, different body traits are combined for identity verification. For example, biometrics such as face, ear, iris, handgeometry, palmprint, palmvein can be combined to form a stronger feature space for verification. Very often, the fusion of independent modalities show improvement of recognition performance with respect to that using a single modality. Depending on the level used for fusion, the dimensionality of the combined features varies.

(6) Hybrid systems: Here, a hybrid system is frequently referred to as a system that integrates several of the above systems. A hybrid system, hence, possesses characteristics inherited from those individual systems adopted.

15.1.3 *Motivation and challenges*

Apart from addressing the above-mentioned issue of nonuniversality, a multibiometric system offers several other advantages too. The following enumerates these advantages in order to motivate the development of such systems.

- Universality: The use of a single or unimodal biometric may not provide an universal coverage of the entire population. For example, the fingerprint- and hand-related technologies (e.g., hand geometry, palmprint, handvein, palmvein, fingervein, etc.) will discriminate against those identities without arms from using the system. This nonuniversality exists too in eye-related technologies (e.g., iris and retina) for blinds. The face-recognition technology, however, requires a fully collaborative user in terms of maintaining a consistent facial appearance such as keeping a similar hair style, mustache, expression, pose, and glasses. The universal usage of face-recognition technology is thus limited to conditions that can comply to these constraints. In short, the use of multiple biometrics for authentication may alleviate the nonuniversality issue in unimodal biometrics.
- Performance: Due to an increase in degree of freedom for each added modality, the performance of a multibiometric system can often be enhanced. The performance

enhancement can be viewed either from an information perspective or from a noise perspective. From the information perspective, an addition of an independent modality implies an increase of an input feature space for decision. From the noise perspective, when multiple modalities are available, a noisy or a less reliable modality can be complemented by another reliable one. Hence, it is commonly agreed that a decision can often be enhanced so long as the multiple modalities adopted are mutually independent.

- Robustness: In terms of physical applications, a failure or breakdown of a unimodal biometric, say due to nonuniversality of the biometric or sensing constraints (such as a dry finger skin), may not be always tolerated by an access control system. The situation can be very different when alternative biometrics are available for authentication. This shows the robustness aspect of a multibiometric system.
- Spoofing: Following a similar line of thought with the above arguments, a multibiometric system provides additional difficulty comparing with an unimodal biometric system in terms of spoofing attack. The underlying assumption is that each different and individual modality assumed a different spoofing effort thereby spoofing of a multibiometric system would require multiple number of such efforts, hence the increased difficulty.

The above gains in adopting a multiboimetric system do not come without any price. The major challenges are enumerated as follows:

- Sensing factors: From the current hardware technology perspective, an acquisition of individual biometric modality often requires a specialized or a customized sensing device for the specific application. For example, in a system combining face and iris recognitions, common existing hardware often calls for two separate cameras with different resolutions. The underlying reason could be viewed from either the cost-constraint perspective or from the optical-constraint perspective. Since an all-in-one system (such as a low cost, large field of view, and super-high resolution camera system in the above example) has yet to be available for such an integrated application, the adoption of multiple modalities remains a challenge, balancing between cost and effectiveness.
- Ergonomics: Another concern related to application is the ergonomics of usage, a scientific discipline concerned with design according to human needs. From a *passive user* point of view, the comfort and ease of use during acquisition of multiple biometric data is important. In general, a concurrent acquisition of multiple modalities would be preferred over separate acquisitions. Depending on the choice of modalities, this can be a challenging task. For instance, acquisition of iris with fingerprint would be more challenging than that of iris with face. From an *active user* point of view, the human computer interaction could be very challenging particularly if a challenge-response mechanism is considered.
- Decision theory: Being core components in a multibiometric system, the methodologies for fusion and decision certainly play an important role towards

development of an accurate system. Here, since the outcome of a fusion system is similar to that of a unimodal authentication system which is either a true match (client or genuine user) or a false match (imposter), the task of fusion and decision can be treated as a binary or two-category classification problem. Hence, those challenges encountered by a typical classification system are inherited to the fusion and decision task in a multibiometric system. Typical challenges include the small sample size problem, the under- and overfitting problems (also called generalization or predictivity under respectively, the classification and the regression scenarios).

- Computational complexity: Without much exception, the additional use of a new biometric modality often incur additional computational or signal-processing effort. Considering the available computing facility today, an addition of such processing requirement has yet to be seen as an effortless task.
- Adaptivity: Another challenge is related to the inherent drift of biometric characteristics due to usage and aging. Attributed to the mostly short-term usage requirement and limited effort towards collection of long-term data, relatively few works can be seen tackling this issue.

Majority of the literatures to date appear to reinstate the above motivating factors rather than addressing those challenges directly. For instance, regarding the challenge related to fusion and decision, much of the existing literature appear to focus on exploring different levels of fusion using well-known decision tools to obtain an enhanced system of multiple biometrics while leaving those underlying challenges of small sample size, generalization, and computational complexity rarely attempted. By viewing those existing developments from a bird's eye perspective, we hope that this chapter contributes to moving towards a clearer picture of real underlying needs and challenges ahead.

15.1.4 *Organization*

The chapter is organized as follows. Sections 15.2 and 15.3 respectively provide an account of the state-of-the-art in terms of fusion and decision methodologies and levels of fusion explored. The remaining parts of this chapter are devoted to some focused areas of interest. Section 15.4 provides a brief review on incorporation of ancillary information into multibiometrics, and Sec. 15.5 provides a brief account on explorations into user-specific information. The need for adaptation is relatively less attempted and this issue is noted in Sec. 15.6. Section 15.7 gives some concluding remarks. The appendices include some recent developments in the field of decision theory for immediate reference.

15.2 Fusion and Decision Methodologies

Similar to the literature in *pattern classification*, the fusion and decision methodologies can be divided into supervised (training based) and unsupervised (non-training-based) methods. Whether or not a fusion and decision methodology adopts supervision depends on the availability of a target label or a teacher. This boils down to the problem treatment and assumption taken at the beginning stage of design.

15.2.1 *Unsupervised methods*

Although the unsupervised methods do not require target labels and there is no explicit training process, the underlying statistical assumption could be rather strong in terms of physical applications. The widely adopted SUM rule (see e.g., Kittler *et al.* 1998) inherently assumes a balanced Gaussian distribution among the multiple biometrics used in fusion. An evidence related to this assumption can be seen from the limitation in fusing a strong modality with a very weak modality where the fusion results often fall between the two modalities and not better. Other commonly adopted unsupervised methods include simple rules such as PRODUCT, MIN, MAX, and MEDIAN rules (see e.g., Kittler *et al.*, 1998; Snelick *et al.*, 2005), AND, OR rules (see e.g., Daugman, 2009), and weighted-SUM rule (Brunelli and Falavigna, 1995). In many cases, these rules are seen to be used in conjunction with some normalization techniques (see e.g., Jain *et al.*, 2005) which attempt to drive the data towards fulfilling the above-mentioned statistical assumption. Strictly speaking, if a normalization process makes use of statistical information such as mean, minimum, and maximum values gathered from training data, the fusion is not considered a fully unsupervised one.

15.2.2 *Supervised methods*

The supervised methods constitute a major component in fusion and decision. Particularly, majority of the rich literature in pattern classification can be adopted in a straightforward manner for fusion and decision. To keep the story short, we shall broadly classify such literature into the following two categories according to their manner of formulating the objective function.

(i) *Indirect performance-driven methods*

The indirect performance driven methods refer to those earlier formulations that do not optimize the desired performance measure directly. For example, the least squares error (LSE) minimization has been frequently used in classification problems with an underlying assumption that the expected regression error matches the expected classification error. However, the available training data is usually limited and we may not have anything close to the expected distribution. Hence, minimization of LSE can be treated as an indirect way of optimizing the regression performance with the hope of achieving a good classification performance as well. Common methods of curve fitting and neural networks learning such as backpropagation (Rumelhart *et al.*, 1986; Bishop, 1995; Ripley, 1996;

Schűrmann, 1996), Newton search (Battiti, 1992), conjugate gradient (Moller, 1993), Levenberg-Marquart methods (Bishop, 1995; Schűrmann, 1996), and steepest descent (Barnard, 1992) belong to this category. The reader is referred to Appendix A for a detailed account of some of the fundamental methods belonging to this category.

(ii) *Direct performance-driven methods*

Since the regression or curve-fitting formulation does not match the classification objective of determining whether a query attempt belongs to a genuine user or an imposter, a direct performance optimization would be desired. Some recent works in the field include a direct minimization of the total error rate (Toh *et al.*, 2008a; Toh and Eng, 2008), a direct optimization of the area under the ROC curve (Toh, 2006; Toh *et al.*, 2008b), and a direct minimization of the equal error rate (Toh, 2008). The reader is referred to Appendix B for a detailed account of these direct performance-driven methods.

15.3 Levels of Fusion

According to the information adopted, the approaches for fusion can be classified into fusion before matching and fusion after matching (Ross *et al.*, 2006). Figure 15.1 illustrates the various levels of fusion before and after matching. As seen from the figure, information adopted in fusion before matching includes those raw data acquired directly from sensing devices and those processed data after the stage of feature extraction. These fusions are respectively called sensor-level fusion and feature-level fusion. For information adopted in fusion after matching, the matching outcomes at score or confidence, rank, and abstract levels can be utilized. The following sections provide a brief account of state-of-the-art developments over recent years.

15.3.1 *Fusion before matching*

(i) *Sensor-level fusion*

The most straightforward fusion at sensor level is via a direct concatenation of images for fusion. This is conditioned on the compatibility among the raw data sources. For example, in Chang *et al.* (2003), a segmented ear image is concatenated with a segmented face image to form an input space for PCA feature extraction in a matching process. Their experimental observations validated the effectiveness of such a fusion.

A more sophisticated way of fusion using raw sensor data is by means of an image mosaicking. Here, an alignment of images is always inevitable and transformations such as translation, rotation, and even stretching, affine or nonaffine, are frequently adopted techniques. In face recognition, attempts can be

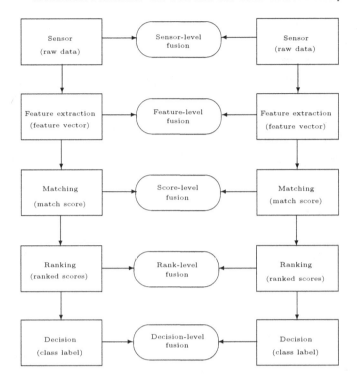

Fig. 15.1.   Fusion levels.

seen to construct either a 3D or a panoramic view in order to gain some global information from the merged image (Aghajanian and Prince, 2008; Yang *et al.*, 2005). In fingerprint recognition, a recent example can be seen in Choi *et al.* (2007) where a fingerprint image mosaicking has been performed to enlarge the effective image region for identity authentication.

(ii) *Feature-level fusion*

The next level of fusion after sensor level but before matching is feature-level fusion. Here, the general approach is to concatenate those compatible extracted features to form a larger feature space for recognition. For example, in one of the cases in Ross and Govindarajan (2005), the feature vectors obtained from two different modalities are concatenated and utilized for subsequent matching.

Other types of fusion at feature level include geometrical alignment, coding means, and series/parallel strategies. In fingerprint recognition dealing with small sensor area (Toh *et al.*, 2001), a geometrical transformation was applied to align the extracted minutia features prior to merging them to form a large minutia template for subsequent matching. In Kong *et al.* (2006), palmprint features extracted based on multiple elliptical Gabor filters at different orientations were merged according to a fusion rule to produce a single feature code where the similarity between two codes was measured by their normalized hamming distance. In Yang *et al.* (2003), a parallel strategy was proposed for handwritten character recognition.

15.3.2 *Fusion after matching*

(i) *Abstract- or decision-level fusion*

This is the highest level of fusion with respect to human interface. In other words, the decision (on whether the query is a genuine user or an imposter) from each biometric system is inferred to make the final decision. Common methods adopted for fusion at this level include majority voting (Lam and Suen, 1997) and AND/OR rules (Daugman, 2009). This level of fusion is often considered to be inferior to score-level fusion due to information loss and hence it is relatively less studied.

(ii) *Rank-level fusion*

A rank-level fusion refers to the use of a subset of sorted possible matches from individual modalities for final decision. Since all outputs of biometric modalities are expressed in terms of a performance ranking, there is no question of compatibility among the fusion features. An example for rank-level fusion is seen in Ho *et al.* (1994) where three methods, namely the highest rank method, the Borda count method, and the logistic regression method, were described for fusion at rank level.

(iii) *Score-level fusion*

Match score-level fusion is also called measurement level- or confidence-level fusion. Due to its preservation of raw decision information, this level of fusion is the most widely adopted among the mentioned levels of fusion. Some examples of score-level fusion can be found in Hong and Jain (1998), Jain *et al.* (2005), Nandakumar *et al.* (2008), Toh *et al.* (2004a), Toh and Yau (2005), and Toh *et al.* (2004c). The learning methods summarized in Appendices A and B are particularly suitable for score-level fusion.

15.4 Fusion of Multiple Factors

Apart from the above fusion among biometrics, the scope of multimodal biometrics has been extended to fuse other factors such as a password, a token, and quality information. The following provides a brief account of developments related to fusion of these multiple factors.

15.4.1 *Fusion of biometrics with soft biometrics and quality information*

Motivated by the additional cost (such as additional sensors, and additional enrollment and verification times which often cause inconvenience) incurred in a fusion system adopting multiple traits or modalities, Jain *et al.* (2004) proposed to incorporate soft identifiers such as gender, ethnicity, height, eye color, etc into a primary biometric-recognition system. For example, the ethnicity and eye color can be detected along with a face-recognition system without the need of an additional sensor. By a similar token, a fingerprint quality measure can be incorporated into a primary fingerprint identification system without an additional hardware (Toh *et al.*, 2004d; Lim *et al.*, 2002, 2004; Fierrez-Aguilar *et al.* 2006). The major challenge here is that fusion of a strong (primary) biometric system with a weak (soft) biometric system may result in a deterioration of accuracy performance with respect to that of the strong modality, particularly when a heavy emphasis or weight is put upon the weak modality (Toh *et al.*, 2008b).

15.4.2 *Fusion of biometrics with other ancillary information*

Apart from the biometric itself and related measures, other external factors such as a control input or code, a password, or even a hardware token can be incorporated into an fusion system to achieve additional security. For example, in Toh *et al.* (2004d), in addition to fusion of a fingerprint recognition system and a voice-recognition system, both fingerprint image quality and deliberate control inputs are incorporated into the fusion system. Other examples include incorporation of factors such as fingerprint index, encryption scheme, or hashing where either the search speed can be improved or the security being enhanced via a user-related random number or cryptographic key (see e.g., Teoh *et al.*, 2006, 2004; Connie *et al.*, 2004; Wang *et al.*, 2007; Han *et al.*, 2007; Hu, 2008).

15.5 User-Specific Fusion

The use of a localized multimodal biometric learning was probably first seen in Jain and Ross (2002) where a user-specific scheme was proposed for the multibiometric parameters. Here, a user-specific matching threshold was computed based on a cumulative histogram of imposter scores for each biometric for each user. The scores for each user-specific-threshold biometric was then averaged to produce the final score label. Alternatively, each user was assigned a specific weight for each biometric, and these weights were estimated using an exhaustive search for minimal error rates over all users.

This treatment of user-specific mutlibiometrics was extended and generalized in Toh *et al.* (2004a) from the learning and decision points of view. Consequently, four learning and decision paradigms were identified as follows: *learn globally–decide globally* (GG), *learn globally–decide locally* (GL), *learn locally–decide globally* (LG), and *learn locally–decide locally* (LL). Other application and analysis of user-specific systems can be found in Poh and Bengio (2007), Poh and Kittler (2008). The reader is referred to Poh (2010) (in this book) for a focused review on this topic.

15.6 Adaptive Fusion

In unimodal biometrics, a study on the use of online fingerprint verification system in Jiang and Ser (2002) suggested that the extracted fingerprint features should be considered as a temporal sequence of data. The authors thus proposed an adaptive method which can update the system using fingerprint samples obtained from day-to-day use in order to enhance the verification performance. This concept can be applied to a multimodal biometric verification system where an adaptive updating scheme shall maintain or enhance the verification performance of the system over time. Moreover, new user registration can be a frequent process in a verification system. It would be efficient to have an updating scheme that can easily adapt the system to new observations (i.e., data come from the new user) rather than retraining the entire system using old and new data whenever an enrolment of a new user takes place. Therefore, an adaptive updating scheme can often enhance the system's performance in terms of time and memory storage.

Due to the painstaking effort in data collection, relatively few studies can be found in the literature tackling this adaptation issue. In Toh and Yau (2004) and Tran *et al.* (2004), an adaptive formulation for multibiometrics was proposed to resolve the sensor decay and frequent new user registration issues. Recently, in Poh *et al.* (2009), a theoretical framework for quality-based multimodal adaptation has been proposed. The basic idea consists of conditionally updating a reference model based on the signal quality. Other examples include works of Veeramachaneni *et al.* (2005) and Chu *et al.* (2003) who considered adaptation in multibiometrics using simulated noise and variations in their system.

15.7 Concluding Remarks

Motivated by issues such as nonuniversality of unimodal biometrics, performance enhancement, robustness, and spoofing, the field of multimodal biometrics has gained considerable attention over recent years. According to the information adopted, the approaches for fusion can be broadly classified into fusion before matching and fusion after matching. Fusion before matching can be further divided into sensor-level fusion and feature-level fusion and fusion after matching can be subdivided into score-level fusion, rank-level fusion, and decision-level fusion. Among these levels of fusion, the score-level fusion appears to be a popular choice due to its preservation of raw decision information. Apart from exploring into levels of fusion, existing works in multibiometrics focus on fusing multiple factors, fusion of user-specific information, and fusion taking into consideration the adaptiveness. Although fusion of multiple biometrics possesses certain capabilities to resolve the above-mentioned issues, there remains much challenges in aspects of sensing factors, ergonomics, decision theory, computational complexity, and adaptivity. This chapter summarizes some recent developments in decision theory in appendices for immediate reference.

15.8 Appendices

A. Indirect performance-driven methods

Simple and weighted sum rules: Consider a multibiometric system which combines the outputs $x_1, \ldots, x_n$ of n biometric systems (which are collectively denoted as $\boldsymbol{x}$). When there is no particular preference over any modality, a *simple sum* or *average* rule such as $g(\boldsymbol{x}) = (x_1 + \cdots + x_n)/n$ can be adopted to combine these biometric outputs. For more general cases, a simple weighting among the modalities can be adopted as $g(\boldsymbol{\alpha}, \boldsymbol{x}) = \alpha_1 x_1 + \cdots + \alpha_n x_2$ where $(\alpha_1, \ldots, \alpha_n)$ correspond to certain weighting coefficients on each of the biometric outputs. This weighting method is often referred to as a *weighted sum rule*. In many applications, $(\alpha_1, \ldots, \alpha_n)$ can be set according to the prior probability of distribution or using some pre-set rules resulted from observation.

Linear fusion classifiers: For the case when $(\alpha_1, \ldots, \alpha_n)$ are to be determined based on some training samples, a linear learning system can be employed. Since the output of a biometric scores fusion system maintains a two-category outcome (genuine user and imposter) similar to that of a single biometric system, the task of training a biometric fusion system can be treated as a binary classification problem.

To train a biometric scores fusion system, a database of biometric samples (typically 1–10 samples) from each modality of each user needs to be collected. The training set is consequently generated from intraidentity and interidentity matchings to obtain the genuine user and imposter scores for each unimodal biometric. Each genuine user can be labelled as "1" and each imposter as "0" to form the classical target labelling system: $y \in \{0, 1\}$.

Given a total of m score samples which consist of genuine-user and imposter training scores, a stacked data matrix $\mathbf{X} = [\boldsymbol{x}_1, \boldsymbol{x}_2, \ldots, \boldsymbol{x}_m]^T$ (recall that each $\boldsymbol{x}_k$, $k = 1, \ldots, m$ is a n dimensional vector which contains the scores of the modalities to be fused) can be formed with a corresponding stacked target label $\mathbf{y} = [y_1, y_2, \ldots, y_m]^T$. When a linear model with a parameter vector $\boldsymbol{\alpha} = [\alpha_1, \alpha_2, \ldots, \alpha_n]^T$ is adopted to learn the fusion system, a minimization can be performed on a distance measure such as $\|\mathbf{y} - \mathbf{X}\boldsymbol{\alpha}\|^2$ to find an appropriate parametric combination among the individual biometric modalities. The least squares solution for $\boldsymbol{\alpha}$ can be written as $\hat{\boldsymbol{\alpha}} = [\mathbf{X}^T\mathbf{X}]^{-1}\mathbf{X}^T\mathbf{y}$ (Toh *et al.*, 2004b). For stability reason, a weight-decay regularization is often adopted and this gives the solution in the form $\hat{\boldsymbol{\alpha}} = [\mathbf{X}^T\mathbf{X} + b\mathbf{I}]^{-1}\mathbf{X}^T\mathbf{y}$.

After having solved for $\hat{\boldsymbol{\alpha}}$, the trained fusion output scores can be written as $\hat{\mathbf{g}}_{tr} = \mathbf{X}\hat{\boldsymbol{\alpha}}$. For unseen test data, another data matrix $\mathbf{X}_t$ will be stacked using the test data. The estimated parameter $\hat{\alpha}$ can then be applied to generate the test output $\hat{\mathbf{g}}_t = \mathbf{X}_t \hat{\alpha}$ for authentication decision, i.e., by applying a threshold process to make a final decision regarding whether the fused output is considered a genuine user or an imposter. Let $\hat{\mathbf{g}}_t = [\hat{g}_{t1}, \ldots, \hat{g}_{tn}]^T$ be the predicted scores for n queries. Then, the threshold process can be written as

$$cls(\hat{g}_{ti}) = \begin{cases} 1 & \text{if } \hat{g}_{ti} \geq \tau, \\ 0 & \text{if } \hat{g}_{ti} < \tau, \end{cases} \quad i = 1, \ldots, n, \qquad (A.1)$$

where τ is the decision threshold, "1" denotes the genuine user, and "0" indicates an imposter.

Linear parametric classifiers: The linear fusion classifier can be easily extended to embed input-nonlinearity to cater for complex decision boundaries. Essentially, the only modification to the above formulation needed is to change the regressor matrices $\mathbf{X}$ and $\mathbf{X}_t$ to a function of $\boldsymbol{x}$ such as $\mathbf{P}(\boldsymbol{x})$ and $\mathbf{P}_t(\boldsymbol{x})$ (polynomial expansion of $\boldsymbol{x}$), respectively. Hence, the estimate becomes $\hat{\alpha} = [\mathbf{P}^T\mathbf{P} + b\mathbf{I}]^{-1}\mathbf{P}^T\mathbf{y}$ and the prediction becomes $\hat{\mathbf{g}}_t = \mathbf{P}_t\hat{\alpha}$. A similar threshold process to Eq. (A.1) can finally be applied to determine whether a query is a genuine user or an imposter.

Remarks: The above methods for fusion are referred to as *indirect performance-driven methods* in this review since there is no direct relation between the performance and the fusion design. The simple sum-rule inherently assumes an equal Gaussian distribution for all modalities while the weighted sum-rule extends the assumption to Gaussians with different sizes. Although the linear fusion classifiers attempt to learn according to data distribution, there remains a gap between the actual performance on error counting and the data density learning.

B. Direct performance-driven methods

Total error rate minimization: In Toh (2006) and Toh *et al.* (2008a), a direct optimization of fusion classifiers according to the desired performance measure has been proposed. Essentially, the proposed method minimizes the total error rate (TER) of system performance with respect to fusion classifier design. When the fusion classifier can be expressed in a linear parametric form, a closed-form solution for minimizing the TER can be obtained. The method was subsequently found to be related to weighted least squares as well as being useful for other classification applications (Toh and Eng, 2008).

Consider a biometric fusion classifier $g(\boldsymbol{x})$ operating on an input vector $\boldsymbol{x}$ whose elements are individual biometric modalities. Denote for variables related to positive and negative examples by respective superscripts $+$ and $-$, then the *false accept rate* (FAR) and *false reject rate* (FRR) for m number of training examples can be written as

$$\text{FRR} = \frac{1}{m^+} \sum_{i=1}^{m^+} 1_{g(\boldsymbol{x}_i^+) < \tau}, \tag{B.1}$$

$$\text{FAR} = \frac{1}{m^-} \sum_{j=1}^{m^-} 1_{g(\boldsymbol{x}_j^-) \geq \tau} \tag{B.2}$$

where τ is a pre-set decision threshold, and the term $1_{g(\boldsymbol{x}) < \tau}$ (alternatively, $1_{g(\boldsymbol{x}) \geq \tau}$) corresponds to a "1" whenever $g(\boldsymbol{x}) < \tau$ (alternatively, $g(\boldsymbol{x}) \geq \tau$), and "0" otherwise.

In Toh (2006), Toh *et al.* (2008a) and Toh and Eng (2008) the counting step function which appears in Eq. (B.1) and Eq. (B.2) was approximated by a quadratic function, giving a differentiable cost function:

$$\text{TER} \approx \frac{1}{2m^-} \sum_{j=1}^{m^-} \left[\epsilon(\boldsymbol{\alpha}, \boldsymbol{x}_j^-) + \eta \right]^2 + \frac{1}{2m^+} \sum_{i=1}^{m^+} \left[\varepsilon(\boldsymbol{\alpha}, \boldsymbol{x}_i^+) + \eta \right]^2 \tag{B.3}$$

where $\eta > 0$ and

$$\epsilon(\boldsymbol{\alpha}, \boldsymbol{x}_j^-) = g(\boldsymbol{\alpha}, \boldsymbol{x}_j^-) - \tau \tag{B.4}$$

$$\varepsilon(\boldsymbol{\alpha}, \boldsymbol{x}_i^+) = \tau - g(\boldsymbol{\alpha}, \boldsymbol{x}_i^+) \tag{B.5}$$

The quadratic approximation is conditioned on all elements of $\boldsymbol{x}$ being normalized within [0,1]. The formulation is differentiated from the conventional methods which used either a monotonic or a sigmoid-like function for step function approximation. The advantage of using a quadratic approximation is that the solution can be obtained in closed form which is also least squares optimal (Toh, 2006; Toh and Eng, 2008).

Suppose the biometric fusion classifier g consists of some d number of adjustable parameters $\boldsymbol{\alpha} = [\alpha_1, \alpha_2, \dots, \alpha_d]^T$ operating linearly on an embedded input (such as $g(\boldsymbol{\alpha}, \boldsymbol{x}) = \boldsymbol{p}(\boldsymbol{x})\boldsymbol{\alpha}$ where $\boldsymbol{p}(\boldsymbol{x})$ is a polynomial expansion of biometric scores $\boldsymbol{x}$. To simplify notations, $\boldsymbol{p}(\boldsymbol{x})$ will be abbreviated as $\boldsymbol{p}$), then a regulated solution to minimizing Eq. (B.3) can be obtained in closed form as follows

$$\hat{\boldsymbol{\alpha}} = \left[b\mathbf{I} + \frac{1}{m^-} \sum_{j=1}^{m^-} \boldsymbol{p}_j^T \boldsymbol{p}_j + \frac{1}{m^+} \sum_{i=1}^{m^+} \boldsymbol{p}_i^T \boldsymbol{p}_i \right]^{-1} \left[\frac{(\tau - \eta)}{m^-} \sum_{j=1}^{m^-} \boldsymbol{p}_j^T + \frac{(\tau + \eta)}{m^+} \sum_{i=1}^{m^+} \boldsymbol{p}_i^T \right] \tag{B.6}$$

After having the parameters ($\boldsymbol{\alpha}$) estimated, the procedure to test prediction is similar to that of a linear parametric classifier (i.e., using $\hat{\boldsymbol{g}}_t = \mathbf{P}_t \hat{\boldsymbol{\alpha}}$ and a threshold process where $\mathbf{P}_t$ is the polynomial regressor obtained from test data).

EER minimization: Consider again, the quadratic error rates approximation adopting a linear parametric model for fusion, the problem of EER minimization (Toh, 2008) can be written as

$$\arg\min_{\boldsymbol{\alpha}} \quad E(\boldsymbol{\alpha}) = \sum_{k=1}^{2} Q_k$$

$$\text{subject to} \quad h(\boldsymbol{\alpha}) = 0 \tag{B.7}$$

where

$$h(\boldsymbol{\alpha}) = Q_1 - Q_2 \tag{B.8}$$

$$Q_1 = \frac{1}{2m^-} \sum_{j=1}^{m^-} [(\boldsymbol{p}_j \boldsymbol{\alpha} - \tau) + \eta]^2 \tag{B.9}$$

$$Q_2 = \frac{1}{2m^+} \sum_{i=1}^{m^+} [(\tau - \boldsymbol{p}_i \boldsymbol{\alpha}) + \eta]^2 \tag{B.10}$$

Solving the Lagrangian results in

$$\frac{1}{m^-} \sum_{j=1}^{m^-} [(\boldsymbol{p}_j \boldsymbol{\alpha} - \tau) + \eta]^2 - \frac{1}{m^+} \sum_{i=1}^{m^+} [(\tau - \boldsymbol{p}_i \boldsymbol{\alpha}) + \eta]^2 = 0 \tag{B.11}$$

and

$$\boldsymbol{\alpha} = \left[\frac{1+\lambda}{m^-} \sum_{j=1}^{m^-} \boldsymbol{p}_j^T \boldsymbol{p}_j + \frac{1-\lambda}{m^+} \sum_{i=1}^{m^+} \boldsymbol{p}_i^T \boldsymbol{p}_i \right]^{-1}$$

$$\times \left[\frac{(1+\lambda)(\tau - \eta)}{m^-} \sum_{j=1}^{m^-} \boldsymbol{p}_j^T + \frac{(1-\lambda)(\tau + \eta)}{m^+} \sum_{i=1}^{m^+} \boldsymbol{p}_i^T \right] \tag{B.12}$$

By substituting Eq. (B.12) into Eq. (B.11), λ can be solved. This λ can be substituted back into Eq. (B.12) for an optimal estimate of $\boldsymbol{\alpha}$ with desired operating condition of FAR=FRR. In practice, solving for an exact λ value may be laborious. Here, we can make λ an adjustable parameter for validation tuning. In addition, a weight decay regularization can be included for stabilizing the inverse term in Eq. (B.12).

AUC maximization: Apart from TER and EER, the receiver operating characteristic (ROC) curve is a common performance indicator in biometric applications. A typical ROC plots $(1 - \text{FRR})$ vs. FAR over a range of decision threshold where the more bow is the curve towards the upper left corner, the better is the performance of a fusion classifier. In other words, the larger the area under the curve (AUC), the better is the *overall* classifier performance.

Consider a random observation pair, one from each pattern class (say labelling them as positive class and negative class), the AUC can be expressed as the probability that the score of the positive class observation is greater than that of the negative class observation (Bamber, 1975; Herschtal and Raskutti, 2004). By denoting the variables $(\boldsymbol{x}, m)$ that correspond to positive and negative examples by respective superscripts $+$ and $-$, it can be seen that the AUC for the given m training examples can be expressed as:

$$A(\boldsymbol{x}^+, \boldsymbol{x}^-) = \frac{1}{m^+ m^-} \sum_{i=1}^{m^+} \sum_{j=1}^{m^-} 1_{g(\boldsymbol{x}_i^+) > g(\boldsymbol{x}_j^-)} \tag{B.13}$$

where the term $1_{g(\boldsymbol{x}_i^+) > g(\boldsymbol{x}_j^-)}$ corresponds to a "1" whenever the elements $g(\boldsymbol{x}_i^+) > g(\boldsymbol{x}_j^-)$ ($i = 1, 2, \ldots, m^+$, $j = 1, 2, \ldots, m^-$), and "0" otherwise (see e.g., Herschtal and Raskutti, 2004; Hanley and McNeil, 1982; Rakotomamonjy, 2004; Yan et al., 2003). Here, we note that Eq. (B.13) is also known as Wilcoxon–Mann–Whitney statistic.

Consider a linear parametric model as before and define a *unit* step function $u(\xi) \triangleq 1_{\xi > 0}$ with $\xi_{ij} = g(\boldsymbol{\alpha}, \boldsymbol{x}_i^+) - g(\boldsymbol{\alpha}, \boldsymbol{x}_j^-)$, then the goal to optimize the fusion classifier's discrimination performance can be treated as to maximize the AUC:

$$\arg\max_{\boldsymbol{\alpha}} A(\boldsymbol{\alpha}, \boldsymbol{x}^+, \boldsymbol{x}^-) = \arg\max_{\boldsymbol{\alpha}} \frac{1}{m^+ m^-} \sum_{i=1}^{m^+} \sum_{j=1}^{m^-} u(\xi_{ij}) \tag{B.14}$$

where $\xi_{ij} = g(\boldsymbol{\alpha}, \boldsymbol{x}_i^+) - g(\boldsymbol{\alpha}, \boldsymbol{x}_j^-)$, $i = 1, 2, \ldots, m^+$, $j = 1, 2, \ldots, m^-$. This maximization problem is usually solved in its dual form, i.e., by minimizing the area above ROC curve (AAC):

$$\arg\min_{\boldsymbol{\alpha}} A(\boldsymbol{\alpha}, \boldsymbol{x}^+, \boldsymbol{x}^-) = \arg\min_{\boldsymbol{\alpha}} \frac{1}{m^+ m^-} \sum_{i=1}^{m^+} \sum_{j=1}^{m^-} u(\xi_{ji}) \tag{B.15}$$

where $\xi_{ji} = g(\boldsymbol{\alpha}, \boldsymbol{x}_j^-) - g(\boldsymbol{\alpha}, \boldsymbol{x}_i^+)$, $j = 1, 2, \ldots, m^-$, $i = 1, 2, \ldots, m^+$.

Similar to that in TER and EER minimization, a quadratic approximation can be adopted when we have all inputs normalized within [0,1] (Toh, 2006; Toh et al., 2008b):

$$\arg\min_{\boldsymbol{\alpha}} A(\boldsymbol{\alpha}, \boldsymbol{x}^+, \boldsymbol{x}^-) \approx \arg\min_{\boldsymbol{\alpha}} \left\{ \frac{b}{2} \|\boldsymbol{\alpha}\|_2^2 + \frac{1}{2 m^+ m^-} \sum_{i=1}^{m^+} \sum_{j=1}^{m^-} \phi(\xi_{ji}) \right\} \tag{B.16}$$

where

$$\phi(\xi_{ji}) = (\xi_{ji} + \eta)^2$$
$$= \left[g(\boldsymbol{\alpha}, \boldsymbol{x}_j^-) - g(\boldsymbol{\alpha}, \boldsymbol{x}_i^+) + \eta \right]^2$$
$$= \left[(\boldsymbol{p}(\boldsymbol{x}_j^-) - \boldsymbol{p}(\boldsymbol{x}_i^+))\boldsymbol{\alpha} + \eta \right]^2 \tag{B.17}$$

for $j = 1, 2, \ldots, m^-$, $i = 1, 2, \ldots, m^+$. Here, we note that a weight decay has been included in the above optimization objective. This is to provide stabilization in case of matrix inversion.

Abbreviating the row polynomial vectors by $\boldsymbol{p}_j = \boldsymbol{p}(\boldsymbol{x}_j^-)$ and $\boldsymbol{p}_i = \boldsymbol{p}(\boldsymbol{x}_i^+)$, the solution for $\boldsymbol{\alpha}$ which minimizes the approximated AAC can be written as (Toh, 2006; Toh *et al.*, 2008b):

$$\hat{\boldsymbol{\alpha}} = \left[b\mathbf{I} + \frac{1}{m^+ m^-} \sum_{i=1}^{m^+} \sum_{j=1}^{m^-} (\boldsymbol{p}_j - \boldsymbol{p}_i)^T (\boldsymbol{p}_j - \boldsymbol{p}_i) \right]^{-1} \left[\frac{-\eta}{m^+ m^-} \sum_{i=1}^{m^+} \sum_{j=1}^{m^-} (\boldsymbol{p}_j - \boldsymbol{p}_i)^T \right]$$

(B.18)

where $\mathbf{I}$ is an identity matrix of $d \times d$ size.

After having the parameters estimated, the procedure to test prediction is similar to that of a linear parametric classifier as described above.

Remarks: According to our empirical observations, most methods work well when there is sufficient training data and when the scores for fusion are comparable. In other words, when the strength of each biometric for fusion does not vary significantly, most methods can yield an improved fusion performance than that before. The sum rule performs particularly well in this respect. However, the sum rule can fail to have performance gain when fusing a strong biometric with a very weak biometric (such as near-random performance). For such an instance, the AUC- and TER-based methods, attributed to their nature of formulation, are preferred over the sum rule.

References

Aghajanian, J. and Prince, S. Mosaicfaces: a discrete representation for face recognition, in *Proc. IEEE Workshop Appl. Comput. Vision*, pp. 1–8, 2008.

Bamber, D. The area above the ordinal dominance graph and the area below the receiver operating characteristic graph, *J. Math. Psychol.* **12**, 387–415, 1975.

Barnard, E. Optimization for training neural nets, *IEEE Tran. Neural Networks* **3**, 2, 232–240, 1992.

Battiti, R. First- and second-order methods for learning: between steepest descent and Newton's method, *Neural Computation* **4**, 2, 141–166, 1992.

Bishop, C. M. *Neural Networks for Pattern Recognition* (Oxford University Press Inc., New York), 1995.

Brunelli, R. and Falavigna, D. Personal identification using multiple cues, *IEEE Trans. PAMI* **17**, 10, 955–966, 1995.

Chang, K., Bowyer, K. W., Sarkar, S., and Victor, B. Comparison and combination of ear and face images in appearance-based biometrics, *IEEE Trans. Pattern Analy. Machine Intelligence* **25**, 9, 1160–1165, 2003.

Choi, K., Choi, H., Lee, S., and Kim, J. Fingerprint image mosaicking by recursive ridge mapping, *IEEE Trans. Syst., Man, Cybernetics — Part B* **37**, 5, 1191–1203, 2007.

Chu, S. M., Yeung, M., Liang, L., and Liu, X. Environment-adaptive multi-chennel biometrics, in *Proc. Int. Conf. Acoustics, Speech, Signal Processing (ICASSP)* (Hong Kong), pp. V788–V791, 2003.

Connie, T., Teoh, A., Goh, M., and Ngo, D. Palmhashing: a novel approach for dual-factor authentication, *Pattern Anal. Appl.* **7**, 3, 255–268, 2004.

Daugman, J. G. Combining multiple biometrics, http://www.cl.cam.ac.uk/~jgd1000/combine/combine.html, 2009.

Fierrez-Aguilar, J., Chen, Y., Ortega-Garcia, J., and Jain, A. K. Incorporating image quality in multi-algorithm fingerprint verification, in *Proc. Int. Conf. Biometrics (ICB)* (Hong Kong), pp. 213–220, 2006.

Han, F., Hu, J., Yu, X., and Wang, Y. Fingerprint images encryption via multi-scroll chaotic attractors, *Appl. Math. Computation* **185**, 2, 931–939, 2007.

Hanley, J. A. and McNeil, B. J. The meaning and use of the area under a receiver operating characteristic (ROC) curve, *Radiology* **143**, 29–36, 1982.

Herschtal, A. and Raskutti, B. Optimising area under the ROC curve using gradient descent, in *Proc. Int. Conf. Machine Learning (ICML 2004)* (Banff, Alberta, Canada), 2004.

Ho, T. K., Hull, J. J., and Srihari, S. N. Decision combination in multiple classifier systems, *IEEE Trans. Pattern Anal. Machine Intelligence* **16**, 1, 66–75, 1994.

Hong, L. and Jain, A. Integrating faces and fingerprints for person identification, *IEEE Trans. on Pattern Anal. Machine Intelligence* **20**, 12, 1295–1307, 1998.

Hu, J. Mobile fingerprint template protection: progress and open issues, in *Proc. IEEE Int. Conf. Ind. Electronics Appl.* (Singapore), pp. –, 2008.

Jain, A. K. and Ross, A. Learning user-specific parameters in a multibiometric system, in *Proc. IEEE Int. Conf. Image Processing (ICIP'2002)* (Rochester, New York), pp. 57–60, 2002.

Jain, A. K., Nandakumar, K., Lu, X., and Park, U. Integrating faces, fingerprints and soft biometric traits for user recognition, in *Proc. ECCV International Workshop on Biometric Authentication (BioAW)*, pp. 259–269, 2004.

Jain, A. K., Nandakumar, K., and Ross, A. Score normalization in multimodal biometric systems, *Pattern Recognition* **38**, 12, 2270–2285, 2005.

Jiang, X. and Ser, W. Online fingerprint template improvement, *IEEE Trans. Pattern Anal. Machine Intelligence* **24**, 8, 1121–1126, 2002.

Kittler, J., Hatef, M., Duin, R. P. W., and Matas, J. On combining classifiers, *IEEE Trans. PAMI* **20**, 3, 226–239, 1998.

Kong, A. W.-K., Zhang, D., and Kamel, M. Palmprint identification using feature-level fusion, *Pattern Recognition* **39**, 3, 478–487, 2006.

Lam, L. and Suen, C. Y. Application of majority voting to pattern recognition, *IEEE Trans. Syst., Man, Cybernetics — Part A* **27**, 5, 553–568, 1997.

Lim, E., Jiang, X., and Yau, W.-Y. Fingerprint quality and validity analysis, in *Proc. IEEE Int. Conf. Image Processing (ICIP'02)*, pp. I:469–I:472, 2002.

Lim, E., Toh, K.-A., Suganthan, P. N., Jiang, X., and Yau, W.-Y. Fingerprint image quality analysis, in *Proc. IEEE Int. Conf. Image Processing (ICIP)* (Singapore), pp. 1241–1244, 2004.

Moller, M. F. A scaled conjugate gradient algorithm for fast supervised learning, *Neural Networks* **6**, 525–533, 1993.

Nandakumar, K., Chen, Y., Dass, S. C., and Jain, A. K. Likelihood ratio based biometric score fusion, *IEEE Trans. Pattern Anal. Machine Intelligence* **30**, 2, 342–347, 2008.

Poh, N. *User-specific Score Normalization and Fusion for Biometric Person Recognition* (World Scientific, Singapore), pp. –, 2007a.

Poh, N. and Bengio, S. Performance generalization in biometric authentication using joint user-specific and sample bootstraps, *IEEE Trans. Pattern Anal. Machine Intelligence* **29**, 3, 492–498, 2007b.

Poh, N. and Kittler, J. Incorporating variation of model-specific score distribution in speaker verification systems, *IEEE Trans. Audio, Speech Language Processing* **16**, 3, 594–606, 2008.

Poh, N., Wong, R., Kittler, J., and Roli, F. Challenges and research directions for adaptive biometric recognition systems, in *Advances in Biometrics, Proceedings of the Third International Conference on Biometrics*, pp. 753–764, 2009.

Rakotomamonjy, A. Optimizing area under ROC curve with SVMs, in *Proc. Int. Workshop ROC Analysis in Artificial Intelligence (ROCAI)* (Valencia, Spain), pp. 71–80, 2004.

Ripley, B. D. *Pattern Recognition and Neural Networks* (Cambridge University Press), 1996.

Ross, A. A. and Jain, A. K. Information fusion in biometrics, *Pattern Recognition Lett.* **24**, 13, 2115–2125, 2003.

Ross, A. A. and Govindarajan, R. Feature level fusion using hand and face biometrics, in *Proc. SPIE Conf. Biometric Technology for Human Identification II* (Orlando, USA), pp. 196–204, 2005.

Ross, A. A., Nandakumar, K., and Jain, A. K. *Handbook of Multibiometrics* (Springer Publisher), International Series on Biometrics, Vol. 6, 2006.

Rumelhart, D. E., Hinton, G. E., and Williams, R. J. Learning internal representations by backpropagating errors, *Nature* **323**, 99, 533–536, 1986.

Schürmann, J. *Pattern Classification: A Unified View of Statistical and Neural Approaches* (John Wiley & Sons, Inc., New York), 1996.

Snelick, R., Uludag, U., Mink, A., Indovina, M., and Jain, A. Large-scale evaluation of multimodal biometric authentication using state-of-the-art systems, *IEEE Trans. PAMI* **27**, 3, 450–455, 2005.

Teoh, A. B., Ngo, D. C., and Goh, A. Biohashing: two factor authentication featuring fingerprint data and tokenised random number, *Pattern Recognition* **37**, 11, 2245–2255, 2004.

Teoh, A. B. J., Goh, A., and Ngo, D. C. L. Random multispace quantization as an analytic mechanism for BioHashing of biometric and random identity inputs, *IEEE Trans. Pattern Analy. Machine Intelligence* **28**, 12, 1892–1901, 2006.

Toh, K.-A. Learning from target knowledge approximation, in *Proc. IEEE Int. Conf. on Industrial Electronics and Applications* (Singapore), pp. 815–822, 2006.

Toh, K.-A. Direct minimization of equal error rate for biometric scores fusion, in *Proc. Int. Conf. on Electronics, Information, and Communication*, pp. –, 2008.

Toh, K.-A. and Eng, H.-L. Between classification-error approximation and weighted least-squares learning, *IEEE Trans. Pattern Anal. Machine Intelligence* **30**, 4, 658–669, 2008.

Toh, K.-A. and Yau, W.-Y. Fingerprint and speaker verification decisions fusion using a functional link network, *IEEE Trans. Syst., Man, Cybernetics — Part C* **35**, 3, 357–370, 2005.

Toh, K.-A. and Yau, W.-Y. Some learning issues in user-specific multimodal biometrics, in *Proc. Int. Conf. on Automation, Robotics and Computer Vision (ICARCV)* (Kunming, China), pp. 1268–1273, 2004c.

Toh, K.-A., Yau, W.-Y., Jiang, X., Chen, T.-P., Lu, J., and Lim, E. Minutiae data synthesis for fingerprint identification applications, in *Proc. Int. Conf. Image Processing (ICIP)* (Greece), pp. 3:262–265, 2001.

Toh, K.-A., Jiang, X., and Yau, W.-Y. Exploiting global and local decisions for multimodal biometrics verification, *IEEE Trans. Signal Processing* **52**, 10, 3059–3072, 2004a.

Toh, K.-A., Tran, Q.-L., and Srinivasan, D. Benchmarking a reduced multivariate polynomial pattern classifier, *IEEE Trans. Pattern Anal. Machine Intelligence* **26**, 6, 740–755, 2004b.

Toh, K.-A., Yau, W.-Y., and Jiang, X. A reduced multivariate polynomial model for multimodal biometrics and classifiers fusion, *IEEE Trans. Circuits and Systems for Video Technology (Special Issue on Image- and Video-Based Biometrics)* **14**, 2, 224–233, 2004d.

Toh, K.-A., Yau, W.-Y., Lim, E., Chen, L., and Ng, C.-H. Fusion of auxiliary information for multi-modal biometrics authentication, in *Proc. Int. Conf. on Biometric Authentication (ICBA)* (Hong Kong), pp. 678–685, 2004e.

Toh, K.-A., Kim, J., and Lee, S. Biometric scores fusion based on total error rate minimization, *Pattern Recognition* **41**, 3, 1066–1082, 2008a.

Toh, K.-A., Kim, J., and Lee, S. Maximizing area under ROC curve for biometric scores fusion, *Pattern Recognition* **41**, 11, 3373–3392, 2008b.

Tran, Q.-L., Toh, K.-A., and Srinivasan, D. Adaptation to changes in multimodal biometric authentication, in *Proc. IEEE Conf. on Cybernetics and Intelligent Systems (CIS)* (Singapore), pp. 981–985, 2004.

Veeramachaneni, K., Osadciw, L. A., and Varshney, P. K. An adaptive multimodal biometric management algorithm, *IEEE Trans. on Systems, Man, and Cybernetics — Part C: Applications and Reviews* **35**, 3, 344–356, 2005.

Wang, Y., Hu, J., and Philip, D. A fingerprint orientation model based on 2D Fourier expansion (FOMFE) and its application to singular-point detection and fingerprint indexing, *IEEE Trans. Pattern Anal. Machine Intelligence, Special Issue on Biometrics: Progress and Directions* **29**, 4, 573–585, 2007.

Yan, L., Dodier, R., Mozer, M. C., and Wolniewicz, R. Optimizing classifier performance via an approximation to the Wilcoxon-Mann-Whitney statistic, in *Proc. Int. Conf. Machine Learning (ICML 2003)* (Washington DC, USA), pp. 848–855, 2003.

Yang, J., Yang, J.-Y., Zhang, D., and Lu, J. Feature fusion: parallel strategy vs. serial strategy, *Pattern Recognition* **36**, 6, 1369–1381, 2003.

Yang, F., Paindavoine, M., Abdi, H., and Monopoli, A. Development of a fast panoramic face mosaicking and recognition system, *Opt. Eng.* **44**, 8, 1–10, 2005.

Chapter 16

USER-SPECIFIC SCORE NORMALIZATION AND FUSION FOR BIOMETRIC PERSON RECOGNITION

Norman Poh

University of Surrey, Guildford, GU2 7XH, Surrey, UK
normanpoh@iccc.org

16.1 Introduction

16.1.1 *Doddington's menagerie*

An automatic biometric authentication system operates by first building a reference model or template for each user (or enrollee). A template is a single enrollment data, whereas a reference model, in a more general context, is a statistical model obtained from one or more enrollment samples. During the operational phase, the system compares a scanned biometric sample with the reference model of a claimed identity in order to render a decision. Typically, the underlying probability distributions of genuine and impostor scores exhibit strong user model dependency. They also reflect the stochastic nature of the biometric matching process. Essentially, these user-dependent components of the distribution determine how easy or difficult it is to recognize an individual and how successfully he solidus she can be impersonated. The practical implication of this is that some reference models (and consequently the users they represent) are systematically better (or worse) in authentication performance than others. The essence of these different situations has been popularized by the so-called Doddington's zoo (Doddington *et al.*, 1998), with individual users characterized by animal names such as:

- **sheep**: persons who can be easily recognized;
- **goats**: persons who are particularly difficult to be recognized;
- **lambs**: persons who are easy to imitate; and
- **wolves**: persons who are particularly successful at imitating others.

Goats contribute significantly to the false reject rate (FRR) of a system while wolves and lambs increase its false acceptance rate (FAR). A more

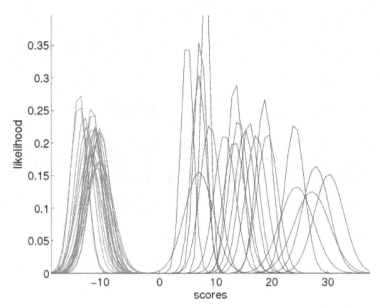

Fig. 16.1. User-specific class-conditional score distributions of a typical speech verification system. Shown here are the distributions of 20 enrollees. The right clusters (in blue) are for the genuine class whereas the left ones (in red) are for the impostor class.

recent work (Yager and Dunstone, 2007) further distinguishes four other semantic categories of users by considering both the genuine and impostor matching scores for the same claimed identity simultaneously.

16.1.2 *User-specific class conditional score distributions*

To motivate the problem, it is instructive to show how the different animals are characterized by their matching scores. In Fig. 16.1, for the purpose of visualization, we fitted a Gaussian distribution to the matching scores originated from a reference model, subjecting to genuine or impostor comparisons. The choice of Gaussian distribution is dictated by the small sample size of the data, especially the genuine matching scores. More discussion about this can be found in Sec. 16.2.

In order to avoid cluttering the figure, we show only the distributions associated with 20 randomly selected enrolled identities (enrollees) out of 200. These scores are taken from the XM2VTS benchmark database (Poh and Bengio, 2005a). Since there is one pair of distribution per enrollee (subjecting to being a genuine and an impostor comparison), there are a total of 40 distributions.

The matching scores used here (as well as throughout the discussion in this chapter) are likelihood ratio scores in the logarithmic domain. A high score implies a genuine user, whereas a low score implies an impostor. Similarity scores can be interpreted in the same way. However, for dissimilarity scores, where a high (resp. low) value implies an impostor (resp. a genuine user), the interpretation is exactly the opposite. In this case, if y is a dissimilar score, one can use $-y$ in order to interpret it as a similarity score. Similarity or likelihood ratio matching scores are thus assumed throughout this chapter.

Referring to our discussion above, sheep (resp. goats) are characterized by high (low) genuine matching scores. Hence, the genuine distributions with high mean values are likely to be sheep. On the other hand, the genuine distributions with low mean values are likely to be goats. Lambs are characterized by high impostor matching scores. This implies that they have high impostor mean values. These characteristics are used in Doddington *et al.* (1998) to identify the animals.

Wolves are not shown in Fig. 16.1. These are persons who "look" similar to all other enrollees in classification sense, i.e., similar in the feature representation. The presence of a large number of wolves will shift the impostor score distribution to the right, closer to the genuine score distributions. This will increase the amount of overlap between the two classes. Consequently, the classification error is increased.

It should be noted that the so-called impostors here refer to *zero-effort* impostors, i.e., these persons do not have any knowledge about the claimed identity, e.g., possessing his/her biometric traits. While this is a common practice to assess biometric performance, in an authentication/verification application, a deliberate impostor attempt would be more appropriate. Examples of deliberate impostor attempts are gummy fingers (Matsumoto *et al.*, 2002), synthesized voice forgery via transformation (Perrot *et al.*, 2005), and animated talking faces (Abboud and Chollet, 2005). This subject is an on-going research topic. For the rest of the discussion, we shall focus on zero-effort impostor attempts.

16.1.3 *Sources of score variability*

We shall refer to the varying user-specific class-conditional distributions illustrated in Fig. 16.1 as *Doddington's menagerie*. Before we discuss techniques that can deal with this phenomenon, it is useful to understand why the score distributions vary from one enrollee to another (i.e., the *between-enrollee* variation) and why variation exists *within* each user/enrollee.

The between-enrollee variation is caused by the fact that a biometric system builds a reference model, which can be a statistical model or a template[*] for each enrollee. If there are N enrollees, there will be N reference models. As a result, all the N reference models will be different in parametrization. Two examples of difference in parametrization are given here.

- In iris recognition, it is common to apply a mask prior to matching the IrisCode (Daugman, 1999) (represented by a bit string) in order to ignore

---

[*]A template is a feature representation, often extracted from a biometric sample, of an enrollee's biometric data. A model is a statistical representation of an enrollee, obtained from possibly *several* biometric samples. Templates are commonly used in fingerprint recognition just as models are commonly used speaker verification. For generality, we shall use term *reference model*.

occlusions such as eyelashes, eyelids, and specular reflections. The mask area is different from one IrisCode to another. This variation can be normalized by postprocessing the scores (Daugman, 2007).

- In speaker verification, it is common to first train a "world" model that can gauge the speech feature distribution of all the speakers. The world model is then adapted to each enrollee upon presentation of a speaker's speech data. This process produces a reference model tailored to each enrollee. Unlike the IrisCode, however, in speaker verification, how the model parametrization affects the matching score is much more complex. A data-intensive approach to normalize against this variation is called Z-norm (Reynolds, 1997). Yet another computational intensive approach is to normalize the score with a set of cohort models (obtained from other enrollees). This is known as T-norm (Auckenthaler *et al.*, 2000).

The within-enrollee variation is due to the fact biometric matching is inherently a stochastic process, i.e., two biometric samples can never be matched perfectly. This is due to noise in the sensed data. One can distinguish three kinds of noise in the sensed data: sensor, channel, and modality-specific noise.

- Sensor noise is the noise that is introduced by the sensor itself. For instance, each pixel in a camera sensor contains one or more light sensitive photodiodes that convert the incoming light (photons) into an electrical signal. The signal is encoded as the color value of the pixel of the final image. Even though the same pixel would be exposed several times by the same amount of light, the resulting color value would not be identical, but have small variation called "noise."
- Channel noise is the result of degradation introduced by the transmission channel or medium. For example, under slightly changed lighting conditions, the same modality may change. The best known example perhaps is in face recognition, where the same face under changing lighting conditions appear *more differently* than two different faces captured under the same lighting condition.
- Modality-specific noise is one that is due to the difference between the captured data and the *canonical* representation of the modality. For instance, it is common to use frontal (mugshot) face to represent the face of a person. As a result, any pose variation in a captured face image can become a potential source of noise.

It is well known that the above variability is amplified when the enrollment and the query biometric samples are collected in different sessions (Martin *et al.*, 2005). The reason for this is that there are always differences between two sessions, e.g., the acquisition environment, the way the user interacts with the device, the channel noise, and temporary alteration of biometric data (e.g., growth of beard). Consequently, samples collected within a single session are always *more similar* than samples collected in different sessions.

16.2 Modeling User-Specific Class Conditional Matching Score Distributions

16.2.1 *Notation*

Let $j \in \mathcal{J}$ to be the *claimed* identity which must come from a set of enrolled users in the *gallery* $\mathcal{J} = [1, \ldots, J]$ and there are J users (enrollees). Each of these users has his/her own reference model. Let $j' \in \mathcal{J}'$ to be the remaining identity not in $\mathcal{J}$, essentially representing non-legitimate users (the rest of the world). Hence, the two populations must be disjoint: $\mathcal{J} \cap \mathcal{J}' = \emptyset$. Matching the two populations simulates an *open-set* recognition task. In contrast, in a closed-set recognition task (i.e., identification), both $\mathcal{J}$ and $\mathcal{J}'$ are the same. Finally, let us further introduce the actual identity $j'' \in \mathcal{J} \cup \mathcal{J}'$ denoting the person who actually submits a biometric query sample. The goal of identification is to identify whether or not j'' is one of $j \in \mathcal{J}$, whereas the goal of authentication/verification is to determine whether j'' is indeed the claimed j. In order to simplify the notation, we also assume that there is only a single reference model associated with each user.

In both the identification and authentication/verification scenarios, one always need to compare all samples belonging to j'' with the model of j in order to obtain a score set $\mathcal{Y}'(j, j'')$ ($\mathcal{Y}$ with a prime). When $j = j''$, the matching score set is genuine, whereas when $j \neq j''$, it is impostor.

We further introduce two *user-specific* score sets, both dependent on the claimed identity: $\mathcal{Y}_j^C \equiv \mathcal{Y}'(j, j)$ (noting $\mathcal{Y}_j^C$ without a prime) for the genuine class, and $\mathcal{Y}_j^I$ for the impostor class. In this study, for the impostor class, the scores are a *union* (or aggregation) of all other users (from $\mathcal{J}'$ and/or $\mathcal{J}$) claiming to be j, i.e., $\mathcal{Y}_j^I \equiv \bigcup_{j'' \in \mathcal{J} \cup \mathcal{J}', j'' \neq j} \mathcal{Y}'(j, j'')$.

16.2.2 *Characterizing the user-specific class conditional scores*

Using the above notation, we shall use the score variable y to represent an element in the set $\mathcal{Y}_j^k$ for a given class $k = \{C, I\}$ (genuine user or impostor) and a given claimed identity j. The unknown distribution from which $\mathcal{Y}_j^k$ was generated is denoted by $p(y|k, j)$. Thus, the system-wide class-conditional score distribution is given by

$$p(y|k) = \sum_j p(y|k, j) P(j|k) \tag{16.1}$$

where $P(j|k)$ is the prior probability of the claiming identity j conditioned on k. As can be observed, the *system-wide* (class-conditional) score distribution is a mixture of *user-specific* score distributions, hence, a *function* of user-specific score distribution. In the following, we shall show that the first and second order of system-wide moments are each a *function* of user-specific moments too, i.e., they are consequences of Eq. (16.1).

The user-specific class-conditional expected value of y is

$$\mu_j^k = \int_y p(y|k,j)ydy \equiv \mathbb{E}_y[y|k,j] \tag{16.2}$$

The system wide class-conditional expected value of y, when written as a function of Eq. (16.2), is

$$\mu^k = \sum_{j=1}^{J} \left(\int_y p(y|k,j)ydy \right) P(j|k)$$

$$\equiv \mathbb{E}_j[\mathbb{E}_y[y|k,j]|k]$$

$$= \mathbb{E}_j[\mu_j^k|k] \tag{16.3}$$

where we have used the following term

$$\mathbb{E}_j[\bullet|k] \equiv \sum_{j=1}^{J} \bullet P(j|k)$$

to denote the expectation over all users (enrollees), conditioned on k. From Eq. (16.3), it is obvious that the system wide μ^k is dependent on the user-specific term μ_j^k.

Let the system-wide variance be defined as $(\sigma^k)^2 \equiv \mathbb{E}_y[(y-\mu^k)^2|k]$ and $\left(\sigma_j^k\right)^2 \equiv \mathbb{E}_y\left[\left(y-\mu_j^k\right)^2|k,j\right]$ be the user-specific variance. It can be shown that these two variances are related by

$$(\sigma^k)^2 = \mathbb{E}_j\left[\left(\sigma_j^k\right)^2|k\right] + \underbrace{\mathbb{E}_j\left[\left(\mu_j^k - \mu^k\right)^2|k\right]} \tag{16.4}$$

The underbraced term effectively is the expected squared difference between a user-specific mean and the system wide mean. We note again that the system-wide variance is a function of user-specific variances.

The dependence of the class-conditional system-wide moments on the user-specific moments is consistent with Eq. (16.1) which says that the system-wide (class-conditional) distribution is effectively a mixture of user-specific score distributions. This has a very important implication in studying Doddington's menagerie. Very often, the user-specific class conditional score distribution $p(y|k,j)$ is unknown, or that it is known but cannot be estimated. For example, the set $\mathcal{Y}_j^C$ that is needed to estimate $p(y|k=C,j)$ is very small in size, i.e., only 2 or 3 genuine in the XM2VTS database (Messer et al., 1999) and an average of 10 in the NIST2005 speaker evaluation databases (Martin et al., 2005). Due to the small sample size, one is constrained to work with low order of moments, since a lower order of moment can always be estimated more accurately than its higher order counterpart. In practice, only the first two orders of moments are used, e.g., (Doddington et al., 1998; Yager and Dunstone, 2007; Poh and Kittler, 2009). The consequence is that $p(y|k,j)$ is approximated by a Gaussian distribution.

An immediate weakness with the above approach is that higher order moments are simply ignored. If the system-level class-conditional score has a skewed distribution, then one can reasonably expect that the user-specific distributions to be skewed too; and the reverse is also true. A justification of this is due to Eqs. 16.3 and 16.4. Intuitively, this means that if one can preprocess the system-wide (class-conditional) matching score distribution to exhibit high central tendency, with zero-skewness (with respect to a Gaussian) and zero kurtosis, one can safely proceed to approximate $p(y|k, j)$ using the first two orders of moment.

An order-preserving transformation to improve the central tendency, when the output of a classifier is bounded in $[a, b]$, is as follows (Dass *et al.*, 2006):

$$y' = \log\left(\frac{y - a}{b - y}\right) \tag{16.5}$$

Note that this is a generalization of the *logit* transform where $a = 0$ and $b = 1$. Another procedure to improve the central tendency is the Box–Cox transform (Box and Cox, 2007). This technique was used to pre-process biometric scores by Poh and Kittler (2008b).

In summary, to ensure that the Gaussian assumption on $p(y|j, k)$ is valid, one needs to ensure that the system-wide class conditional distribution $p(y|k)$ is normal. This can be achieved using Eq. (16.5) or the Box–Cox transform.

16.3 User-Specific Score Normalization Procedures

16.3.1 *Existing user-specific score normalization procedures*

In the previous section, we have justified a moment-based approach that effectively models the matching score distributions by

$$p(y|k, j) = \mathcal{N}\left(y|\mu_j^k, \left(\sigma_j^k\right)^2\right)$$

where $\mathcal{N}$ is a Gaussian distribution with mean μ_j^k and standard deviation σ_j^k for $k \in \{C, I\}$ and $j \in \mathcal{J}$ (the enrolled identity).

Among the user-specific score normalization procedures, the earliest one is possibly due to Furui (1981):

$$y_j^Z = y - \mu_j^I \tag{16.6}$$

This method does not consider the impostor variance term. When this is taken into account, the normalization is called the Z-norm (Reynolds, 1997):

$$y_j^Z = \frac{y - \mu_j^I}{\sigma_j^I} \tag{16.7}$$

The Z-norm (as well as its predecessor) is *impostor*-centric because it relies only on the impostor distribution. In fact, it can be verified that after applying Z-norm the resulting expected value of the impostor scores will be zero across all the models j

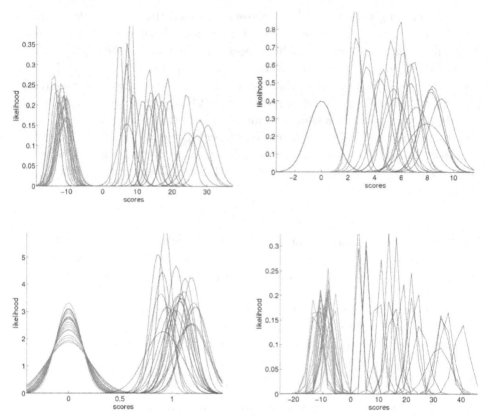

Fig. 16.2.   User-specific class conditional distributions of (a) a GMM-based speaker verification system, its normalized scores using (b) the Z-norm, (c) the F-norm, and (d) the likelihood-ratio based normalization. Only the distributions of 20 users are shown here. Blue curves (on the right clusters) denote genuine score distributions; and red curves (the left clusters), impostor distributions. For illustration purpose, the distributions here are plotted using Gaussian and are rescaled to highlight two phenomena: the dependence of distributions on a particular user, and the effect of user-specific normalization on the resultant distributions.

(Fig. 16.2). The net effect is that applying a global threshold to Z-normalized scores will give better performance than doing so with the unprocessed scores.

A client-centric version of Z-norm was reported in Garcia-Romero et al. (2003). While such a solution may be effective, it requires a lot genuine score samples, making such an approach impractical.

Yet another approach is to use both the genuine and impostor information simultaneously. This method is thus *client-impostor* centric. Examples of this approach are the EER-norm (Fierrez-Aguilar et al., 2004b) and the F-norm (Poh and Bengio, 2005b). The EER-norm has the following two variants

$$y^{TI1} = y - \Delta_j^{\text{theo}} \tag{16.8}$$

$$y^{TI2} = y - \Delta_j^{\text{emp}} \tag{16.9}$$

where $\Delta_j^{\text{theo}} = \frac{\mu_j^I \sigma_j^C + \mu_j^C \sigma_j^I}{\sigma_j^I + \sigma_j^C}$ is a threshold found as a result of assuming that the class-conditional distributions, $p(y|j,k)$ for both k, are Gaussian and Δ_j^{emp} is found empirically. In reality, the empirical version Eq. (16.9) cannot be used when only one or two user-specific genuine scores are available.

Another study conducted by Toh *et al.* (2004) used a rather heuristic approach to estimate the user-specific threshold. This normalization is defined as

$$y^{\text{mid}} = y - \underbrace{\frac{\mu_j^I + \mu_j^C}{2}} \tag{16.10}$$

The rest of the approaches in Toh *et al.* (2004) can be seen as an approximation to this one. The under-braced term is consistent with the term Δ_j^{theo} in Eq. (16.8) when one assumes that $\sigma_j^C = \sigma_j^I = 1$.

A significantly different normalization procedure than the above two is called *F*-norm (Poh and Bengio, 2005b). It is designed to project scores into another score space where the expected client and impostor scores will be the same, i.e., one for client and zero for impostor, across all J models. Therefore, *F*-norm is also client-impostor centric. This transformation is

$$y_j^F = \frac{y - \mu_j^I}{\gamma \mu_j^C + (1 - \gamma)\mu^C - \mu_j^I} \tag{16.11}$$

where γ has to be tuned. Two sensible default values are 0 when μ_j^C cannot be estimated because no data exists and at least 0.5 when there is only a single user-specific sample. γ thus accounts for the degree of reliability of μ_j^C and should be close to 1 when abundant genuine samples are available. According to Poh and Kittler (2007), $\gamma = 0.5$ is recommended for the *F*-norm when there is only a one genuine matching score.

A more recent normalization is based on the log-likelihood ratio test:

$$y^{\text{norm}} = \Psi_j(y) = \log \frac{p(y|j, \text{C})}{p(y|j, \text{I})} \tag{16.12}$$

We will assume that $p(y|j,k)$ is a Gaussian, i.e., $p(y|j,k) = \mathcal{N}(\mu_j^k, (\sigma_j^k)^2)$. In this case, $\Psi_j(y)$ can be written as

$$\Psi_j(y) = \frac{1}{2(\sigma_j^C)^2}(y - \mu_j^C)^2 - \frac{1}{2(\sigma_j^I)^2}(y - \mu_j^I)^2 + \log \frac{\sigma_j^C}{\sigma_j^I} \tag{16.13}$$

Equation (16.13) is theoretically optimal in Neyman Pearson sense, i.e., resulting in the lowest Bayes error, when

(1) the class-conditional scores can be described by the first- and second-order statistics, and
(2) the parameters μ_j^k, σ_j^k for $k \in \{\text{C}, \text{I}\}$ and for all j are estimated correctly.

The first condition can be fulfilled by converting any score such that the resulting system-wide score distribution confirms better than a Gaussian distribution, e.g., using Eq. (16.5).

The second condition is unlikely to be fulfilled in practice because there is always lack of user-specific training data $(\mathcal{Y}_j^k)$, especially the genuine scores. In order to compensate for the paucity of data affecting the reliability of the estimated parameter, in Poh and Kittler (2007), the following *adapted* parameters was proposed instead:

$$\mu_{\text{adapt},j}^k = \gamma_1^k \mu_j^k + \left(1 - \gamma_1^k\right)\mu^k \tag{16.14}$$

$$\left(\sigma_{\text{adapt},j}^k\right)^2 = \gamma_2^k \left(\sigma_j^k\right)^2 + \left(1 - \gamma_2^k\right)\mathbb{E}_j\left[\sigma_j^k\right]^2 \tag{16.15}$$

so that $p(y|j,k) = \mathcal{N}(y|\mu_{\text{adapt},j}^k, (\sigma_{\text{adapt},j}^k)^2)$. Note that γ_1^k weighs the first moment and γ_2^k weighs the second moment of the user-specific class-conditional scores. The term $\mathbb{E}[\sigma_j^k]^2$ is also found in Eq. (16.4). γ_t^k thus provides an *explicit* control of contribution of the user-specific information against the user-independent information.

Because of the paucity of the genuine data, but not of the impostor one, in Poh and Kittler (2007), the following values are recommended:

$$\gamma_1^{\text{I}} = 1, \quad \gamma_2^{\text{I}} = 1, \quad \gamma_1^{\text{C}} = 0.5, \quad \gamma_2^{\text{C}} = 0 \tag{16.16}$$

The rationale for using the first two constraints in Eq. (16.16) is that the user-specific statistics μ_j^{I} and σ_j^{I} can be estimated reliably since a sufficiently large number of simulated impostor scores can be made available by using a development population of users. The rationale of the third and fourth constraints in Eq. (16.16) is exactly the opposite of the first two, i.e., due to the lack of user-specific genuine scores, the statistics μ_j^{C} and σ_j^{C} cannot be estimated reliably. Furthermore, between these two parameters, the second order moment $\left(\sigma_j^{\text{C}}\right)$ is more severely affected by the small sample size problem than its first-order counterpart $\left(\mu_j^{\text{C}}\right)$. As a result, if one were to fine tune γ_t^k, the most likely one should be γ_j^{C}. The effectiveness of Eq. (16.13) with constraints shown in Eqs. (16.14)–(16.16)was reported in Poh and Kittler (2007).

16.3.2 *Empirical illustration*

It is instructive to measure the effectiveness of various user-specific score normalization. For this purpose, we carried out some experiments on the XM2VTS score database (Poh and Bengio, 2005a). The experiment involves training the parameters of a given normalization procedure on a development (training) set and applied them to an evaluation (test) set. The following procedures are used: Z-norm, F-norm, and the likelihood-based normalization, i.e., Eq. (16.12). We then plotted the user-specific class conditional distribution of the *normalized* scores, $p(y^{\text{norm}}|j,k)$, for all j's and the two k's. The distributions are shown in Fig. 16.2. Since there are 200 users in the experiment, each subfigure would show 200 Gaussian fits on the impostor distributions (the left cluster) and another 200 on the client distributions (right cluster). However, in order to avoid cluttering the figures, only the distributions of 20 users are shown here.

Prior to any normalization, in (a), the user-specific class-conditional score distributions are very different from one model to another. In (b), the impostor score distributions are aligned to center close to zero. In (c), the impostor distributions center around zero, whereas the client distributions center around one. Shown in (d) is the LLR normalization. Its resulting optimal decision boundary is located close to zero. This is a behavior similar to EER (not shown here). Since the distributions in (b), (c), and (d) are better aligned than that of (a), improvement is expected.

As a case study to compare the effectiveness of various user-specific score normalization procedures, we use the publicly available XM2VTS benchmark score database (Poh and Bengio, 2005a).[**] There are altogether seven face and six system outputs. The scores of these systems have been obtained by following strictly the two defined experimental protocols, called Lausanne Protocols I and II (LP1 and LP2), respectively. These protocols differ by the way training and validation data sets are partitioned. However, in both the protocols, a *common* test set is used. The training dataset is used to build the baseline systems, whereas the scores obtained by running the systems on the validation dataset is used to train the user-specific parameters. Finally, the test set is set apart uniquely for testing the resultant systems (with user-specific score normalization). It is important to note that there are 3 genuine matching scores for training a user-specific score normalization procedure in LP1, whereas only two are available for LP2. The details of this experiment.

Since there are 13 sets of experiment scores, there is a need to summarize the 13 experiments into a single statistic with confidence intervals. One way to do so is to compute the *relative* change of equal error rate (EER), which is defined as

$$\text{rel. change of EER} = \frac{\text{EER}_{\text{norm}} - \text{EER}_{\text{orig}}}{\text{EER}_{\text{orig}}} \tag{16.17}$$

where EER_{norm} is the EER of a user-specific score normalization procedure and EER_{orig} is the EER of the original system output. Negative (resp. positive) change of EER implies improvement (resp. performance degradation) whereas zero change implies no change in performance.

By comparing the performance with the original system, Eq. (16.17) actually takes into consideration the fact that if the original EER is very small, the expected improvement possible on the dataset will also be difficult. Consequently, this statistic normalizes against the performance difference of the original systems.

One way to collate the 13 matching scores of the relative change of EER is by using a boxplot. This is essentially a non-parametric approach showing the median, the first and third quarters, as well as the fifth and 95th percentiles of the data.

[**]Available for download at http://personal.ee.surrey.ac.uk/Personal/Norman.Poh/fusion.

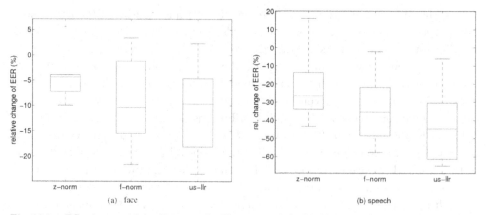

Fig. 16.3. Effectiveness of the Z-norm, the F-norm, and the likelihood ratio-based normalization (labelled as US-LLR) compared to the baseline system, applied to (a) the 7 face systems and (b) the 6 speaker verification systems of the XM2VTS benchmark score database. Negative change of EER implies improvement over the baseline system.

Figure 16.3 reports the relative change of EER for the 7 face system in (a) and 6 speech systems in (b) in boxplots.

The following observations can be made:

- Since the median values of all the systems are less than zero, it can be concluded that the user-specific normalization procedures examined here, i.e., the Z-norm, the F-norm, and the LLR normalization, improve, in general, over the baseline system.
- Between the face and speech systems, the improvement is much more significant for the speech systems. For instance, for the LLR normalization, the median of relative change of EER is about -50%, hence it has reduced the original system error by at least half. In comparison, the median value for the face system is only around -10%. Our ongoing (unpublished) studies also show that a minutia-based fingerprint matching system can also benefit from a user-specific score normalization procedure. It is still an ongoing research why some biometrics can benefit more from a user-specific score normalization procedure than others.
- The F-norm and the LLR normalization procedure outperforms the Z-norm. An explanation of this is that the Z-norm is impostor-centric, whereas the F-norm and LLR-norm are client-impostor centric. Therefore, it is beneficial to exploit the genuine matching score information.
- The LLR-norm slightly outperforms the F-norm. However, further experiments on other databases show that both normalization attain somewhat similar performance (Poh and Kittler, 2008a). Although the likelihood ratio approach is arguably more advantageous, its reliance on the second-order moments can be a weakness. In comparison, the F-norm is a much simpler approach as it does not require the estimate of the second-order moments. As a result, the F-norm is more useful under small training sample size.

A more extensive comparison of different user-specific score normalization procedures can be found in Poh and Kittler (2008a).

16.4 Effects of User-Specific Score Normalization on Fusion

Let $y_i \in \mathbb{R}$ be the output of the ith expert and there are N expert outputs, i.e., $i \in \{1, \ldots, N\}$. In the literature, the conventional fusion classifier, f, can be written as

$$f : y_1, \ldots, y_N \to y_{\text{com}}$$

where $y_{\text{com}} \in \mathbb{R}$ is a combined score.

In contrast, a user-specific fusion classifier, f_j, takes the following form

$$f_j : y_1, \ldots, y_N \to y_{\text{com}}$$

where j is the claimed identity and there are J claimed identities/reference models. Examples of this approach includes Jain and Ross (2002), Snelick *et al.* (2005), Fierrez-Aguilar *et al.* (2004a, 2005), Kumar and Zhang (2003), and Toh *et al.* (2004). Directly designing a user-specific classifier is nontrivial. For example, in order to combine N system outputs, if one uses a Gaussian classifier, one will need at least $N + 1$ user-specific genuine scores in the training set in order to guarantee a non-singular covariance matrix. Since N is severely limited by the number of available training sample, such an approach is not scalable to combining a large number of systems. Furthermore, even if this condition is satisfied, the estimate of the covariance matrix may still not be reliable.

In order to overcome the small training sample size problem, one solution is to apply the user-specific score normalization for each system output individually and then combining the resultant output using a common (under-indepedent fusion classifier) (Poh and Kittler, 2008a):

$$f : y_{1,j}^{\text{norm}}, \ldots, y_{N,j}^{\text{norm}} \to y_{\text{com}} \tag{16.18}$$

where $y_{i,j}^{\text{norm}} \in \mathbb{R}$ is a result of a score normalization procedure specific to the claimed identity j, which is defined as

$$\Psi_j : y_i \to y_{i,j}^{\text{norm}} \quad \text{for } i \in \{1, \ldots, N\}$$

Note that although the fusion classifier, f, in Eq. (16.18) is user independent, the resultant fusion classifier is still *user specific*. This is because its input are normalized scores which differ from one claimed identity to another.

We shall give an intuitive explanation regarding why applying a user-specific score normalization procedure to each individual system output *prior to fusion* is beneficial. Figure 16.4 shows the fitted densities of 10 claimed identities subjecting to being a genuine user or an impostor class. Prior to applying the F-norm, the distributions are not well aligned. However, after applying the F-norm, the impostor mean score is centered on the origin whereas the genuine mean score has been projected close to $(1,1)$. This projection is, nevertheless, not perfect because the

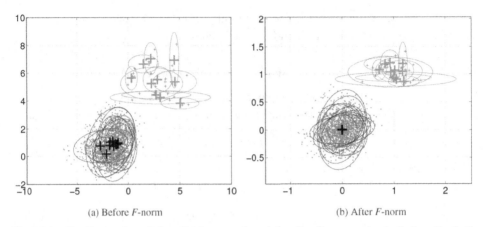

(a) Before *F*-norm   (b) After *F*-norm

Fig. 16.4. An illustration of the effectiveness of applying the *F*-norm prior to fusion. For both figures, the *X*- and *Y*-axes are the output score-space of face and speech systems, respectively. The upper right clusters are client accesses, whereas the lower left clusters are impostor accesses. In each figure, the scores of ten users (out of 200 available) are shown here in order to avoid cluttering the figure. This results in $10 \times 2 = 20$ Gaussian fits, i.e., a pair of user-specific class-conditional scores for each of the 10 reference models.

user-specific genuine mean score still cannot be estimated reliably. A perfect user-specific normalization would require that all user-specific class-conditional score distributions after transformation to be the same for every enrollee.

Despite the somewhat imperfect normalization, Poh and Kittler (2008a) showed that applying user-specific score normalization using the *F*-norm prior to fusion can reduce the fusion error (with respect to not using the normalization) by as much as 70%. More results supporting this claim can be found in Poh (2006).

16.5 Conclusions and Open Issues

User-specific score normalization is a current topic in biometrics. It is strongly related to Doddington's menagerie, although early literature in this direction rarely refers to this phenomenon. By applying user-specific score normalization, an improved decision in terms of FAR and FRR is often observed. Furthermore, by applying user-specific score normalization prior to fusion, the design of a *user-specific fusion classifier* is greatly simplified (Poh and Kittler, 2008a).

There still remain some open issues:

- **Effectiveness of user-specific normalization across all biometrics**: It is generally believed that Doddington's menagerie occurs in all biometric (Yager and Dunstone, 2007; Poh and Kittler, 2009). Therefore, it is reasonable to expect that a user-specific score normalization procedure to be able to improve over the baseline systems. However, not all biometrics benefit from the user-specific score normalization to the same degree. This requires a thorough investigation.
- **User ranking**: Due to Doddington's menagerie, in principle, it is possible to estimate the user-specific performance and then rank the users according to their

performance. In Poh and Kittler (2009), the d-prime statistic, the F-ratio, and the two-class Fisher-ratio were examined. Ability to rank the users according to their performance has at least two important applications. First, this allows the system designer to control the quality of data collected in an enrollment session. Second, in the context of multimodal fusion, instead of using all the biometric modalities, one can select only a subset of the most discriminative biometric traits for each person to perform fusion.

- **Normalization under deliberate impostor attempts**: All user-specific score normalization procedures developed in the literature assume zero-effort impostor. In an authentication scenario, it is reasonable to expect deliberate impostor attacks. It is still an on-going research issue regarding how well a user-specific score normalization can withstand such an attack; and if not, how such an approach can be improved.

Acknowledgments

This work is supported by the advanced researcher fellowship PA0022_121477 of the Swiss National Science Foundation and by the EU-funded Mobio project grant IST-214324.

References

Abboud, B. and Chollet, G. Appearance based lip tracking and cloning on speaking faces, in *Proc. Int. Symposium Image and Signal Processing and Analysis*, pp. 301–305, 2005.

Auckenthaler, R., Carey, M., and Lloyd-Thomas, H. Score normalization for text-independant speaker verification systems, *Digital Signal Processing (DSP) J.* **10**, 42–54, 2000.

Box, G. E. and Cox, D. R. An analysis of transformations, in *Proc. IEEE Workshop on Automatic Identification Advanced Technologies*, pp. 211–246, 2007.

Dass, S. C., Zhu, Y., and Jain, A. K. Validating a biometric authentication system: sample size requirements, *IEEE Trans. Pattern Anal. Machine Intelligence* **28**, 12, 1902–1319, 2006.

Daugman, J. *How Iris Recognition Works* (Kluwer Publishers), 1999.

Daugman, J. New methods in iris recognition, *IEEE Trans. Syst., Man, Cybernetics, Part B* **37**, 5, 1167–1175, 2007.

Doddington, G., Liggett, W., Martin, A., Przybocki, M., and Reynolds, D. Sheep, Goats, Lambs and Wolves: a statistical analysis of speaker performance in the NIST 1998 speaker recognition evaluation, in *Int. Conf. Spoken Language Processing (ICSLP)* (Sydney), pp. –, 1998.

Fierrez-Aguilar, J., Garcia-Romero, D., Ortega-Garcia, J., and Gonzalez-Rodriguez, J. Exploiting general knowledge in user-dependent fusion strategies for multimodal biometric verification, in *Proc. IEEE Int. Conf. Acoustics, Speech, and Signal Processing (ICASSP)* (Montreal), pp. 5:617–620, 2004a.

Fierrez-Aguilar, J., Ortega-Garcia, J., and Gonzalez-Rodriguez, J. Target dependent score normalisation techniques and their application to signature verification, in *Proc. Int. Conf. Biometric Authentication (ICBA), LNCS 3072* (Hong Kong), pp. 498–504, 2004b.

Fierrez-Aguilar, J., Garcia-Romero, D., Ortega-Garcia, J., and Gonzalez-Rodriguez, J. Bayesian adaptation for user-dependent multimodal biometric authentication, *Pattern Recognition* **38**, 1317–1319, 2005.

Furui, S. Cepstral analysis for automatic speaker verification, *IEEE Trans. Acoustic, Speech and Audio Processing / IEEE Trans. on Signal Processing* **29**, 2, 254–272, 1981.

Garcia-Romero, D., Gonzalez-Rodriguez, J., Fierrez-Aguilar, J., and Ortega-Garcia, J. U-Norm likelihood normalisation in PIN-based speaker verification systems, in *Proc. 4th Int'l. Conf. Audio- and Video-Based Biometric Person Authentication (AVBPA 2003), LNCS 2688* (Guildford), pp. 208–213, 2003.

Jain, A. and Ross, A. Learning user-specific parameters in multibiometric system, in *Proc. Int. Conf. Image Processing (ICIP 2002)* (New York), pp. 57–70, 2002.

Kumar, A. and Zhang, D. Integrating palmprint with face for user authentication, in *Proc. Workshop on Multimodal User Authentication (MMUA 2003)* (Santa Barbara), pp. 107–112, 2003.

Martin, A., Przybocki, M., and Campbell, J. P. *The NIST Speaker Recognition Evaluation Program* (Springer), 2005.

Matsumoto, T., Matsumoto, H., Yamada, K., and Hoshino, S. Impact of artificial gummy fingers on fingerprint systems, in *Proc. SPIE 4677: Biometric Techniques for Human Identification*, pp. 275–289, 2002.

Messer, K., Matas, J., Kittler, J., Luettin, J., and Maitre, G. Xm2vtsdb: the extended m2vts database, in *Proc. Second International Conference on Audio and Video-based Biometric Person Authentication*, pp. –, 1999.

Perrot, P., Aversano, G., Blouet, R., Charbit, M., and Chollet, G. Voice forgery using alisp: indexation in a client memory, in *Proc. IEEE Conf. Acoustics, Speech, and Signal Processing*, pp. 1:17–20, 2005.

Poh, N. *Multi-system Biometric Authentication: Optimal Fusion and User-Specific Information*, Ph.D. thesis, Swiss Federal Institute of Technology in Lausanne (Ecole Polytechnique Fédérale de Lausanne), 2006.

Poh, N. and Bengio, S. Database, protocol and tools for evaluating score-level fusion algorithms in biometric authentication, *Pattern Recognition* **39**, 2, 223–233, 2005a.

Poh, N. and Bengio, S. F-ratio client-dependent normalisation on biometric authentication tasks, in *Proc. IEEE Int. Conf. Acoustics, Speech, and Signal Processing (ICASSP)* (Philadelphia), pp. 721–724, 2005b.

Poh, N. and Kittler, J. On the use of log-likelihood ratio based model-specific score normalisation in biometric authentication, in *Proc. IEEE/IAPR Int'l Conf. Biometrics (ICB'07), LNCS 4542* (Providence, R.I.), pp. 614–624, 2007.

Poh, N. and Kittler, J. Incorporating variation of model-specific score distribution in speaker verification systems, *IEEE Trans. Audio, Speech Language Processing* **16**, 3, 594–606, 2008a.

Poh, N. and Kittler, J. On using error bounds to optimize cost-sensitive multimodal biometric authentication, in *Proc. 19th Int. Conf. Pattern Recognition (ICPR)*, pp. –, 2008b.

Poh, N. and Kittler, J. A biometric menagerie index for characterising template/model-specific variation, in *Proc. 3rd Int'l Conf. on Biometrics*, pp. 816–827, 2009.

Reynolds, D. Comparison of background normalization methods for text-independent speaker verification, in *Proc. of EUROSPEECH*, pp. 963–966, 1997.

Snelick, R., Uludag, U., Mink, A., Indovina, M., and Jain, A. Large scale evaluation of multimodal biometric authentication using state-of-the-art systems, *IEEE Trans. Pattern Anal. Machine Intelligence* **27**, 3, 450–455, 2005.

Toh, K.-A., Jiang, X., and Yau, W.-Y. Exploiting global and local decision for multimodal biometrics verification, *IEEE Trans. Signal Processing* **52**, 10, 3059–3072, 2004.

Yager, N. and Dunstone, T. Worms, chameleons, phantoms and doves: new additions to the biometric menagerie, in *Proc. IEEE Workshop on Automatic Identification Advanced Technologies*, pp. 1–6, 2007.

Chapter 17

MULTIBIOMETRIC AUTHENTICATION

Michael Wagner
National Centre for Biometric Studies
Faculty of Information Sciences & Engineering
University of Canberra, ACT 2601, Australia
Michael.Wagner@canberra.edu.au

17.1 Introduction

While some biometrics, such as fingerprints, handwritten signatures or facial photographs, have been used in forensics for a good century or longer, modern biometric technology, both for person authentication and for forensic applications, has come to the fore as part of the rapidly expanding capabilities of computer technology in the final decades of the 20th century. A recent review of the history of speaker recognition begins with the words "research in automatic speaker recognition has now spanned four decades" (Furui, 2005), and other biometrics such as face, iris or finger recognition, have been topics for intensive research for about the same period. Only more recently, however, these technologies have moved out of the research labs and into commercial applications, having first required considerable progress in the signal processing and pattern recognition fields to address the difficulties that are inherent in the various biometrics.

The main problem in the development of algorithms for the automatic identification or verification of persons is the within-subject variability of the different biometrics. All biometrics show a long-term aging effect, which may be more pronounced in a biometric like face recognition and, for example, less in one like iris recognition. Some biometrics have strong behavioural components and thus significant within-person variation, such as speech, handwritten signature, or facial appearance; and all biometrics are subject to variations in the capture of the person's biometric features, starting from the environmental conditions, in which the biometric is captured, and the variability of the biometric sensor, through to the distortions in any transmission channel and in the digitization of the analogue sensor data, as shown in Fig. 17.1.

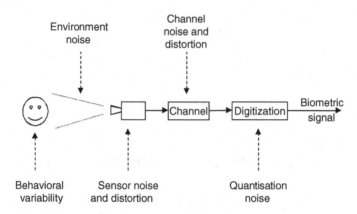

Fig. 17.1.   Sources of variability in biometric systems.

In order to increase the reliability of biometric technology in the face of within-subject variability, researchers have long proposed to combine different biometrics, especially pairs of biometrics that provide apparently mutually independent information on the individual, such as the face and the voice, or a fingerprint and the signature. Systems that use more than one biometric are known as multibiometric, multichannel, or multimodal systems, and examples of such systems are face-voice recognition (Brunelli and Falavigna, 1995; Chetty and Wagner, 2006a), face-iris recognition (Morizet and Gilles, 2008), voice-and-handwriting recognition (Vielhauer and Scheidat, 2005), face-and-palmprint recognition (Feng et al., 2004), finger-and-iris recognition (Baig et al., 2009), face-fingerhand recognition (Ross et al., 2001) and many more. The motivation for the development of such combinations may range from curiosity to–very importantly–the availability of suitable multi-biometric data corpora and to the suitability of those combinations for real-world applications such as border control or Internet banking.

Another motivation to combine particular biometrics derives from the fact that changing environmental conditions may affect the different biometrics of a multibiometric authentication system in different ways. For example, the face recognition component of a face-voice authentication system may not work well in adverse lighting conditions, while the voice recognition component may break down when there is much background noise. In either situation, the biometric that is less affected by the environmental conditions may be able to compensate for the performance loss of the other.

A further concern in many biometric systems is the assurance that the biometric information is actually provided by the true client at the place and time of the authentication and is not a replay of an earlier recording or is channelled surreptitiously into the authentication system. Any authentication system, irrespective of the specific biometrics used, is vulnerable to the attacks illustrated in Fig. 17.2 (Wagner, 2009).

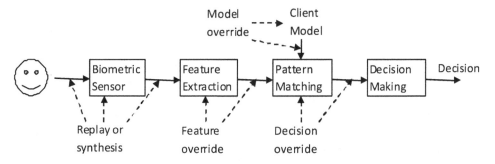

Fig. 17.2. Biometric system vulnerabilities to replay, synthesis, and software engineering attacks (adapted from (Wagner, 2009)).

Attacks through access to an inner component of the authentication system between the sensor and the decision-making module can be prevented by means of sufficient physical security for the system and appropriate software-engineering techniques, which guard against hacker attacks. However, attacks on the system that replay recorded information, such as a photograph of a face or a tape recording of a voice, directly to the biometric sensor, may require a second, independent, modality to enhance the assurance of liveness of the biometric information provided. Examples may be the detection of the constriction of the iris that is expected in response to a brief flash of light in an iris recognition system (Toth, 2005) or a combined face-voice recognition system, which ascertains the proper match of the speech sounds and the respective corresponding facial appearances (Chetty and Wagner, 2004).

Not only can different biometrics be combined in multimodal systems, but sometimes it can be advantageous to let separate classifiers analyze one and the same biometric. One case in point is the application of two separate commercial speaker recognition systems, each providing its own authentication of telephone callers (Wagner *et al.*, 2006; Australian, 2009), where the two authentication scores are combined using a suitable fusion algorithm. The reason for separate unimodal use of the biometric information in this case is that each subsystem will use its own, commercially confidential, algorithm and studies have shown that the combined system will achieve better performance than each individual system (NCBS, 2005).

A further motivation for a unimodal biometric system may be the extraction of disparate feature sets from the one modality, which lend themselves more successfully to being processed through separate classifiers before the separate authentication scores are finally combined by a suitable fusion algorithm. An example of such a system is a unimodal emotion detector, which uses both linguistic and acoustic features, extracted from speech utterances, in order to detect those utterances that were spoken in anger (Polzehl *et al.*, 2009). Such a unimodal system benefits from the separate use of separate classifiers because the two feature sets–spectral information for the acoustic signal and semantic information for the recognized words–are disparate and hence difficult to combine at the feature level, using currently known normalization techniques.

For both multimodal and unimodal biometric authentication systems, there are essentially three different ways of combining the information from the different feature sets (Ross et al., 2001). First, the different feature sets can be combined in a suitable manner before the joint features are further processed through the classification and decision algorithms of the system ("feature fusion" or "early fusion").

Another way of fusing information from different modalities–or from different feature sets of the same modality–is to employ separate classifiers on each set of features. Instead of performing a joint classification on a combined feature set, each feature set is processed by a separate classifier, which calculates a recognition score based on its own feature set. The information fusion can then take place either at the level of the separate recognition scores ("score fusion") or, if each classifier makes its own independent accept-reject decision, at the level of those separate decisions ("decision fusion)." Together, these two alternatives are also known as late fusion.

Feature fusion, score fusion, and decision fusion are illustrated in Fig. 17.3.

The remainder of this chapter is organized as follows: The next section gives an overview of different multibiometric combinations reported in the literature, including face and voice, face and iris, voice and handwriting, face and palmprint, finger and iris, face, finger and hand; and a four-way typing-writing-pointing-speaking authentication system proposed for continuous authentication at the workstation. In the following two sections, there will be a discussion of any robustness enhancements achieved by multibiometric systems and an overview over multibiometric systems with liveness assurance. The next two sections present examples of the use of fusion in unimodal systems with separate decision channels and evaluations of different fusion algorithm, followed by a conclusions section.

17.2 Combinations of Pairs of Biometrics for Authentication

Research into combining speaker recognition and face recognition for multimodal person authentication was motivated by the maturing of both technologies towards the end of the 20th century, by the prospect of gaining performance through the combination of two largely independent feature sets, and perhaps at the time also by the newly introduced integration of cameras into consumer mobile telephones.

An early proposal for combining acoustic and visual information in a person identification system was made by Brunelli and Falavigna (1995). Their system contains two acoustic classifiers and three visual classifiers. The acoustic subsystem is based on mel-frequency cepstra (MFC) and their derivatives ($\triangle$MFC) obtained from overlapping frames of the speech signal after eliminating frames that do not contain speech. The 8D "static" MFC vectors and the 8D "dynamic" $\triangle$MFC vectors for the training data are clustered independently into speaker-dependent static and dynamic codebooks, using a vector quantization algorithm (Huang et al., 2001). The static codebooks are adapted to the recording conditions of the test data

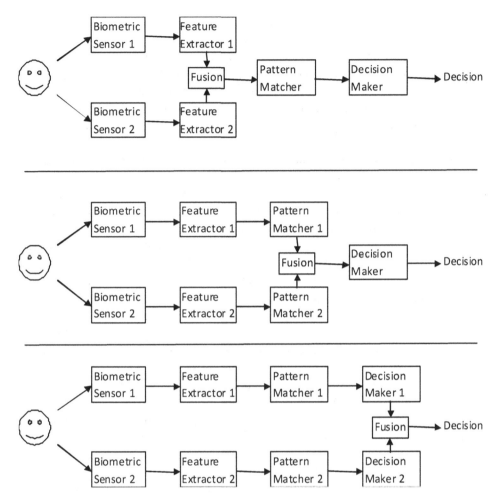

Fig. 17.3. Fusion options in multibiometric systems; Top: feature fusion; Middle: score fusion; Bottom: decision fusion.

using a "few utterances," while the dynamic codebooks are not adapted. Test data are evaluated against the MFC and $\triangle$MFC codebooks using the negative mean Mahalanobis distance, yielding a static acoustic similarity score, and a dynamic acoustic similarity score for each test utterance.

The visual subsystem described by Brunelli and Falavigna (1995) normalizes the frontal-view pixel matrices to a coordinate system of the interocular axis and the vertical symmetry axis, scaled to the interocular distance. A local contrast operator is used on the images to increase robustness against lighting variations, and for each facial image, three regions of interest (ROI) are identified: the eyes, nose, and mouth. Finally, a similarity measure based on the L_1 norm between test vector and template vector is obtained, yielding three visual similarity scores between a template and a test image: one for each of the three ROIs.

The five scores, two acoustic and three visual, are normalized, first, to be distributed with zero mean and unit variance and, second, by means of a hyperbolic tangent transform into the interval $(0, 1)$ (Hampel et al., 1986). The fusion of the two acoustic scores yielded a recognition error rate of 12% on a database of 89 persons, and the fusion of the three visual scores yielded a recognition error rate of 9%. The fusion of all five scores reduced the recognition error rate to 2%.

A second fusion strategy was also proposed for this system, which uses the best integrated score, the ratio between the best and second-best integrated scores, and 16 statistics derived from the ranking of the five subsystem scores for the two best candidates as input to a linear classifier in $\mathcal{R}^{18}$. This strategy, which also allows rejection of out-of-set (OOS) data, yielded error rates of 0.5% for OOS persons falsely recognized, 1.5% for in-set persons falsely rejected and no identification errors for in-set persons. Finally, the authors proposed a third fusion strategy, where combining the outputs of the five classifiers is seen as a learning task and the scores of the classifiers and their ranks are mapped into the interval $(0, 1)$ by means of a HyperBF network. For a specific set of thresholds, the authors reported no false identifications of in-set persons, a 3% false-rejection rate of in-set persons and a 0.5% false-acceptance rate of OOS persons (Poggio and Girosi, 1990).

A comparison between score fusion and feature fusion for a face-voice authentication system was presented by Chetty and Wagner (2006a). The facial features are extracted from parallel multiperspective video sequences in the VidTIMIT and AVOZES audio-video databases (Sanderson and Paliwal, 2004; Goecke and Millar, 2004). A set of 15 facial anchor points is extracted automatically from each video frame and their 3D coordinates estimated from the different perspectives. Using the corresponding anchor points of a generic 3D head model, the shape of that model is then aligned precisely with the 2D data. Next, the facial texture of the 2D data is projected onto the 3D model, and finally the shape and texture information for a set of 128 vertices of the model yields two (128×3)-D feature vectors, where the shape information is the set of 3D coordinates of the vertex, and the texture information is the color value of the vertex. Principal component analysis (PCA) reduces the shape space to 6 dimensions ("eigenshapes") and the texture space to 3 dimensions ("eigentextures)." The corresponding acoustic feature vector comprises the first 8 components of the MFC of a 30-ms acoustic frame, normalized through cepstral-mean normalization, and the fundamental frequency (F0), extracted from the frame through autocorrelation analysis (Huang et al., 2001).

Chetty and Wagner (2006a) combined the 6 eigenshapes, 3 eigentextures, 8 cepstral components, and the F0 value to form an 18D audiovisual feature vector for early-fusion verification experiments on the VidTIMIT and AVOZES databases. For comparison, the nine facial features and the nine speech features were also processed by separate classifiers in score-fusion experiments on the same data, where the two scores for each test were simply combined with equal weights. The verification results were presented in the form of equal-error rates (EERs) with feature fusion achieving EERs of 0.64% and 1.24%, respectively, for the two databases, while score fusion achieved EERs of 0.92% and 1.53%, respectively, a relative advantage of between 18% and 31% for the feature fusion over the score fusion.

Data corpora are not always readily available for multibiometric combinations, and researchers sometimes use "chimeric"* databases where a virtual person is synthesized as a combination of two or more real persons, one whose Biometric A has been collected in Database A, and another whose Biometric B is found in Database B, etc. This method can be used where the biometrics used are not–or at least not significantly–correlated. Morizet and Gilles (2008) constructed a chimeric face–iris database from the FERET and CASIA databases (Phillips *et al.*, 2000; Casia, 2005) in order to investigate an adaptive combination approach to score fusion for the face and iris biometrics.

For each target, the impostor scores are normalized to zero mean and unit variance, which allows them to be treated as Gaussian noise when mixed with a "signal" consisting of the genuine scores. Based on this premise, the noisy "signals," which comprise collections of both genuine and impostor scores in each modality, can be reduced in noise by transformation to, and thresholding in, the wavelet domain, which is reported to result in a better separation of genuine scores and impostor scores. The scores for the modalities, thus filtered, are then fused by weighted summation where the weights are chosen so as to maximize both the skewness and the kurtosis of the two score distributions, thereby increasing the separation distance between genuine and impostor scores. The proposed method is reported to reach a genuine acceptance rate of 100% at a false acceptance rate of 0.0007%.

A combination of the face and palmprint biometrics was proposed by Feng *et al.* (2004), a study motivated, among other factors, by the fact that face recognition has "less than desirable accuracy." The study uses feature fusion and shows that the results of the combined system are significantly better than those of either individual biometric. The dimensionality of the face and palm images is reduced either through PCA or through independent-component analysis (ICA) before combining the two feature vectors. The classification uses a nearest-neighbor algorithm. The combined system achieves a recognition accuracy of 95.83%, compared to 70.83% and 85.83%, respectively, for the face and palmprint subsystems when both vectors are reduced by PCA, and 99.17% compared to 85.0% and 92.5%, when both vectors are reduced by ICA.

The relatively large variability of the face is also addressed in a study by Kisku *et al.* (2009) by combining it with a biometric that "does not change in shape over [···] time due to change in expressions or age," namely the shape of the ears. Landmarks are used to detect eyes and mouth in the facial images and to detect the

---

*The Chimera is a fearsome creature of ancient Greek mythology. Homer describes it in the Iliad as "a thing of immortal make, not human, lion-fronted and snake behind, a goat in the middle, and snorting out the breath of the terrible flame of bright fire" (Wikipedia, 2010).

pinna in the aural images, before both images are cropped and intensity normalized. The images are convolved with 40 wavelets–five frequencies and eight orientations– and the resulting spectral densities for face and ear images are represented as Gaussian mixtures models (GMM). Unknown vectors are classified using Dempster-Shafer fusion (Wilson, 2000) of the two likelihoods into a belief value, which is then thresholded to obtain a verification decision. The study reports the results in terms of verification EER with the combined face–ear system achieving 4.47% compared with EERs of 8.04% and 6.65%, respectively, for the stand-alone face recognition and ear recognition subsystems.

A combination of two biometrics that already perform well individually, because both are physical rather than behavioral, is that of iris and fingerprint. The Hamming distance, already used for the comparison of iris patterns, is proposed by Baig *et al.* (2009) as the single distance measure for the combined fingerprint–iris biometrics. Fingerprint minutiae are coded in a bit pattern comprising coordinates, angle and minutia type and allowing the Hamming distance score to be calculated efficiently by a single scoring module for both biometrics.

17.3 Multibiometric Combinations

Different fusion strategies at the score level were researched by Ross *et al.* (2001) using a chimeric database of face, fingerprint, and hand geometry verification scores. Face verification scores were determined through PCA and the L_2-norm in the low-dimensional eigenface space. Fingerprint verification scores were determined on the basis of comparing minutia patterns (Jain *et al.*, 1997); and hand geometry scores were based on the L_2-norm between feature vectors of various geometric measures of hand, fingers and palm (Jain *et al.*, 1999). All scores were normalized into the interval $[0, 100]$, and three simple classifiers were evaluated: a sum rule with equal weights, a decision tree generated from training data scores, and linear discriminant analysis (LDA) between genuine scores and impostor scores in the 3D score space. The experimental results showed that the sum rule outperformed both the decision tree and the LDA classifiers and that the combination of the three biometrics produces lower error rates than any single biometric. The authors also report on conducting a feature fusion experiment between the face and fingerprint biometrics, where face image vectors and fingerprint image vectors were combined and classified together with results surpassing the score-level fusion results.

Chaudhari and Nath (2009) report on a multibiometric system with palmprint, fingerprint, and face biometrics, using score-level fusion. Palm-print features are derived from a specific region of interest in the image, PCA and projection into a low-dimensional subspace and a Euclidean distance in that "eigenpalm" space. Fingerprint recognition proceeds through image enhancement, minutia detection, and a similarity score based on the matching of minutia pairings. Face recognition also uses PCA and eigenface projection with a Euclidean distance between the eigenface coefficients of the different faces. All three scores are minimum-maximum normalized and mapped into the interval $[0, 1]$. The fingerprint similarity score is converted to a distance score by the transformation $x' = 1 - x$, and the three scores are then combined by a weighted sum with weights optimized for each user so as to minimize error rates. The results show that the three-way score fusion reduces error rates compared with each individual biometric.

A different approach to multibiometric score fusion is taken by Ma *et al.* (2005). The original database, which comprises face, hand, and finger scores, is partitioned and a decision tree is generated for each bootstrap sample, creating overall a random forest of trees. The final authentication decision is then made by voting of all the decision trees in the forest. The authors report that "voting among the trees built from different bootstrap samples of the original data stabilizes the classifier and improves the performance of the forest over a single tree." The experimental results are reported as "encouraging."

A multibiometric system with continuous real-time scoring of four different biometrics was developed by the TRUST Project (Technology for Robust User-conscious Secure Transactions) at the Australian National University (Millar *et al.*, 1994). The system was designed for anticipated desktop computers with typing, pointing, speech, and handwriting input modalities. Each of these modalities, when activated by the user, would be subject to continuous scoring against the user model in that modality and would trigger an alarm if the user would fail to be authenticated. Fusion strategies for the system were aimed at the flexibility of utilizing different multibiometric combinations as the corresponding input modalities were active and at algorithms that would treat a much less reliable biometric like pointing–the idiosyncratic manner in which a mouse is moved from one point on the screen to another–as providing some limited complementary support to the more reliable biometrics like voice or typing (Barrelle *et al.*, 1995; Mahar *et al.*, 1994; Wagner *et al.*, 1994).

17.4 Unimodal Authentication with Separate Channels

In some biometric authentication systems, it has been considered useful to conduct late fusion, either score or decision fusion, after a single modality was processed through separate channels. A system, which uses both the fusion of two different biometrics and the fusion of different channels within one of those biometrics, was proposed by Vielhauer and Scheidat (2005). That system combines the voice biometric and the handwritten signature biometric, and within the signature biometric four different classifiers are fused in a multialgorithmic, but unimodal fusion process. For the signature modality, features are extracted by means of the biometric hash method, but distances between features are calculated in four different ways: the Canberra distance, Hamming distance, and the L_1 and L_2 norms. The four individual handwriting scores are then fused into an overall handwriting score, before the latter is finally fused with the speaker verification score. The authors reported an increase in recognition accuracy of 15% with this hierarchical unimodal/multimodal fusion paradigm.

Mian *et al.* (2006) investigated unimodal fusion at score level of 3D nose matching, 3D forehead matching as well as 2D and 3D whole-face matching. The different scores are mapped to the interval [0, 1] using minimum-maximum normalization and are then combined by either a product rule or a weighted-sum rule. The fused score is reported to outperform the baseline system for both fusion rules, but with the product rule performing slightly better than the weighted-sum rule.

In the fingerprint domain, authentication systems are divided between the image comparison and the minutia detection paradigms. The study by Ito *et al.* (2005) proposes unimodal fusion between the two paradigms. Two fingerprint images are compared with respect to their texture by means of a band-limited variant of the cross-phase spectrum. With respect to their minutiae, the two fingerprints are compared by, first, an automatic extraction of the minutiae and their representation as vectors comprising coordinates, orientation, and type of each minutia; second by establishing corresponding minutiae in the two fingerprints by comparing their surrounding "local structures;" and third by finding the best-matching minutia pair as a set of reference coordinates in each of the two finger images. A small image region centered at each matching minutia pair is then scored with the same band-limited cross-phase spectrum that is already used in the texture paradigm, and the minutia matching score is compounded from the local scores of all matching minutiae. The overall classification then follows an algorithm that declares a match (score $= 1$) when the minutia match is above a given threshold, a no-match (score $= 0$) when there are fewer than three matched minutiae, and a score calculated from the compounded local-region scores in all other cases ($0 <$ score < 1). The EER of the proposed algorithm is reported to be lower than both the texture paradigm and the minutia-based paradigm.

A different example for an authentication system with unimodal fusion is the roll-out of a speaker recognition system for telephone-based authentication for the clients of Centrelink, an Australian government agency, which receives some 28 million calls per year (Australian, 2009). The system, which became operational in 2009, is based on the combination of two separate commercial speaker recognition systems performing parallel authentications on the incoming telephone speech data and fusing the resulting scores for an overall speaker score (Wagner *et al.*, 2006).

17.5 Liveness Assurance

All biometric authentication systems are vulnerable to replay or synthesis attack. A replay attack is an attempt by an impostor to defraud the system by presenting to it the biometric of a genuine client that has been recorded at an earlier time. Holding a photograph of a genuine client in front of the system camera, playing a recording of a genuine client voice to the system microphone, or placing a rubber replica of a genuine client's fingerprint on the system finger scanner are all examples of replay attacks (Wagner, 2009). Synthesis attacks are attempts to defraud the system by an impostor who uses a client model generated from previously collected client biometric data in order to synthesize biometric data that are indistinguishable from real client data. Examples of synthesis attacks are a speech synthesizer that utilizes an acoustic model generated from previously recorded client speech data, and an audiovisual synthesis program, which creates a speaking face on a laptop screen, generated by means of a hidden Markov model constructed from audiovisual speech data collected from a client previously (Wagner, 2009).

It is essential for biometric systems to provide an assurance that the biometric signals are given to the system live, i.e., at the time and at the place of the authentication request. While some systems could achieve such an assurance from a human supervisor who could ascertain at the point of authentication that a client voice has not been presented by way of a tape recorder or laptop computer, a client face not by way of a photograph, and a client video has not been synthesized and presented the system by way of a laptop computer.

When human supervision of the client-system interaction is not possible, e.g., when clients telephone a call center from their home, multibiometric system can be designed to provide good liveness assurance. Such a system has been investigated by Chetty and Wagner (2004). The system tests the correlation and synchrony of the speaker's phonemes and visemes, namely images of the lip area of the face taken at the time the corresponding phonemes are enunciated. For liveness assurance, it is essential to preserve the synchrony of phonemes and visemes, which requires that scoring uses the integrated features and rules out that the audio or the video subsystem integrates the features separately over time. Fusion for bimodal liveness assurance, therefore, requires the combination of the feature vectors from the different biometrics before computing a combined score.

The system proposed by Chetty and Wagner (2004) extracts eight MFC coefficients c_1 to c_8 (leaving out c_0) at a frame rate of 100 Hz and either six, ten or 16 visual features of the lip region-of-interest (ROI) at a frame rate of 50 Hz. The 6D visual feature vector comprises four geometric heights and two geometric widths of the mouth shape, all derived by means of an automatic algorithm, while the 10D visual vector consists of the first ten eigenlip coefficients derived by means of PCA. The 16D visual vector is simply the combination of the two. The combination of acoustic and visual feature vectors compensates for the differing frame rates by including two consecutive acoustic vectors for each visual vector, thus yielding a combined feature vector of 22, 26, or 32 dimensions. Gaussian mixture models were generated for the audiovisual features from the training data. Assuming an attack scenario with audio recording together with still photographs, the system was tested with data that comprised the original audio together with a single frame repeated throughout the utterance. The results show EERs of 5.1% for the 6D lip-shape features, 2.2% for the 10D eigenlip textures, and 1.0% for the 16D combination of shape and texture. Similar experiments were also undertaken for attack scenarios involving more sophisticated (and difficult) audio-video synthesis tools (Chetty and Wagner, 2006b). The lip movements corresponding to each audio waveform were synthesized and projected onto a synthetic face using the XFace toolkit (Xface, 2010). The resulting synthetic speaking faces were then used for replay attacks, resulting in equal-error rates between 1.5% and 4.6% for distinguishing synthetic impostors from genuine clients in four different gender and text-dependence/independence conditions.

17.6 Evaluation of Multibiometric Fusion

A number of researchers have undertaken evaluations of the different fusion paradigms as applied to different combinations of biometrics. (Kittler *et al.*, 1998) examined a selection of fundamental formulas for classifier fusion at the score level, namely the product rule; sum rule; max, min, and median rules; and the majority-vote rule. These algorithms were compared for a bimodal face-voice authentication task and a unimodal multialgorithm handwritten-digit recognition task. The authors concluded that the sum rule outperformed the other rules and that it was the most resilient of the different schemes against estimation errors.

Poh and Bengio (2005) proposed to incorporate both client-dependent information and confidence information for the given biometric subsystem, or "expert," into the fusion algorithm between the different biometrics. Client-dependent information is often applied to normalize score distributions by means of algorithms such as Z-norm, T-norm, or F-norm, while confidence information may be derived in the form of the margin $|FAR(y) - FRR(y)|$ between the false-acceptance and false-rejection rates for a given score y of the particular biometric. An experiment in bimodal authentication using 32 fusion datasets from the XM2VTS database shows that a fusion algorithm that incorporates for each biometric (1) the original score, (2) the client-dependent information in the form of an F-norm-transformed score, and (3) the margin-related confidence information for the score, outperforms fusion that only uses the original scores as well a fusion that incorporates only one of the two additional information sources. The concept of multibiometric fusion using both scores and score-related confidences is further examined by Poh *et al.* (2009) who used a database of face, finger, and iris biometrics with some 500 persons to confirm the hypothesis that classifiers, which incorporate confidence information for the different subsystems, outperform those that do not incorporate such confidence information.

The most general score fusion strategies include classifiers that take the set of subsystem scores derived from a development dataset as an input vector and are trained to minimize a given error criterion, such as EER or detection-cost function. Examples of such general score classifiers include artificial neural networks (ANNs) and support-vector machines (SVMs). A study evaluating the use of an SVM to fuse scores from an appearance-based face verification system, a minutia-based fingerprint system and an online signature verification system, based on hidden

Markov models (HMM) to model the temporal functions of the pen dynamics, is reported by Fierrez-Aguilar *et al.* (2003). An SVM transforms the score vectors into a higher-dimensional space, where a hyperplane can be found that separates client scores from impostor scores. The authors chose a radial-basis-function (RBF) kernel for their SVM and generated a chimeric database of 50 virtual persons from XM2VTS (faces) and the MCYT multimodal database (fingerprints and signatures). In order to extend the available data, the score distributions are modelled by means of Gaussian mixture models and more scores are generated synthetically according to the distribution of the real scores. A baseline system is established, which achieves an EER for the three-way fusion of 0.5% as against EERs of 10%, 4%, and 3%, respectively, for the face, signature, and fingerprint subsystems. Compared with the baseline, the SVM-based three-way fusion achieves EERs of 0.3% where a single SVM is used for all users and of 0.05% where user-dependent SVMs are used.

17.7 Conclusions

An overview has been presented over a variety of contemporary multibiometric authentication systems and the information fusion paradigms that derive a single authentication decision from the combinations of biometrics. Examples of biometric combinations with two or more subsystems were given. Other examples span fusion paradigms used between different classifiers used on a single biometric in order to achieve better authentication, as well as fusion strategies for multibiometric systems that are used for enhanced liveness assurance. The examples, particularly those on fusion algorithm evaluation and comparison in the previous section, provide important clous on the future directions of multibiometric authentication.

References

Australian. Centrelink goes biometric, *The Australian*, 26 May 2009.

Baig, A., Bouridane, A., and Kurugollu, F. Fingerprint-iris fusion based identification system using a single Hamming distance matcher, in *Proc IEEE Symposium on Bio-inspired Learning and Intelligent Systems for Security*, pp. 9–12, 2009.

Barrelle, K., Laverty, W., Henderson, R., Gough, J., Wagner, M., and Hiron, M. User verification through indirect pointing device control characteristics: an exploratory examination, in *Proc Int. Conf on Human Computer Interaction (HCI International 95)* (Tokyo), 1995.

Brunelli, R. and Falavigna, D. Person identification using multiple cues, *IEEE Trans Pattern Analysis and Machine Intelligence* **17**, 10, 955–966, 1995.

Casia. Center for biometrics and security research, http://www.cbsr.ia.ac.cn/IrisDatabase.htm, 2005.

Chaudhari, S. and Nath, R. A multimodal biometric recognition system based on fusion of palmprint, fingerprint and face, in *Proc. IEEE Int Conf on Advances in Recent Technologies in Communication and Computing*, pp. 596–600, 2009.

Chetty, G. and Wagner, M. 'Liveness' verification in audio-video authentication, in *Proc. Int Conf on Spoken Language Processing (ICSLP-04)*, 2004.

Chetty, G. and Wagner, M. Face-voice authentication based on 3D face models, in *LNCS 3851* (Springer Verlag, Berlin, Heidelberg), pp. 559–568, 2006a.

Chetty, G. and Wagner, M. Speaking faces for face-voice speaker identity verification, in *Proc. Int Conf on Spoken Language Processing (Interspeech 2006)* (Pittsburgh), 2006b.

Feng, G., Dong, K., Hu, D., and Zhang, D. When faces are combined with palmprints: a novel biometric fusion strategy, in *LNCS 3072* (Springer Verlag, Berlin, Heidelberg), pp. 701–707, 2004.

Fierrez-Aguilar, J., Ortega-Garcia, J., Garcia-Romano, D., and Gonzalez-Rodriguez, J. A comparative evaluation of fusion strategies for multimodal biometric verification, in *LNCS 2688* (Springer Verlag, Berlin, Heidelberg), pp. 830–837, 2003.

Furui, S. 40 years of progress in automatic speaker recognition, in *LNCS 5558* (Springer Verlag, Berlin, Heidelberg), pp. 1050–1059, 2005.

Goecke, R. and Millar, J. The audio-video Australian English speech data corpus AVOZES, in *Proc 8th International Conference on Spoken Language Processing (INTERSPEECH 2004)*, pp. 2525–2528, 2004.

Hampel, F., Ronchetti, E., Rousseeuw, P., and Stahel, W. *Robust Statistics — The Approach Based on Influence Functions* (Wiley), 1986.

Huang, X., Acero, A., and Hon, H.-W. *Spoken Language Processing* (Prentice Hall, Inc., Upper Saddle River, New Jersey), 2001.

Ito, K., Morita, A., Aoki, T., Nakajima, H., Kobayashi, K., and Higuchi, T. A fingerprint recognition algorithm combining phase-based image matching and feature-based matching, in *LNCS 3832* (Springer Verlag, Berlin, Heidelberg), pp. 316–325, 2005.

Jain, A., Hong, L., Pankanti, S., and Bolle, R. An identity authentication system using fingerprints, *Proc IEEE* **85**, 1365–1388, 1997.

Jain, A., Ross, A., and Pankanti, S. A prototype hand geometry-based verification system, in *Proc. Second Int Conf on Audio and Video-Based Biometric Person Authentication*, pp. 166–171, 1999.

Kisku, D., Sing, J., and Gupta, P. Multibiometrics belief fusion, in *IEEE Second Int Conf on Machine Vision*, pp. 37–40, 2009.

Kittler, J., Hatef, M., Duin, R., and Matas, J. On combining classifiers, *IEEE Trans Pattern Analysis and Machine Intelligence* **20**, 3, 1998.

Ma, Y., Cukic, B., and Singh, H. A classification approach to multi-biometric score fusion, in *LNCS 3546* (Springer Verlag, Berlin, Heidelberg), pp. 484–493, 2005.

Mahar, D., Henderson, R., Laverty, W., Lawrie, K., Hiron, M., Gough, J., and Wagner, M. Typist identity verification: a comparison of the utility of overall reference profile and digraph-specific estimates of digraph latency variability, in *Proc. Int. Conf. on Human Computer Interface (HCI'94)* (Glasgow), 1994.

Mian, A., Bennamoun, M., and Owens, R. 2D and 3D multimodal hybrid face recognition, in *LNCS 3953* (Springer Verlag, Berlin, Heidelberg), pp. 344–355, 2006.

Millar, J., Chen, F., Macleod, I., Ran, S., Tang, H., Wagner, M., and Zhu, X. Overview of speaker verification studies towards technology for robust user-conscious secure transactions, in *Proc. Int Conf on Speech Science and Technology* (Perth, Australia), 1994.

Morizet, N. and Gilles, J. A new adaptive combination approach to score level fusion for face and iris biometrics combining wavelets and statistical moments, in *LNCS 5359* (Springer Verlag, Berlin, Heidelberg), pp. 661–671, 2008.

NCBS. National Centre for Biometric Studies, University of Canberra, Unpublished report, 2005.

Phillips, P., Moon, H., Rizvi, S., and Rauss, P. The feret evaluation methodology for face-recognition algorithms, *IEEE Trans Pattern Analysis and Machine Intelligence* **22**, 1090–1104, 2000.

Poggio, T. and Girosi, F. Networks for approximation and learning, *Proc. IEEE* **78**, 1481–1497, 1990.

Poh, N. and Bengio, S. A novel approach to combining client-dependent and confidence information in multimodal biometrics, in *LNCS 3546* (Springer Verlag, Berlin, Heidelberg), pp. 1120–1129, 2005.

Poh, N., Bourlai, T., Kittler, J., Allano, L., Alonso-Fernandez, F., Ambekar, O., Baker, J., Dorizzi, B., Fatukazi, O., Fierrez, J., Ganster, H., Ortega-Garcia, J., Maurer, D., Ali Salah, A., Scheidat, T., and Vielhauer, C. Benchmarking quality-dependent and cost-sensitive score-level multimodal biometric fusion algorithms, *IEEE Trans Inf. Forensics Security* **4**, 4, 849–866, 2009.

Polzehl, T., Sundaram, S., Ketabdar, H., Wagner, M., and Metze, F. Emotion classification in children's speech using fusion of acoustic and linguistic features, in *Proc. 10th Annual Conference of the Int. Speech Communication Assoc. (Interspeech-2009)*, 2009.

Ross, A., Jain, A., and Qian, J.-Z. Information fusion in biometrics, in *LNCS 2091* (Springer Verlag, Berlin, Heidelberg), pp. 354–359, 2001.

Sanderson, C. and Paliwal, K. Identity verification using speech and face information, *Digital Signal Processing* **14**, 5, 397–507, 2004.

Toth, B. Biometrics, *Information Security Bulletin* **10**, 291–297, 2005.

Vielhauer, C. and Scheidat, T. Multimodal biometrics for voice and handwriting, in *LNCS 3677* (Springer Verlag, Berlin, Heidelberg), pp. 191–199, 2005.

Wagner, M. Liveness assurance in voice authentication, in S. Li and A. Jain (eds.), *Encyclopedia of Biometrics* (Springer Verlag), 2009.

Wagner, M., Chen, F., Macleod, I., Millar, B., Ran, S., Tridgell, A., and Zhu, X. Analysis of type-ii errors for vq distortion based speaker verification, in

Proc. ESCA Workshop on Automatic Speaker Recognition, Identification and Verification (Martigny), pp. 83–86, 1994.

Wagner, M., Summerfield, C., Dunstone, T., Summerfield, R., and Moss, J. An evaluation of 'commercial off-the-shelf' speaker verification systems, in *Proc IEEE Speaker and Language Recognition Workshop Odyssey*, p. CD, 2006.

Wikipedia. Chimera (mythology), http://en.wikipedia.org/wiki/Chimera_(mytho logy), 2010.

Wilson, N. *Algorithms for Dempster-Shafer Theory* (Oxford Brookes University), 2000.

Xface. Open source facial animation engine, http://xface.itc.it/, 2010.

Part IX

Security and Others

Chapter 18

CANCELABLE BIOMETRICS: MULTIPLE RANDOM PROJECTIONS AND ITS EXTENSIONS

Andrew Beng Jin Teoh

Biometrics Engineering Research Center (BERC)
Yonsei University, Seoul, South Korea
E-mail: bjteoh@yonsei.ac.kr

18.1 Introduction

Although biometrics is a powerful tool against repudiation and has been widely deployed in various security systems, biometric characteristics are largely immutable, resulting in permanent biometric compromise when stolen. The concept of cancellable biometrics was introduced (Ratha *et al.*, 2001) to make a biometric template cancellable and replaceable, as well as being unique in every application. Cancellable biometrics requires storage of a transformed version of the biometric template, which provides a high privacy level by allowing multiple templates to be associated with the same biometric data. This helps to promote nonlinkability of user's biometric data stored across various databases.

Cancellable biometrics is a relatively new direction of research, spurred on by the privacy invasion and biometrics non-revocable issues. To formally define the concept, four objectives were highlighted as follows (Teoh *et al.*, 2006):

(1) Diversity: no same cancellable template can be used in two different applications.
(2) Reusability: straightforward revocation and reissue in the event of compromise.
(3) Noninvertibility: noninvertibility of template computation to prevent recovery of biometric data.
(4) Performance: the formulation should not deteriorate the recognition performance.

18.2 Related Works

The first attempt towards this direction was recorded by Davida *et al.* (1998) but the concrete idea of cancellable biometrics was furnished by Ratha *et al.*

(2001). This research area is growing rapidly and numerous new techniques have been proposed since then. These methods generally fall into three categories: (1) error-correcting based, (2) integration of external factors and biometrics, and (3) non-invertible transforms.

In error-correcting code scheme, codeword and decoding functions are established from the biometric templates during enrolment. The codeword value can be used either as a key or hash. At the authentication stage, the input biometric data is used to compute or recover the codeword. For instance, Davida et al. (1998) proposed a majority decoding scheme for iris biometrics. In their scheme, a pair of related binary representations of iris code, the input, and test template which is 2048 bit in length was extracted through the majority decoding scheme and matched by using hamming distance. Subsequently, algebraic decoding was applied in order to rectify the offset of the test data using the help of offline checksums. To certain extent, the scheme may preserve user privacy as the biometric template was nonrecoverable. However, neither the issues of reusability/cancellability nor practical work were addressed.

Juels et al. (Juels and Wattenberg, 1999 and Juels and Sudan, 2002) generalized and improved Davida et al. (1998) scheme through a modification in error-correcting codes, and hence the code size is reduced and with a higher resilience. Hao et al. (2006) proposed an improved fuzzy commitment scheme based on the hybrid error-correction techniques that reported a very low false reject rate (FRR) around 0.47% and 0% false accept rate (FAR). Clancy et al. (2003) implemented the technique of a fuzzy vault scheme. In Clancy's work, a group of minutia points were extracted from input fingerprint to bind in a locking set using polynomial-based secret sharing scheme. Subsequently, a non-related chaff point were added intentionally to "shadow" the key for maximizing the unlocking computational complexity, where the secret key could only be recovered if there is a substantial overlap between the input and testing fingerprint. The method has been theoretically proven secure in protecting the secrecy of fingerprint, but is beyond the level of practical use due to the high FRR at 20–30% and huge storage requirement. Juels and Sudan's fuzzy vault scheme has spurred the great interest among the researchers, there are a few methods such as Geometrics Hashing (Chung et al., 2005) and Yang and Verbauwhede (2005) were proposed to solve the template–query alignment issue.

Linnartz and Tuyls (2003) assumed that a noise-free template X of a biometric identifier is available at the enrolment time and use this to enrol a secret S to generate a helper data W. They assume that each dimension of the template is quantized at q resolution levels. In each dimension, the process of obtaining W is equivalent to finding residuals that must be added to X to fit to odd or even grid quantum depending upon whether the corresponding S bit is zero or one. At verification time, the (noise-prone) biometric template Y is used to obtain S', which is approximately the same as S. It is hoped that the relatively few errors in S' can be corrected using error-correction techniques. The proposed technique assumes that the noise in each dimension is relatively small compared to the quantization Q.

Tuyls *et al.* (2005) described a practical system based on the proposed scheme, achieving equal error rates around 5.3% and 4.5% for two datasets reported. However, the secret bit length generated (40 bits) is still low for most security applications.

Another possible way is to combine two or more factor authenticators. A common multifactor authenticator is an ATM card, which combines a token with a secret (PIN). Combination of password or secret with a biometrics is of not so favorable, since one of the liabilities of biometrics is to get rid of the task of memorizing the password. As a user has difficulty remembering the secret, a token may be combined with a biometrics. A token is a physical device that can be thought of as a portable storage for authenticator, such as ATM card, smart card, or an active device that yields time-changing or challenged-based passwords. The token can store human-chosen passwords, but an advantage is to use these devices to store longer codewords or pseudorandom sequence that a human cannot remember, and thus they are much less easily attacked. This kind of approach of integration was first addressed by Soutar *et al.* (1999). They described a different approach for generating a cancellable biometrics from fingerprints using optical computing techniques for integration. With a few fingerprint images and a set of random numbers for training, the algorithm creates a complex-valued correlation filter function which is mathematically optimized to possess both distortion tolerance and discrimination properties. An output pattern c_0 is also generated via correlation between the training fingerprint image and the correlation filter. This output pattern will then be binarized using a simple threshold-based decision and used to derive cryptographic key using redundant error correction code resulting in a lookup table T. However, the method does not carry rigorous security guarantees and the resulting FAR and FRR are unknown.

Similarly, Savvides *et al.* (2004) proposed a cancellable biometrics scheme that encrypts the training images used to synthesize the correlation filter for biometrics authentication. They demonstrated that convolving the training images with any random convolution kernel prior to building the biometric filter does not change the resulting correlation output peak-to-sidelobe ratios, thus preserving the authentication performance. However, the security will be jeopardized via a deterministic deconvolution with a known random kernel. Most recently, Boult (2006) introduced the biometrics-based tokens that support robust distance computations, which provide cryptographic security such that it can be canceled or revoked and replaced with a new one.

In non-invertible transformed-based approach, instead of storing the original biometric, the biometric is transformed using a one-way function. The transformation occurs in the same signal or feature space as the original biometric. For example, Bolle *et al.* (2002) introduced an intentional distortion of a biometrics signal based on a chosen transform function. The biometrics signal was distorted in the same fashion at each presentation, i.e., during enrolment and for every subsequent authentication. With this approach, every instance of enrolment can use a different transform function thus rendering cross-matching impossible. Furthermore, if one variant of the biometrics is compromised, then the transformation can simply be changed to create a new variant for reenrolment. However, it is not an easy task to design such a function due to the limiting characteristics of the feature vector. Generally, extracted features take different values and changing within some range depending on the type of biometrics used and feature extractor, rather than taking precise values. Therefore, a transform function has to satisfy some smoothness criteria. While providing robustness against to variability of a same user's biometric data, that transformation must also distinguish among different users successfully. An interesting realization of this approach can be found in Ratha *et al.* (2007). Sutcu *et al.* (2005) realized this idea by proposing a sum of weighted and shifted Gaussian functions as a noninvertible and scalable transformation function. However, their preliminary results showed that the method was not so favorable in term of recognition performance. Ang *et al.* (2005) proposed a similar technique with a key-dependent transformation so that the matching can be done in the transformed domain. Yet, both transforms degrade the matching accuracy significantly in the altered domain.

18.3 Motivations

In this chapter, we report a technique whereby biometrics template refreshment can be done through a set of user-specific random numbers from biometrics data. However, the generic two-factor noninvertible mixing process is carried out by linear subspace projection, which is known as multispace random projections (MRPs) (Teoh and Chong, 2007). The random subspace is constituted by the independent, zero mean, and unit variance Gaussian distributed random bases, which can be generated from the user-specific pseudorandom numbers (PRNs). Since different users hold their own set of PRN, the formulation can be extended to include multiple users or applications to produce multiple random subspaces. MRP inspires a two-factor authentication mechanism by introducing the traditional biometrics recognition system a secondary authentication factor–a private token that constitutes the user PRN. A two-factor authentication system has the advantage of avoiding any attack with single factor–attempting with a stolen token or a fake biometrics that works with the traditional system. This is the typical attack to the traditional token-based system where a hacker intrudes the system with a stolen or dictionary-generated password. MRP fortifies the security level of the system where a legitimate access requires a valid token and a genuine face's feature.

From the performance perspective, we consider three different scenarios when MRP is applied:

(1) Legitimate-token scenario in which the genuine's biometrics is mixed with the user-specific token.

(2) Stolen token: in which an imposter has access genuine token and used by the imposter to claim as the genuine user.
(3) Stolen biometrics: in which an imposter possesses intercepted biometric data of sufficiently high quality to be considered genuine.

We show that MRP satisfies the performance requirement in these three scenarios and fulfills all the others cancellable biometrics criteria, such as diversity, reusability, and non-invertible properties, either theoretically or experimentally. We utilize face biometrics as the subject of study since there is an established and standardized database for comparison.

18.4 Overview of MRPs Formulation

MRP comprises of two stages: feature extraction and multispace random projections. In the feature extraction stage, an individual's biometric image, $\mathbf{i}$ is transformed to a fixed length feature vector with length n by using a feature extractor, $\mathbf{x} \in \Re^n$. The biometric feature vector, $\mathbf{x}$ is further projected onto a random subspace as determined from an externally derived pseudorandom sequence, $\mathbf{R} \in \Re^{mn}$, where $m \leq n$. The random projection (RP) vector, $\mathbf{v}$, is described as follows

$$\mathbf{v} = \sqrt{(1/m)}\mathbf{R}\mathbf{x} \tag{18.1}$$

where $\mathbf{R}$ is a $m \times n$ random matrix and $m \leq n$, n is the biometrics feature length. In the literature, RP is a simple yet powerful dimension-reduction technique (Kaski, 1998) that uses random matrices, $\mathbf{R}$, to project the raw data into low-dimensional spaces.

RP theory is addressed by means of the Johnson-Lindenstrauss (JL) lemma (Johnson and Lindenstrauss, 1984):

J-L lemma: For any $0 < \varepsilon < 1$ and any integer k, let m be a positive integer such that $m \geq \frac{4\ln k}{\varepsilon^2/2-\varepsilon^3/3}$. Then, for any set S of $n = |S|$ data points in $\Re^n$, there is a map $f : \Re^n \to \Re^m$ such that for all $\mathbf{x}, \mathbf{y} \in S$

$$(1 - \varepsilon)\|\mathbf{x} - \mathbf{y}\|^2 \leq \|f(\mathbf{x}) - f(\mathbf{y})\|^2 \leq (1 + \varepsilon)\|\mathbf{x} - \mathbf{y}\|^2$$

The lemma states that any set of k points in n-dimensional *Euclidean space* can be embedded into an $O(\frac{\ln k}{\varepsilon^2})$ dimensional space, such that the pairwise distance of any two points are maintained within an arbitrarily small factor. This pleasant property implies that it is possible to alter the data's original form and yet preserves its statistical characteristics.

The basic formulation can be extended to include g users to generate g different RP features, i.e., multiple random subspaces, $\mathbf{R}^k$ which render a set of unique feature vectors

$$\mathbf{v}^k = \sqrt{(1/m)}\mathbf{R}^k\mathbf{x}^k \quad \text{where } k = 1,\ldots,g \tag{18.2}$$

18.5 Multispace Random Projections

In this section, we analyze the MRP in term of its feature's intra- and interclass variations. Independently to JL lemma, we first show that the statistical properties–mean and variance, of feature's intraclass variation are preserved exactly just like in the feature vector level (before random projection is performed), while amplifying interclass variations via projecting onto uncorrelated random subspaces in legitimate-token and stolen-biometrics scenarios. On the other hand, we show that the recognition performance retained as sole biometrics performance in stolen-token scenario, through the choice of dissimilarity measure–normalized inner product that governs the statistics preservation transformation. For these to be done, we need to understand the statistical properties of the product of random matrices.

18.5.1 *Statistical properties of the product of random matrices*

Let $\mathbf{R}$ be a $m \times n$ $(m < n)$ random matrix such that each entry r_{ij} of $\mathbf{R}$ is independent and identically (i.i.d) drawn from Gaussian distribution with mean, $E[r_{ij}] = 0$ and variance, $\text{Var}[r_{ij}] = 1$, and ε_{ij} be the entry of $\mathbf{R}^T\mathbf{R}$, then $r_{ij} = \sum_{k=1}^{m} r_{ki}r_{kj}$, and hence its expectation Liu *et al.* (2006) is

$$E[\varepsilon_{ij}] = E\left[\sum_{k=1}^{m} r_{ki}r_{kj}\right] = \sum_{k=1}^{m} E[r_{ki}r_{kj}] = \begin{cases} \sum_{k=1}^{m} E[r_{ki}]E[R_{kj}], & \text{if } i \neq j \\ \sum_{k=1}^{m} E[r_{ki}^2], & \text{if } i = j \end{cases}$$

Note that $E(r_{ij}) = 0$ and $E(r_{ij}^2) = 1$, hence

$$E[\varepsilon_{ij}] = \begin{cases} 0, & \text{if } i \neq j \\ m, & \text{if } i = j \end{cases} \quad \text{or} \quad E[\mathbf{R}^T\mathbf{R}] = m\mathbf{I} \tag{18.3}$$

or if each column vector of $\mathbf{R}$ is normalized to have a unit length, we have

$$E[\varepsilon_{ij}] = \begin{cases} 0, & \text{if } i \neq j \\ 1, & \text{if } i = j \end{cases} \tag{18.4}$$

The above result suggests that column vectors of $\mathbf{R}$ are orthogonal to each other and this is specifically true in a high-dimensional space. This observation was also verified by Hecht-Nielsen (Hecht-Nielsen, 1994): in a high-dimensional space, there exists a much larger number of almost orthogonal than orthogonal directions. Thus, vectors having random directions might be sufficiently close to orthogonal, and equivalently $\mathbf{R}^T\mathbf{R}$ would approximate an identity matrix. Note that $\mathbf{R}$ has not undergone orthonormalization process such as Gram-Schmidt's procedure due to its heavy computation, which will jeopardize the MRP for practical use.

From Eq. (18.3), since $E[\varepsilon_{ii}] = m$ and it can be proved that $E[\varepsilon_{ii}^2] = (2m + m^2)$, thus $\text{Var}(\varepsilon_{ii}) = 2m, \forall i$. Similarly, we have $E(\varepsilon_{ij}^2) = m$ and $E(\varepsilon_{ij}) = 0$, thus $\mathrm{Var}(\varepsilon_{ij}) = m, \forall i, j, \ i \neq j$. Collectively

$$\mathrm{Var}(\varepsilon_{ij}) = \begin{cases} m, & \text{if } i \neq j \\ 2m, & \text{if } i = j \end{cases} \tag{18.5}$$

For MRP formulation, individual random subspace can be easily extended to include g users with g PRN sets to generate g random subspaces. For instance, let $\mathbf{R}$ and $\mathbf{S}$ be two $m \times n$ ($m < n$) uncorrelated random matrices such that each entry $r_{ij} \in \mathbf{R}$ and $s_{ij} \in \mathbf{S}$ are independent and identically (i.i.d) drawn from the standard Gaussian distribution, and η_{ij} be the entry of $\mathbf{R}^T\mathbf{S}$, then $\eta_{ij} = \sum_{k=1}^{m} r_{ki}s_{kj}$. Thus

$$E[\eta_{ij}] = E\left[\sum_{k=1}^{m} r_{ki}s_{kj}\right] = \sum_{k=1}^{m} E[r_{ki}s_{kj}]$$

Since $r_{ij} \in \mathbf{R}$ and $s_{ij} \in \mathbf{S}$ are uncorrelated. Hence $E(r_{ij}) = 0$ and $E[\eta_{ij}] = \sum_{k=1}^{m} E[r_{ki}]E[s_{kj}]$, $\forall i, j$. Thus, we have

$$E[\eta_{ij}] = 0 \ \forall i, j \quad \text{or} \quad E[\mathbf{R}^T\mathbf{S}] = 0 \tag{18.6}$$

and

$$\mathrm{Var}[\eta_{ij}] = m \ \forall i, j \tag{18.7}$$

18.5.2 *MRP's genuine and imposter distributions analysis*

The nature of biometrics system offers two possible error outcomes known as FAR and FRR. By manipulating the decision criteria, the relative probabilities of these two outcomes can be adjusted in a way that reflected their associated cost and benefits. The interdependency of FAR and FRR is regulated by the system threshold value t, as indicated in Fig. 18.1. As t moves to the right, the FAR will decrease but FRR will increase and this results in more conservative system. On the other hand, moving t to the left will cause FRR to decrease, but FAR will rise to cause more imposters attempting to access the system. Based on Fig. 18.1, the decidability of the system accuracy is determined by how much overlap there is between the two distributions–genuine and imposter distributions which represent the quantitative measurement of intra-class and interclass variations, respectively.

Here, we employ normalized dissimilarity measures, $\nu = 1 - \mathbf{x}^T\mathbf{y}$ in the analysis, where $\mathbf{x}$ and $\mathbf{y}$ are the face feature vector. Note that if the feature vector is properly normalized, the inner product, $1 - \mathbf{x}^T\mathbf{y}$ that is used in the demonstration is directly related to the similarity measures such as cosine angle, and dissimilarity measure, Euclidean distance of the vectors, and thus their statistical properties are remained (Liu *et al.*, 2006). For instance

(1) $\cos\vartheta = \mathbf{x}^T\mathbf{y}$

(2) $\varepsilon(\mathbf{x}, \mathbf{y}) = \sqrt{\sum_i (x_i - y_i)^2} = \sqrt{\sum_i x_i^2 \sum_i y_i^2 - 2\sum_i x_i y_i} = \sqrt{2 - 2\mathbf{x}^T\mathbf{y}}$

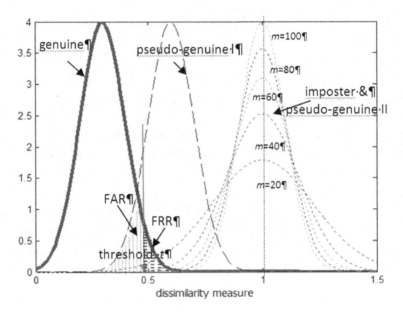

Fig. 18.1.   Theoretical genuine, imposter, pseudogeninue type I and II distributions for MRP.

Next, we show that the dissimilarity measures are preserved after random projection in genuine distribution whereby the face features from an individual are compared. On the other hand, the interclass (imposter distribution) is amplified if different random subspaces are engaged (legitimate token scenario). Then, we combine all the observations together to infer the recognition performance of an MRP in three different scenarios, i.e., legitimate-token, stolen-token, and stolen-biometrics scenarios.

(a) Genuine distribution

We let $\mathbf{u} = \sqrt{(1/m)}\mathbf{R}\mathbf{x}$ and $\mathbf{v} = \sqrt{(1/m)}\mathbf{R}\mathbf{y}$, $\nu_R = 1 - \mathbf{u}^T\mathbf{v}$, $\nu = 1 - \mathbf{x}^T\mathbf{y}$ and $\delta = (\nu - \nu_R)$. Thus, we have

$$\delta = (\mathbf{u}^T\mathbf{v} - \mathbf{x}^T\mathbf{y} = (1/m)\mathbf{x}^T\mathbf{R}^T\mathbf{R}\mathbf{y} - \mathbf{x}^T\mathbf{y}$$

Then

$$E[\delta] = (1/m)\mathbf{x}^T E[\mathbf{R}^T\mathbf{R}]\mathbf{y} - \mathbf{x}^T\mathbf{y}$$

From Eq. (18.3), we have

$$E[\delta] = 0 \tag{18.8}$$

For $\mathrm{Var}[\delta] = \mathrm{Var}[\mathbf{u}^T\mathbf{v} - \mathbf{x}^T\mathbf{y}]$, there is

$$\mathrm{Var}[\delta] = \frac{1}{m}\left[\sum_{i=1}^{m} x_i^2 y_i^2 + \sum_{i=1}^{m} x_i^2 \sum_{j=1}^{m} y_j^2\right] \tag{18.9}$$

If both $\mathbf{x}$ and $\mathbf{y}$ are normalized to unit length, thus $\sum_i x_i^2 \sum_j y_j^2 = 1$ and $\sum_i x_i^2 y_i^2 < 1$, then we have

$$\text{Var}[\delta] < 2/m \tag{18.10}$$

The proof of Eq. (18.9) is given in Teoh and Chong (2007).

The above equation shows that the error δ of the dissimilarity measures produced by the random projection technique is zero on average and the variance is less than the inverse of m, the dimension of RP multiply by 2 if the feature vectors, $\mathbf{x}$ and $\mathbf{y}$ are normalized. This indicates that the genuine distribution will remain the same before and after random projections, especially when m is large. According to JL Lemma, the lower bound of m for this to be happened is $m = (4 \ln k)/(\varepsilon^2/2) - (\varepsilon^3/3)$. However, in our experiments, we find that when $m \approx n$, where n is the dimension of feature vector, the preservation effect is attained. This analysis applies to genuine distributions in legitimate-token, stolen-token as well as stolen-biometrics scenarios.

(b) Imposter distribution

To the other spectrum, we consider the imposter distribution behavior in legitimate-token and stolen-biometrics scenarios where difference subspaces, $\mathbf{R}$ and $\mathbf{S}$ are used. Note that imposter distribution for stolen-token scenario would be identical to the genuine distribution discussed above.

For instance, let $\mathbf{u} = \sqrt{(1/m)}\mathbf{R}\mathbf{x}$ and $\mathbf{v} = \sqrt{(1/m)}\mathbf{S}\mathbf{y}$, then $\nu_R = 1 - \mathbf{u}^T\mathbf{v}$, thus, imposter distribution mean

$$\mu_i = E[\nu_i] = E[1 - \mathbf{u}^T\mathbf{v}] = E[1 - (1/m)\mathbf{x}^T\mathbf{R}^T\mathbf{S}\mathbf{y}] = 1 - (1/m)\mathbf{x}^T\mathbf{y}E[\mathbf{R}^T\mathbf{S}]$$

From Eq. (18.6), we obtain

$$\mu_i = 1 \tag{18.11}$$

and from the imposter distribution variance $\sigma_i^2 = \text{Var}[\nu_i] = \text{Var}[1 - \mathbf{u}^T\mathbf{v}] = \text{Var}[\mathbf{u}^T\mathbf{v}]$, we have

$$\sigma_i^2 = \frac{1}{m}\left[\sum_{i=1}^{m} x_i^2 \sum_{j=1}^{m} y_j^2\right] \tag{18.12}$$

If both $\mathbf{x}$ and $\mathbf{y}$ are normalized to unit length, $\sum_{i=1}^{m} x_i^2 \sum_{j=1}^{m} y_j^2 = 1$, hence

$$\sigma_i^2 \leq \frac{1}{m} \text{ or standard deviation } \sigma_i = \sqrt{1/m} \tag{18.13}$$

The proof of Eq. (18.12) is given in Teoh and Chong (2007).

In the legitimate-token scenario, we anticipate that the genuine curve will remain and the imposter curve will be centered at 1 and its profile envelope is being shrunk when m grows large, as depicted in Fig. 18.1. Therefore, the genuine and imposter distributions become separated as m increases. The clear separation of the genuine-imposter distribution indicates zero FAR and FRR, and hence leads to zero error rate in the legitimate-token scenario.

Conversely, when the token is stolen, it means that a different **x**s are projected into a random subspace, **R**. Note that this is similar to the genuine analysis in part (a) except the feature vectors are from different users. It is obvious that the impostor (*pseudogenuine type I distribution* hereafter) distribution will revert to its original state as the dissimilarity measures are preserved, as indicated in Fig. 18.1. This is true when m is large.

On the other hand, for the stolen-biometrics scenario, the net effect essentially equivalent to projection of the compromised biometrics features onto multiple random subspaces, and hence it is expected the imposter distribution (*pseudogenuine type II distribution* hereafter) will peak at 1 and its standard deviation follows $1/\sqrt{m}$. We verify all the assertions in the following section.

18.5.3 *Analysis on non-invertible property of MRP*

To preserve the privacy of the users, it is expected that no information can be disclosed if the stored biometrics template is compromised. In other words, the formulation must be noninvertible. Due to the randomness of MRP's projection matrix, the user's information cannot be revealed if only the template is compromised. However, if the projection matrix is also revealed, then an adversary can estimate the original biometrics data. For a robust privacy preserving mechanism, the estimated individual elements in the data vector should not be exactly the same as original signals. Furthermore, the global characteristics of the estimated data vector should be far apart from the genuine data vector up to some similarity functions.

The analysis can be carried out by looking at Eq. (18.1), $\mathbf{v} = \mathbf{Rx}$ where $\mathbf{R}$ is an $m \times n$ orthonormal random matrix and $m \leq n$. $\mathbf{v}$ can be regarded as a set of underdetermined systems of linear equations (more unknowns than equations). Therefore, it is impossible to find the *exact values of all the elements* in $\mathbf{x}$ by solving an underdetermined linear equation system in $\mathbf{v} = \mathbf{Rx}$ if $m < n$, based on the premise that the possible solutions are infinite (Demmel and Higham, 1990). However, it is possible that an adversary can estimate partial of the real values, and therefore reveal partial of the user's information. To solve this problem, the projected dimensionality should satisfy $m \leq (n + 1)/2$, such that each unknown variable is disguised by $m-1$ other variables (Liu *et al.*, 2006). Since it is impossible to find $m-1$ linearly independent equations that involves this $m-1$ variables, the solutions to each of the unknown variable is infinite, and therefore it is impossible to find the exact value of any element in the original data vector.

18.5.4 *Analysis on reusability property of MRP*

We also examine the cancelable property of MRP by evaluating whether a MRP A and a MRP B (with same PCA feature) are correlated. In other words, we wish to avoid the old MRP from falling into the region of acceptance of the refreshed MRP. In this case, we let $\mathbf{u} = \sqrt{(1/m)}\mathbf{R}\mathbf{x}$, $\mathbf{v} = \sqrt{(1/m)}\mathbf{S}\mathbf{x}$ and $\mathbf{R} \neq \mathbf{S}$, then the correlation of $\mathbf{u}$ and $\mathbf{v}$ is

$$\mathbf{u}^T\mathbf{v} = (1/m)\mathbf{x}^T\mathbf{R}^T\mathbf{S}\mathbf{x}$$

According to Eq. (18.8), there are $E[\mathbf{u}^T\mathbf{v}] = 0$ and $\text{Var}[\mathbf{u}^T\mathbf{v}] = 1/m$. This implies there is no correlation for old MRP and refreshed MRP when m is large. Experimentally, the evaluation is exactly the same as the imposter distribution of the stolen-biometrics scenario, where different PRNs are mixed with the same PCA feature.

18.6 Evaluations

18.6.1 *Experiments setup*

In the experiments, eigenface (Turk and Pentland, 1991) is adopted as the face feature extractor and $\nu = 1 - \mathbf{x}^T\mathbf{y}$ is used as the dissimilarity measure, where $\mathbf{x}$ and $\mathbf{y}$ are normalized. For the eigenbasis training, we use 400 images (40 subjects with 10 images per each) from ORL Face Database (http://www.uk.research.att.com/facedatabase.html). We evaluate the assertions by using the publicly available FERET Face database (Phillips *et al.*, 1997). For the experiment, we randomly selected a subset of 600 users, each having 4 essentially frontal images with variations in pose (i.e., within 15 angles rotation out of plane), scale and illumination. Many of these images were taken over an extended period, and are highly varied i.e., in terms of eyewear (absence and presence thereof) and illumination.

As the focus is on the efficacy with respect to genuine vs. imposter classification, it is important to incorporate pre-processing mechanisms that contribute to recognition robustness. To this end, we performed geometrical normalization in order to establish correspondence between face images to be compared. The procedure is based on automatic location of the eye positions, from which various parameters (i.e., rotation, scaling, and translation) are used to extract the central part of the face from the original dataset image. For the following experiments, all faces were subjected to DynaFace geometric normalization (Ngo *et al.*, 2004).

To generate the impostor distribution, the first MRP of each subject is matched against the first MRP of all other subjects, and the same matching process was repeated for subsequent MRPs, leading to $(600 \times 599)/2 \times 4 = 718,800$ impostor attempts. For the genuine distribution, each MRP of each subject is matched against all other MRPs of the same subject, leading to $3,600((3 \times 4)/2$ attempts of each subject $\times 600)$. For the pseudogenuine I distribution, we take the worst case where the impostors always manage to steal the genuine token. In other words, only a set of PRN is mixed with all the facial images and the matching is performed according to the impostor match described above. Pseudogenuine II distribution is generated by taking other biometrics features from the data set mixed with the corresponding imposter PRN (imposter's own token). Besides that, PCA and PCAMRP-m denote eigenface and MRP, respectively, with m feature length. Note that the feature length of PCA, n is 110 for this experiment. The experimental data is acquired for MRP with lengths 20, 40, 60, 80, and 100.

18.6.2 *Performance evaluation*

From Figs. 18.2(a) and 18.2(b), the genuine distribution's mean and standard deviation of PCAMRP-m are identical to PCA at $m = 100$. This suggests that the genuine distributions of MRP are preserved when $m \approx n$. On the contrary, the large deviation in the genuine's means and standard deviations for small m, like $m = 20$ indicates the distortion as discussed in Sec. 18.3.

On the other hand, the experimental values of the impostor's and pseudogenuine II's mean are packed around theoretical mean of 1 regardless of m (Fig. 18.2(c)). The empirical values of the impostor's standard deviation for various m are also tightly tagged to the theoretical value, $\sqrt{1/m}$ and closely followed by the pseudogenuine II's standard deviation, as indicated in Fig. 18.2(d). The observation leads to the conclusion that the impostor and the pseudogenuine II distribution of MRP is independent to the feature extractor, and it solely rely on the MRP

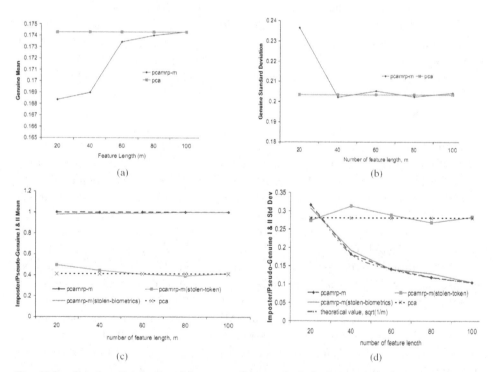

Fig. 18.2. Genuine distribution (a) means, (b) standard deviation variations and imposter distribution, (c) means, and (d) standard deviation variations according to MRP feature length, m (Teoh and Chong, 2007).

bitlength, m. This implies that the amplification of the interclass variation (the impostor/pseudogenuine II distribution) of MRP is controllable as long as $m < n$.

For the stolen-token scenario, we see that the pseudogenuine I distribution's mean is very close to PCA and the $\sqrt{1/m}$ rule is destroyed in standard deviation as depicted in Figs. 18.2(c) and 18.2(d). This vindicated the inference described in Sec. 3.2–the performance maintains the same in the feature vector level (EER = 31.23%), which is one of the important requirements in cancellable biometrics formulation.

Figure 18.3 illustrates the genuine vs. imposter and genuine vs. pseudogenuine I distributions of PCA and their MRP counterparts, respectively. We observe that the genuine and imposter distributions of PCA are highly similar to their corresponding MRP's genuine and pseudogenuine I distributions, respectively, with slightly small m compared to n ($m = 100, n = 110$ in the experiments).

From the above discussion, we observed that MRP fulfills the requirement of cancellable biometrics in term of performance, even in stolen-token scenario whereby the performance is retained as at feature vector level. In practice usage, we should set the system threshold t, which is used to decide the acceptance/rejection of the users according to the feature level performance (or stolen-token performance profile), instead of other scenarios. Nevertheless, recall that our results to be an important contribution to help preserve the privacy of the biometrics data and enable the enrolled template to be replaced in the event of template compromise.

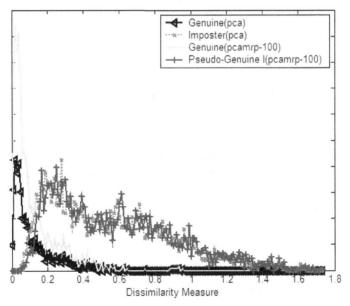

Fig. 18.3. Genuines, imposters for PCA and pseudogenuine I distributions and PCAMRP-100 (Teoh and Chong, 2007).

In one implementation scenario, an MRP feature can be stored on an off-line token or centered database during enrollment, and then used as reference for user authentication. If the token is stolen or lost, it can be simply reenrolled using another PRN sequence to produce a refreshed template. The adopted PRN sequence is generated using a seed from a tamper-proof physical device (USB token or smartcard), which can be its serial number. Note that PRN sequence is unique if they are generated from different seeds. During the verification stage, the biometrics feature is mixed with the legitimate PRN and the resulting MRP template is compared with the enrolled template. However, more secure two-factor MRP deployment can be done by using challenge-response and secret-sharing techniques or some cryptographic protocols such as the extension of the Diffie-Hellman protocol, Schnorr signature, and Zheng signcryption protocols, as reported in Goh and Ngo (2003).

The MRP is indeed not restricted to the user-specific PRN, but also can apply in common PRN setting. In this formulation, we use one set of PRN to conceal all biometrics feature to eliminate the stolen-token concern and ready to apply in the identification configuration. However, it would be susceptible to an attack which enables recovery of the biometrics feature through multiple extraction of the MRP template.

One may argue that the PRN overpowers the biometrics in the MRP formulation and resulting biometrics role is nullified. However, we content both components (PRN + biometrics) play equally important roles in MRP. For instance, if the PRN overtakes biometrics, the most apparent effect is the zero mean and standard deviation occurrences in the genuine distribution. Furthermore, without the presence of PRN, sole biometrics suffers from nonrevocable and privacy invasion issues, which are the primary concerns of the cancellable biometrics, whilst sole token usage is susceptible to repudiation.

18.7 Binarization of Multiple Random Projections

In this section, we present the extensions of MRP, namely quantized MRP (Teoh et al., 2006) and $2^\wedge N$ quantized MRP (Teoh et al., 2007) which resulting in bit string representation, **b**. Despite of the primary motivation of biometric binarization is for privacy protection, it also merit fast matching and compressed storage, facilitating a variety of applications utilizing low-cost storage media. Furthermore, it is a critical immediate stage in generating biometric private key for cryptographic keys applications (Teoh and Toh, 2008).

18.7.1 *Quantized multiple random projections*

MRP can be easily binarized by reformulating Eq. (18.1) with

$$\mathbf{b} = \text{Sig}(\mathbf{R}\mathbf{x} - \tau) \tag{18.14}$$

where Sig($\cdot$) is defined as a signum function and τ is a preset threshold, which is normally set to $\tau = 0$.

For quantized MRP, RP is quantized to binary bit string by thresholding τ such that on average 50% of the projections have absolute value greater than τ; while the remaining 50% have absolute value less than τ. Equation (18.13) only applies to a user who holds $\mathbf{R}$ (the user-specific random vectors), and thus the formulation can be extended to

$$\mathbf{b}^k = \text{Sig}(\mathbf{R}^k \mathbf{x}^k - \tau) \quad \text{with } k = 1, \ldots, g \tag{18.15}$$

where g is the total number of users k in the system.

Since quantized MRP is a bit string thus the matching is done in hamming metric, the genuine distribution of quantized MRP could not be identical (in terms of its mean and standard deviation) to the genuine distribution of $\mathbf{x}$ as discussed in Sec. 5.2 due to the loss of information during the quantization process. Nonetheless, the deviation is not significant.

As for imposter distribution, we conceive quantized MRP as the failure of a test of statistical independence, similar to the prescription on IrisCode described in Daugman *et al.* (Daugman, 2003). This test is statistically inclined to succeed when templates computed from different individuals are compared, and correspondingly to fail when templates of the same individual are compared. The statistical property of g quantized MRP, which are constructed using uncorrelated and distinctive $\mathbf{R}^k$, is the outcome of a Bernoulli trial. Therefore, the impostor distribution corresponds to a binomial distribution having mean hamming distance (HD), $d_{\text{HD}} = 0.5$, and degree of freedom, $\nu = m$, the length of $\mathbf{b}$

$$f(x) = \frac{\gamma!}{\lambda!(\gamma - \lambda)!} p^\lambda (1 - p)^{(\gamma - \lambda)} \tag{18.16}$$

with expectation $= p$ and standard deviation $= \sqrt{\frac{p(1-p)}{m}}$ where $x = \lambda/\gamma$ is the outcome fraction of ν Bernoulli trials and $p = 0.5$. In our case, x is the HD, the fraction of bits that happens to agree when two different quantized MRP from two different individuals are compared. This implies that the impostor distribution will be centered at 0.5, and the standard deviation will decrease as m increases to yield a steeper slope as shown in Fig. 18.4.

As illustrated in Fig. 18.5, the impostor distribution is shifted to the right and centered at 0.5; while the standard deviation (the impostor distribution profile) shrinks according to $0.5/\sqrt{m}$. Conversely, when the token is stolen, it means that a different $\mathbf{x}^k$ is projected onto the single random subspace, $\mathbf{R}$. It is obvious that the impostor (*pseudogenuine type I* hereafter) distribution will revert to its original state (or become poorer due to the quantization process) as the pairwise distances are only preserved to a certain extent, as indicated in Fig. 18.4. Again, this is only true for $m \approx n$, where n is biometrics feature dimension. On the other hand, for the stolen-biometrics scenario, the net effect

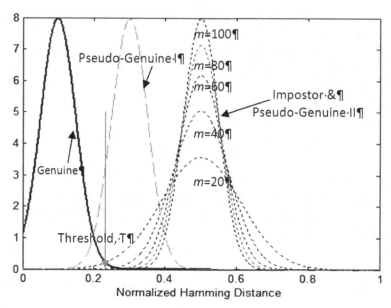

Fig. 18.4. Theoretical genuine, impostor, pseudogenuine type I and II distributions for quantized MRP.

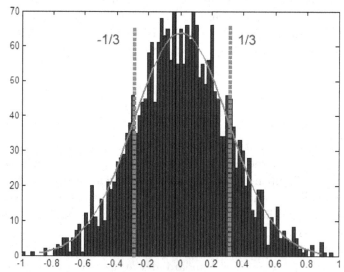

Fig. 18.5. Distribution of v_i is close to $N(0, 1/3^2)$. The red line represents $N(0, 1/3^2)$ (Teoh *et al.*, 2009).

is essentially equivalent to projection of the compromised biometrics features onto multiple random subspaces, and hence the impostor distribution (*pseudogenuine type II* hereafter) is expected to peak at 0.5 while its standard deviation would be $0.5/\sqrt{m}$.

The non-invertibility property of quantized MRP is inherited from MRP as discussed in Sec. 5.3, but the difficulty of inversion is aggravated by means of bit string representation. This is because the conversion of the real-valued random projection is a lossy discretization step which is not easily inverted.

18.7.2 $2^{\wedge}N$ *quantized multiple random projections*

The performance of quantized MRP in stolen-token scenario is often poorer than its original counterpart due to high loss of information when transforming from real to binary space. This is because as shown in early paragraph in Sec. 18.6.1, the discretization method is just a simple binary thresholding scheme. In order to enhance the distinguishability of random projected features, $\mathbf{v} = \mathbf{R}\mathbf{x}$ such that each transformed feature is discernible to separate the genuine user from potential impostor users, we propose to transform the random projection features, $\mathbf{v} = v_i | i = 1, \ldots, m$ such that each transformed feature is discernible to separate the genuine user from potential impostor users. Specifically, we transform v_i from the real into the index space and convert the resultant indices to gray code. We assume that v_i is distributed according to normal distribution, $v_i \sim N(0, 1/3^2)$ and the element values fall within twice of user-dependent standard deviation from the mean value. The feature element space is then divided into 2^N segments by adjusting the user-dependent standard deviation, σ_{ij}. The $v_i \sim N(0, 1/3^2)$ assumption is verified by using 2400 samples of $\mathbf{v}$ which described in Sec. 6.1. This leads to a distribution of $\{\bar{\mathbf{v}} = \frac{1}{m} \sum_{i=1}^{k} \mathbf{v}_i^k | k = 1, \ldots, 2400\}$ with mean and standard deviation being $0.0006 \approx 0$ and 0.29, respectively. As shown in Fig. 18.5, the histogram distribution closely approaches $N(0, 1/3^2)$.

The implementation is outlined below:

(1) At enrolment, we compute the standard deviation of v_i of user j, $\sigma_{ij} = \sqrt{\frac{1}{r} \sum_{k=1}^{r} (v_{ijk} - \bar{v}_{ij})^2}$, $i = 1, \ldots, m$ where r is the number of training samples and $\bar{v}_{ij}$ is the mean of v_{ij}.

(2) For a user j, $\mathbf{v}'$s feature space with range $[LR]$ is divided into 2^w segments where w denotes the segment width. In this case, L and R are the left and right boundaries of entire feature space and they take the values $-\pi$ and π, respectively, due to the observation that $v_i \sim N(0, 1/9)$. The corresponding segment width of v_{ij} is defined as $w_{ij} = \frac{R-L}{2^{N_{ij}}}$ where $N_{ij} \in Z^+$. To determine the most suitable w_{ij} that fits to v_{ij}, N_{ij}^* can be obtained by minimizing the following cost function

$$N_{ij}^* = \arg \min_{N_{ij}} \left(\frac{R - L}{2^{N_{ij}}} - 2\sigma_{ij} \right) \tag{18.17}$$

After that, $\mathbf{N}^* = \{N_{ij}^* | i = 1, \ldots, p\}$ of user j is stored. Figure 18.6 illustrates the idea how to determine N_{ij}^* based on the cost function in Eq. (18.17).

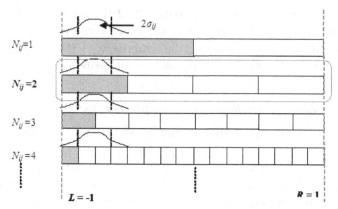

Fig. 18.6.   The illustration shows how to select a segment width which is best to describe the inner-product mixing feature, v_i of user j. From the above example, $N_{ij}^* = 2$ gives the smallest error to Eq. (18.17) (Teoh $et\ al.$, 2009).

(3) At verification, given a fresh $\mathbf{v}_j$ and the corresponding $\mathbf{N}_j^*$, the $genuine\ segment$ $index\ d_{ij}$ can be obtained from $d_{ij} = [(\frac{v_{ij}-L}{R-L})2^{N_{ij}^*}]$. Its binary representation of v_{ij} is rendered by gray coding, $b_{ij} = \text{gray}(d_{ij})$. The reason for using gray coding is to enable each v_{ij} provides multiple bits instead of one bit. The number of bits is determined by N_{ij}^*. Therefore, the resultant bit string with length $\nu_j = \sum_{i=1}^m N_{ij}^*$ can be generated by cascading all gray-encoded indices of genuine segments from the m-dimensional $\mathbf{v}_j$. Here, the maximum values of N_{ij}^* is arbitrarily limited to 10 to avoid too many bits used for one representative.

The non-invertibility property of $2^\wedge N$ quantized MRP lies in two important dispositions: (1) irreversible random projection, this was elaborated in Sec. 5.3 and (2) transformation from real-valued biometric feature to index space and finally to binary bit strings. The noninvertible property of the latter can be proved as follows: let the discretization process be defined in term of a composition function, $g \circ h$ where $g : (-1, 1)^m \rightarrow Z_{2^N}^m$ and $h : Z_{2^N}^m \rightarrow \{0, 1\}^\nu$ with $\nu > m$. Since g involved a transformation from real-to-index space, information will be lost. In particular, the continuous to discrete entropy lost is about $\sum_i \log(2^{N_i^*})$ based on individual $\mathbf{N}^*$ (Cover and Thomas, 1991). Hence, the $2^\wedge N$ quantized MRP is irreversible.

The overall effect of $2^\wedge N$ quantized MRP is a non-invertibility transformation based on the product principle of Shannon (Cover and Thomas, 1991), which stated the systematic cascading of different types of ciphers in a single cryptosystems will increase the cipher strength provided that the product ciphers are associative but not commutative. We let individual inner-product mixing be defined as f: $\mathfrak{R}^p \times \mathfrak{R}^p \rightarrow (-1, 1)^m$ and let discretization be $k : (-1, 1)^m \rightarrow \{0, 1\}^\nu$ with $\nu > m$. Obviously, $f \circ k$ is associative but not commutative since the domain and range cannot be interchanged. Since f and k are noninvertible and due to the product principle, $f \circ k$ is noninvertible.

18.7.3 *Comparisons*

In this section, we compare the performance of MRP, quantized MRP, and $2^\wedge N$ quantized MRP in legitimate, stolen-token, and stolen-biometrics scenarios. In order to assess the performances systematically, we use equal error rate (EER) for fair comparisons. The genuine vs. imposter distributions and the genuine vs. pseudogenuine I and II distributions enable us to calculate the EER for the legimate-token, stolen-token, and stolen-biometrics scenarios. However, since stolen-biometrics and legitimate-token scenarios are identical, we omit the stolen-biometrics for the sake of simplicity. For every experiment, we repeat the same process 20 times and the results are averaged to reduce the statistical frustration caused by the different set of random numbers.

From Fig. 18.7, we notice that MRP and both extension of MRPs are performed well in legitimate scenario where near-zero EER can be attained. Among the three, $2^\wedge N$-quantized MRP outperformed the others and followed by MRP and quantized MRP. On the others hand, $2^\wedge N$-quantized MRP still performs the best in stolen-token scenario as its complex discretization mechanism alleviates the loss of information while MRP reverts back to the original technique i.e., PCA. The quantized MRP performs the worst as expected due to loss of information.

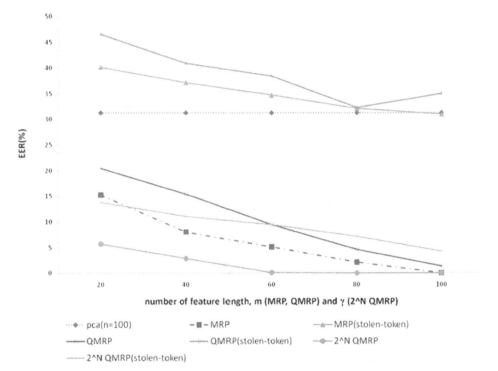

Fig. 18.7.   The performance comparisons for PCA and their MRP counterparts genuine-token, stolen-token, and stolen-biometrics scenarios.

Table 18.1:   The comparisons of MRP, quantized MRP, and $2^{\wedge}N$-quantized MRP

Techniques	MRP	Quantized MRP	$2^{\wedge}$N-Quantized MRP
Metric space	Real (normalized inner product)	Binary (normalized hamming distance)	Binary (normalized hamming distance)
Performance in legitimate-token/stolen-biometrics scenario	• Genuine distribution is approximately preserved as its original counterpart. • Imposter distribution peaks at 1 with variance $1/m$. • The performance is generally better than its original counterpart.	• Genuine distribution is deviated from its original counterpart. • Imposter distribution peaks at 0.5 with variance $0.25/m$. • The performance is generally better than its original counterpart.	The performance is generally much better than its original counterpart.
Performance in stolen-token scenario	• Genuine and imposter distributions are preserved. • The performance is similar to its original counterpart.	• Genuine and imposter distributions are deviated from its original counterpart. • The performance deteriorates in general.	The performance is generally much better than its original counterpart.
Noninvertibility	Weak	Moderate	Strong
Reusability	Good	Good	Good
Complexity	Low	Low	High

We summarize the characteristics of three techniques in Table. 18.1. In term of noninvertibility, it is obvious that $2^{\wedge}N$-quantized MRP is the strongest compared to quantized MRP and MRP as mentioned in Sec. 7.2.2. However, $2^{\wedge}N$-quantized MRP is relatively complex compared to the others.

18.8 Conclusion

In this chapter, we describe a cancellable biometrics technique known as MRP. MRP involves transformation of raw biometrics data into a low-dimension feature space representation, and subsequently reprojecting these user-specific feature vectors onto a sequence of random subspaces specified by the tokenized random vectors. The end result is a two-factor authenticator which integrates biometric data with token in a noninvertible manner, thereby protecting sensitive biometric data. MRP is cancellable via straightforward revocation and a refreshment of the token, thereby protecting against interception of biometric data or even physical fabrication of the biometric feature.

In terms of recognition performance, MRP also offers significant advantage, namely possibility of achieving zero error rates when the genuine tokens are used. This is accomplished through an ensemble of the random projections capable of preserving intraclass variations, while amplifying the interclass variations via a projection onto uncorrelated random subspaces. Performance of MRP reverts to the original state when the genuine token is stolen and used by the impostor to claim as the genuine user.

We also report two binarized MRPs, namely quantized MRP and $2^\wedge N$-quantized MRP. This enables binarized MRPs to be used as cryptographic keys, thereby addressing application scenarios beyond identity verification.

Acknowledgment

This work was supported by the Korea Science and Engineering Foundation (KOSEF) through the Biometrics Engineering Research Center (BERC) at Yonsei University. (Grant Number: R112002105080020).

References

Ang, R., Rei, S. N., and McAven, L. Cancelable key-based fingerprint templates, in *Proc. 10th Australasian Conference on Information Security and Privacy (ACISP 2005)* (Brisbane, Australia), pp. 242–252, 2005.

Bolle, R. M., Connel, J. H., and Ratha, N. K. Biometrics perils and patches, *Pattern Recognition* **35**, 2727–2738, 2002.

Boult, T. Robust distance measures for face-recognition supporting revocable biometrics token, in *Proc. 7th Int. Conf. on Automatic Face and Gesture Recognition*, pp. 560–566, 2006.

Chung, Y. W., Moon, D., Lee, S. J., Jung, S. H., Kim, T. H., and Ahn, D. S. Automatic alignment of fingerprint features for fuzzy fingerprint vault, in *Proc. First SKLOIS Conference on Information Security and Cryptology, CISC 2005, LNCS 3822*, pp. 358–369, 2005.

Clancy, T. C., Kiyavashand, N., and Lin, D. J. Secure smartcard-based fingerprint authentication, in *Proc. ACM SIGMM 2993 Multimedia, Biometrics Methods & Applications Workshop*, pp. 45–52, 2003.

Cover, T. M. and Thomas, J. A. *Elements of Information Theory* (JohnWiley & Sons, New York), 1991.

Daugman, J. The important of being random: Statistical principles of iris recognition, *Pattern Recognition* **36**, 279–291, 2003.

Davida, G., Frankel, Y., and Matt., B. J. On enabling secure applications through off-line biometrics identification, in *Proceeding Symposium on Privacy and Security*, pp. 148–157, 1998.

Demmel, J. W. and Higham, N. J. Improved error bounds for underdetermineded system solvers, Technical Report CS-90-113, Computer Science Department, University of Tennessee, Knoxville, TN, 1990.

Goh, A. and Ngo, C. L. D. Computation of cryptographic keys from face biometrics, in *Proc., LNCS, 2828*, pp. 1–13, 2003.

Hao, F., Anderson, R., and Daugman, J. Combining crypto with biometrics effectively, *IEEE Trans. Comput.* **55**, 9, 1081–1088, 2006.

Hecht-Nielsen, R. *Context vectors: general purpose approximate meaning representations self-organized from raw data* (Imitating Life), pp. 43–56, 1994.

Johnson, W. B. and Lindenstrauss, J. Extension of lipschitz mapping into a hilbert space, in *Proc. Amer. Math. Soc. Conf. in Modern Analysis and Probability* (Providence, R.I.), pp. 189–206, 1984.

Juels, A. and Sudan, M. A fuzzy vault scheme, in *Proc. ACM Conference on Computer and Communications Security*, pp. 408–, 2002.

Juels, A. and Wattenberg, M. A. Fuzzy commitment scheme, in *Proc. ACM Conference on Computer and Communications Security*, pp. 28–36, 1999.

Kaski, S. Dimensionality reduction by random mapping, in *Proc. Int. Joint Conf. on Neural Networks*, pp. 1:413–418, 1998.

Linnartz, J. P. and Tuyls, P. New shielding functions to enhance privacy and prevent misuse of biometric templates, in *Proc. 4th Int. Conf. on Audio- and Video-Based Biometric Person Authentication. LNCS 2688*, pp. 393–402, 2003.

Liu, K., Kargupta, H., and Ryan, J. Random projection-based multiplicative data perturbation for privacy preserving distributed data mining, *IEEE Trans. Knowledge Data Engineering* **18**, 1, 92–106, 2006.

Ngo, C. L. D., Goh, A., and Teoh, A. B. J. Front-view facial feature extraction using dynamic symmetry, Technical report, Multimedia University, 2004.

Phillips, P., Moon, H., Rauss, P., and Rizvi, S. The feret database and evaluation methodology for face recognition algorithms, in *Proc. IEEE Conf on Computer Vision and Pattern Recognition*, pp. 137–143, 1997.

Ratha, N., Connell, J., and Bolle, R. M. Enhancing security and privacy in biometrics-based authentication systems, *IBM Syst. J.* **40**, 3, 614–634, 2001.

Ratha, N. K., Chikkerur, S., Connell, J. H., and Bolle, R. M. Generating cancelable fingerprint templates, *IEEE Trans. Pattern Anal. Machine Intelligence* **29**, 4, 561–572, 2007.

Savvides, M., Kumar, B. V., and Khosla, P. K. Cancelable biometrics filters for face recognition, in *Proc. Int. Conf. of Pattern Recognition*, pp. 3:922–925, 2004.

Soutar, C., Roberge, D., Stoianov, A. R., Gilroy and Kumar, B. V. Biometrics Encryption, in R. Nichols (ed.), *ICSA Guide to Cryptography* (McGraw-Hill, New York), pp. 649–675, 1999.

Sutcu, Y., Sencar, H. T., and Memon, N. A secure biometric authentication scheme based on robust hashing, in *Proc. the 7th Workshop on Multimedia and Security* (New York, USA), pp. 111–116, 2005.

Teoh, A. B. J. and Chong, T. Y. Cancellable biometrics realization with multispace random projections, *IEEE Trans. SMC Part B — Special Issue on Recent Advances in Biometrics Systems* **37**, 5, 1096–1106, 2007.

Teoh, A. B. J., Goh, A., and Ngo., D. C. L. Random multispace quantisation as an analytic mechanism for biohashing of biometric and random identity inputs, *IEEE Trans. Pattern Anal. Machine Intelligence* **28**, 12, 1892–1901, 2006.

Teoh, A. B. J. and Toh, K.-A. Secure biometric-key generation with biometric helper, in *Proc. 3rd IEEE Conf. on Industrial Electronics and Applications (ICIEA 2008)* (Singapore), pp. 3–5, 2008.

Teoh, A. B. J., Toh, K.-A., and Yip, W. K. 2^n discretisation of biophasor in cancellable biometrics, in *Proc. Int. Conf. on Biometrics, LNCS 4642*, pp. 435–444, 2007.

Teoh, A. B. J., Yip, W., and Toh, K. Cancellable biometrics and user-dependent multi-state discretization in biohash, *Pattern Anal. Appli.*, pp. –, 2009.

Turk, M. and Pentland, A. Eigenfaces for recognition, *J. Cognitive Neuroscience* **13**, 1, 71–86, 1991.

Tuyls, P., Akkermans, A., Kevenaar, T., Schrijen, G. J., Bazen, A., and Veldhuis, R. Practical biometric template protection system based on reliable components, in *Proc. 5th Int. Conf. on Audio- and Video-Based Biometric Person Authentication. LNCS 3546*, pp. 436–446, 2005.

Yang, S. and Verbauwhede, I. Automatic secure fingerprint verification system based on fuzzy vault scheme, in *Proc. IEEE Int. Conf. Acoustics, Speech, and Signal Processing (ICASSP 2005)*, pp. 609–612, 2005.

Chapter 19

BIOMETRIC AUTHENTICATION FOR MOBILE COMPUTING APPLICATIONS

Fengling Han[*,‡], Jiankun Hu[*,§], and Ramamohanarao Kotagiri[†,¶]

School of Computer Science and Information Technology
Royal Melbourne Institute of Technology, VIC 3001 Australia
†*Department of Computer Science and Software Engineering*
University of Melbourne, Australia
‡*fengling.han@rmit.edu.au*
§*jiankun@cs.rmit.edu.au*
¶*kotagiri@unimelb.edu.au*

19.1 Introduction

Today's mobile devices offer many benefits to enterprises in the sense of extending desktop computing systems to mobile devices (Whitepaper, 2006). These devices have become very popular because of their convenience and portability, and are available anytime and anywhere.

Provision of fully available and reliable services is a main target for any enterprise. In mobile computing applications, a reliable access to the mobile devices and protection of sensitive information over the air are paramount. Biometrics can help to authenticate a genuine user. It will play an imperative role in the next generation m-commerce services. This chapter introduces the biometric authentication schemes for the mobile computing applications.

19.2 Introduction to Mobile Computing and Mobile Commerce

Mobile computing devices include cellular/mobile telephones, laptops, personal digital assistants (PDAs), as well as mobile electronic devices that are capable of storing, processing, displaying, and communicating. Mobile computing is one of the fastest growing sectors. This section introduces the development of mobile communication and mobile commerce.

19.2.1 *The development of mobile communication*

The first generation of wireless mobile communication is based on analog signaling, which is designed for voice instead of data. The second generation (2G) of the wireless mobile networks is built mainly to provide voice services to subscribers, which is based on low-band digital data signaling. 2G systems use digital multiple access technology, such as TDMA (time division multiple access) and CDMA (code division multiple access). Global system for mobile communications, or GSM, uses TDMA technology to support multiple users. It can handle some data capabilities such as fax and short message service at a data rate of up to 9.6 to 14.4 kbps. The move into the 2.5G begins with general packet radio service (GPRS). 2.5G systems enable data speed of up to 115 to 384 kbps. The third generation (3G) wireless technology, also known as the universal mobile telecommunication system (UTMS), can meet the requirements of transmission of video images. 3G systems use a completely new radio access technology based on wideband CDMA which provide high levels of bandwidth. It can provide 144 kpbs for full mobility applications, 384 kbps for limited mobility applications in macro- and microcellular environments, and 2 Mbps for low-mobility applications in micro- and pico-cellular environments (Umar, 2004).

Mobile communications technology has evolved amazingly during the last dozen years to meet a very demanding market. In the year of 2006, Pyramid Research published a report of mobile subscriber growth and forecast by region between the year of 2001 and 2010 (Pyramid Research, 2007) as shown in Fig. 19.1. Currently, there are over 3.5 billion mobile phones in use across the globe; this figure is set to double in the next decade. Further, another forecast shows that the increasing trend will peak in the following years as shown in Fig. 19.2 (Wireless Week, 2007).

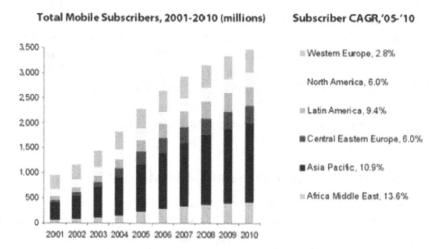

Fig. 19.1.   Mobile subscriber growth and forecast 2001–2010 (Pyramid Research, 2007).
Source: Pyramid Research Mobile Communications Forecasts, 1Q2006.

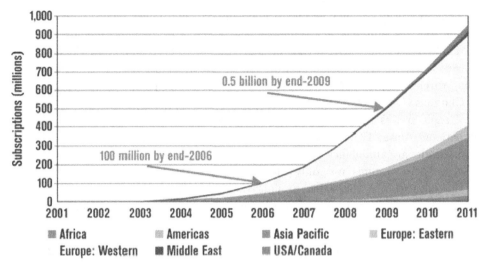

Fig. 19.2.   Mobile subscriber growth and forecast 2001–2011 (Wireless Week, 2007).

19.2.2 *Mobile commerce (m-commerce)*

Mobile commerce (m-commerce) is the next generation of e-commerce. It can be defined as the conduct of business transactions over the Internet-enabled wireless devices (Grami and Schell, 2004). Current m-commerce is mainly in healthcare, finance, and government service domains, which aim at achieving a better quality of service in mobile environment. These applications will be introduced in the following sections.

19.2.2.1 *Mobile healthcare*

Mobile and ubiquitous healthcare technologies (m-healthcare and u-healthcare) typically refers to portable devices with the capability to create, store, retrieve, and transmit data in real time between end users for the purpose of improving patient safety and quality of care (Istepanian *et al.*, 2005). This represents the evolution of e-healthcare systems from traditional desktop telemedicine platforms to wireless and mobile configurations.

Time and space constitute barriers between healthcare providers and their patients, and among healthcare providers. Telemedicine, especially m-healthcare technologies have presented themselves as a powerful tool to break the barriers (Tachakra *et al.*, 2003) which will eventually contribute to improving the quality of healthcare for everyone (Xiao and Chen, 2008). Following are three examples that can illustrate the benefits of the m-healthcare technology:

Example 1   Ambulance emergency services (Chu and Ganz, 2005; Xiao and Chen, 2008).

Ambulance emergency service system in Xiao and Chen (2008) consists of a mobile unit for ambulance installation and a receiving base station for hospital Intranet connection. The real-time patient vital signs data, audio and video images of care activities from inside an ambulance are transmitted to a trauma center using wireless digital cellular communications and in-hospital Intranet technology. In Chu and Ganz (2005), the mobile device enables transmitting real-time patient vital signs (refers to a set of readings that can express the basic health status of patients) data, ECG waveform, medical images, and real-time video images from inside an ambulance over a 3G wireless link and Internet to a trauma center. These systems not only allows the hospital to prepare for the arrival of the patient, but they also provide the emergency medical technicians with specialist's advice before arriving which can improve the patient's chance for a full recovery.

Example 2 On-line access and transmit the medical information (Montoni *et al.*, 2002; Tachakra *et al.*, 2003).

Most of the medical records are stored in digital format. In turn, digital transmission and exchange of medical information has become possible. Online transmission of patient data, X-ray, ECG, microscopic images, and vital parameters of a patient to other parts of the world will become increasingly common. It can be used in circumstances as a monitoring device for individual who suffer from chronic disease or a service for providing remote consultation to physicians by allowing medical consultations to be done independent of the local infrastructure. This technology can also be used to conduct direct simultaneous video conferencing between different sites, to consult remote requests, and to teach in mobile telemedicine community. It can alleviate the shortage of qualified doctors, and poor health coverage in rural areas.

Example 3 Post-trauma care and nursing home, elderly person surveillance (Hackney, 2005; Xiao and Chen, 2008).

Cardiovascular disease and stroke are the world's leading causes of death. Many of these deaths can be prevented by reliable monitoring and response systems. In addition, supervision remotely of patients in post-trauma care and elderly persons by healthcare professionals, are one of the best way to improve their life expectancy and the quality of living. Wearable or handheld devices can be used in home healthcare, for example, to fight diabetes (Xiao and Chen, 2008) or cardiac monitoring (Hackney, 2005). In these scenarios, data collection is either done by patients or mobile health clinicians which tours the communities, and specialists in central hospitals help to analyze the data, provide supervised autonomy and make therapeutic decisions.

M-healthcare systems allow patients to have frequent medical consultations without the need to travel to see their doctors. From the above examples, the potential benefits of integrating Internet and mobile technology can be summarized as follows (Chu and Ganz, 2005):

(1) It provides rapid response to critical medical care regardless of geographic barriers. Therefore, severely injured patients can be treated locally, and access to a specialist wirelessly.
(2) Flexible and rapid access to expert opinion and advice at the point of care without delay, and better management of medical resources.
(3) Interactive medical consultation environment and communication links of medical images, video data over Internet links in complete mobility and in global coverage and connectivity.
(4) In rural and underserved areas, healthcare could be greatly improved using these technologies.
(5) Normally local hospitals may suffer from less qualified medical and nursing staff, these technologies will help in managing seriously ill patients.

Electronic transmission of medical records must follow ensure security and privacy governed by laws (Hu *et al.*, 2009; Lee *et al.*, 2008). In addition, efficient and secure transmission large volume of digital medical images is a very challenging issue (Hu and Han, 2009).

19.2.2.2 *Mobile banking and mobile payment*

Finance-related services offered by employing mobile telecommunication technologies are often referred to as "Mobile financial services" (MFS). They can be divided into two categories: "Mobile payment" and "Mobile banking" (Tiwari *et al.*, 2006). Mobile payment (m-payment) addresses retail payment transactions such as micropayments. These technologies provide the ability to pay for products, vending, ticketing, mobile content service, and games or gambling (Ciccarelli *et al.*, 2007). Mobile banking (m-banking) is a term used for performing balance checks, account transactions, payments, funds transfer etc. via a mobile device such as a mobile phone (Owens and Anna, 2006). Mobile banking presents an opportunity for banks to retain their existing technology-savvy customer base by offering value-added, innovative services, and to attract new customers from corresponding sections of the society (Tiwari *et al.*, 2006).

Australia's largest bank, Commonwealth Bank of Australia (CBA) launched a mobile banking service with Vodafone as early as November 1999. But it was shut down in 2005 after a lukewarm response (Sharma, 2008). From 2003 to 2007, banks across the globe have invested billions of dollars to build sophisticated Internet banking capabilities (Owens and Anna, 2006). Australia and New Zealand Bank (ANZ) launched first mobile phone banking service on 29th January 2008 (Rellos, 2008). One year later, all the big four banks in Australia, CBA, Westpac, National Australia Bank (NAB), Australia and New Zealand Bank (ANZ), as well as some other banks, have begun to offer some form of mobile banking services for their customers.

Bank transactions are predominately text, numeric, and tables based and like, which are not likely to consume a huge amount of bandwidth (Tiwari *et al.*, 2006). Financial institutions use a variety of mobile media channels including short message service (SMS), mobile web, and mobile client applications. M-banking through SMS-based service would require the lowest amount of effort in terms of cost and time. However, SMS is not considered secure. It requires the addition of full encryption, both on the handset and over the air (Mobile Marketing Association, 2009). A hybrid solution: combination of SMS with mobile web, SMS with a mobile client application exhibits expanding functionality and increasing security to customers (Mobile Marketing Association, 2009).

The dual slot solution is used for m-payment (Sadeh, 2002) to address the security issue. In this technology, subscriber identity module (SIM) card is used to identify the mobile device, a second card, such as wireless identity module (WIM) issued by bank, credit card company, or a third party, integrated within a mobile phone.

19.2.2.3 *Mobile government*

E-government is about using information and communication technologies (ICTs) to improve the activities of public sector organizations (Kumar and Sinha, 2007). E-government has in many cases boosted the capability of more efficient gathering and processing of data. ICTs in governmental organizations have reduced cost, redundancies, and errors significantly, thus speeding up the handling of services (Roggenkamp, 2004). Mobile government (m-government) will be the next inevitable direction of evolution of e-government. M-government can help make public information and government services available anytime and anywhere. Generally speaking, m-government has three levels of mobility (Kumar and Sinha, 2007):

(1) device mobility,
(2) user mobility, and
(3) service mobility.

Several examples of m-government are (Kumar and Sinha, 2007):

Example 4 Police officers are likely to use a PDA or a laptop connected to the Internet wirelessly. When officers spot a suspicious vehicle, they can search the databases immediately which can provide information on who owns the vehicle, whether it has been reported stolen or has been reported at a crime scene, and whether the owner is in the wanted list etc.

Example 5 Citizens can update their electoral information, such as the parliamentary and state constituencies where they are to vote, using SMS.

Alternatively, citizens can request that real-time information is sent to their mobile phone or PDA as an e-mail or text message.

Example 6 California state government in the United States has established a Web page where citizens can register to receive wireless PDA and cell phone notification services for energy alerts, lottery results, traffic updates, and articles from the governor's press room.

For the m-government, device and service mobility is of big concern in order to fulfill the proposition of delivering the right thing at the right time and right place to the right person (Roggenkamp, 2004).

19.3 Access Control and Biometric Authentication in M-commerce

Mobile service can be available anywhere and anytime that addresses the convenience and reduces complexity. The portability of mobile devices is attractive but also increases the risk of exposing data to opponents. This section introduces the importance of access control and why biometric authentication is necessary in m-commerce.

19.3.1 *Access control in m-commerce*

Many portable devices such as smartphones and PDAs are lost every year. The risk of sensitive information falling into the wrong hands also increases and the data stored on the device may be of great value to competitors and criminals. These devices can store large amounts of sensitive data, which could cause harm if accessed by unauthorized users. Mobile devices also have the potential to provide unauthorized users with access to corporate networks and to introduce viruses and other harmful software into these networks (Aissi *et al.*, 2006).

In the preceding section, the application of m-healthcare was introduced. In m-healthcare applications, the patients' information should be obtained by healthcare professionals from any given location. Access to patient histories, pharmaceutical information, and medical resources with mobile devices can improve the quality of patient care. However, health information is inherently sensitive. United States law mandates that medical devices meet the privacy requirements of the 1996 Health Insurance Portability and Accountability Act (HIPAA). Therefore, keeping such sensitive information private is an important issue.

Access control is especially important when using mobile devices. The access control has three aspects (Whitepaper, 2006):

(1) Access to the device: Because the small size of mobile devices makes them susceptible to being lost or stolen, devices need to verify that the person attempting to access them is a legitimate user.
(2) Access to stored data: The storage cards that fit into the pocket PC's or smartphone's expansion slots heighten the concern that all this data can be

easily fallen into the wrong hands. The data stored on the device may be of value to competitors and criminals.

(3) Access to wireless networks: Wireless connectivity achieved through expansion cards, external jackets, or integrated wireless chips provides remote access to sensitive information stored on personal, local, and wide area networks. Security is needed at this point to prevent unauthorized access to information stored on these networks.

The importance of access control is to ensure that only people granted access to any of the component systems are those authorized to do so.

19.3.2 *Biometrics solution for control access remotely*

Access control is usually represented as authentication. Three different characteristics are normally used to authenticate someone's identity:

(1) Something you know, like a password or a personal identification number (PIN);
(2) Something you have, like a smart-card or a token; and
(3) Something you are, like behavioral or biological characteristics.

Password/PIN is a simple access control method. They are usually used to authenticate the user to control the initial access to the mobile devices. Experience shows that password/PIN is weak in the sense that they are often poorly chosen, such as their name or their date of birth, and that they are easy to forget. Biometrics has the character of uniqueness and unchanged, or acceptably changed, over the lifetime of the individual. Biometrics authenticate individuals based on what you are by using behavioral or biological characteristics rather than by what you have or what you know, which are believed to have a stronger level of authentication. Biometric authentication has been serving a wide range of commercial and government applications effectively (Wang *et al.*, 2007; Hou *et al.*, 2008; Lam *et al.*, 2009).

With the improvement of technology, biometrics, such as fingerprint, face, iris, and voice recognition, has been incorporated in some mobile devices. Figure 19.3 illustrates some methods of biometric authentication (MIS Biometrics, 2008).

The iris of each eye is different; even identical twins have different iris patterns. The iris remains constant over a person's lifetime. Built from elastic connective tissue, the iris is a very rich source of biometric data. Complex patterns include striations, rings, furrows, a corona, and freckles (Daugman, 1999). Iris recognition is currently claimed and perhaps widely believed to be the most accurate biometric, especially when it comes to false acceptance (FA) rates. It maintains stability of characteristic over a lifetime. However, gathering iris pattern requires much user cooperation or complex, expensive input devices (Bolle *et al.*, 2004). Iris recognition has been used as a mainstay technology for controlling access to highly secure government facilities (National Preparedness, 2002).

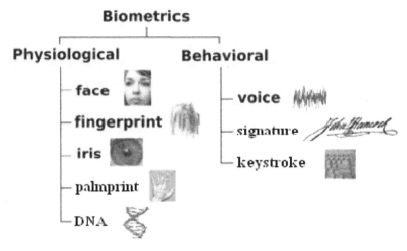

Fig. 19.3. The type of biometric authentication (MIS Biometrics, 2008).

Face recognition uses digital images of face, features such as eye sockets, cheekbones, and the side of the mouth (Vacca, 2007), comparing the live image against a reference template usually stored. One advantage is that it could be used to recognize people "passively," without their knowledge or cooperation (Bowyer, 2004). Face authentication suffers high false accept rate and high reject rate than other biometric technology because it can not distinguish identical siblings. Among many different biometric techniques, facial recognition may not be the most reliable and efficient but its great advantage is that it does not require aid from the test subject.[*]

Fingerprint recognition is one of the most used and familiar biometric methods. Most of the automatic fingerprint matching systems rely on ridge endings and ridge bifurcations, which are called minutiae. A minutia is usually described by its position (x, y coordinates) and the direction (θ) of the ridge. Federal Bureau of Investigation (FBI) in the United States claims that no two individuals can have more than eight common minutiae (Rerd, 2004). Fingerprint authentication has been proven to be high reliable and accurate, which appears to be the best technology to use today in mobile applications (Owens and Anna, 2006).

Voice recognition is a biometric process of validating a user's claimed identity using characteristics extracted from their voices. Successful voice recognition depends on background noise, handset/microphone and channel quality and the users' healthy condition (such as a cold or throat infection). In relation to other biometrics systems, the voice recognition technique is less expensive. It is, however, not the most perfect system. It is best to use voice recognition in conjunction with

---

[*]http://en.wikipedia.org/wiki/Facial_recognition_system

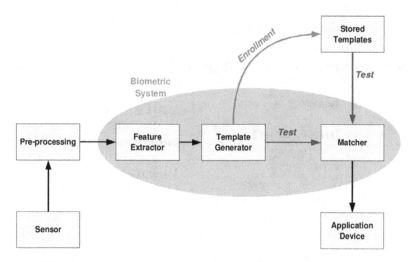

Fig. 19.4. Biometric authentication system (MIS Biometrics, 2008).

a more secure system such as fingerprint recognition (Fogie, 2005; Toh and Yau, 2004; Toh *et al.*, 2004; Toh and Yau, 2005; Shabeer and Suganthi, 2007).

19.3.3 *Biometric authentication in mobile systems*

Biometric authentication/verification systems are essentially pattern recognition systems. The main operations that a system can perform include enrollment and authentication/verification. Acquisition devices such as cameras and scanners are often used to capture (most of the time they are) images, then preprocess the images, followed by feature extraction. During the enrollment stage, multiple biometric samples from an individual are obtained and processed, then a template is stored somewhere (on a card or within a database or both). A vector of numbers or an image with particular properties is used to create a template. During the authentication/verification stage, a query biometric sample is detected, processed, and compared against a stored template. The matcher output is used for the decision whether the query template fits to a reference template. A biometric authentication system mainly comprises the following function units, which is shown in Fig. 19.4.

Currently, there is a number of fingerprint sensor- or camera-equipped mobile devices in market. In these applications, recognition sensor requires no additional hardware. Users register their own biometric (face or fingerprint) images to their mobile devices. The system will automatically detect the user and unlock the unit upon successful authentication. For the face recognition, a report shows that the identification process takes less than a second from snapping the photograph.[**]

It is noted that the driving force for incorporating biometrics in mobile computing is used as a supplementary to the current security measures, rather than

---

[**]Omron Corporation, (2008), http://www.japancorp.net/Article.asp?Art_ID=9494

replacement. It would be fraud prevention and not the emphasis on high security. Accuracy, reliability, acceptability, susceptibility to fraud, ease of enrollment, cost are the main issues when considering which biometrics to be deployed. Technically, the use of biometrics is entirely feasible in mobile applications but the mobile biometric template itself has become a critical issue of security (Hu *et al.*, 2008).

19.4 Security Issues in Mobile Computing Applications

A typical mobile network includes a network operator and mobile users. For m-commerce applications, usually an independent application service provider provides service to the mobile users via their mobile device (Tin *et al.*, 2004). Protecting mobile devices and services are two major concerns in such applications. Access control can protect access to the mobile devices while an infrastructure can guarantee the protection of services.

19.4.1 *Security vulnerabilities and security infrastructure in mobile systems*

There are fewer physical assets to protect in wireless computing environment; nor locked door on the air wave, so it is far easier to hack (Randall and Panos, 2002). Therefore, if connected to computers or communication networks, one must make sure: (1) to prevent attacks and unauthorized access to data, typically through various cryptographic techniques and (2) to detect these occurrences when they happen and take whatever steps are necessary to recover, minimize the damage, and prevent the same thing from happening again in the future (Yu *et al.*, 2008).

Further security vulnerabilities raised in m-commerce involve mobile devices and wireless communications. Take mobile banking as an example, the potential threats include (Mobile Marketing Association, 2009):

(1) Clone: copying the identity of one mobile phone to another which could give the hacker an access to the victim's financial account.
(2) Hijacking: taking control of a communication session between two entities, masquerade as one of them.
(3) Malicious code: software in the form of a virus, worm, or other malware, which is loaded to perform unauthorized process.
(4) Malicious software (Malware): software inserted covertly into system, with the intent of compromising the confidentiality, integrity or availability, or otherwise annoying or disrupting the victim.
(5) Man-in-the-middle attack: During the authentication, the attacker himself sits in between the claimant and the verifier and presents as the verifier to the claimant, and the claimant to the verifier.
(6) Phishing: tricking a victim into disclosing sensitive personal information or downloading malware through an e-mail or a malicious website.

(7) Redirecting: intercepting a communication session by substituting a fraudulent address or identity, potentially by using a man-in-the-middle attack.

(8) SMS phishing: using SMS to facilitate bogus requests for sensitive personal information.

(9) Spoofing: sending a network packet that appears coming from a source different from its actual source.

(10) Voice and phishing: tricking the victims into disclosing sensitive personal information through telephone communication.

Access control on a mobile device is one of the most important steps for enhancing the security. In the wireless m-commerce application, where communications rely on the open and public transmission media, some threats are more likely to occur, such as hijacking attack, man-in-the-middle attack, etc. Establishing a security infrastructure using a combination of following security services can protect the service:

(1) Authentication: verifying a user's identity, it can be one way or mutual.

(2) Confidentiality: protection of data from disclosure to an unauthorized person. Encryption is usually used.

(3) Authorization: verifying whether a user has the right to access to some protected resources.

(4) Nonrepudiation and Integrity: nonrepudiation can ensure that the sender and the receiver should not be able to deny the communication and the content of the massage later. Integrity is the assurance that data can not be changed or destroyed.

Another privacy issue is the location of a mobile user in mobile systems. In order to be able to establish communication links to mobile terminals, the terminals' positions need to be scanned and entered in corresponding registers. If a call is initiated, the current position of the mobile device is read from these registers and a connection to the appropriate base station is established. For the users of mobile services, this means that their location is permanently monitored as long as they carry a switched-on terminal with them. If the factual location does not correspond with the location given to a family member or employer, troubles may arise.

19.4.2 *Mobile network security*

All GSM (or 2G) devices have a special kind of smart card called a SIM card. The security functions of the GSM can be described as (Federrath, 1999):

(1) Access control by using the SIM card and PIN.

(2) Authentication of the users towards the network carrier and generation of a session key in order to prevent abuse.

(3) Encryption of communication on the radio interface, i.e., between mobile station and base station.

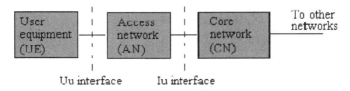

Fig. 19.5. Basic structure 3G/GSM architecture (Kasera and Narang, 2004).

(4) Concealing the users' identity on the radio interface, i.e., a temporary valid identity code (TMSI) is used to identify a mobile user.

The cryptographic algorithms deployed are based on symmetric cryptography, i.e., both the network carrier and the mobile user (more precisely, the user's SIM card) share a secret key K_i (unique for each user). All security parameters (encryption key, authentication data) are derived from K_i.

Lack of mutual authentication is a considerable vulnerability in GSM systems. The UTMS (or 3G) network is based on the same principles as that in GSM (2G) and GPRS (2.5G) networks, while 3G networks use a completely different air interface and modulation techniques compared with that of the 2G and 2.5G systems, which can provide mutual authentication. The basic structure of 3G architecture is as shown in Fig. 19.5:

(1) The user equipment (UE) is used by a subscriber/user to access network services. The UE includes two logical parts: The mobile equipment (ME) and the universal subscriber identity module (USIM).
(2) The access network (AN) performs functions required for the access of air interface.
(3) The core network (CN) provides various network features and services. It also performs other networking functions like mobility management, call control, switching, session management, routing, authentication, and equipment identification (Kasera and Narang, 2004).

Security management in 3G networks provides both access security and network security, which is as shown in Fig. 19.6. The security function includes (Kasera and Narang, 2004):

(1) User domain security: making ensure that only an authenticated user can gain access to a mobile station.
(2) Network access security includes:

   • Mutual authentication process based on a challenge-response protocol.
   • Data confidentiality and integrity: Generation of the ciphering key and integrity key to provide confidentiality and data integrity over the air interface.

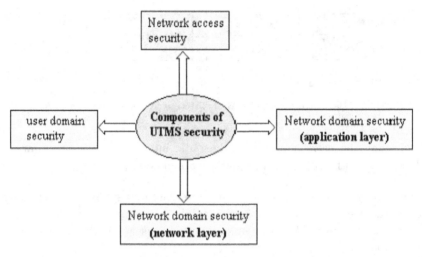

Fig. 19.6.   Basic functional blocks of 3G security (Kasera and Narang, 2004).

- User identity confidentiality: the user identity is kept confidential and that it cannot be eavesdropped on the radio access link by using cryptographic encryptions.

(3) Network domain security at the application layer and network layer is used for interdomain communication. It is assumed that the network for intradomain communication is secure.

3G communications can offer further security enhancements on the radio link, which supports integrity protection and mutual authentication (Kasera and Narang, 2004). The user identity is authenticated locally in the USIM with a PIN. Mutual authentication between USIM and the mobile operator (MO) is performed by a challenge and response protocol utilizing two pre-stored values. User and signaling data confidentiality is suggested but not mandatory. KASUMI is a block cipher used as the underlying crypto algorithm in the confidentiality (f8) and integrity algorithms (f9) for 3G mobile communications. The developed middleware supports most popular ciphers and hashes such as AES, DES, KASUMI, and SHA, as well as asymmetric operations such as RSA and PKI algorithms for signature and verification. Elliptic curve cryptography is also supported. For more discussions on the basic security concepts, interested readers are referred to (Hu et al., 2008).

19.5 Cryptographic Key Binding with Fingerprint Template

Implementation of security services can be done in several ways, such as cryptographic algorithms and key management techniques (Verschuren, 2002; Khadraoui and Herrmann, 2007). In modern mobile networks, network carrier and the mobile users share symmetric keys. Mobility management in 3G systems ensures that the identity of the user is kept confidential and that only authenticated users

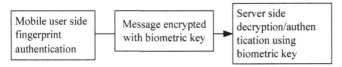

Fig. 19.7. A biocrypto system architecture incorporating biometric authentication and cryptography.

can obtain network services (Aissi *et al.*, 2006). In the era of 3G, there are still risks in mobile business communications because many networks will not offer a consistent level of encryption that meets the confidentiality requirements for m-commerce (Gindraux, 2002). In addition, 3G networks reduce the whole security infrastructure to a simple PIN mechanism (Dimitriadis and Polemi, 2005), which is vulnerable to attacks. Biometric authentication is especially necessary in such a circumstance where the identity of a claimed user should be verified. Biometric authentication can make sure that only the legitimate users are using the device and services. We propose a biometric authentication and cryptographic key binding architecture as shown in Fig. 19.7.

This is a multilayer authentication architecture. During registration stage, the mobile user registers his/her fingerprint template in the server and the mobile. When in use, a user has to pass fingerprint authentication in order to gain access to the mobile device. Then, the sensitive information will be encrypted by the biometric key generated from the matched fingerprint minutia and sent to the server. On the server side, it can generate the corresponding biometric key based on the IDs of the fingerprint minutia. Details are illustrated in the following sections.

19.5.1 *User side fingerprint authentication*

As we know, fingerprint minutiae are unique but unreliable. Even though prints of the same finger are likely to be close, but two prints are rarely identical. Multiple impressions from the same finger are slightly different, called intrauser variation. The unreliability of fingerprint includes:

(1) missing of genuine minutiae and presence of spurious minutiae; and
(2) rotation and translation.

On the other hand, cryptography demands exactness in every digit. Bridge the gap between uncertainty in biometric features and exactness in cryptographic key is still an unsolved research topic (Han *et al.*, 2007a,b; Hu, 2008).

We propose the architecture that fingerprint authentication as the first layer access control. In this architecture, a mobile equipped with a fingerprint scanner and processing system as shown in Fig. 19.8(a) is employed. When the user requests access to the mobile system, his/her fingerprint is scanned, and the query fingerprint X_Q is processed, then compared against the stored template X_T as shown in Fig. 19.8(b). If more than eight minutiae were matched, then the

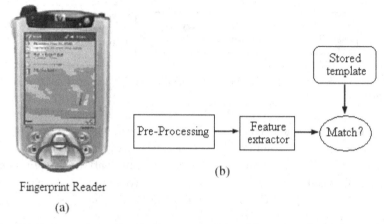

Fingerprint Reader

(a)

(b)

Fig. 19.8.   Mobile fingerprint authentication system. (a) mobile equipped with fingerprint reader, and (b) processing and matching.

authentication is complete and a positive authentication will be granted. Otherwise, the authentication is failed.

For the purpose of replacing password/PIN, biometric authentication via local matching should suffice in terms of security (Loretta, 2008). Fingerprint authentication can assure that the legitimate users are accessing the mobile system.

User fingerprint authentication is the first layer access control, which controls the access to the device and the data stored on the mobile device.

19.5.2 *User side biofeature transmission*

Assume that there are eight minutiae on the query fingerprint image have matched against those on the template. Each minutia is described with its coordinates and direction (x, y, θ) of ridge. The matched eight minutiae information released from template are $\{(x_i, y_i, \theta_i), i = 1, \ldots, 8\}$, which are given by

$$\{x_i, y_i, \theta_i\} = \left\{ \begin{array}{l} (57, 164, 132°) \\ (91, 110, 22°) \\ (123, 286, 92°) \\ (122, 200, 110°) \\ (152, 152, 70°) \\ (180, 173, 12°) \\ (185, 280, 45°) \\ (197, 135, 5°) \end{array} \right\} \quad i = 1, \ldots, 8 \qquad (19.1)$$

We can express each element x, y, or θ with a 12-bit binary stream, thus one minutia can be described with a triple 12-bit binary stream. Then, the binary representation of the eight minutiae is

$$
\{x_i, y_i, \theta_i\} = \left\{ \begin{array}{l}
(000001010111, 000101100100, 000100110010) \\
(000010010001, 000100010000, 000000100010) \\
(000100100011, 001010000110, 000010010010) \\
(000100100010, 001000000000, 000100010000) \\
(000101010010, 000101010010, 000001110000) \\
(000110000000, 000101110011, 000000010010) \\
(000110000101, 001010000000, 000001000101) \\
(000110010111, 000100110101, 000000000101)
\end{array} \right\} \tag{19.2}
$$

which is a group of 8×36-bit binary stream.

After successful matching, the labels of these 8 matched minutia expressed in Eq. (19.1) and the sensitive message encrypted with key extracted (e.g., use the last eight digits of each element) from Eq. (19.2) are sent to the central server.

To enhance the security strength of application domain, a transformed version of user template is stored in mobile devices. This can be achieved by encrypting the template using a local key k_1 (the pre-stored password). Unless having obtained both the correct password and genuine fingerprint information, an attacker is not able to gain access to the mobile device. During the fingerprint matching procedure, the system should decrypt the stored template, followed by comparing query fingerprint X_Q against the template X_T.

19.5.3 *Server side biometric key construction*

When successful passing of the local fingerprint matching, the matched minutiae from template are encrypted and sent to the central server. The second layer authentication is based on the matched minutiae from template which is accurate in every digit.

The message received by the server contains the ID of the user and the labels of the minutia, which are protected. Central server has rich computational resources. With the knowledge of the user ID and the labels of the minutia, the central server can construct a biometric key the same way as the mobile device did.

The construction of biometric key at the server side is equivalent to a second layer access control. Upon successful reconstruction, the further steps at the central server can proceed.

Discussion. It is very challenging to generate a stable key from biometric fingerprints due to the random uncertainty. The main contribution of this proposed architecture is that the biometric key is generated from the matched fingerprint minutia stored in the template, which is consistent all the time. Due to the randomness, the input fingerprint minutia matched with the template tends to be random. Compared with conventional symmetric key that is fixed and prestored, the biometric cryptographic key generated by our proposed scheme retains some randomness, which effectively increases the entropy. By the knowledge of the user ID and the labels of minutia, the server can easily construct back the exact biometric key from the stored template, which has been used by the mobile user. The user ID and the labels of the minutia are not protected. However, hackers are not able to construct the same biometric key as they just know the labels of the minutia but without any further information of actual minutia.

19.6 Conclusion

We have experienced a rapid growth in consumer adoption of mobile applications. However, the success of m-commerce depends much on the security of the underlying applications.

In this chapter, biometric authentication for enhancing the security in mobile computing applications is discussed. Security architecture, in which fingerprint authentication is used to control access to the mobile devices and the sensitive information stored in the central database, has been proposed. Instead of directly generating biometric key from the input fingerprint which tends to be uncertain, we propose to output the matched minutiae information extracted from the template which is accurate in every digit. The information is then encrypted and sent to the central server. This new architecture makes the whole mobile system secure and robust.

Public key infrastructure (PKI) provides a strong authentication to verify the identities of each entity. Integrating PKI into a single SIM handset is a research topic (Sadeh, 2002). The proposed security architecture may open a new branch in enhancing the security of m-commerce, such as combining fingerprint authentication and ring authentication.

References

Aissi, S., Dabbous, N., and Prasad, A. R. *Security for Mobile Networks and Platforms* (Artech House, Boston, London), 2006.

Bolle, R., Connell, J. H., Pankanti, S., Ratha, N. K., and Senior, A. W. *Guide to Biometrics* (Springer), 2004.

Bowyer, K. Face recognition technology: security versus privacy, *IEEE Technol. Soc. Magzine* **23**, 1, 9–20, 2004.

Chu, Y. and Ganz, A. Mobile telemedicine systems using 3g wireless network, *Business Briefing: U.S. Health Strategies*, pp. 2–6, 2005.

Ciccarelli, P., Faulkner, C., FitzGerald, J., Dennis, A., Groth, D., and Skandier, T. *Networking Basics* (Wiley Pathways), 2007.

Daugman, J. Recognizing persons by their iris patterns, in A. Jain, R. Bolle and S. Pankanti (eds.), *Biometrics: Personal Identification in Networked Society* (Kluwer Academic), pp. 103–120, 1999.

Dimitriadis, C. K. and Polemi, D. Biometric-enabled authentication in 3g/wlan systems, in *Proc. 39th Int. Carnahan Conf. on Security Technology*, pp. 164–167, 2005.

Federrath, H. Protection in Mobile Communications, in G. Muller and K. Rannenberg (eds.), *Multilateral Security in Communications* (Addison Wesley-Longman), pp. 349–364, 1999.

Fogie, S. Security reference guide, access control systems, part 3, http://www.informit.com /index.aspx, 2005.

Gindraux, S. From 2g to 3g: a guide to mobile security, in *Proc. of IEEE Int. Conf. on 3G Mobile Communication Technologies* (London), pp. 308–311, 2002.

Grami, A. and Schell, B. Future trends in mobile commerce: service offerings, technological advances and security challenges, in *Proc. of Conf. on Privacy, Security and Trust (PST'04)* (Fredericton), pp. 1–14, 2004.

Hackney, D. Wireless telemedicine for nursing homes and retirement centres, B.S thesis, University of Virginia, 2005.

Han, F., Hu, J., He, L., and Wang, Y. Generation of reliable pins from fingerprints, in *Security Symposium, Proc. of IEEE Int. Conf. on Communication* (Glasgow, Scotland), pp. 1191–1196, 2007a.

Han, F., Hu, J., Yu, X., and Wang, Y. Fingerprint images encryption via multi-scroll chaotic attractors, *Appl. Math. Computation* **185**, 931–939, 2007b.

Hou, Z., Li, J., Lam, H. K., Chen, T. P., Wang, H. L., and Yan, W. Y. Fingerprint orientation analysis with topological modelling, in *Proc. of Int. Conf. on Pattern Recognition*, pp. 1–4, 2008.

Hu, J. Mobile fingerprint template protection: Progress and open issues, in *Proc. IEEE Conf. ICIEA* (Singapore), pp. 2133–2138, 2008.

Hu, J. and Han, F. A pixel-based scrambling scheme for digital medical images protection, *J. Network Comput. Appl.* **32**, 4, 788–794, 2009.

Hu, J., Bertok, J., and Tari, Z. Taxonomy and framework for integrating dependability and security, in Y. Qian (ed.), *Information Assurance: Dependability and Security in Networked Systems* (Elsevier), pp. 149–170, 2008.

Hu, J., Chen, H. H., and Hou, T. W. A hybrid public key infrastructure solution (hpki) for hipaa privacy/security regulations, *Computer Standards & Interfaces (Special Issue on Information and Communications Security, Privacy and Trust: Standards and Regulations)*, 2009.

Istepanian, S., Laxminarayan, S., and Pattichis, C. *M-health: Emerging Mobile Health Systems* (Springer), 2005.

Kasera, S. and Narang, N. *3G Mobile Networks* (McGraw-Hill Publishing Company), 2004.

Khadraoui, D. and Herrmann, F. *Advances in Enterprise Information Technology Security* (Hershey, New York), 2007.

Kumar, M. and Sinha, O. Towards next generation E-government, in J. Bhattacharya (ed.), *Computer Society of India* (Hyderabad), pp. 294–301, 2007.

Lam, H., Hou, Z., Yau, W., Chen, T., Li, J., and Sim, K. Reference point detection for arch type fingerprints, in *Proc. of Int. Conf. on Biometrics*, pp. 666–674, 2009.

Lee, C., Luo, X., and Warkentin, M. Perceptions of security and privacy when using mobile communication systems, in *Proc. of the National Decision Sciences (DSI) 39th Annual Conf.*, pp. 4281–4286, 2008.

Loretta, M. Biometric security for mobile banking, World Resource Institute, Markets Enterprise, White Paper, Washington USA, 2008.

MIS Biometrics Mis biometrics home, http://misbiometrics.wikidot.com/, 2008.

Mobile Marketing Association. Mobile banking overview, http://www.mmaglobal.com/mbankingoverview.pdf, 2009.

Montoni, M., Villela, K., Rocha., A., and Rabelo, A. Telecardio mobile: development of platform-independent telemedicine applications, in *Proc. of 2nd Conf. Mobile Computing* (Heidelberg, Germany), 2002.

National Preparedness. Technologies to secure federal buildings, Rept # GAO-02-687T 116, U.S. General Accounting Office, 2002.

Owens, J. and Anna, B.-H. *Catching the Technology Wave: Mobile Phone Banking and Text-A-Payment in the Philippines* (Chemonics International Inc), 2006.

Pyramid Research. Global mobile subscribers to top out over 2.6bn by ye2006, www.pyr.com/mbl_may17_mobsub.htm, 2007.

Randall, K. and Panos, C. *Wireless Security, Models, Threats, and Solutions* (McGraw-Hill TELECOM), 2002.

Rellos, K. Media release, http://www.anz.com/resources/1/2/12ef0c804d2faac283 f9b7766a918285/ANZ-MediaRelease-20080129.pdf, 2008.

Rerd, P. *Biometrics for Network Security* (Prentice Hall PTR), 2004.

Roggenkamp, K. Development modules to unleash the potential of mobile government, in *Proc. 4th European Conf. on e-Government* (Zurich, Switzerland), pp. 1–13, 2004.

Sadeh, N. *M-Commerce: Technologies, Services, and Business Models* (John Wiley & Sons, Inc), 2002.

Shabeer, H., and Suganthi, P. Mobile phones security using biometrics, in *Proc. Int. Conf. on Computational Intelligence and Multimedia Applications*, pp. 270–272, 2007.

Sharma, M. http://www.australianit.news.com.au/story/0,24897, 23401288-15321, 00.html, 2008.

Tachakra, S., Wang, X., Istepanian, R., and Song, Y. Mobile e-health: the unwired solution of telemedicine, *J. e-Health* **9**, 3, 247–257, 2003.

Tin, Y., Vasanta, H., Boyd, C., and Nieto, J. Protocols with security proofs for mobile applications, in *Proc. 9th Australasian conf. ACISP (LNCS 3108)*, pp. 358–369, 2004.

Tiwari, R., Buse, S., and Herstatt, C. Customer on the move: strategic implications of mobile banking for banks and financial enterprises, in *Proc. 8th IEEE Conf. on E-Com. Tech.* (San Francisco), pp. 522–529, 2006.

Toh, K. and Yau, W. Combination of hyperbolic functions for multimodal biometrics data fusion, *IEEE Trans. Syst., Man, Cybernetics, Part B* **34**, 2, 1196–1209, 2004.

Toh, K., Yau, W., and Jiang, X. A reduced multivariate polynomial model for multimodal biometrics and classifiers fusion, *IEEE Trans. Circuits Syst. for Video Technol. (Special Issue on Image- and Video-Based Biometrics)* **14**, 2, 224–233, 2004.

Toh, K. and Yau, W. Fingerprint and speaker verification decisions fusion using a functional link network, *IEEE Trans. Syst., Man, Cybernetics, Part C* **35**, 3, 357–370, 2005.

Umar, A. Mobile computing and wireless communications: applications, networks, platforms, architectures, and security, NGE Solutions, U.S.A, 2004.

Vacca, J. *Biometric Technologies and Verification Systems* (Butterworth-Heinemann, Burlington), 2007.

Verschuren, J. Assessing the security strength of mobile applications endorsed by smart cards, in *Proc. Workshop on Requirements for Mobile Privacy and Security* (Royal Holloway, University of London), pp. 16–17, 2002.

Wang, Y., Hu, J., and Philip, D. A fingerprint orientation model based on 2d fourier expansion (fomfe) and its application to singular-point detection and fingerprint indexing, *Special Issue on Biometrics: Progress and Directions, IEEE Transactions on Pattern Analysis and Machine Intelligence*, pp. 573–585, 2007.

Whitepaper. Windows mobile devices and security: protecting sensitive business information, www.microsoft.com/windowsmobile/, 2006.

Wireless Week. Mobile subscriber growth and forecast, http://www.wirelessweek.com/uploaded Images/WW/articles/020108-UMTS-2.gif, 2007.

Xiao, Y. and Chen, H. *Mobile Telemedicine, A Computing and Network Perspective* (CRC Press), 2008.

Yu, W., Gummadikayala, R., and Mudumbi, S. A web-based wireless mobile system design of security and privacy framework for u-healthcare, in *Proc. 10th IEEE conf. on e-Health Networking, Appl. Serv.*, pp. 96–101, 2008.

Chapter 20

DISCRIMINATIVE FRAMEWORK OF NEURAL
ACTIVATION ANALYSIS WITH fMRI

Yang Wang[*,†,¶] and Jagath C. Rajapakse[‡,§,∥]

*National ICT Australia
†School of Computer Science and Engineering,
University of New South Wales
‡School of Computer Engineering and BioInformatics
Research Centre, Nanyang Technological University
§Department of Biological Engineering,
Massachusetts Institute of Technology
¶yang.wang@nicta.com.au
∥asjagath@ntu.edu.sg

20.1 Introduction

Functional brain mapping becomes a more and more popular topic of brain biometrics, which is used in various application areas such as person authentication, lie detection, and mind reading (Bourbakis and Makrogiannis, 2003; Ravi and Palaniappan, 2005; Sitaram *et al.*, 2008). Particularly, the functional magnetic resonance imaging (fMRI) is probably the most important technique that noninvasively studies brain functions under numerous cognitive and behavioral tasks. Functional brain studies acquire a time series of brain scans while the subject is alternatively performing an experimental task and a baseline task (so that the input stimulus to the brain takes the form of an on-off box-car pattern). Brain regions of interest are then detected through measuring the oxygenation level variations in blood vessels near the neurons activated by the input stimulus, i.e., the blood oxygenation level dependent (BOLD) contrast. The detection of brain activation provides functional maps exhibiting which brain regions correspond to specific sensory or cognitive tasks. In fMRI experiments, the BOLD signal (or the hemodynamic response) changes resulted from neural activities follow the pattern of input stimulus, but are usually contaminated by high-level noises (Bandettini *et al.*, 1993). Hence, it is important to develop analysis methods that can robustly detect activated brain regions from the noisy fMRI time series.

For neural activation detection with functional brain imaging, both model-based and data-driven (model-independent) approaches have been extensively studied to classify or segment brain voxels (points in the scan image) into active and inactive areas. In model-based methods, a statistical parametric map of brain activation is built by examining the time-series response of each voxel in the brain, given the information about the stimulation and activation temporal response. The significance of activation is assessed using various statistical models including correlation analysis (Bandettini et al., 1993; Friman et al., 2001), t-test or F-test (Friston et al., 1995b), permutation (Nichols and Holmes, 2001), and mixture model (Everitt and Bullmore, 1999; Woolrich et al., 2005). Recently, probabilistic graphical models such as Bayesian network and hidden semi-Markov event sequence model have also been employed to characterize fMRI time series (Faisan et al., 2005; Marrelec et al., 2003). On the other hand, data-driven methods such as clustering analysis (Goutte et al., 1999), principal component analysis (Hansen et al., 1999), and independent component analysis (Calhoun et al., 2001) attempt to reveal components of interest from the fMRI data without requiring the knowledge of the activation temporal response. However, the physiological meaning of the results is usually hard to explain, and it is difficult to perform statistical significance analysis based on data-driven methods.

Furthermore, functional integration study describing how functionally specialized areas interact when the brain is performing a specific task has attracted more and more attention in recent years. Various techniques have been proposed to use functional brain imaging data to characterize the effective connectivity, i.e., the influence that one region exerts on another. With the detection of the brain activation, the activity of each activated region is represented by the average of the time series of hemodynamic responses of neurons in the brain region, and the connectivity of the neural system is encoded by the dataset containing activities of all activated brain regions. The structural equation modeling (SEM) is a commonly used method that analyzes the effective connectivity among brain regions by finding the maximum likelihood (ML) parameters of connection (McIntosh and Gonzalez-Lima, 1994; Penny et al., 2004b). The information about functional interactions is extracted by exploring the covariances between activated brain regions. The multivariate autoregressive (MAR) approach models activated brain regions as multiple variables in a causal, dynamical, and linear system (Goebel et al., 2003; Harrison et al., 2003). Fully connected models, in which each region is linked to all the other regions, are usually employed (Cosman and Wells, 2005). More recently, the dynamic causal model (DCM) has been introduced to describe the functional interactions at the neuronal level (Friston, 2003; Penny et al., 2004a). The DCM comprises of a bilinear model and an extended balloon model describing neurodynamics and hemodynamics, respectively. An exploratory approach that does not require a prior model has also been proposed to derive effective connectivity based on Bayesian networks (Zheng and Rajapakse, 2006). Furthermore, dynamic Bayesian networks are employed to explicitly take into account temporal characteristics of image time series during brain activation analysis (Rajapakse *et al.*, 2008; Rajapakse and Zhou, 2007).

Besides local information measured at individual brain voxels, the strategy to effectively fuse contextual information in functional imaging data is a key factor for the analysis of brain activation (Hartvig and Jensen, 2000; Wang and Rajapakse, 2006). For instance, it is known that the regions of interest usually consist of a number of contiguous brain voxels (Cosman *et al.*, 2004). Since neighboring sites are likely to belong to the same class, spatial smoothing or filtering can be used in the preprocessing of fMRI data to enhance the overall signal-to-noise ratio (SNR) in activated regions. However, the linear filtering suppresses high-frequency information in fMRI data and may cause small activated regions undetectable. Markov random field (MRF) has been introduced to encourage contiguous results of activity detection by defining pairwise potentials between neighboring segmentation (activated/inactive) labels (Descombes *et al.*, 1998; Salli *et al.*, 2001; Rajapakse and Piyaratna, 2001). In these MRF approaches, spatial regularization and activity detection are simultaneously handled to enhance the performance of fMRI data analysis. Markov random field has also been employed to impose smoothness constraints on brain regions with different characteristics of hemodynamic response function (HRF) (Svensen *et al.*, 2000).

However, conditional independence of observations is usually assumed in MRF approaches so that the interactions among observed data are ignored when segmentation labels are given. Because of the interconnection within brain areas, the time series of an activated brain voxel is highly dependent on its activated neighbors. Therefore, the strong assumption of conditional independence is too restrictive for the modeling of functional activities in fMRI analysis. Compared to generative models including Markov random field, the conditional random field (CRF) models the contextual dependencies in a probabilistic discriminative framework that directly considers the posterior distribution over labels given observations (Lafferty *et al.*, 2001), which relaxes the strong independence assumption and captures neighborhood interactions among observations. Originally proposed for 1D text sequence labeling, CRF has been applied to image and video labeling recently (Kumar and Hebert, 2004; Wang and Ji, 2005; Wang *et al.*, 2006).

Based on the conditional random field, this work presents a probabilistic approach for the analysis of brain activity from fMRI data. The contextual dependencies of both segmentation labels and observed data of brain voxels are unified in a probabilistic discriminative framework where the interaction strength is adaptively adjusted according to a similarity measure between neighboring sites. Given the observed data, the posterior distribution over the segmentation labels is maximized by variational approximation. The effective connectivity is then derived from the activities of detected brain regions. Experimental results show that the proposed approach effectively integrates contextual constraints in functional images and robustly performs brain activation analysis with fMRI data.

20.2 Contextual Model

For a point x (a point could be a pixel within a 2D image or a voxel within a 3D image), the observed data and segmentation label of the point are denoted by d_x and l_x, respectively. The observation d_x consists of measured information at the site x. The label l_x assigns each point x to one of K regions (or classes) composing the scene, and $l_x = e_k$ if point x belongs to the kth class, where e_k is a K-dimensional unit vector with its kth component equal to one. Here $K \in N(K = 2$ in this chapter), $x \in X$, and X is the spatial domain of the scene (scan image). The entire label field and observed data over the scene are compactly expressed as l and d, respectively.

Given the observed data, there are two ways to estimate the segmentation labels (Kumar and Hebert, 2004). In the probabilistic generative framework, both the prior model of the label field and the likelihood model of the observed data are formulated to estimate the joint distribution over observations and labels. Alternatively, in the probabilistic discriminative framework the posterior distribution of the label field is directly formulated. In this work, the contextual constraints of activity detection are imposed through a discriminative framework of statistical dependencies among neighboring sites.

To incorporate interactions among both segmentation labels and observed data into the detection of brain activation, the posterior probability $p(l|d)$ is formulated by a CRF. The CRF approach relaxes the strong assumption of conditional independence for contextual modeling of functional imaging data. CRF is originally proposed in the discriminative framework avoiding the formulation of observation model. The definition of CRF is given by Lafferty *et al.* (2001). For observed data d and corresponding labels l over the scene, (l, d) is a conditional random field if, when conditioned on d, the random field l obeys the Markov property: $p(l_x|d, \{l_y\}_{y \neq x}) = p(l_x|d, \{l_y\}_{y \in N_x})$, where set N_x denotes the neighboring sites of point x (e.g., Fig. 20.1). Using the Hammersley-Clifford theorem and considering up to pairwise clique potentials, the posterior distribution can be expressed as a

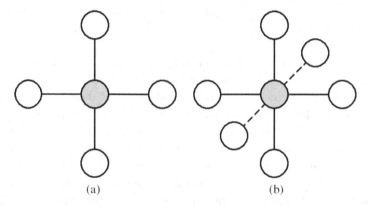

(a)   (b)

Fig. 20.1.   (a) The 4-pixel neighborhood. (b) The 6-voxel neighborhood.

Gibbs distribution with the following form (Besag, 1986)

$$p(l|d) \propto \exp\left(-\sum_{x \in X}[V_x(l_x|d) + \sum_{y \in N_x} V_{x,y}(l_x, l_y|d)]\right) \quad (20.1)$$

The one-pixel potential $V_x(l_x|d)$ imposes the local constraint for a single site. Meanwhile the two-pixel potential $V_{x,y}(l_x, l_y|d)$ models the contextual information (or pairwise constraint) between neighboring sites. According to the expression, strength of the constraints (potentials) is dependent on the observed data. The potential functions are further expressed as

$$V_x(l_x|d) = V_x^l(l_x) + V_x^{l|d}(l_x|d)$$
$$V_x(l_x, l_y|d) = V_{x,y}^l(l_x, l_y) + V_{x,y}^{l|d}(l_x, l_y|d) \quad (20.2)$$

In the one-pixel potential, the first term reflects the prior knowledge for different label classes, and the second term reflects the observed information from individual sites (see the next section). In the two-pixel potential, the first term imposes the connectivity constraint independent of the observations, and the second term imposes the neighborhood interaction dependent on the observed data. The dependencies of data in functional MRI may come from spatial coupling of hemodynamic responses or correlated noises. Thus, during the segmentation process both the data-independent and data-dependent contextual dependencies are unified in a probabilistic discriminative framework based on the conditional random field. The CRF approach will degenerate into an MRF approach when the data-dependent pairwise potential is ignored, which is equivalent to the conditional independence assumption of the observed data used in previous approaches. However, the connectivity of neural systems makes the observation from a brain voxel highly dependent on its neighboring sites of the same class. In the discriminative framework, the interaction strength between neighboring sites can be adaptively adjusted in terms of their similarity, which enables the proposed approach further explore the contextual information in functional images.

To encourage contiguous segmentation, the connectivity constraint is imposed by the following data-independent pairwise potential:

$$V_{x,y}^l(l_x, l_y) \propto -\frac{1}{\|x - y\|} l_x \cdot l_y \quad (20.3)$$

where $\cdot$ denotes the inner product, and $\|\|$ is the Euclidean distance. The pairwise smoothness constraint is imposed only when the two segmentation labels are different. Thus, neighboring points are more likely to belong to the same class than to different classes. Moreover, the strength of the connectivity constraint decreases with the increasing distance between neighboring points.

The data-dependent pairwise potential can be expressed in the following to encourage data similarity between two neighboring sites when they have the same segmentation label:

$$V_{x,y}^{l|d}(l_x, l_y|d) \propto -\frac{1}{\|x-y\|} \frac{l_x \cdot l_y}{|d_x - d_y|/\delta + 1} \tag{20.4}$$

where $\delta > 0$. The pairwise potential models the neighborhood interaction dependent on the observed data. Naturally, the potential imposes an adaptive contextual constraint that adjusts the interaction strength according to the similarity between neighboring observations. However, under heavy noises, neighboring sites may become quite different even though they belong to the same class. When dealing with noisy fMRI data, the regulation term δ is used in the data-dependent pairwise potential to prevent such problem. The data-dependent constraint will be too sensitive to noises when the value of δ is too small. On the other hand, if the value of δ is too high, the constraint will be insensitive to the data difference between neighboring sites. In this work, the regulation term is set as $\delta = \frac{1}{|N_x|}\sum_{z\in N_x}|d_x - d_z| + \frac{1}{|N_y|}\sum_{z\in N_y}|d_y - d_z|$, where for a set of points M, $|M|$ denotes the size (number of points) of the set.

20.3 Activation Detection

In an fMRI time series with total T $(T \in N)$ image scans, the time-series response of a point x is represented by $(r_x(1), r_x(2), \ldots, r_x(T))$, and the input stimulus to the brain is denoted by a binary time series $(s(1), s(2), \ldots, s(T))$. The expression of observation d_x is given later in this section. For the detection of brain activity, each voxel x in the brain is labeled as either activated or inactive. The segmentation label equals e_1 if the site is inactive, otherwise the label equals e_2.

The one-pixel potential function is set as $V_x(l_x|d) = -\ln p(l_x|d_x)$ so that the posterior distribution $p(l|d)$ becomes the product of local posterior probability $p(l_x|d_x)$ at each site if the two-pixel potential $V_{x,y}(l_x, l_y|d)$ is ignored. Since $p(l_x|d_x) \propto p(l_x, d_x) = p(l_x)p(d_x|l_x)$, the two terms in the one-pixel potential become $V_x^l(l_x) = -\ln p(l_x)$ and $V_x^{l|d}(l_x|d) = -\ln p(d_x|l_x)$. The prior information of individual classes can be expressed by the following data-independent one-pixel potential

$$V_x^l(l_x = i) = -\ln p(l_x = i) = \alpha_i \tag{20.5}$$

The smaller the α_i is, the more likely a site x will be labeled as the ith class.

In the detection of brain activity, the temporal response from regions of interest should be impacted by the stimulus signal. Consider the correlation coefficient between the stimulus and the response at a site x: $c_x = \frac{\sum_t[s(t)-\bar{s}][r_x(t)-\bar{r}_x]}{\sqrt{\sum_t[s(t)-\bar{s}]^2\sum_t[r_x(t)-\bar{r}_x]^2}}$, where $\bar{s} = \frac{1}{T}\sum_t s(t)$, $\bar{r}_x = \frac{1}{T}\sum_t r_x(t)$, c_x is the correlation coefficient, and $-1 \leq c_x \leq 1$. The value of correlation coefficient will be positive if the brain voxel is activated by the input stimulus. Otherwise its value will be close to zero for an inactive brain voxel. Considering the hemodynamic response of neuron activities, the input stimulus is replaced by the convolution of the stimulus signal and synthetic hemodynamic response function (the HRF used in the statistical parametric mapping software from http://www.fil.ion.ucl.ac.uk/spm/) when calculating correlation coefficients. The multiple correlation analysis or canonical correlation analysis is employed to compute the correlation coefficient when dealing with varying hemodynamic response functions and multiple stimulus conditions (Friman *et al.*, 2001). We represent the observation by using the Fisher's Z transformation: $d_x = \frac{1}{2} \ln \frac{1+c_x}{1-c_x}$. As exhibited in Ardekani and Kanno (1998), the posterior probability of the observation can be approximated by a zero-mean Gaussian distribution when the site is inactive. Hence

$$V_x^{l|d}(l_x = e_1|d) = -\ln p(d_x|l_x = e_1) \approx -\ln N\left(d_x; 0, \frac{1}{T-3}\right) \qquad (20.6)$$

where $N(z; \mu, \sigma^2)$ represents a Gaussian distribution with argument z, mean μ, and variance σ^2. When the site is activated by the input stimulus, the posterior is simply approximated by a uniform distribution since the true distribution of the activated voxels is not known:

$$V_x^{l|d}(l_x = e_2|d) = -\ln p(d_x|l_x = e_2) \approx -\ln \frac{1}{c} \qquad (20.7)$$

where $d_x \in (0, c]$, $c = \frac{1}{2} \ln \frac{1+c_{\max}}{1-c_{\max}}$, and $c_{\max} = \max_{x \in X} c_x$.

Combining Eqs. (20.3)–(20.5), the potential functions of the posterior probability $p(l|d)$ are expressed as the following

$$V_x(l_x|d) = \begin{cases} -\ln N\left(d_x; 0, \frac{1}{T-3}\right), & \text{if } l_x = e_1, \\ \alpha + \ln c, & \text{if } l_x = e_2, \end{cases}$$

$$V_{x,y}(l_x, l_y|d) = -\frac{\beta_1}{\|x-y\|} l_x \cdot l_y - \frac{\beta_2}{\|x-y\|} \frac{l_x \cdot l_y}{|d_x - d_y|/\delta + 1} \qquad (20.8)$$

where $\alpha = \alpha_1 - \alpha_0$. α controls the sensitivity of activity detection, β_1 and β_2 respectively weigh the importance of data-independent smoothness constraint and data-dependent neighborhood interaction. To balance the potential terms for the contextual constraints, we assume that

$$\frac{1}{|X|} \sum_{x \in X} \sum_{y \in N_x} \beta_1 = \frac{1}{|X|} \sum_{x \in X} \sum_{y \in N_x} \beta_2 = \gamma^2.$$

The parameters α and γ are manually determined to reflect the influences of prior information for brain activation and contextual information from neighboring sites. The smaller the value of α, the more easily activated regions will be detected. Meanwhile, the higher the value of γ, the stronger contextual constraints are utilized. In our experiments, it is found that $1 \leq \alpha \leq 2$ and $1 \leq \gamma \leq 3$ produce the visually optimal activation pattern for the analysis of fMRI data. Given the one-pixel and two-pixel potential functions, the maximum a posteriori (MAP) estimation of the label field is given by $\hat{l} = \arg\max_l p(l|d)$.

20.4 Variational Approximation

Given the potential functions, the optimization of the posterior probability of the label field is generally difficult due to the data-dependent interactions among neighboring sites. Here, a variational algorithm scheme is employed to get an estimate of the label field (Marrelec *et al.*, 2003). The variational method minimizes the Kullback-Leibler (KL) divergence between the approximating distribution and the true posterior, which yields the best lower bound on the probability of observed data in the family of approximations. It is known that the Kullback-Leibler divergence $KL(q(l|d)\|p(l|d)) = \sum_l q(l|d) \ln \frac{q(l|d)}{p(l|d)}$, where the approximating distribution $q(l|d) = \prod_{x \in X} q(l_x|d)$. In order to optimize the KL divergence, the local approximating probabilities $\{q(l_x|d)\}$ should be given by the mean field equations. For the label at site x

$$q(l_x|d) = \frac{1}{Q_x} \exp\{E_q[\ln p(l|d)|l_x]\}$$

$$Q_x = \sum_{l_x} \exp\{E_q[\ln p(l|d)|l_x]\} \tag{20.9}$$

where $E_q\{|\}$ stands for the conditional expectation with respect to the variational distribution $q(l|d)$, Q_x is the local normalization constant for $q(l_x|d)$:

$$E_q[\ln p(l|d)|l_x] = \sum_{l \setminus l_x} \left[\prod_{y \neq x} q(l_y|d) \ln p(l|d) \right]$$

$$= -V_x(l_x|d) - \sum_{y \in N_x} \sum_{l_y} q(l_y|d) V_{x,y}(l_x, l_y|d) \tag{20.10}$$

During the computation, additive constant is ignored since the term will not take effect after the normalization. It can be seen that in order to find the local approximating probability of a site, one has to know the probabilities of its neighbors. Therefore the approximating probabilities can be iteratively estimated by Eqs. (20.9) and (20.10). For each site x, $\hat{l}_x = \arg\max_{l_x} q_x(l_x|d)$.

20.5 Effective Connectivity

Given the labels of activation detection, each cluster of active brain voxels represents an activated region in this work. The activity of an activated brain region is represented by the average of the time-series responses in the region, which is denoted as $r_i = (r_i(1), r_i(2), \ldots, r_i(T))$ for the ith region. The region activities for the entire neural system are compactly expressed as $R = \{r_1, r_2, \ldots, r_N\}$, where N is the number of activated regions. The form of brain connectivity is specified by linear regression that describes how the activity in one region is related to the activities of other regions via a set of path coefficients (Penny *et al.*, 2004b). The influence that the ith region exerts on the jth region (i.e., see the directed connections in

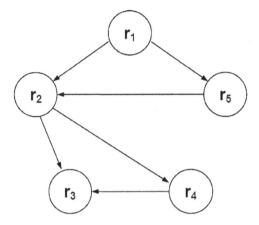

Fig. 20.2.   Illustration of effective connectivity among activated regions.

Fig. 20.2) is denoted by coefficient $c_{i,j}$, and the set for effective connectivity among all the activated regions is represented by matrix C. At each time instant t, the connectivity of the neural system is expressed as

$$R_t = CR_t + n_t \qquad (20.11)$$

where $R_t = (r_1(t), r_2(t), \ldots, r_N(t))^T$ denotes the vector of the region activities at time t, and n_t is the zero mean Gaussian noises with diagonal covariance Σ. It can be known that the likelihood of observed region activity becomes

$$p(R_t|C) = N(R_t; 0, (I - C)^{-1}\Sigma(I - C)^{-T}) \qquad (20.12)$$

where I is the identity matrix. The observation likelihood for the region activities over time is factorized as $p(R|C) = \prod_t p(R_t|C)$. Thus the parameters of effective connectivity can be estimated through likelihood maximization. In this work, the Metropolis-Hastings algorithm is employed to search the space of effective connectivity (Jordan, 1999), with the Bayesian information criterion (BIC) as score function to find optimal connectivity model. $\hat{C} = \arg\max_C \ln p(R|C) - \frac{1}{2}s \ln T$, where s is the number of non-zero connections within the neural system.

20.6 Results and Discussion

In the experiments, the present approach was tested on both synthetic and real functional time series and compared with the statistical parametric mapping (SPM) algorithm (Friston *et al.*, 1995b). The detected activation by SPM is given by significance values using t-test, whereas those by CRF are given by the probabilities of activation. The 24-pixel neighborhood for 2D images and 124-voxel neighborhood for 3D images were utilized in the experiments. All the fMRI data were corrected for motion artifacts as described in Friston *et al.* (1995a). Spatial smoothing was performed with a Gaussian filter of 6 mm FHWM in the SPM approach.

20.6.1 *Synthetic data*

A 2D dataset with 64×64 pixels per image scan was generated by using the synthetic functional time series. The synthetic data totally had 96 images, where the input stimulus consisted of six cycles, each having eight rest samples followed by eight task samples, and the duration between two scans was 2 seconds (TR $= 2$ s). A box-car time series was designed for activated pixels, while inactive pixels remained unchanged over time. Here, a neural system was simulated with synthetic time series where interactions among the brain regions are represented by a linear system with regression equations describing how the activity of one region is related to the activities of the other regions with a set of linear coefficients: $R_t = CR_t + n_t$, where R_t denotes the vector of region activities at time t, and n_t is the vector of zero mean Gaussian innovation. The interaction structure is shown in Fig. 20.2, and the non-zero elements of the linear coefficient matrix C are $c_{1,2} = 0.9$, $c_{1,5} = 1.1$, $c_{2,3} = 0.7$, $c_{2,4} = -0.8$, $c_{4,3} = 1.2$, $c_{5,2} = -1.0$. The response of the activated pixels in region 1 was generated by convolving the box-car time series with a gamma hemodynamic response function (lag $= 5$ s and dispersion $= 5$ s). Gaussian random noises were then added to the time series of both activated and inactive pixels. Pixel intensities of one image scan are shown in Fig. 20.3. The SNR is defined as $SNR = \frac{h^2}{\sigma^2}$, where h is the amplitude of the box-car time series, and σ is the standard deviation of the noise. The SNR was set as 1.2 in the synthetic experiment.

Figure 20.4 shows the activation detection results by SPM and CRF approaches for the synthetic functional data. Although most activated points are detected by the SPM approach, boundary details (or high-frequency information) of activated regions are blurred by statistical parametric mapping. The conditional random field approach generates relatively contiguous segmentation results by simultaneously performing activity detection and spatial regularization. By incorporating interactions of both segmentation labels and observed data, the

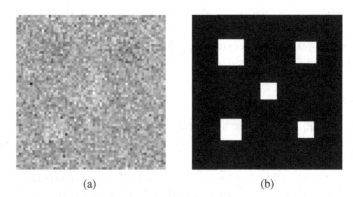

(a)   (b)

Fig. 20.3. Synthetic functional images with five activated regions: (a) one image scan and (b) the activation pattern. (The central activation represents region 1 of the connectivity model in Fig. 20.2, the top-left, bottom-left, top-right, and bottom-right ones, respectively represent activation region 2, 3, 4, and 5).

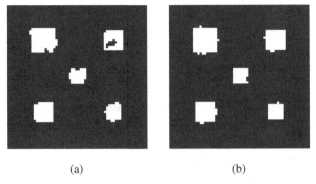

(a)   (b)

Fig. 20.4. (a) Detected activation from synthetic functional data by the SPM algorithm. (b) Detected activation from synthetic functional data by the proposed algorithm.

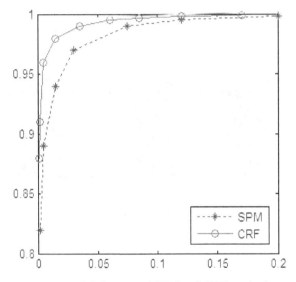

Fig. 20.5. ROC curves of SPM and CRF methods.

accuracy of activity detection is significantly improved by the proposed approach under noisy environments.

The detection results were also evaluated quantitatively by comparing to the ground-truth image shown in Fig. 20.3 (a). The corresponding receiver operating characteristic (ROC) curves for the two algorithms are shown in Fig. 20.5, where the vertical axis and horizontal axis represent the true positive rate (the portion of activated points that are detected) and the false negative rate (the portion of inactive points that are misclassified), respectively. Compared to the SPM approach, the CRF approach takes advantage of data-dependent neighborhood interactions, which helps accurately keep high-frequency information in functional images and relaxes the strong assumption of conditional independence among observations. The substantial increase of the detection accuracy indicates that the CRF approach effectively fuses contextual constraints in functional images.

20.6.2 *Functional MRI data*

In an experiment with memorial retrieval task, for each subject an fMRI time series of 864 brain scans with eight slices ($64 \times 64 \times 8$ voxels per scan) was acquired using a gradient-echo EPI sequence (TR $= 1$ s, TE $= 40$ ms). In the experiment, subspan sets of 3–6 alphabet letters excluding the letter Y were presented visually for 2 seconds, then a probe letter appeared after a variable delay length. Subjects were required to decide if the probe letter belonged to a previously presented subspan set. All trial combinations were presented randomly in a single run, at an intertrial interval of 18 s. Further details of the experiments can be found in Kruggel *et al.* (2000).

Figure 20.6 shows the detected activation from fMRI data gathered on the memory retrieval task by the proposed approach and the statistical parametric mapping approach. Expected brain areas such as middle frontal gyrus (BA 9/46), inferior frontal gyrus (BA 44/45), superior parietal cortex (BA 5/7), supplementary

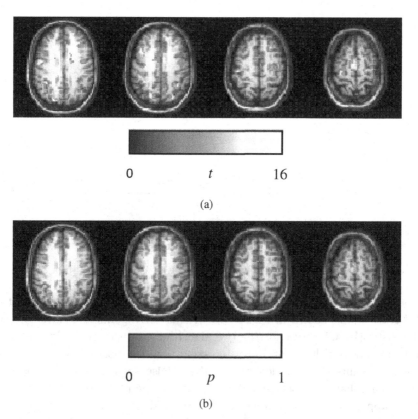

Fig. 20.6. Detected activation on four axial brain slices by (a) SPM and (b) CRF methods from fMRI data of a representative subject performing the memory retrieval task.

motor area (BA 6), and primary motor cortex (BA 4) were detected by both methods. As seen, compared to the results by SPM, the activated areas detected by the CRF approach are relatively contiguous and concentrative. Furthermore, the activation patterns detected by the proposed method contain less spurious noises.

In another experiment with silent reading task, for each subject 360 brain scans with 35 slices ($64 \times 64 \times 35$ voxels per scan) were acquired using an EPI sequence (TR = 3.15 s, TE = 40 ms). The experimental task involved alternative reading of words and pseudowords with variable presenting frequencies, and the resting condition involved fixating a cross in the middle of the screen. Each trial lasted 21 s and was followed by a resting period of 16 s. More details of the experiments can be found in Penny *et al.* (2004a).

Figures 20.7 and 20.8 show the results of activity detection from fMRI data gathered on the silent reading task by the CRF approach and the SPM approach.

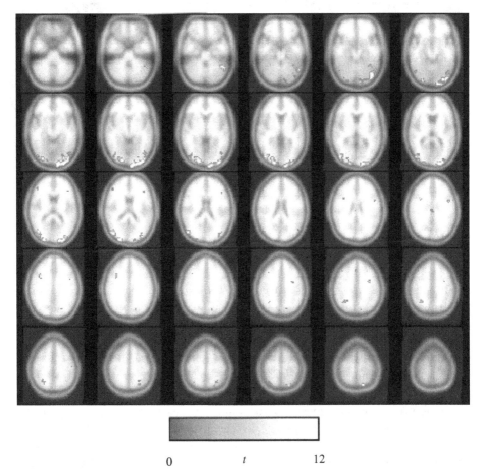

$$0 \qquad t \qquad 12$$

Fig. 20.7.   Detected brain activation by SPM method from fMRI data of a representative subject performing the silent reading task.

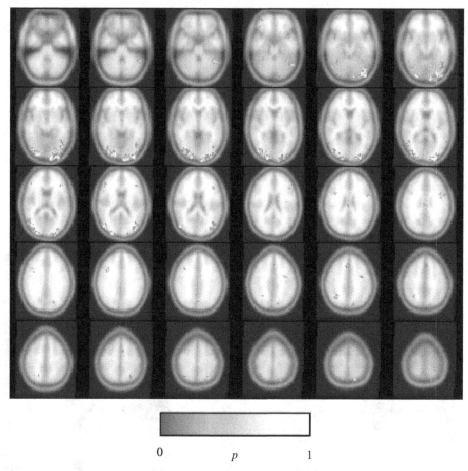

Fig. 20.8.   Detected brain activation by CRF methods from fMRI data of a representative subject performing the silent reading task.

It can be seen that the detection results by the proposed algorithm are consistent with those by the statistical parametric mapping method. Expected activation in related brain regions including extrastriate cortex (VEC, BA 18/19), superior parietal lobule (SPL, BA 7), middle temporal cortex (MTC, BA 21/22), inferior frontal gyrus (IFG, BA 44/45), and middle frontal gyrus (MFG, BA 9/46) were found by both methods.

Figure 20.9 shows the estimated interaction network of effective connectivity. To simplify the computation, only activated regions in the left brain are used for connectivity estimation since the left hemisphere has been the focus of the neural activities for reading tasks. The VEC plays the important role of visual representation in word processing. The connection from VEC to SPL forms the dorsal stream of visual analysis, performing the perception of visual word form. Meanwhile, the connection from the VEC to prefrontal cortex including MFG

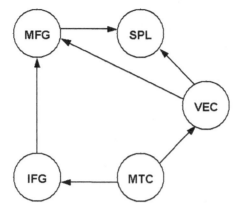

Fig. 20.9. The neural system derived from fMRI data of the silent reading task.

represents the information flow for the processing of semantic analysis and decision. Furthermore, the MTC involved in our model is the general association cortex that integrates the input from the lower level auditory and visual areas for retaining in the memory. The connection from MTC to VEC is associated with the retaining and recalling of words from the memory. The SPL plays the role of visual analysis and makes efferent connection to the prefrontal cortex, providing more elaborate information. The functional links from VEC to SPL via prefrontal cortex form the dorsal visual pathway of language processing. The MFG is involved in tasks that require executive control, such as the selection of behavior based on short-term memory. The connection between SPL and MFG is found with reversed direction; the reversed direction may be due to the bidirectional characteristic of the connectivity. The IFG is most active for phonemic decisions and receives inputs from MTC. The detected activation and connectivity pattern derived from our method are overall consistent with the information flow in the reading task as evidenced by previous cognitive neuroscience study (Zheng and Rajapakse, 2006).

20.7 Conclusion

This work presents a probabilistic discriminative approach to fuse contextual constraints in functional images based on the conditional random field and applied it to the analysis of brain activation from both synthetic and real fMRI data. The CRF provides an effective approach to model the contextual dependencies of both labels and data. Compared to earlier work such as SPM, the CRF approach takes the advantage of data-dependent interactions within the segmentation process and significantly improves the performance of the detection of brain activity: In the experiment with synthetic data, the ROC curves showed that detection accuracy was substantially increased. With the real fMRI data, the detection results by the proposed method were visually either similar or better in the sense of details and localization to cortical areas. The brain connectivity among activated regions was also effectively derived from real fMRI data. The improvement indicates that it is important to consider contextual dependencies of the observations in addition to those among the labels or neural activities when studying fMRI data.

Acknowledgment

The authors thank Dr. F. Kruggel for providing the memory retrieval experiment data at the Max-Planck-Institute of Cognitive Neuroscience, Leipzig, Germany. The silent reading dataset is supported by fMRIDC (The fMRI Data Center, Dartmouth College, USA, http://www.fmridc.org). NICTA is funded by the Australian Government as represented by the Department of Broadband, Communications and the Digital Economy and the Australian Research Council through the ICT Centre of Excellence program.

References

Ardekani, B. A. and Kanno, I. Statistical methods for detecting activated regions in functional MRI of the brain, *Magn. Reson. Imaging* **16**, 1217–1225, 1998.

Bandettini, P. A., Jesmanowicz, A., Wong, E. C., and Hyde, J. S. Processing strategies for time-course data sets in functional MRI of the human brain, *Magn. Reson. Medi.* **30**, 161–173, 1993.

Besag, J. On the statistical analysis of dirty pictures, *J. Roy. Stat. Soc. B* **48**, 259–302, 1986.

Bourbakis, N. and Makrogiannis, S. An l-g & spng based model for brain biometrics, in *Proc. Int. Conf. Tools with Artificial Intelligence*, pp. 628–635, 2003.

Calhoun, V. D., Adali, T., Pearlson, G. D., and Pekar, J. J. Spatial and temporal independent component analysis of functional MRI data containing a pair of task-related waveforms, *Hum. Brain Mapp.* **13**, 43–53, 2001.

Cosman, E. R. and Wells, W. M. Bayesian population modeling of effective connectivity, in *Proc. Information Processing in Medical Imaging Conf.*, pp. 39–51, 2005.

Cosman, E. R., Fisher, J. W., and Wells, W. M. Exact map activity detection in fMRI using a GLM with an ising spatial prior, in *Proc. Int. Conf. Medical Image Computing and Computer-Assisted Intervention*, pp. 2:703–710, 2004.

Descombes, X., Kruggel, F., and von Cramon, D. Y. Spatio-temporal fMRI analysis using markov random fields, *IEEE Trans. Med. Imaging* **17**, 1028–1039, 1998.

Everitt, B. S. and Bullmore, E. T. Mixture model mapping of brain activation in functional magnetic resonance images, *Hum. Brain Mapp.* **7**, 1–14, 1999.

Faisan, S., Thoraval, L., Armspach, J.-P., Metz-Lutz, M.-N., and Heitz, F. Unsupervised learning and mapping of active brain functional MRI signals based on hidden semi-Markov event sequence models, *IEEE Trans. Med. Imaging* **24**, 263–276, 2005.

Friman, O., Cedefamn, J., Lundberg, P., Borga, M., and Knutsson, H. Detection of neural activity in functional MRI using canonical correlation analysis, *Magn. Reson. Med.* **45**, 323–330, 2001.

Friston, K. J. Dynamic causal modeling, *Neuroimage* **19**, 1273–1302, 2003.

Friston, K. J., Ashburner, J., Frith, C. D., Poline, J.-B., Heather, J. D., and Frackowiak, R. S. J. Spatial registration and normalization of images, *Hum. Brain Mapp.* **3**, 165–189, 1995a.

Friston, K. J., Holmes, A. P., Poline, J.-B., Grasby, P. J., Williams, S. C. R., Frackowiak, R. S. J., and Turner, R. Analysis of fMRI time-series revisited, *NeuroImage* **2**, 45–53, 1995b.

Goebel, R., Roebroeck, A., Kim, D.-S., and Formisano, E. Investigating directed cortical interactions in time-resolved fMRI data using vector autoregressive modeling and granger causality mapping, *Magn. Reson. Imaging* **21**, 1251–1261, 2003.

Goutte, C., Toft, P., Rostrup, E., Nielsen, F. A., and Hansen, L. K. On clustering fMRI time series, *Neuroimage* **9**, 298–310, 1999.

Hansen, L. K., Larsen, J., Nielsen, F. A., Strother, S. C., Rostrup, E., Savoy, R., Lange, N., Sidtis, J., Svarer, C., and Paulson, O. B. Generalizable patterns in neuroimaging: how many principal components? *NeuroImage* **9**, 534–544, 1999.

Harrison, L., Penny, W. D., and Friston, K. Multivariate autoregressive modeling of fMRI time series, *NeuroImage* **19**, 1477–1491, 2003.

Hartvig, N. V. and Jensen, J. L. Spatial mixture modeling of fMRI data, *Hum. Brain Mapp.* **11**, 233–248, 2000.

Jordan, M. I. *Learning in Graphical Models* (MIT Press), 1999.

Kruggel, F., Zysset, S., and von Cramon, D. Y. Nonlinear regression of functional MRI data: an item recognition task study, *NeuroImage* **12**, 173–183, 2000.

Kumar, S. and Hebert, M. Discriminative fields for modeling spatial dependencies in natural images, in *Advances in Neural Information Processing Systems*, pp. 1351–1358, 2004.

Lafferty, J., McCallum, A., and Pereira, F. Conditional random fields: probabilistic models for segmenting and labeling sequence data, in *Proc. Int. Conf. Machine Learning*, pp. 282–289, 2001.

Marrelec, G., Ciuciu, P., Pelegrini-Issac, M., and Benali, H. Estimation of the hemodynamic response function in event-related functional MRI: directed acyclic graphs for a general bayesian framework, in *Proc. Conf. Information Processing in Medical Imaging*, pp. 635–646, 2003.

McIntosh, A. R. and Gonzalez-Lima, F. Structural equation modeling and its application to network analysis in functional brain imaging, *Hum. Brain Mapp.* **2**, 2–22, 1994.

Nichols, T. E. and Holmes, A. P. Nonparametric permutation tests for functional neuroimaging: a primer with examples, *Hum. Brain Mapp.* **15**, 1–25, 2001.

Penny, W. D., Stephan, K. E., Mechelli, A., and Friston, K. J. Comparing dynamic causal models, *NeuroImage* **22**, 1157–1172, 2004a.

Penny, W. D., Stephan, K. E., Mechelli, A., and Friston, K. J. Modelling functional integration: a comparison of structural equation and dynamic causal models, *NeuroImage* **23**, s264–s274, 2004b.

Rajapakse, J. C., and Piyaratna, J. Bayesian approach to segmentation of statistical parametric maps, *IEEE Trans. Biomed. Eng.* **48**, 1186–1194, 2001.

Rajapakse, J. C. and Zhou, J. Modeling effective brain connectivity with dynamic bayesian networks, *NeuroImage* **37**, 749–760, 2007.

Rajapakse, J. C., Wang, Y., Zheng, X., and Zhou, J. Probabilistic framework for brain connectivity from functional mr images, *IEEE Trans. Med. Imaging* **27**, 825–833, 2008.

Ravi, K. V. R. and Palaniappan, R. Recognising individuals using their brain patterns, in *Proc. Int. Conf. Information Technology and Applications*, pp. 520–523, 2005.

Salli, E., Aronen, H. J., Savolainen, S., Korvenoja, A., and Visa, A. Contextual clustering for analysis of functional MRI data, *IEEE Trans. Med. Imaging* **20**, 403–414, 2001.

Sitaram, R., Weiskopf, N., Caria, A., Veit, R., Erb, M., and Birbaumer, N. fMRI brain-computer interfaces, *IEEE Signal Processing Magazine*, pp. 95–106, 2008.

Svensen, M., Kruggel, F., and von Cramon, D. Y. Probabilistic modeling of single-trial fMRI data, *IEEE Trans. Med. Imaging* **19**, 25–35, 2000.

Wang, Y. and Ji, Q. A dynamic conditional random field model for object segmentation in image sequences, in *Proc. IEEE Conf. Computer Vision and Pattern Recognition*, pp. 1:264–1:270, 2005.

Wang, Y. and Rajapakse, J. C. Contextual modeling of functional MR images with conditional random fields, *IEEE Trans. Med. Imaging* **25**, 804–812, 2006.

Wang, Y., Loe, K.-F., and Wu, J.-K. A dynamic conditional random field model for foreground and shadow segmentation, *IEEE Trans. Pattern Anal. Machine Intelligence* **28**, 279–289, 2006.

Woolrich, M. W., Behrens, T. E. J., Beckmann, C. F., and Smith, S. M. Mixture models with adaptive spatial regularization for segmentation with an application to fMRI data, *IEEE Trans. Med. Imaging* **24**, 1–11, 2005.

Zheng, X. and Rajapakse, J. C. Learning functional structure from fMR images, *NeuroImage* **31**, 1601–1613, 2006.